The Coming of the Kingdom

The Coming of the Kingdom explores the experiences of the Indigenous Muisca peoples of the New Kingdom of Granada (Colombia) during the first century of Spanish colonial rule. Focusing on colonialism, religious reform, law, language, and historical writing, Juan F. Cobo Betancourt examines the introduction and development of Christianity among the Muisca, who from the 1530s found themselves at the centre of the invaders' efforts to transform them into tribute-paying Catholic subjects of the Spanish crown. The book illustrates how successive generations of missionaries and administrators approached the task of drawing the Muisca peoples to Catholicism at a time when it was undergoing profound changes, and how successive generations of the Muisca interacted with the practices and ideas that the invaders attempted to impose, variously rejecting or adopting them, transforming and translating them, and ultimately making them their own. This title is also available as Open Access on Cambridge Core.

Juan F. Cobo Betancourt is Assistant Professor at the University of California, Santa Barbara. He is the author of *Mestizos heraldos de Dios* and co-editor (with Natalie Cobo) of *La legislación de la arquidiócesis de Santafé*. He co-founded Neogranadina, a Colombian non-profit devoted to digitising endangered archives and promoting digital history in Latin America.

CAMBRIDGE LATIN AMERICAN STUDIES

General Editors
KRIS LANE, Tulane University
MATTHEW RESTALL, Pennsylvania State University

Editor Emeritus
HERBERT S. KLEIN
Gouverneur Morris Emeritus Professor of History, Columbia University and Hoover
Research Fellow, Stanford University

Other Books in the Series

137 *The Coming of the Kingdom: The Muisca, Catholic Reform, and Spanish Colonialism in the New Kingdom of Granada*, Juan F. Cobo Bettencourt

136 *The Shamanism of Eco-tourism: History and Ontology among the Makushi in Guyana*, James Andrew Whitaker

135 *Fallen from Heaven: The Enduring Tradition of Europeans as Gods in the Americas*, Nicholas Griffiths

134 *Global Servants of the Spanish King: Mobility and Cosmopolitanism in the Early Modern Spanish Empire*, Adolfo Polo y La Borda

133 *Plebeian Consumers: Global Connections, Local Trade, and Foreign Goods in Nineteenth-Century Colombia*, Ana María Otero-Cleves

132 *Peopling for Profit in Imperial Brazil: Directed Migrations and the Business of Nineteenth-Century Colonization*, José Juan Pérez Meléndez

131 *Being the Heart of the World: The Pacific and the Fashioning of the Self in New Spain, 1513–1641*, Nino Vallen

The Coming of the Kingdom

The Muisca, Catholic Reform, and Spanish Colonialism in the New Kingdom of Granada

JUAN F. COBO BETANCOURT
University of California, Santa Barbara

CAMBRIDGE
UNIVERSITY PRESS

Shaftesbury Road, Cambridge CB2 8EA, United Kingdom

One Liberty Plaza, 20th Floor, New York, NY 10006, USA

477 Williamstown Road, Port Melbourne, VIC 3207, Australia

314–321, 3rd Floor, Plot 3, Splendor Forum, Jasola District Centre, New Delhi – 110025, India

103 Penang Road, #05-06/07, Visioncrest Commercial, Singapore 238467

Cambridge University Press is part of Cambridge University Press & Assessment, a department of the University of Cambridge.

We share the University's mission to contribute to society through the pursuit of education, learning and research at the highest international levels of excellence.

www.cambridge.org
Information on this title: www.cambridge.org/9781009314053
DOI: 10.1017/9781009314046

© Juan Fernando Cobo Betancourt 2024

This publication is in copyright. Subject to statutory exception and to the provisions of relevant collective licensing agreements, with the exception of the Creative Commons version the link for which is provided below, no reproduction of any part may take place without the written permission of Cambridge University Press & Assessment.

An online version of this work is published at doi.org/10.1017/9781009314046 under a Creative Commons Open Access license CC-BY-NC 4.0 which permits re-use, distribution and reproduction in any medium for non-commercial purposes providing appropriate credit to the original work is given and any changes made are indicated. To view a copy of this license visit https://creativecommons.org/licenses/by-nc/4.0

When citing this work, please include a reference to the DOI 10.1017/9781009314046

First published 2024

A catalogue record for this publication is available from the British Library.

Library of Congress Cataloging-in-Publication Data

NAMES: Cobo Betancourt, Juan Fernando, author.
TITLE: The coming of the kingdom : the Muisca, Catholic reform, and Spanish colonialism in the new Kingdom of Granada / Juan F. Cobo Betancourt, University of California, Santa Barbara.
DESCRIPTION: Cambridge, United Kingdom ; New York, NY : Cambridge University Press, [2024] | Includes bibliographical references and index.
IDENTIFIERS: LCCN 2024025185 (print) | LCCN 2024025186 (ebook) | ISBN 9781009314053 (hardback) | ISBN 9781009314039 (paperback) | ISBN 9781009314046 (epub)
SUBJECTS: LCSH: Chibcha Indians–Colombia–History–17th century. | Chibcha Indians–Religion. | Colombia–Discovery and exploration–Spanish. | Colombia–History–To 1810. | Catholic Church–Misssions–Colombia–History. | Ethnic relations–Religious aspects–Catholic Church.
CLASSIFICATION: LCC F2270.2.C4 C63 2024 (print) | LCC F2270.2.C4 (ebook) |
DDC 986.1/46–dc23/eng/20240605
LC record available at https://lccn.loc.gov/2024025185
LC ebook record available at https://lccn.loc.gov/2024025186

ISBN 978-1-009-31405-3 Hardback

Cambridge University Press & Assessment has no responsibility for the persistence or accuracy of URLs for external or third-party internet websites referred to in this publication and does not guarantee that any content on such websites is, or will remain, accurate or appropriate.

Justice removed, then, what are kingdoms but great bands of robbers? What are bands of robbers themselves but little kingdoms? The band itself is made up of men; it is governed by the authority of a ruler; it is bound together by a pact of association; and the loot is divided according to an agreed law. If, by the constant addition of desperate men, this scourge grows to such a size that it acquires territory, establishes a seat of government, occupies cities, and subjugates peoples, it assumes the name kingdom more openly. For this name is now manifestly conferred upon it by not by the removal of greed, but by the addition of impunity.

—Augustine, *On the City of God*, book IV, ch. 4. Trans. R. W. Dyson

Being asked by the Pharisees when the kingdom of God would come, he answered them, 'The kingdom of God is not coming in ways that can be observed, nor will they say, "Look, here it is!" or "There!" for behold, the kingdom of God is in the midst of you'.

—Luke 17:20–21 (ESV)

Contents

List of Figures		*page* ix
Acknowledgements		xi
List of Abbreviations		xv
	Introduction	1
1	The Muisca and the Problem of Religion	19
2	The Settlers, Rescript Government, and the Foundations of the Kingdom	73
3	The Failure of Colonial Governance and the Breaking of Indigenous Authority	124
4	The Friends of Ceremony and the Introduction of Reform	172
5	Language Policy and Legal Fiction	223
6	Indigenous Confraternities and the Stakeholder Church	262
	Conclusion: The Coming of the Kingdom	305
References		311
Index		335

Figures

I.1 Gaspar de Figueroa, 'San Nicolás de Tolentino y
las Ánimas', 1656 *page 2*

1.1 Joseph Mulder, title page to Lucas Fernández de
Piedrahita, *Historia general* 24

1.2 Painted textile fragment of a luxury blanket (*manta*),
Colombia, Eastern Cordillera, 800–1600 CE (Muisca period) 44

1.3 Ceramic figure with facial decoration and gold alloy
nose ring (*santuario?*), Colombia, Eastern Cordillera,
800–1600 CE (Muisca period) 64

1.4 Tripod offering bowl with human and bird guardians,
containing votive figures (*tunjos*) and emeralds,
Colombia, Eastern Cordillera, 800–1600 CE
(Muisca period) 65

3.1 Votive figure (*tunjo*) of Indigenous ruler (*cacique*)
in residential enclosure (*cercado*), Colombia,
Eastern Cordillera, 800–1600 CE (Muisca period) 125

3.2 Offering of thirty-two votive figures (*tunjos*) and
one unworked gold lump, Colombia, Eastern
Cordillera, 800–1600 CE (Muisca period) 152

6.1 Anonymous, mural portrait of Indigenous donor,
Church of San Juan Bautista, Sutatausa, Colombia, c. 1630 301

Acknowledgements

The research, writing, and rewriting of this book was a collective effort that would have been impossible without the extraordinary generosity and support of a number of people and institutions. It began as the subject of my doctorate at the University of Cambridge, which was funded by the Lightfoot Scholarship in Ecclesiastical History, the Arts and Humanities Research Council, and Peterhouse. At Cambridge I incurred a great debt of gratitude to Gabriela Ramos for her rigorous criticism and patient support. It was Gabriela who first asked me many of the questions that this book has sought to answer, and its title, in part, pays homage to her work.[1] I am also indebted to Magnus Ryan, Patrick Zutshi, Scott Mandelbrote, and Peter Linehan for their mentorship and for providing me with tools that would later shed old light on a new context. I am also very grateful to Simon Ditchfield and Aliocha Maldavsky for their thoughtful observations and generous encouragement as examiners, which led me to broaden the scope of this project considerably, and for their support and advice as colleagues as I found my feet as a young academic.

I am profoundly grateful for the support I received from several institutions in Colombia. I was welcomed as a visiting scholar at the Pontificia Universidad Javeriana by Juana Marín and Jorge Enrique Salcedo SJ. Diana Bonnett invited me to spend some time as a visiting scholar at the Universidad de los Andes, where I was also grateful to discuss my work with Carl Langebaek and Mauricio Nieto. At the Instituto Colombiano

---

[1] Gabriela Ramos, ed., *La venida del reino: religión, evangelización y cultura en América, siglos XVI–XX* (Cuzco: Centro de Estudios Regionales Andinos "Bartolomé de las Casas", 1994).

xii *Acknowledgements*

de Antropología e Historia, Jorge Gamboa and Guillermo Sosa gave me valuable advice, and with Bibiana Castro and her colleagues in the publications department also supported the production of *La legislación de la Arquidiócesis de Santafé,* one of the many detours and parallel roads I travelled in the journey to this book. Another has been Neogranadina, the non-profit foundation Santiago Muñoz, Natalie Cobo, and I set up in 2015 to contribute to rescue, protect, and promote the holdings of endangered archives and libraries in Colombia and elsewhere in Latin America, and to develop digital and public history initiatives to bring them to new audiences. Seven major digitisation initiatives, multiple digital platforms and projects, and many hundreds of thousands of images later, Neogranadina has become a major part of my life and scholarship. I am profoundly grateful to them, to our colleagues Andreína Soto, María del Pilar Ramírez Restrepo, Jairo Melo Flórez, and María Gabriela Betancourt, and to the dozens of students, interns, volunteers, and users around the world who have contributed in different ways to make possible Neogranadina's work in Colombia, Peru, and online. Since 2016 I have also had the immense privilege of participating in the intellectual community of Department II of the Max Planck Institute for Legal History and Legal Theory in Frankfurt, where my work has benefitted immeasurably from conversations with Thomas Duve, Benedetta Albani, María del Pilar Mejía, Otto Danwerth, Max Deardorff, Manuela Bragagnolo, Osvaldo Moutin, José Luis Egío, Christiane Birr, and other colleagues. Research stays at the institute were integral to rethinking important aspects of this book.

In 2016 I joined the faculty of the History Department of the University of California, Santa Barbara, where I found a nurturing and supportive intellectual community. I have an enormous debt of gratitude to Sherene Seikaly and Utathya Chattopadhyaya, who painstakingly read and engaged with every word of this book and gave me generous comments, thoughtful insights, and much needed encouragement. So too to Cecilia Méndez Gastelumendi for her unwavering support of me and of this project and for our long conversations on Andean politics past and present. I am also very grateful to Manuel Covo for his support and thoughtful engagement with different chapters of this book. Alicia Boswell provided company and solidarity that made the lonely task of writing and editing much more enjoyable. Thank you to Hilary Bernstein, Beth Digeser, Erika Rappaport, Adam Sabra, Luke Roberts, Stephan Miescher, and Sarah Cline, who asked crucial questions and provided valuable advice at different junctures. I am also very grateful for the time I was able to spend at the John Carter Brown Library, with support provided by the Donald L. Saunders Fellowship, which allowed me to consult material that became

Acknowledgements

xiii

central to this project – it was there, after all, that I first encountered Juan Sanz Hurtado – and afforded me crucial time to write and rewrite. I am grateful to Neil Safier, Bertie Mandelblatt, Domingo Ledesma, and Pedro Germano Leal for their support and advice, and to my fellow fellows, particularly Tessa Murphy and Franco Rossi, for reading and commenting on sections of this work, even after the coming of the pandemic.

This book relies on material from collections in Bogotá, Tunja, Seville, Rome, London, Cambridge, Oxford, and Providence. I would like to thank the many archivists and librarians that made my research possible, especially Francisco Molinero Rodríguez and Luis Emilio Calenda at the Archivo General de Indias (AGI), Mauricio Tovar at the Archivo General de la Nación (AGN), María Rósula Vargas de Castañeda at the Archivo Histórico Regional de Boyacá (AHRB), and Germán Mejía and Alma Miranda at the Archivo Histórico Javeriano 'Juan Manuel Pacheco'. I was also very fortunate to have been granted access to three ecclesiastical archives in Bogotá after many unsuccessful attempts. Fr. Antonio Balaguera OP was instrumental in helping me access the Archivo de la Provincia de San Luis Beltrán de Colombia, where archivist Martha Hincapié went beyond the call of duty to help me find what I needed. The rector and staff of the Colegio de San Bartolomé generously allowed me to spend many hours in their archive and trusted me with their materials. I had no such luck at the Franciscan archive in Bogotá, but I must thank Fr. Augusto Duque OFM for his valiant efforts to help me gain access. Fabián Leonardo Benavides, Andrés Mauricio Escobar, and their colleagues at the Universidad de Santo Tomás kindly included me in their project to commemorate the 450th anniversary of the Archdiocese of Bogotá, which afforded me a little access to the archives of the cathedral chapter.

Along the way, I presented portions of this project in different conferences and venues where it benefitted from the comments and insights of multiple scholars. I learned more than I can say from Beth Penry and Tom Abercrombie, generous mentors and kindest of colleagues, about confraternities, religious institutions, Indigenous politics, and much more beyond research. Aliocha Maldavsky, Roberto Di Stefano, Marie-Lucie Copete, and Ariane Boltanski generously included me in their research groups on lay sponsorship of the sacred and encouraged me to rethink the engagement of Indigenous elites and commoners with Christian institutions. Diana Magaloni invited me to participate in the preparation of the *Portable Universe* exhibition at the Los Angeles County Museum of Art, and with Julia Burtenshaw helped me to think about the persistent influence of colonial stereotypes and categories. Alcira Dueñas encouraged me to think more deliberately about the shape of the archive. Guillermo

xiv   *Acknowledgements*

Wilde and Andrés Castro Roldán provided me with invaluable suggestions concerning language policy, Jesuit strategies, and missionary politics. Yanna Yannakakis gave me feedback on my efforts to historicise the *cacicazgo*. Juan Carlos Estenssoro, whose work inspired this project from the outset, was always generous with his comments and acute observations. I am especially grateful to Santiago Muñoz Arbeláez, my closest colleague, for his generous engagement with my work, invaluable advice, continuous encouragement, sharp insights, and friendship.

I am indebted to Kris Lane for believing in this project from its infancy. An earlier version of Chapter 5 appeared as an article in the *Colonial Latin American Review* and benefitted greatly from his input and advice. I am also very grateful to him and Matthew Restall for encouraging me to bring the manuscript to Cambridge University Press and for supporting me through the publication process. I am also indebted to Cecelia Cancellaro and Victoria Philips for their assistance, and to the anonymous reviewers of the manuscript for their insights and suggestions. Carrie Gibson, who was there at the very beginning of this project, also saw it to the end – rigorously copy-editing the final manuscript, just as she did its earlier incarnations, and providing thoughtful insights and patient comments. Esther González helped me tie up loose ends at the AGI, Yezid Pérez at the AGN, and Pilar Ramírez among AHRB materials from Tunja. María Alicia Uribe and her colleagues at the Museo del Oro aided me in obtaining permission to include the images of the objects in their collection that appear throughout this book. Julia Burtenshaw helped me obtain the images of objects in Los Angeles County Museum of Art and in a private collection whose owners, who wished to remain anonymous, kindly allowed me to include. Mercedes López provided valuable advice in the task of obtaining an image of Gaspar de Figueroa's canvas in Cómbita, which Santiago Medina photographed for me with the kind authorisation of Hernán David López, parish priest. Andrés Cuervo took me to Sutatausa to see and photograph its striking murals many years ago, and he, Nohora, and Daniel put me up in Bogotá countless times and supported me in many different ways as I researched this book. Rosa Andalón, Andrea Conde, and Ximena Garzón helped us look after Sebastián while I wrote and rewrote.

This project would not have been possible without the limitless support and generosity of my family. I am grateful to my cousins, my brother, my grandparents, my aunts, my stepfather, and my wonderful mother, whom I will never be able to thank enough. My father, who always gave me the gift of his boundless encouragement, sadly did not get to see this book in print, but I will treasure the memory of the days we spent together working on its maps, images, and proofs. Finally, I will be forever grateful to Natalie Cobo, my closest collaborator, frequent co-author, sharpest reader, constant companion, and most generous supporter. This book is for her.

Abbreviations

AGI	Archivo General de Indias, Seville
AGN	Archivo General de la Nación, Bogotá
AHJ	Archivo Histórico Javeriano Juan Manuel Pacheco, SJ, Pontificia Universidad Javeriana, Bogotá
AHRB	Archivo Histórico Regional de Boyacá, Tunja
AHSB	Archivo Histórico, Fundación Colegio Mayor de San Bartolomé, Bogotá
AHT	AHRB, Fondo Archivo Histórico de Tunja
APSLB	Archivo Histórico, Provincia de San Luis Beltrán de Colombia, Bogotá
ARSI	Archivum Romanum Societatis Iesu, Rome
C&I	AGN, Sección Colonia, Fondo Caciques e Indios
C&O	AGN, Sección Colonia, Fondo Curas y Obispos
CJ	AGN, Sección Colonia, Fondo Criminales Juicios
E	AGN, Sección Colonia, Fondo Encomiendas
FI	AGN, Sección Colonia, Fondo Fábrica de Iglesias
NR&Q	ARSI, Provincia Novi Regni et Quitensis
PB	AGN, Sección Archivos Parroquiales, Archivos Parroquiales de Boyacá
RH	AGN, Sección Colonia, Fondo Real Hacienda
SF	AGI, Sección Gobierno, Serie Audiencia de Santafé
VB	AGN, Sección Colonia, Subfondo Visitas de Boyacá
VC	AGN, Sección Colonia, Subfondo Visitas de Cundinamarca

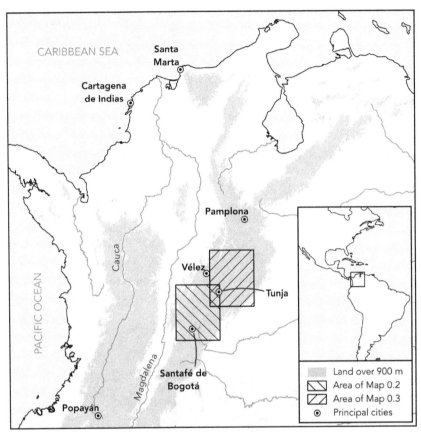

MAP I The Northern Andes, showing the principal Spanish cities of the New Kingdom of Granada and of the Archdiocese of Santafé[1]

---

[1] These maps attempt to show the sites and communities studied in this book across the highlands of the Northern Andes. In most cases, I have mapped them in the locations that they occupied by the middle of the seventeenth century – a pragmatic choice that reflects when documentation is most abundant, particularly Rodrigo Zapata de Lobera's 1663 summary of the civil visitations of the first half of the seventeenth century (discussed in Chapter 6). I have tried to be exhaustive, but this has not been entirely possible because many sites are no longer extant today. Indeed, by 1663, many had already been abandoned, or amalgamated with their neighbours as a result of trends discussed in the chapters that follow. Where no location could be ascertained, I have tried to indicate an approximate location in relation to mapped sites and landmarks in the main text, where I also sought to distinguish between settlements with identical names. All maps were drawn by me, using ASTER Global Digital Elevation Data and the *Diccionario Geográfico de Colombia* and *Colombia en mapas* data sets of the Instituto Geográfico Agustín Codazzi (IGAC). I am grateful to Santiago Muñoz for his thoughtful feedback, as well as for information on the location of sites in the Valley of Ubaque, published in *Costumbres en disputa*.

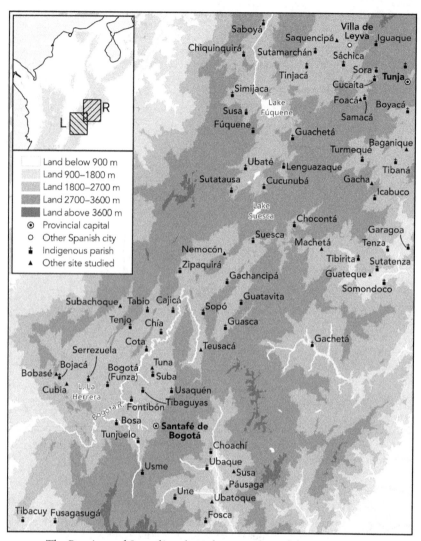

MAP 2 The Province of Santafé and southern reaches of the Province of Tunja, c. 1650, showing cities, towns, and other settlements studied in this book

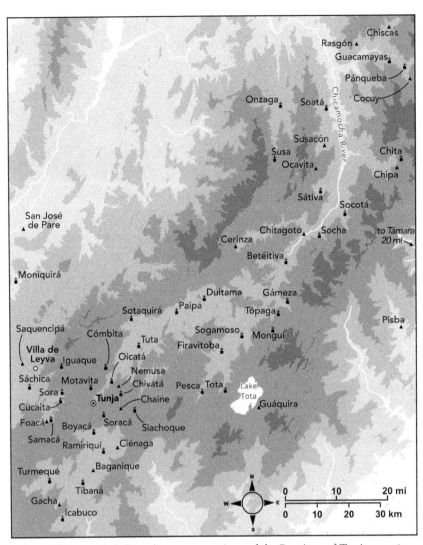

MAP 3 The central and north-eastern portions of the Province of Tunja, c. 1650, showing cities, towns, and other settlements studied in this book

Introduction

In the parish church of Cómbita, in what is now the Department of Boyacá, Colombia, hangs a large canvas completed in 1656 by the Neogranadian painter Gaspar de Figueroa (Figure I.1). It depicts, in a series of overlapping and interconnected scenes, the imagined interplay between the Catholic Church of this corner of the Andes and its conception of the sacred. The painting portrays a well-known Catholic subject, the Mass of Saint Gregory, showing the miracle of the apparition of Christ as the 'Man of Sorrows' during the mass, as Pope Gregory I utters the words of consecration – a visual statement of the Catholic doctrine of the real presence of Christ in the Eucharist, reaffirmed at the Council of Trent.[1] In the background is a depiction of Purgatory, and above it, presiding over the entire painting, are the two remaining persons of the Christian Trinity and the Virgin Mary in Heaven. They are surrounded by angels, some of whom are helping a select few souls escape their torment by pulling them out with black leather belts, associated with the devotion to Saint Monica, to whom the parish church was dedicated.[2] A final

---

[1] On the theme of the Mass of Saint Gregory in Catholic art in this period, see, for example, Lee Wandel, 'The Reformation and the Visual Arts'. In *The Cambridge History of Christianity. Vol. 4: Reform and Expansion, 1500–1660*. Edited by R. Po-Chia Hsia, 343–370 (Cambridge: Cambridge University Press, 2007).

[2] Depictions of purgatory are common in Neogranadian churches in this period, as Natalia Lozada Mendieta notes in *La incorporación del indígena en el Purgatorio cristiano: estudio de los lienzos de ánimas de la Nueva Granada de los siglos XVI y XVII* (Bogotá: Ediciones Uniandes, Universidad de los Andes, 2012), 80. A common theme is the rescue of souls in torment using an object associated with a particular devotion, often the rosary. For other examples, see María del Rosario Leal del Castillo, 'El purgatorio en la plástica neogranadina'. *Alarife: Revista de arquitectura*, no. 18 (2009): 85–95. The

FIGURE I.1 Gaspar de Figueroa, San Nicolás de Tolentino y las Ánimas, 1656. Parroquia de la Inmaculada Concepción, Cómbita, Boyacá. Photograph by Santiago Medina

element further unites the two scenes, and gives the painting its name: the inclusion of Saint Nicholas of Tolentino, the figure in the black Augustinian habit towards the centre of the painting, associated both

parish church of Cómbita is now dedicated to a different devotion, the Immaculate Conception.

Introduction

with the souls of Purgatory and with the Augustinian order that ran the parish. At first sight, this seems largely to reflect the interests and priorities of the European missionaries charged with Christianising the Indigenous peoples of this region, then known as the New Kingdom of Granada.

A closer look, however, reveals additional elements that reflect the hopes and concerns – both spiritual and material – of the Indigenous people of the town, whose painting, and church, this was. Most striking of all is the inclusion of members of the Indigenous laity among the figures portrayed behind Saint Nicholas, who appear to have processed into the frame. Their depictions are individualised, and we know that they are the leaders of the Confraternity of the Souls of Purgatory of the parish of Cómbita, which commissioned and funded the painting. The confraternity was, in one sense, an entirely local institution, and the painting responded to very local concerns. The town of Cómbita had been created in 1601 by forcibly bringing together three different communities – Cómbita, Motavita, and Suta. The confraternity depicted here was associated with the community of Cómbita, which was making a visible claim to an important position within the life of the town with this painting, in the face of the other two groups with which it shared it, and their rival confraternity.[3] As Mercedes López Rodríguez has shown, the individuals depicted here are don Pedro Tabaco, the *cacique*, or Indigenous ruler, of Cómbita, and his family. Tabaco was using the institution of the confraternity as a means to reassert his position of leadership within his community, which was facing unprecedented pressures as a result of colonial impositions – a generalised phenomenon afflicting Indigenous authorities throughout the region in the early seventeenth century.[4] At the same time, this confraternity was only a local instance of a cult integrating Saint Monica, the Souls of Purgatory, and Saint Nicholas of Tolentino that the Augustinians had promoted in many contexts since the fifteenth century, making this isolated parish in the Neogranadian highlands part of a far-reaching, global devotion.[5]

---

[3] The resettlement and confraternities of Cómbita are discussed in Chapter 6.

[4] Mercedes López Rodríguez traces the situation faced by don Pedro in relation to the increasing relative wealth and importance and his former subordinates in 'La memoria de las imágenes: Donantes indígenas en el Lienzo de las Ánimas de San Nicolás de Tolentino'. In *Historia e imágenes: Los agustinos en Colombia, 400 años*. Edited by José Antonio Carbonell Blanco (Bogotá: Museo Nacional de Colombia, 2002), 29–32.

[5] The Archconfraternity of Our Lady of Consolation and Cincture, or of the Black Leathern Belt of Saint Monica, Saint Augustine, and Saint Nicholas of Tolentino. On the role of such local-global devotions in this period, such as the Madonna of the Snows, see Simon

4 *Introduction*

The painting is catechetical, and the ideas it depicts – the Trinity, the mechanics of the afterlife, the immortality of the soul, the value and role of the sacraments – were all, like the model and style of the painting itself, introduced by the European invaders of the New Kingdom of Granada and the missionaries who followed them. Some of the ideas and practices it promotes – the centrality of the Eucharist, the efficacy of the cult of saints, the procession of the confraternity – reflect the priorities of Catholic reformers in the aftermath of the Council of Trent, including those who, in its train, sought to implement crucial reforms to the missionary project of the New Kingdom. However, here, all these features have also been appropriated by the parish laity, who used not only the iconographic language of the painting but also the institutions and practices of this Tridentine Catholicism for their own purposes. The painting provides a lens on the incorporation of the Indigenous peoples of the New Kingdom of Granada into Christianity, the subject of this book.

The chapters that follow trace the experience of the peoples today known as the Muisca – a number of groups characterised, before the European invasion, by their great linguistic, political, and religious diversity – over the course of the century or so after the Spanish invasion of the Northern Andes, from the foundation of the city of Santafé de Bogotá in 1538 to the final years of the archiepiscopate of Cristóbal de Torres (d. 1654), the last in a series of reforming archbishops of Santafé. In this period, successive generations of priests and administrators sought to incorporate the Muisca into Catholicism and transform them into Christian subjects of the Spanish monarchy. By preparing Indigenous people for the coming of the kingdom of God, missionaries and officials sought to realise a colonial normative, political, and religious order, the New Kingdom of Granada, whose self-declared justification and purpose, and the basis of its Indigenous tributary and extractive economy, was – like that of the rest of the Spanish empire – Christianisation.

On both sides of the Atlantic, and in Southeast Asia, the Spanish monarchy placed a special emphasis on the incorporation of its subjects into its vision of Christianity, a position that was broadly derived from two interconnected lines of historical development. The first was the consolidation of the identity of 'Spain' and Spanishness that accompanied the political unification of Castile and Aragon. Especially after the capture

Ditchfield, 'Romanus and Catholicus: Counter-Reformation Rome as Caput Mundi'. In *A Companion to Early Modern Rome, 1492–1692*. Edited by Pamela M. Jones, Barbara Wisch, and Simon Ditchfield, 131–147 (Leiden: Brill, 2019).

Introduction

of Granada in 1492, this identity became increasingly characterised by ideas of cultural unity, most often expressed in religious terms, eventually leading to a growing obsession with 'purity' of blood (*limpieza de sangre*). The second was the development of a justification for the conquest and possession of the New World based initially on the need for Christian evangelisation, from the *Inter caetera* bulls onwards,[6] and later on the preservation of orthodoxy. As a result, Christianisation, ultimately, was rooted in coercion: incorporation into Christianity, all theological niceties aside, was an unavoidable imperative for people under Spanish rule.

Time and time again, these designs were tempered by local conditions, the shortcomings of colonial administrators, and, most importantly, the contestations of Indigenous people as they navigated profound changes, dramatic demographic collapse, and ever-growing colonial impositions. However, by the middle of the seventeenth century, despite complaints to the contrary of some contemporary observers and modern scholars, Catholicism had spread widely and taken root among the Indigenous inhabitants of the highlands of the New Kingdom of Granada. What I mean by this is not the fulfilment of a predefined strategy that simply unfolded over this period, or indeed the crossing of some watershed in a linear process of conversion involving the progressive abandonment of one 'religion' and the adoption of another. Instead, what the chapters that follow trace are a series of interconnected processes – contingent, faltering, contested, and subject to reversals – that fundamentally transformed the lives of Indigenous people across the region, and created the space and conditions that allowed them to engage with Christianity in diverse ways. Indigenous people adapted and adopted what Christianity had to offer them, incorporating many of its features into their lives for multiple reasons and purposes, of which only a few are visible to us in the historical record. Those processes, and these interactions, created and sustained the New Kingdom of Granada. Like the scenes in Figueroa's painting, the story is partly one of missionaries and settlers, but also, and at its heart, it is an Indigenous story, involving a diverse cast of actors firmly rooted in local contexts and dynamics while connected to, and shaped by, global trends.

---

[6] *Inter caetera*, 3 and 4 May 1493, in Josef Metzler, ed., *America Pontificia: Primi saeculi evangelizationis, 1493–1592. Documenta Pontificia ex registris et minutis praesertim in Archivo Secreto Vaticano existentibus*, vol. 1 (Vatican: Libreria editrice vaticana, 1991), 71–75 and 79–83.

6   *Introduction*

The focus of this book is the highland region of the eastern range of what are now the Colombian Andes. This is a territory of roughly 10,000 square miles broadly corresponding to the highlands of the modern-day Colombian *departamentos* of Cundinamarca and Boyacá, composed of the high plateau known as the *altiplano cundiboyacense*, located at an average altitude of about 2,500 metres above sea level, and its surrounding highland valleys. Its inhabitants, first encountered by Europeans in 1536, lived across a multitude of settlements of different sizes, were organised in a variety of political groupings of various configurations, and spoke a range of languages. They are known to us as the Muisca. In the years that followed the European invasion, this region was organised into two colonial provinces: Santafé and Tunja. These became the focus of Spanish settlement in the Northern Andes and eventually the core of a Spanish colonial realm known as the New Kingdom of Granada, which covered – at least on paper – much of the region of northern South America that is now the Republic of Colombia. Over the period with which this book is concerned, the Muisca peoples – like so many other Indigenous groups – suffered catastrophic demographic collapse as a result of colonial impositions and the ravages of successive waves of epidemics. Estimates of the size of their population before the invasion remain largely informed guesses, but figures for the colonial period – although inexact and based on patchy documentation – suggest that the population crashed from about 280,000 individuals around 1560 to tens of thousands by the 1630s, a collapse of around 80 per cent by some measures.[7]

This New Kingdom of Granada was at the margins of Spanish power in America. It lacked the status and resources of the two viceregal centres, New Spain and Peru. It attracted far fewer European immigrants, it received much less attention from the Spanish crown, and its civil and ecclesiastical institutions developed at a slower pace. European explorers and missionaries had been active in the region's Caribbean coast from the first decade of the sixteenth century, but their exploration and settlement of the interior and the establishment of the institutions of government and the church lagged behind similar developments in New Spain and Peru.

---

[7] Figures derived from this and every other colonial visitation in this period are discussed in the chapters that follow. For a survey of the long history of human occupation of this region, see Marta Herrera Ángel, 'Milenios de ocupación en Cundinamarca'. *In Los muiscas en los siglos XVI y XVII: Miradas desde la arqueología, la antropología y la historia*. Edited by Jorge Augusto Gamboa (Bogotá: Universidad de los Andes, 2008), 1–39.

Introduction

Europeans only ventured inland in the late 1530s, when news of the invasion of Peru prompted expeditions to find an overland route to connect it with the Caribbean. The city of Santafé was not founded until 1538, and the region then remained a Caribbean hinterland, governed from Santa Marta and Santo Domingo, until the arrival of its own *Audiencia* (royal court and chancery) in 1550. Its first bishop, for his part, would not reach the highlands until 1553, and the region only became its own ecclesiastical province in 1564. Indeed, it even had to wait until the eighteenth century for its own printing press. These events occurred years, decades, and in the latter case centuries, after similar developments in Mexico and Peru. As a result, scholars of colonial Latin America, and even of 'the Andes', especially those writing in English, have tended to overlook the New Kingdom's early colonial history. For too long, the region has been assumed to have followed a similar trajectory to the viceregal centres, if more slowly and at a smaller scale, with little to add to our understanding of broader trends.[8]

These assumptions have a long history and are, in fact, rooted in the distinctive ways in which writing about the New Kingdom and its peoples took shape from the sixteenth century. From early explorers to chroniclers, missionaries, and officials, successive generations of authors – writing across different genres and registers, in works of history, legislation, linguistic observation, and bureaucratic documentation, occasionally in collaboration with Indigenous informers – applied models and assumptions derived from more central regions to understand conditions on the ground and to explain them to foreign audiences. This framing continued

---

[8] This is beginning to change, and the history of the New Kingdom of Granada in the sixteenth and seventeenth centuries is beginning to enjoy significant interest in English-language scholarship. In the last two decades, Kris Lane highlighted the region's connectedness to early modern global networks of exchange in *Colour of Paradise: The Emerald in the Age of Gunpowder Empires* (New Haven, CT: Yale University Press, 2010). J. Michael Francis examined the Spanish invasion in *Invading Colombia: Spanish Accounts of the Gonzalo Jiménez de Quesada Expedition of Conquest* (University Park: Penn State University Press, 2007), alongside translations of key sources. Joanne Rappaport and Tom Cummins set their study of Indigenous literacy, *Beyond the Lettered City: Indigenous Literacies in the Andes* (Durham, NC: Duke University Press, 2012), in the Northern Andes, noting the historiographical relevance of exploring colonial Andean culture in a non-Incaic setting. Rappaport has also examined the emergence, development, and ambiguities of *mestizaje* in colonial Santafé and Tunja in multiple works, most notably *The Disappearing Mestizo: Configuring Difference in the Colonial New Kingdom of Granada* (Durham, NC: Duke University Press, 2014). All these works coincide in highlighting the distinctive perspective of this region to explore broader questions usually considered from the perspective of the viceregal centres.

8   *Introduction*

in scholarly writing about the region long after Colombian independence: rather than exploring the historical, for decades much of the historiography took part in perpetuating the categories, perspectives, and fictions in which colonial authors were invested.

There were certainly important commonalities with central regions. In Mexico and Peru, as elsewhere in Spanish America, missionaries and administrators faced the common task of Christianising Indigenous peoples. They struggled with the problems posed by Indigenous languages and the settlement patterns of the people under their jurisdiction. They faced common challenges regarding how best to employ limited manpower and resources in religious instruction, which methods to use to impart the mysteries of the Christian faith, which devotions and practices to promote among their catechumens – and how to determine whether the message they sought to impart was being received in the way they intended. All of this intensified when, in 1564, Philip II accepted the decrees of the Council of Trent in the Crown of Castile and ordered their implementation across its dominions, and civil and ecclesiastical authorities across the monarchy had to face the common task of reforming the churches under their care along Tridentine lines – and more immediately of trying figure out what it was exactly that these were supposed to be. The details and contours of these problems were, of course, always local, but some broad features were universal, so that these shared experiences need not be a distorting influence. Indeed, the contributions and perspectives of scholars who have examined the Christianisation of Indigenous peoples in those regions and elsewhere around the early modern world offer important insights that frame the questions this book explores.

In fact, the New Kingdom of Granada occupied a distinctive place in the Spanish empire. It was marginal and received little attention from the Spanish crown, and yet it was firmly embedded in the networks of exchange and movement of people, goods, ideas, and knowledge that spanned the early modern world. Deposits of gold, emeralds, and other precious resources attracted significant numbers of immigrants. Between 1550 and 1650, New Granada produced over 55 per cent of all the gold extracted in Spanish America.[9] Neogranadian emeralds, originating primarily in the mines of the region of Muzo in the province of Tunja,

---

[9] 55.58 per cent (85.914 kg, of 154.557 kg) between 1550 and 1650. For these figures, and more information about Neogranadian gold production, see John J. TePaske, *A New World of Gold and Silver*. Edited by Kendall W. Brown (Leiden: Brill, 2010), 37–40, 56, and 261–270.

quickly became a global commodity traded as far afield as South Asia.[10] The discovery and extraction of these and other resources resulted in the establishment of significant administrative and commercial centres in the interior of New Granada from the 1530s, which in turn prompted the creation and development of other industries to sustain the growing colonial population. Moreover, the region was at the geographic centre of the Spanish presence in America, and its Caribbean port of Cartagena de Indias was an important nexus in the network of trade and communication on which it depended, not least through its status as the principal Spanish American port in the trans-Atlantic slave trade in this period.[11]

Ambitious priests and administrators may have had their sights on more distinguished regions, but many passed through New Granada on their way to higher office in the colonial administration or church, where they often discovered that they had a greater freedom of action and were further removed from royal supervision than their contemporaries elsewhere. The New Kingdom's dearth of resources and manpower, the weakness of its institutions in the face of personal ambition and private interest, and its limited oversight often resulted in catastrophe, especially in the sixteenth century. At the same time, the lack of resources and supervision opened possibilities for experimentation and innovation, forcing local actors to find creative solutions to issues that in other regions could be approached with greater financial, technical, or human resources.

One such experiment, an ambitious reform programme inaugurated at the beginning of the seventeenth century, is the pivotal moment of this book. Partly as a response to multiple crises and failures of governance of the sixteenth century, and partly as a result of the changing priorities and preoccupations of religious reformers, an ambitious archbishop, a determined president, and an exiled cohort of Jesuits, with the broad support of the kingdom's leading settlers, came together to concoct a plan to overhaul the missionary project. The plan focused on the introduction of the most current devotions, practices, and institutions in Catholicism at a global level, creating new avenues for Indigenous people to engage with Christianity and setting the New Kingdom on a distinctive course. This book explores this experiment from a variety of perspectives, focusing on

---

[10] These are the subject of Lane, *Colour of Paradise*.

[11] See David Wheat, 'The First Great Waves: African Provenance Zones for the Transatlantic Slave Trade to Cartagena de Indias, 1570–1640'. *Journal of African History* 52, no. 1 (2011): 1–22.

10   *Introduction*

how the Indigenous inhabitants of the region experienced, negotiated, and participated in these efforts. It shows how collaboration among Indigenous people, priests, administrators, and the Spanish laity, albeit uneven and asymmetrical, both consolidated and assured the very survival of the colonial project. As a result, the coming of Christianity to this region, and the coming of the New Kingdom of Granada, were complex, collective, and negotiated processes.

This book also advances several methodological arguments. The first concerns the use of sources. This is a region whose sixteenth- and seventeenth-century history is not as well documented as others in Spanish America. It lacks the vast Indigenous-language archives of regions of Mesoamerica, and a few petitions aside – crucial and revealing though these certainly are – there is no surviving body of Indigenous writing in Spanish of the sort that scholars of the Central Andes and other regions have studied so fruitfully. Even more mundane colonial records are comparatively scarce for a number of reasons, including the relative inefficacy of the institutions of its colonial administration, which this book explores; the destruction by fire of significant portions of what was by then the viceregal palace of Santafé in 1785 and with them large sections of the *Audiencia*'s archive; and the unavailability to researchers – and possible loss – of key ecclesiastical archives, such as those of the now Archdiocese of Bogotá.[12] One genre of documentation central to this book, visitations, provides a good illustration. For a start, it is clear that these were never carried out as often or as thoroughly as they were supposed to be. Most of the records of those that were completed by the civil authorities – as far as we can tell from summaries and excerpts sent to Spain or held in other archives – have been lost, leaving just a fraction. And an entire body of sources, the records of ecclesiastical visitations, with the exception of the handful considered in this book, have never been available to researchers. Like historians everywhere, we know that there are questions that we simply cannot answer with the sources available to us, but in the context of the New Kingdom – whose history and historiography developed in the shadow of better documented regions – this limit has overdetermined what and how we can know.

---

[12] On the destruction of the viceregal palace, Robert Ojeda Pérez, Adriana Castellanos Alfonso, and Sebastián Torres. 'Incendio del palacio virreinal en Santafé: Resonancia histórica y patrimonial'. *Módulo Arquitectura CUC* 12 (2013): 163–181. To this we might add the loss of additional materials held in other collections in central Bogotá on 9 April 1948 and the days that followed.

Introduction

We also need to tread carefully in using a significant set of the sources we do have: the works of colonial chroniclers and other such authors. Historians of the New Kingdom do not have a convincing answer to how to read these sources judiciously, with the appropriate criticism, carefully, or however else different scholars, who recognise some or most of their limitations, have proposed. This book shows how this register of colonial writing developed for the consumption of foreign audiences for a broad range of purposes, including immediate personal gain, spiritual edification and promotion, even the advancement of what, in a different period, might be described as 'patriotic' projects, and many more besides. In doing so, these authors appropriated the histories, languages, and other features of Indigenous peoples, erasing or overlooking their specificity and diversity, and repackaged them according to foreign models and expectations in pursuit of their objectives. As Chapters 1 and 2 explore, their descriptions of Indigenous peoples and their politics, social structures, ritual practices and ideas, and cultural features before the European invasion and in the early years that followed are deeply problematic, and have had a profoundly distorting effect. The same is also the case with the early history of Spanish colonial rule and missionary activity, which underwent a similar refashioning in the minds and pens of successive colonial authors for similar reasons. As a result, in this book, I treat these texts – in common with all other sources – as reflective of the historical present in which they were written, and not as privileged insights into a pre-Hispanic or early colonial past.

In response to the difficulty and paucity of sources, I have tried to be as exhaustive as possible with what does exist. The chapters that follow are the result of my reading of many hundreds of individual items held in archives and libraries in Colombia, Spain, Rome, the United Kingdom, and the United States. These range from scores of letters, reports, petitions, and rescripts, to dozens of extensive files, such as visitation reports, each comprised of multiple witness interviews, descriptions, charges, appeals, sentences, and supporting information. Out of the same concern I have sought to understand, and to explain, how it was that these materials came to be. My contention is that only by understanding the shape of the archive can we really understand the mechanics of colonisation and Christianisation. For this reason, in this book, I reflect on the workings of petitions, rescript, royal and local legislation, synods and provincial councils, civil and pastoral visitations, resettlement, land and *encomienda* titling, tribute collection and taxation, *corregidores* and other local officials, the creation and staffing of parishes, Indigenous political and social structures, and all the other elements of the normative ordering and reordering of the kingdom studied in the pages that follow. Reading across these diverse archival objects has necessitated a fuller and deeper reckoning with the internal instability, contingency, and anxiety at the heart of the creation of the New Kingdom of Granada and its missionary project. These anxieties are all too easily ignored if we assume an already complete, singular, uniform, colonial state that simply unfolds from 1538 until it begins to come undone in the late eighteenth century. Only by unpacking and narrating the granular, quotidian, and ever-shifting experience of colonial rule can we understand the coming of the New Kingdom of Granada and processes like it. A granular approach must be a methodological imperative in these archives and others like them.

These arguments unfold over six chapters, arranged into two chronological parts. The first three chapters focus on the sixteenth century, from the establishment of the Spanish cities of Santafé and Tunja in the 1530s and the arrival, in the 1550s, of the principal institutions of colonial government – the *Audiencia* and the secular church – through to the long period of *sede vacante* that followed the death of the New Kingdom's first reforming archbishop, fray Luis Zapata de Cárdenas, in 1590. This section has a double focus. The first is unpacking the misunderstandings and mischaracterisations about Indigenous people, and particularly their religious practices, that have had a long hold on scholarship, and which have their roots in colonial visions and assumptions. The second is the distance between the claims and aspirations – the fictions – of colonial officials and other observers about the state and development of the kingdom and reality on the ground, a distance that colonial authorities ignored at their peril.

The first chapter explores the contours of the religious practices of the Muisca in the early decades after the European invasion. To do so unravels a series of overlapping fictions, stereotypes, and assumptions about the functioning of 'religion', social organisation, and political economy among these groups. Even as recent scholars have debunked the traditional portrayal of the Muisca as a relatively homogenous and centralised Indigenous 'nation' governed by a handful of despotic leaders, much of the historiography continues to take for granted that these people constituted a pagan laity led in the worship of a transcendental religion by a hierarchy of priests who performed sacrifices in temples. This chapter reveals these long-held narratives as fictions originating in the earliest descriptions of the region, later embellished and developed by seventeenth-century chroniclers for multiple reasons. Instead, drawing on the latest work on the Muisca, key recent contributions on the anthropology and sociology of religion, and a large corpus of colonial observations, it reassesses what we know about Indigenous peoples in this region. The picture that emerges is of highly localised immanentist religious practices, centred on the maintenance of lineage deities that Spaniards called *santuarios* and a sophisticated ritual economy of reciprocal exchange, that were intimately connected to the workings of political power and economic production.

Chapter 2 explores the early history of colonial rule in the New Kingdom of Granada, and of the priests and officials first tasked with introducing Christianity to the Indigenous peoples of the region. This too involves unravelling a series of powerful assumptions and stereotypes entrenched in the historiography that insist on the dominance and efficacy colonial officials and institutions. Instead, by carefully examining the workings and limitations of the procedures and praxis of early modern Spanish colonial governance, and by drawing on a broad range of often-overlooked sources, this chapter shows that the ability of colonial officials, missionaries, and institutions on both sides of the Atlantic to effect change on the ground remained fleeting, contingent, and inconstant. To do so, the chapter explores the participatory nature of the royal administration and judiciary, both at an imperial and a local level, and its reliance on petitioners, supplicants and rescript; reassesses the role of the legislative projects of local officials, whose efficacy is so often taken for granted; and tests the real impact of these institutions and their claims on the lives of Indigenous people through a careful re-reading of all surviving records of early visitations, showing that for decades royal control remained an illusion and that in practice power remained far from the hands of its officials in the New Kingdom, and instead rested, ultimately, on the all too fragile foundations of the authority of Indigenous rulers.

Far from the established story of a gradual and triumphant consolidation of colonial institutions by the final decades of the sixteenth century, Chapter 3 shows that this was instead a period of deep, overlapping, and abiding crisis for the New Kingdom as a result of the limitations and failures of colonial governance. At its core was the unravelling of the authority of Indigenous rulers, who found themselves pulled in two unreconcilable directions. They remained reliant on maintaining the Indigenous ritual economy that sustained their authority, at the same time as they were pressured to participate in its dismantling. This is because colonial authorities understood and interpreted Indigenous politics by drawing on European concepts, particularly natural law, and thus felt free to try to conscript and transform Indigenous rulers into intermediaries for

14   *Introduction*

governing, taxing, and Christianising the people that they ruled. Engrossed
in increasing competition over the leadership of the colonial project, the
second archbishop of Santafé, Luis Zapata de Cárdenas, and his civil
counterparts tried to pursue increasingly belligerent policies to reform the
lives of Indigenous people in the final decades of the century. Their rivalries,
venality, and misunderstanding of local conditions and of the limitations of
their own power spilled out of the realm of correspondence and unleashed
a brutal campaign of violence and dispossession on Indigenous communities in the late 1570s, with harrowing results. The blow they struck to
Indigenous political structures, and through them to the colonial tributary
and extractive economy, brought the kingdom to its knees.

The second half of the book focuses on the seventeenth century, when a
dramatic ideological change transformed the priorities and methods of
the missionary project. Chapter 4 focuses on this pivotal moment, when
religious policy in the kingdom came to be in the hands of a determined
new *Audiencia* president, Juan de Borja y Armendía, and an ambitious
archbishop, Bartolomé Lobo Guerrero. With the support of an influential
group of Jesuits effectively exiled from the Central Andes, headed by
Diego de Torres Bollo and Martín de Funes, and the backing of a broad
coalition of the kingdom's *encomenderos*, these authorities took
Christianisation in a different direction. Better known as an advocate of
a forceful approach to evangelisation, as one of the architects of the first
systematic campaigns of extirpation of Indigenous 'idolatry' of the
Archdiocese of Lima, Lobo Guerrero's earlier career in New Granada
was in fact marked by an entirely different approach. Here, he and his
allies moved decidedly away from the failed punitive policies of their
predecessors, and instead promoted the regular and frequent participation in a range of quotidian Catholic practices and institutions that had
generally been discouraged or withheld from Indigenous people, particularly popular celebrations, confraternities, and public ceremony. This
began in a handful of parishes entrusted to these Jesuit reformers, who
had a very particular understanding of the role of 'external' manifestations of piety, and who used these sites as testing grounds for new
approaches to Christianisation. These ultimately had the effect of
affording Indigenous people space and opportunities to engage with
Christianity in new – if, for the reformers, not always desirable – ways,
laying the foundations for the reformation of the kingdom.

Chapter 5 focuses on the history of language policy and the treatment
of Indigenous languages. In addition to refocusing Christianisation on to
everyday practice, the reformers of the early seventeenth century laid to

Introduction

rest a long-running dispute among missionaries and administrators in the region concerning the role that Indigenous languages should play in religious instruction. In the sixteenth century, the Spanish crown had twice sought to impose a universal solution to the challenges posed by linguistic heterogeneity across its American territories, based on the petitions and feedback of actors in the two viceregal centres: first to suppress Indigenous languages and teach Castilian, and later to focus on the 'general language' of each region, such as Quechua in Peru and Nahuatl in Central Mexico. These imperial ambitions were defeated in the New Kingdom, where the linguistic landscape even among Muisca groups was overwhelmingly heterogeneous, and where the power of the crown and its officials was limited and fleeting. Nevertheless, the authorities of the *Audiencia* and secular church, eager to employ the disciplinary mechanisms of the imperial language legislation for their own purposes, created and maintained the fiction that a single Muisca language existed and could be used for religious instruction. By the end of the century, this manoeuvring had resulted in the emergence and entrenchment of a bitter opposition to the use of Indigenous languages in Christianisation. A key contribution of the seventeenth-century reformers, therefore, was to overcome this division and establish a consensus around Indigenous language instruction. How they did so, in practice, had the opposite effect to what royal legislation had intended – serving to reinforce, and not overcome, linguistic heterogeneity – but still contributed to bring Christianity to the diverse multilingual environments that were the parishes of the New Kingdom.

These parishes are crucial sites to understand the transformation of religious life on the ground in the first half of the seventeenth century. Chapter 6 traces how, in the aftermath of these reforms, the Neogranadian church, at the parish level, became an Indigenous and grassroots organisation. One aspect of this transformation was institutional, as it came to be better staffed, organised, and equipped. Another was ideological, as the lessons of the Jesuit experiments with missionary methods were extended across the archdiocese, centring everyday practice, popular devotion, and social institutions. But the most significant aspect was led by Indigenous people themselves, as the shift away from punitive policies and towards a more inclusive Christianisation, coupled with the implementation of a more effective language policy, created space and opportunities for people in rural parishes to interact with Christianity in new ways. Many Indigenous authorities who survived the crises of the sixteenth century, like don Pedro Tabaco, found in participation in religious confraternities and in the sponsorship of

Christian art, artefacts, and public celebrations new ways to maintain their positions of leadership and to offer support to their subjects. In other communities, where traditional hierarchies had collapsed, these same mechanisms allowed commoners to step in when new leadership was most needed. Through a meticulous analysis of surviving civil and ecclesiastical visitation records, and the information they provide about the financing and provision of parish churches, the chapter shows how the voluntary fees, donations, and alms paid by Indigenous people engaged in these voluntary activities came to constitute a large part of the funding of parishes and their priests, fundamentally altering the relationship between the church, at a local level, and its Indigenous stakeholders. This went much further than the authorities had intended, as they learned when they sought to rein in and control the activities of confraternities, only to discover that these changes had long since outrun them.

Together, these chapters address a number of historiographical trends. The first is the position that religious questions have occupied in the historiography of the New Kingdom of Granada. Reflecting on the historiography of the church and religion in Spanish America, and especially Guatemala, Adriaan van Oss concluded that the perspective of most scholarship 'has served to isolate the Church from the historiographic mainstream', and called for 'a more holistic view of Catholicism in colonial society'.[13] The intervening years since his 1986 observation have indeed seen the publication of important studies that have transformed our understanding of the role of religion in colonial Latin America, and, within this, the role of religion in the consolidation and maintenance of colonial rule. This has not, however, been the case in the historiography of the New Kingdom of Granada. Generations of historians of the church of this region largely wrote it into a historiographic cul-de-sac, where it remained for decades.[14]

The authors of the earliest histories of the New Kingdom of Granada were concerned with presenting the church and religion as the antithesis

---

[13] Adriaan C. van Oss, *Catholic Colonialism: A Parish History of Guatemala, 1524–1821* (Cambridge: Cambridge University Press, 1986), xiv.

[14] A relatively recent survey of the historiography of New Granada is further testimony to this neglect. Published in the 1990s and reflecting on the major trends that had marked the historiography of the colonial period over the previous century and a half, it devoted a total of two paragraphs in its 114 pages to the historiography of the church and religion. Bernardo Tovar Zambrano, 'La historiografía colonial'. In *La historia al final del milenio: ensayos de historiografía colombiana y latinoamericana* (Bogotá: Editorial Universidad Nacional, 1994), 42–43.

Introduction

of a colonial state, as the moderator of the evils of the crown and its agents, the rival of the conquerors, and the defender of Indigenous people. In these depictions, the church was not – or, at most, was only reluctantly – an arm of Spanish power, a key ingredient in colonialism, or an agent of the transformation of the Indigenous peoples of the New World into Christian subjects of the Spanish monarchy. This perspective emerged in nineteenth-century efforts to reposition the Catholic Church in the new Colombian republic by distancing it from the colonial past, as in the work of José Manuel Groot, but has had a long legacy: not only among the multitude of later studies that perpetuated the image of the church as the counterweight to the excesses of the colonial regime, without problematising what was in fact a much more complex history, but also the works that took the diametrically opposite perspective, with equally unhelpful results.[15]

These trends contributed to isolate this field from the historiographical mainstream. For example, when the first generation of university-trained professional historians began to emerge in Colombia in the mid-twentieth century, they left religious issues aside almost completely. Even social histories that explored the origins of the social and racial divisions of Colombian society and of economic inequality, including those that examined the treatment of Indigenous people, treated the church largely from an economic perspective, as a landowner and landlord. When in 1978 Jaime Jaramillo Uribe edited the *Manual de Historia de Colombia*, a three-volume work meant to bring together the work of this first cohort, it lacked a single chapter devoted to religious issues.[16] There were, of course, some exceptions to this general trend, such as the pioneering work of Juan Friede, and the tide has begun to turn in recent years with exciting new works, cited in the pages that follow, nourished by the work of scholars of Spanish America and beyond.

Against the disinterest of historians of the New Kingdom of Granada in religious issues, this book argues that it is not just anachronistic but impossible to separate ecclesiastical and civil affairs – or, worse still, a colonial church and a colonial state. We cannot make sense of the

---

[15] For a striking statement of Groot's perspective on these issues see *Historia eclesiástica y civil de Nueva Granada* (Bogotá: Ministerio de Educación Nacional, Ediciones de la Revista Bolívar, 1953), xi.

[16] The closest was a chapter in volume 2, devoted to the nineteenth century, by Fernando Díaz Díaz devoted to the expropriation of church property by the new republican regime. Jaime Jaramillo Uribe, *Manual de historia de Colombia* (Bogotá: Instituto Colombiano de Cultura, 1976).

development and consolidation of the New Kingdom of Granada without centring Christianisation, and the relentless challenges it posed, as a generative site of contention and negotiation integral to the coming of the kingdom. Equally, the concern here is not the success or failure of a missionary project. I do not read the stories of successive archbishops of Santafé, Jesuit reformers, or myriad lesser-known actors to assess their success or failure in conversion, a process whose core definitions, goal-posts, and priorities were in any case never fixed. I read them instead to trace their role in shaping conditions that made it possible for Indigenous people to engage with Christianity, even within deeply unequal circumstances ultimately rooted in coercion.

Studies of religious change and of the imposition of colonial rule in Latin America, with a few exceptions, have tended to focus on imperial centres, or on a handful of other regions that for different reasons received significant attention from colonial authorities. These were sites where Spanish institutions were better staffed, had greater resources, and where – to different degrees – they were better able to realise their claims and designs. Most of colonial Latin America and the Philippines, however, looked a great deal more like the provinces of Santafé and Tunja than Mexico City and Lima: little places, with small Spanish populations, few resources, weak institutions, patchy governance, and perpetual crisis, reliant on creative solutions by local actors and the participation of broad groups to function. The story of the coming of the New Kingdom of Granada, in other words, resonates with those other peripheral spaces, and contributes to the work of provincialising imperial centres. In the same vein, if we are truly to decentre the Catholic Reformation – as recent scholars have urged – then we not only need to look at contexts beyond Europe, but also shift the object of our study: to see that the story of the people of places like Cómbita can shed valuable light on what it was to be an early modern Catholic. The portraits of don Pedro Tabaco and his family, looking out to us from Figueroa's striking canvas, invite us into a process and a history that was diverse, uneven, adaptive, and global.

I

The Muisca and the Problem of Religion

The earliest accounts of Spanish encounters with the Indigenous inhabitants of the highlands recorded some extraordinary rumours. Conquistadors and early observers wrote that the plateaux and high valleys of the eastern range of the Northern Andes were inhabited by a people called the Muisca, ruled by powerful lords who sponsored lavish religious practices. There was talk of a great house 'dedicated to the sun', where 'certain sacrifices and ceremonies' took place, full of 'an infinity of gold and stones'.[1] There were 'temples in each town', chapels in 'mountains, paths, and diverse parts', an impressive infrastructure of causeways and avenues, and a range of sacred 'forests and lakes consecrated to their false religion', sites of a variety of nefarious practices, including 'sacrifices' of blood and children. That every individual, 'poor as they might be', possessed 'one or two or three or more idols' – some, elaborate gold figures, others humbler wooden objects – which they carried with them at all times, even into battle. Although it was largely unknown to whom these buildings and sites were dedicated, or what purpose the rituals and paraphernalia served, one thing was certain: Early observers agreed that religion played a crucial role in the lives of these people. The Muisca appeared to be, in the words of one, 'in their erroneous manner,

---

[1] This according to the earliest surviving account of the first Spanish expedition to the region: Juan de San Martín and Antonio de Lebrija, 'Relación del Nuevo Reyno: Carta y relación para su magestad que escriben los oficiales de v(uest)ra m(ages)t(ad) de la provincia de Santa Marta [1539]'. In *Relaciones y visitas a los Andes, s. XVI. Vol. III: Región Centro-Oriental.* Edited by Hermes Tovar Pinzón (Bogotá: Colcultura, Instituto de Cultura Hispánica, 1993), 108–109.

20   *The Muisca and the Problem of Religion*

extremely religious'.[2] That the authors of these early sources made this claim is easily explained: It was a common trope among Spanish observers of Indigenous societies around the New World and Southeast Asia keen to highlight their potential to embrace Christianity while underscoring the need for colonial rule and evangelisation.[3] Making sense of what they observed is another matter.

This chapter explores some of the contours of the religious practices of the peoples who came to be known as the Muisca in the early decades after the European invasion. This is not a straightforward task: It involves unpicking a series of powerful stereotypes, assumptions, and elaborations – fictions, some more rooted in reality than others – that emerged and became entrenched over the course of the colonial period in two distinct but interconnected registers of writing about the New Kingdom of Granada and its Indigenous inhabitants. The first is the influential corpus of materials produced largely for foreign audiences that comprised early descriptions, chronicles and works of history, important civil and ecclesiastical legislation, and key linguistic works; the second, the corpus of bureaucratic writing produced by local observers, priests, and bureaucrats in the service of colonial institutions. More subtly, exploring these practices also requires us to unpick some of our own assumptions about the functioning of religious traditions, economic production, social organisation, and political power among Indigenous peoples.

The picture that emerges is one of complex ritual practices deeply embedded in local contexts, where they performed crucial roles in the functioning of key aspects of everyday life for Muisca individuals and communities. This is a far cry from the visions of Muisca 'religion' in colonial texts and much of the historiography, and it is key to exploring how these groups would interact with the developing colonial church and its programme of evangelisation in the decades to come. To make sense of it, we need to start at the root of these misunderstandings.

---

[2] According to the anonymous 'Epítome de la conquista del Nuebo Reino de Gra(na)da [ca. 1544]'. In Tovar Pinzón, *Relaciones y visitas*, 138.

[3] Harking back to the Augustinian and Thomist idea that all men are implanted with a natural inclination to seek God, a key theme in the writings of Las Casas. See Pierre Duviols, *La lutte contre les religions autochtones dans le Pérou colonial; 'l'extirpation de l'idolâtrie' entre 1532 et 1660* (Lima: Institut français d'études andines, 1971), 21–22, and D. A. Brading, *The First America: The Spanish Monarchy, Creole Patriots, and the Liberal State, 1492–1867* (Cambridge: Cambridge University Press, 1991), 90–91.

OVERLAPPING FICTIONS

Few early accounts of the European exploration and conquest of the region that became the New Kingdom of Granada have survived, and none were ever produced of the volume and scale of those from Mexico and Peru. Europeans had been active in the Caribbean coast of the region from the turn of the sixteenth century, but it was not until the late 1530s that they set about exploring the interior. The catalyst was news of the invasion of Peru, which prompted three expeditions – from Santa Marta in the north, Venezuela in the east, and Popayán in the south-west – that sought an overland connection from the Central Andes to the Caribbean. The first of these was an expedition south along the Magdalena River led by Gonzalo Jiménez de Quesada, which set off in April 1536, climbed the Eastern *Cordillera* and first encountered the Indigenous groups that inhabited its highlands, and culminated in the foundation of Santafé de Bogotá in August 1538.

There are only two known accounts by people involved in this expedition: One by Jiménez de Quesada and another by two of his men. The first is now lost, but was used in the sixteenth century by a number of authors as the basis for their own retelling of these events. The second, known as the 'Relación del Nuevo Reino', was a letter written by Juan de San Martín and Antonio de Lebrija from Cartagena in 1539, while they waited to return to Spain. The following decade two additional texts of disputed authorship appeared that narrated the Jiménez de Quesada expedition and described the inhabitants of the highlands. The first, which seems to have been composed between 1545 and 1550, is known as the 'Relación de la conquista de Santa Marta y Nuevo Reino de Granada' and may have also been written by one of Jiménez de Quesada's men. The second is the more famous 'Epítome de la conquista del Nuevo Reino de Granada', the authorship of which remains the subject of debate.[4]

These first Europeans who arrived in the high valleys and plateaux of the Eastern *Cordillera* encountered a variety of agricultural societies, inhabiting a multitude of settlements of various sizes, and organised in different political configurations. As in other regions of the Andes, their basic units were matrilineal kinship groups – each with its own languages,

---

[4] Critical editions of these three texts can be found in Tovar Pinzón, *Relaciones y visitas*, 93–143. For an English-language introduction to this history and these early texts, with translations of important passages, see Francis, *Invading Colombia*.

resources, deities, and leaders – which had come together with others to form composite political units of different sizes, but without this resulting in the political unification of the region. Some of these composite groups were large and their leaders rich and powerful, such as Bogotá, whose name came to be given to the largest of these highland valleys, while others were more modest and their rulers less distinguished. This diversity and lack of centralisation surprised and disappointed the invaders, whose ambition was to find societies similar to those of Central Mexico and Peru, and who had great difficulty in understanding and explaining what they encountered on the basis of those models and expectations. One aspect that was particularly challenging was the religious landscape, as is clear from their earliest descriptions of these groups, which are full of rumours of rich temples full of gold and precious stones, run by a hierarchy of priests who performed frightening rituals.[5]

The authors of these early accounts, like their contemporaries in other regions of Spanish America and South-east Asia, relied on categories and frames of reference derived from their European past and present to understand and describe what they observed. This is one reason why they identified Indigenous leaders with European princes and assumed that religious practices were performed by priests and directed to transcendental deities. However, they were also invested in presenting the disparate groups they encountered as a coherent and unified people, following the model of the Inca and Mexica, whose encounter by Europeans a few years earlier had motivated these expeditions. In fact, accounts of the expeditions of Hernán Cortés and Francisco Pizarro, and of the Indigenous societies they encountered, served not just as inspiration but even as practical models or scripts to imitate.[6] It is not surprising that their accounts, written in the model of the accounts of the expeditions of their more distinguished contemporaries, emphasised the prowess and bravery of the small band under Jiménez de Quesada and the power and sophistication of the enemy they faced.[7] Would-be conquering heroes, after all, needed fitting opponents, and to justify their actions, their struggle needed a moral and legal cause. It was for this reason that these early accounts

---

[5] San Martín and Lebrija, 'Relación del Nuevo Reyno', 108–109.

[6] On this 'scripted conquest', see Santiago Muñoz Arbeláez, 'The New Kingdom of Granada: The Making and Unmaking of Spain's Atlantic Empire, 1530–1620'. PhD dissertation, Yale University, 2018, 31.

[7] This vision of expeditions of 'a handful of adventurers' succeeding against all odds had already become a standard trope, as is well known. See Matthew Restall, *Seven Myths of the Spanish Conquest* (Oxford: Oxford University Press, 2004), 1–26.

Overlapping Fictions

also sought to cast Indigenous leaders as despots, drawing on established European discourses of good government, and contrasting the virtuous, Christian rule of the Spanish monarchy with the excesses of Indigenous tyrants.[8]

With time, these images developed in scope and ambition, as successive authors in New Granada writing primarily for foreign audiences, occasionally in collaboration with Indigenous elites, sought to render the pre-Hispanic societies of the region all the more impressive, in a bid to highlight the prestige of their homeland or in pursuit of other objectives.[9] By the late seventeenth century, these authors had produced richly detailed accounts of an imagined history of the Muisca before the arrival of Spaniards, complete with detailed descriptions of powerful centralised political structures culminating in two great kings – the Zipa of Santafé and the Zaque of Tunja – and a common, unified transcendental religion run by a hierarchy of priests. Lucas Fernández de Piedrahita's 1688 *Historia general* of New Granada – in many ways the colonial culmination of this register of writing – was thus full of confident assertions concerning a Muisca 'religion' with a pantheon of deities, creation stories, and visions of the afterlife, led from great temples by high priests – some of whom were pictured, at great expense, in three richly illustrated title pages that accompanied his book (e.g. Figure 1.1).[10]

The story of the Muisca has been one that has grown in the telling and retelling, and the stereotypes and images that came to characterise this register of writing have not been easy to dispel. Part of their enduring power is that they continue to be key to the way we Colombians have imagined the roots of our nation since independence. Since the early nineteenth century, generations of writers and scholars continued to

---

[8] Drawing on classical ideas of government as interpreted and developed in the works of Augustine and Thomas Aquinas. On this phenomenon in general, and especially in the case of the 1582 chronicle of Pedro de Aguado, see Jaime Humberto Borja Gómez, *Los indios medievales de fray Pedro de Aguado: construcción del idólatra y escritura de la historia en una crónica del siglo XVI* (Bogotá: Centro Editorial Javeriano, 2002), 118–128. It was, of course, hardly unique to accounts of New Granada.

[9] For example, Juan Rodríguez Freyle (c. 1566–1642), whose chronicle of 1636–1638, *El carnero* (Caracas: Biblioteca Ayacucho, 1979) served as a platform for one of his informants, the then *cacique* of Guatavita, to aggrandise the history of his ancestors. See Jorge Augusto Gamboa, *El cacicazgo muisca en los años posteriores a la Conquista: del sihipkua al cacique colonial* (Bogotá: Instituto Colombiano de Antropología e Historia, 2010), 26–27.

[10] Its title pages were directly modelled on those of Antonio de Herrera y Tordesillas, *Historia general de los hechos de los castellanos en las islas i Tierra Firme del Mar Oceano* (Madrid: En la Emplenta Real, 1601).

FIGURE 1.1 Joseph Mulder, title page to Lucas Fernández de Piedrahita, *Historia general de las conqvistas del Nuevo Reyno de Granada, a la S.C.R.M. de D. Carlos Segvndo*. [Madrid & Antwerp]: Por Iuan Baptista Verdussen, 1688. Courtesy of the John Carter Brown Library

Overlapping Fictions

reproduce and further embellish the claims of these colonial texts in works of history, theatre, and art, as the Muisca above all other Indigenous groups became integral to the construction of the identity of the Colombian Republic.[11] Still today, images of the Muisca and their material culture appear everywhere from banknotes to public buildings, as we continue to appropriate the Muisca – in the words of Carl Langebaek – as 'the official "tribe" of the Colombian nation' and a sort of 'local version of the Aztecs and the Incas'.[12] In the process, the colonial circumstances of the production of these images and stereotypes have faded from view, and these elaborations have come to be taken as reliable reflections of the pre-Hispanic past, to the point of being used to inform not just historical research but even the analysis of archaeological and linguistic findings.

This has begun to change in recent years, but in piecemeal fashion. One important recent area of focus for historians has been the Spanish invasion itself, as recent works have questioned the traditional Eurocentric triumphalist story – found everywhere from the first accounts of the early expeditions, through seventeenth-century chronicles, to the nineteenth-century historical works that they inspired – of a small band of Spaniards, led by brave and pious leaders, overcoming overwhelming odds to 'conquer' the region in brief episodes of military conflict.[13] Another, as we will see shortly, is the notion of political centralisation among Muisca groups at the moment of contact. But the religious landscape described in this register of writing has received much less critical attention.[14]

[11] On this, see Carl Henrik Langebaek, *Los herederos del pasado: Indígenas y pensamiento criollo en Colombia y Venezuela* (Bogotá: Universidad de los Andes: Ediciones Uniandes, 2009), and Luis Fernando Restrepo, *El estado impostor: Apropiaciones literarias y culturales de la memoria de los muiscas y la América indígena* (Medellín: Editorial Universidad de Antioquia, 2013).

[12] Carl Henrik Langebaek, 'Buscando sacerdotes y encontrando chuques: De la organización religiosa muisca'. *Revista de Antropología y Arqueología* 6, no. 1 (1990): 81. See also Roberto Lleras Pérez, 'Los Muiscas en la literatura histórica y antropológica. ¿Quién interpreta a quién?' *Boletín de Historia y Antigüedades* 92, no. 829 (2005): 307–338, and Gamboa, *El cacicazgo*.

[13] Francis, *Invading Colombia*; Jorge Augusto Gamboa, *Los muiscas y su incorporación a la monarquía castellana en el siglo XVI: Nuevas lecturas desde la Nueva Historia de la Conquista* (Tunja: Universidad Pedagógica y Tecnológica de Colombia, 2016); Muñoz Arbeláez, 'The New Kingdom', pt. 1.

[14] As recently as 2004, for example, the anthropologist François Correa analysed 'Muisca religion' and its impact on politics based on a reading of Muisca mythology as produced in colonial chronicles, in *El sol del poder: Simbología y política entre los Muiscas del norte de los Andes* (Bogotá: Universidad Nacional de Colombia, Facultad de Ciencias Humanas, 2004).

26   *The Muisca and the Problem of Religion*

The influential, if increasingly fanciful, images of the Muisca and of the New Kingdom that can be found in this register of writing diverge from those of the second register that developed in the region over the colonial period: the internal documentation of the colonial bureaucracy. While the authors who wrote about the region and its supposed past for foreign audiences could ignore or gloss over local realities, those in charge of constructing colonial institutions and incorporating Indigenous people into colonial rule at a local level had no choice but to try to make sense of them, if only in order to overcome and take advantage of them. This began in earnest with the establishment of the kingdom's civil and ecclesiastical government, with the arrival of the *Audiencia* of Santafé in 1550 and of the first bishop in 1553, which are the focus of Chapter 2.[15] By the time Fernández de Piedrahita's *Historia general* was published in 1688, these local bureaucrats and missionaries had produced a large corpus of written sources that documented their continued interactions with Indigenous communities and individuals. These sources are no more objective than the writings of the chroniclers, but they do provide an alternative perspective from which to reassess a great many established ideas and stereotypes about Indigenous societies, and especially the Muisca, who, as the groups closest to the centres of Spanish settlement, received the greatest attention from colonial officials. The authors of this bureaucratic register of writing were no less reliant on imported categories and frames of reference than the chroniclers, and they too tended to assume, at least initially, that the Indigenous inhabitants of the highlands constituted a single 'people' or 'nation' with a common language, that Indigenous rulers worked in a manner comparable to European lords, and that Indigenous people constituted a pagan laity engaged in the worship of a demonic religion with temples, priests, and sacraments. In short, another fiction, perhaps less grandiose, but still far removed from local realities. Backed by the power of colonial institutions, and constituting the bulk of the colonial archive, this bureaucratic register constituted not only a privileged perspective on what it purported to describe but also in important ways a legal reality – what recent scholars of the New Kingdom of Granada have termed a *papereality* or a 'kingdom on paper', whose assumptions and explanatory power are all too easily taken for granted.[16]

---

[15] For a recent history of the *Audiencia*, see Fernando Mayorga García, *La Audiencia de Santafé en los siglos XVI y XVII*. 2nd edition (Bogotá: Imprenta Distrital, Secretaría General de la Alcaldía Mayor de Bogotá, 2013).

[16] The first term is used by Joanne Rappaport, following David Dery, to explore the way that colonial visitations do not just claim to represent what they record but themselves constitute a legal reality. See Joanne Rappaport, 'Letramiento y mestizaje en el Nuevo

Politics, Power, and Social Organisation

Despite these obstacles, recent scholarship on the Muisca from different disciplines has been scrutinising this second register of writing, alongside archaeological and linguistic findings, and offering new insights that allow us to explore the contours of Indigenous political and religious features at the time of first contact with Europeans and through the first decades of the colonial period. The result is a very different picture indeed: far from a unitary and homogenous society ruled by one or two great kings and with a centralised religion of priests and temples, the picture that emerges is a rich tapestry of enormous diversity and local specificity that deserves much greater attention.

POLITICS, POWER, AND SOCIAL ORGANISATION

The starkest change so far in our understanding of the Muisca has concerned their political organisation and the power of elites. Among the chroniclers, early reports of the wealth and power of two important Indigenous leaders soon gave rise to the notion that the Muisca had been consolidated into two large kingdoms, led by the rulers of Bogotá and Tunja. This idea, first advanced in the 1570s by the Franciscan chronicler Pedro de Aguado, would reach its most elaborate colonial formulation in the work of Fernández de Piedrahita a century later, whose history of the two kingdoms included details of dynastic conflict, warfare, and intrigue between these two rival states.[17] The model of political organisation that emerged in these works, of an extremely hierarchical and centralised society organised into just two large political units, was enthusiastically taken up by historians in the nineteenth century and long remained influential, even as it shed its more obviously early modern terminology and the Muisca 'kingdoms' of the Zipa and the Zaque became 'confederations'.[18]

Reino de Granada, siglos XVI y XVII'. *Diálogo andino* no. 46 (2015): 9–26, and David Dery, '"Papereality" and Learning in Bureaucratic Organizations'. *Administration & Society* 29, no. 6 (1998): 677–689'. Santiago Muñoz, for his part, explores how the production of bureaucratic writing played a central role in the creation of the New Kingdom of Granada, by serving to enact the designs, philosophical ideas, and religious policies of diverse colonial officials. See Muñoz Arbeláez, 'The New Kingdom', ch. 2.

[17] Pedro de Aguado, *Recopilación historial*. Edited by Juan Friede (Bogotá: Empresa Nacional de Publicaciones, 1956).

[18] See, for example, Juan A. Villamarín and Judith E. Villamarín, 'Chiefdoms: The Prevalence and Persistence of "Señoríos Naturales", 1400 to European Conquest'. In *The Cambridge History of the Native Peoples of the Americas. Vol. 3: South America, part 1*. Edited by Frank Salomon and Stuart B. Schwartz (Cambridge:

28   *The Muisca and the Problem of Religion*

This model of two states has long been criticised, first as historians identified a handful of other large Indigenous polities and more recently as the consensus has moved further away from ideas of centralised political organisation altogether. Indeed, the latest research across a variety of fields suggests that the Muisca at the time of contact with Spaniards were organised into a large number of political units of different configurations and sizes. As in other regions of the Andes, all political units were at their core composed of basic matrilineal kinship groups that came together with each other in different ways to form composite units, which often came together again to form larger units still.[19] Scholars since the 1970s have argued that the larger Muisca political units were essentially nested amalgamations of subunits down to the level of the household, but recent research, especially the work of Jorge Gamboa, has moved further in emphasising that these associations were far more flexible and loose than previously thought, and that the component units were largely economically autonomous and self-contained – a situation that made them especially adaptable to changing circumstances.[20]

Cambridge University Press, 1999), 584–586. Some early critics aside, this model of political organisation only began to come under sustained criticism from the 1970s, when other important polities began to come to light. One key work in this process was Manuel Lucena Salmoral, 'El indofeudalismo chibcha como explicación de la fácil conquista quesadista'. In *Estudios sobre política indigenista Española en América. Vol. 1*, 111–160 (Valladolid: Seminario de Historia de América, Universidad de Valladolid, 1975). For an outline of these developments, see Gamboa, *Los muiscas y su incorporación*, 35–55.

[19] This was proposed as early as in Guillermo Hernández Rodríguez's 1949 study of Muisca social organisation, *De los chibchas a la colonia y a la República; del clan a la encomienda y al latifundio en Colombia* (Bogotá: Universidad Nacional de Colombia, Sección de Extensión Cultural, 1949), 60. Some linguists have labelled each of these kinship groups a 'güe', from their analysis of colonial Muisca grammars and dictionaries, a word related to the concept of the household, but – as Chapter 5 argues – Muisca societies were far from linguistically homogenous, and colonial grammars and dictionaries only record the language spoken by communities near Santafé. See Hope Henderson and Nicholas Ostler, 'Muisca Settlement Organization and Chiefly Authority at Suta, Valle de Leyva, Colombia: A Critical Appraisal of Native Concepts of House for Studies of Complex Societies'. *Journal of Anthropological Archaeology* 24, no. 2 (2005): 148–178.

[20] For an early example of this interpretation of Muisca organisation, see Juan A. Villamarín and Judith E. Villamarín, 'Kinship and Inheritance among the Sabana de Bogotá Chibcha at the Time of Spanish Conquest'. *Ethnology* 14, no. 2 (1975): 174. An excellent example of the new emphasis on flexibility is the work of Jorge Gamboa, who draws on James Lockhart's model of 'cellular or modular' organisation of Nahua groups. See Gamboa, *El cacicazgo*, 55–67, cf. James Lockhart, *The Nahuas after the Conquest: A Social and Cultural History of the Indians of Central Mexico, Sixteenth through Eighteenth Centuries* (Stanford, CA: Stanford University Press, 1992), especially 438ff. Drawing on research on other Andean groups, and most immediately on

Politics, Power, and Social Organisation

As in so many other regions, the violence and disruption unleashed by the arrival of Europeans resulted in fundamental changes to the political landscape. The Spanish invasion of the Muisca territories, like those of other regions, was not a straightforward series of military engagements, but a gradual process that took shape over a prolonged period, made possible by the making and remaking of alliances with Indigenous groups. As a result of Spanish pressure, some of the larger conglomerations of Muisca political units – including Bogotá and Tunja, and many more – broke into their component parts in order to react efficiently to changing conditions.[21] Even what Spaniards saw as the most solid of political ties proved to be more flexible than they had anticipated. The ruler of Chía, for example, who had been observed to have an especially close relationship to his uncle Bogotá – as his subordinate and perhaps even designated successor – showed that he was willing to align himself with Spaniards against his superior when it suited his purposes.[22]

Indeed, recent work on the history of this early period has begun to focus on the structural features of Muisca hierarchies that explain their inability to resist the Spanish invasion as a concerted whole, and at the same time allowed individual Muisca groups to realign themselves to best adapt to the changes that it represented.[23] This situation raises interesting questions concerning the mechanics of the imposition of Spanish rule elsewhere in Spanish America, because New Granada once again does not fit the model of other regions. On one hand, there exists the notion that the more sophisticated political apparatuses of the Inca and the Mexica rendered Peru and Central Mexico easier to dominate, because by capturing the Tenochca Tlatoani or the Sapa Inca Spaniards could

---

anthropological research on the U'wa, some scholars have argued for a model of Muisca organisation along asymmetric symbolic halves (moieties), e.g. Roberto Lleras Pérez, 'Las estructuras de pensamiento dual en el ámbito de las sociedades indígenas de los andes orientales'. *Boletín del Museo del Oro* no. 40 (1996): 10ff; and Correa, *El sol del poder*, 63ff. For an outline, see Carl Henrik Langebaek, 'De las palabras, las cosas y los recuerdos: el Infiernito, la arqueología, los documentos y la etnología en el estudio de la sociedad muisca'. In *Contra la tiranía tipológica en arqueología: una visión desde Suramérica*. Edited by Cristóbal Gnecco, Axel E. Nielsen, and Carl Henrik Langebaek (Bogotá: Universidad de los Andes, Facultad de Ciencias Sociales-CESO, 2006), 225–228.

[21] For an overview of some of these processes, see Gamboa, *El cacicazgo*, 191–252 and 275ff.

[22] Their close relationship was noted in accounts as early as that of San Martín and Lebrija, who speculated about a succession arrangement. San Martín and Lebrija, 'Relación del Nuevo Reyno', 105. Later writers elaborated on this speculation.

[23] On these trends in New Granada, see Gamboa, *El cacicazgo*, 214ff.

30 *The Muisca and the Problem of Religion*

hijack the political systems that they dominated; and on the other, the idea that political fragmentation and a lack of centralisation among Indigenous groups, such as the Mapuche, rendered regions more difficult to subjugate.[24] Neither model applies here.

From 1539, the Spanish arrivals began to assemble the institutions of colonial civil and ecclesiastical government. At its root, as elsewhere, was the system of *encomiendas* – grants of the right to collect tribute from Indigenous communities – which were distributed to individual Spaniards. As in other regions, these grants took advantage of the existing social and political structures of Indigenous communities, so that Muisca groups were assigned to *encomenderos* as self-contained political and economic units, each headed by an Indigenous ruler. Because some groups were still much larger than others, as in other regions, this process also involved simplifying and homogenising the diverse political landscape, 'dismembering' – as contemporaries put it – the larger political units into more manageable pieces, and identifying the rulers of each one, who were to collect tribute from their subjects and pay it up the chain to their *encomenderos*.[25]

This started with the 105 *encomiendas* that Jiménez de Quesada granted his followers and collaborators shortly after the foundation of Santafé. By 1560, the records of the first visitation conducted by the *Audiencia* indicate that 171 *encomiendas* had been granted, composed of some 88,000 tribute-paying individuals and their families.[26] By the 1570s, by one estimate, all Muisca polities had been distributed to *encomenderos*. Initially, insurrections against the new *encomenderos* were common, but none surpassed the level of the purely local, of an alliance of two or three Indigenous leaders and their subjects, reflecting the political fragmentation of the region.[27] The effects of this reorganisation will be explored later in this book, but the point is that the basic building blocks of Muisca societies – the matrilineal kinship groups and the

---

[24] Still, these mainstays of the historiography continue to be questioned. See Restall, *Seven Myths of the Spanish Conquest*, 71ff; and Peter Bakewell, 'Conquest after the Conquest: The Rise of Spanish Domination in America'. In *Spain, Europe, and the Atlantic World: Essays in Honour of John H. Elliott.* Edited by Richard L. Kagan and Geoffrey Parker (Cambridge: Cambridge University Press, 1995), 296–315.

[25] On this process, see Santiago Muñoz Arbeláez, *Costumbres en disputa: los muiscas y el Imperio español en Ubaque, siglo XVI* (Bogotá: Universidad de los Andes, Facultad de Ciencias Sociales, Departamento de Historia, 2015), 30–53.

[26] This visitation, and these figures, are discussed in Chapter 2.

[27] Gamboa, *El cacicazgo*, 309, 287–288.

Politics, Power, and Social Organisation

composite units of different configurations that they had long come together to form – not only remained in place, but became the foundations of the colonial tributary system.

To write of 'kinship groups' and 'composite units' may seem inelegant, but we lack a better political vocabulary to describe these different structures before the European invasion.[28] Spaniards at the time were less concerned with documenting and understanding Indigenous political organisation than transforming it for their own purposes. In addition to dismembering the larger composite units into distributable parts, Spaniards sought to simplify the complex political structures of different groups into something more akin to what they were used to seeing in other regions. After the initial work of political dismemberment was complete, Spaniards mapped a two-tiered system of political organisation on to Indigenous communities, labelling those leaders who seemed to govern whole groups '*caciques*' and their polities '*cacicazgos*' – a political vocabulary they had obtained and brought with them from the Caribbean – and those who governed only subordinate units '*capitanes*', or captains, and their units '*capitanías*', '*parcialidades*' or simply '*partes*', parts. This Spanish system of Indigenous political organisation rode roughshod over what were undoubtedly more nuanced and varied relations, but it would do for their purposes.[29]

Positions of leadership and other responsibilities within the matrilineal kinship groups that made up Muisca societies were generally held by men but transmitted along matrilineal lines, usually from the incumbent to the eldest son of his eldest sister. At the same time, certain kinship groups played specific roles within the larger units of which they were

---

[28] Scholars have sought to recover Muisca terminology for different composite units since at least the 1960s, with one influential proposal labelling component parts 'uta' and composite units 'sybyn' – the former appearing in a handful of visitation records for some sites. Since this terminology continues to be unclear and its use by scholars has been variable, and in light of our growing appreciation of the linguistic diversity of these societies, this book avoids it. For an outline of this terminology, and some theories of what these terms might refer to, see Eduardo Londoño, 'El lugar de la religión en la organización social muisca'. *Boletín del Museo del Oro* no. 40 (1996): 63; Ana María Boada Rivas, 'Organización social y económica en la aldea muisca de El Venado (Valle de Samacá, Boyacá)'. *Revista Colombiana de Antropología* 35 (1999): 127–128; François Correa, 'Fundamentos de la organización social muisca'. In *Los chibchas: adaptación y diversidad en los Andes Orientales de Colombia*. Edited by José Vicente Rodríguez Cuenca (Bogotá: Universidad Nacional de Colombia, 2001), 26; and Langebaek, 'De las palabras', 225–226.

[29] For a compelling recent proposal of how some of these groups may have come together, see Gamboa, *El cacicazgo*, 55–67.

32 *The Muisca and the Problem of Religion*

part – including exercising leadership – so that specific positions in a composite group were transmitted within a specific component part.[30] This has long been known, but what has been much less clear is how Indigenous leaders maintained and exercised power over their communities and what their precise functions were, in large part owing to the distorting weight of imported stereotypes.

Early colonial sources wrote of the exaggerated reverence and shows of respect shown by the Muisca to their leaders, in part as an effort to portray many of them as tyrants in need of being deposed. The very earliest Spanish account of Muisca societies, by San Martín and Lebrija, told of how Muisca leaders were greatly revered, describing specifically how Bogotá was 'honoured excessively by his vassals, because, truth be told, in this New Kingdom the Indians are greatly subjected to their lords'.[31] In this and later texts no one doubted that Indigenous rulers exercised power in a manner comparable to European princes. Indeed, as Chapter 3 explores, in Spanish law, Indigenous leaders were understood to be natural lords, whose power was derived from natural law and ancient custom. By the late seventeenth century, Fernández de Piedrahita and his fellow authors were writing of great Muisca kings and despots, of electors in the manner of those of the Holy Roman Empire, and of dukes and nobles in the manner of European aristocrats, whose hereditary power over subordinate groups was taken for granted.[32] These accounts and legal frameworks created the impression these figures exercised power in a manner comparable to how European lords held power over their subjects: controlling land, labour, and exchange.[33]

Most recent research on the Muisca from across a range of fields has sought to reassess these ideas and better understand the foundations of the power of authorities. For example, archaeologists have, for some time, shown that political power among the Muisca was not based on direct control of fertile lands or labour, and that economic inequality between

---

[30] The succession pattern was identified as early as the 1940s, in Hernández Rodríguez, *De los chibchas a la colonia*, 60.

[31] San Martín and Lebrija, 'Relación del Nuevo Reyno', 98.

[32] Lucas Fernández de Piedrahita, *Historia general de las conquistas del nuevo reyno de Granada: A la S. C. R. M. de D. Carlos Segundo, Rey de las Españas, y de las Indias. Por el doctor d. Lvcas Fernandez Piedrahita, Chantre de la Iglesia Metropolitana de Santa Fé de Bogotá, Calificador del Santo Oficio por la Suprema y General Inquisición y Obispo electo de Santa Marta* (Madrid and Antwerp: Por Juan Baptista Verdussen, 1688), book 1.

[33] The catastrophic consequences of this misunderstanding are the subject of Chapter 3 of this book.

Politics, Power, and Social Organisation

elites and the rest of the population was limited.[34] They note, for example, that the Muisca region is conspicuous among other areas of what is now Colombia for its lack of lavish burial offerings that could distinguish elite burials from those of commoners.[35] Archaeologists have also found little evidence that elites could appropriate resources to the point of resulting in nutritional problems among the rest of the population in times of dearth, further questioning the notion that political power was based on economic disparities.[36] Indeed, most recent archaeological research coincides in highlighting that the basic units that composed Muisca polities were to a very great degree economically self-sufficient, and that the leaders of the larger political units that they formed had little direct control over production.[37]

---

[34] This is the conclusion of Carl Henrik Langebaek in *Regional Archaeology in the Muisca Territory: A Study of the Fúquene and Susa Valleys [Arqueología regional en el territorio muisca: estudio de los valles de Fúquene y Susa]* (Pittsburgh: University of Pittsburgh; Bogotá: Universidad de los Andes, 1995), and more recently 'Fiestas y caciques muiscas en el infiernito, Colombia: Un análisis de la relación entre festejos y organización política'. *Boletín de Arqueología* no. 9 (2005): 281–295. He discussed the methodology and assumptions of Colombian archaeologists in 'De las palabras'.

[35] Ana María Boada Rivas, *The Evolution of Social Hierarchy in a Muisca Chiefdom of the Northern Andes of Colombia [La evolución de jerarquía social en un cacicazgo muisca de los Andes septentrionales de Colombia]* (Pittsburgh: University of Pittsburgh, Department of Anthropology; Bogotá: Instituto Colombiano de Antropología e Historia, 2007), 11.

[36] This is from an analysis of the incidence of anaemia and hypoplasia (associated with malnutrition) in elite and non-elite remains. Carl Henrik Langebaek et al., 'Condiciones de vida y jerarquías sociales en el norte de Suramérica: El caso de la población muisca en Tibanica, Soacha.' *Indiana* no. 28 (2011): 15–34.

[37] Langebaek, 'Fiestas y caciques', 291–292, and Langebaek, 'Buscando sacerdotes'. On this phenomenon more broadly, Andrea M. Cuéllar, 'The Archaeology of Food and Social Inequality in the Andes'. *Journal of Archaeological Research* 21, no. 2 (2013): 123–174. There is, nevertheless, a contrary argument that seems increasingly untenable: that the basis of the power of Muisca leaders was related to control of access to productive lands, and that elites were able to institutionalise this control. This is the position, for example, of Ana María Boada in her study of the remains of a pre-Hispanic village in the valley of Samacá, on the basis of access to deer meat, 'Organización social y económica'. Based on related data, Michael H. Kruschek argued that some elite dwellings in the site of Funza controlled access to productive lands, in 'The Evolution of the Bogotá Chiefdom: A Household View' (PhD dissertation, University of Pittsburgh, 2003). Boada has also argued that Muisca elites gradually appropriated and monopolised communal infrastructure such as raised beds to the same effect. See Ana María Boada Rivas, *Patrones de asentamiento regional y sistemas de agricultura intensiva en Cota y Suba, Sabana de Bogotá (Colombia)* (Bogotá: Fundación de Investigaciones Arqueológicas Nacionales, Banco de la República, 2006), 167. For an outline of archaeological research on the Muisca, see Robert D. Drennan, 'Chiefdoms of Southwestern Colombia'. In *The Handbook of South American Archaeology*. Edited by Helaine Silverman and William Harris Isbell (New York: Springer, 2008), 392–396.

34   *The Muisca and the Problem of Religion*

It is difficult at first sight to understand the position of Indigenous authorities in their societies in light of this evidence, but as scholars have reassessed the relative importance of factors such as the control of land and labour in explaining the place and role of Indigenous authorities, other elements have become more prominent – especially those related to their ritual and religious practices. Indeed, the records of civil and ecclesiastical visitations and inquiries carried out among different Muisca groups over the course of the sixteenth century reveal how it was the sponsorship and administration of the sacred that was at the root not just of the position of authorities, but of the very functioning of economic production and exchange. To understand how, it is best to see it action.

The corpus of colonial sources that describe Indigenous religious practices is not vast or systematic. As we will see, changing attitudes among the civil and ecclesiastical authorities of New Granada concerning the most effective means of Christianisation in the seventeenth century meant that they launched few enquiries to investigate Indigenous religious practices, and certainly nothing as systematic as the punitive inquisitorial models that emerged in the centres of empire.[38] What they did produce, however, provides revealing glimpses of the existence of complex and multi-layered practices, firmly rooted in local communities and kinship groups.

RITUAL ECONOMY AND LEADERSHIP

On Christmas Eve 1563, news reached Santafé that a great ceremony was taking place in an Indigenous town some thirty miles to the south-east of the kingdom's capital.[39] Reports stated that large numbers of people had

---

[38] The documentation that emerged from the so-called extirpation of idolatry in the archdiocese of Lima is comparatively vast and has received a great deal of scholarly attention. So too in Central Mexico. This divergence will be discussed and contrasted in greater detail, but for a basic illustration of the magnitude of the documentation concerning accusations of idolatry in the dioceses of Mexico and Oaxaca in the colonial period, see David Eduardo Tavárez, *The Invisible War: Indigenous Devotions, Discipline, and Dissent in Colonial Mexico* (Stanford, CA: Stanford University Press, 2011), 18ff. For an outline of the investigative model that emerged in the archdiocese of Lima, drawing on an earlier inquisitorial model, see Duviols, *La lutte*, 211ff.

[39] The documentation of the resulting enquiry survives as AGI Justicia 618, fols. 1395r–1438v. These records were published as Clara Inés Casilimas Rojas and Eduardo Londoño, eds, 'El proceso contra el cacique de Ubaque en 1563'. *Boletín del Museo del Oro* no. 49 (2001): 49–101, and discussed in Clara Inés Casilimas Rojas, 'Juntas, borracheras y obsequias en el cercado de Ubaque'. *Boletín del Museo del Oro* no. 49 (2001): 13–48; and Eduardo Londoño, 'El proceso de Ubaque de 1563: La última ceremonia religiosa pública de los muiscas'. *Boletín del Museo del Oro* no. 49 (2001):

Ritual Economy and Leadership

been summoned by Ubaque – the ruler of the community and town of the same name – who had called together not only his subjects but also the leaders and representatives of multiple other groups from as far afield as the province of Tunja, and even some of the Indigenous inhabitants of the city of Santafé.[40] Even though the majority of Indigenous people involved were not Christians, the authorities were especially concerned about the deleterious effect that the celebrations would have on those who were.[41] There was talk of feasting, dancing, and processions for 'the cult and veneration of the devil' and even of ritual homicide, all on the capital's doorstep and – as the authorities repeatedly noted – at Christmas of all times, 'in mockery of the mysteries of our holy faith'.[42] The *Audiencia* took it upon itself to investigate, dispatching one of its members, the *oidor* Melchor Pérez de Arteaga, to the town.[43] That it was a civil authority and not an ecclesiastical one that was investigating these allegations is significant, as we will see, and a reminder that the authority and leadership of the church over the religious affairs of the kingdom would take years to be consolidated. The proceedings at Ubaque were to be the last large public religious celebration held openly by a Muisca group that was recorded by Spanish observers.

Pérez de Arteaga arrived in the town three days later to find that the celebrations were still ongoing. A great number of people were present, certainly hundreds and perhaps even thousands, including a number of Indigenous leaders, *caciques* and captains from around the region – from communities such as Suba, Tuna, Bogotá, Cajicá, and Fontibón, which we will be visiting later.[44] One Spanish official reported that there were as many as five or six thousand people present, while another explained that these barely amounted 'to a third of the Indians who were expected to come'.[45] Most of the people were 'singing and dancing with banners', processing in groups along a long causeway marked off in front of the *cacique*'s *cercado*, his residential compound, which had been decorated with feather standards. Each group carried 'banners before them and [were] dressed in different ways', some wearing masks and headdresses, 'playing flutes and conches and other instruments' and 'singing sorrowful

---

1–12. This episode has also been examined by Correa, *El sol del poder*, 104ff; Gamboa, *El cacicazgo*, 492–500; and most thoroughly Muñoz Arbeláez, *Costumbres*, chs 3 and 4.

[40] As Santiago Muñoz Arbeláez explains, the names of Indigenous leaders, 'in the native tradition, were complex concepts that described at once a territory, a political formation, and a person', in 'The New Kingdom', 62.

[41] Documents pertaining to the case of Ubaque, 1563, AGI Justicia 618, 1409r.

[42] Ibid., 1396r–1397r. [43] Ibid., 1397r. [44] Ibid., 1400r. [45] Ibid., 1400r–1403v.

36 *The Muisca and the Problem of Religion*

songs in a language that could not be understood'.[46] The groups of dancers were observed processing along the causeway and entering the *cacique*'s compound, where the celebrations continued, in particular the consumption of food and drink. Pérez de Arteaga called the *caciques* together and told them to stop, and persuaded them, 'with gentle words' to remain in the town and not to hide or dispose of the objects they were using, so that he could investigate. Or so he recorded in his account of the proceedings.[47]

The following day, when the celebrations finally stopped, Pérez de Arteaga was able to interrogate a number of Indigenous leaders and to confiscate a large number of masks, musical instruments, gold jewellery, and feather adornments. He later had a number of buildings that seemed to be integral to the celebrations destroyed, and took a number of *caciques* and other people with him to Santafé for further interrogation.[48] That he was able to do this is extraordinary given the vast disparity in numbers between those present and the *oidor* and his entourage, but it is not easily explained by the documentation itself, which takes the imposition and efficacy of Spanish power for granted. In addition to participants in the celebrations, Pérez de Arteaga also interrogated Spanish observers in Ubaque and, back in Santafé, a number of other Indigenous leaders who had apparently refused to attend despite being invited. The investigation continued into the early days of 1564, but was dropped after the continued detention of Indigenous rulers resulted in a strike among labourers working on the construction of the cathedral of Santafé, who refused to work whilst their leaders were detained. A few days later, bishop Juan de los Barrios persuaded the *Audiencia* to release the prisoners so construction could resume, and the records stop.[49]

The report of Pérez de Arteaga's investigation is an intriguing document, testimony to the attempts of Spanish authorities to understand what was taking place and the issues this involved, and to their efforts to make sense of the diverse perspectives of the people they interrogated. Part of the confusion arose from the fact that even though the authorities described the celebration as a single event, the celebrations actually comprised a variety of individual practices related to different aspects of the community's life, including several to do with the agricultural cycle and others with succession to the office of ruler and the preparation of the

---

[46] Ibid., 1400v.   [47] Ibid., 1401r.   [48] Ibid., 1425r–1425v.
[49] On 8 January 1564. Ibid., 1436r. It is unclear whether the case was simply closed. See also Gamboa, *El cacicazgo*, 493.

Ritual Economy and Leadership

next incumbent. Many of these elements would be documented in other sites around the region in greater detail over the following decades. For this reason, the events of Ubaque in 1563 provide an excellent starting point for examining some of the workings of a number of different practices.

A good place to start is the feasting and drinking that so concerned Spanish observers. The proceedings of Ubaque, in common with a broad range of Indigenous celebrations in New Granada and elsewhere, were described by Spanish authorities with the denigrating terminology of 'borrachera' or drunken revelry, as an expression of Indigenous intemperance and an affront to natural reason. This was a very old trope in Christian writing about non-Christians, present from early critiques of so-called pagans in the Mediterranean in late antiquity.[50] Augustine, for example, identified drunken excess as one of the hallmarks of the influence of false deities, denouncing drunkenness as means through which they induced their worshippers 'to become the worst of men'.[51] As with so much of the late-antique Christian repertory on paganism, drunkenness looms large in early modern characterisations of Indigenous people across the New World.[52] That it was a Spanish obsession, however, should not distract us from recognising the importance of the consumption of certain foods and drink in celebrations of this sort. These were much more significant than Spaniards realised, if for different reasons.

Pérez de Arteaga recorded seeing large numbers of gourds and other vessels of *chicha*, maize beer, provided by Ubaque to his guests, and the consumption of this beer was clearly central to the celebrations.[53] Indeed, Indigenous witnesses reported that this was one of the principal reasons

---

[50] See Sabine MacCormack, *Religion in the Andes: Vision and Imagination in Early Colonial Peru* (Princeton, NJ: Princeton University Press, 1991), 235. On the construction of the totalising categories of 'pagan' and 'paganism' in late antiquity, see Christopher P. Jones, *Between Pagan and Christian* (Cambridge, MA: Harvard University Press, 2014).

[51] Augustine, *The City of God against the Pagans*. Edited and translated by R. W. Dyson (Cambridge: Cambridge University Press, 1998), II.6, 56.

[52] This denigrating terminology is intimately connected with developing characterisations of Indigenous people as 'wretched' (*miserabilis*) and in need of special tutelage and supervision. This discourse, integral to the justification of colonial rule, will be scrutinised later. For now, see Juan Carlos Estenssoro Fuchs, 'El simio de Dios: Los indigenas y la Iglesia frente a la evangelización del Peru, siglos XVI–XVII'. *Bulletin de l'Institut Français d'Études Andines* 30, no. 3 (2001): 455–474. For an outline of discourses on drunkenness in the sixteenth century and beyond, see Rebecca Earle, 'Indians and Drunkenness in Spanish America'. *Past and Present* 222, suppl. 9 (2014): 81–99.

[53] Documents pertaining to the case of Ubaque, 1563, AGI Justicia 618, 1423r.

38 *The Muisca and the Problem of Religion*

they had come. Riguativa, a captain from the town of Fontibón, reported that he had been invited 'to celebrate and to drink', and explained flatly that 'this is why this witness had come to the town of Ubaque'. Others reported that Ubaque had promised them gifts as well. Xaguaza, the leader of Tuna, explained that Ubaque had 'said he would give [him] gold and *mantas*', blankets of cotton cloth.[54] But what was behind Ubaque's largesse?

Celebrations of this sort were not unusual. Indeed, Spanish witnesses reported having seen multiple celebrations in Ubaque alone. Nicolás Gutiérrez, who lived nearby, explained that he had seen 'three *borracheras* like this one now', even if none had been 'as solemn as this'.[55] Observers coincided in saying that what made this ceremony so striking was its scale. Even older Indigenous witnesses explained that they had never seen anything like it since the days of the old ruler of Bogotá, before the Spanish invasion.[56] This seems to have been deliberate. The statements of Spanish and Indigenous witnesses, and Pérez de Arteaga's record of the many distinguished Indigenous leaders who participated, make it clear that the celebration at Ubaque in 1563 was, on an important level, a bid for regional pre-eminence and a display of wealth before other regional leaders, including the successor to the now less prominent polity of Bogotá.[57] When questioned, Ubaque eventually explained that it had taken him six months of planning.[58] It was clearly an investment of significant labour and resources in a bid for regional pre-eminence. But how to pay for all of this?

The answer is that this was not a one-way exchange. When Ubaque was interrogated, he explained that he had also received gold and other gifts from the participants. 'Each *cacique* and captain who came', he explained, 'has given a piece of gold, some worth 10 pesos and some worth 5'.[59] When asked about this, some Indigenous witnesses confirmed they had brought gifts. Chasquechusa, described as a captain of Bogotá, reported having brought Ubaque two *mantas*.[60] This was not simply a display of generosity, but an occasion for exchange, and through this exchange for the making and remaking of political allegiances in a period of profound political change.

These gifts aside, it was clear even to Spaniards that it was the community of Ubaque that had provided the resources and labour for the celebration. News of the celebrations had reached Santafé through a

---

[54] Ibid., 1426v, 1417v.   [55] Ibid., 1407r.   [56] Ibid., 1431r.   [57] Ibid., 1400r.
[58] Ibid., 1415v.   [59] Ibid., 1416v.   [60] Ibid., 1434v.

Ritual Economy and Leadership 39

number of Dominican friars active in the area, including one Francisco Lorenzo, who testified before Pérez de Arteaga. His testimony is a litany of the regime's worst fears – ritual homicide, adultery, incest, the summoning of demons, and dancing – but it also expressed concern about the misuse of the community's resources by Ubaque. Lorenzo explained how these sorts of celebrations involved the collection of vast amounts of '*mantas*, gold, and maize', which, he speculated, probably placed an unsustainable financial burden on Ubaque's subjects and would doubtless cause them to flee the town to escape their ruler's unreasonable demands.[61] Viewed through the lens of European political categories, the celebration was understood by Spaniards to be an expression of excess and ill government by the ruler at the expense of his subjects. This perspective was clear in Pérez de Arteaga's questions to Spanish witnesses, which asked them specifically to comment on 'whether they know Ubaque to be evil and perverse and idolatrous'. As one apparently replied, 'these *borracheras* can only be at the expense of innocents'.[62]

Spaniards took for granted the power of Indigenous leaders to compel their communities to work and to provide them with resources. So ingrained was their understanding of Indigenous leaders as natural lords that they built the colonial tributary system on the assumption that these figures had the power to require their subjects to pay and to work. Lorenzo and other Spaniards gave little thought to how Ubaque had mobilised his subjects, and Pérez de Arteaga never thought to ask them. Instead, the proceedings only served to confirm their assumptions about the tyranny and despotism of Muisca leaders. What they failed to see was that the celebration itself was integral to Ubaque's ability to mobilise his community.

The timing of the celebration, which so offended the authorities, provides a clue. While news of the proceedings only reached Santafé on Christmas Eve, by the time Pérez de Arteaga arrived it was clear that it had been going on for several days. They had begun around the time of the winter solstice, 22 December 1563, which marked the beginning of the dry season, when work on raised beds and planting took place, before the rains resumed in March.[63] In fact, a crucial aspect of the proceedings involved preparation for the agricultural cycle ahead. Witnesses

---

[61] Ibid., 1402v. [62] Ibid., 1408r.

[63] François Correa and others have noted the importance of the agricultural cycle in explaining the timing of a number of Muisca celebrations. See Correa, *El sol del poder*, 118.

40   *The Muisca and the Problem of Religion*

interrogated at Ubaque mentioned that celebrations of this kind took place precisely for the preparation of fields, raised beds, and irrigation canals. Indeed, in his testimony, the Spaniard Nicolás Gutiérrez explained that although some ceremonies, in his view, were held 'to invoke demons and for idolatry', Indigenous leaders also held feasts for the community 'when they dig', preparing ditches and raised beds for planting. Gutiérrez remarked that although idolatrous practices should of course be banned, the latter should be allowed because these 'have no purpose other than eating and celebrating and working and no other thing'.[64]

Gutiérrez's observations are corroborated by a significant body of complaints by Indigenous leaders half a century later, when they turned to Spanish authorities to complain that their subjects had by then ceased to perform this essential labour. Significantly for them, this was not just how leaders had directed communal efforts, but how they had survived: it was in exchange for the provision of food, drink, and certain special products that their subjects had built and maintained their leaders' residential compounds, planted their food, and harvested their crops. This was made clear, for example, by don Pedro, the *cacique* of the town of Suba, who in 1605 explained to the authorities that Muisca *caciques* obtained labour and tribute from their subjects in exchange for their provision of banquets and celebrations.[65]

The practice of feasting has long been seen by archaeologists as an indicator of the emergence of elites.[66] In the case of the Muisca, archaeological research shows that feasting intensified in many regions during the Early Muisca period (800–1200 CE), as evidenced by the appearance, in ever growing numbers, of vessels for the preparation and consumption of *chicha* among archaeological findings.[67] But how this relates to political and economic centralisation has been a matter of debate. Some scholars have taken the growing prevalence of feasting as evidence that Muisca societies grew increasingly centralised and their elites better able to

---

[64] Documents pertaining to the case of Ubaque, 1563, AGI Justicia 618, 1407r.

[65] Unfortunately for don Pedro, his subjects were now refusing to uphold their end of the bargain. We will return to this case in Chapter 3, which examines the broader political and economic crisis of which it was a symptom. Suit of don Pedro, *cacique* of Suba, 1605. AGN, Misceláneo 137 d. 43, 330r–332v.

[66] See, for example, John E. Clark and Michael Blake, 'The Power of Prestige: Competitive Generosity and the Emergence of Rank Societies in Lowland Mesoamerica'. In *Factional Competition and Political Development in the New World*. Edited by Elizabeth M. Brumfiel and John W. Fox. New Directions in Archaeology (Cambridge: Cambridge University Press, 1994), 17–30.

[67] Langebaek, 'Fiestas y caciques', 282.

Ritual Economy and Leadership

exercise control over economic production, using their control over land and labour to produce the food and drink provided at these celebrations.[68] Indeed, some hold that feasting was a key mechanism through which these elites attained this economic centralisation.[69] But more recent analyses of archaeological evidence of feasting in pre-Hispanic Muisca societies suggests there was no positive correlation between evidence of feasting and control of land or labour, and that it could instead be related to a broader range of social processes – not least serving as occasions for Muisca leaders to justify their pre-eminent positions.[70]

Informed by work on Indigenous authorities elsewhere in the Andes, archaeologists have for some time been arguing that the principal role of Muisca leaders was redistribution. Far from controlling the means of production and appropriating surpluses for themselves, Muisca leaders received goods and services from their communities, and their neighbours, which they then returned to them through mechanisms of redistribution – in a way that is comparable, if smaller in scale, to what occurred in other Andean societies. In the late 1980s, for example, Langebaek argued that Indigenous leaders were 'specialists in the storage and distribution of communal surpluses' to satisfy collective needs, and valuable intermediaries performing essential functions.[71] These 'collective needs' could be broad, and also included the organisation and direction of communal efforts for a range of purposes.[72] How this redistribution

---

[68] Boada Rivas, 'Organización social y económica', 139–140.

[69] If feasting was recognised as a means through which economic centralisation was attained, it was less clear how elites obtained the means to hold these feasts in the first place. This circular argument is criticised by Langebaek, 'Fiestas y caciques', 282.

[70] Ibid., 291–293.

[71] This, which has become perhaps the most widely accepted model of the functioning of power and authority within Muisca communities, was first proposed by Carl Henrik Langebaek in *Mercados, poblamiento e integración étinca entre los muiscas: Siglo XVI* (Bogotá: Banco de la República, 1987), especially 47–52. Langebaek drew on the model of the 'vertical archipelago' developed by John Murra for Peru and adapted to Ecuador by Udo Oberem, in which a particular group takes advantage of plots of land distributed along different altitudes at relatively short distances. For an overview of archaeological literature on redistribution, see Craig Morris, 'Storage, Supply and Redistribution in the Economy of the Inka State'. In *Anthropological History of Andean Polities*. Edited by John V. Murra, Nathan Wachtel, and Jacques Revel (Cambridge: Cambridge University Press, 1986), 60.

[72] What in other contexts has been described as social power, 'the capacity to control and manage the labour and activities of a group to gain access to the benefits of social action'. Elizabeth DeMarrais, Luis Jaime Castillo, and Timothy Earle, 'Ideology, Materialization, and Power Strategies'. *Current Anthropology* 37, no. 1 (1996): 15, following the model

42 *The Muisca and the Problem of Religion*

worked, and how Indigenous leaders inserted themselves in the centre of these exchanges, was less clear.

Recent research by anthropologists and historians on colonial records such as those of the celebrations of Ubaque has been throwing important light on this question. The latest work on the distribution of land, labour, and resources among the leaders of the different groups that composed each Muisca *cacicazgo* in the first decades of the colonial period has been highlighting the inability of Indigenous leaders to exercise direct control over the economic affairs of their communities.[73] The documentation of visitations, tax assessments, and population surveys in this period show very clearly that the groups directly under the control of Indigenous rulers – that is, what Spaniards called the *parcialidad* or *parte* of the *cacique* – tended not to have the largest populations, control over the largest parcels of land, or the greatest economic production. On the contrary, in many cases they were smaller and poorer than the *parcialidades* of other community leaders, the people Spaniards called *capitanes*, who were somehow still their subordinates.

As Santiago Muñoz Arbeláez's work on the valley of Ubaque has shown, this was not a simple matter of numerical inequality, but one of specialisation. A civil visitation carried out in the nearby town of Pausaga in 1594, for example, recorded that the community there was by then composed of ten *parcialidades*, nine of which were headed by captains and the tenth by the *cacique*.[74] Of these, the *cacique*'s was, with one exception, the smallest. But what these detailed records reveal is that most of the adults of the *cacique*'s group were '*indias del servicio*', female servants, and other women, while none were '*indios útiles*', or working men, in contrast to the other *parcialidades*, most of which had no '*indias del servicio*' and all of which had large numbers of working men. What Muñoz's analysis shows is that these women were specialists in the production of *chicha* and other special foods, and that this production was concentrated in the *parcialidad* of the ruler – something he also observed in Ubatoque and other towns in the area.[75] This growing specialisation is corroborated by the archaeological record, which shows that the brewing of *chicha* and the preparation of certain foods consumed in feasts – such as deer meat – came to be concentrated in elite dwellings

---

of Michael Mann, *The Sources of Social Power* (Cambridge: Cambridge University Press, 1986).

[73] E.g. Gamboa, *El cacicazgo*, 55–67.

[74] Muñoz Arbeláez, *Costumbres*, 143; based on records of Miguel de Ibarra's visitation of the *encomiendas* of Alonso de Olmos in 1594, AGN VC 8, d. 3, 341r–358r.

[75] Ibid., 143–145.

Ritual Economy and Leadership

from as early as the Early Muisca period (c. 800–1200 CE), even as it shows that it did not result in nutritional deficiencies among the rest of the population, suggesting that the food prepared in these sites was consumed by the broader community as well.[76]

This is what was happening in Ubaque in 1563. It was the community that provided the maize and the raw materials for the celebration, which the *cacique* processed in special ways and distributed back to the community – and in this case also to neighbouring elites. In exchange, the community also came together to perform works of communal labour for the benefit of all, such as the building of raised beds for planting and channels for irrigation. Moreover, as Gutiérrez's distinction suggests, the communal labour performed on these occasions could be limited to infrastructure and agricultural work – as was also the case in Suba in 1605 – but it could also go beyond this. Indeed, at Ubaque in 1563 the proceedings also involved the performance of ritual labour, not least divination of the agricultural cycle ahead. As Gutiérrez also explained, an individual, dressed all in white, was placed on the causeway that had been constructed outside of the *cacique*'s compound, along which processions took place. He stood there from sunrise to sunset, and if he remained perfectly still it was a sign that it would be a fertile year. 'If he moved', the witness added, 'there is to be hunger'.[77]

The other activity closely associated with Indigenous leaders and their immediate kinship groups around the Muisca region was the production of special dyed and painted cotton *mantas* (e.g. Figure 1.2). The raw materials for these were the cotton blankets that so many of these communities produced. The production of *mantas* was such an important part of the regional economy that cotton cloth was one of the basic units of exchange in which colonial authorities set the standard rates for the payment of the tribute owed by these groups to their *encomenderos*, and through them to the crown. These textiles were woven by members of individual kinship groups and collected by their leaders, who paid them up the chain to leaders of the composite units to which their groups belonged, all the way to the ruler. In exchange, the ruler returned a portion of these *mantas* to other community leaders, but only after having had them decorated and painted by carefully controlled specialists. In 1594, as Muñoz noted, don Antonio, *cacique* of Pausaga described

---

[76] Boada Rivas, 'Organización social y económica', 134.
[77] Documents pertaining to the case of Ubaque, 1563, AGI Justicia 618, 1406r.

FIGURE 1.2 Painted textile fragment of luxury blanket (*manta*), Colombia, Eastern Cordillera, 800–1600 CE (Muisca period). Museo del Oro, Banco de la República, Bogotá. 35 x 59.5 cm. T00054. Photograph by Clark M. Rodríguez

how this system worked. Before the coming of the Spaniards, he explained, the captains had paid the *cacique* 'fifteen or twenty *mantas*' in tribute, while commoners had paid him 'one or two, according to their ability, and in addition to this tribute did his planting and [constructed] buildings and *cercados*'. In exchange, the leader marked the captains with a dye, 'which was an honour among them', presented them with 'one painted and one coloured *manta*', and provided commoners and captains alike with food and drink.[78]

---

[78] Muñoz Arbeláez, *Costumbres*, 138. A number of similar declarations by Indigenous witnesses are discussed in Chapter 4.

Ritual Economy and Leadership 45

This brief description from Pausaga may be one of the clearest explanations of the functioning of these exchanges, but we can also see examples of these practices throughout the Muisca region. In Ubaté in 1592, don Pedro, the *cacique*, explained how he had heard that in the old days, each captain would pay '4 or 5 *mantas* and 2 or 3 pesos, and common and ordinary Indians would pay one plain *manta* and half a peso of gold and work our fields and build our houses and *cercados*'. In turn, 'the captains would receive one painted *manta* in recompense, called *chicate*, and the rest would be fed and given deer meat'.[79] In 1594, in Fontibón, some eight miles to the west of Santafé, witnesses explained that individuals close to the *cacique* were trained in the decoration of 'good and rich' *mantas*, which were then given by the *cacique* to select individuals, along with other objects and special foods, as they put it, 'in confirmation of office'.[80] These could only be granted by Indigenous leaders in specific ritual contexts, and could only be used or consumed by the individuals whom they chose. Everyone else, the witnesses explained, was forbidden to wear or use them. The same was the case with the food that was prepared and distributed by the *caciques*. The community provided the ingredients, but only the *cacique* and his household could transform them into the special foods and drink served at the feasts. As don Antonio Saquara, the leader of Teusacá, explained in 1593, the preparation of special food, which in his household was done by six women, 'is the custom and authority of *caciques*, so that we may be obeyed'.[81]

In other words, Muisca leaders may have lacked direct control of the means of economic production, but they maintained a monopoly on key means of *ritual* production, and this was central to their position at the head of their communities, and a key instrument through which they projected their power beyond them. This is what rendered the asymmetrical exchanges that were at the centre of community life, and which were the foundation of political hierarchies, – in an important sense – symmetrical.

These conclusions are supported by a careful reading of the final series of practices that Pérez de Arteaga's report documented at Ubaque in 1563, which were to do with the office of the ruler itself. There, some of the proceedings appeared to be related to the succession of the office of leader of Ubaque. They centred around a special building, described as a

---

[79] Visitation of Ubaté by Bernardino de Albornoz, May 1592, AGN VC 5 d 2, 212r.
[80] Visitation of Fontibón by Ibarra, 18 May 1594. AGI SF 17, 92a, 1r–1v.
[81] Visitation of Teusacá by Ibarra, 14 February 1593, AGN VC 5 d. 3, 577v.

coyme, where the heir to Ubaque was said to prepare for his position, and the celebrations also involved an aspect of mourning for the current incumbent, even though he was still alive.[82] Rumours circulated about what occurred in the interior of the building, not least because few witnesses had any experience of what went on inside. A priest active in the area, Francisco Lorenzo, claimed that *coymes* were 'houses of their sanctuaries', where the Muisca buried deceased notables, and speculated that the buildings were also the sites of grisly sacrifices – something akin, in short, to an inverted Christian church.[83] Spaniard Nicolás Gutiérrez, for his part, claimed it was the site of the most excessive drinking, that he had heard it was where the devil himself appeared before them and gave them instructions.[84] Armed with this information, Pérez de Arteaga asked Indigenous witnesses to confirm whether 'some idolatry' had taken place inside, and particularly whether they had summoned the devil – confident, as ever, in the universality of these Christian categories. Eventually Susa, the elderly leader of a nearby community of the same name, disappointed the Spaniards by explaining that it was something much less scandalous. It was for the preparation of Ubaque's heir: 'the heir is put inside for six years', he explained, and 'does nothing more than sit by the fire, and that there is no drinking or summoning of the devil'. This, he added, 'is the truth, as I am too old to lie'.[85] As it would turn out, this sort of ritual enclosure for an extended period followed by celebrations was not unique to this incident. What was unique, as so often with this case, was its scale.

Accounts of this practice of ritual enclosure abound from the earliest European accounts of the Muisca. Even the anonymous author of the 'Epítome' explained that 'those who are to be *caciques* or captains ... are placed when they are young in certain houses, [and] enclosed there for some years', depending on the office they were to inherit.[86] In 1569, when the *Audiencia* sent someone to investigate allegations of illicit ritual practices among the people of Suba and Tuna, a few miles north-west of the city of Santafé, a variety of witnesses described how the *caciques* and captains of the town made use of these structures to prepare their successors for office.[87]

---

[82] Documents pertaining to the case of Ubaque, 1563, AGI Justicia 618, 1418v.
[83] Ibid., 1402r.   [84] Ibid., 1406v–1407r.
[85] Ibid., 1431v. This Susa, located in the Valley of Ubaque, is not to be confused with the settlement of the same name near Lake Fúquene, discussed in Chapter 6.
[86] Anonymous, 'Epítome', 135.
[87] Inquiry concerning Suba and Tuna, 1569, AGN C&I 27, doc. 23, 660r–667v. Witnesses ranged from Spanish residents of the town, such as the priest, to Indigenous servants and enslaved Africans in the household of the *encomendero*.

Ritual Economy and Leadership

There was disagreement as to how long the individuals concerned remained enclosed, and what they did whilst inside, but witnesses agreed that great celebrations took place when the process came to an end.[88] Without this ritual enclosure, they asserted, they could not succeed to the office.[89] In the town of Tota, some forty miles west of Tunja, witnesses interrogated in 1574 described a similar celebration. One explained how there was someone currently enclosed, but that the period of enclosure was to come to an end at the time of the upcoming maize harvest. Then, the *cacique* would hold a great celebration, for which he had 'prepared much maize and called together all the land' and had readied 'many feathers and adornments for the said celebration'.[90]

The clearest description of the purpose of this ritual enclosure comes from the report of an investigation carried out by the *Audiencia* in 1594 in the town of Fontibón. The report, compiled on the basis of the declarations of a number of Indigenous witnesses, makes it clear that at least there it was not only Indigenous rulers who were enclosed, but that this was also a means by which other individuals were prepared for other positions of responsibility.[91] For example, witnesses described how these buildings were where certain ritual practitioners, described as *xeques*, prepared their nephews to become their successors.[92] Those who were to become *xeques*, the report explained, were placed in these buildings in groups of three or four, from around the age of ten, where they were to remain enclosed for four or six years. Far from the drunken excess that witnesses in Ubaque imagined, they spent this time observing a strict diet, 'eating very little, and with no salt', and limiting their foods to 'toasted maize and small potatoes, which have little substance, and some wild leaves', and 'drinking chicha only once a day, and very moderately', all of which was provided through a small hatch cut into the building. Their

---

[88] Ibid., 664r–664v.   [89] Ibid., 660v, 662v, 664r.

[90] Documentation of the suit between the *cacique* and *encomendero* of Tota, 1574–1575, AGN C&I 29, doc. 1, 179r.

[91] AGI SF 17, n 92a, 1r.

[92] Following the now familiar Muisca inheritance pattern. Report on rites and ceremonies, Fontibón, April 1594, AGI SF 17, no. 92a. The term '*jeque*' or '*xeque*' appears frequently in colonial records and in later dictionaries and chronicles. Variants in other local languages, and in alternative Spanish transliterations – some of which are cited later in this chapter – included 'rrique' and 'chuque'. It was generally translated by contemporaries as '*sacerdote*' or priest. In the glossary to his 1626 chronicle, for example, Pedro Simón explained that a 'Ieque [sic] is a priest of idols, who fasts and makes the offerings'. Simón, *Noticias historiales de las conquistas de tierra firme en las Indias occidentales* (Bogotá: Casa editorial de Medardo Rivas, 1892), 1627 [p. 705].

only visitors were 'their uncles, the old *xeques* whom they are to succeed, [who] give them their law and teach them how to make their sacrifices and burnt offerings'. Crucially, the report explains, they also 'teach them how to paint and weave *mantas* of the good and rich kind that they make'.[93] In 1608, similar practices were described by Jesuit observers in Cajicá, who also associated them with the training of Indigenous 'priests'.[94] In both cases, the conclusion of the period of enclosure was followed by celebrations and additional rituals by which local rulers confirmed the practitioners in their office.[95]

These *xeques*, and the broader effort of colonial authorities to identify Indigenous priests, will be scrutinised later, not least because they became a recurring obsession of colonial officials. For now, it is key to note that these practices of ritual enclosure were the means through which Indigenous leaders and their close associates acquired the knowledge and status that allowed them to produce the special *mantas* and organise the celebrations that were central to the functioning of the ritual economy that powered production and exchange in their communities, and which was central to their social and political hierarchies.

Other mainstays of the received image of a centralised and homogenous Muisca society also take on a new significance with these considerations in mind. The protocol and distance observed by the Muisca towards their rulers that so concerned early observers is a good example. Shortly after first contact, San Martín and Lebrija had observed that the Indigenous peoples of the highlands were 'greatly subjected to their lords'. A few years later, the anonymous author of the 'Epítome' added further details, explaining how the Muisca were forbidden from facing their *caciques* when addressing them, and also had to offer other elaborate marks of respect and submission.[96] This treatment of Indigenous leaders was corroborated by a multitude of observations in colonial records. For example, when the enemies of the controversial *mestizo* don Diego de Torres, *cacique* of Turmequé, sought to support their assertion that he was encouraging his subjects to rebel against Spanish rule and to turn away from Christianity in 1564, they claimed that he 'made them turn their backs [to him] following their ancient rites, and does not face them

---

[93] AGI SF 17, no. 92a, 1r.

[94] Jesuit *littera annua* for 1608–1609, 1609-09-20, ARSI NR&Q 12 I, at 49r. These buildings are also discussed in Londoño, 'El lugar'.

[95] For an outline of other examples of ritual enclosure among the Muisca, see Gamboa, *El cacicazgo*, 488ff.

[96] Anonymous, 'Epítome', 134.

Muisca 'Priests', 'Temples', and 'Sanctuaries' 49

when he talks to them or allows them to look him in the face', in a manner befitting '*caciques* who are not political or Christian'.[97]

It is not surprising that descriptions of these Indigenous customs contributed to the impression that Muisca rulers were despotic, because they were intended by Spanish observers to do just that, contrasting this Indigenous despotism with righteous government under Spanish rule. From the 1560s, Spanish authorities began to attempt to ban what they perceived as these exaggerated customs in successive rounds of visitations in an effort to bring Indigenous leaders more in line with their own conceptions of righteous and legitimate rulers should behave, for the sake of political stability. But given what we now know about the dynamics of the power of Indigenous authorities, and of the real distance – at least in economic terms – between them and their subjects, these behaviours take on a different significance. They are less the marks of vassalage and tyranny, and more the symbolic means through which an Indigenous political and economic order, with strong ritual dimensions, was made material. And it was on these non-Christian ritual foundations – which the authorities were already working to undermine – that colonial government and the colonial tributary economy, through their reliance on Indigenous leaders, were actually built.

MUISCA 'PRIESTS', 'TEMPLES', AND 'SANCTUARIES'

It should already be clear that these highly localised ritual practices are a far cry from the depictions of Indigenous religion in colonial historical texts, such as the writings of chroniclers like Fernández de Piedrahita. But reading administrative records such as those of Pérez de Arteaga also shows that bureaucrats and missionaries also tended to misunderstand Indigenous religious practices by relying on imported frames of reference. In this way, they tended to assume that religious practices were the province of a small and specialised section of the population, a clergy, whom they labelled *xeques* or 'sorcerors'. In the language of a typical report, such as that prepared by the *oidor* Miguel de Ibarra after carrying out an investigation in Fontibón in 1594, the Muisca were thought to hold these *xeques* 'in the same reverence as Christians do their bishops and archbishops'.[98] This hierarchy of priests, bishops, and archbishops,

---

[97] Suit between *cacique* don Diego de Torres and his *encomendero*, Pedro de Torres, 1564–1575, AGN E 21, doc. 9, 404v.

[98] Letter of Miguel de Ibarra to the King, 18 May 1574, AGI Santa Fe 17, no. 92, fol. 1r.

50 *The Muisca and the Problem of Religion*

based in temples consecrated to the devil rather than to God, were assumed to carry out 'rites and ceremonies' in a manner that was the inverse, but otherwise entirely similar, to their Christian counterparts.[99] These ideas were taken up by colonial chroniclers, who further elaborated these assumptions, just as they did with Muisca rulers. For example, writing in the 1570s, the Franciscan chronicler Pedro de Aguado (born c. 1538) described how they were 'held in great veneration and feared spiritually and temporally' by the Muisca, even by *caciques*, because they exploited their anxieties with 'great fears and threats of the punishment of the wrath of their gods'.[100]

These images of Muisca religious leaders were in part a reflection of the very well-established Christian tendency to focus on false prophets and perceived corrupters of the flock, which was influential across a multitude of missionary theatres.[101] Confronted with the unknown and unfamiliar, early modern Spaniards reached for familiar concepts, confident in the applicability of the categories and frameworks of biblical and classical sources and Christian history, which held themselves to be universally applicable.[102]

The assumption of commensurability is ubiquitous in colonial documentation, and it was often even ascribed to non-Christian Indigenous witnesses by translators and scribes. For example, in Ubaque in 1563, Xaguara, the leader of Tuna, was asked whether 'in that building they summoned the devil', referring to the *coyme*, and was recorded saying that 'he believed that they summoned him because that is the custom among them' – or at least that was what was written by the scribe Luis de Peralta on the basis of the translation of the interpreter Lucas Bejarano. Ubaque himself, when asked why he had organised the celebration, through the

---

[99] On this phenomenon elsewhere in the New World, see Carmen Bernand and Serge Gruzinski, *De la idolatría: Una arqueología de las ciencias religiosas* (Mexico City: Fondo de Cultura Económica, 1992), 11–37.

[100] To the extent that he held them responsible for early resistance to the imposition of Spanish rule by Indigenous people, as the architects of a 'general conspiracy'. Aguado, *Recopilación historial*, vol. 1, book 4, ch. 4, 340.

[101] This idea, and its impact, will be discussed in greater detail in Chapters 3 and 4. For an example of its influence in missionary strategies, see Duviols, *La lutte*, 189–200.

[102] Anthony Pagden, *The Fall of Natural Man: The American Indian and the Origins of Comparative Ethnology* (Cambridge: Cambridge University Press, 1982), 5; and Sabine MacCormack, 'Limits of Understanding: Perceptions of Greco-Roman and Amerindian Paganism in Early Modern Europe'. In *America in European Consciousness, 1493–1750*. Edited by Karen Ordahl Kupperman (Chapel Hill: University of North Carolina Press, 1995), 79–129.

Muisca 'Priests', 'Temples', and 'Sanctuaries'

same interpreter and scribe, was recorded to have said 'that when God made the Indians he gave them this as their Easter, as he gave the Christians their own'.[103]

It is not that Spaniards were blind to the fact that that Indigenous people perhaps might not be familiar with European concepts and categories. Records of conversations with Indigenous people in this early period generally relied on translators, especially when witnesses were not Christians and had little contact with Spaniards and colonial institutions. Because the documentation recorded the answers given by the interpreters, who were sworn to render an accurate translation, and never the responses of the Indigenous witnesses themselves, the work of translation itself is generally rendered invisible. We generally do not know how translators explained concepts and ideas or how these were received and understood by Indigenous witnesses. Indeed, as we will see, surviving bilingual works such as vocabulary lists and more elaborate dictionaries all date to a later period, and most to the seventeenth century. But a handful of records do make visible some efforts to determine the accuracy of communication.

Visitations carried out by the *Audiencia* in this same period in regions further removed from the centres of Spanish settlement, such as the northern reaches of the province of Tunja, show a clear sensibility to the fact that key concepts might not be universal. In his 1571 visitation of the *encomiendas* held by Jiménez de Quesada, for example, the *oidor* Juan López de Cepeda needed to determine how many *mantas* and other products local communities paid Jiménez de Quesada, and how this compared to the rates that the *Audiencia* had set. In each case, when questioning local Indigenous leaders, Cepeda was not content simply to record the numbers and quantities that the translator relayed. In Pisba, for example, when a group of captains explained that each year they paid twenty *mantas*, Cepeda made sure that they were all on the same page. 'They were ordered to take kernels of maize and count out 20 kernels' in front of him, 'and they said that this was 20'. To be certain, the scribe recorded in the margin 'they know what 20 is'.[104] He repeated the

---

[103] Documents pertaining to the case of Ubaque, 1563, AGI Justicia 618, 1418v, 1415v–1416r.

[104] On similar practices in the Central Andes, see Marco Curatola Petrocchi and José Carlos de la Puente, 'Contar concertando: Quipus, piedritas y escritura en los Andes coloniales'. In *El quipu colonial: Estudios y materiales*. Edited by Marco Curatola Petrocci and José Carlos de la Puente (Lima: Pontificia Universidad Católica del Perú, 2013), 193–243. Visitation of the *encomiendas* of Gonzalo Jiménez de Quesada by Juan López de Cepeda, 1571, AGNC Visitas Boyacá 2 d 1, 76v.

52 *The Muisca and the Problem of Religion*

procedure each time: 'captain Sasa said he has 23 Indians ... using 23 kernels of maize; Captain Yuramico said he has 36 Indians who are his subjects ... which he said with 36 kernels of maize'. All the accounts were accurate, the scribe recorded, because 'the said *caciques* and captains said it and gave accounts in maize'.[105] They repeated the procedure time and again.

Cepeda recognised that there might be difficulties communicating something as basic as a measurement, and took pains to ensure that the records his visitation produced were accurate. But he also took for granted the universality of religious concepts. These same witnesses, whom we are told again and again were not Christians and could not speak Castilian, were nevertheless asked whether they had 'sanctuaries and sacrifices', and whether 'they speak to the devil'. The intelligibility of these concepts was taken for granted. Often Indigenous witnesses were recorded saying that they did not. Others, like Quesmecosba, captain of Tabaquita, in Pisba, went a little further, explaining that 'they do not have sanctuaries, that they are poor, and that there is no gold in their land', suggesting he had caught on to what the authorities were really after.[106] Clearest of all was Atunguasa, *cacique* of Mama, who explained that 'he does not know what a sanctuary is'.[107] No matter: Cepeda continued asking after them, ordering 'that those who are not Christians become so', and commanding them 'to leave their evil rites and ceremonies', whatever those might actually turn out to be.[108]

The reality was rather different, and to appreciate it we need to look at a broader range of colonial documentation. The great celebrations that took place in Ubaque in 1563 were to be among the last of their kind. Perhaps the last was a smaller celebration that took place in the town of Tota, news of which reached the authorities in 1574, in a suit between the Indigenous leader and his *encomendero*, who reported having stumbled upon a celebration in which he claimed some 2,000 people from around the region participated.[109] One witness explained that it consisted of three

---

[105] Ibid., 88r.　　[106] Ibid., 80r.　　[107] Ibid., 115v.　　[108] Ibid., 28r.

[109] Many of the details of the celebration are unclear, but the *encomendero* claimed that he had been told that this was to do with the death by suicide of a woman after a row with her husband. This episode is cited by Gamboa in *El cacicazgo*, 489, and discussed in greater detail in Jorge Augusto Gamboa, 'Caciques, encomenderos y santuarios en el Nuevo Reino de Granada: Reflexiones metodológicas sobre la ficción en los archivos: El proceso del cacique de Tota, 1574–1575.' *Colonial Latin American Historical Review* 13, no. 2 (2004): 113–145. The documentation of the case can be found in AGN C&I 29, doc. 1, fols. 1r–327v. Other information recorded in the suit between the *encomendero* and the *cacique* of Tota is also considered later in this chapter and in Chapter 2.

Muisca 'Priests', 'Temples', and 'Sanctuaries'   53

or four days of dancing and various ceremonies in the *cacique*'s *cercado*, which included sorrowful chanting.[110]

As in other parts of the New World, these large, public celebrations were the first to succumb to colonial pressures.[111] Early rumours of a regional network of hidden temples and of trade in child victims for ritual homicide, so common in the first texts about the Muisca, disappeared from the written record by the time the *Audiencia* arrived in 1550.[112] They continued to be considered in successive chronicles, but do not appear in the documentation of the colonial bureaucracy, beyond questions asked of Indigenous witnesses by officials like Pérez de Arteaga, who were sorely disappointed. Instead, the records that he and his colleagues produced show glimpses of increasingly modest, but no less important, religious practices.[113] This was not simply because colonial pressures made large-scale celebrations increasingly difficult, but because the religious practices recorded as the colonial period developed came to be set in the context of the smaller social and political units that replaced what larger conglomerations had existed before the arrival of Spaniards.[114]

---

[110] Ibid., 178v.

[111] In Peru, these were the great cults and religious sites of the Inca state cults, which were nevertheless a relatively recent imposition in much of the region. MacCormack, *Religion in the Andes*, 143–181.

[112] The author of the 'Epítome' proposed that there was an elaborate network of exchange in place to provide sacrificial victims for various Muisca groups around the region. The author proposed that individual *caciques* tended to have two or three 'young priests' attached to their individual religious buildings, who performed a number of functions, not least communicating with the sun, and who were apparently eventually sacrificed to the solar deity when they reached puberty. Anonymous, 'Epítome', 137. On the European obsession with 'human sacrifice' among non-Europeans in this period, and the related concern with antropophagy, see Pagden, *Fall of Natural Man*, especially at 80–93.

[113] Similar processes occurred elsewhere. In Peru, as 'the religion of the Andean present began to diverge from the Inca past', so too 'the task of historians who recorded this past … began to diverge from the task of the missionaries and secular officials who administered the viceroyalty of Peru', and who required an understanding of present conditions in the localities. MacCormack, *Religion in the Andes*, 145.

[114] Langebaek, for example, has proposed a distinction between horizontal and vertical shamanism in Muisca society: the former associated with informal and less important practices, and the latter with a more carefully organised hierarchical structure of greater prestige. In his analysis, the latter declined with the imposition and consolidation of colonial rule. Carl Henrik Langebaek, 'Resistencia indígena y transformaciones ideológicas entre los muiscas de los siglos XVI y XVII'. In *Muiscas: Representaciones, cartografías y etnopolíticas de la memoria*. Edited by Ana María Gómez Londoño (Bogotá: Editorial Pontificia Universidad Javeriana, 2005), 30ff.

54 *The Muisca and the Problem of Religion*

The core of Muisca religious practices – at least in a number of instances for which documentation survives – appears to have been the interaction of individuals and kinship groups with deities or metapersons that Spanish observers described as *santuarios*. The records of colonial officials mention only one by name, Bochica, who appears on three occasions in the proceedings of 1563, as a *santuario* belonging to Ubaque. Bochica was variously described by witnesses as a building, which Pérez de Arteaga had destroyed, as the father of a 'tiger' – perhaps a puma or jaguar – that had recently been attacking travellers on local roads, and as an 'idol'. When asked who Bochica was, Ubaque replied that 'he is a wind' – '*un viento*' – and that he was in the site of the building that the Spaniards had destroyed.[115]

Bochica aside, all the other *santuarios* of the colonial record appear to have been lineage deities that inhabited portable objects. Although the term *santuario* can be translated as 'sanctuary', and the near-contemporary Sebastián de Covarrubias defined the term as 'a religious place', *santuarios* were not sites or buildings, as Spaniards generally expected.[116] They varied somewhat in shape and composition, but shared some basic characteristics. Each was the figure of an ancestor and was firmly rooted in the kinship group that maintained it. They fulfilled a range of purposes and were integral to the identity of its group and its grounding in a particular location. Just as some of the kinship groups that formed part of a particular Muisca polity occupied a position of responsibility or leadership over the rest of the composite whole, some *santuarios* had spheres of action that embraced entire communities. And, naturally, there were differences in the use to which these practices were put by different groups within Muisca communities, most obviously Indigenous leaders, who used them to cement and enhance their prestige and authority. To understand their operation, it is best, once again, to consider them in action.

In 1594, rumours that don Alonso, the *cacique* of the town of Fontibón, was determined to maintain various heterodox ritual practices among his community prompted another investigation by the *Audiencia*.[117]

---

[115] Documents pertaining to the case of Ubaque, 1563, AGI Justicia 618, 1409v, 1416r.

[116] Sebastián de Covarrubias, *Tesoro de la lengua Castellana o Española* (Madrid: Luis Sánchez, impressor del Rey N. S., 1611), pt. 2, 21v.

[117] Reports on rites and ceremonies, Fontibón, April–May 1594, AGI SF 17, nos 91, 92, 92a, 92b, 93, 95, 96, and 99. The last of these documents was published by Eduardo Londoño as 'Memorias', who examined it in 'El lugar'. It was also analysed by Carl Langebaek in 'Buscando sacerdotes', 87. Once again, the assumption was that don Alonso was at the head of a competing religious hierarchy.

Muisca 'Priests', 'Temples', and 'Sanctuaries'

Led by the *oidor* Miguel de Ibarra, *Audiencia* officials arrived in the town searching for what they assumed were the pillars of Indigenous religion, priests and temples, but what they found was quite different. By the end of the sixteenth century, the idea that the Muisca were misled in religious matters by a self-perpetuating cohort of Indigenous priests was firmly established, and Ibarra's report, as we have seen, compared the place they occupied among the Muisca to that of Christian bishops and archbishops, and went as far as to distinguish between different ranks of religious practitioners. Ibarra, for example, distinguished between '*xeques* and *tibas*, with *xeques* being the priests and *tibas* the sacristans'.[118] This focus by the colonial authorities on these perceived corrupters of the flock was common throughout the New World, and was rooted in biblical notions of false prophets. Whether or not they held the influence that was ascribed to them, they were repeatedly blamed for the persistence of non-Christian practices, and legislation was put in place to target them specifically.[119]

The presence of Indigenous priests was so well established a trope that it was guaranteed to trigger a reaction from the authorities. In 1569, for example, the *encomendero* of Suba and Tuna, some ten miles north-west of Santafé, forwarded a complaint by a priest he had hired to provide instruction, Andrés de San Juan, to the *Audiencia*.[120] It described how the priest was struggling to hold his catechism classes and to impose his authority over local people, complaining that 'all of this is caused by the *xeques*'.[121] Witnesses, all closely connected to the priest, described an entire hierarchy of Indigenous priests who were not only determined to sabotage his efforts, but who ran their own programme of counter-indoctrination with the cooperation of the Indigenous rulers of the town.[122] Their testimonies

---

[118] Report by Miguel de Ibarra on the rites and ceremonies of the Indians, Fontibón, 1594, AGI SF 17, n. 99a, fol. 1v.

[119] On these issues and their treatment in legislation in the archdiocese of Lima, see Duviols, *La lutte*, 189–200, and Kenneth Mills, *Idolatry and Its Enemies: Colonial Andean Religion and Extirpation, 1640–1750* (Princeton, NJ: Princeton University Press, 1997), 95ff. Equivalent legislation for New Granada will be discussed in Chapters 3 and 4.

[120] Inquiry concerning Suba and Tuna, 1569, AGN C&I 27, doc. 23 652r–667v. Most of these documents were also published as Eduardo Londoño, 'Documento sobre los indios de Fontibón y Ubaque: Autos en razón de prohibir a los caciques de Fontibón, Ubaque y otros no hagan las fiestas, borracheras, y sacrificios de su gentilidad'. *Revista de Antropología y Arqueología* 7, nos 1–2 (1991): 130–156.

[121] Fray Andrés de San Juan to *encomendero* Antonio Días Cardoso, October 1569, AGN C&I 27, doc. 23 657v–659v, at 658r.

[122] Report of the investigation in Suba and Tuna, 1569-10-23, AGN C&I 27, doc. 23 660r–665r.

56   *The Muisca and the Problem of Religion*

resemble a catalogue of the regime's worst fears: heresiarchs, human sacrifice, murder, and intrigue. No evidence to prove these allegations was uncovered, but that hardly mattered. What was really going on was that most of the people of Suba and Tuna had refused to remain in the site of a new planned town to which they had been forced to resettle and had returned to their previous settlements, and the *Audiencia* had failed to do anything to stop it. The scandal served the priest and the *encomendero* to compel the authorities to take action to bring them back together.[123]

In Fontibón in 1594, the authorities set about finding these individuals, but what they found shocked them: 'as it turned out', one of the officials later reported, 'there were one hundred and thirty-five *xeques*'.[124] The numbers simply did not add up: even though Fontibón was then one of the largest *encomiendas* in the region, home to 507 tribute-paying men, these records suggested that over 20 per cent of the adult male population was a *xeque*.[125] Fontibón was not unique. The following year, an inquiry into non-Christian practices conducted in the more distant town of Iguaque, in the province of Tunja, offered a similar picture.[126] The town was much smaller, but the proceedings resulted in the prosecution of seven Indigenous authorities – *caciques* and captains – and fifteen others, here including women, for 'having *santuarios* in the usage of their gentility'.[127] Rather than a specialised group of people devoted exclusively to religious functions, the picture that emerges suggests that these were simply individuals who held responsibility over certain ritual functions within their communities.[128] Above all, they were responsible for the

[123] Summary of the case of Suba and Tuna, 1569, AGN C&I 27, doc. 23 665v.

[124] AGI SF 17, no. 92, 1r.

[125] These inquiries of 1594–1595 took place within the broader framework of a visitation of the province of Santafé by Miguel de Ibarra, discussed in Chapter 4. The statistics are from the documentation of the visitation, which recorded a total population of 1,831 individuals.

[126] Inquiry concerning Iguaque, April–May 1594, AGN C&I 58, doc. 2, 16r–43v. This was also published as Carl Henrik Langebaek, 'Santuarios indígenas en el repartimiento de Iguaque, Boyacá: Un documento de 1595 del Archivo Histórico Nacional de Colombia'. *Revista de Antropología* 4, no. 2 (1988): 201–227.

[127] AGN C&I 58, doc. 2, 37r. A 1635 visitation recorded a total population of 406 individuals. Record of the tributaries of provinces of Santafé, Tunja, Vélez, and Pamplona, 1635–1636, at APSLB Conventos Tunja, 3/2/16, 66r–75v, at 72r.

[128] Both of these episodes have been examined by scholars to question received ideas about the characteristics and functions of supposed Muisca 'priests'. See Langebaek, 'Buscando sacerdotes', 87; Londoño, 'El lugar'. Both speculate about possible hierarchies of Indigenous religious practitioners, and their role in their societies, but both agree that the picture is nevertheless different to earlier characterisations of such figures in the mould of Christian priests.

Muisca 'Priests', 'Temples', and 'Sanctuaries'

maintenance of the *santuarios*. And here too things were not as the authorities expected.

The documentation of Iguaque and Fontibón, which has received the most scholarly attention, does not describe *santuarios* or the functions of these religious practitioners in detail, but a less studied report of that same year from Lenguazaque, a town in the same province, offers more.[129] The inquiry was launched when news reached the authorities that an Indigenous authority in town, Pedro Guyamuche, had used some gold from a hidden *santuario* to purchase some sheep and wheat from local Spaniards.[130] As a result, the visitor paid special attention to learning about them. He soon learned that 'all captains have their *santuarios*', but that they were not the only ones.[131] Other witnesses, including individuals who were not Indigenous authorities, also revealed that they had their own in their homes.[132] Eventually, officials came to a surprising realisation: *santuarios* were not buildings or places. Spaniards were asking for Indigenous temples, but Indigenous witnesses were instead producing portable objects. This became clearer to the visitor as the investigation progressed. He had initially referred to *santuarios* as places, such as when he accused Guyamuche of 'having a *santuario* and idolising and adoring in it', but he was soon asking about the materials out of which the *santuarios* were made: not bricks and mortar, but 'cotton, or wood, or gold'.[133]

This important insight shines new light into the well-thumbed records of Iguaque and Fontibón. There too, *santuarios* seemed to be everywhere, and were kept by people of all stations. In Iguaque, for example, while the authorities were concerned to find 'the great sanctuary of this repartimiento', they were instead presented with a variety of objects that made little sense to them.[134] In all cases, witnesses explained that they had

---

[129] Inquiry concerning Lenguazaque, August 1595, AGN C&I 16, doc. 5, 563r–616v. In the visitation of 1635–1636, Lenguazaque was found to have a population of 655 people. Record of the tributaries of provinces of Santafé, Tunja, Vélez, and Pamplona, 1635–1636, at APSLB Conventos Tunja, 3/2/16, 73r.

[130] Pedro Guyamuche, who explained that he had inherited it from his family, who were now all dead. Inquiry concerning Lenguazaque, August 1595, AGN C&I 16, doc. 5, 572v.

[131] As witness don Alonso Saltoba, himself a captain, explained. Ibid., 566r.

[132] As was the case with Pedro Chuntaquibiguya, 'private inhabitant of this town', or Hernando Cunsaneme, a self-described poor member of the community. Ibid., 578r.

[133] Inquiry concerning Lenguazaque, August 1595, AGN C&I 16, doc. 5, 572v. Another was asked whether his were of gold, or blankets, or other metals, at 570v.

[134] Inquiry concerning Iguaque, April to May 1594, AGN C&I 58, doc. 2, 20r.

58 *The Muisca and the Problem of Religion*

inherited them through their families or close relations.[135] They were, most probably, lineage deities, and they bear some resemblance to the *chancas* of the central Andes – small portable objects often found in the dwellings of the individuals who inherited their care, and revered by their extended family or kinship group.[136]

The people identified by Spaniards and prosecuted as *xeques* in these inquiries were largely the men and women who cared for these objects, who seemed to fulfil this function on behalf of their kinship groups. In Fontibón, for example, the authorities prosecuted 100 inhabitants of the town, who were listed in the documentation by their membership of each of the ten *capitanías* that composed the *cacicazgo*.[137] The catalogue resembles a list of each of the component subunits of each *capitanía*, of each of the matrilineal kinship groups that were the building blocks of the town, and it seems likely – as several scholars have proposed – that each kinship group included individuals responsible for maintaining its *santuario* and other sacred objects.[138]

Santuarios performed a range of functions. Some were as basic as subsistence. In 1571, for example, Moniquirá, *cacique* of the community of the same name, complained to the *Audiencia* that one of his captains, Ucarica, had left the town and moved elsewhere with a number of his subjects. The *cacique* explained that the reason for his disappearance was that he had burnt the captain's *santuario*, 'which provided him with maize, potatoes, and *mantas*'.[139] In 1574, Indigenous witnesses in Tota explained that their *cacique* encouraged them to maintain their *santuarios*

---

[135] In Iguaque, García Aguicha, and Pedro Pacacoca admitted inheriting them, whilst Luis Aguaquén and Juan Neaquenchía specified that they had received them from their uncles. Ibid., at 20v, 29v, 30r, and 21v, respectively. In Lenguazaque, similar statements were recorded from Pedro Guyamuche, Andrés Juyesa, Gonzalo Nesmeguya, Hernando Consaneme, Pedro Chuntaquibiguya, Juan Biatoque, and Diego Nearva. Inquiry concerning Lenguazaque, August 1595, AGN C&I 16, doc. 5, at 564v, 569v, 571r, 572r, 577v, 578r, 578v, and 579r, respectively.

[136] For a description of these chancas, see Mills, *Idolatry*, 78ff, 75–76.

[137] Report on rites and ceremonies, Fontibón, April–May 1594, AGI SF 17, no. 92b, 1v–2v.

[138] For example, based on the documentation of Iguaque and Fontibón, Langebaek proposed a distinction between 'major' and 'minor' *xeques* and sanctuaries and their activities, the former connected to the *cacique* and the latter to individuals and *capitanías*. See 'Buscando sacerdotes', especially from 93. The evidence of Lenguazaque, however, suggests the situation was more flexible still. Londoño, for his part, argued that alongside the political hierarchy of *caciques* and captains there was a parallel religious one, of priests who administered a network of temples – a conclusion that now seems difficult to sustain. Londoño, 'El lugar'.

[139] Complaint of the *cacique* of Moniquirá, 1571-11-13, AGN VB 5, doc. 3, 382r, 384v.

Muisca 'Priests', 'Temples', and 'Sanctuaries'

to secure the success of their crops, for the benefit of the entire community. One witness even reported how the *cacique* had explained that if the appropriate devotions were not performed for his *santuario* his subjects would not be able to harvest cotton.[140] At the same time, the *santuarios* were closely connected to the identity of the group, and to the maintenance of social and political hierarchies.

Nor were all *santuarios* equal. Some were clearly more exalted than others, in the same manner as the kinship groups with which they were associated were not equal. *Caciques* and some captains, for example, had dedicated staff and buildings for the maintenance of their particular *santuarios*, in a way that suggests that their positions of prestige and authority were connected to the resources and effort that they were able to employ in maintaining them on behalf of their communities. In Fontibón, *cacique* don Alonso was found to have four individuals to care for his *santuario*, with one holding it on his behalf.[141]

In fact, *caciques*, captains, and a handful of others also had some special buildings known as '*cucas*'. In Lenguazaque, witnesses described how 'all the captains of this town have houses of feathers, which are called *cucas*', while in Iguaque others had them also.[142] The association between possession of these structures and political power has long been noted by historians of the Muisca.[143] They were also transmitted through certain lineages, and entry into the *cucas* was restricted to the individual responsible for maintaining it and subject to a strict protocol. Curiously, in Lenguazaque, it was only the individuals responsible for maintaining these structures who were described as '*rriques*' or *xeques*.[144] In some cases, the *xeques* were the individuals who owned the structures, but – once again – the wealthier and more important individuals outsourced the maintenance of these structures to others too.[145]

---

[140] Suit between the *encomendero* and *cacique* of Tota, 1574–1575, AGN C&I 29, doc. 1, 178v.

[141] Report on rites and ceremonies, Fontibón, April–May 1594, AGI SF 17, no. 92b, 1v.

[142] Inquiry concerning Lenguazaque, August 1595, AGN C&I 16, doc. 5, 571v. In Iguaque, several people came forwards to say that they had these structures who were not part of the Indigenous nobility. Inquiry concerning Iguaque, April–May 1594, AGN C&I 58, doc. 2, 18v–19r.

[143] Who have nevertheless thought of them as temples. See Langebaek, 'Buscando sacerdotes'; Londoño, 'El lugar'.

[144] For example, in Lenguazaque, one Pedro Guyamuche explained that only 'rriques' alone could enter these buildings and had to fast before doing so. Inquiry concerning Lenguazaque, August 1595, AGN C&I 16, doc. 5, 572v, 574r.

[145] Such as *cacique* don Juan of Lenguazaque, whose *cuca* was maintained by Alonso Sistoba. In contrast, captain don Pedro Guarcavita was the '*rrique*' of his own building. Ibid., 574r, 593v.

60 *The Muisca and the Problem of Religion*

Crucially, these structures do not seem to have been straightforwardly temples or the sites of devotions, but rather special buildings where feathers and adornments were kept for use in a variety of celebrations and rituals by the group headed by the *cacique* or captain in question. Some were perhaps associated with the cult of the *santuarios*, and there is evidence that offerings of feathers and feather adornments were common. Others were used for public celebrations, such as the welcoming of visitors, or participation in regional festivities.[146] Featherworks were indeed prominent in the catalogue of objects observed and confiscated at Ubaque in 1563, which ranged from masks and costumes to the standards borne by visiting *caciques* and their representatives.[147] They were also among the objects that don Diego, *cacique* of Tota, was said to have ready for the celebration he was to hold in 1575.[148] Such featherworks were, perhaps, communal sacred resources controlled and administered by Indigenous leaders for the benefit of their communities, and to cement their own positions of leadership and authority.

The *santuarios* themselves also reflected the inequalities and hierarchies of the different lineages of the community. Few descriptions of the objects survive because Spaniards often overlooked them in their search for objects that were more familiar or easy to understand, notably the myriad votive objects of gold described as '*tunjos*' or '*santillos*' that they were so concerned with locating and confiscating.[149] For example, when Juan Neaquenchía of Iguaque led the authorities to his *santuario*, which he kept on a hilltop some distance away from the town, the scribe who described what they found wrote that there was a 'white bundle', containing 'a gold *santillo* and two golden eagles ... which seems to be of good gold ... another small *santillo*, and another like a fastener [*apretador*], of low gold, and five little cotton blankets which were rotten, which were not worth anything'.[150] The focus in the text was of course on the

---

[146] Some witnesses at Lenguazaque held that feathers were not even related to the cult of *santuarios*, but used exclusively for public celebrations, such as when important visitors came to the town. Ibid., 573r, 606r.

[147] The latter included a captain of Fontibón, Riguativa, who explained he was the father of the *cacique*. Documents pertaining to the case of Ubaque, 1563, AGI Justicia 618, 1412v–1415v, and 1426r.

[148] Suit between the *encomendero* and *cacique* of Tota, 1574–1575, AGN C&I 29, doc. 1, 178v.

[149] Indeed, early in the proceedings at Lenguazaque, the authorities took to asking whether 'the feathers and house are called sanctuary'. Inquiry concerning Lenguazaque, August 1595, AGN C&I 16, doc. 5, 581r.

[150] Inquiry concerning Iguaque, April–May 1594, AGN C&I 58, doc. 2, 21v.

objects made of precious stones and metals, carefully weighed and appraised, and yet it is likely that the lineage deity was in fact the cotton bundle. This is made clearer by other descriptions.

On one end of the spectrum seem to have been the deities of the more important kinship groups, who tended to occupy positions of leadership and responsibility in their wider communities. In Iguaque, for example, investigators were led to a cave some distance from the town where the *santuario* of the *cacique* was kept. There, they found a large bundle of cotton wool, which was found to contain 'the body and bones of the old *cacique* which they have as a sanctuary'. The remains were wrapped with 'five or six cotton blankets', and kept together with 'a small fastener [*apretadorcillo*] of gold'.[151]

Archaeological evidence suggests that mummification continued well into the colonial period, and at least four mummies have been identified that can be dated to the period after Spanish invasion, including the well-studied mummy found near Pisba.[152] Funerary practices were of particular interest to many of the earliest observers of the Muisca, and some of their descriptions closely resemble the findings at Iguaque and elsewhere.[153] Indeed, the anonymous author of the 'Epítome' described the embalming of notables and their preservation in bundles of blankets.[154] The interest in funerary practices of the authors of these texts is not unique, but was a frequent feature of other early accounts and chronicles

[151] Ibid., 25v.
[152] Scholars have used radiocarbon analysis to date the mummy of Pisba to 1400–1650 CE, but further analysis of the blankets used to wrap the mummy revealed they were made of wool, a material unavailable before the arrival of Spaniards. See Felipe Cárdenas Arroyo, 'La momia de Pisba Boyacá'. *Boletín del Museo del Oro* no. 27 (1990): 3–13. On mummification in the region, Carl Henrik Langebaek, 'Competencia por el prestigio político y momificación en el norte de Suramérica y el Itsmo, siglo XVI'. *Revista Colombiana de Antropología* 29, no. 1 (1992): 4–27.
[153] On descriptions of embalming practices in chronicles of the Muisca, and an analysis of their significance, see Correa, *El sol del poder*, 66ff.
[154] San Martín and Lebrija described elaborate funerary practices among the subjects of Tunja, whose notables 'are not buried, but placed above the ground', in their 'Relación del Nuevo Reyno', 100. The author of the 'Epítome' explained that the Muisca disposed of important members of their communities by embalming them, using gold and precious objects, and depositing the mummies 'in some sanctuaries that they have dedicated for this purpose of the dead'. Others were said to be laid to rest at the bottom of lakes and rivers, with coffins full to bursting with gold and precious objects, much to the irritation of conquistadors hungry for treasure who lamented they were thus placed forever out of their reach. 'Epítome', 139.

62 *The Muisca and the Problem of Religion*

on the Indigenous peoples of the New World.[155] Evidence of the persistence of the practice of mummifying certain individuals and of the preservation and ritual maintenance of ancestors also appears scattered in various colonial records, often unrelated to reports of investigations into Indigenous religious practices. In 1583, for example, don Diego, *cacique* of Guáneca (near Garagoa, in the province of Tunja), denounced a man before the authorities for having stolen some jewels and other objects from his uncle. Closer examination revealed that the victim of the theft was in fact 'long dead, kept embalmed, dry on a bed', and that the jewels had been adorning his remains.[156]

Santuarios of human remains were nevertheless rare, and all the documentary evidence suggests that they were the province of only the most exalted of Indigenous lineages, even if they were maintained by them on behalf of the broader communities that they led and represented. Detailed descriptions of them are rarer still. In Iguaque, for example, another inhabitant of the town later produced two sets of remains that had been buried in a field, 'and which were kept as *santuarios* in this town' since before the arrival of Spaniards.[157] No further details were recorded of their characteristics, and he was not a member of the Indigenous nobility, but he implied that the two bundles were revered by the community as a whole. Further down the social scale, the *santuarios* of less prominent individuals and their kinship groups are remarkably similar. Perhaps most obviously, the humble *santuario* of Juan Neaquenchía was a smaller-scale representation of a mummy like that of his *cacique*, constructed as it was of blankets bound tightly together, and secured with a fastener of gold. This sort of smaller-scale replication was far from

---

[155] One notable example is the chronicle of Pedro Cieza de León, who despite not having visited the Muisca territories did pass through the western range of what are now the Colombian Andes, and wrote of the burial of Indigenous leaders in province of Anserma and the mummification of Indigenous leaders in the Cauca Valley. See Pedro de Cieza de León, *Crónica del Perú: el señorío de los incas*. Edited by Franklin Pease (Caracas: Fundación Biblioteca Ayacucho, 2005), 53, 78, 118, respectively. For Sabine MacCormack, Cieza's interest in funerary practices 'conformed to a well-established rubric of ethnographic inquiry by Greek and Roman historians, whom Cieza had read, and the preoccupations of missionaries working among the Muslims of Granada'. See *Religion in the Andes*, 89. On Cieza's treatment of funerary rituals, see also Gabriela Ramos, *Death and Conversion in the Andes: Lima and Cuzco, 1532–1670* (Notre Dame, IN: University of Notre Dame Press, 2010), 11.

[156] Suit of *cacique* don Diego of Guáneca, 1583, AGI Escribanía 824A, no. 6, 292r. This example was identified by Jorge Gamboa in *El cacicazgo*, 487.

[157] Inquiry concerning Iguaque, April–May 1594, AGN C&I 58, doc. 2, 31v.

Muisca 'Priests', 'Temples', and 'Sanctuaries' 63

unique. In Fontibón in 1594, one captain Lorenzo surrendered his sanctuary at the beginning of the investigation. He had kept it in its own building, which he took apart, 'and took out of it a section of a stick of about three spans [*cuartas*] long, wrapped in some white cotton *mantas*'. The wooden object had been made into 'a figure with a sort of face and hands and feet, and in the stomach was placed a small nugget of fine gold'.[158] In Tota, the *cacique* was found to have a *santuario* that Spanish observers described as 'a stick made into a bust ... wrapped in a *manta*', with a hole containing a small golden votive object.[159]

Offerings were also made to these smaller-scale *santuarios*, and of the same sort as those offered to the mummies. In Fontibón in 1594, don Lorenzo, for example, produced three or four vessels containing 164 golden figurines of various sizes, along with a few emeralds, 'which he had offered to the said idol'.[160] Other offerings were humbler. In Tota, witnesses described seeing *cacique* don Diego offering a single gold votive object, a '*santillo*', to his sanctuary on one occasion, and burning turpentine before it on another.[161] When Gonzalo Niatonguya surrendered his sanctuary to the authorities in Fontibón, it was found to be a small 'figure of cotton string with parrot feathers', but even then it was the object of offerings of feathers and small objects of gold.[162]

Examples of these sanctuaries abound, but they are sometimes difficult to identify because the Spanish investigators who recorded their existence often failed to see them for what they were. For example, many were bundles of cloth that contained small objects in their folds, so that Spaniards treated them as wrappings or containers, especially if what they found inside was made of precious materials. Or they ignored cloth, wood, or ceramic objects altogether (such as, perhaps, the object in Figure 1.3), instead focusing on what were in fact votive objects and other paraphernalia that were offered to them (Figure 1.4). In Sogamoso in 1577, for example, *cacique* don Juan was compelled to hand over his sanctuary by representatives of the *Audiencia*. They meticulously recorded the various golden objects that he produced, and practically ignored the 'net bag [*mochila*] full of small

---

[158] Report on rites and ceremonies, Fontibón, April–May 1594, AGI SF 17, no. 92b, 1r–1v.
[159] Suit between the *encomendero* and *cacique* of Tota, 1574–1575, AGN C&I 29, doc. 1, 177r.
[160] Report on rites and ceremonies, Fontibón, April–May 1594, AGI SF 17, no. 92b, 1v.
[161] Suit between the *encomendero* and *cacique* of Tota, 1574–1575, AGN C&I 29, doc. 1, 177r.
[162] Inquiry concerning Lenguazaque, August 1595, AGN C&I 16, doc. 5, 564v.

FIGURE 1.3 Ceramic figure with facial decoration and gold alloy nose ring (*santuario?*), Colombia, Eastern Cordillera, 800–1600 CE (Muisca period). Note the geometric design painted on the body of the figure, likely depicting a painted manta. Private collection. Photograph by Julia Burtenshaw

FIGURE 1.4 Tripod offering bowl with human and bird guardians, containing votive figures (*tunjos*) and emeralds, Colombia, Eastern Cordillera, 800–1600 CE (Muisca period). Los Angeles County Museum of Art, the Muñoz Kramer Collection, gift of Camilla Chandler Frost and Stephen and Claudia Muñoz-Kramer. Photograph © Museum Associates/LACMA

rags and wrapped cotton, all smoked', that was probably the object of all of these offerings.[163]

The colonial officials who recorded these observations, like their contemporaries across the early modern Americas and South-east Asia, were poorly equipped to understand what they observed, and their documentation is frequently a record of defeated expectations and misunderstanding.

---

[163] Proceedings of *santuario* seizures in the province of Tunja, 1577, AGN RH 21, 732r. On archaeological evidence of burnt resins found on Muisca mummies, see Felipe Cárdenas Arroyo, 'Moque, momias y santuarios: Una planta en contexto ritual'. *Revista de Antropología y Arqueología* 6, no. 2 (1990): 37–59.

66   *The Muisca and the Problem of Religion*

Often, as in the earlier cases, their assumptions were challenged by what they encountered in practice, and the documents they produced provide a glimpse into local realities. And yet, the circumstances of the New Kingdom of Granada were such that this knowledge often had little effect. Because it lacked a printing press until the first half of the eighteenth century, it was also a manuscript culture in the age of print. Knowledge produced in the region – including but not limited to information about Indigenous peoples – only circulated with great difficulty, while works in printed form coming from imperial centres such as Mexico and Peru did so with comparative ease.[164] In this way, local legislation – such as the constitutions of the synods and provincial council of the church in Santafé, which are scrutinised in the following chapters – reflects imported stereotypes drawn from printed legislation produced in imperial centres, rather than local findings. Those texts not only reproduced ethnographies and models of social and religious organisation derived from the observation of societies in the central Andes and Central Mexico but – beyond the inclusion of a handful of local products and terms – lack any information derived from investigations carried out in the New Kingdom of Granada.[165] Inquiries, like those considered earlier, tended to start from the same premises, make the same mistakes, and reach the same conclusions again and again. The power of these fictions was difficult to dispel. But so are our own expectations – and this brings us to the thorny problem of 'religion'.

THE PROBLEM OF RELIGION

Colonial bureaucrats and missionaries have hardly been alone in taking for granted the applicability of European religious concepts to understand and explain Indigenous societies. In the decades that followed, these imported stereotypes and assumptions also served as the basis for increasingly elaborate formulations of an imagined Muisca religion in the writings of successive colonial chroniclers, especially as the initial encounter with the Muisca and the first decades of colonial rule faded from living memory. Writing in the 1570s, the chronicler Pedro de Aguado had

---

[164] Printing presses were established in Mexico in 1539 and Peru 1581, but would take another century and a half to reach the New Kingdom. José Toribio Medina, *La imprenta en Bogotá, 1739–1821* (Amsterdam: N. Israel, 1964).

[165] And as we will see, the imported stereotypes and assumptions of this normativity would serve as the basis for later investigations and civil and ecclesiastical visitations, perpetuating this cycle of misinformation. See Juan Fernando Cobo Betancourt and Natalie Cobo, eds, *La legislación de la arquidiócesis de Santafé en el periodo colonial* (Bogotá: Instituto Colombiano de Antropología e Historia, 2018), xxvii–xxix.

The Problem of Religion

claimed that *xeques* were pagan bishops and archbishops, but by the 1620s they had been recast, in the etymological speculations of his fellow Franciscan Pedro Simón (1574–1628), into a local manifestation of a global lineage of false priests stretching back into the distant past, perhaps to the ruler Geque of the Kingdom of Mazagan in Morocco or to the false priests of Persia. Simón also reimagined ritual enclosure, the *coyme*, into an institution like 'an Academy or University'.[166] Ubaque's *santuario*, Bochica, for his part, became a creator god, who created the rainbow and used it to drain the flooded valley of Bogotá, and was worshipped across the region alongside an elaborate pantheon of other deities, all headed by the sun.[167] By the 1680s, in the writings of Fernández de Piedrahita, who sought to incorporate the region and its inhabitants further into Christian history, Bochica had also become a civilising hero, descending to earth to found the Muisca religion – or perhaps he had actually been the apostle Bartholomew, introducing Christianity to the Northern Andes in antiquity, only for it to wither and grow corrupt under the influence of Satan.[168] The story, in short, grew more elaborate with each retelling, and an ever closer fit into the framework of Christian ideas.

This urge to understand the Muisca with Christian categories is not unique to the colonial period. Anthropologists have for some time highlighted the European and Christian genealogies of much of the 'conceptual apparatus' used by generations of scholars to make sense of the religious practices of societies around the world.[169] Our very concept of 'religion' in its modern sense, and the frameworks we use to compare religious traditions, as several scholars have argued, are precisely the product the interaction of European Christians with non-European societies from the sixteenth century on, and with each other through the

---

[166] Simón, *Noticias historiales*, 1892, pt. 2, cuarta noticia, ch. 5, p. 291.

[167] Ibid., pt. 2, cuarta noticia, ch. 10, p. 311.

[168] Fernández de Piedrahita, *Historia general*, 19. On contemporary ideas of a pre-Hispanic evangelisation elsewhere in the Andes, see Juan Carlos Estenssoro Fuchs, *Del paganismo a la santidad: la incorporación de los indios del Perú al catolicismo 1532–1750*. Translated by Gabriela Ramos (Lima: Pontificia Universidad Católica del Perú, 2003), 196–198.

[169] See Talal Asad, *Genealogies of Religion: Discipline and Reasons of Power in Christianity and Islam* (Baltimore: Johns Hopkins University Press, 2009). This is not to say that these concepts are therefore analytically useless, but rather that we need to approach them deliberately and critically. On this, see Alan Strathern, *Unearthly Powers: Religious and Political Change in World History* (Cambridge: Cambridge University Press, 2019), 11–14. This is comparable to the use of the developmental models concerning the origin and evolution of political and social structures. See, for example, Bernand and Gruzinski, *De la idolatría*.

68   *The Muisca and the Problem of Religion*

Reformation and Counter-Reformation.[170] As a result, one consequence of the overlap of the interpretative lens of colonial sources and the conceptual categories of modern scholarship has been the notion that the Muisca adhered to a relatively homogenous and centralised religion, involving some agreement around a series of core beliefs, even if scholars rejected the more outrageous inventions of colonial authors.[171] The illusion was further reinforced by the rich mythology and complex cosmology that these successive chroniclers ascribed to the Muisca, which continues to have a powerful hold on scholars, some of whom continue to resort to it in an effort to make sense of pre-Hispanic and colonial Indigenous societies.[172] So what, then, is 'Muisca religion'?

One influential model for understanding religious change among Indigenous societies in colonial Latin America has been that proposed by Nancy Farriss in her magisterial 1984 study of the Yucatec Maya, in which she argued that Christianity and Indigenous religious practices – 'Mesoamerican paganism' – were both 'complex, multi-layered systems' that 'confronted each other as total systems and interacted at a variety of levels'.[173] In order to understand how this occurred in practice, Farriss proposed a three-tiered model for the operation of religious beliefs and practices and the interaction of different traditions. At its core, the model held that both traditions could be organised into three categories: the universal, the corporate or parochial, and the private.[174] Because both

---

[170] Which of course is not to say that what came to be described in these terms had not been there all along in different societies, or that people before the early modern period had no means to recognise or label the religious practices of others. See Guy G. Stroumsa, *A New Science: The Discovery of Religion in the Age of Reason* (Cambridge, MA: Harvard University Press, 2010); and 'The Scholarly Discovery of Religion in Early Modern Times'. In *Cambridge World History. Vol. 6, part 2.* Edited by Jerry H. Bentley, Merry E. Wiesner-Hanks, and Sanjay Subrahmanyam (Cambridge: Cambridge University Press, 2015), 313–333.

[171] To paraphrase David Tavárez's criticism of employing the terminology of 'indigenous religion', in *Invisible War*, 4.

[172] A clear example is the work of François Correa, who sought to analyse this mythology to explore Muisca social organisation and the foundations of power, in *El sol del poder*. It is not unlikely that these sources contain some grounding in the stories, ideas, and traditions of some Muisca groups in colonial New Granada, and through them some memory of pre-Hispanic ones, but this book prefers to treat these accounts as reflections of the colonial present in which they were written, rather than attempting to untangle countless layers of interpretation, embellishment, and reimagination.

[173] Nancy Farriss, *Maya Society under Colonial Rule: The Collective Enterprise of Survival* (Princeton, NJ: Princeton University Press, 1984), 294–295.

[174] The model was a reinterpretation of Robin Horton's analysis of voluntary conversion from 'traditional' belief systems to 'universal' ones, which posited a difference in the

The Problem of Religion

operated on all three levels, and confronted each other as 'complete systems', interaction surely took place across each of them. More recently, in his analysis of Nahua and Zapotec religious practices, David Tavárez proposed a revised model, in which ritual labour and ritual exchanges take place in two spheres, the collective and the elective, both of which are intrinsically integrated with the universal.[175] But what, really, is the universal?

In his recent study of religious change in world history, Alan Strathern argues that 'religion' is a difficult concept to pin down in part because it 'strains to cover two distinctive phenomena'. On one hand, 'the tendency to imagine that the world plays host to supernatural forces and beings with whom we must interact in order to flourish', what he describes as 'immanentism', and on the other, those traditions that seek to overcome or escape the mundane, 'transcendentalism'.[176] The former is 'a universal feature of religion, found in every society under the sun', whilst the latter is associated with a much more limited range of traditions, including Christianity.[177] This is not to suggest that one is superior to the other, more rational, sophisticated, or advanced, but rather to highlight that the handful of traditions with the greatest number of adherents today – what other scholars have termed 'world religions' – are in fact historical exceptions rather the norm.[178] Instead, the object of this distinction is to break from teleological assumptions that see transcendentalist religious traditions as the culmination of human development or of cognitive

---

spheres of operation of these two kinds of belief system – a microcosm and a macrocosm, respectively. Instead, she sought to move away from this evolutionary model by seeing the microcosm and macrocosm as two ends of a continuum, throughout which religion operated – whether Christianity or Mesoamerican paganism. See Ibid., 294–296, based on Robin Horton, 'African Conversion'. *Africa: Journal of the International African Institute* 41, no. 2 (1971): 85–108, 'On the Rationality of Conversion: Part I'. *Africa: Journal of the International African Institute* 45, no. 3 (1975): 219–235, and 'On the Rationality of Conversion: Part II'. *Africa: Journal of the International African Institute* 45, no. 4 (1975): 373–399.

[175] Tavárez, *Invisible War*, 9–13.   [176] Strathern, *Unearthly Powers*, 3–6.

[177] For a detailed description of both concepts, see Ibid., ch. 1.

[178] This is in part an effort to overcome the shortcomings of earlier dichotomies that distinguished 'world' religions from traditions that have been variously described as "pagan', 'primitive', 'primal', 'local', 'communal', or 'traditional'. Strathern, following Robert Bellah, locates this divergence in the notion of an 'Axial Age', an increasingly popular organising principle in the historical sociology of religion. Ibid., 7, 19–26. For the Axial Age in Robert Neelly Bellah's thought, see his final book, *Religion in Human Evolution: From the Paleolithic to the Axial Age* (Cambridge, MA: Harvard University Press, 2011).

achievement.[179] In other words, to underscore that the notion that religious practices are necessarily directed to overcoming the mundane – to obtaining salvation, transcendence, or enlightenment – is not applicable except in a limited number of traditions. And yet, these ideas are usually at the centre of conceptions of the 'universal' or the 'macrocosm'. Put simply, we cannot assume that transcendentalism was a feature of religious practices among the Muisca and take this as the starting point for exploring religious change, without evidence that it actually was.

Instead, what the records of the colonial bureaucracy do allow us to glimpse are a series of complex practices firmly embedded in local contexts, where they played key roles in the functioning of a variety of aspects of everyday life for individuals and communities. At the scale of whole communities, it was the ritual economy that was organised and made possible by Indigenous rulers and their close associates, whose ability to transform mundane foods and objects into extraordinary feasts and gifts of key ritual significance brought the community together and made possible the flow of labour and exchange. Just as significantly, the matrilineal kinship groups that were the foundation of Muisca societies were bound together by familial ties, collective interest, and a common identity, closely connected to their lineage deities, which passed down through generations of their members, embodying their common heritage and their connection to the land. When these kinship groups came together with others to form larger ones, and when these composite units amalgamated to form larger units still, they were all held together by similar dynamics; and in this context too the maintenance of the lineage deities of certain privileged groups within the community for the benefit of all played a fundamental part.

As this chapter has shown, the latest historical, anthropological, and archaeological research on the Muisca has all questioned long-standing stereotypes about the configuration of these societies, beginning with the idea that they constituted a centralised, homogenous 'nation', ruled by leaders with vast powers over their societies. The picture that is emerging is more subtle, of societies composed of largely self-sufficient units coming together to pursue collective interests, led by elites whose position of leadership was in constant need of negotiation and reinforcement through ritual means. Social differentiation and stratification existed, but not straightforwardly in terms of the accumulation of material resources. Instead, hierarchy and leadership depended on the possession of symbolic power and its deployment for the benefit of the collective. This is why

---

[179] Strathern, *Unearthly Powers*, 18–19.

The Problem of Religion

some Indigenous leaders such as Ubaque and Tota held large celebrations for their communities, and provided stores of featherworks and adornments for certain occasions, and why others maintained their own exalted sanctuaries, some with dedicated staff and buildings.

The precise reasons why Muisca groups preserved the remains of their ancestors or made objects in their images are unclear, but scholarship on the cult of ancestors in other regions highlights the breadth of its functions in different contexts. It could be central to the representation and exercise of authority, as the case of Muisca leaders illustrates so clearly, but also in a variety of different situations. Lineage deities could aid their descendants in the pursuit of specific objectives, such as securing a steady supply of food as in the case of Moniquirá, or of cotton in Tota; in ensuring the health and well-being of the group, as in Iguaque and Lenguazaque; or even in appropriating and controlling land and territory, embodying the connection of a group to a particular place.[180]

This chapter has focused on analysing what glimpses of the practices of different Muisca groups can be seen in colonial documentation, but it is clear that this is only one part of what was undoubtedly a larger picture, a picture that may be beyond the scope afforded by surviving evidence to reconstruct. Earlier analyses of Muisca religious features focused on the descriptions of Muisca cosmology and mythology of the colonial chroniclers and later writers, sources of questionable reliability, and used them to make sense of Muisca social, political, and religious features during the colonial period.[181] François Correa, for example, has used these descriptions to argue that the symbolic power of Indigenous leaders, so central to the stratification of Muisca society, was the result of notions of solar descent.[182] And yet, much in the same way as the writers of these colonial chronicles sought to find Indigenous equivalents to Christian ideas of God, creation, the afterlife, and other concepts, and to describe their manifestation in practice, this methodology seems to take us in the opposite direction to understanding what was really going on.

What we can glean from the documentation of colonial bureaucrats about Indigenous religious practices highlights important considerations

---

[180] To paraphrase Gabriela Ramos, who provides an outline of ethnographic and anthropological research on the cult of ancestors and an analysis of its features in the central Andes in *Death and Conversion*, 9–10ff.

[181] Clara Inés Casilimas Rojas and María Imelda López Ávila, 'El templo muisca'. *Maguaré* 5 (1987): 127–150; Carlos Eduardo Mesa Gómez, 'Creencias religiosas de los pueblos indigenas que habitaban en el territorio de la futura Colombia'. *Missionalia Hispanica* 37, nos 109–111 (1980): 111–142.

[182] Correa, *El sol del poder*, 276ff, 340–345.

to take forwards in exploring Spanish efforts to incorporate Muisca societies into Christianity. Most recent analyses of religious change among Indigenous societies in the New World highlight that it is a complex process of adaptation and transformation, and emphasise the centrality of the role of Indigenous individuals and their communities in navigating and negotiating this change.[183] They also emphasise that change took place as a series of mutual exchanges across different contexts of religious practice and experience.

Practices such as those described in this chapter played important roles in Muisca communities, they were central to the foundations of the power of Indigenous leaders, to the production of food and necessary resources, to the identity and configuration of kinship groups and communities, and in many other such contexts and dimensions – some of which will remain inaccessible to scholars. Significantly, they were performed and maintained because they remained relevant in these diverse ways. This is how they were firmly embedded in the fabric of everyday life. The colonial authorities' effort to introduce Christianity, and to displace Indigenous religious practices, would therefore pose a multi-dimensional challenge to the very fabric of Indigenous societies. Considering just the role of religious practices in relation to Indigenous leaders, it is clear that conversion would endanger the very foundations of their power and authority, and jeopardise the colonial tributary economy that Spaniards sought to build on the back of Indigenous labour.

For evangelisation to be effective, it would have to engage with the needs of individuals and communities across all these different contexts. To do this, missionaries could draw from the rich and multi-layered landscape of everyday religion in Catholic Europe: a landscape of diverse traditions steeped in immanentism, of popular devotions, local ceremonies, participatory institutions, and everyday practice. For the rest of the century, however, the authorities of the New Kingdom of Granada did not avail themselves of much of this store of everyday practice. As a result in part of their preoccupations and priorities and in part of local conditions, their response for decades was in fact to withhold it, and to focus instead on undermining the existing religious landscape – with devastating results.

---

[183] See Farriss, *Maya Society*; Mills, *Idolatry*; Estenssoro Fuchs, 'Simio de Dios' and *Paganismo*; Ramos, *Death and Conversion*; and Tavárez, *Invisible War*.

2

The Settlers, Rescript Government, and the Foundations of the Kingdom

In July 1582, in the middle of a bitter lawsuit, the *mestizo* priest Alonso Romero de Aguilar told the *Audiencia* of Santafé the story of the coming of Christianity to the region half a century before. 'In the beginning of the planting of the faith', he explained, 'many friars came to this New Kingdom.' These Franciscans and Dominicans learned the local language 'most perfectly', and used it to preach in Indigenous towns, markets, and various public places. 'These Indians', he continued, 'thus began to understand and be persuaded that the coming of the Spaniards to this land was principally so they could teach them doctrine', and many had converted to Christianity. But this golden age of evangelisation had not lasted. Before long, the friars had abandoned their study of languages, interpreters had become scarce, and 'these Indians, whose faith was not yet well imprinted, apostatised and placed their faith in idolatry'.[1] Romero was a secular priest, ordained a few years before by the second archbishop of Santafé, Luis Zapata de Cárdenas, who had recently ignited a conflict with the religious orders over the distribution of Indigenous parishes.[2] It was in this context that Romero and some of his fellow secular priests, all of whom were bilingual, had taken their case to the *Audiencia*, arguing that the mendicants were not fit to run such parishes because of their neglect of Indigenous languages – a fact made all the more scandalous by their supposed early history – and that in any case

[1] Alonso Romero de Aguilar to the *Audiencia* of Santafé, 10 July 1582, AGI SF 234, n. 47, 24r.
[2] The precise details of this controversy, which concerned the use of Indigenous languages in catechisation, are scrutinised in Chapter 5.

73

74   The Settlers, Rescript, and the Foundations of the Kingdom

they were no longer needed now that there was a functioning diocesan hierarchy and plenty of secular priests to go round.[3]

Conflicts of this kind between the secular and regular church will be familiar to many scholars of colonial Spanish America and the Philippines. When the Spanish crown needed to deploy clerical manpower overseas, only the mendicant orders could provide it: they had sufficient numbers, indeed far outnumbering their secular counterparts in Iberia in the sixteenth century; a long tradition of missionary activity in Europe and the further reaches of the world known to Europeans; and, above all, they were the only people in the church with the institutional organisation and experience required. These were circumstances and qualities that the secular clergy lacked.[4] The regulars, in turn, generally did not have many of the powers necessary to minister to the laity, a task from which they had traditionally been excluded, so a number of these were granted to them by the papacy to make their participation in this missionary enterprise possible.[5] Rooted in earlier concessions designed to facilitate the conduct of missions outside of Europe during the middle ages, these grants empowered the regulars not just to run parishes and administer the sacraments to the laity in the absence of secular priests but even, as a collective, to perform functions usually reserved to bishops.[6] As a result, in many regions, the evangelisation of Indigenous people was initially in

---

[3] The suit also concerned the more immediate issue of the payment of the salary of the holder of the chair of Muisca language, Gonzalo Bermúdez, which had been withheld by the *Audiencia* at the request of the regular authorities as part of this broader conflict. This is also discussed in greater detail in Chapter 5.

[4] The Spanish crown funded the passage to Spanish America of over 15,000 regulars between 1493 and 1822, to destinations from California to Patagonia. Of these, around 1,150 were dispatched to destinations in New Granada. Detailed records survive of these subsidies, which have been analysed in detail in Pedro Borges Morán, *El envío de misioneros a América durante la época española* (Salamanca: Universidad Pontificia, 1977), 477–540.

[5] For a discussion of these privileges, see Antonio García García, 'Los privilegios de los franciscanos en América'. *Archivo Ibero-Americano* 48, no. 48 (1988): 369–390; and Jorge E. Traslosheros, 'Audiencia Episcopal (Episcopal Court)'. *Max Planck Institute for Legal History and Legal Theory Research Paper Series 2021* no. 12 (2021), 13–15.

[6] In 1521, for example, they had been authorised to administer even confirmation and ordination (up to minor orders), to consecrate chapels, altars, chalices, and other objects; appoint ministers for churches and other benefices; grant indulgences; and other powers usually reserved to 'bishops in their dioceses'. See *Alias felicis recordationis*, 25 June 1521, in Metzler, *America Pontificia*, vol. 1, 161–162. Subsequent grants extended these privileges. On earlier, medieval, concessions, see James Muldoon, *Popes, Lawyers and Infidels: The Church and the Non-Christian World, 1250–1550* (Philadelphia: Penn State University Press, 1979).

The Settlers, Rescript, and the Foundations of the Kingdom   75

their hands and so, when the secular church finally arrived years later – the story goes – it had the difficult task of carving a place for itself on an already crowded table, which often resulted in administrative and jurisdictional conflict.[7]

These are the broad coordinates within which the early institutional history of Christianisation in New Granada has usually been laid out, from early descriptions such as Romero's, through the writings of successive chroniclers, to the work of generations of historians. First, a haphazard, mendicant evangelisation from the late 1530s, followed by a painful but effective transition to a second stage characterised by the growing leadership of the secular church, which sought, with royal support, to centralise and homogenise the missionary enterprise – variously collaborating or clashing with the civil authorities on the ground.[8] The trouble, as is so often the case with the New Kingdom of Granada, is that much of what we think that we know about this early history is, like Romero's sketch of the early mendicants of Santafé, mostly misconception, wishful thinking, or illusion. In reality, there was no golden age of mendicant evangelisation in New Granada: when the first bishop, Juan de los Barrios, arrived in Santafé in 1553 there were but two Franciscans in the entire highlands and one of them was in jail, the lone Augustinian had

---

[7] In Mexico, the religious orders enjoyed a period of relative autonomy in which to experiment with a variety of missionary models, without the guidance or pressure of a centralised ecclesiastical hierarchy – until one began to take shape in the 1530s and to seek to curtail their independence. In Peru, invasion and conquest came later, and were followed by a period of instability and civil war, during which evangelisation was also largely in the hands of regulars, with the secular church lagging behind. In both contexts, the tide began to turn in the 1550s, with the promulgation of the first comprehensive legislation of the secular church at the first provincial councils of Mexico and Lima, which notably sought to circumscribe the role of the regulars. The trend then accelerated with the conclusion of the Council of Trent in 1563 and royal legislation to strengthen episcopal control over evangelisation from 1574. For an introduction to this broad chronology, see John Frederick Schwaller, ed., *The Church in Colonial Latin America* (Lanham, MD: Rowman & Littlefield Publishers, 2000), especially xvii–xviii. On the Peruvian context, see Estenssoro Fuchs, 'Simio de Dios', 459–461 and *Paganismo*, 31–34 and 47–53. On Mexico, Ryan Dominic Crewe, *The Mexican Mission: Indigenous Reconstruction and Mendicant Enterprise in New Spain, 1521–1600* (Cambridge Latin American Studies. Cambridge: Cambridge University Press, 2019), especially ch. 6.

[8] For this perspective, see, for example, Groot, *Historia eclesiástica y civil*; Mario Germán Romero, *Fray Juan de los Barrios y la evangelización del Nuevo Reino de Granada* (Bogotá: Academia Colombiana de Historia, 1960); Juan Manuel Pacheco, *La evangelización del Nuevo Reino, siglo XVI. Historia extensa de Colombia. Vol. 13, part 1* (Bogotá: Academia Colombiana de Historia, 1971); and Luis Carlos Mantilla, *Los franciscanos en Colombia (1550–1600)* (Bogotá: Editorial Kelly, 1984).

76   *The Settlers, Rescript, and the Foundations of the Kingdom*

gone in search of El Dorado, and the Dominicans were in crisis. Almost no one had learned Indigenous languages. And few Indigenous people had ever had contact with Christianity – let alone embraced the new religion in droves. Nor was the arrival of the secular church and its civil counterpart, the *Audiencia* of Santafé, a straightforward watershed. The introduction of these institutions of royal government was in fact haphazard, chaotic, and ineffective, and both would struggle for decades to make their claims and designs material.

This chapter explores the early history of colonial rule in the New Kingdom of Granada, and of the friars, secular priests, bishops, and royal officials tasked with introducing Christianity to Indigenous people in the middle decades of the sixteenth century. If understanding the workings of the social and political organisation of Muisca groups, and especially their religious practices, required unpicking a series of entrenched stereotypes and powerful assumptions, making sense of this history requires a comparable effort. Once again, it is not just the colonial chronicles, so favoured by earlier generations of historians, that are misleading – in this case, conventual histories that gloss over the complexity of this early period or understand it as the gradual unfolding of a fully formed missionary church and colonial administration.[9] In fact, early descriptions of missionary activity in petitions and letters are, like the accounts of the invasion analysed before, rife with exaggeration and misconception, designed more to elicit support and reward than to record or document. These and later sources also tend to take the efficacy of the power of the kingdom's civil and ecclesiastical authorities for granted, when in reality their ability to effect change remained fleeting, contingent, and inconstant.

To understand the limitations of early Spanish colonial governance in New Granada, this chapter reflects on the particularities of three of its

---

[9] This is the case in the very first Franciscan chronicle, produced in the 1580s by the then head of the order in Santafé, fray Esteban de Asensio, *Memorial de la fundación de la provincia de Santa Fe del Nuevo Reino de Granada del orden de San Francisco 1550–1585* (Madrid: Librería General de Victoriano Suárez, 1921). The first conventual chronicles and histories of the Dominicans in Santafé, which appeared in print as part of a larger work in 1619, also largely skipped the period between their formal establishment in 1551 and the activities of some of their more notable members after 1565. See Antonio de Remesal, *Historia de la provincia de S. Vicente de Chyapa y Guatemala de la orden de nuestro glorioso padre sancto Domingo*, (Madrid: F. de Angulo, 1619) book 9, 549–556. It would take until the 1690s for a Dominican chronicle specifically focused on the New Kingdom to appear, in the form of Alonso de Zamora, *Historia de la provincia de San Antonino del Nuevo Reino de Granada*. Edited by Caracciolo Parra and Andrés Mesanza (Bogotá: Editorial ABC, 1945).

principal areas of action. First, it re-examines the establishment and consolidation of Santafé as an administrative centre in civil and ecclesiastical affairs by exploring the participatory and contingent nature of the royal administration and judiciary, at both an imperial and a local level, and its reliance on petitioners, supplicants, and rescript. Then it reassesses the role of legislation in shaping the development of the kingdom and the incorporation of Indigenous peoples into colonial rule, by exploring the legislative projects and designs of Bishop Barrios and his civil counterparts. Finally, it tests the efficacy and real impact of these institutions and their claims on the lives of the over 280,000 Indigenous inhabitants of the provinces of Santafé and Tunja through a careful re-reading of the records of early visitations, showing that for decades royal control remained an illusion, and in practice power remained far from the hands of the kingdom's civil and ecclesiastical authorities.

'PAPER AND GOOD WORDS'

That the early history of Christianisation in the New Kingdom was so easily reimagined in the 1580s is in part a reflection of the comparative lack of sources produced in the region before the arrival of the two principal institutions of royal government in the middle of the century: the *Audiencia* – or royal court and chancery – of Santafé de Bogotá; and the bishop and his curia, its counterpart in ecclesiastical affairs.[10] The two served as judicial authorities in their respective spheres of action, hearing cases, conducting enquiries, and resolving conflicts.[11] They received petitions and complaints and took action to address them, either by themselves or by issuing writs and instructions empowering others to do so on their behalf. Both also issued legislation, according to the extent of their jurisdictions and in different capacities. They exercised – at least on paper – executive authority in their share of government, to a greater or

---

[10] On the development and characteristics of Spanish colonial *audiencias*, see Carlos Antonio Garriga Acosta, 'Las audiencias: Justicia y gobierno de las Indias'. In *El gobierno de un mundo: Virreinatos y audiencias en la América Hispánica*. Edited by Feliciano Barrios (Cuenca: Ediciones de la Universida de Castilla-La Mancha, 2004), 711–794.

[11] In the case of the bishops, on cases pertaining to spiritual affairs broadly understood, from matters of canon law and doctrine, to issues concerning the clergy and certain issues pertaining to the behaviour and customs of the laity. For an excellent recent introduction to the organisation and functioning of episcopal courts (*audiencias episcopales*) in Spanish America, see Traslosheros, 'Audiencia Episcopal'. Unfortunately, the archive of the episcopal court of the Archdiocese of Santafé has never been available to researchers, and may well have been lost.

78   The Settlers, Rescript, and the Foundations of the Kingdom

lesser extent in representation of the distant monarch. And they too, in turn, acted as informants, petitioners, suppliants, and generally prolific correspondents with their superiors on the other side of the Atlantic. As a result, the bulk of the colonial archive, whether now held in Colombia, Spain, Rome, or elsewhere, was generally produced by, mediated through, or at the very least involved, one of these two institutions. But Santafé had not always been an administrative centre, and the story of how it became one, although more difficult to reconstruct, deserves attention.

Since its foundation in 1538, Santafé and the other highland cities established in the wake of the European invasion had fallen under the jurisdiction of the Caribbean city and province of Santa Marta in both civil and ecclesiastical affairs. The first expedition to reach the highlands, under Gonzalo Jiménez de Quesada, had set off at the initiative and under the authority of Santa Marta's governor, Pedro Fernández de Lugo, and so the newly settled regions fell under its jurisdiction – despite Jiménez's ultimately unsuccessful efforts to claim an independent title to the new discoveries. Santafé's early development, then, was as an offshoot. After Lugo's death in 1536, the government of Santa Marta had fallen to interim governor Jerónimo Lebrón, who was in Santa Marta when Jiménez and some of his men, including San Martín and Lebrija, passed through in June 1539 on their way back to Castile to petition the king to recognise their claims and settle their conflicts. Lebrón promptly set about organising his own expedition to the interior, which arrived in the highlands in the summer of 1540s, not least to sell the newly rich settlers a full complement of European imports.[12] His successor, Fernández de Lugo's son and heir Alonso, would do the same shortly after, once he was confirmed in his late father's titles.

In ecclesiastical matters, the highland interior also fell under the jurisdiction of the diocese of Santa Marta, the first in the region of modern-day Colombia, which had been established in 1534. Its bishop, Juan Fernández de Angulo, thus sent *maestrescuela* Pedro García Matamoros with Lebrón's expedition, to minister to Spaniards in the new highland cities as his representative.[13] As Santafé began to expand and develop as an economic centre, the balance between the Caribbean lowlands and the

---

[12] His ostensible aim, to have the settlers of Santafé recognise him as their governor, was less successful. José Ignacio Avellaneda Navas, *The Conquerors of the New Kingdom of Granada* (Albuquerque: University of New Mexico Press, 1995), 40–44.

[13] Alberto Lee López, 'Clero indígena en el Arzobispado de Santafé en el siglo XVI'. *Boletín de Historia y Antigüedades* 50, nos 579–581 (1963): 9.

'Paper and Good Words' 79

Andean highlands began to shift in its favour, and this was reflected in the growing interest of successive ecclesiastical authorities to relocate to Santafé. In the mid 1540s, Fernández de Angulo's successor, Martín de Calatayud, passed through the city on his way to being consecrated in Lima, and began to petition the king to ask the pope to move the seat of his diocese there permanently.[14] The change would take another eight years to take effect, but this was how Calatayud's successor, Juan de los Barrios, found himself arriving in the city in April 1553 as bishop of Santa Marta and New Kingdom of Granada, as the diocese was now known.[15] That the Spanish crown was so closely involved in this is a reflection of the special privileges that the Spanish monarchy had come to enjoy over the church in the previous decades: the succession of papal concessions known collectively as *patronato*, or royal patronage, which granted the crown wide powers over ecclesiastical affairs and, in certain key respects, made the secular church answerable to the monarch.[16]

Barrios and his secular church were one part of a larger effort to transform the highlands from Caribbean hinterland into northern South America's colonial core.[17] The other was the establishment of the *Audiencia* to serve as the kingdom's chief executive authority and highest court of appeal.[18] The bishop and the *Audiencia* were to work to overhaul their respective spheres of action but also to collaborate in the pursuit of even their most central objectives. The *Audiencia* was to help the bishop construct an effective missionary project, exercising a number of the powers of royal *patronato*. The bishop, for his part, was to help the *Audiencia* implement recent empire-wide legislation on the treatment of Indigenous people and the reform of the *encomienda*, the famous New

---

[14] His petition was referenced in the king's reply, the royal rescript or *cédula* of 5 February 1549, AGI SF 533, lib. 1, 13r–13v.

[15] See also Pacheco, *La evangelización*, 168; Luis Carlos Mantilla, *Historia de la arquidiócesis de Bogotá: Su itinerario evangelizador, 1564–1993* (Bogotá: Arquidiócesis de Bogotá, 1994), 8.

[16] For an outline of these papal concessions, see Juan Fernando Cobo Betancourt, *Mestizos heraldos de Dios: La ordenación de sacerdotes descendientes de españoles e indígenas en el Nuevo Reino de Granada y la racialización de la diferencia, 1573–1590* (Bogotá: Instituto Colombiano de Antropología e Historia, 2012), 32–35.

[17] These imperial designs, and their implementation, are the subject of Muñoz Arbeláez, 'The New Kingdom'.

[18] The precise date of the creation of the *Audiencia* of Santafé is unclear and remains the subject of debate, and could, on paper, have been as early as May 1547, when its first *oidores* were appointed. For an overview, see Mayorga García, *La Audiencia*, 453 n. 8.

80   *The Settlers, Rescript, and the Foundations of the Kingdom*

Laws of 1542–1543. And each was to keep an eye on the other and alert the king if they went astray.[19]

This new *Audiencia* was given power and jurisdiction not just over the highland interior but also over the older Caribbean districts, *gobernaciones*, of Santa Marta and Cartagena – a change that was matched in ecclesiastical affairs in 1564, when the diocese of Santafé was elevated to the rank of archdiocese and made the metropolitan of the older dioceses of Cartagena and Popayán. Santafé's transformation into an ecclesiastical capital was completed in 1577, when the old region of Santa Marta was spun off as an independent diocese once more, but now under Santafé's jurisdiction.[20] This territorial refocusing from the Caribbean to the Andes was also reflected in the expansion of the term 'New Kingdom of Granada', initially used to describe only the highland interior, but which came to be applied to the entire region of northern South America under the rule of the *Audiencia* of Santafé, including the older Caribbean districts. In theory and in legislation, then, this New Kingdom developed very rapidly indeed. In practice it would take a great deal more than ink and paper.

It is tempting to understand these developments as the implementation of a design by the Spanish crown: first to impose its authority and power over the region's inhabitants through the creation of institutions of civil and ecclesiastical government, and then to use these institutions to implement royal policy. Intuitive as this may seem to modern eyes, this perspective in fact obscures the complex and participatory nature of the workings of early modern government and legislation – and its most fundamental limitations. Although in theory and in law colonial governance was a top-down affair, involving the delegation of power and jurisdiction from the monarch through successive rungs of the administrative hierarchy, in practice, the relationship between the crown and its subjects in most spheres of activity was in many ways the opposite, as it was local actors and officials who brought the monarchy's authority to bear on the issues that affected them through petitions (*peticiones*) and reports (*memoriales*).[21] In them, petitioners and supplicants provided the distant monarch, or his more

---

[19] As was made clear to Barrios on his appointment. See his letter from Prince Philip, 10 November 1551, AGI SF 533, lib. 1, 176v.

[20] The historiographical consequences of this change are discussed in Chapter 3.

[21] For an excellent survey of colonial Spanish American diplomatic, see José Joaquín Real Díaz, *Estudio diplomático del documento indiano* (Seville: Escuela de Estudios Hispanoamericanos, 1970), which discusses petitions and their handling in the royal chancery at 58–72.

'Paper and Good Words' 81

immediate representatives, with a vision of local affairs and usually suggested a course of action to resolve the issue at hand.[22]

Such petitions could be requests to the monarch for a favour, a *merced*, in response to a particular need, great or small: from asking the pope to move the seat of the diocese of Santa Marta to Santafé, to rewarding a young bilingual priest for his merits and service. Or they could be requests for the monarch or his representatives to rule in the resolution of a conflict or a suit. Petitions could be answered straight away, or they could prompt an inquiry, a *consulta*, requiring the input of other administrators and counsellors, whether at court or elsewhere in the monarchy, before issuing a decision or ruling.[23] Responses to petitions and requests then took the form of royal letters of decree – *reales provisiones, cédulas*, or other *despachos* – which constitute much of Spanish colonial law.[24] These responses then empowered a given petitioner or official to take action in a specific way, but also generally left them the initiative and responsibility for doing so. Not only was this administration by response, but also, because these decrees tended to reproduce the content of the original petitions, it was also administration by *rescript*. The language of supplicants became the language of the king, and in the process, their appeals and petitions served to make – however fleetingly – the monarch's authority and power a reality on the ground.[25]

This is clear in the emergence of Santafé as a colonial centre. Within a year of the city's foundation in 1538, confident that 'this city will be the most important in the whole province', the settlers who made up Santafé's

[22] Although the usefulness and purpose of this early modern information-gathering should not itself be taken for granted. See Kathryn Burns, *Into the Archive: Writing and Power in Colonial Peru* (Durham, NC: Duke University Press, 2010), 12; and Arndt Brendecke, 'Informing the Council: Central Institutions and Local Knowledge in the Spanish Empire'. In *Empowering Interactions: Political Cultures and the Emergence of the State in Europe 1300–1900*. Edited by Wim Blockmans, André Holenstein, and Jon Mathieu (Farnham: Routledge, 2017), 236–237.

[23] On the functioning of these *consultas*, see the introduction to Antonia Heredia Herrera, ed., *Catálogo de las consultas del Consejo de Indias (1529–1591)* (Madrid: Dirección General de Archivos y Bibliotecas, 1972).

[24] On the taxonomy of the documents (*despachos*) issued by the royal chancery, from the most solemn (*provisiones*) to the least (*cédulas*), see Real Díaz, *Estudio diplomático*, 147–187.

[25] For an overview of rescript government in Spanish America, and its role in the development and spread of categories and ideas of race and difference concerning *mestizos*, see Cobo Betancourt, *Mestizos heraldos de Dios*, especially ch. 1. More recently, Adrian Masters explored similar trends in 'A Thousand Invisible Architects: Vassals, the Petition and Response System, and the Creation of Spanish Imperial Caste Legislation'. *Hispanic American Historical Review* 98, no. 3 (2018): 377–406.

82 The Settlers, Rescript, and the Foundations of the Kingdom

brand new *cabildo*, or municipal council, began to petition the crown to make their city the administrative capital of the region, whether by relocating the provincial administration from Santa Marta or by creating an independent administration in Santafé. It was they who petitioned the king from as early as 1539 'to call, and command others to call, this city and kingdom "the New Kingdom of Granada"', to establish a mint and other government offices, and to foster its church. The king, they requested, should provide priests for Santafé and neighbouring cities, build churches and endow them with 'ornaments and other sundries', and also send friars and other 'expert men' to engage in the conversion of Indigenous people to Christianity.[26] Along the way, the settlers of Santafé also petitioned for favourable rates of taxation on the importation of cattle and other necessities, the extraction of gold and precious stones, Indigenous tribute, and other concerns. In the best style of rescript government, these petitions soon gave rise to a whole string of royal legislation, echoing their petitions, and variously granting, tempering, or rejecting their requests.

Rescript government was by no means unique to the early modern Spanish administration but was a recurring feature of many premodern governments. In the European context, it has received perhaps the most attention as a key contributor to the expansion and consolidation of papal authority from the twelfth century and the production of canon law.[27] There, too, a chancery received an ever-growing flood of petitions and appeals requesting a ruling or response. These were issued by papal officials, often echoing the wording of the request, and ideally, if not always, ensuring that the response was in accordance with the law and earlier responses.[28] In the process, the act of petitioning itself contributed to make the papacy's broad claims of jurisdiction a reality, at least for those concerned.[29] As Colin Morris noted, rescript government was

---

[26] This in a 1539 petition to the king from the *cabildo* of Santafé (AGI SF 60, n. 1, 2r).

[27] For a recent outline of this historiography, see Thomas William Smith, *Curia and Crusade: Pope Honorius III and the Recovery of the Holy Land: 1216–1227* (Turnhout: Brepols Publishers, 2017), 21–24. I remain indebted to Patrick Zutschi for this insight on the parallels between the chanceries of the twelfth- and thirteenth-century papacy and of early modern Spanish royal courts.

[28] On this problem, see Arndt Brendecke, *Imperio e información: funciones del saber en el dominio colonial español.* 2nd edition (Madrid: Iberoamericana, 2016), 110–112.

[29] Patrick Zutshi, 'Petitioners, Popes, Proctors: The Development of Curial Institutions, c. 1150–1250'. In *Pensiero e sperimentazioni istituzionali nella Societas Christiana, 1046–1250: Atti della sedicesima Settimana internazionale di studio, Mendola, 26–31 agosto 2004.* Edited by Giancarlo Andenna (Milan: Editrice Vita e Pensiero, 2007), 287.

'Paper and Good Words' 83

particularly well suited to contexts in which governments lacked the means to enforce their authority evenly – especially over vast geographies – but could offer 'a jurisdiction to which parties could turn'.[30] Conversely, it was a system that was ill suited to proactive or consistent policymaking – especially policy that ran counter to the interests of the supplicants and petitioners on whom the system depended. Contrary to the top-down, universal claims of the papacy, in practice the formulation, content, and direction of papal decisions and their subsequent implementation, scholars have shown, is better understood from the opposite direction, as the result of the influence and participation of countless petitioners and supplicants.[31]

There is significant distance from the medieval papal Curia to the early modern Spanish court, but not much in this regard. What the monarchy offered its subjects in distant geographies and contexts was a jurisdiction that they could invoke in the pursuit of their own affairs. On its own, this was little more than 'paper and good words' – to paraphrase Gonzalo Fernández de Oviedo on the contribution of the king to conquest – but still words that local actors could enact into reality.[32] In the process they also helped to establish precedents and patterns that shaped and moulded – or more accurately, *translated* – the law to better respond to the conditions of their diverse developing contexts and circumstances. In this way, rescript administration was also a key component behind perhaps the most distinctive characteristic of colonial Spanish American law, what legal historians since at least Víctor Tau Anzoátegui have described as its emphasis on casuistry rather than on systematic principles – that is, the fact that the law was predominantly rooted in the particularities of each individual case, rather than on abstract norms or legal doctrines.[33] With the exception of a handful of specific areas, which

---

[30] As a result, for Colin Morris, 'at the heart of what may seem a very active administration the pope or king was passive, responding to applications without, in many cases, any real capacity to assess the situation'. See *The Papal Monarchy: The Western Church from 1050 to 1250* (Oxford: Clarendon Press, 1989), 211–213.

[31] Even, as Thomas Smith recently argued, in areas such as the organisation of the crusades, which were well beyond 'quotidian ecclesiastical business'. See *Curia and Crusade*, 24.

[32] Gonzalo Fernández de Oviedo y Valdés, *Historia general y natural de las Indias, islas y tierra-firme del mar Océano* (Madrid: Real Academia de la Historia, 1851), book 35, ch. 4 (=vol. 3, 597). The phrase was analysed by Alfonso García Gallo in 'La ley como fuente del derecho en Indias en el siglo XVI'. *Anuario de historia del derecho español* 21–22 (1951), 608.

[33] Víctor Tau Anzoátegui, *Casuismo y sistema: Indagación histórica sobre el espíritu del derecho indiano* (Buenos Aires: Instituto de Investigaciones de Historia del Derecho, 1992). For a recent discussion of Tau's contributions to early Ibero-American legal history, and his distinction between casuistry and system, see Thomas Duve and Heikki

84   *The Settlers, Rescript, and the Foundations of the Kingdom*

will be discussed in a moment, it is difficult, therefore, to write of pro-active policymaking on the part of the monarchy, or of the development of systematic principles beyond identifying patterns in the response to multiple petitions over time. This was a challenge with which the successive jurists, academics, and administrators who sought to compile and codify royal legislation struggled time and time again, as Tau and others showed, because overcoming casuistry and arriving at a fixed and uniform legal system in fact involved trying to read coherence and structure into the law retroactively.[34]

The other driver of rescript government was the resolution of conflicts, which was also key for the development of public law and imperial institutions. The establishment of the *Audiencia* of Santafé is a case in point. In the years after their first petitions to the monarch, the settlers of Santafé and nearby Tunja had begun to struggle with the expense and inconvenience of taking their suits and cases to authorities in the Caribbean, let alone across the Atlantic. A key issue was the growing number of disputes among the settlers over the spoils of the invasion. The city's founder, Gonzalo Jiménez de Quesada, had made the first distribution of *encomiendas*, grants of Indigenous tribute, and in the process had favoured his own followers over those of Nikolaus Federmann and Sebastián de Belalcázar, the leaders of the two expeditions that had arrived in the highlands shortly after his own.[35] This gave rise to conflicts over uneven access to tribute and resources, while even those who had received *encomiendas* from Jiménez felt insecure in their titles and sought royal guarantees of their permanence, fearing that subsequent governors might take them away in favour of their

---

Pihlajamäki, eds, *New Horizons in Spanish Colonial Law. Contributions to Transnational Early Modern Legal History* (Frankfurt: Max Planck Institute for European Legal History, 2016), and especially the chapter by Brian Philip Owensby, 'The Theater of Conscience in the "Living Law" of the Indies', 125–149.

[34] See Tau Anzoátegui, *Casuismo y sistema*, 152. Tau also discusses the earliest of these efforts, by Juan de Ovando from 1569 (at 393–394). An excellent survey of this and subsequent efforts of compilation and codification of Spanish American law remains Juan Manzano Manzano's two-volume *Historia de las recopilaciones de Indias: siglo XVI* (Madrid: Ediciones Cultura Hispánica, 1950).

[35] According to María Ángeles Eugenio Martínez, Jiménez granted *encomiendas* to 105 of the 289 Spaniards who arrived in the three initial expeditions, of whom 72 were his followers. See *Tributo y trabajo del indio en Nueva Granada (de Jiménez de Quesada a Sande)* (Seville: CSIC, 1977), 13.

'Paper and Good Words' 85

own clients.[36] This was, predictably, precisely what Alonso Luis de Lugo proceeded to do after he displaced Jiménez as *adelantado* and governor of the region in the early 1540s, when the crown ruled that Santafé should belong to the governorship of Santa Marta that Lugo had inherited from his father Pedro.[37]

Matters were further complicated by the crown's promulgation of the famous New Laws in 1542–1543 that, among other matters, sought to reform and curtail the institution of the *encomienda*.[38] Their implementation was the principal task entrusted to Miguel Díez de Armendáriz, a royal official first sent to the region in March 1543 to conduct a general visitation in response to the petitions and complaints of the settlers, and who would later displace Lugo as the first royal governor of the New Kingdom.[39] His promulgation of the New Laws in Santafé in early January 1547 poured fuel on the fire of settler discontent, especially as he started to investigate and reverse some of his predecessors' grants of *encomiendas* and to make his own.[40] Appeals to the crown to intervene in resolving their various conflicts, and indeed to suspend the application of hated aspects of the New Laws, were slow and frustrating, but the kingdom's settlers had their eyes on another solution, even if the price was steep.[41]

The New Laws had redrawn the political geography of much of Spanish America, disbanding the *Audiencia* of Panama and creating new *audiencias* in Lima and Guatemala. This reorganisation bypassed northern South America, which remained under the jurisdiction of the *Audiencia* of Santo Domingo, although the settlers soon set to work to

[36] For example, in the petition of the *cabildo* of Santafé, 1539, AGI SF 60, n. 1, 2r.

[37] After years of failed litigation by Jiménez to hold on to these positions, the crown eventually ruled that the new discovery fell under the terms of a 1535 *capitulación* it had signed with the governor of Santa Marta, Pedro Fernández de Lugo. Lugo had died in 1536, so these titles and powers were awarded to his son and heir Alonso, who proceeded to take his own expedition of settlers from Spain in 1542–1543. For an English-language outline of this history, complete with translations of key documents, see Francis, *Invading Colombia*.

[38] An excellent overview of those aspects pertaining to the *encomienda* remains Lewis Hanke, *The Spanish Struggle for Justice in the Conquest of America* (Boston; Toronto: Little, Brown and Company, 1949), 91–105.

[39] See the inventory of the various items of legislation that either empowered Díez to act on a matter, or that he was required to implement, dated 22 March 1543, which included not just a decree empowering him to do so, but also six freshly printed copies of the legislation, AGI Patronato 195, r. 10, 29v.

[40] See Eugenio Martínez, *Tributo y trabajo*, 3, 33–40.

[41] If not entirely ineffective, as the settlers had managed to obtain a two-year suspension of the New Laws until 1549. See Ibid., 22–33, 131–133.

86   The Settlers, Rescript, and the Foundations of the Kingdom

change this. A few of these petitions survive, such as an extensive report of 3 February 1547 by procurators for Santafé, Tunja, and other highland cities on the various ills that afflicted their constituents – chief among them the *encomienda* clauses of the New Laws and actions of governor Armendáriz – in which they argued that they should be given an *Audiencia* of their own to better resolve their suits and grievances. Getting petitions to Santo Domingo was 'hard work and a great expense', while Santafé was an ideal site for an *Audiencia*, being at the centre of several provinces and boasting the best climate and the most abundant supplies of food. With this, they added, 'we will not be aggrieved and bothered by governors, as we have until now'.[42] In the same vein, two weeks later, the *cabildo* of Santafé wrote to the king directly, reiterating the arguments they had been making for almost a decade – that their city should be an administrative centre as 'land so healthful and abundant' – but now explicitly arguing for the need to establish an *Audiencia* there, and as soon as possible.[43]

It could hardly have been a surprise to the settlers, after their requests were granted, that the *oidores* that began to be appointed to set up the new *Audiencia* of Santafé later that year were given express instructions to implement the dreaded New Laws on arrival, as they duly did on the inauguration of the *Audiencia* in April 1550, but at least now they could appeal and negotiate with the king's representatives more directly and also take advantage of the new institution to pursue their claims and resolve their conflicts.[44] Notably, the *Audiencia* also arrived with instructions to implement a series of reforms concerning everything from tribute collection schedules to different aspects of the extraction and taxation of emeralds – all in answer to requests from the settlers and their representatives, such as a twenty-nine-point petition by Jiménez himself, which alone resulted in no less than twelve rescripts instructing the *Audiencia* to take action on specific issues.[45] In other words, the coming of the *Audiencia* was at least as much the policy of the settlers of Santafé as it

---

[42] Petition of the procurators of Santafé, Tunja, Vélez, and los Panches, 3 February 1547, AGI Patronato 195, ramo 1, 181r.

[43] Letter of the *cabildo* of Santafé to the king, 15 February 1547, AGI SF 60, n. 4, 1v.

[44] Admittedly, the fact that in 1545 the king had revoked the most controversial clause, forbidding the granting of new *encomiendas* and ordering that they all revert to the monarch on the death of their holders, had taken some of the sting out. Hanke, *The Spanish Struggle for Justice*, 101.

[45] The petition, on these issues and more, can be found in AGI Patronato 196, r. 30, and its rescripts in AGI SF 533, 62v–73v.

'Paper and Good Words'

was of the king, for it was they who had been working to persuade the monarchy to turn Santafé into a colonial administrative centre, invited the *Audiencia* into their city, provided it with much of its agenda, and invoked and enacted the king's claims of jurisdiction in pursuit of their own interests and for the resolution of their grievances and conflicts – even if it meant submitting, at least in theory, to life under a tighter leash.

It is all too easy to take the effectiveness of the jurisdiction and power of the Spanish crown for granted, precisely because the sources this system produced, of petitions and rescripts, are predicated on accepting its claims and, as we have seen, served to enact them in specific contexts. But, in practice, the administration was greatly dependent on the continued participation of its supplicants and informants, and not just at the level of the court of the king. The receipt of appeals and petitions was also the principal mode of operation for the Spanish imperial administration at a local level. *Audiencias* in Spanish America and the Philippines were not just courts of law where cases were heard, but just as fundamentally chanceries, *chancillerías*, that received and answered appeals and petitions as correspondence.[46] Supplicants, like Romero de Aguilar, addressed their requests to the *Audiencia* of Santafé as if to the king ('Most powerful Lord', in the singular) and it in turn issued rescripts, *reales provisiones*, in response, written in the king's stead ('Don Carlos, by the divine clemency Emperor', etc.) and with his seal.[47] This is how most of the cases discussed in Chapter 1, concerning ritual practices, came to the attention of the authorities – with the notable exception of cases encountered in the course of periodic rounds of visitation, which will be examined later.

More often, news reached the *Audiencia* in the form of a petition or as part of a dispute and, if the case merited it, it would then open an investigation, either summoning witnesses or commissioning someone to investigate and report back. If nothing was reported, however, short of stumbling upon a matter whilst doing something else, the *Audiencia* remained oblivious. And matters were further complicated by the system's reliance on the quality of petitions and appeals. If the information they provided was inadequate or inaccurate, so were the results it generated as it moved through the bureaucracy, and so too the impression left to today's scholars in the bureaucratic archive. This is made clear by the

---

[46] On this function, see Antonio Dougnac Rodríguez, *Manual de historia del derecho indiano* (Mexico City: Universidad Nacional Autónoma de México, 1994), 160.

[47] On these, see Real Díaz, *Estudio diplomático*, 194–198.

88   *The Settlers, Rescript, and the Foundations of the Kingdom*

early history of Christianisation in the New Kingdom, which is overdue a re-examination.

'THE BEGINNING OF THE PLANTING OF THE FAITH'

A total of twenty priests accompanied the six expeditions that constituted the European invasion of the highlands of the Northern Andes, from Jiménez de Quesada's initial expedition of 1536 through to that of Alonso Luis de Lugo, which reached Santafé in May 1543.[48] Most of these priests did not stay in the highlands, returning to Castile with the leaders of the expeditions or moving elsewhere. Contrary to what the experience of other regions might lead us to expect, those who stayed were mostly secular priests, rather than friars. Evidence survives for five secular priests and two regulars remaining in Santafé and Tunja, and what limited records exist all suggest that they were largely devoted to ministering to the Spanish population of the two cities.[49] A little issue like a lack of sources, of course, was not going to get in the way of chroniclers and their readers from telling a good story, and by the 1690s, the Dominican Alonso de Zamora had not only transformed one of these early, fleeting figures – Domingo de las Casas OP, who had left in 1539 – into a central player in the invasion of the Muisca territories and the foundation of Santafé, but had also written at length about the ministry of a further four distinguished members of his order who had been active throughout this period converting key Indigenous leaders through the power of their preaching, but who are nowhere to be found in the historical record.[50]

These early arrivals aside, it was not until the middle of the century that priests began to arrive in earnest. The Franciscans were the first to do so, with a dozen friars dispatched to New Granada in 1549. Those that reached Santafé were led by one Jerónimo de San Miguel, who proved to

---

[48] Two in each of the first three expeditions, under Jiménez, Belalcázar, and Federmann, eight under Lebrón, one under Montalvo de Lugo, and three under Alonso Luis de Lugo. See Avellaneda Navas, *The Conquerors*, 134–135.

[49] These were the secular priests García Matamoros, Juan Esteban Verdero, Juan Gómez de Córdoba, Juan Cetino (or Patiño), and Diego de Riquelme; the Dominican Juan de Torres (or Aurres); and the Augustinian Vicente de Requejada. A further five priests settled in other cities of the interior. See Ibid., 135.

[50] These were Pedro Durán, Juan de Montemayor, Lope de Acuña, and Antonio de la Peña, in Zamora, *Historia*, book 2, 272–314. Cf. Avellaneda Navas's careful tallying of members of the expeditions, in *The Conquerors*, 134–135.

'The Beginning of the Planting of the Faith' 89

be an effective petitioner, promptly complaining to the king about what he claimed to have found, and requesting royal intervention.[51] When his petitions were received and processed in the royal chancery, in the best style of rescript government, multiple decrees were dispatched to the New Kingdom instructing the *Audiencia* and *encomenderos* to provide funding for the friars, ordering *encomenderos* not to get in their way, and authorising friars to tell Indigenous people about royal legislation that benefitted them – in each case repeating San Miguel's claims as fact and following his suggestions for their resolution.[52] Most strikingly, in September 1551 the king, at San Miguel's request, ordered the secular priests of Indigenous towns in the province of Santafé to stop preventing the friars from entering their towns to preach.[53] Except, of course, in reality, there were no such secular priests. Of the original five, one, Juan Esteban de Verdero, had died in 1542. The trail also runs cold for a second, Juan Gómez de Córdoba, who was appointed sacristan to the *cabildo* of Santafé that year. The other three were employed in ministering to the Spaniards of the cities of Santafé and Tunja.[54]

---

[51] To summarise San Miguel's first letter to the king, 20 August 1550, AGI SF 233, ramo 1, d. 7. On this early history of Franciscan petitions, see Juan Friede, 'Los franciscanos en el Nuevo Reino de Granada y el movimiento indigenista del siglo XVI'. *Bulletin Hispanique* 60, no. 1 (1958): 5–29.

[52] See the decrees ordering the *Audiencia* to find funding for friars of 4 September 1550 (AGI SF 533, lib. 1, 234v–235r); and the decrees ordering *encomenderos* to admit them in their *encomiendas* (11 August 1551, Ibid., 233r), to let them share news of royal legislation (10 November 1551, ibid, 175r), and to provide them with stipends (8 August 1552, Ibid., 259r).

[53] Royal rescript on allowing the friars to preach in Indigenous towns, 4 September 1551, AGI SF 533, lib. 1, fol. 168v.

[54] Much of this was pieced together by Avellaneda Navas from the few documents that survive of the records of the *Cabildo* of Santafé for this early period, most of which were lost to a fire in May 1900. See José Ignacio Avellaneda Navas, 'The Conquerors of the New Kingdom of Granada' (PhD dissertation, University of Florida, 1990), 291–292, 312, 315, 326, and 329. Some are accounts sent to Spain, which document, for example, Cetino collecting his wages as parish priest of Santafé in 1552, and others are surviving fragments of *Cabildo* deliberations, recording, for example, Gómez's appointment as sacristan on 20 May 1542 (published as Guillermo Alba, 'Primicia documental del archivo de la ciudad de Bogotá'. *Boletín Cultural y Bibliográfico* 11, no. 10 (1968): 61). On Verdero's death, see José Ignacio Avellaneda Navas, *La expedición de Gonzalo Jiménez de Quesada al mar del sur y la creación del Nuevo Reino de Granada* (Bogotá: Banco de la República, 1995), 224. Matamoros was parish priest of Santafé until September 1541, when he moved to Tunja to replace Vicente de Requejada, where he remained until October 1552. See Lee López, 'Clero indígena', 11, and Ernesto Porras Collantes, 'Historia del primer templo mayor de Tunja, nombrado de Nuestra Señora de Guadalupe'. *Anuario Colombiano de Historia Social y de la Cultura* no. 31 (2004): 37. Porras also identified a further two priests, possibly in minor orders, although it is unclear

90   *The Settlers, Rescript, and the Foundations of the Kingdom*

Equally, contrary to what these petitions and later sources led scholars to believe, there were also strikingly few friars. As we saw, when Barrios arrived in 1553 there were just two Franciscans left in the New Kingdom. One was Juan de Santo Filiberto, who had arrived a few months before as the new head of the order in Santafé, only to find that all his fellows had left for greener pastures – although not before, as he put it to the king, 'having infected the land with their poor examples'. The other, San Miguel, had been prevented from escaping by the *Audiencia*, for 'his actions were too grave', and was instead jailed pending his removal to Spain for trial.[55] The Dominicans were doing almost as poorly. One, fray Juan de Torres, had arrived with Lebrón in 1540, and was still working as a priest in Santafé a few years later.[56] He was joined by a few more Dominicans by 1550, who established convents in Santafé that year and in Tunja in 1551.[57] But by 1553, at least according to Barrios, these too were struggling, their leaders 'sick people' and their fledging order on the brink of collapse under the strain of their poor leadership.[58] The Augustinians would take a little longer to arrive, only establishing their first convent in Santafé in 1575.[59] In the meantime, the only member of their order in the New Kingdom, Vicente de Requejada, who had arrived with Federmann in 1538 and briefly served as the founding parish priest of Tunja, had ditched the highlands altogether in 1541 to take part in a failed attempt to find El Dorado, and later a botched attempt to loot a

---

when they arrived in the highlands. These were Vicente de Ruesga and one unidentified 'fray Francisco', both employed as sacristans in Tunja from 1545 to 1552 (at 38, n. 26).

[55] It is unclear what these were exactly, even if later authors imagined them to have been heroic. Asensio, writing in the 1580s, skipped over the details (in *Memorial*, 14), but by the 1680s Piedrahita had recast him as a brilliant theologian whose temper occasionally got the better of him (*Historia general*, 474–475). In the 1950s, Friede speculated that his fate was the result of his 'combative pro-indigenous position', in 'Los franciscanos y el movimiento', 14, but this seems wishful thinking on the basis of little evidence. Cf. Juan de Santo Filiberto's letter to the king of 3 February 1553 (AGI SF 188, fol. 33r).

[56] José Ignacio Avellaneda Navas, *La jornada de Jerónimo Lebrón al Nuevo Reino de Granada* (Bogotá: Banco de la República, 1993), 241–242.

[57] For a recent outline of this history, see William Elvis Plata, 'Frailes y evangelización en el Nuevo Reino de Granada (s. XVI). Vicisitudes de un proceso conflictivo y no muy exitoso'. *Franciscanum* 58, no. 165 (2016): 263–302.

[58] Letter of Juan de los Barrios to the Council of the Indies, 15 April 1553, AGI Patronato 197, r. 26, 123r–126r.

[59] Fernando Campo del Pozo, 'Los agustinos en la evangelización del Nuevo Reino de Granada'. In *Provincia Agustiniana de Nuestra Señora de Gracia en Colombia: Escritos varios*. Vol. 3. Edited by José Pérez Gómez OSA (Bogotá: Provincia Agustiniana de Nuestra Señora de Gracia en Colombia, 2000), 402.

'The Beginning of the Planting of the Faith' 91

lowland town that resulted in the deaths of some 400 people.[60] A golden age of evangelisation this was not.

Finally, a careful reading of early sources confirms that this was not an age of secular-regular conflict either, as historians have tended to assume. Far from the image of rivalry and competition between secular priests and friars conveyed in San Miguel's letters and other sources, under Barrios's watch the secular and regular church trundled together. The bishop, a former Franciscan, took an active interest in the internal affairs of the religious orders, complaining in his correspondence with the crown that that the friars of New Granada were 'dissipated and destroyed', their leaders 'ill and unsuitable', and their ranks full of 'renegade friars' that should be removed from their positions, even if it meant 'leaving churches deserted and forsaken'.[61] But his principal interest, throughout his term, was to reform rather than displace them. His interference in the affairs of the friars prompted a handful of complaints to the king in the late 1550s, which resulted in rescripts admonishing him to 'in no manner bother them' and to 'treat them lovingly'.[62] These, in turn, elicited the bishop's indignation and complaints in his own letters to the king, which have often been quoted for their ferocious language, such as when he complained of the quality of the friars by comparing them, in helpfulness, to 'corpses washed up on our shore', or, more often, to 'scum and filth that Spain discards' – but these were only paper and bitter words that have tended to be blown out of proportion by historians.[63]

In fact, the principal issue afflicting the church in this period was a lack of manpower. This is difficult to overstate. When in 1556 Barrios called the first synod, or ecclesiastical assembly, of his diocese the priests who gathered in Santafé were not so much the representatives of the secular clergy of the kingdom as the clergy in its entirety. It consisted of Barrios, two members of his cathedral chapter (one of whom was Pedro García

---

[60] On this episode, see J. Michael Francis, 'The Muisca Indians under Spanish Rule, 1537–1636' (PhD dissertation, University of Cambridge, 1998), 225–226. Requejada would later return to the highlands in the second half of the 1550s, settling in Tunja once again. For a recent, rather hagiographical, biography of Requejada, see Fernando Campo del Pozo, *Fray Vicente de Requejada: Biografía y mito de un agustino quijotesco* (Tunja: Academia Boyacense de Historia, 2012).

[61] Letter of Juan de los Barrios to the Council of the Indies, 15 April 1553, AGI Patronato 197, r. 26, 124r.

[62] This in a royal rescript to Barrios of 29 October 1559, AGI SF 533, lib. 2, 149r.

[63] The first in his letter to the king of 10 June 1561 (AGI SF 188, 337r) and again in 1564, the second, a recurring formula, in that of 15 April 1553 (AGI Patronato 197, r. 26, 125r) and in at least two subsequent letters in the 1560s. Cf. Pacheco, *La evangelización*, 179.

92 The Settlers, Rescript, and the Foundations of the Kingdom

Matamoros), and eight further priests who ministered to the inhabitants of six Spanish cities across the interior of New Granada.[64] Only Santafé and Tunja had more than one priest – a fact confirmed by a string of petitions to the king from the *cabildos* of the other cities around this time asking to have two priests as well.[65] Barrios would do little to improve this situation: before his death in 1569 he had ordained just four more secular priests, and the secular church continued to minister principally to Spaniards.[66] His focus instead was on bringing more (and better) friars to the New Kingdom. For this he had brought four Franciscans with him when he arrived; dispatched the remaining Franciscan he found in Santafé, Juan de Santo Filiberto, to Spain to plead for reinforcements; and requested more friars be sent in practically every letter he sent to the king.[67] And not just Franciscans: at least two Dominicans participated in the synod, and a further seven would be sent to New Granada the following year.[68] This trickle would soon become a larger flow – one discussed in Chapter 3. But how to sustain all these priests?

LEGISLATION FOR THE KINGDOM

A key clause of the New Laws that travelled to the New Kingdom with Armendáriz was the requirement that royal authorities establish a *tasa*, or standard assessment of the tribute that each Indigenous community should pay its *encomendero*. This was, as is well known, a response to a multitude of petitions and complaints the crown had received, whether because the tributes *encomenderos* levied were excessive, or because *ad hoc* arrangements made keeping track of the resulting tributary obligations of *encomenderos* themselves more difficult.[69] For this the officials of

---

[64] 'Constituciones sinodales hechas en esta ciudad de Santafé por el señor don fray Juan de los Barrios, primer arzobispo de este Nuevo Reino de Granada, que las acabó de promulgar a 3 de junio de 1556'. In *La legislación de la arquidiócesis de Santafé en el periodo colonial*. Edited by Juan Fernando Cobo Betancourt and Natalie Cobo (Bogotá: Instituto Colombiano de Antropología e Historia, 2018), 136.

[65] This is mentioned in their rescript of 29 October 1556, AGI SF 533, lib. 2, 5r.

[66] It is crucial to highlight that these numbers are not unproblematic, given the poor records for this period. Lee López, 'Clero indígena', 30.

[67] Ibid., 16.

[68] Juan Méndez and Jerónimo de Vidas. See 'Constituciones sinodales 1556', 136.

[69] As Chapter 38 of the New Laws itself explained. In its initial formulation, it in fact sought to cut *encomenderos* out of tribute collection entirely, by requiring tribute to be collected by royal officials, who would then pay the *encomendero* their allotted share. This was particularly contentious, and entirely unrealistic in most regions, and was soon moderated. See Silvio Zavala, *La encomienda indiana*. 3rd edition. Biblioteca Porrúa 53

Legislation for the Kingdom

the four *Audiencias* of Spanish America were ordered to conduct inquiries about the economic conditions of Indigenous people in their districts and set tribute rates that they could comfortably afford. The idea, at least in the law, was that these should be 'less than what they used to pay in the time of their *caciques* and lords before becoming our subjects, so that they may know that we wish to relieve and favour them'. The resulting rates were to be carefully recorded in their archives, copies were to be given to *encomenderos* and Indigenous leaders, and an account of everything was to be sent to the Council of the Indies.[70]

In the New Kingdom, which still lacked an *audiencia* in the 1540s, this task fell to the embattled Armendáriz, who was also commissioned with conducting a visitation of the cities and towns of Santa Marta and the New Kingdom, and completed neither.[71] This, despite the fact that the settlers of the principal cities of the New Kingdom, led by one Juan Ruiz de Orejuela, petitioned Armendáriz, and through him the king, to suspend the application of most of the New Laws, but still establish a *tasa* – at least provided the king dropped the plan to make tribute less than before the coming of Europeans ('which we know for certain was much less than the tributes and services they currently give Spaniards', and which were already too low for their liking). Revealingly, they also petitioned that he establish stricter penalties for people failing to pay – ideally imprisonment, because, in their words, 'the Indians of this kingdom are so ill disposed and reticent in paying' that they needed to be 'forced and compelled' to do so, something with which many *encomenderos* clearly already needed help.[72]

At the end of the decade the tasks of setting a *tasa* and a carrying out a visitation were inherited by the three founding *oidores* of the *Audiencia* of Santafé, who would themselves be in no rush to complete them, despite

---

(Mexico City: Editorial Porrúa, 1992), 82, 102–105. The idea would finally be realised in the form of *corregidores* later in the century, as examined in Chapter 4.

[70] *Leyes y ordenanças nueuame[n]te hechas por Su Magestad, p[ar]a la gouernacion de las Indias y buen tratamiento y conseruacion de los indios: Que se han de guardar en el consejo y audie[n]cias reales q[ue] en ellas residen: Y por todos los otros gouernadores, juezes y personas particulares dellas* (Fueron impressas ... en la villa de Alcala de Henares: En casa de Joan de Brocar, 1543), 11v–12r.

[71] Armendáriz's commission was among the items given to him on his appointment, 22 March 1543, AGI Patronato 195 r 10, 29v.

[72] Petitions of procurators of the New Kingdom to the king, 3 February 1547, AGI Patronato 195, r. 15, 187r, 186v.

94　*The Settlers, Rescript, and the Foundations of the Kingdom*

repeated admonitions from the king.[73] Of the three, two – Francisco Briceño and Beltrán de Góngora – were immediately seconded to the Caribbean and Popayán, respectively, leaving only Juan de Galarza, who did little. A fourth *oidor*, Juan de Montaño, was dispatched in 1552, and tasked with conducting a *residencia*, or inquiry into how Góngora and Galarza conducted themselves in office, which resulted in both being suspended, arrested, and sent back to Spain to answer charges – only to drown when their ship sank on the way.[74] Montaño would fare no better, developing an intense rivalry with Briceño, and later becoming the first of only two *oidores* ever sentenced to death for their conduct in office in the history of Spanish America. We will meet the other, Luis Cortés de Mesa, also *oidor* in Santafé, in Chapter 3.[75] To say that the *Audiencia* of Santafé was a mess in this period would be a generous understatement.

As a result, the first visitations of the Indigenous communities of the New Kingdom, which finally began in the early 1550s, were in fact carried out by the settlers themselves, for their own purposes. In the province of Tunja the task fell to none other than Juan Ruiz de Orejuela, who had led the charge against the implementation of the New Laws in 1547 and was now the newly minted *alcalde mayor*, or magistrate, of the city and province, which he set off to inspect in July 1551. His counterparts in Santafé did the same there the following year.[76] The resulting records are lost, although the Franciscan chronicler Pedro de Aguado, writing in the 1570s, seems to have to have consulted those for Tunja and described the procedure followed by Orejuela in some detail.[77] In any case, the visitors' observations made their way into the settlers' petitions, whether to complain of

---

[73] They were first given the tasks in the royal rescript to the *Audiencia* of Santafé, 4 September 1549, AGI SF 533, lib. 1, 90v–92v. These instructions would be reiterated twice in 1551, and in 1552 and 1553. See respectively, AGI SF 533, lib. 1, 153v and 156v–158r; Indiferente 532, 52v–53r; and SF 533, lib. 1, 284v–296v.

[74] On the former, see the royal decree commissioning Juan de Montaño, 11 July 1552 (AGI SF 533, lib. 1, 221v); on the latter, which included giving *encomiendas* to their friends and relatives, see the royal decree briefing Francisco Díaz de Arbizo, appointed president of the *Audiencia*, of 25 September 1555 (Ibid., 399v). Arbizo would drown on the way to take up his post.

[75] For a brief account of both, see Ernst Schäfer, *El consejo real y supremo de las Indias: Su historia, organización y labor administrativa hasta la terminación de la Casa de Austria. Vol. 2* (Seville: Imprenta M. de Carmona, 1935–1947), 128–129, notes 205 and 206. I am grateful to Santiago Muñoz for bringing this to my attention.

[76] See Eugenio Martínez, *Tributo y trabajo*, 133–137.

[77] Aguado, *Recopilación historial*, vol. 1, book 4, ch. 16, 403–409. The population figures cited by Aguado, and their use by scholars, are discussed in J. Michael Francis, 'Nature

Legislation for the Kingdom

the inefficacy of the *oidores* or the plight of *encomenderos*, and into the royal rescripts that these prompted, such as a 1552 royal decree that confidently asserted that it was Indigenous leaders (and, by implication, not downtrodden *encomenderos*) who were oppressing their subjects with excessive tributes and levies.[78] A proper visitation by royal officials would not take place until the following decade.

Remarkably, in the middle of this chaos, Briceño and bishop Barrios managed to come together to set the first *tasa* in 1555, based on those early haphazard visitations. Few records of this process survive and much remains unclear. For example, although royal officials reported in 1555 that Briceño and Barrios, taking advantage of a brief absence by Montaño to the coast, had 'set rates for most of this land', it is not known exactly how much of it they actually managed to cover.[79] Records are clearest for the province of Tunja, for which a summary of the rates for 103 communities was included as part of a later suit over their adjustment in 1562.[80] This has received significant attention for its demographic and economic information, but for our purposes it is the original *tasa* decrees issued by Briceño and Barrios that are the most revealing, if also the rarest and least often examined. These have survived for just seven communities in Tunja and Santafé, copied into the proceedings of later visitations.[81]

One such community was Cota, located some twenty miles north-west of Santafé, whose *cacique* of the same name and *encomendero* Francisco de Tordehumos appeared before Barrios and Briceño in January 1555 and duly received the rates of goods and services the pair had set. Each year, Cota and his subjects were to provide Tordehumos with 400 *mantas*, various amounts of timber, firewood, hay, and, if they hunted, game; to grow potatoes, wheat, barley, and maize for him (with his seeds);

and Quality of Early-Colonial Tribute Records in Colombia's Eastern Highlands, 1560–1636'. *Jahrbuch Für Geschichte Lateinamerikas* 49, no. 1 (2012).

[78] Royal decree of 31 January 1552, AGI SF 533, lib. 1, fol. 202v.

[79] Treasurer Andrés López de Galarza and other officials to the king, 1 October 1555, AGI SF 68.

[80] In the suit of the *encomenderos* of Tunja against the *visita* and *retasa* of Diego Angulo de Castejón, 1563–1567, AGI Justicia 511 d 1, 3r–56v, which was collated in Francis, 'The Muisca', 283–330 alongside later rates, and discussed in Gamboa, *El cacicazgo*, 408–409.

[81] In addition, as Germán Colmenares noted, in at least forty of the *encomiendas* visited by Tomás López in 1560, in the visitation discussed later, the 1555 *tasa* was at least mentioned, even if copies of the decrees had been lost. See Germán Colmenares, *La provincia de Tunja en el Nuevo Reino de Granada; ensayo de historia social, 1539–1800* (Bogotá: Universidad de los Andes, Facultad de Artes y Ciencias, Departamento de Historia, 1997), 94 note 7.

96   *The Settlers, Rescript, and the Foundations of the Kingdom*

and to provide two people to work as his shepherds, two as farmhands, and six more in his household (whom Tordehumos was to feed and clothe). If the community failed to meet its obligation, they would incur fines and any outstanding amounts would be doubled, with the municipal authorities of Santafé empowered to confiscate the property of the *cacique* and community to settle their debts. These penalties were not as harsh as those that the settlers had requested in 1547, but it was their own *cabildo* that was given power and responsibility to enforce them. If Tordehumos overcharged the people of Cota he was to make restitution, in full the first time, quadruple the second, and forfeiting the *encomienda* on the third offence – a penalty left to the *Audiencia* to enforce.[82] Almost identical arrangements, with different amounts and products – including, sometimes, gold – are recorded in the decrees for the communities of Ubaté, Suesca, and Tunjuelo in Santafé, and Ramiriquí, Cucaita, and Moniquirá in Tunja, and were established for many others too.[83]

Most significantly for us, the *tasa* also served as an opportunity for Barrios to establish, at least on paper, the rudiments of a system of funding for religious instruction. All surviving decrees contain a section, left out of the 1562 summary, imposing additional tributary obligations on each community for this purpose. The *tasa* for Cota, for example, noted that until 'there are tithes from which to support a priest or friar', the people of Cota should provide food and sustenance for a priest in the interim: four *fanegas* of maize per month, plus ten birds per week or, during Lent and other fasts, a dozen eggs and some fish. Each day they were also to provide a small vessel of *chicha* (maize beer), some firewood, and – if the priest had a mount – some hay as well.[84] The legislation assumed priests would be itinerant and required the community to pay only 'during the time when the said priest was actually resident', before moving on.[85]

---

[82] 1555 *tasa* for Cota, copied in Diego Villafañe's 1563 visitation of the *encomienda* of Francisco de Tordehumos, AGN E 12, d 8, at 228r–229v.

[83] The 1555 *tasas* for Ubaté, Suesca, and Tunjuelo survive as part of Diego de Villafañe's 1563 visitation of those communities. See AGN VC 5 d 5, 991r–992r; 5 d 6, 950r–951r; and 5 d 6, 957r–958v, respectively. In Tunja, those for Ramiriquí, Cucaita, and Moniquirá survive as part of the records of the 1571 visitation by Juan López de Cepeda. See AGN VB 9 d 3, 774r–775r; 14 d 12, 876r–877r; and 5 d 3, 388r–389r.

[84] A *fanega* is a unit of volume equivalent (at least in Castile) to about 55 litres. *Equivalencias entre las pesas y medidas usadas antiguamente en las diversas provincias de España y las legales del sistéma métrico-decimal* (Madrid: Imprenta de la Dirección General del Instituto Geográfico y Estadístico, 1886), 7.

[85] 1555 *tasa* for Cota, AGN E 12, d 8, 228v.

Legislation for the Kingdom

We can only speculate as to whether Briceño and Barrios actually believed that this procedure, and the pieces of paper they duly gave the *encomendero* and the *cacique* – at least one of whom could not read – would actually settle the thorny questions of tribute collection or of the provision of resources for Christianisation, especially as the *tasa* was to be enforced by justices in the employ of the *encomenderos* and other settlers who made up the *cabildos* of these provinces. This was, not, however, the only aspirational legislation to which Barrios put his name in this period, or even the most ambitious. That was the legislation he issued at the first synod, or ecclesiastical assembly, of priests of the diocese, held in his half-built cathedral the following year, and which sought to establish a firm foundation for the development of the church and its programme of Christianisation.

The constitutions of the first synod of Santafé comprise 135 chapters, arranged thematically into ten books.[86] We will explore several of these in more detail later, but for now what is most significant is the first book, which concerns how religious instruction should take place and what it should contain. Its provisions were by no means sophisticated. In practical terms, the legislation differed from the approach of the 1555 *tasa*, which had bypassed *encomenderos* entirely and required communities to provide food and other provisions to priests directly, and now echoed royal requirements that dictated that it should be *encomenderos* who were to make provision for the instruction of the people under their jurisdiction. For this *encomenderos* were ideally to provide a priest, failing this a lay 'Christian and virtuous Spaniard' certified as such by the bishop or at least a nearby priest, or – as a final resort – teach their subjects themselves. Failure to do so was to be punished by a modest fine, increasing for repeat offenders, half of which was to be given to whoever brought these breaches to the authorities' attention, in recognition of their limited ability to police the behaviour of *encomenderos* or indeed anyone else.[87] The synod also ordered churches be built, at least in the larger settlements where *caciques* resided, with bells to call the people together for regular religious instruction. For this, the legislation outlined a programme of frequent catechisation, with all priests in the diocese, even members of the cathedral chapter, required to teach Christian doctrine to

---

[86] For an overview, see Cobo Betancourt and Cobo, *La legislación*, li.
[87] Starting at ten pesos, and increasing by a further ten on each offence, tit. 1, ch. 4, 17–18.

98   *The Settlers, Rescript, and the Foundations of the Kingdom*

Indigenous people on Sundays and feast days, on pain of a fine of two pesos.[88]

Also key was an easily ignored section, tucked away at the very end of the last book, among chapters concerned with procedural matters, of short but radical chapters concerning the controversial question of restitution.[89] These considered if and to what extent the dispossession of Indigenous people was licit – whether in the initial invasion of the region or subsequently through the *encomienda* and other means – and how and in what way Spaniards were obliged to make restitution for what they had illicitly taken.[90] Chapter 9 thus considered the question of whether *encomenderos* who 'have failed to provide instruction for their Indians or taken care to teach and indoctrinate them' as required were obliged to make restitution of the tribute they had received from them. For this Barrios quoted a long section from one of the first assemblies of bishops of New Spain, the *Junta eclesiástica* of 1546, which detailed the obligation of *encomenderos* to provide religious instruction to their subjects in place of the monarch, which entailed not just someone to instruct them but everything else required for the proper functioning of the local

---

[88] Ibid., tit. 1, ch. 4, 24–25. Many of these requirements will be familiar to historians of other regions of the Andes, for they were drawn from recent legislation issued in Lima. Legislation of this sort was never produced in a vacuum, but drew on a broad range of legal, theological, and pastoral sources from a variety of different geographic and temporal contexts. In this case, in addition to the First Provincial Council of Lima (1551–1552), Barrios's synod drew from that of Mexico (1555), and earlier legislation still from that of Seville of 1512. The circulation and translation of knowledge and ideas in ecclesiastical legislation is a central theme in Cobo Betancourt and Cobo, *La legislación*.

[89] I am indebted to Aliocha Maldavsky for first encouraging me to explore the question of restitution in the New Kingdom of Granada. For her work on restitution in Peru, in particular in relation to the *encomienda*, see, most recently, 'Teología moral, restitución y sociedad colonial en los Andes en el siglo XVI'. *Revista Portuguesa de Filosofia* 75, no. 2 (2019): 1125–1148.

[90] The first of these chapters (ch. 8) thus began with the biggest issue of all, the Spanish invasion of the region, but concluded that it exceeded the jurisdiction of the synod and referred the matter to the Spanish court and, of all places, the Council of Trent. 'Constituciones sinodales 1556', tit. 10, ch. 8, 125–126. This was less radical than the almost contemporaneous effort by the bishop of Popayán, Juan del Valle, who in the 1560s took his grievances to the king's court in person, and – finding no resolution – set off to the Council of Trent himself, making it as far as France before his death in 1561. See Juan Friede, *Vida y luchas de don Juan del Valle, primer obispo de Popayan y protector de indios* (Popayán: Editorial Universidad, 1961).

churches, including ornaments and consumables.[91] If they failed to provide this, the Mexican *junta* recommended, 'in addition to incurring and remaining in grievous fault, they are to make restitution of everything they should have justly spent on these matters' – a penalty that should increase if they had also obstructed the task of priests and other missionaries. How much was to be up to the ordinary (i.e. the bishop) and until they had made this restitution their confessors were to deny them absolution, an instruction that Barrios now gave to confessors across his diocese.[92]

The idea of centring restitution in the regulation of the *encomienda* was not new, nor was using an ecclesiastical sanction to enforce civil legislation.[93] But here, after a faltering start, it would be transformative. On one hand, the synod centred the provision of religious instruction in how the authorities should assess the conduct of *encomenderos*, going further than contemporary royal legislation, which was largely concerned with tributes exceeding pre-Hispanic precedent or established rates.[94] For Barrios, a failure to provide adequate religious instruction automatically forfeited at least a portion of any tribute owed. On the other, it also went further than the Mexican *junta*, extending ecclesiastical sanctions to *encomenderos* who overcharged their subjects, ignoring the official rates

---

[91] The assembly had been called by the royal visitor-general Tello de Sandoval to discuss the application of the New Laws in New Spain. On this and the other *juntas eclesiásticas* that preceded the first provincial council of Mexico, see Fernando Gil, 'Las juntas eclesiásticas durante el episcopado de Fray Juan de Zumarraga (1528–1548): Algunas precisiones históricas'. *Teología: Revista de la Facultad de Teología de la Pontificia Universidad Católica Argentina* no. 54 (1989): 7–34.

[92] 'Constituciones sinodales 1556', tit. 10, ch. 9, 127–130.

[93] As Natalie Cobo notes, Bartolomé de las Casas – who had himself been subject to the denial of absolution as a young *encomendero* – had already gone much further in his 1545 *Avisos y reglas* in arguing for restitution *in solidum*, that is, that the entire group of *encomenderos* was liable for the damage caused by any and all of their members, even if these were now dead. She also explores how this more radical idea was taken up in the Philippines by bishop Domingo de Salazar OP in the Synod of Manila (1582–1586), which she situates in the broader context of the spread and development of the ideas of the School of Salamanca at a global level. Salazar also went much further than Barrios in considering the thorny question of the legality of the Spanish title to the Philippines himself. See 'Creating Authority and Promoting Normative Behaviour'. In *The School of Salamanca: A Case of Global Knowledge Production*. Edited by Thomas Duve, José Luis Egío, and Christiane Birr (Leiden: Brill, 2021), 210–244. For a recent English-language edition of the *Avisos*, see David Thomas Orique, *To Heaven or to Hell: Bartolomé de Las Casas's Confesionario* (University Park: Penn State University Press, 2018).

[94] E.g. royal decree on conducting a visitation, 20 December 1553, AGI SF 533, lib. 1, 294v–296v.

100   *The Settlers, Rescript, and the Foundations of the Kingdom*

that he and Briceño had set the previous year, as well as to those Spaniards who had looted Indigenous graves and other sites and stolen gold and precious objects.[95] Failure to obey the law, or to make appropriate restitution after doing so previously, would now not only incur the sanctions and penalties already laid out in royal legislation that the settlers of New Granada were proving so able to ignore: it would exclude them from salvation.

The sanctions stung. There are few details of how many *encomenderos* incurred them, but by the end of the decade their complaints were pouring into the royal chancery through their allies and representatives. The magistrate Juan de Penagos of Santafé, for example, wrote to the king in 1559 and 1560 complaining of Barrios, who 'like a shepherd gone to war with his own sheep' had 'agitated and upset the citizens of this kingdom with excommunications and censures', and urged him to intervene 'before something terrible happens'.[96] Less vague and threatening was his argument that Barrios was overstepping his jurisdiction – an idea that he and his friends in the *cabildo* of Santafé also took to the *Audiencia*, which, in October 1560, ruled that it pertained not to the bishop's jurisdiction but to its own to enforce restitution. It then commanded Barrios to absolve 'all the citizens and persons he has excommunicated, and lift any and all censures'.[97] Chastised but undeterred, Barrios continued to apply and enforce ecclesiastical sanctions, prompting repeated complaints to the king and repeated rescripts ordering him to stop excommunicating people altogether until shortly before his death in 1569.[98] As for the synod, in 1561 the crown ruled that its application (and that of those of other regions) should be suspended altogether, pending their review at court, in case they did indeed overstep the fuzzy boundaries of royal patronage.[99]

---

[95] 'Constituciones sinodales 1556', tit. 10, chs. 10 and 11, 130.

[96] *Alcalde mayor* Juan de Penagos to the king, 15 September 1559, AGI SF 188, 226r.

[97] Decree of the *Audiencia* of Santafé, 19 October 1560, quoted in Zamora, *Historia*, book 3, ch. 6, 69–70.

[98] Royal rescript ordering Barrios not to excommunicate people, 27 August 1560, reiterated on 4 November 1568 (AGI SF 534, lib. 3, 151v).

[99] Royal decree on the publication of synods, 31 August 1560 (Diego de Encinas, *Cedulario indiano Recopilado por Diego de Encinas. Reproduccion facsimil de la edicion unica de 1596*. Edited by Alfonso García Gallo (Madrid: Ediciones Cultura Hispánica, 1945), vol. 1, 137). This decree, which also affected other regions, is also discussed in Ismael Sánchez Bella, *Iglesia y estado en la América Española* (Pamplona: Ediciones Universidad de Navarra, 1991), 32.

'To Learn and Investigate'

What was not suspended, but in fact wholly embraced and appropriated by the *Audiencia*, was the idea of using restitution as a tool to enforce the *tasa* and to require *encomenderos* to make provision for religious instruction. Regardless of who wielded it, in other words, the instrument of restitution served to give royal authorities, perhaps for the very first time, some teeth. To understand how, we need to turn away from the realm of legislation and consider what was happening on the ground.

'TO LEARN AND INVESTIGATE'

Just as the promulgation of ecclesiastical legislation in synods and councils was a rare instance of proactive policymaking for bishops in this period, their counterparts in the *Audiencia* too had occasional, if more limited, opportunities to break from their usually reactive role in rescript government. Of these few were more important for our purposes than the periodic visitations they were supposed to conduct of the region under their care. These '*visitas ordinarias*' or '*de la tierra*' were tours of inspection, carried out by a member of the *Audiencia*, that served to observe and record information about a given region, its population, and their affairs.[100] To quote one such visitor's standard explanation of their purpose, they were opportunities 'to learn and investigate' by interviewing local people, usually elites, following a standard questionnaire. Visitors usually carried out a census of the population (or at least of men of working age), their economic activities, and the resources at their disposal, making possible the establishment and periodic updating of standard tribute rates. They were also there to listen: to investigate local affairs and resolve conflicts, without having to wait for petitioners, supplicants, or litigants to bring these affairs to Santafé, or indeed for them to be able to meet the cost and effort of doing so. Visitors explicitly asked people about the conduct of local officials and particularly *encomenderos*, providing an often-valuable opportunity for them to bypass local authorities and deal directly with a higher instance. In doing so, visitations also served a pedagogical purpose, instructing Indigenous people, or at least

---

[100] These are not to be confused with the 'general' visitations that were dispatched to investigate the conduct of the colonial administration in response to specific issues, such as that carried out by Armendáriz in the 1540s, or those that followed later in the century, discussed in Chapter 3. An excellent survey of the literature on both kinds of civil visitations is Tamar Herzog, *Ritos de control, prácticas de negociación* (Madrid: Fundación Ignacio Larramendi, 2000), 5–6 notes 2–3, and 11–12, which itself focuses on the former.

102 *The Settlers, Rescript, and the Foundations of the Kingdom*

their elites, of the role of the institutions they represented, royal legislation that affected or protected them, and of practical aspects about the functioning of the bureaucracy and judiciary and how they might be of use. They were also rare opportunities for the *Audiencia* to proactively introduce reforms or policies, to ascertain whether earlier initiatives were bearing fruit, and to take corrective action. Finally, visitations were also carefully choreographed affairs, in which the visitor and his retinue conjured up a tangible vision of the monarchy before its subjects. Visitors were there not just to see, in other words, but also to be seen.[101]

After the haphazard visitations of the early 1550s, the first comprehensive visitation of the provinces of Santafé and Tunja was finally carried out in 1560 by the *oidor* Tomás López Medel, who had recently arrived to replace Juan de Galarza. This was part of a broader visitation of the highlands of the New Kingdom that he was commissioned to perform by the *Audiencia* in November 1559, following a similar tour in neighbouring Popayán.[102] Summaries of his findings began to circulate soon after, most notably as part of a detailed anonymous description of the

---

[101] Visitations of this sort – and their ecclesiastical counterparts, pastoral visitations, considered in Chapter 6 – have thus received significant scholarly attention across Spanish America and the Philippines. Historians have explored their institutional development from medieval precedents, serving to bring the king's most fundamental function, the administration of justice, to his subjects on the ground, for example, Carlos Antonio Garriga Acosta, 'La expansión de la visita castellana a Indias: Presupuestos, alcance y significado'. In *XI Congreso del Instituto Internacional de Historia del Derecho Indiano: Buenos Aires, 4 al 9 de septiembre de 1995. Actas y estudios*. Vol. 3 (Buenos Aires: Instituto de Investigaciones de Historia del Derecho, 1997), 51–80. Others, such as Armando Guevara Gil and Frank Salomon, have studied their role as instances of 'political theatre', performing claims of power and jurisdiction, in 'A "Personal Visit": Colonial Political Ritual and the Making of Indians in the Andes'. *Colonial Latin American Review* 3, nos 1–2 (1994): 3–36. Others still have reviewed them as spaces of negotiation between colonial institutions and the people ostensibly under their rule, such as Gabriela Ramos, who focused on ecclesiastical visitations in 'Pastoral Visitations: Spaces of Negotiation in Andean Indigenous Parishes'. *The Americas* 73, no. 1 (2016): 39–57. On visitations in New Granada, see Muñoz Arbeláez, 'The New Kingdom', 111–118, who pays special attention to the materiality of the visitation – the caravan of the visitor and his retinue and its physical presence on the land – and of the paper artefacts that resulted from its efforts. Visitation of Suta by Tomás López, 15 April 1560, AGN VB 18 d 2, 199r.

[102] In his previous position as *oidor* of the *Audiencia* of Guatemala, López had also carried out extensive visitations in Chiapas and Yucatán. For a detailed study of his career there and in the New Kingdom, see Berta Ares Queija, *Tomás López Medel: Trayectoria de un clérigo-oidor ante el Nuevo Mundo* (Guadalajara: Institución Provincial de Cultura 'Marqués de Santillana', 1993), 588–591, which includes a copy of his 1559 commission.

'To Learn and Investigate' 103

territories and inhabitants of both Popayán and the New Kingdom that López had visited, which collated statistics on the numbers of tributaries belonging to each community, their tribute obligations, and their economic activities, which has received significant scholarly attention.[103] These counted a total of some 35,482 tributaries in Santafé and 52,564 in Tunja, and it is on the basis of these records that successive historians have sought to estimate the size of the broader population, calculating – with some agreement around Germán Colmenares's proposal of a multiplier of 3.2 individuals per tributary – a total of some 280,000 individuals in the two provinces.[104] The records of López's visitation of individual *encomiendas*, from which these summaries were produced, are less well studied. Of the 171 documented across the two provinces in 1560, visitation records survive only for 41 *encomiendas* in the province of Tunja, comprising some 63 individual communities, whose leaders appeared before López between April and August of 1560. Equivalent records for towns in Santafé have not survived, except as quoted in the records of a 1563 visitation of that province by the *oidor* Diego de Villafañe, which we will come to in a moment.

With tight deadlines and scant funding, López's enquiries rarely took place in the settlements where his Indigenous interlocutors actually lived. Instead López remained largely stationary, and the visited came to him. In the province of Tunja most inquiries took place in the city itself, with a handful more in Sogamoso, the centre of an *encomienda* belonging to the crown in the northern reaches of the province. As a result, his inspections are devoid of observations about local conditions. Instead Indigenous leaders of different ranks, and the occasional Indigenous commoner, appeared before the *oidor* in quick succession to answer a short list of

[103] This anonymous *relación*, held at the Real Academia de la Historia in Madrid, is the closest equivalent to the famous *relaciones geográficas* of other regions that was ever produced in New Granada. It was published as Hermes Tovar Pinzón, 'Visita de 1560'. In *No hay caciques ni señores* (Barcelona: Sendai Ediciones, 1988), 21–120.

[104] These figures, which are, as ever, likely inexact, are from Ibid., 78–81 and 94–96. Tovar's sums, as J. Michael Francis noted (in 'Población, enfermedad y cambio demográfico, 1573–1636. Demografía histórica de Tunja: una mirada crítica'. In *Muiscas: Representaciones, cartografías y etnopolíticas de la memoria*. Edited by Ana María Gómez Londoño (Bogotá: Editorial Pontificia Universidad Javeriana, 2005), 120), were slightly off. I am grateful to Jorge Camargo Hernández, who as a student intern at Neogranadina worked in collating and mapping this and other demographic data. Colmenares proposed his multiplier of 3.2 in *La provincia*, 50, on the basis of later visitations and of visitations of neighbouring provinces that did include non-tributaries. For a discussion of this multiplier, see Francis, 'Población', 118–123.

104 *The Settlers, Rescript, and the Foundations of the Kingdom*

questions about their treatment by their *encomenderos* and their Spanish neighbours, labour conditions, the rates and specie of their tributes, and the provision of religious instruction. That so many Indigenous authorities travelled significant distances to appear before the *oidor* is not explained by the sources, which, as ever, take the efficacy of royal authority for granted, but in many cases, it seems the opportunity to voice grievances against *encomenderos* or other Spaniards was very welcome. At the end of the visitation, in August and September of 1560, the *oidor* summoned each *encomendero* and asked them to provide information on their titles to the *encomienda*, tribute arrangements, and any grievances voiced by their subjects. In complex cases he carried out new inquiries, interrogated more witnesses, and wrote new reports. And in the end, he issued each *encomendero* with a sentence, imposing fines or penalties for the specific charges resulting from the investigations, which in some cases resulted in appeals and further legal action.

López is an intriguing figure. He was already an experienced administrator, cutting his teeth as *oidor* in the *Audiencia* of Guatemala in the aftermath of the promulgation of the New Laws, where he conducted extensive visitation tours in Chiapas and Yucatán, before arriving in the Northern Andes and doing the same in Popayán. He was also a distinguished humanist, educated at Alcalá de Henares and Seville, where he obtained a doctorate in canon law and was admitted to holy orders.[105] A prolific writer, after his time in the New Kingdom he would go on to write texts on the failings and reform of evangelisation, on the need for regulars to engage in missionary activity, a manual for confessors, a catechism, and a pathbreaking treatise on the natural history of the New World and the history and politics of its Indigenous inhabitants, among others.[106] It is tempting to focus on his ideas and designs for the reform of Indigenous peoples in Guatemala and the New Kingdom, which have long drawn historians. To do so properly, however, it is first

---

[105] López was long the focus of the work of Berta Ares Queija. On his education and early career, see her excellent biography, *Tomás López Medel*, 24–55.

[106] The first was 'Tratado intitulado "Matalotaje espiritual"', composed around 1562; the second, 'Apologia o defensión para persuadir la pasada de los religiosos a las Indias', for which the date is unclear. The confession manual and catechism, which perhaps date to the 1570s, when he was offered – but declined – the job of bishop of Guatemala, are unfortunately lost. The final text is his famous treatise, Tomás López Medel, *De los tres elementos: Tratado sobre la naturaleza y el hombre del Nuevo Mundo*. Edited by Berta Ares Queija (Madrid: Quinto Centenario: Alianza, 1990). On these and other texts, see Ares Queija, *Tomás López Medel*, 196–235.

'To Learn and Investigate'

essential to understand the shape and limitations of the power that he wielded, and of the institution that he represented. For this we need to examine the records of his visitation of Tunja.

If a careful recounting of the numbers of priests active in the highlands in this period began to chip away at the notion of even a basic programme of religious instruction for Indigenous people in the middle decades of the sixteenth century, the records of López's interviews with Indigenous authorities up and down the province demolish it. Of the sixty-three communities for which records survive, only five had their own priest at the time of the visitation. The first of these, Sogamoso, had reverted to the crown a few years before and – as the local *cacique*, don Alonso, explained – had then become home to a few friars.[107] Gonzalo Suárez Rendón, the founder of Tunja, who held Tibaná and Icabuco, had provided the two communities with a priest between them for two or three years, according to Quecamucha, *cacique* of the latter, who added that a few people had become Christians, although he himself had not.[108] In Suta, where the *cacique* was a minor, his guardian, Cuyacucha, explained that the new *encomendero*, Antón de Santana, had brought a priest when he took over, although Tibagüenza, another captain, explained that it had only been for stretches of a few months at a time, adding that 'usually the Indians die without having become Christians, although a few have'.[109] The *encomendero* of Chita, Pedro Rodríguez Salamanca, had provided a priest since taking over the *encomienda* some six or seven years before, and the *cacique*, don Miguel, explained that 'many Indians', himself included, 'had become and continue to become Christians'.[110] What exactly this meant is a question for later.

The other fifty-eight communities whose leaders were questioned had no such provision. Some, like Boyacá, had a priest previously, but no longer. A few received the odd traveller, while others were occasionally visited by priests based in the five communities that had them or in Tunja. This included six whose leaders reported occasionally hosting friars from Sogamoso, and a few more from Chita, which had emerged as small-scale, *de facto* centres of religious instruction.[111] Sometimes their visits may

---

[107] Visitation of Sogamoso by Tomás López, 13 April 1560, AGN VB 8 d 4, 775r.

[108] Visitation of Tibaná, Icabuco, and Guáneca by Tomás López, 10 and 11 April 1560, AGN VB 7 d 6, 398v.

[109] Visitation of Suta by Tomás López, 18 April 1560, AGN VB 18, d 2, 200r.

[110] Visitation of Chita by Tomás López, 12 July 1560, AGN VB 19 d 10, 582r.

[111] From Sogamoso, Satoba, Chámeza, Pesca, Guáquira, Tota, and Socotá; from Chita, Ura, Cocuy, and Cheva.

106   *The Settlers, Rescript, and the Foundations of the Kingdom*

have been organised by the *encomendero*, like Luis de Sanabria, who held Firavitoba and Cormechoque, and claimed he had arranged for priests from Sogamoso to visit his communities every so often.[112] His neighbour, Diego Montañez, *encomendero* of Tota and Guáquira, recalled the names of several priests from Sogamoso whom he apparently paid to make the journey to his *encomienda*.[113] Elsewhere, arrangements seem to have been more spontaneous, perhaps at the initiative of priests themselves or even of Indigenous people. For example, in Chaine, near Tunja, Cuyiava, the *cacique*, explained to the visitor that his subjects often had business in the city, building stone walls, and sent 'the youths' to the city's Franciscan convent while they worked.[114] So did some of the people of Moniquirá, at least occasionally – as Sastoque, the *cacique*, explained – 'and some of the Indians have become Christians, but others have died without being so'. The onus, it seems, was on them.[115]

The lack of priests was not just a local problem. There were, as we saw, strikingly few in the New Kingdom in the 1550s, and their numbers would not increase substantially until the following decade. As a result, a typical example was the community of Chivatá, located less than ten miles from Tunja, where indoctrination was largely in the hands of lay Spaniards. There, *cacique* Neausipa explained that a priest had been with them for three or four months, 'otherwise never', but that 'a few Spaniards have taught the Indians doctrine'. Overall, he noted, 'usually most die without becoming Christians'. The *encomendero*, Pedro Bravo de Ribera, blamed the shortage of priests, which was corroborated by other *encomenderos* and citizens of Tunja whom he called to declare in his favour when López drew a number of charges against him. Instead, Bravo explained, he had hired various laymen, including his teenage son, and even stepped in himself.[116] In all, a full twenty communities had apparently never had a priest to indoctrinate them at all.

For some *encomenderos* it was a question of resources. Susaba, captain of Rasgón, explained that his late *encomendero*, Francisco de Sierra, had always taught them Christian doctrine himself, and that after his death his

---

[112] Visitation of Cormechoque and Pirabita by Tomás López, 7 August 1560, AGN VB 9 d 9, 871r.

[113] Although 'how much he could not recall'. Visitation of Tota and Guáquira by Tomás López, 18 August 1560, AGN VB 19 d 5, 533r.

[114] This was the case in Bagajique, Chaine, Soracá, Viracachá and Neacachá.

[115] Visitation of Moniquirá (de Sánchez Ropero) by Tomás López, 18 July 1560, AGN VB 18 d 10, 311r.

[116] Visitation of Chivatá by Tomás López, 15 April 1560, AGN VB 18 d 6, 265v, 270r.

widow, María de Sotelo, got her brother to do so. When interrogated, she explained that she received no more than two dozen *mantas* a year as tribute, so could afford nothing else.[117] This was roughly the value of the annual bonus that the *encomendero* Bartolomé Camacho claimed that he paid one of his workers to teach his community of Pánqueba.[118] But for other *encomenderos* it was clearly something else. Francisco de Velandia, *encomendero* of Chitagoto, received 2,000 *mantas* a year in tribute, but decided a layman would do just fine. After all, his subjects, including *cacique* don Francisco, who said he was a Christian, could not tell the difference.[119] Nor could don Antonio, *cacique* of Somondoco, also apparently a Christian, who reported 'that a man has been teaching them, but he does not know whether he is a priest or not'.[120]

Although it is common for historians to refer to these sites in this period as *doctrinas*, Indigenous parishes, and to imagine them to have been organised into some sort of institutional structure, controlled – even ostensibly – by the bishop, they were no such thing.[121] In reality, these were *ad hoc*, haphazard arrangements that were out of the authorities' hands. The bishop was powerless even when called in to intervene. In Cucaita, for example, the *encomendero*, Gregorio Suárez, reported that he had employed the Dominican fray Juan de Zúñiga for a whole four and half years, only for his order to move him and replace him with one Bartolomé de Ojeda, who had barely turned up. The disgruntled Suárez and Zúñiga had gone to Barrios in 1559 to ask him to force the Dominicans to reinstate him, but the bishop had no success.[122]

Legislation was no different. Even its most basic requirements proved unenforceable. While the synod of 1556 had made provision for laymen to be in charge of instruction when no priests could be found, it had also required that they be vetted and that they follow the synod's prescribed

---

[117] Visitation of Rasgón by Tomás López, 2 August 1560, AGN VB 8 d 6, 796v, 798v.

[118] Visitation of Pánqueba and Neacachá by Tomás López, 1 August 1560, AGN VB 9 d 4, 823v.

[119] Visitation of Chitagoto by Tomás López, AGN VB 19 d 11, 595v, cf. 1555 *tasa* in Francis, 'The Muisca', 291.

[120] Visitation of Somondoco by Tomás López, 27 August 1560, AGN VB 19 d 4, 517v.

[121] E.g. most recently, Jorge Iván Marín Taborda, *Vivir en policía y a son de campana: El establecimiento de la república de indios en la provincia de Santafé, 1550–1604* (Bogotá: Instituto Colombiano de Antropología e Historia, 2022), 373–374, apparently following the late seventeenth-century chronicler Zamora. Even on paper, such positions would only become benefices from 1574, as Chapter 3 discusses.

[122] Visitation of Cucaita by Tomás López, 12 April 1560, AGN VB 19 d 7, 549r.

108 *The Settlers, Rescript, and the Foundations of the Kingdom*

materials – on pain of various fines and the denial of absolution.[123] Of the fifty-eight communities without a priest, only in three had the *encomendero* followed the requirement. One was Velandia, in Chitagoto. In Súnuba (near Guateque), *encomendero* Diego Paredes explained he had hired a carpenter called Andrés, who had been examined 'as the bishop commands'.[124] And in Socha the *encomendero*, Gerónimo de Carvajal, followed the synod's requirements with unusual care, explaining he had a layman 'examined by the priest of the city [of Tunja] in accordance with the synod', and adding that he had voluntarily relaxed the tribute obligations of his subjects by 100 or 200 *mantas* – up to a third of their annual obligation – 'for the lack of proper instruction, to allay his conscience'.[125]

Where arrangements existed, in other words, they were down to *encomenderos*, and reflected the disparate resources at their disposal and, perhaps especially, their widely varying interest and concern for Christianisation. Barrios could legislate all he wanted, but the initiative and control remained with them, and very few bothered. On one end of the spectrum were *encomenderos* like Carvajal, or indeed Luis de Sanabria, *encomendero* of Firavitoba and Cormechoque, who claimed not only to have brought visiting priests to provide instruction but also to have hired a layman expressly for this purpose, at the cost of some 300 pesos over four years.[126] On the other, *encomenderos* who seemed to have made something up on the spot when confronted, perhaps for the first time, by an authority with the power to sanction them in any meaningful way. This seems to have been the case with the *encomendero* Cristóbal de Roa of Tenza, who was questioned by López after the *cacique*, Neamuechequa, revealed that 'there has never been a secular priest or friar to teach the Indians doctrine'. Thinking on his feet, Roa denied that he had been negligent because, actually, 'one of his sons, aged about 10 or 11, teaches the Indians doctrine' – likely an illegitimate son, whose age he struggled to remember, and whose name he could not even recall, living with his Indigenous mother.[127] Somewhere in between were

---

[123] 'Constituciones sinodales 1556', tit. 1, ch. 3, 17–18.

[124] Visitation of Súnuba and Bagajique by Tomás López, 12 April 1560, AGN VB 9 d 6, 842r.

[125] Visitation of Socha by Tomás López, 24 October 1560 (AGN VB 8 d 9, 832v), cf. its 1555 *tasa*, of 600 *mantas* and other products, as compiled in Francis, 'The Muisca', 315.

[126] Visitation of Cormechoque and Pirabita by Tomás López, 7 August 1560, AGN VB 9 d 9, 871r.

[127] Visitation of Tenza by Tomás López, 8 April 1560, AGN VB 9 d 10, 884v, 888v.

'*To Learn and Investigate*'

people like Martín Sánchez Ropero, *encomendero* of Moniquirá and Socotá, who claimed he had always provided someone, although it had often been '*indios ladinos*' – that is, able to speak Spanish – 'to say the doctrine to the other Indians'.[128]

The synod of 1556 seems to have gone practically unnoticed, as had the efforts of the crown and *Audiencia* to the same effect. For instance, the synod had also ordered that churches be built, at least in the larger towns, but of the sixty-three only one – Martín Sánchez's Moniquirá – seems to have had anything approaching one, and it was only just under construction.[129] In fact, Barrios's main impact on the development of Christianisation on the ground may instead have come in an entirely different form. If his long-time critic, the magistrate Penagos, can be believed, Barrios may have been unwittingly responsible for unleashing a catastrophic epidemic that devastated the population of the highlands from 1558. In a complaint to the king of September 1559, Penagos claimed that the epidemic, which he calculated had already killed over 40,000 people, had arrived in the region borne by a number of enslaved Africans, whose names were not recorded, recently brought from Santo Domingo by Barrios for his service.[130]

Whether a consequence of Barrios's actions or not, the epidemic, which contemporaries speculated may have been of both smallpox and measles, certainly resulted in the deaths of thousands, making it, according to Michael Francis, likely the deadliest to hit the region in the entire colonial period.[131] While we lack any concrete figures of the death toll before López's visitation, records for a reassessment of tribute rates in the province of Tunja carried out in 1562 by the *oidor* Diego Angulo de Castejón, suggest that of the 52,564 men of working age counted by López in 1560, only 35,480 survived two years later.[132] As many as

---

[128] Visitation of Socotá and Moniquirá (de Sánchez Ropero), 12 August 1560, AGN VB 18 d 10, 317r.

[129] Visitation of Moniquirá (de Sánchez Ropero) by Tomás López, 18 July 1560, AGN VB 18 d 10, 311r.

[130] Juan de Penagos to the King, 15 September 1559, AGI SF 188, 226r–229r.

[131] The death toll, as with other demographic data, is inevitably imprecise. The most thorough analysis of demographic change in the region remains the work of J. Michael Francis, who focuses on the province of Tunja, where the data is most abundant. See 'Población'.

[132] The first figure is from the anonymous report discussed earlier (Tovar Pinzón, 'Visita de 1560', 94–96). Records for Angulo's individual inspections have largely not survived, but a summary of the resulting reassessment can be found at AGN C&I 5, d. 2, 574–592. This was published as 'Retasa de la provincia de Tunja', in Hermes Tovar

110 *The Settlers, Rescript, and the Foundations of the Kingdom*

17,000 tributaries had perished in Tunja alone in the intervening two years, perhaps reflecting a drop of 31 per cent of the overall population.[133] Unsurprisingly, it was the epidemic, and not anything the authorities had done, that had been the real watershed for the people López interviewed and had the greatest impact on the development of Christianity in the region.

The epidemic had disrupted much of what little religious instruction was taking place, worsening the shortage of priests. Multiple communities reported that they had had some sort of provision only until it hit. In Bagajique (near Soracá), the eponymous *cacique* explained 'there has not been a friar or other priest since the smallpox'.[134] In Moniquirá, Nimpiqui, a captain, explained 'after the smallpox there has been no instruction'.[135] Their counterparts in at least another seven *encomiendas* made similar reports. Some, like Boyacá, which had had their own resident priest, had lost them – 'and since the smallpox no priest has been to our town', as Sichabón, the *cacique*, explained.[136] In others, like Socha, where priests had only ever visited, these visits stopped. As Tobagia, the *cacique*, put it, 'before the smallpox some priests would come to our town to teach the Indians, and stay two or three days', but no longer.[137] Nemchía, *cacique* of Samacá, reported that our acquaintance Vicente de Requejada, having abandoned his Augustinian habit, had turned up every so often in his community, but had not been seen since.[138] We do not know precisely what was happening in the province of Santafé at this time, but there are suggestions that things there were no different. Alonso de Grajeda, a recently arrived *oidor*, complained to the king in October

---

Pinzón, 'Apéndice documental: Estado actual de los estudios de demografía histórica en Colombia'. *Anuario Colombiano de Historia Social y de la Cultura* no. 5 (1970): 115–117. The reliability of both sets of figures is discussed in Francis, 'Tribute Records'.

[133] See Francis, 'Población', 75, 103–104. The epidemic is also briefly discussed with reference to the province of Santafé in Juan A. Villamarín and Judith E. Villamarín, 'Epidemic Disease in the Sabana de Bogotá, 1536–1810'. In *Secret Judgments of God: Old World Disease in Colonial Spanish America*. Edited by Noble David Cook and W. George Lovell (Norman: University of Oklahoma Press, 1991), 118.

[134] Visitation of Súnuba, Sochaquirá, and Bagajique by Tomás López, AGN VB 9 d 6, 839v.

[135] Visitation of Moniquirá (de Chinchila) by Tomás López, AGN VB 11 d 9, 817v.

[136] Visitation of Boyacá by Tomás López, AGN VB 18 d 9, 305v.

[137] Visitation of Socha by Tomás López, AGN VB 8 d 9, 830v.

[138] Visitation of Samacá by Tomás López, AGN VB 8 d 12, 856v.

'To Learn and Investigate'   III

1559 that the Dominicans there had apparently hidden away in their convent, refusing to come out.[139] The epidemic also interrupted many of the informal arrangements by which Indigenous people would travel to nearby towns and cities to receive instruction. Tocavita, captain of Susacón, explained that 'he and his youths would go to the *repartimiento* of Soatá', where there was a priest, but 'after the smallpox they have not returned and there is no instruction'.[140] In Soracá, Anbarja, the *cacique*, reported that 'before the smallpox the youths would come to Tunja to the Franciscan convent', but that this had stopped with the epidemic. 'After the smallpox there has been no instruction, and some Indians in the town die having been baptised, but others without.'[141]

At the same time, it was during the crisis that some *encomenderos* and priests had organised large-scale efforts to baptise Indigenous people before they perished. Alonso, brother of the *cacique* of Turmequé, explained that in his community 'at the time of the smallpox many Indians became Christians', and his *encomendero*, Juan de Torres, explained that he had 'brought men to baptise and tend to them'.[142] Simbaumba, a commoner from Tunquirá, explained that in his community they had never had a priest, 'except in the time of the smallpox, when a priest came'. Neubasia, his captain, explained that the priest 'made the dying Christians'.[143] In Motavita, Saacha, a captain, explained that it was 'in the time of the smallpox that many Indians became Christians'. Indeed, when different witnesses reported that members of their communities had 'become Christians' by the time of the visitation, it had often been the result of such efforts. This was the case in Boyacá, the only one of the sixty-three communities where witnesses reported 'that most of the Indians of the town are Christians, as are those who have died'. As Sichabón, the *cacique*, explained, 'in the time of the smallpox all the Indians who died became Christians', and many more besides.[144] Beyond being baptised, however, these conversions appear to have made little impact on the lives of these people, as we will see.

---

[139] Alonso de Grajeda to the king, 22 October 1559, AGN SF 188, 234r.

[140] Visitation of Susacón by Tomás López, AGN VB 8 d 7, 809v.

[141] Visitation of Soracá by Tomás López, AGN VB 11 d 7, 777v.

[142] Visitation of Turmequé by Tomás López, AGN VB 18 d 5, 236v, 247r.

[143] Visitation of Tunquirá (Baganique) by Tomás López, AGN VB 18 d 4, 212v, 214v.

[144] Visitation of Boyacá by Tomás López, AGN VB 18 d 9, 306v, 307v.

'SATISFACTION AND RESTITUTION'

The sentences that López issued *encomenderos* all conformed to a standard template that reflected the visitor's priorities. This included a general admonition to treat their subjects well and to follow 'the laws, *cédulas*, and *provisiones* that his majesty has issued in their favour'. But the bulk of the sentences concerned issues of religious instruction. *Encomenderos* were ordered, within six months, 'to construct in the said town a church of the most permanent construction possible', a task with which the Indigenous community was, vaguely, 'to help'. The church's dedication was to be selected by the bishop, or at least by a local priest. *Encomenderos* were to purchase a bell of a specified weight, depending on the size of the community; a reredos, 'whether carved and painted or just a decorated canvas'; and all the vestments and ornaments required for mass and the administration of the sacraments. And, of course, they were to provide 'sufficient instruction by a secular priest or friar, as the law requires'.[145]

It is striking how much of what López sought to enforce in his visitation had been the policy promoted by Barrios in his synod and in the years leading up to the visitation. López and his colleagues in the *Audiencia* could complain about Barrios invading their jurisdiction, but they clearly embraced his priorities and made them their own. In fact, López's sentence referred to Barrios, noting how 'the bishop of this kingdom has long been concerned with the satisfaction and restitution that must be made of tributes and other things that have been collected without the provision of instruction', and ordered *encomenderos* to make restitution as per the terms of the synod, 'beseeching their conscience' to comply, but also adding that failure to do so would incur penalties from the *Audiencia* too, including large fines. In this vein, Juan de Torres, *encomendero* of Turmequé, was ordered to return 300 *mantas* to his subjects.[146] In similar terms *encomenderos* were ordered to stick to the standard *tasa*, not to alter or commute the obligations without permission, and not to force their subjects to work or send them to the mines in the lowlands.

Although absent from those issued in Tunja, we also know from a 1563 visitation of the province of Santafé by Diego de Villafañe, which

---

[145] See, for example, the terms issued in the visitation of Tutasá by Tomás López, AGN VB 11 d 8, 814r.

[146] Visitation of Turmequé by Tomás López, AGN VB 18 d 5, 262v.

'Satisfaction and Restitution'

we will examine shortly, that López also used his sentences to introduce a further reform, the mass resettlement of Indigenous communities into nucleated towns. This was by no means a new initiative, and legislation had been in place in parts of the viceroyalty of New Spain for this purpose since the 1530s, which López had helped to implement in his visitation of Yucatán earlier in the 1550s.[147] This was something that the crown had ordered the *Audiencia* to pursue from its foundation, but which had been generally neglected until López issued a set of instructions in 1559 to outline how towns were to be laid out and people resettled.[148] López's legislation conformed to what was by now a standard model, aiming to congregate dispersed populations into gridded towns of a standard size and shape, which has been examined in detail by scholars of New Granada and other regions, and which we will explore in greater detail later, when the initiative finally gained some traction under López's successors at the end of the century.[149] For now it was yet another item in López's aspirational list, and was added to his sentences too.

Finally, the sentences imposed fines and penalties for specific offences committed by each *encomendero*. Pedro Bravo de Ribera, *encomendero* of Chivatá, was found guilty of mistreating his subjects and was ordered to return some land that he had seized. Juan de Torres, in Turmequé, was also found guilty of abusing his former subjects when he was *encomendero* of Bosa, banished from their town, and ordered to pay compensation

---

[147] This was pioneered in Hispaniola and detailed legislation was later issued for this purpose in Guatemala in the 1530s. It was later adopted as a priority by the first congregation of bishops held in Mexico in 1546, and extended elsewhere. See Pierre Duviols, *La lutte*, 248; Farriss, *Maya Society*, 161ff; and Francisco de Solano, *Ciudades hispanoamericanas y pueblos de indios* (Madrid: Consejo Superior de Investigaciones Científicas, 1990), 43, 337–338. Much of the legislation on this process in New Spain and Peru is compiled in Francisco de Solano, *Cedulario de tierras: compilación de legislación agraria colonial, 1497–1820* (Mexico City: Universidad Nacional Autónoma de México, Instituto de Investigaciones Jurídicas, 1991).

[148] Royal decree on the congregation of indigenous people, 9 October 1549, AGI SF 533, lib. 1, 99r. Instructions issued by Tomás López, 1559, AGN C&I 49, doc. 97, 751r–780v.

[149] For New Granada, most recently by Guadalupe Romero Sánchez, *Los pueblos de indios en Nueva Granada* (Granada: Editorial Atrio, 2010). On the better known resettlement programme of the Central Andes, see Jeremy Ravi Mumford, *Vertical Empire: The General Resettlement of Indians in the Colonial Andes* (Durham, NC: Duke University Press, 2012), and S. Elizabeth Penry, *The People Are King: The Making of an Indigenous Andean Politics* (Oxford: Oxford University Press, 2019).

114 *The Settlers, Rescript, and the Foundations of the Kingdom*

to the current *cacique*.[150] Finally, *encomenderos* were generally sentenced to pay small fines plus the costs of any legal procedure or investigation resulting from their charges – in the case of Bravo, ten gold pesos, and of Torres, fifteen. These small fines were often paid quickly, as is frequently noted in the documentation of the visitations themselves. The report for Chivatá, for example, finishes with a short line by the scribe noting that Bravo 'paid the fine'.[151] So too with Diego Montañez, *encomendero* of Tota and Guáquira, who was ordered to pay ten pesos and costs, and with many others.[152]

In general, the *encomenderos* and Indigenous authorities that interacted with the visitor all acknowledged his authority and the validity of his power – at least according to the scribes, officials, and interpreters who travelled with him. There are, for example, almost no examples of *encomenderos* visibly interfering with the visitation as it was happening. One was Pedro Bravo de Ribera, of Chivatá, who had apparently sought to prevent the *cacique*, Neausipa, from speaking to López. As Neausipa explained, Bravo had come to his house and confronted him about his plans to see López in Tunja and particularly to show him the *tasa* and the weights that Bravo had given him to weigh the gold for his tribute. 'He said we must not bring them, and took them, and would not let us.' Realising the game was up, Bravo had returned with two other men and tried to force the *cacique* and two of his captains to pay their tribute early, before López corrected the rate and weights, with threats and eventually violence.[153] If other *encomenderos* tried something similar then perhaps they were more discrete. The imminent arrival and presence of López, and through him, the *Audiencia*, clearly had some effect. But for how long after he left?

'THE POWER IN OUR HANDS'

One way to assess the effectiveness of López's visitation is to examine the records of the next one, carried out in the province of Santafé by the *oidor* Diego de Villafañe in 1563. These survive only for nine *encomiendas*, but at least tend to be more detailed than those of López because Villafañe travelled to where his Indigenous interlocutors lived. Of the nine, only

---

[150] Visitation of Turmequé by Tomás López, AGN VB 18 d 5, 262v.
[151] Visitation of Chivatá by Tomás López, AGN VB 18 d 6, 286v.
[152] Visitation of Tota and Guáquira by Tomás López, AGN VB 19 d 5, 535v.
[153] Visitation of Chivatá by Tomás López, AGN VB 18 d 6, 266v–267v.

'The Power in Our Hands'

one, Ubaté, had a resident priest, who had been there for the last eight months, and another before him for a shorter period. As the *cacique*, Orencipa, explained, both had run a programme of religious instruction for young and old alike.[154] A second community, Suesca, had seen a stream of priests, most recently Franciscans, including the future chronicler Pedro de Aguado, who had done the same, although no one was currently in residence.[155] Elsewhere the picture was much the same as it had been in Tunja three years before. Witnesses in a couple of towns reported occasional visits from priests based in Santafé or communities for which visitation records are lost. The longest were four- and five-month stays in Cota and a month-long stay in the community of Gachancipá.[156] The rest were occasional visits lasting no more than a few days, or even a few hours. Some were spontaneous, as in Suta and Tausa, where the odd priest had come for the day on five occasions since López's visitation; others by arrangement of the *encomendero*, as in Choachí, which received a five- or six-day visit from neighbouring Ubaque twice a year.[157] Elsewhere, as the eponymous leader of Tunjuelo reported, 'never in this town have we seen a secular priest or friar to teach the Indians doctrine', whether before or after López's visitation.[158]

López seemed to have fared a little better in his command that churches be built – at least in part. Of the communities for which records survive, Suesca, Ubaté, and Gachancipá had properly appointed churches, which the scribe often described in the records, all apparently built after López's visitation.[159] Only two towns, Simijaca and Tunjuelo, were still without a church. In the rest, each Indigenous community had done its part and built a church, of thatch or adobe, but *encomenderos* had not done theirs, so that these basic buildings lacked ornaments, a reredos, or an altar cloth. In at least one case, Cota, the *encomendero* had rushed to acquire some of these things before Villafañe turned up.[160] These empty churches, largely unused, lay in various states of disrepair, and two – in Choachí

[154] Visitation of Ubaté by Diego de Villafañe, AGN VC 5, d 7, 986v.
[155] Visitation of Suesca by Diego de Villafañe, AGN VC 5, d 6, 942v.
[156] Visitations of Cota and Gachancipá by Diego de Villafañe, AGN E 12 d 8, 218r, and VC 7 d 14, 670v.
[157] Visitations of Choachí and Suta and Tausa by Diego de Villafañe, AGN VC 4 d 11, 973r, and 12 d 11, 1039r.
[158] Visitation of Tunjuelo and Unjica by Tomás López, AGN VC 5 d 6, 940r.
[159] See AGN VC 5 d 6 943r–943v; 5 d 7, 978r; and 7 d 14 617r–617v, respectively.
[160] Visitation of Cota by Villafañe, AGN E 12 d 8, 219v.

116 *The Settlers, Rescript, and the Foundations of the Kingdom*

and Tenjo – had already burned down or collapsed. Villafañe's visitations also ended on similar terms to López, with a standard template containing much the same as his predecessor's instructions: *encomenderos* were to build or finish churches, appoint them with adequate ornaments and materials, and provide proper instruction by secular priests or friars. He also appealed to the consciences of negligent *encomenderos*, ordered that they make restitution for ill-gotten gains, imposed small fines for this and that, and reiterated the same threats of stripping their *encomiendas* for repeated offences that surely, by now, were ringing hollow.

It is for this reason that restitution, ordered not just under the threat of the deprivation of office but also ecclesiastical sanction, is especially interesting. Few *encomenderos*, as we saw, followed the letter of the law unprompted. Gerónimo de Carvajal, *encomendero* of Socha, was alone among the *encomenderos* visited by López in voluntarily reducing the tribute he collected from his subjects to compensate for his inability to find them a priest. But others did follow López's command, such as Nicolás de Sepúlveda, *encomendero* of Gachancipá, who settled his debt to the people under his charge by reducing their tribute obligations for a time.[161] Some took a little longer to obey, only making arrangements for restitution on their deathbeds, perhaps moved by the bishop's command that they be denied of absolution by their confessors if they failed to do so. This was the case with Diego Rodríguez de Valderas, the late *encomendero* of Ubaté, who had been ordered by López to reimburse his subjects 200 pesos in *mantas*, and finally did so in his will, as his executors confirmed.[162] Even so, it was no magic solution. Some remained unmoved, such as Diego Montañez, of Tota, who was sentenced to make restitution by López and perhaps also by later visitors, but who in the 1570s was at the centre of a suit with the *cacique* in which it emerged that even though he had eventually repaid what he had been ordered – 3 pots of gold containing some 160 pesos – he had promptly stolen 2 of them back, and was trying to recover the third.[163]

An older historiography on the *encomienda* might lead us to expect relations between *encomenderos* and their subjects to be like that of

---

[161] Visitation of Gachancipá by Villafañe, AGN VC 7 d 14, 962v, 700v.

[162] Visitation of Ubaté, AGN VC 5 d 7, 1029v. 1032v. Villafañe, notably, ordered his widow to make further restitution, as it was insufficient and had not been done according to law, at 1053v.

[163] Suit of Diego Montañez against don Diego, *cacique* of Tota, 3 December 1574, AGN C&I 29, d. 1, 82v–83r. The gold had been given to don Diego's predecessor, presumably the same Unicón who appeared before López in 1560.

'The Power in Our Hands' 117

Montañez and the people of Tota, in no small measure because this is also how royal legislation, the rhetoric of colonial officials, and the writings of polemicists such as Las Casas generally characterised them.[164] Some certainly were, such as that of *encomendero* Antonio Bermúdez and his subjects in Choachí. There, witnesses came forwards to report myriad abuses to Villafañe: these included the murder of a young man; beatings, with the visitor shown the resulting bruises, broken bones, and scars; and multiple instances of the theft, damage, or destruction of land and other property. To cap things off, Villafañe discovered that Bermúdez had also been able to depose Fosatiba, the *cacique*, and replace him with his own man, Guanecipa. Bermúdez had enough retainers to run the old *cacique* out of town with threats of violence after they quarrelled, declared he had abandoned his office, and appointed Guanecipa his replacement. The new leader 'mistreats the Indians', Fosatiba complained, 'for I have seen him beating them with whips and canes, and this is why Bermúdez likes him: he forces the other Indians to do as he says'.[165]

Other relationships, however, were quite the opposite, built on collaboration and community of interest, such as that between Bermúdez's neighbours, *encomendero* Juan de Céspedes and his subject Ubaque, the

[164] The historiography on the *encomienda* is vast, especially since the publication of Silvo Zavala's 1935 study, *La encomienda indiana*, subsequently much revised and expanded in multiple editions. For a survey of the historiography of the institution in Perú, see Teodoro Hampe Martínez, 'La encomienda en el Perú en el siglo XVI (ensayo bibliográfico)'. *Histórica* 6, no. 2 (1982): 173–216. Two recent approaches that constructively engage with this historiography and encourage us to rethink its assumptions are the works of Santiago Muñoz, whose work on the *encomiendas* of the valley of Ubaque, *Costumbres*, is discussed later; and Aliocha Maldavsky, who examines the complex ways in which *encomenderos* in Peru participated in religious change even beyond the curtailment of the *encomienda*, through restitution, charity, and the sponsorship of the sacred. On this, see her articles, 'Les encomenderos et l'évangélisation des Indiens dans le Pérou colonial: "Noblesse", charité et propagation de la foi au XVIe siècle'. In *Le Salut par les armes: Noblesse et défense de l'orthodoxie (XIIIe–XVIIe siècle)*. Edited by Ariane Boltanski and Franck Mercier (Rennes: Presses Universitaires de Rennes, 2011), 239–250'; 'De l'encomendero au marchand: Charité et évangélisation dans le Pérou colonial, xvie–xviie siècles'. *Cahiers des Amériques latines* 2011, no. 67 (2012): 75–87; 'Giving for the Mission: The *Encomenderos* and Christian Space in the Late Sixteenth-Century Andes'. In *Space and Conversion in Global Perspective*. Edited by Giuseppe Marcocci, Wietse de Boer, Aliocha Maldavsky, and Ilaria Pavan (Leiden: Brill, 2014), 260–284; and 'Encomenderos, indios y religiosos en la región de Arequipa (siglo XVI): Restitución y formación de un territorio cristiano y señoril'. In *Invertir en lo sagrado: salvación y dominación territorial en América y Europa (siglos XVI–XX)*. Edited by Aliocha Maldavsky and Roberto Di Stefano (Santa Rosa: Universidad Nacional de la Pampa, 2018).
[165] Visitation of Choachí by Villafañe, 28 March 1563, AGN VC 12 d 11, 1041r.

118 *The Settlers, Rescript, and the Foundations of the Kingdom*

ruler of the community of the same name. This was clear in the great celebration held by Ubaque in late 1563, discussed in Chapter 1, which had been so resoundingly condemned by the authorities, but which had in fact been organised with the support of Céspedes. News of Ubaque's plans had first reached the *Audiencia* through witnesses who had apparently seen people from Ubaque travelling around the region inviting Indigenous authorities to participate in the celebration. Several reported that their movement was facilitated by Céspedes's involvement, such as Gonzalo García Zorro the elder, *encomendero* of Fusagasugá, who explained that the couriers were bearing a note, signed by Céspedes, reading 'Christians, let these Indians through for they are messengers', with the implication that they were travelling on Céspedes's business – which, in a sense, they were. When questioned, Ubaque later explained Céspedes had made fourteen such writs for him, to aid with the preparations.[166] This was just one example of the complex relationship between Céspedes and Ubaque, which has been studied in detail by Santiago Muñoz, who also details other ways in which Céspedes advocated for Ubaque against *Audiencia* officials and supported his ambitions over neighbouring communities.[167] Indeed, a careful examination of these and other records of the actions of *encomenderos* in this period reveals a broad range of attitudes, priorities, and concerns.

Conversely, to recognise that the powers of the *Audiencia* and the bishop were profoundly limited should not be understood to imply that the power of *encomenderos* was not. Some may have been able to resist or ignore the command of the king's representatives, especially outside of the formal setting of a visitation or hearing, but so too could their own subjects ignore theirs. The power of *encomenderos* itself was tenuous, contingent, and fleeting. This is clear from Villafañe's findings concerning López's policy of resettlement, which reflected not only the varying interest and willingness of *encomenderos* to participate in implementing the policy, but more fundamentally their ability to compel their subjects to obey them. A couple claimed to Villafañe that they had managed it, although it is unclear what they had actually done, as in Cota, where none of the Indigenous witnesses seemed to know anything about having been resettled. Others had tried and failed. Florentina de Escobar, the acting *encomendera* of Tenjo, explained that her late husband had tried,

---

[166] Documents pertaining to the case of Ubaque, 1563, AGI Justicia 618, 1398r–1398v, 1417r.
[167] Muñoz Arbeláez, *Costumbres*, 44–53.

'but afterwards they left the settlement and went back to their old houses', and he had been powerless to stop them.[168] In Gachancipá, *encomendero* Nicolás Sepúlveda had gone as far as to burn their old houses, as the *cacique* complained.[169] Leonor Maldonado, acting *encomendera* of Ubaté, spelled it out for the visitor: 'the Indians do not want it, because it would be to their detriment', and to force them, quite simply, 'would take the strength and authority to execute justice, to command, to arrest, and to imprison, and neither my late husband nor any *encomendero* can do it, because it exceeds the power in our hands'. Pushing too hard would only drive them 'to flee elsewhere, so that we will not be able to collect tribute, and they will be lost'.[170] The others, it seems, had avoided it altogether. 'I did not try to congregate or compel or force them', Gonzalo de León, *encomendero* of Simijaca, explained, adding that it should be a matter for the *Audiencia* 'and not for me to do on my own'.[171] But what could the *Audiencia* do?

Uprooting and relocating entire communities clearly exceeded the power of many *encomenderos*, but so too did some of the everyday business of their *encomiendas*. Even their most basic function, the collection of tribute, required negotiation and compromise. A key question in both visitations was whether *encomenderos* had commuted any of the terms of the *tasa*, perhaps exchanging the obligation to provide a certain kind of product with another or altering the quantities. Officials asked this question because they were concerned, often rightly, that *encomenderos* might do this in order to increase their profits to the detriment of their charges, as some certainly did. But the visitations also reveal the opposite: *encomenderos* who had no choice but to accept tribute in different forms to those prescribed by their *tasa*, or not receive it at all. In Suta, the *cacique*, Cupachilagua, reported that instead of paying Gonzalo de León the gold and *mantas* in their *tasa*, they grew some wheat for him, while his neighbour, Fosquiraguya, *cacique* of Tausa, had agreed to pay *mantas* but not gold.[172] Leonor Maldonado was candid on the subject, explaining that her late husband had negotiated with the *cacique* to reduce the number of *mantas* they paid him, in exchange for doing some more agricultural work, 'because *encomenderos* are forced to accept

---

[168] Visitation of Tenjo Villafañe, AGN E 6, d 18, 505r.
[169] Visitation of Gachancipá by Villafañe, AGN VC 7 d 14, 692r.
[170] Visitation of Ubaté by Villafañe, AGN VC 4 d 7, 1000v.
[171] Visitation of Simijaca by Villafañe, AGN VC 4 d 11, 997r.
[172] Visitation of Suta and Tausa by Villafañe, AGN VC 4, d. 11, 973v, 974v.

120   *The Settlers, Rescript, and the Foundations of the Kingdom*

whatever the Indians give them, for they never fulfil or pay what is contained in the *tasa*'. This was an exaggeration, no doubt, but not entirely. She and many other *encomenderos*, she added, had complained to the authorities, 'but they have not forced them to pay'.[173] And how could they?

Indigenous leaders in turn relied on a delicate balance of ritual, reciprocity, and participation to exercise what power they had. In those rare instances when commutations went through the official channels, leaving us with more of a paper trail, Indigenous leaders reported having the same problems as *encomenderos*. Just two years after the 1555 *tasa* was issued, for example, the leaders of Tibaná in Tunja petitioned Briceño to commute their obligation to pay their *encomendero*, the mighty Suárez Rendón, 330 pesos of low gold, into *mantas*: 'we cannot give gold because we do not have any and cannot get it, and if we were to demand it of the Indians of our town they would flee and abandon it'.[174] And who, indeed, could prevent it?

THE FOUNDATIONS OF THE KINGDOM

Reading the records of the first visitations of the provinces of Santafé and Tunja against the better thumbed legislation and correspondence surrounding the introduction of the *Audiencia* and first bishop to the New Kingdom reveals a series of striking parallels. Both, at first sight, seem to be expressions of increasingly confident and effective monarchical power. Indeed, an earlier historiography understood the introduction of the *Audiencia* as the first step in the progressive unfolding of a colonial state over the settlers and Indigenous peoples, one that allowed the Spanish crown, at least for a time, to strengthen its grip on local affairs and impose its authority on unruly local elites.[175] It was common for historians to understand the centuries that followed as the story of collaboration with, or resistance against, the monarchy by local elites: of 'imperial centralization and colonial decentralization', in the words of John Leddy Phelan.[176] The historiography on the New Kingdom was by no means unique in this

---

[173] Visitation of Ubaté by Diego de Villafañe, AGN VC 4 d 7, 1001v.
[174] Visitation of Tibaná by Tomás López, AGN VB 7 d 6, 406r.
[175] For Jaime Jaramillo Uribe, for example, it was with the *Audiencia* and the New Laws that 'the monarchy, the Spanish state, assumed control and exercised its full sovereign rights over the new territories'. See *Manual de historia de Colombia*, 1:350.
[176] John Leddy Phelan, *The People and the King: The Comunero Revolution in Colombia: 1781* (London: University of Wisconsin Press, 1978), xviii.

The Foundations of the Kingdom

regard. As Tamar Herzog has shown, much of the historiography on early modern government in Spain and Spanish America has focused on royal projects of state-building, in which 'the state', a public administration understood to be the monarchy or its royal bureaucracy, 'gradually affirmed itself against opposition'.[177] In these readings, royal officials such as *oidores* are understood to be fundamentally distinct and separate to the people they are sent to govern, concerned primarily with state-building.

In this interpretation, visitations become primarily opportunities for gathering information in the service of this state, implementing policy, and bringing wayward subjects to heel: mechanisms, through which 'the state' intrudes on the localities and their people, to observe, command, and discipline. These conclusions are easy to draw from the documentation itself, which after all takes for granted the visitors' ability to do all these things themselves and more. Indeed, the very records they produced often presented these visitations as watersheds. Some claimed to draw a line under a period of lawlessness and inaugurate one of better government, as in the case of López, whose sentences repeatedly explained that 'failures and excesses will be punished with all rigour *from now on*', or that transgressions of different sorts would be tolerated no longer; while others, such as those of Villafañe and his successors, announced new and stricter standards for the future.[178] It is, in other words, easy to read these claims and imagine that the purpose and effect of the visitations was to tighten the vice of royal control one inspection at a time.

As this chapter has shown, however, a careful reading of both sets of records reveals a very different picture. It was not just the establishment of the *Audiencia* of Santafé, or the coming of the bishop, that must be understood within the context of the operation of rescript government, as the result of multiple petitions by the settlers of the New Kingdom to turn their principal city into an administrative and ecclesiastical capital, in pursuit of their own interests. So too must their continued operation and ability to function, as institutions themselves dependent on the participation of litigants, supplicants, informants, and diverse other actors, whether at home in their chambers in Santafé or out in the field in a

---

[177] Indeed, as she notes, this historiography is predicated on the existence of multiple binaries, 'state versus society, institutions and bureaucrats versus local elites, law versus its implementation, tyranny versus flexibility, public versus private spheres'. See Tamar Herzog, *Upholding Justice: Society, State, and the Penal System in Quito (1650–1750)* (Ann Arbor: University of Michigan Press, 2004), 5–8.

[178] As in López's visitation of Chivatá, AGN VB 11 d 8, 814r. My italics.

122 *The Settlers, Rescript, and the Foundations of the Kingdom*

borrowed room or a visitor's tent. Instead of the image of a constant, universal authority confidently projecting its power from the courts of the bishop and *Audiencia* on to Spanish and Indigenous subjects that is embedded in the triumphant rhetoric of royal legislation and administrative records, what the visitations show is patchy, fleeting, and contingent: flickering spots of power and jurisdiction moving across the landscape like fireflies in the night, following a visitor as he interacted with local people on a visitation, surrounding an official as he carried out an inquiry, or invoked by different actors in the resolution of a suit or conflict, before fading into the darkness and disappearing once more. Because everything in the bureaucratic archive is illuminated by this light, it is easy to imagine that it shone over everything and that it was always on, but we must not lose sight of its fleeting, incomplete, and partial nature.

What is more, in practice, royal authority was not something for a bureaucrat to impose, but rather something that was collectively brought into being by the interaction of the monarch's subjects, whether or not they were one of the tiny handful of salaried royal officials. They did so when they sent the monarch or his representatives a petition or request, appeared before a magistrate or official, testified in a visitation, or obeyed – or indeed appealed – a sentence or ruling. Visitations facilitated many of these interactions, by bringing the *Audiencia* or the bishop to the localities, and making it easier, for example, for the people of Tota to denounce Diego Montañez and obtain restitution. Without the participation of witnesses and informants, the *Audiencia* would have remained unaware of his abuse. But they were no magic solution: lacking the means to compel Montañez in the long term, he was able to reverse course once the visitor left and steal the money back. Other *encomenderos*, of course, did not, but not because the nature of their sentences, the threats of pecuniary or spiritual sanctions, or the claims of power and jurisdiction of the authorities over them were any different. What changed was the nexus of social relations, obligations, reciprocity, expectations, beliefs, priorities, and much more besides, that shaped the actions of each *encomendero*, and their relations to their subjects, neighbours, and different authorities. This complex web is often invisible in the documentation, which so stubbornly prioritises hierarchy above all else, but it is essential in understanding how the power of the monarchy functioned in practice.

The records of the visitations show how, time and time again, the visitors overestimated not just their own authority, but also that of the people with whom they interacted. They thought little of ordering

The Foundations of the Kingdom 123

encomenderos to take on enormous tasks and seemed to believe they would achieve them if only they did as they were told. But these same records, as we saw, are also revealing of the limits of the power of those local actors. They show how *encomenderos* were aware of the limitations of their power, and how they devised diverse strategies and compromises to pursue their interests. These in turn remind us of the fragility of the authority of the Indigenous leaders with whom they interacted, which the Chapter 1 explored, and which constituted the very foundations of the kingdom and its tributary economy. Seen from above the authority and power of the *Audiencia*, bishops, and even *encomenderos* may seem solid and unshakeable, but seen from the ground up they are revealed to be as delicate, contingent, and fragile as the power of Muisca leaders. In pursuing their ambitions, the bishops of Santafé and their civil counterparts would have done well to see that the New Kingdom was built on sand. Instead, over the following decades, both would grow increasingly belligerent, and push the kingdom to breaking point.

3

The Failure of Colonial Governance and the Breaking of Indigenous Authority

In late January 1605, don Pedro, *cacique* of Suba, a town some twelve miles north of Santafé, went to the *Audiencia* for redress. His grievance was not with his *encomendero*, his parish priest, or his Spanish or Indigenous neighbours. Instead, it was with his own subjects, who had stopped obeying him. They no longer went to his *cercado*, or residential complex, which had previously been the centre of the political, economic, and social life of the community (Figure 3.1). His subordinates, the *capitanes*, had stopped recognising him as their superior, and two were directly trying to replace him. Recently, he had asked his subjects to harvest his crops and to erect a building on his lands, and for this he had held a banquet, as was the custom of Muisca rulers. His subjects had come, eating the special foods and drinking the *chicha* he had provided, but they had not built anything, and even though they had harvested the maize from his fields, they had taken it with them and kept it. Left with no other choice, don Pedro now asked the *Audiencia* to force his subjects to recognise him as 'natural lord and principal *cacique*' and show him 'respect and obedience', and to punish them for their insubordination 'because otherwise they will not want to obey'.[1] Don Pedro's was just the latest of a multitude of similar complaints that had been reaching the *Audiencia* of Santafé over the previous decade, whether in the form of petitions presented in Santafé or in interviews carried out by members of the *Audiencia* while out on visitation.

Across the region, the authority of Indigenous rulers was crumbling as the complex ritual economy that had underpinned it – explored in

---

[1] Petition of don Pedro, *cacique* of Suba, AGN Miscelánea 137, d. 43, 330r–330v.

The Failure of Colonial Governance 125

FIGURE 3.1 Votive figure (*tunjo*) of an Indigenous ruler in a residential enclosure (*cercado*), Colombia, Eastern Cordillera, 800–1600 CE (Muisca period). Museo del Oro, Banco de la República, Bogotá. 7.9 x 7 cm, O12065. Photograph by Clark M. Rodríguez

126   *The Failure of Colonial Governance*

Chapter 1 – teetered on the brink of collapse. This was not just a problem for people like don Pedro of Suba, but for the entire colonial project, which remained wholly dependent on the permanence of Indigenous social and political structures for its lifeblood. It was an issue so serious that it had prompted the *Audiencia*, in its general visitations of the region, to issue legislation to require Indigenous communities to obey their *caciques* and to fulfil their traditional obligations, and ordinary Spaniards, through their municipal councils, to appeal to the monarch for a wholesale reform of the administration and religious instruction. The crisis threatened the twin engines of the kingdom's colonial economy: the *encomienda* tribute of highland communities, and the extraction of gold from deposits in the lowlands, itself reliant on the continuous flow of provisions and labour from the highlands. As don Juan, the beleaguered *cacique* of Fontibón put it in his own, similar petition to the *Audiencia* a few years earlier: 'without the greatest punishment' from the *Audiencia*, his subjects would 'lose all respect' for him, 'and then who will collect the *demora* and the royal fifths?'[2]

At the heart of the problem were the actions of the civil and ecclesiastical authorities, who pursued policies that directly undermined the power of Indigenous leaders, just as they sought to take advantage of that power for their own purposes – to conscript and transform Indigenous rulers into intermediaries through which to govern, tax, and Christianise the people that they ruled. This meant that people like don Pedro were pulled in two unreconcilable directions: needing to maintain the Indigenous ritual economy in order to preserve their positions of leadership, but at the same time being pressured to participate in its dismantling. Then, chaffing against the limitations of their power and engrossed in increasing competition over the leadership of the colonial project, in the final decades of the sixteenth century the archbishop and *Audiencia* of Santafé pursued increasingly belligerent policies to reform the lives of Indigenous people, with catastrophic results. It was in this way that Indigenous leaders increasingly found themselves, at the turn of the century, in the paradoxical position of having to petition the Spanish authorities to coerce their own subjects to treat them as the natural lords

---

[2] The *demora* was the Neogranadian term for was the tribute paid by Indigenous people to their *encomenderos*. The royal fifth was the 20 per cent tax Spaniards were required to pay the crown on all precious metals and other commodities they extracted, including any *demoras* received, but in this context, the mention of a fifth it could also refer to the *requinto*, a new poll tax discussed in Chapter 4. Petition of don Juan, *cacique* of Fontibón, October 1595, AGN C&I 9 d. 13, 457r.

'No Church ... or Anything Else'

that Spaniards claimed they were: to make the fiction of the Spanish understanding of Indigenous politics a reality. This was not, as we will see, because the archbishop or the *Audiencia* had become able enforce the claims they made about Indigenous leaders, or, indeed, about themselves: don Pedro and his fellows simply had nowhere else to turn.

This chapter explores the final decades of the sixteenth century. Contrary to the established story of the gradual and triumphant consolidation of colonial institutions, it shows that this was a period of deep, overlapping, and abiding crisis for the New Kingdom of Granada: personal crises for Indigenous leaders and commoners, as their communities unravelled in the face of ever greater colonial pressures and unrelenting waves of epidemics; crises for *encomenderos* and other settlers, who struggled to wrest a profit from them and preserve their own positions; and crises for the archbishop and members of the *Audiencia*, whose rivalries, venality, and misunderstanding of local conditions brought the kingdom to its knees. To understand how this came to be, we must begin with the man at the very heart of the crisis: the second archbishop of Santafé, fray Luis Zapata de Cárdenas, and the circumstances of his arrival in 1573.

'NO CHURCH ... OR ANYTHING ELSE'

On Juan de los Barrios's death in February 1569 the New Kingdom of Granada still lacked a programme of religious instruction. Barrios and his civil counterparts had issued ambitious legislation, as we saw, and had sought to compel *encomenderos* to reform the people under their charge and to provide them with the rudiments of Christianity in three tours of inspection, with little success. In practice, however, efforts to Christianise Indigenous people remained haphazard and inconstant for the rest of the decade, entirely reliant on the interest and means of individual *encomenderos*, and the *Audiencia* and Barrios could do little more than observe.

One notable change in the 1560s, at least at first sight, was a greater number of friars departing Spain for destinations in the New Kingdom than ever before. Because their Atlantic crossing was generally subsidised by the crown, records were kept by the *Casa de Contratación* that show that 41 Franciscans and 149 Dominicans left Spain for destinations in the New Kingdom over the course of the decade.[3] These passage records do not indicate how many of these went to the highlands on arrival, or

---

[3] These numbers would only continue to increase after Barrios's death: a further 84 Franciscans, 117 Dominicans, and – from 1575 to 1777 Augustinians were sent to the

128   *The Failure of Colonial Governance*

indeed how many merely used a Neogranadian port as a stepping stone to greener pastures, but other sources provide some clues. Among the Dominicans, it seems the largest contingent to make it to the highlands was a group of nineteen friars that arrived towards the middle of the decade, led by one Francisco de Carvajal, who sought to find his fellows easy employment shortly after their arrival by petitioning the king to appoint them all to minister to just three royal *encomiendas* in the province of Santafé – Cajicá, Fontibón, and Guasca – which he claimed 'need six friars per town'.[4] When this was rejected, the new arrivals took to wandering around the province begging for alms and refusing to obey Carvajal, who attracted complaints from Barrios and the settlers, was investigated for malfeasance, and eventually left the highlands for Cartagena.[5] It is less clear how many Franciscans made it to the highlands in this period, in part because their actions attracted fewer complaints. In 1568, they petitioned the king for financial support and further reinforcements, explaining there were by now twenty friars in the area and that they had established convents in the principal Spanish cities.[6] That year they also dispatched the head of their convent of Santafé, fray Francisco de Olea, to court to lobby in support of these requests.[7]

What the new arrivals actually did in Indigenous communities is more difficult to piece together. Local sources are scarce, not least because the *Audiencia* had gone back to neglecting its obligation to conduct regular visitations of Indigenous communities after those of the beginning of the decade. It would take nine years for the province of Tunja to get its next visitation, under the *oidor* Juan López de Cepeda in 1571–1572, and records, as ever, are patchy.[8] Detailed reports survive just for eleven *encomiendas*, although brief summaries for a further eighteen survive among the papers of a general inspection of the *Audiencia* that was carried out the following decade.[9] Combined, these concern fewer than

---

New Kingdom before the end of the century. These figures are all from the detailed appendices to Borges Morán, *El envío de misioneros*, 485–498.

[4] According to the king's rescript, 2 April 1566, AGI SF 534 L3, 1v.

[5] See the king's instructions to the *Audiencia* concerning Carvajal, 17 August 1568, AGI SF 534, 183r.

[6] Franciscan authorities to the king, 1 January 1568, AGI SF 188, 697r.

[7] On Olea's time in Spain, see the rescripts issued at his prompting between October and December 1568, in AGI SF 534, L3, 206r, 221r, and 237v.

[8] All the more so because Cepeda appears not to have sent a final report of his visitation to Spain. See Francis, 'The Muisca', 160.

[9] The latter is the Juan Prieto de Orellana's report of towns visited in the districts of Santafé and Tunja, 1584, AGI SF 56A n. 17 pt 12.

'No Church ... or Anything Else'

half of the *encomiendas* held by the seventy or so *encomenderos* that the *cabildo* of Tunja reported among its citizens around this time, but they still comprise some forty-eight different Indigenous communities distributed across much of the province – from Oicatá and Nemusa, scarcely five miles north of Tunja, to the distant communities that made up the vast *encomienda* of Chita, held by Gonzalo Jiménez de Quesada himself, that straddled the northern reaches of the province and the eastern slopes of the Andes.[10] There are no contemporaneous visitation records for the province of Santafé, which would have to wait until the 1590s for a new inspection tour of its own.

Cepeda's inspection shows that churches had become more common, but they remained scarce. Of the forty-eight communities for which records survive, twenty-seven had still never had one, and a further two had lost theirs to disuse and neglect.[11] As might be expected, a few of the communities without churches were small, like Guachetá, which had scarcely seventy-six tributaries and provided its *encomendero* with little income.[12] Others were located in remote settlements, such as Tecasquirá, in the further reaches of Chita, whose *cacique*, Chugame, explained 'that in his land there is no church or instruction or Christian Indians or priest or anything else'.[13] Just as before, however, distance from the centres of Spanish power, or the availability of resources, did not explain why some *encomenderos* obeyed the requirement to build churches and others did not. Some of the largest and richest *encomiendas* in the land, like Turmequé, with its 872 tributaries, and Icabuco and Tibaná, with a combined 1,500, remained without churches twelve years after Tomás López had punished their holders for their negligence and threatened further sanctions. This was also the case in some the most centrally located *encomiendas* of the province, such as Soracá, a stone's throw away from Tunja.[14] The inverse was also true: the eighteen communities

[10] See the rescript to a petition of the cabildo of Tunja on the number of encomiendas in the province, issued 20 October 1568 (AGI SF 534 L3, 213r). On this *encomienda*, see Pablo Fernando Pérez Riaño, *La encomienda de Chita, 1550–1650* (Bogotá: Academia Colombiana de Historia, 2021).

[11] These were in Pedro Chinchilla's Moniquirá (AGN VB 5 d. 3) and Juan Prieto's Tinjacá (AGI SF 56A d. 17 n. 12, 6v). I specify the names of the *encomenderos* to avoid confusion, as there were at least a further two communities called Moniquirá and three called Tinjacá in this period, often located far from one another, and each assigned to a different *encomendero*.

[12] Report of recent visitations, AGI SF 56A n. 17 pt 12, 21r.

[13] Visitation of Tecasquirá by Cepeda, AGN VB 2 d. 1, 130v.

[14] Report of recent visitations, AGI SF 56A n. 17 pt 12, 14r, 2r, and 14v, respectively.

130 *The Failure of Colonial Governance*

that did have churches were as diverse in size and location as those that lacked them.[15] Even small and remote Chipa in the *encomienda* of Chita, with just 111 tributaries, had 'a little adobe church, with a *manta* hanging inside and some paper pictures', as don Felipe, its *cacique*, declared before Cepeda.[16]

Of the sixteen churches extant in 1572, only three were properly appointed, solid buildings of brick or stone. One was in Sáchica, where the visitor described 'a small, well-constructed brick church, lime washed on the inside, wooden doors with a lock and key, and a bell to call to mass'. Inside were a few images, including a painting of the Crucifixion as the altarpiece, and a couple of statues, all provided by the *encomendero*.[17] The others, as before, tended to be basic buildings of adobe and thatch, constructed by the community itself, with more or less support from their *encomendero*. In Cucaita, the visitor recorded that *encomendero* Gregorio Suárez had provided everything required: a well-dressed altar with all necessary linens and cloths, vestments, a chalice and paten, missal, a few prints, and a small painting.[18] Others were much less fortunate, as in Soatá, where *cacique* don Juan declared that their *encomendero* had ordered them to build a 'a hut for a church' two months before, 'but it has no doors or images', or Chiscas, where *cacique* Guascaryara declared that their church had neither 'an altar, images, or a bell'.[19] Most were somewhere in between, lacking only a few things, as in Pisba and Támara, whose churches had no bells and doors, but had been provided with 'some mantas and two papers with pictures' to hang behind the altar, as Guayquen, *cacique* of the latter, explained to the visitor.[20] Some churches also performed a dual function, serving – perhaps primarily – *encomenderos* and resident Spaniards, as with the chapel that Diego Montañez, the awful *encomendero* of Tota and Guáquira, introduced in Chapter 2, had built next to his house in the latter, which he claimed to share with the community.[21]

---

[15] We lack information about whether the final community mentioned in the sources, Iguaque, had a church in this period.

[16] Visitation of Chipa by Cepeda, AGN VB 2 d. 1, 144v.

[17] Visitation of Sáchica by Cepeda, AGN VB 18 d. 27, 773r.

[18] Visitation of Cucaita by Cepeda, AGN VB 14 d. 12, 875r.

[19] See Cepeda's visitation of Soatá (AGN VB 12 d. 12, 938r) and of Chiscas (Ibid., 2, d. 1, 21r).

[20] Visitation of Pisba by Cepeda, AGN VB 2 d. 1, 80r.

[21] The visitor was not convinced and ordered him to build a proper one, and to provide one for Tota too. Visitation of Tota and Guáquira by Cepeda, AGN VB 4 d. 5, 388r.

'No Church ... or Anything Else'

Priests remained rarer still, despite the growing numbers crossing the Atlantic. We lack information for seven of the forty-eight communities, but a full twenty-three had never had as much as a fleeting visit from a passing priest, at least according to Indigenous witnesses.[22] In fact, only ten of the forty-eight were found by Cepeda to have had an adequate provision of instruction.[23] Eight of these had a priest at the time of the visitation, whether living there full-time, as in Chita, where the Franciscan Pedro Palomino had resided for a number of years, or at least spending extended periods in a community on a regular basis, as in Gonzalo Suárez Rendón's Tibaná and Icabuco, which had long shared a priest between them, despite lacking a church.[24] Of these almost half – Chita, Tibaná, Icabuco, and Cucaita – had this provision since Tomás López's visitation over a decade before. Five more – Ramiriquí, Onzaga, Sáchica, Oicatá, and Saquencipá – had since been provided with a priest for most of the year.[25] Details on the tenth, Sora, are vague, but Cepeda still deemed it to have 'a good church and sufficient instruction'.[26] The visitor found that two other communities, Guáquira and Gacha, had a priest for a total of about four months a year, which he found inadequate.[27] A further six communities barely hosted the occasional priest, whether for a couple of weeks every now and then, as in Diego Alonso's Tinjacá; just three times in nine years, as in Pisba; or even more sporadically in others, like Támara.[28] We do not know where the dozens of Dominicans and Franciscans who apparently landed on the New Kingdom's shores in this period were going, but it was certainly not here.

---

[22] These were ten communities in the encomienda of Chita: Chiscas, Gueycuro-Chuaqueue, Guyamite, Mimite-Guacete-Cubacute, Motavita, La Sal, Tecasquirá, Susuchey, Mona, and Mama (AGN VB 2 d. 1, 21r, 238v, 283r, 285v, 6v, 282v, 284v, 284v, 283r, 283v, respectively); Nemusa (AGN VB 5 d. 5 451v); Soatá (AGN VB 17 d. 12, 938r); Tota (AGN VB 4 d. 5); Chinchilla's Moniquirá (AGN VB 5 d. 3, 376v); Castro's Tinjacá, Vélez's Tinjacá, Turca-Gachantivá, Suta, Mojica's Moniquirá, Guachetá, Sasa, Sorocotá, and Cucaita-Meacha (AGI SF 56A n. 17 pt 12, 20v, 19r, 18r, 7r, 15r, 21r, 17r, 18v, 16r, respectively).

[23] Sora (AGI SF 56A n. 17, pt 12, 15v), Suárez's Icabuco and Tibaná (Ibid., 2r), Oicatá (AGN VB 5 d. 5 451r), Chita (AGN VB 2 d. 1, 158v), Cucaita-Gacha (AGN VB 14 d. 12, 888v), Onzaga (AGN VB 17 d. 12, 906v), Sáchica (AGN VB 18 d. 27, 785r), Saquencipá (AGN VB 7 d. 10, 562v), and Ramiriquí (AGN VB 9 d. 3, 781r).

[24] Report of recent visitations, AGI SF 56A n. 17 pt 12, 14r, 2r.

[25] See Cepeda's visitations of Oicatá, AGN VB 5 d. 5, 447v.

[26] Report of recent visitations, AGI SF 56A n. 17 pt 12, 15v.

[27] See Cepeda's visitations of Guáquira (AGN VB 4 d. 5, 429r) and Gacha (Ibid., 7 d. 11, 684r).

[28] On Tinjacá, AGN VB 13 d. 24, 1090v; on Pisba and Tamara, AGN VB 2 d. 1 80r and 122r.

132   *The Failure of Colonial Governance*

As the disruption of the 1558 epidemic faded, some places were emerging once more as *ad hoc* hubs of religious instruction for their neighbours. Some served as bases for itinerant priests, like the notorious former Augustinian Vicente de Requejada, still active in the region, whom witnesses reported was based in Foacá, where the *encomendero* had ceded him the *encomienda*'s income, but who was also seen in Barrera's Moniquirá and other places, where he could earn additional cash.[29] Others served as centres for Indigenous people to travel for instruction, such as the people of Sasa, who went to Samacá, the people of Mona to Pisba, or those of Nemusa to Oicatá.[30] And others still went to Tunja, where different priests plied their services. Don Juan, *cacique* of Soatá, explained how his people used to go to the Franciscan convent there for instruction every Sunday, but had switched to the new church of San Laureano a year before. There they only had to pay the priest 'one load of firewood and another of hay' each time, although, he added, they were punished for missing sessions 'and the priest fines them a *manta* or a bit of gold for not coming'.[31]

Where these records do depart from earlier visitations is in their detail, allowing a few glimpses, often for the very first time, of the everyday practice of religious instruction among Indigenous communities. The records are clearest for Chita, where one captain, don Francisco, explained that the youths of the community came together every day to be instructed by their Franciscan priest, Pedro Palomino, and that the adults did so on feast days. Cepeda's questionnaire also asked witnesses about the care of the sick, and witnesses in Chita explained that this was a key part of the priest's role. As don Miguel, one of four *caciques*, explained, 'the priest brings them to his house and feeds them until they recover'; another, don Pablo, added that they always called him when they were sick, 'and he bleeds and cures them and gives them whatever they need'. If they failed to notify the priest and someone died without the chance to become Christian or say their confession – added don Gonzalo,

---

[29] Although by then he had apparently not been seen in Foacá for at least four years. See Cepeda's visitation of Foacá (AGN VB 7 d. 11, 680v, 698r) and of Juan de la Barrera's Moniquirá (AGN VB 7 d. 10, 571r), which he visited three or four times for months at a time.

[30] See AGI SF 56A n. 17 pt 12, 17r; AGN VB 2 d. 1, 103v; and Ibid., 5 d. 5, 453r, respectively.

[31] Visitation of Soatá by Cepeda, AGN VB 17 d. 12, 938r–938v.

'No Church ... or Anything Else'   133

a captain – the community's leaders would be punished.[32] It was in these
moments near death that most Indigenous people had been admitted to
baptism during the 1558 epidemic, as we saw in Chapter 2, so that those
people who identified as Christians in the visitations of the 1560s tended
to have been baptised in these exceptional circumstances. This was in line
with the legislation that Barrios had promulgated in 1556, which had
been clear in ordering that except when death was imminent no
Indigenous person over the age of eight should be admitted to the sacrament without at least two months of prior instruction, and then only after
having been examined in the basic prayers and tenets of doctrine.
Children were not to be baptised either, except if one of the parents was
already Christian, or if unbaptised parents clearly and explicitly
consented.[33]

The prevalence of baptised Christians among Indigenous communities
may therefore also serve as a measure of the general provision of religious
instruction beyond the witnesses' quick declarations to the visitor, showing which towns had enough provision to make satisfying these requirements possible. Among the communities for which records survive, only
Chita had a majority Christian population. There *cacique* don Pablo
explained that 'the Indians who want to become Christians are baptised',
and that he said mass regularly and heard confessions. Don Gonzalo, a
captain, added that as a result 'in this *repartimiento* almost everyone is a
Christian' – something that Cepeda corroborated in a book of parish
records that he inspected.[34] This was remarkable, given Chita had some
400 tributaries, suggesting its total population was somewhere over 1,200
people.[35] But Chita was very much an outlier. In Oicatá, which also had
detailed parish records, and where witnesses too spoke of frequent
instruction and confessions, its Dominican priest had admitted a mere
seventy people to baptism out of a total population not much

---

[32] Ibid., 161r, 166r, 163v. There were, unusually, a total of seven *caciques* in Chita at this
point, as another, don Pablo, explained to Cepeda (at 164r).

[33] In this Barrios had drawn on the legislation of the First Provincial Council of Lima of
1551–1552, and the Council of Seville of 1512. This attitude contrasts sharply with early
missionary efforts in Mexico. See 'Constituciones sinodales 1556', 20–23. On this see
Osvaldo F. Pardo, *The Origins of Mexican Catholicism: Nahua Rituals and Christian
Sacraments in Sixteenth-Century Mexico* (Ann Arbor: University of Michigan Press,
2004), ch. 1.

[34] Visitation of Chita by Cepeda, AGN VB 2 d. 1, 158v, 165r, 163v, 182v.

[35] Using Colmenares's proposed multiplier of 3.2, discussed in Chapter 2. For a compilation
of tributary figures for Tunja throughout this period, see Francis, 'Población', where
Chita appears at 133.

134   *The Failure of Colonial Governance*

smaller – although this might well reflect differing standards between the two priests.[36] Everywhere else, even in those towns deemed by the visitor to have adequate instruction, baptism continued to be largely restricted to the dying. In Ramiriquí, even the *cacique*, who said he hoped to become a Christian, was still waiting for admission.[37]

Cepeda's records also provide a clearer picture of the arrangements made with the religious orders by those *encomenderos* who provided a priest to the people under their care. When Sebastián García, *encomendero* of Gacha, was charged with having failed to provide sufficient instruction, he presented Cepeda with a series of receipts recording his family's dealings with the Dominicans of Tunja since the mid 1560s. Every so often, a member of his family, usually his mother, Brígida Díaz, would go to the Dominican convent in Tunja and arrange for a priest to go to Gacha, paying the Dominicans for their trouble. These ranged from the 106 pesos and four *tomines* that she paid for six months' instruction in 1569, to ten and a half for a few days' work the previous year, with most payments in the region of eighteen pesos. The same Dominicans – Gabriel de Robles, Francisco de Medina, Gonzalo Carrera, and Bernardino de Figueroa – come up time and time again, not just in the receipts for Gacha but also in the statements of Indigenous and Spanish witnesses across the province.[38] Figueroa, for example, was the priest in residence in Oicatá during Cepeda's inspection, likely hired in a similar arrangement.[39] The limited records that survive of priests present in Indigenous towns in Santafé in this period, most of which were discussed in Chapter 1, paint a similar picture, of the occasional site of with a permanent or semipermanent presence, and otherwise fleeting figures moving across the province at the request of *encomenderos*, staying in a community for a few days or weeks at a time, and moving on. Little change, then, since the early 1560s, and nothing to do with the diocesan or *Audiencia* authorities.

This stasis on the ground contrasts sharply with the rapid development and expansion of the kingdom's central institutions in the same period in

---

[36] Visitation of Oicatá by Cepeda, AGN VB 5 d. 5, 454r–454v, cf. the 383 tributaries recorded for Oicatá and neighbouring Nemusa, which formed part of the same encomienda. See Ibid., 134.

[37] Visitation of Ramiriquí by Cepeda, AGN VB 9 d. 3, 780v–781r.

[38] Visitation of Gacha by Cepeda, AGN VB 7 d. 11, 686r–693r.

[39] Unfortunately, the earliest surviving accounts for the Dominican convents of Tunja and Santafé date to 1600 and 1611, APSLB Conventos Tunja 1/3/92 and Conventos Bogotá 1/1/1.

'No Church ... or Anything Else'   135

legislation and on paper. It was during this same period that the *Audiencia* of Santafé obtained its definitive shape, with the appointment of its first president, Andrés Díaz Venero de Leiva, who arrived in 1563 equipped with the same 'powers and faculties of government' – if not title and status – as the viceroy of Mexico.[40] This was part of a reorganisation meant to limit the scope of action – and disruption – of the *oidores*, who henceforth were to be excluded from the executive functions of government, in particular anything to do with the granting of *encomiendas* and other privileges to settlers, and thus better able to focus on the administration of justice, whether at home in Santafé or on visitation.[41] Shortly after, in 1564, the diocese of Santafé was also reorganised, elevated to the rank of archdiocese, and made the centre of a new ecclesiastical province that also included the older Caribbean dioceses of Cartagena and Popayán, which had until then had been under the archdioceses of Santo Domingo and Quito, respectively.[42] As a result, scholars have tended to see the 1560s as another watershed in the expansion and consolidation of colonial rule in the region, the beginning of a new era of government – even, for one, 'the golden age of the colonial period'.[43]

In fact, as we have seen, little had changed in practice. The newly unencumbered *oidores* showed no greater interest in going out on visitation than before, the newly promoted archbishop was as just unconcerned with the everyday business of the Christianisation of Indigenous people, and the president was uninterested in involving himself in the internal affairs of *encomiendas* and the provision of religious instruction.[44] Barrios, in fact, spent much of the 1560s trying, unsuccessfully, to leave the New Kingdom and retire.[45] Indeed, by the time of his death in 1569, he had ordained a mere four priests, all of whom ministered to

---

[40] Royal decree (*cédula*) appointing Venero de Leyva, 3 October 1562, AGI SF 533, lib. 2, fol. 260v. This in response to petitions from, among others, Barrios himself, as early as his letter to the king of 31 January 1554, AGI SF 230.

[41] Mayorga García, *La Audiencia*, 37.

[42] Pius IV, *In suprema dignitatis Apostolicae specula*, 22 March 1564, compiled in Metzler, *America Pontificia*, vol. 2, 733–739.

[43] To quote Juan Manuel Pacheco, for whom, Venero's arrival 'inaugurated a period of peace and progress', in *La evangelización*, 182.

[44] The latter, despite the 'great care' that the former magistrate Juan de Penagos reported he apparently felt for the missionary enterprise, in his letter to the king of April 1564 (AGI SF 188, 430r), which had no practical effect.

[45] Going as far as absconding in 1562 and trying to sail back to Spain, and later through multiple petitions to the king to let him leave. On the former, see the complaint of the Franciscans to the king, 12 June 1562, AGI SF 188, 455r. On the latter, see the king's final rescript denying his request, January 1569, AGI SF 534 L3, 252r.

136   *The Failure of Colonial Governance*

Spaniards.[46] The crown, for its part, appeared content with the status quo. Two petitions that reached the royal chancery in 1568 from the *cabildos* of Tunja and Santafé complained of the difficulty *encomenderos* had in compelling friars to work for them, to stay put once appointed, or to remove them if they failed to do their jobs, which resulted in rescripts empowering them to this effect.[47] Whether out of a lack of interest, or an awareness of the limitations of their power and authority, the civil and ecclesiastical authorities continued as before. That is, at least, until the reverberations of events on the other side of the Atlantic began to be felt in Santafé.

IN THE TRAIN OF CATHOLIC REFORM

The 1560s were a period of profound change at the centres of the Spanish monarchy and of Roman Catholicism. The final session of the Council of Trent finally concluded in early December 1563, and by July of the following year Philip II had accepted its decrees in the crown of Castile and ordered their implementation across its dominions, leaving the civil and ecclesiastical authorities of Spanish America with the task of reforming the churches under their care along Tridentine lines.[48] This was easier said than done. As recent scholarship on the council has shown, contrary to the 'myth of Trent' as a prescriptive monolith and ready-made comprehensive project for reform, much of what scholars have generally associated with the council was in fact ignored, deliberately sidestepped, or barely treated in its sessions, and a great deal more was instead the product of diverse, often radically different, efforts by subsequent reformers in different contexts, in Europe and beyond, over the years and decades that followed.[49] Far from providing a clear way

---

[46] Lee López, 'Clero indígena', 30.

[47] The first, for Tunja, on 30 July 1583 (AGI SF 534 L3 172v–173r), the second, for Santafé, on 22 August (Ibid., 187r).

[48] Copies of this decree circulated widely, and were compiled and published alongside the constitutions of the council, including López de Ayala's influential translation of the council, Ignacio López de Ayala, *El sacrosanto y ecuménico Concilio de Trento* (Madrid: La Imprenta Real, 1785), Appendix 8, pp. XLIX.

[49] Notably the work of John W. O'Malley. See 'The Council of Trent: Myths, Misunderstandings, and Misinformation'. In *Spirit, Style, Story: Essays Honoring John W. Padberg*. Edited by Thomas M. Lucas (Chicago: Jesuit Way/Loyola Press, 2002) 205–226; and O'Malley, *Trent: What Happened at the Council* (Cambridge, MA: Harvard University Press, 2013), especially at 20ff. See also Simon Ditchfield, 'Tridentine Catholicism'. In *The Ashgate Research Companion to the Counter-Reformation*. Edited by Alexandra Bamji, Geert H. Janssen, and Mary Laven (Farnham: Ashgate, 2013), 17ff.

In the Train of Catholic Reform 137

forwards, then, the conclusion of the council in many ways inaugurated a period of adjustment and disruption around the Catholic world, as different actors, great and small, jostled in its wake in defence and pursuit of their varied interests. The New Kingdom was no exception, as its civil and ecclesiastical authorities scrambled to use the council's constitutions (or what they had heard of them) to their advantage, or at least to protect themselves from others trying to do so. As early as April 1566, for example, the Dominicans of Santafé began to complain to the king that 'after the Council of Trent was promulgated here' Barrios had been using its constitutions 'as a weapon to destroy us', apparently citing it to interfere in their affairs.[50] The following year, the Franciscans complained that the Dominicans, 'like restless, obstinate rebels, not only fail to follow it [Trent] but interpret it however they like' to suit their purposes.[51] This would continue for years.

Opportunistic friars in Santafé were in illustrious company, as no one, save perhaps for the pope, devoted more effort and concern to ensuring that the promulgation of the Council of Trent served his interests than the king of Spain himself. It was in this way that Philip II had dispatched agents to Trent to report on proceedings during council sessions, petitioned it with requests, instructed his representatives to keep an eye on the composition of sensitive decrees, and sought to shelve problematic issues.[52] On its conclusion, he held off from accepting its decrees while his counsellors pored over them to ensure they did not threaten his rights of patronage over the church, surveyed bishops returning from the council on questions of interpretation, and worked to ensure that it would be he who oversaw the application of reform. Indeed, even the decree by which he accepted its constitutions in the Crown of Castile, as Ignasi Fernández Terricabras has argued, was a carefully worded affair that minimised the role of the papacy in rendering the council valid and that placed his own authority at the centre of its execution.[53] In the years that followed, Philip II worked carefully to control Trent's definition and application across the monarchy. In Spanish America, the crown saw Tridentine reform as an instrument through which it could obtain greater

---

[50] Dominicans of Santafé to the king, 16 April 1566, AGI SF 188, 543v.
[51] Franciscans of Santafé to the king, 27 December 1567, AGI SF 188, 666r.
[52] Most notably the proposed decrees on the 'reform of princes'. See Ignasi Fernández Terricabras, *Felipe II y el clero secular: la aplicación del Concilio de Trento* (Madrid: Sociedad Estatal para la Conmemoración de los Centenarios de Felipe II y Carlos V, 2000), 72–73.
[53] Ibid., 103–116.

138 *The Failure of Colonial Governance*

control over ecclesiastical affairs, and through them bring local actors, including the religious orders, *encomenderos*, and other authorities under closer supervision. The idea was to use the secular church, over which it already had, at least on paper, extensive control, as the means for this royal power grab.

In Mexico, these reforms were pursued by viceroy Martín Enríquez and archbishops Alonso de Montúfar and Pedro Moya de Contreras; in Peru, by the influential viceroy Francisco de Toledo – who had previously served as one of Philip II's ambassadors to Trent – and archbishops Jerónimo de Loayza and especially Toribio de Mogrovejo.[54] Reform was by no means straightforward in either of the two centres of empire – to characterise reform there as simply the strengthening of the secular church and a movement away from an evangelisation dominated by the religious orders belies a far more complex situation.[55] But at least in both viceregal centres reformers could generally rely on substantial clerical manpower, the ability to hold provincial councils and synods, the funds to establish seminaries and educational institutions, and effective judicial and disciplinary bodies. They could even promulgate sophisticated legislation and issue systematic catechetical corpora in print, having recourse to presses – introduced in Mexico by fray Juan de Zumárraga in 1539, and more recently to Peru, in 1581, in advance of the Third Provincial Council of Lima.[56] But in New Granada, although the Spanish crown showed similar ambitions, local conditions made the situation rather different.

The man sent to replace Barrios and implement reform in the New Kingdom was fray Luis Zapata de Cárdenas (1515–1590), an administrator with a proven track record of ruthless efficiency. Born into an aristocratic military family, Zapata had spent his youth as an officer in the Spanish armies fighting in Germany, Italy, and Flanders, before

---

[54] Estenssoro Fuchs, *Paganismo*, 32ff, 245ff.

[55] As Stafford Poole notes considering the Mexican case, even there the idea of displacing the regulars entirely was unrealistic, and in practice the only clear trend was the increase in the involvement and authority of the crown over religious issues, through a 'devious, but ultimately successful, policy of both restricting the religious and gaining control over the bishops'. Stafford Poole, *Pedro Moya de Contreras: Catholic Reform and Royal Power in New Spain, 1571–1591* (Berkeley: University of California Press, 1987), 167.

[56] Luis Resines, *Catecismos americanos del siglo XVI* (Salamanca: Junta de Castilla y León, Consejería de Cultura y Turismo, 1992), vol. 2, 236–237; Ángel Rosenblat, 'La hispanización de América. El castellano y las lenguas indígenas desde 1492'. In *Presente y futuro de la lengua española: actas de la asamblea de filología del I Congreso de Instituciones Hispánicas* (Madrid: Ediciones Cultura Hispánica, 1964), vol. 2, 89.

In the Train of Catholic Reform

becoming a Franciscan. Aided by family connections and his record of military service, he had rapidly risen up the ranks, becoming the prior of various Franciscan convents in his native Extremadura, before being dispatched across the Atlantic in 1561 as *comisario general* of the Franciscan province of Peru – with the task of investigating and disciplining the Franciscans of the province at a time when it covered all of Spanish South America and when the order was at the peak of its influence in the region. Zapata spent his time as *comisario* conducting visitations of even the furthest reaches of the province to enforce stricter disciplinary standards, personally travelling as far as Chile and sending deputies to other regions, including the New Kingdom, and devoting much of his time to defending the privileges of his order against efforts by local bishops to interfere in their affairs.[57]

Zapata struck a delicate balance, becoming popular both with the authorities critical of his order and with his fellow Franciscans, and his reputation spread among both. Dissatisfied with Barrios, the Franciscans of Santafé had begun to petition the king to replace him with Zapata as early as June 1562.[58] By the mid 1560s, the civil and ecclesiastical authorities of Peru were also recommending that he be made a bishop.[59] By the end of the 1560s Zapata had returned to Spain and been rewarded with the job of provincial of the Franciscans of Extremadura, but the king had his own ideas, and in 1569 offered him the position of bishop of Cartagena. Shortly after, when news reached court that Barrios had died, he was offered that job instead. The idea was that Zapata's experience reforming the Franciscans from within might serve him well in fulfilling Philip II's desire to reorganise the church of the New Kingdom – at least provided he did as he was told. Zapata accepted and, all necessary

---

[57] On Zapata's early life and the Franciscan stage of his career, see Luis José Garrain Villa, 'Documentos sobre Fray Luis Zapata de Cárdenas y otros evangelizadores llerenses en los archivos de Llerena'. In *Extremadura en la evangelización del Nuevo Mundo, actas y estudios: congreso celebrado en Guadalupe durante los días 24 al 29 de octubre de 1988*. Colección Encuentros. Serie Seminarios (Madrid: Turner, Junta de Extremadura, 1990), 379–400; and Luis Arroyo, *Comisarios generales del Perú* (Madrid: Consejo Superior de Investigaciones Científicas, Instituto Santo Toribio de Mogrovejo, 1950), 39–54.

[58] Franciscans of Santafé to the king, 12 June 1562, AGI SF 188, 455r.

[59] See the letter of archbishop Loayza to the king of 2 August 1564, and that by the influential *oidor* Lope García de Castro to the king of 23 September 1565, compiled, respectively, in Rubén Vargas Ugarte, *Biblioteca peruana: Manuscritos peruanos del Archivo de Indias* (Lima: Tall. Tip. de la Empresa Periodística La Prensa, 1938), vol. 2, 85; and Roberto Levillier, *Gobernantes del Perú, cartas y papeles, siglo XVI: documentos del Archivo de Indias* (Madrid: Sucesores de Rivadeneyra, 1921), vol. 3, 94–110.

140 *The Failure of Colonial Governance*

arrangements complete, arrived in Santafé on 28 March 1573. What he found was a mess.

THE CREATION OF INDIGENOUS PARISHES

We glimpsed, as much as sources allow, what conditions were on the ground among Indigenous communities in the early 1570s, but it is worth briefly turning our attention to the state of ecclesiastical institutions at the centre of the kingdom. For a start, there was no money. Most Spaniards in New Granada 'had little experience in paying tithes', as Zapata's new cathedral euphemistically explained to him in one of their first letters, and what little money there was to be made in ministering to Indigenous people was going to the religious orders. These had long been unruly, but things had been made worse by the confusion introduced by Trent, 'which they interpret however they like', and by the absence, since Barrios's death, of whatever influence he had exerted.[60] The Franciscans, for example, had been sent a new provincial – their old procurator, Francisco de Olea – to conduct a visitation and investigate reports of misconduct, but by June 1572 Olea had reported that he had been assaulted by the friars he had tried to discipline, had his papers burnt, and his seal of office stolen – and that with this seal they had deposed him and made one of their number provincial instead.[61] As a result, local actors had been petitioning the crown to intervene for years, and to force the friars of the New Kingdom, as *Audiencia* president Venero put it, to stop 'acting like little kings and popes', and instead force them 'to live as friars do in Mexico and Peru'.[62] In the best style of rescript government, the reform of the religious orders became central to the agenda Zapata was given by the monarch, and a key priority on his arrival.[63]

Not content with his predecessor's strategy of half-heartedly pressuring the regular authorities to keep their subjects in check through occasional threats and choleric letters to the king, Zapata instead pursued an ambitious two-pronged approach: to push the regulars back into their convents and away from the Christianisation of Indigenous people, and to

[60] Cathedral chapter of Santafé to Archbishop Zapata, 4 May 1571, AGI SF 231, no. 2.
[61] Letter of the Franciscan visitor, Francisco de Olea, to the king, 12 June 1572, AGI SF 233, ramo 3.
[62] President Venero to Zapata, 16 May 1571, AGI SF 16, ramo 15, no. 32, IV.
[63] For which he was also given extensive powers to reform the Franciscans on arrival. See king to Zapata, 7 August 1572, AGI SF 534, lib. 4, 23v–24r.

The Creation of Indigenous Parishes

replace them with a properly trained and disciplined secular clergy answerable to himself. For the first part of his strategy he could draw on a key initiative by the crown. In addition to appointing trusted reformers to episcopal posts across Spanish America, the other pillar of Philip II's strategy to seize the opportunities provided by Trent was the promulgation of a legal framework, based on the broad and often nebulous patchwork of privileges and powers of royal patronage over the church that he and his predecessors had acquired, that strengthened and regulated the power of the diocesan hierarchy and civil authorities over ecclesiastical affairs. This came in the form of the so-called *Cédula magna*, or Great Decree, of royal patronage of 1 June 1574, sent to every diocese in Spanish America.[64]

The new legislation began by reiterating the king's monopoly over ecclesiastical patronage, not only as a result of papal grants but also, as the legislation declared, by virtue of having endowed and funded all manner of ecclesiastical institutions, before issuing twenty-three articles on a broad range of issues on the basis of these rights. Some, such as a new emphasis on the use of Indigenous languages in religious instruction, will be explored later, but for now two aspects are particularly important. First, the legislation introduced a precise system for filling ecclesiastical positions at every level – from positions in cathedral chapters, which, with their bishops, ran entire dioceses, all the way down to minor positions in local churches or hospitals – that placed diocesan and civil authorities at the centre. From now on, the local bishop or archbishop was to advertise a position, receive and evaluate applications according to the requirements for each job, and produce a shortlist of two candidates, from which the viceroy or president was to make the final selection, for which the legislation also provided guidelines and desired criteria.[65]

This done, the legislation declared that this procedure was to apply 'in the *repartimientos* and places of Indians' even if these had not been formally constituted as benefices before. From now on, it would be the

---

[64] *Cédula magna del patronato*, issued on 1 June 1574, and received in Santafé on 24 February 1575, AGI Indiferente 427, lib. 30, 255–259r. There is a significant literature on this legislation in Mexico, where it is often referred to as the 'ordenanza del patronazgo'. See, Robert Charles Padden, 'The Ordenanza del Patronazgo, 1574: An Interpretative Essay'. *The Americas* 12, no. 4 (1956): 333–354; and John Frederick Schwaller, 'The *Ordenanza del patronazgo* in New Spain, 1574–1600'. *The Americas* 42, no. 3 (1986): 253–274. The decree, split into its constituent parts, later became codified as much of *Recopilación* 1.6: 'Del patronazgo real de las Indias'.

[65] *Cédula magna del patronato*, AGI Indiferente 427, lib. 30, 256(b)v–257r.

142   *The Failure of Colonial Governance*

responsibility of the archbishop and the president to select and appoint priests to minister to Indigenous people, for these positions were now going to be proper benefices with cure of souls (known as curacies or '*beneficios curados*'). The 1574 legislation, in other words, transformed, at a stroke, the growing numbers of churches that *encomenderos* and Indigenous people had been building in their communities over the previous two decades into parish churches, *doctrinas*, for the first time. In doing so, it also transformed the job of running these churches into curacies that had to be filled, according to the new rules, with qualified candidates by Zapata and Venero, and not with random friars by *encomenderos* or their mothers, whose only role now was to hand over a portion of the tributes they collected to fund their salaries. The religious orders, for their part, were to have no power over these positions either, for their members would have to be nominated and vetted by the archbishop and president in the normal way. Finally, the legislation further limited their autonomy by ordering the heads of the religious orders to keep records of all convents and friars in their provinces and to submit annual reports to the authorities. *Audiencias* were to receive lists of all active friars, 'with their names, ages, qualities, offices, and occupations', and especially of all friars engaged in ministering to Indigenous people, which they should share with the archbishop, in the same way as they were to share responsibility for the broader missionary project.[66]

How exactly the archbishop and his civil counterparts were to share the responsibility of overseeing and regulating the new parishes – and who should be in charge of the overall direction of the enterprise – was much less clear in law. However, relations between the two started cordially enough. In August 1574, Zapata and the *Audiencia* came together to issue legislation establishing a basic stipend for Indigenous parishes. The two decreed that priests were to receive a stipend of 50,000 *maravedís* per year (about 111 gold pesos, by Zapata's own calculation), to be taken directly from *encomienda* tribute, plus a number of additional payments in kind – wheat, maize, potatoes, pigs, rams, and chickens – at different times of the year from the *encomenderos*, *caciques*, and Indigenous commoners.[67] The following year, the *Audiencia* reiterated

---

[66] Ibid., 257r–258r.

[67] August 1574 ordinances, AGI Patronato 196, r. 8, 105v–106r. The conversion of 50,000 *maravedís* to gold pesos is Zapata's, as per his letter to the king of 8 March 1575, in which he complained it was too little, and that 200 pesos would be more appropriate, AGI SF 266, n. 5, 4r.

The Creation of Indigenous Parishes

the requirements in a well-known set of ordinances issued for the province of Tunja, introducing a system for keeping track of payments to parish priests by *encomenderos*, and also outlining a process for joining smaller communities together into single parishes of two or three towns so that they could share the cost of a priest's salary. These ordinances also instituted a number of guidelines for the management of the parishes themselves, and ordered all '*doctrina* priests' to obtain and use a catechism that Zapata was preparing.[68] This collaboration would not last long.

Zapata's plan was to displace the friars, and for this he needed to be able to replace them with a properly organised and regulated diocesan church. Seeing that provincial councils were being held in Mexico and Peru, he sought to do the same, calling one for August 1583.[69] And he attempted to issue a standardised catechetical corpus for his priests to use, like his counterparts elsewhere. He also attempted to establish a diocesan seminary, in accordance with the requirements of the Council of Trent, in 1581.[70] But Zapata faced an uphill struggle. This was, in part, as a result of the circumstances of the New Kingdom. His attempt to hold a provincial council fell victim to a jurisdictional dispute with the archdiocese of Lima, when the bishop of Popayán – exiled in Quito owing to disputes with the civil authorities of his province – refused to recognise Zapata as his metropolitan, and the whole council had to be called off in March 1584.[71] Even his attempt to establish a seminary ultimately failed, having to close in 1586 owing a lack of funds.[72]

Even so, many of the problems Zapata faced were of his own making. To provide the kingdom with a secular clergy, he turned to the mass ordination of secular priests, ordaining at least 124 men to the priesthood before his death in 1590, in order to place them in the newly instituted Indigenous parishes – often in places where the religious orders had previously been active. To justify doing so, he took advantage of the fact that the 1574 legislation ordered all authorities involved in the selection and appointment of candidates to benefices, whether in making the nominations or selecting the final appointee, to prefer – all else being equal – candidates with a command of Indigenous languages and 'the children of Spaniards who have served us in those parts'.[73] While the

---

[68] This in the so-called Ordinances of Tunja, 7 December 1575, AGI Patronato 196, r. 8, 107r, 108v.

[69] Archbishop Zapata to the king, 26 March 1583, AGI SF 226, no. 44, 5r.

[70] Archbishop Zapata to the king, 12 May 1582, AGI SF 226, no. 40.

[71] Archbishop Zapata to the king, 7 March 1584, AGI SF 226, no. 49.

[72] On its closure, see Zapata's letter to the king of 21 January 1586, AGI SF 226, no. 57.

[73] *Cédula magna del patronato*, AGI Indiferente 427, lib. 30, 258r.

144 *The Failure of Colonial Governance*

overwhelming majority of friars were European-born, thirty-nine of Zapata's new priests were *criollos*, the American-born descendants of Spaniards, and a further twenty-two of them were *mestizos*. The religious orders reacted forcefully to Zapata's efforts to displace them and sought to stop him, working to enlist the support of the civil authorities and various settlers. They later came to focus their efforts on the most controversial aspects of Zapata's reforming efforts: language policy (the subject of Chapter 5), and his ordination of *mestizos*, which grew into a huge controversy in its own right that came to pit the archbishop against the king himself, who repeatedly ordered him to stop, and to even involve the pope, as Zapata repeatedly defied the monarch and his officials.[74]

Unlike his predecessor, Zapata chaffed against the limitations of his power, and sought every opportunity to implement the reforms he desired, regardless of the cost. This was also clear in his appointment of his secular priests to the newly created Indigenous parishes. Already by 1583 Zapata reported that he had installed thirty-two in Indigenous parishes in the provinces of Santafé and Tunja, and he sought to increase their number at every opportunity.[75] These efforts quickly became a bitter conflict that derailed any chance of meaningful reform in the archdiocese, as the friars fought back fiercely, on the ground and at court, and increasingly obtained the support of the *Audiencia*, whom Zapata soon alienated too. The archbishop's belligerence proved counterproductive, as it eroded much needed support from his civil counterparts and the monarch for his other initiatives. In 1586, for example, the king suspended the application of legislation favouring the appointment of secular priests over friars to vacant parishes, after Zapata had simply declared all regular parishes vacant, and forced him to return them.[76] The Dominicans recovered twenty-one parishes, only for Zapata to take them again two years later, and for the king to give them back, to Zapata's annoyance.[77] By 1594, four years after Zapata's death, the Dominicans still held on to their twenty-one parishes in the provinces of Santafé and Tunja, the Franciscans to eighteen, and the Augustinians, who only arrived in earnest from 1575, to ten.[78]

---

[74] The controversy over Zapata's ordinations, and what they reveal about emerging ideas and categories of difference is the subject of Cobo Betancourt, *Mestizos heraldos de Dios*.

[75] Zapata to the king, 26 March 1583, AGI SF 226, n. 44.

[76] King to Zapata, 9 March 1586, AGI SF 528 L1, 111v–112r.

[77] Fernando de Porras OP to the king, February 1594, AGI SF 236, n. 4, 1r, 76v–77r.

[78] Report on convents, friars, and rents, 24 April 1594, AGI SF 237, unnumbered. 1r, 3r, 55–55v.

'To Build and to Plant'   145

This was the context of division and controversy in which bilingual *mestizo* priests such as Alonso Romero de Aguilar, whom we met in Chapter 2, found themselves enveloped in the 1580s, as easier objects of scorn and criticism than their archbishop. For this reason, they advanced different visions of the history of Christianisation of the region that sought to place them in a tradition of language usage independent of Zapata, in order to find allies and stay afloat in the midst of the conflict between the kingdom's leaders. Romero and his fellows, however, were far from the most vulnerable group to have been left exposed by Zapata in pursuit of his designs and ambitions. His actions, and his conflicts with his civil counterparts, would soon spill out of the realm of correspondence and legal procedure, and over the towns and homes of Indigenous people, with catastrophic results. To understand how, we need to look more closely at Zapata's understanding of Christianisation, through the very text that the *Audiencia* had heralded in its 1575 ordinances.

'TO BUILD AND TO PLANT'

While his contemporaries in Mexico and Lima were able to produce sophisticated conciliar legislation and comprehensive catechetical materials translated into Indigenous languages, Zapata had to make do with what we could write himself, composing a *Catechism with rules and documents for the priests of Indians* in 1576, which circulated in manuscript. Part didactic text, body of law, practical manual, and reference work, Zapata's text was intended not only as a legal framework for the reform of the church of the New Kingdom, but as a toolkit for the everyday practice of religious instruction at a parish level. Divided into seven sections, the text contained a catechism, that is, a summary of doctrine, in the form of a dialogue of questions and answers, designed to teach Indigenous people the basics of Christian doctrine – but this was far from its focus. It also contained detailed legislation on instruction, the conversion of Indigenous people, and how priests should perform their duties. To ensure uniformity in practice – and to make up for the lack of a proper seminary for the training of priests – the text also contained detailed reference materials for the administration of the sacraments, including transcriptions of necessary Latin texts, and model sermons to preach and to utilise in the production of pedagogical materials.

What is most striking, however, is the breadth of its legislation concerning the lives of Indigenous people. Its starting point was the idea that they had fallen into 'all manner of sins, rites, and gentile ceremonies, sacrifices, and evil customs pertaining to the cult of the devil' because they had been evangelised so little and so poorly.[79] The means it proposed to overcome this was not simply to provide more religious instruction, but rather to reform the lives of Indigenous people along European lines to create the conditions that would make Christianisation possible. Following an Old Testament metaphor, Zapata highlighted the need to prepare the ground for planting, to give Christianity the best chance of taking root.[80] The text thus began with 'what pertains to corporeal civility [policía], which serves as a stepping-stone to spiritual matters', in the form of twelve chapters devoted to reforming practically every aspect of life – from the way people should be resettled into planned, urban towns and how these should be laid out; how they should dress, eat, and sleep; how communal lands should be apportioned and how they should be worked, and what crops and animals they should keep; what magistrates and officers they should appoint, and how conflicts should be resolved; how their houses, jails, and hospitals should be constructed and maintained; how the sick and elderly should be cared for, and children taught; and who should be allowed to live among them.[81] Some of these measures were similar to the policies that Tomás López had sought to implement in the New Kingdom sixteen years before, discussed in Chapter 2, and to a number of provisions in the *Audiencia*'s ordinances of 1575, but much more ambitious and detailed in scope.

It was only after these matters had been addressed that the text discussed questions pertaining to catechisation proper and the running of the church: how and what priests should teach, what sacraments to administer and how, and what to preach and when. While Barrios had imagined a system of itinerant friars visiting Indigenous communities fleetingly, both in his 1555 *tasa* and in the synod that followed, with much of the work of instructing Indigenous people carried out by (ideally 'Christian and virtuous') laymen, Zapata's text outlined a permanent parish-centred system of instruction.[82] Priests were to keep detailed records of all parishioners,

---

[79] Luis Zapata de Cárdenas, 'Catecismo, en que se contienen reglas y documentos para que los curas de indios les administren los santos sacramentos, con advertencias para mejor atraerlos al conocimiento de nuestra santa fe católica [1576]'. In *La legislación de la arquidiócesis de Santafé en el periodo colonial*. Edited by Juan Fernando Cobo Betancourt and Natalie Cobo (Bogotá: Instituto Colombiano de Antropología e Historia, 2018), 145–146.
[80] Quoting Jeremiah 4:3, 'Break up your fallow ground, and sow not among thorns' (ESV).
[81] Zapata de Cárdenas, 'Catecismo', 148–152.
[82] Cf. 'Constituciones sinodales 1556', 17–18.

'To Build and to Plant' 147

identifying the Christians and those not yet baptised, and recording everyone by age, and to which *caciques* and captains they answered. They were to hold a daily catechism school for children, training a number of them as assistants to help with the instruction of others less advanced. Adults were to receive weekly catechism classes, but they too were to be encouraged to make visiting the church an integral part of their daily routine. And 'because our aim is uniformity in all things', the text explained, it also established a set curriculum for instruction, 'laying out the order that should be followed in teaching even the most basic principles of Christianity' – from the motions and gestures of crossing oneself, to the basic catechism, commandments, articles of faith, sacraments, and prayers.[83] It was, at least on paper, a fundamental departure from the haphazard arrangements that had characterised religious instruction in the New Kingdom so far.

In addition to improving the quality of religious instruction and expanding the remit and scope of what Christianisation should involve, there was a third, darker, side to Zapata's strategy to incorporate the Indigenous peoples of the New Kingdom into Christianity. Making the ground ready 'to build and to plant' involved not only tilling but 'rooting up and tearing down, destroying and demolishing'.[84] As he explained, 'before we build a house for God we must tear down the buildings and houses that have been built for the devil'.[85] This idea was far from new, of course, and scholars of the Christianisation of Indigenous peoples in Spanish America have long noted its influence in the formulation of missionary strategies. The improvement of catechisation and the removal of impediments were two sides of the same coin, rooted in an understanding of heterodoxy as the result not only of ignorance but also of the agency of malign influences that needed to be removed for Christianisation to succeed.[86]

---

[83] Zapata de Cárdenas, 'Catecismo', 156–164.
[84] Ibid., 146, paraphrasing Jeremiah 1:10.   [85] Ibid., 146.
[86] This distinction had a long history in Christian theology, and was already clear in the work of Thomas Aquinas, who in *Summa* IIaIIae 94 argued that idolatry was partially the fault of men, resulting from 'misdirected affection' towards a person 'beyond reason'; from being seduced by the beauty of crafted objects; or simply from 'ignorance of the true God'. But that it was also the fault of demons, who – wishing to be adored as gods – '[gave] answers in the idols, and [did] things which to men seemed marvellous' (Thomas Aquinas, *Summa Theologiae: Latin Text and English Translation, Introductions, Notes, Appendices and Glossaries*. Edited by Thomas Gilby. Translated by the Fathers of the English Dominican Province (London: Blackfriars; Eyre and Spottiswoode, 1964–1981), vol. 40, 33–35). Scholars as early as Hanke (in *The Spanish Struggle for Justice*) examined

148   *The Failure of Colonial Governance*

What exactly these were was much less clear, as Zapata was no closer to grasping the workings of Indigenous practices than his predecessors. Predictably, perhaps, he resorted to established stereotypes, focusing on 'sanctuaries', by which he meant temples and sacred spaces; Indigenous 'priests'; and 'gentile ceremonies' akin to inverted sacraments. To deal with the first, parish priests were to 'enquire about where sanctuaries are located', and then notify diocesan authorities, who with the help of the *Audiencia* would 'destroy and raze them entirely, so that there may be no memory of them'. The second, '*xeques, mohanes,* and sorcerers', who counteracted whatever progress Christian priests made in evangelisation, so that 'when the priest has finished preaching, they say and preach the opposite ... claiming that what the priests teach are lies', were to be identified and dealt with. The same approach was to be taken regarding the 'innumerable rites and ceremonies with which the devil has occupied these people'. Priests were to report their existence to the authorities, and this would somehow result in their removal. Whatever ceremonies and celebrations remained were to be closely monitored by parish priests, in case they turned out to be malignant. At the same time, Zapata warned of specific substances known to be involved in certain ceremonies, such as *moque*, a plant burnt in the manner of incense, which caution advised should be banned altogether.[87]

Reading Zapata's *Catechism*, and indeed the 1574 *Cédula magna* that served as the foundation for his designs and ambitions, it is all too easy to lose sight of the fact that this entire legislation was aspirational and that these reforms existed almost exclusively in the realm of paper. In practice, the churches of Indigenous communities might now be benefices and parishes in law but they remained as incomplete and underfunded as when they had been mere churches. The archbishop, president, and *oidores* wielded no more real power than they had a few years before. They were just as unable to compel Indigenous people to radically alter their ways of life as they had been in 1573 and as powerless to impose their will on the settlers, while the power of *encomenderos* and Indigenous leaders remained as contingent and limited as it had always been. But Zapata was going to try anyway. Resettling tens of thousands

---

these two divergent, but complementary, positions through the contrasting emphases of Bartolomé de las Casas and José de Acosta – a device later taken up by and expanded by Pierre Duviols (*La lutte*, 23), Anthony Pagden (in *Fall of natural Man*, chs. 6 and 7), and Sabine MacCormack (in *Religion in the Andes*, chs. 5 and 6).

[87] Zapata de Cárdenas, 'Catecismo', 152–154.

'Rooting Up and Tearing Down'

of Indigenous people into gridded towns by sheer force of will might take a while, but there were other things with which he could occupy himself in the meantime.

'ROOTING UP AND TEARING DOWN'

As early as April 1575, Zapata reported to the king that he had started to conduct his own visitations of Indigenous communities near Santafé. No records survive for these, if any were kept, but Zapata reported having visited the towns of Fontibón and Bogotá (modern-day Funza), ten and fifteen miles north-west of Santafé, respectively, where he had found evidence that 'idolatry is as alive today in this whole kingdom as it had been before Spaniards arrived, or even more'. Claiming that this was the principal impediment to Christianisation, he petitioned the king for support in investigating further, confiscating ritual objects, and punishing those involved.[88] When the royal chancery issued a rescript in response in November 1576, the archbishop's words became those of the king, who now ordered that these 'rites and ceremonies' – whatever they might be – be eliminated, and 'the idols and shrines [*adoratorios*] extirpated and removed', for which he entrusted the task to Zapata, and dispatched a decree to the *Audiencia* with orders to aid him.[89] Once these rescripts arrived in Santafé in 1577, Zapata sought to enlist the support of the *Audiencia* in a series of meetings and letters in late April and early May. By now, as he explained, further inquiries had allowed him to determine that a key aspect of Indigenous ritual practice was the maintenance of 'idols of wood and cotton in the form of human figures' – the *santuarios* discussed in Chapter 1 – 'which they perfume with something called *moque*' and, crucially, to which people 'frequently offer great quantities of gold and emeralds'.[90] His plan now was to 'destroy the *santuarios*' but to keep the offerings, and 'apply the gold and emeralds we find to pious

---

[88] Zapata to the king, 22 April 1575, AGI SF 226, n. 7, 1v.

[89] King to Zapata, 2 November 1576, AGI Patronato 27 r 28§4, 13r–13v.

[90] As we saw in Chapter 1, this was not the first time someone in the New Kingdom's administration came close to seeing the wooden or cotton objects at the centre of the ritual practices of many Muisca groups and individuals for what they were, but, once again, it would not be the last time someone had to work this out from scratch. Zapata, for his part, argued these figures were made 'in remembrance' of a pantheon 'of certain false and alien gods whom they believe and understand created the visible things of this world, and that it from them that they obtain health and the remedy of their necessities'. Zapata to the *Audiencia*, 2 May 1577, AHSB L2, 14r–14v.

150 *The Failure of Colonial Governance*

works and church building, after paying the royal fifth and other taxes'. This he justified because his inquiries had also apparently yielded the unlikely conclusion – at least in light of all surviving evidence – that most of the people involved had been baptised and were therefore guilt of apostasy, an offense squarely in his ecclesiastical jurisdiction.[91]

Not that Zapata had actually waited for anyone's approval. Already in late March 1577, he had sent his cathedral treasurer, Miguel de Espejo, to various towns near Santafé to begin 'punishing the Indians who keep *santuarios*' and particularly to confiscate associated valuables. How Espejo managed this was not recorded, but witnesses later reported that the bishop's agents were 'abusing them with stocks and other means'. News of this violence spread quickly and prompted neighbouring people to seek out Spaniards they knew to ask for their help, including a number of mid-ranking officials in the *Audiencia*. For example, when news reached the *cacique* of Une, to the south-east of Santafé, that Espejo was in nearby Fusagasugá, he approached Lope de Rioja, *relator* in the *Audiencia*, who had served as his godfather when he had been baptised a few years before, and gave him about 'seventy-eight pesos in *santillos*', votive figurines belonging to his subjects. In exchange for a share of the gold, Rioja took the figures to the royal treasury to be smelted, assayed, weighed, taxed, and stamped, and thus turned into legal tender, which he then returned to the *cacique* and his community, later reportedly giving away his own portion as alms during Holy Week. So too with the people of nearby Unecipá, who contacted Rioja through a Spaniard they knew, Diego de Alcalá, explaining they did not want to lose their gold 'to priests and friars and other strangers'. They gave Rioja 'sixty-eight pesos in *santuarios*, give or take', which he had processed in the same way.[92] Diego de Vergara, who also worked in the *Audiencia*, was approached by the leaders of Queca, and eventually entrusted with various objects, including what Vergara described as 'some clay figures of the devil', which he saw people digging up from their fields and bringing out from their homes, totalling 'about 507 pesos worth of gold', which they asked him to look after.[93] Further afield, in Cubia, thirty miles west of Santafé, news of the confiscations prompted the *cacique* to turn for help to

---

[91] Ibid., 14v.
[92] Declarations of Lope de Rioja and Diego de Alcalá, 15 April 1577, AHSB L2, 5v, 4v, 6r.
[93] Declaration of Diego de Vergara, 15 April 1577, AHSB L2, 3r.

Casilda de Salazar, mother of the *encomendero*, who reported receiving ninety pesos worth of *santuario* gold.[94]

It was in fact something of an open secret among Indigenous leaders and their *encomenderos* that communities up and down the highlands had caches of gold and precious stones in the form of *santuario* offerings, ritual objects, and grave goods (Figure 3.2). As early as 1539, the settlers of Santafé had been petitioning the king to allow them to seize this gold, whether found 'in their graves or as other treasures under ground', as well 'gold found above ground among the Indians', perhaps in the form of 'sacrifices'.[95] When this was denied, they spent the 1540s, petitioning, unsuccessfully, for the right not to have to 'account for where and how they obtained gold and precious stones' that they brought in to be assayed and taxed, so that the authorities might at least turn a blind eye to their looting and grave-robbing.[96] In the 1550s, the question of determining how best to tax the extraction of gold from Indigenous burials was among the first tasks entrusted to the new *Audiencia*.[97] Then, when standard *tasas* were introduced from 1555, and reassessed and adjusted through the 1560s, these often required Indigenous communities to pay their *encomenderos* in gold – and it was often from these caches that they obtained it.[98]

This was because, as Spanish authorities would eventually come to realise, despite what the rich and ancient gold-working traditions of Muisca groups and other highland peoples in the northern Andes might at first sight suggest, gold deposits here – then as now – are generally found only at lower altitudes.[99] What gold there was to be found in the highlands had reached them through Indigenous trade networks over generations before the European invasion, and fresh supplies were becoming increasingly difficult to obtain as these networks broke down and Spaniards came to control the extraction of lowland gold directly. This

---

[94] Casilda de Salazar to the *Audiencia*, 18 April 1577, AHSB L2, 11r.

[95] Settlers of Santafé to the king, 1539, AGI SF 60, n. 1, 1r–1v.

[96] Cabildo of Santafé to the king, 30 September 1543, AGI SF 60, n. 8.

[97] *Audiencia* of Santafé to the king, 10 November 1551, AGI Patronato 197, r. 24, 115v.

[98] Even decades later, as in the case of the Iguaque, where in 1595 the authorities investigated rumours of a hidden mine that had allowed people there to meet tribute obligations and enjoy a comfortable standard of living 'without having to farm or trade or leave the town to work as herders', which was later revealed to have been a sacred spring where a substantial amount of gold had accumulated in the form of offerings made by their ancestors over generations, and not a natural deposit. AGN C&I 58, d. 2, 41v–42r.

[99] Despite some vague references to small highland deposits, discussed in Langebaek, *Mercados*, 88–91.

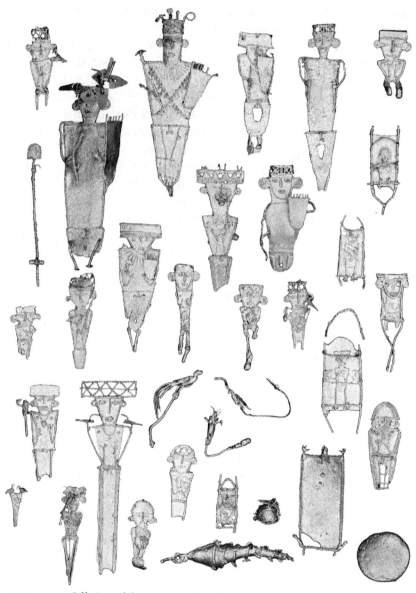

FIGURE 3.2 Offering of thirty-two votive figures (*tunjos*) and one unworked gold lump, Colombia, Eastern Cordillera, 800–1600 CE (Muisca period). Museo del Oro, Banco de la República, Bogotá. Varying sizes (10.3 x 4.6 to 1.6x 19 cm), O33278–309, O33311. Photograph by Clark M. Rodríguez.

'Rooting Up and Tearing Down' 153

was a frequent complaint of Indigenous witnesses to *encomenderos* and officials when their *tasas* were set in the metal.[100] By the 1570s, then, *encomenderos* were quietly receiving gold from these sources as tribute as a matter of course. It was in no one's interest for Zapata to draw attention to these stores of gold or these arrangements, or for the *oidores* and others to come looking for them. But this is exactly what happened.

When the *Audiencia* received its instructions from the king to aid Zapata, it too launched an investigation into the valuables associated with the 'idols and shrines'. It was in this way that the actions of treasurer Espejo, and the efforts of Lope de Rioja and the other Spaniards on behalf of various Indigenous communities came to light, weeks before Zapata formally approached the *Audiencia* to enlist its support. This investigation also revealed that in the first four months of 1577 alone, a whole 937 pesos of '*santuario* gold jewellery' had been handed into the royal treasury for processing into legal tender. This was a significant amount money – almost eight-and-half years' salary for a parish priest in an Indigenous town as per the recent rules – and we can only speculate as to how much more had been received and not handed in for processing. Treasury records showed that those responsible were not only Zapata's officials, Rioja, and the others who collaborated with Indigenous leaders, but also various other people who had already started descending on Indigenous communities in search of a quick profit. So it was with Nicolás Gutiérrez, who was found to have dug up and stolen a cache of *santuario* offerings in Usme, where he found ninety-one pesos worth of gold and some small emeralds that shattered as he tried to pry them out of the wooden figures they adorned.[101] Even the newly arrived Augustinians had decided to have a go, seizing gold from a *santuario* in one of their parishes, and bringing it to Santafé to be turned into legal tender.[102]

The *Audiencia* confiscated the gold still making its way through the treasury pending further inquiries, published edicts forbidding private parties from receiving or seizing *santuario* gold, and ordered anyone

---

[100] For example, as Guecha, *cacique* of Gachancipá, explained during Villafañe's visitation in 1563 (AGN VC 7 d. 14, 692r).

[101] Declaration of Nicolás Gutiérrez before the *Audiencia* of Santafé, 15 April 1577, AHSB L2, 4r. Gutiérrez had been one of the witnesses interrogated by Melchor López de Arteaga in Ubaque in 1563.

[102] Extract from the *Libro de fundición*, AHSB L2, 7r. The Augustinians later claimed the gold had been a gift from their grateful parishioners, after they had 'persuaded them' to abandon their sanctuaries. Baltazar Ortiz OSA to *Audiencia*, 7 May 1577, AHSB L2, 121r.

154   *The Failure of Colonial Governance*

having done so to come forward – but this only served to spread the news, fear, and opportunism further afield. By the end of the month, reports began reaching it of more *encomenderos*, friars, and other Spaniards in the two provinces depriving Indigenous people of their valuables. In Cota, *encomendero* Francisco de Tordehumos took sixty figurines from his subjects when he heard Zapata was in nearby Bogotá.[103] In Usaquén, just north of Santafé, the Franciscans who ran the parish were found to have obtained, somehow, 189 pesos worth of *santuario* gold, having beaten Luis Cardoso, the *encomendero*, to it.[104] Determined not to miss out again, Cardoso went to Suba and Tuna, also in his *encomienda*, where he was seen 'removing *santuarios*' before anyone else got them first.[105] It was at this point, on 2 May, that Zapata finally presented a concrete proposal to the *Audiencia*, requesting that it send officials to accompany cathedral treasurer Miguel de Espejo on his rounds. Treasury official Gabriel de Limpias was dispatched, along with a scribe, who recorded their visit later that week to the towns of Bogotá and Fontibón, where Zapata's campaign had started. In Bogotá, they summoned 'the captains and *xeques*', and interrogated various witnesses concerning the location of their *santuarios* with the help of interpreter Juan de Lara. They dug up and seized a cache belonging to *cacique* don Francisco, worth 164 pesos, and several more belonging to other nobles, for a total of over 548 pesos. The captains who owned these had fled, and *cacique* don Francisco was apparently too ill to travel, but they arrested his heir and sent him to Santafé to face trial.[106] Similar efforts in Fontibón yielded 306 pesos' worth of objects, and 'three *xeques* and *mohanes* of the *cacique*' who were arrested and taken to Santafé for trial.

Behind the scenes, the *Audiencia* was also preparing to join what was fast becoming a feeding frenzy. A few days later, on 9 May, it appointed one of members, the *oidor* Francisco de Auncibay, 'to go to all the *repartimientos* of this province of Santafé in pursuit of the removal of *santuarios*'. Having gathered a small commission, including a constable, scribe, and interpreter, Auncibay set off to the north of the city, descending on multiple Indigenous settlements over the next month,

---

[103] Documents of the *santuario* seizures of Francisco de Auncibay, May 1577, AHSB L2 47r.

[104] Declaration of the Franciscans of Santafé before Francisco de Auncibay, 9 May 1577, AHSB L2 25r.

[105] Decree for the arrest of Luis Cardoso, AHSB L2, 21r.

[106] Santuario inquiry, Fontibón, 3 May 1577, AHSB L2, 15v–18r.

apprehending Indigenous leaders and seizing their valuables.[107] In Suba and Tuna, where *encomendero* Luis de Cardoso had already taken some gold, he seized a further 503 pesos worth of jewellery and figures. In Cota, he seized '12 or 14 clay pots containing a large quantity of *tunjos* and figurines', weighing 110 pesos; in Zipaquirá, multiple 'small *tunjos* and gold jewellery'; in Chía, fourteen pesos' worth; in Cajicá, twenty-five; in Sopó, thirty-four; in Tibaguyas, seventy-three.[108] By the end of May, in just three weeks, Auncibay had confiscated objects worth 918 pesos.[109] His colleague *oidor* Antonio de Cetina, who conducted similar inquiries in Bosa, to the south-west of Santafé, with Bartolomé de Clavijo, archdeacon in the cathedral chapter, had seized a further 261 'in *santillos* and gold figures of all sorts'.[110] Gonzalo Bermúdez, a priest working nearby who would later become the first chair of Muisca language, handed in a further '64 pieces shaped like thick pins' and other objects he had seized, found to be worth about eighteen pesos once melted down. This was only the beginning.

HOW TO STEAL A MILLION PESOS

A number of scholars have characterised inquiries such as these, as well as those examined in Chapter 1, as examples of campaigns for the 'extirpation of idolatry', in the model of the well-known idolatry visitations conducted by the Peruvian church in the Archdiocese of Lima in the seventeenth century, but events in Santafé were a far cry from those of the Central Andes.[111] Those visitations were, at least in theory, carefully choreographed operations governed by increasingly detailed guidelines and built on long-established inquisitorial models to produce what was, at its core, a judicial process. The proceedings revolved around an investigation into illicit religious practices, involved the drawing up of charges,

---

[107] Appointment of Francisco de Auncibay, AHSB L2, 41r–43v.   [108] Ibid., 45r–55r.

[109] Receipt for Auncibay's confiscations, 30 May 1577, AHSB L2, 72r–72v.

[110] Receipt for Cetina's confiscations, 19 May 1577, AHSB L2, 29r–31r.

[111] For example Eduardo Londoño, 'Memorias de los ritos y ceremonias de los muiscas en el siglo XVI'. *Revista de Antropología y Arqueología* 6, no. 1 (1990): 229–250, and 'El lugar'; Correa, *El sol del poder*, 67ff; Sylvia Marguerite Broadbent, *Los chibchas. Organización socio-política* (Bogotá: Universidad Nacional de Colombia, Facultad de Sociología, 1964), 13; Pacheco, *La evangelización*, 216ff; and Francis, 'The Muisca', 215ff. Francis also presents the investigation in Iguaque in 1595 in similar terms, in Richard Boyer and Geoffrey Spurling, *Colonial Lives: Documents on Latin American History, 1550–1850* (Oxford: Oxford University Press, 2000), 39–53.

156   *The Failure of Colonial Governance*

preaching, judgement, and culminated with the application of penalties to those convicted and the public destruction of ritual objects in front of local communities.[112] They may be remembered chiefly for their destructive aspects, but at their core they were intended – however misguidedly – as a pedagogical exercise, which involved not just removing Indigenous ritual objects, but denigrating, countering, and explaining away associated ritual practices and ideas to contribute to the success of Christianisation.

The events in Santafé are striking for the general absence of these elements. With the exception of the inquiries into Bogotá and Fontibón, where people were arrested and taken to Santafé for trial, the inquiries rarely resulted in a judicial process – and even in those cases, we have no further records of any legal action taken. With the exception of one or two mentions of a member of the cathedral chapter 'saying a sermon', as Clavijo did in Bosa, or of a civil official giving a vague admonition 'of the disservice the *caciques*, captains, and Indians do to God our lord with their idolatry, *santuarios*, and offerings to their gods and idols', as Auncibay did in Suba and Tuna, there was no preaching or instruction.[113] Instead, the records for these inspections read like account books, recording little more than the number, materials, perceived quality, and weight of seized objects, because all the authorities were really after were valuables. This became even clearer in the waves of dispossession that followed.

The *Audiencia* of Santafé was in a moment of transition. Its second president, Francisco Briceño – who earlier in his career had been one of its founding *oidores* – had died in 1575 and his replacement was yet to arrive. The most senior *oidor*, Francisco de Auncibay, had received orders to prepare to move to the *Audiencia* of Quito, pending the arrival of his replacement, while the junior *oidores*, Antonio de Cetina and Luis Cortés

---

[112] For a description of these processes, see Duviols, *La lutte*, 211–217; MacCormack, *Religion in the Andes*, 389ff; and Mills, *Idolatry*, 267–285. For a near-contemporary inquisitorial model in Europe, see Gustav Henningsen, *El abogado de las brujas: brujería vasca e Inquisición Española* (Madrid: Alianza Editorial, 1983), 66–74. Practical guidelines for the conduct of these investigations in Peru were produced first by Pablo José de Arriaga and later by Archbishop Villagómez. See Pablo José de Arriaga, *Extirpacion de la idolatria del Piru. Dirigido al Rey N. S. en su Real Consejo de Indias* (Lima: Gerónimo de Contreras, Impresor de libros, 1621); and Pedro de Villagómez, *Carta pastoral de exortacion e instruccion contra las idolatrias de los indios del arçobispado de Lima* (Lima: Por Jorge Lopez de Herrera, impressor de libros, en la calle de la carcel de Corte, 1649).
[113] Santuario inquiry, Suba and Tuna, 11 May 1577, AHSB L2, 45r.

de Mesa, were being investigated for illegally marrying into local families and shady business dealings, for which they were likely going to be transferred elsewhere, too.[114] These three ambitious *oidores*, free from the supervision, or interference, of a superior for a few months yet and soon to be leaving the New Kingdom, had seen at first-hand how lucrative these seizures could be, and spotted an opportunity.

In early July 1577, they launched a larger campaign to seize Indigenous objects. First, they dug up a 1526 rescript from their archives that declared 'idolatry' was forbidden and committed the civil authorities of the New World to seize associated property in the territories under their jurisdiction.[115] With this in hand, they issued a royal ordinance, on behalf of the monarch and with his seal, commanding the archbishop of Santafé not to interfere 'in this business of idolatries'.[116] A few days later, taking advantage of the fact that thirty-one *caciques* and captains were gathered in Santafé for the feast of Corpus Christi, they gathered them together, read them the old rescript, and announced their intention punish 'idolatries, sacrifices, and offerings' by 'the pain of death by fire, the forfeiture of all their goods, and other penalties'.[117] In particular, they emphasised, 'all *santuarios* and offerings that have been made' were to be confiscated, brought before the *Audiencia*, melted down, and the proceeds 'used for public utility'.[118] A few days later the *Audiencia* commissioned two treasury officials to carry out thorough inspections of the two provinces: in Tunja, *factor* Diego Hidalgo de Montemayor, and in Santafé Juan Antonio de Vilches, who was to be accompanied by father Gonzalo Bermúdez. These were joined at different points by the *oidores* themselves – Cortés de Mesa in Tunja, and Auncibay and Cetina in Santafé. Dissatisfied with the *oidores* displacing him, Zapata spent the next few months arguing with the *Audiencia* and appealing to the king

---

[114] The order to transfer Cetina and Mesa would finally come on 11 April 1578. See Mayorga García, *La Audiencia*, 41–42.

[115] This decree of 16 June 1523 had originally been issued for New Spain but had been reissued in 1538 and 1551 and extended to the rest of Spanish America. It was this last version that the *Audiencia* of Santafé incorporated into their decree of 3 July 1577 (AHSB L2 63r–64v, or AGN RH 21, 728r). It was later compiled as *Recopilación* 1.1.7. The same decree had also been invoked by Toledo in Peru to argue that cases involving Indigenous religious practices should also be the purview of civil magistrates, and to justify his investigation of these issues in his general visitation of the 1570s. See Duviols, *La lutte*, 49, 212.

[116] Royal decree of the *Audiencia* of Santafé, 3 July 1577, AHSB L2 63r–64v.

[117] Documents concerning the visitation of Tunja, 1577, AGN RH 21, 728v.

[118] Which 'public' is a question for later. Ibid., 729v.

158 *The Failure of Colonial Governance*

that he should be in charge of the investigations and his projects be the primary recipients of seized funds. Eventually, he embarked on a visitation of his own with Archdeacon Bartolomé de Clavijo, following Hidalgo in Tunja and sending delegates and commissioners to other sites. What followed was a brutal goldrush.

Details of Hidalgo's campaign in the province of Tunja are well known, especially after the surviving documentation of his inspection in Colombian archives was transcribed and published by Vicenta Cortés in 1960, and again by Ulises Rojas in his influential 1965 biography of don Diego de Torres, the famous *mestizo cacique* of Turmequé, alongside the much more revealing statements of surviving witnesses, held in Spain, recorded during the general visitation of the *Audiencia* that was sent by the king the following decade to sort through the rubble of the events of the late 1570s.[119] Records for Vilches's investigation in Santafé were unknown until now.[120] All make utterly harrowing reading.

The records for Tunja detail how from July 1577 bands of armed men, led by Hidalgo, Cortés de Mesa, or their agents, descended on Indigenous communities around the province and systematically terrorised and tortured Indigenous leaders, variously beating, whipping, and stringing them by their genitals until they produced gold and other valuables. Humiliated and badly injured, *caciques* were put in stocks and heavy collars and dragged by their necks to neighbouring towns to frighten their neighbours into submission. They seized gold in the form of figures, jewellery, dust, or nuggets – it hardly mattered. There are even reports of Indigenous communities quickly having gold cast into figurines to satisfy the officials, such as in the cases of the torture of the *caciques* of Paipa and Duitama, who had no such objects to give but thought that the authorities would not be satisfied until they obtained them. In fact, they also took *mantas*,

---

[119] Ulises Rojas, *El cacique de Turmequé y su época* (Tunja: Departamento de extensión cultural de Boyacá, 1965); Vicenta Cortés Alonso, 'Visita a los santuarios indígenas de Boyaca en 1577'. *Revista Colombiana de Antropología* 9 (1960): 199–273. Torres received news of the violence unleashed by Hidalgo while at court in Spain, where he had travelled to petition the monarch for redress of grievances he had received from the *Audiencia* in person, and passed on the reports he received of the brutality suffered by his fellow *caciques* and their subjects. Together with a growing chorus of complaints about the *Audiencia*'s actions, Torres's petitions prompted the king to commission a general visitation to investigate the actions of the *Audiencia* of Santafé, carried out by Juan Bautista Monzón and Juan Prieto de Orellana in the early 1580s.

[120] These survive in a mislabelled, uncatalogued, and previously unexamined volume in the library of the Colegio de San Bartolomé in Bogotá: AHSB Libro 2, 'Autos y diligencias 1565' (sic.).

How to Steal a Million Pesos

food, clothes, conch shells – anything of value. In the 1580s, Juan Bautista Monzón, the first of two visitors-general dispatched to investigate the actions of the authorities of the New Kingdom in these years, estimated that the gold seized just in 1577 by the three *oidores* and their delegates, Zapata and his cathedral chapter, and a handful of priests and friars, amounted to a total of 44,129 gold pesos – not counting the myriad emeralds and other valuables also seized, and any sums that they did not hand in.[121] For scale, when the half-built cathedral of Santafé sank into the city's soft soil and collapsed in late 1567, detailed estimates for a new building – the largest construction project in the highlands – placed the cost at 25,000 gold pesos.[122]

The records of the general visitation are replete with stories of extreme violence and dispossession, and not just by Cortés and Hidalgo, for their thugs had agendas of their own. A particularly cruel example is that of Luisillo, an Indigenous interpreter from Gachetá who travelled with them, who was later frequently reported by Hidalgo's victims to have black-mailed them, threatening to render false translations guaranteed to elicit further tortures if he was not personally rewarded by their already broken victims. Survivors then faced the prospect of additional raids by Zapata's agents or by other Spaniards, keen to strip them of anything they had left. So it was with *cacique* don Juan of Duitama, who was tortured for days by *oidor* Cortés de Mesa and Hidalgo; chained and dragged north to Cerinza and then south-east to Sogamoso, a journey of thirty-six miles, when he had nothing left to give; and threatened and blackmailed by his *encomendero*, Alonso Maldonado, as he lay agonising after his ordeal. He died by suicide a few days later. After a few months Archbishop Zapata appeared in his town and demanded more gold figures from his successor.[123] As before, as news spread of what was happening others decided they wanted a share: *encomenderos*, parish priests, and minor officials all joined in. In the town of Betéitiva, for example, *cacique* don Juan later explained that he had been tortured by Hidalgo's associates, who had taken five nuggets of gold and two *mantas*. But once these men had left, the parish priest decided he too wanted some of the spoils, and threatened to go to Zapata and report them if they did not produce something for him too. He gave him two conch shells and

---

[121] Rojas, *El cacique*, 359.
[122] King to *Audiencia* of Santafé, 18 April 1568, AGI SF 534 L3, 82v.
[123] The incidents at Paipa and Duitama are cited in Rojas, *El cacique*, at 374 and 365–367, respectively.

160 *The Failure of Colonial Governance*

five gold nuggets – everything they had left.[124] Similar cases abound in the documentation.[125]

In the province of Santafé, Vilches, Bermúdez, and their associates carried out two circuits of visitations, in July and September 1577, terrorising the people of the province and extracting hundreds of pesos of gold and valuables.[126] Decades later, while petitioning for high office, Father Bermúdez would boast that he had been personally responsible for 'removing over 300,000 idols of wood or feathers and gold, and many *santuarios*, and with them the occasion for idolatry' from the Indigenous peoples of the region, 'for their own good, the service of God and his majesty, and the profit of the royal treasury'.[127] In October 1577 the *Audiencia* sent interpreter Juan de Lara to a further twenty-six communities across the province of Santafé, ordering *caciques* to collect what *santuario* gold remained from their subjects and to take it to the capital, on pain of sending out another commission. Lara's records are a pitiful testimony of dispossession, as in town after town Indigenous leaders replied that they had nothing more to give. In Subachoque, *cacique* don Pedro said their valuables had already been taken by their *encomendero* Cristóbal Arias de Monroy, and what was left by *oidor* Auncibay. In Fúquene, the *cacique*, also named don Pedro, explained all their gold had been taken by their priest, Domingo de Guevara, and complained they now had no way of meeting their tribute obligations.[128] Terrified, many nevertheless scrambled to take something to Santafé, handing in a further 1,537 pesos worth of gold, 31 of copper, and 57 emeralds in December 1577. A few months later, perhaps dissatisfied with the slim pickings left by Hidalgo and Vilches, Zapata apparently proposed exhuming the remains of Indigenous people buried in rural churches to check for evidence of apostasy and seize associated valuables, although it is not clear that he ever followed through.[129]

---

[124] Ibid., 370–374.

[125] The text recording the visitation of Tunja is in AGN RH 21, 726r–802v. Significant portions of the text of Monzón's investigation were cited and published in Rojas, *El cacique*, 347–399.

[126] The first to Chocontá, Suesca, and other towns in the north-east of the province; the second, in September, to twenty-eight communities, in a great circuit from the valley of Ubaque in the south-east of Santafé, all the way to Suta and Tausa at the northern end of the province. AHSB L2, 69r–71v, 84r–84v.

[127] Petition of Gonzalo Bermúdez for a canonry, 2 March 1610, AGI SF 242, 1r.

[128] Records of Juan de Lara's summons, 20 October 1577, AHSB L2 110r–114v.

[129] At least according to the *Audiencia*, in its letter to the king of 15 October 1578, AGI Patronato 27, r. 28§4, 15r.

How to Steal a Million Pesos

It is tempting to understand this brutal violence as an expression of the growing power of colonial institutions in the New Kingdom of Granada, as many historians, even writing decades apart, have tended to do: to imagine that it was a concerted policy that was planned and executed by a strong colonial government increasingly able to make its claims and designs material.[130] And yet, what seems clearest from these harrowing records of senseless violence is the utter absence of power.[131] No one was really in charge, at any level. Drunk with delegated authority, waving royal rescripts from their archives, and making ever greater claims, Zapata and the *Audiencia* unleashed the violence, but neither had control over what happened next. Zapata could not stop the *oidores* from interfering, and the *Audiencia* could not actually prevent the archbishop from organising his own campaign. Both had little real control over their agents, or these over their subordinates. Even Hidalgo was powerless to control his own thugs, who were there to line their own pockets. And all were powerless to prevent other people – priests, *encomenderos*, random settlers, and other Indigenous people – from joining in and picking over what they left. All that the different actors, great and small, could do was to rush and scramble over one another to grab a share of the spoils for themselves before someone else took it first.

This absence of power is even clearer in the attempted cover-up that followed. In October 1577, as stolen *santuario* gold poured into Spanish pockets, the *Audiencia* issued a short amnesty on the payment of the tax of the royal fifth due on gold brought into the royal treasury to be smelted, assayed, and hallmarked as legal tender, effectively allowing the *oidores* and their henchmen to launder their ill-gotten gains. Chaos ensued as people poured into the treasury to have their gold stamped and its provenance erased. Treasury officials worked non-stop to stamp as much gold as they could, but they struggled to keep up, and in the confusion the royal hallmark was stolen, apparently by a man enslaved by Gaspar Núñez, who together with his friends took to hallmarking anything and everything, turning not only the spoils of *santuarios* into legal tender but transforming brass chamber pots and candlesticks, at least in law, into fine gold. As Esperanza Gálvez described in her detailed

---

[130] Cf. Cortés Alonso, 'Visita a los santuarios', 201; and Francis, 'The Muisca', 257, 222.

[131] This is in fact reminiscent of Hannah Arendt's famous dictum that 'Power and violence are opposites; where the one rules absolutely, the other is absent. Violence appears where power is in jeopardy, but left to its own course it ends in power's disappearance.' *On Violence* (New York: Harcourt, Brace & World, 1970), 56.

162   *The Failure of Colonial Governance*

study of the investigation that followed, people interrogated by the visitor-general a few years later recalled queuing for days to have a turn with the hallmark, while treasury officials later estimated that the amnesty had cost the crown some 200,000 pesos in lost taxes, dwarfing the 44,129 seized by the authorities, and putting the total stolen and laundered somewhere closer to a million: 'the golden age of the colonial period' indeed.[132]

'THIS KINGDOM ... IS A FICTION'

The investigation that followed was far from straightforward. The authorities of Santafé fiercely resisted the first visitor-general in charge, Juan Bautista Monzón, who was jailed by the *Audiencia* and excommunicated by the archbishop on dubious charges of plotting a rebellion with the *mestizo cacique* don Diego de Torres, blasphemy, and witchcraft.[133] His replacement, Juan Prieto de Orellana, was more successful, and it is the witness statements that he eventually managed to compile that allow us to reconstruct this story. Apart from Cetina, who had been transferred to the *Audiencia* of Guatemala before the assay scandal and the worst of the violence and managed to remain in office there until his death in 1586, all the *oidores* were eventually prosecuted. Francisco de Auncibay, who had made it out of the kingdom and to his new post in Quito, was fired, fined 9,000 ducats, barred from royal office for the rest of his life, and exiled from the Indies. He died suddenly shortly after.[134] His replacement in Santafé, Juan Rodríguez de Mora, who had covered for him, was eventually suspended and imprisoned, where he died of pneumonia. Luis Cortés de Mesa became the second and last *oidor* to be sentenced to death and executed in colonial Latin America, but this was at the hand of his own colleagues in the *Audiencia* on charges of sodomy and the murder of a witness, before the visitor-general could send him to Spain for interrogation and trial there over the *santuarios* and assay scandal, perhaps to prevent him from incriminating them further.[135] The new president, Lope Díez de Aux y Armendáriz, who had arrived in August 1578, was suspended for his part in the scandal too, and died in 1585 still appealing the sentence.[136] By then the entire *Audiencia* of Santafé had

---

[132] Esperanza Gálvez Piñal, *La visita de Monzón y Prieto de Orellana al Nuevo Reino de Granada* (Seville: Escuela de Estudios Hispano-Americanos, 1974), 71–75.
[133] Ibid., 88–99.   [134] Mayorga García, *La Audiencia*, 456 n. 116.
[135] Ibid., 176, 168–169.
[136] Not to be confused with his son of the same name, viceroy of New Spain (1635–1640).

'This Kingdom ... Is a Fiction'

been sacked and replaced.[137] But this was no real justice: for Indigenous people there was no restitution or redress, and for *caciques* there was only decline.

The violence and dispossession of the late 1570s struck a deadly blow to the ability of Indigenous rulers to maintain their positions of authority and to hold their communities together. Colonial pressures had already been making it increasingly difficult for Indigenous leaders to hold the feasts and ceremonies that had been crucial to the organisation of communal labour and the flow and redistribution of surpluses through their communities. Now their decline gathered in pace. In the next round of visitations of Santafé and Tunja, in the 1590s, many Indigenous witnesses looked back on the late 1570s as a watershed. In Chocontá, near Santafé, in 1593, *cacique* don Pedro explained how before the coming of the Spaniards and up to the time of the previous *cacique*, don Alonso, in the late 1570s, his predecessors used to receive 'six or seven good mantas and a piece of gold worth nine or ten pesos' from each captain each year and a plain *manta* from every commoner. Now, though, 'these captains and Indians, his subjects, pay him very little tribute – each captain a plain manta each year, and others half a peso of gold, and among the commoners no one has paid anything, except occasionally they plant a field of maize for him'.[138] In Suta, *cacique* don Juan Quechantocha told a similar story in 1594, describing having seen the system in operation under his uncle but lamenting how 'this has now been lost, so that two or three years go by without this witness getting anything in tribute, and when he does he gets two or three *tomines* or half a peso and they work some land'. Don Diego Neamenguya, a captain, remembered how he and his predecessors had paid their *caciques* tribute, and recalled receiving 'a good *manta*' in exchange, but explained that 'the custom was recently lost'. In Tausa, captain don Diego Tenasichiguya said his uncles had paid their *cacique* in the same manner as they had before the coming of the Spaniards, but that this had since ceased, and now his people only worked a small plot for their *cacique*, don Alonso.[139]

Deprived of their remaining gold and valuables, Indigenous communities began to feel more sharply than ever the twin pressures of continuing demographic collapse and growing Spanish tribute obligations – including draft labour, the *alquiler general* or *mita*, in Spanish cities,

---

[137] Gálvez Piñal, *La visita*, 137 n. 27, 88–99.
[138] Visitation of Chocontá by Miguel de Ibarra, 1593, AGN VC 11 d. 1, 148r.
[139] Visitation of Suta and Tausa by Ibarra, AGN VB 17 d. 5, 1594-08-10, 302v, 322r, 316r.

164   *The Failure of Colonial Governance*

public works, and, to a lesser extent, lowland mines.[140] Their *caciques*, unable to help, increasingly became a hindrance and a burden. In Pausaga, where the *cacique* lamented the collapse of a similar system, captain don Diego Tenentiba explained that even providing him a token amount of labour in tribute 'is also falling out of usage, for we have too many obligations to meet'.[141] In Cucunubá, *cacique* don Pedro Neachasenguya reported that the tribute he received was dwindling 'day by day, because the Indians are tired of the tributes and salaries they have to pay'.[142] In Sisatiba, in the province of Santafé, captain don Pedro Conbafurguya listed all his subjects' obligations – the priest, the *encomendero*, the *alquiler general*, and other burdens – explaining that 'for all these reasons we cannot pay the tribute to the *cacique* how we used to', adding that 'back when we did, the *cacique* gave us captains a good *manta*, and gave all the Indians food and drink, and that is why they were respected, but no longer'.[143]

In many other towns up and down the two provinces, witnesses in this period reported no longer paying their *caciques* any tribute at all. In Tibacuy in 1595, don Francisco Chicaguentiba, a captain, explained all the ways in which his people had paid tribute to their *cacique*'s predecessors, before and after the coming of the Spaniards, 'which has now all ceased'.[144] In Guáquira, Felipe Queasocha, a commoner, said that they 'do not give them anything', adding that 'the *caciques* do not ask for anything either'.[145] In Pesca, *cacique* don Juan Quigacha lamented that people 'no longer give anything to their *caciques*'.[146] It would only get worse – by the time of the visitations of the 1630s, discussed in Chapter 6, not only had almost all communities ceased to pay their *caciques* tributes, but several had shed them altogether, replacing them

---

[140] On the *alquiler general*, the Neogranadian version of the *mita*, introduced by President Antonio González from 1590, see Eugenio Martínez, *Tributo y trabajo*, 506–528. Records of Ibarra's 1593–1595 visitation of Santafé showed that as few as 0.55 per cent of the population were engaged in mining at the time of the visitation. This proportion would later increase. See J. Michael Francis, 'The Resguardo, the Mita, and the Alquiler General: Indian Migration in the Province of Tunja, 1550–1636'. *Colonial Latin American Historical Review* 11, no. 4 (2002): 375–406; and Julián Bautista Ruiz Rivera, *Encomienda y mita en Nueva Granada en el siglo XVII* (Seville: CSIC, 1975), 31.
[141] Visitation of Pausaga by Ibarra, 1594, AGN VC 8, d. 3, 386r.
[142] Visitation of Cucunubá by Ibarra, 1594, AGN VC 4 d. 1, 26v.
[143] Visitation of Sisatiba by Ibarra, 1595, AGN VB 17 d. 6, 454r.
[144] Visitation of Tibacuy by Ibarra, 1595, AGN VC 4 d. 8, 877v.
[145] Visitation of Guáquira by Egas de Guzmán, 1596, AGN VB 4 d3, 324v.
[146] Visitation of Pesca by Egas de Guzmán, 1596, AGN VB 4 d. 1, 497r.

'This Kingdom ... Is a Fiction'

with Indigenous governors in charge of collecting *encomienda* tributes and little else. As don Francisco, governor of Tabio, told *oidor* Gabriel de Carvajal in 1638, 'he had heard that in ancient times the Indians gave their *caciques* gold and *mantas* in *tamsa* [tribute], but now they do not pay them tributes because they do not have *caciques*'.[147] Like the old celebrations, their traditional leaders too were becoming, for many, a thing of the past.

This was not supposed to happen. Spanish officials had felt free to pursue increasingly ambitious policies to Christianise Indigenous people because they were convinced that these would only strengthen the political and fiscal structures on which colonial rule depended, particularly the authority and leadership of the people they called *caciques*. In fact, they were blind to the fragile, contingent, and limited nature of the power that Indigenous rulers exercised over their communities through their maintenance of the ritual economy of redistribution and their participation in the cult of *santuarios*, and instead made sense of it by drawing on their own European concepts and categories. This is why they expected Indigenous rulers to have the same power to compel their subjects to reform their ways of life as European lords had over theirs. This was not simply a matter of dismissing or misunderstanding Indigenous politics, but also a reflection of something more fundamental. The delicate, reciprocal, and limited power that Indigenous rulers actually wielded, and the ways in which power worked within their communities, were actually inaccessible and inconceivable with the conceptual tools that the colonial authorities had at their disposal.

Early modern Spaniards, like many other Europeans, had come out of the Middle Ages with a broadly naturalistic understanding of politics.[148] They made sense of the political and legal structures of Indigenous peoples, and their rulers, by drawing on the concept of *ius naturale* (natural law), norms thought to be common to all as a result of natural

---

[147] Visitation of Tabio by Gabriel de Carvajal, 27 September 1638, AGN VC 13 d 4, 639r.

[148] Broadly, an understanding of politics that ascribed a fundamental role to nature and natural law. The concept of natural law was a key concept in medieval political thought even before the reintroduction of Aristotle's *Politics* from thirteenth century, which then provided a variety of authors, notably Aquinas, with new ideas to theorise the origins of power and dominium. For an introduction to these questions, see David E. Luscombe, 'The State of Nature and the Origin of the State'. In *The Cambridge History of Later Medieval Philosophy: From the Rediscovery of Aristotle to the Disintegration of Scholasticism, 1100–1600*. Edited by Norman Kretzmann, Anthony Kenny, and Jan Pinborg (Cambridge: Cambridge University Press, 1982), 757–770.

166   *The Failure of Colonial Governance*

instinct, and the closely related concept of *ius gentium* (law of nations or peoples), customary law produced on the basis of natural law that was also thought to be common to everyone.[149] Crucially, both sorts of law, in this understanding, were already complete and immutable. Natural law was innate and unchanging, while the *ius gentium* had emerged from it – firmly in the past tense – and was no longer being produced.[150] This is why they assumed that the power and jurisdiction of Indigenous rulers was 'derived from antiquity, inherited from their forebears', and therefore grounded on an immutable foundation. It was this that made it a 'legitimate title' – to quote typical language concerning these figures in Spanish law – and indeed as secure, deeply rooted, and immutable as they imagined the power of their own European princes, for their understanding of their own politics was based on the very same ideas.[151]

[149] These were very old ideas in European thought indeed. Both were key in Roman law, where they were defined as two of the three divisions of the private law in Dig. 1.1.1.2–4 (the third was the *ius civile*). On this see Max Kaser, *Ius gentium*. Translated by Francisco Javier Andrés Santos (Granada: Comares, 2004), who traces the evolution of the expression in Roman law in Antiquity, and who discusses this tripartite division at 82–85. For a brief outline of the evolution of these two concepts beyond Antiquity, see David E. Luscombe, 'Natural Morality and Natural Law'. In *The Cambridge History of Later Medieval Philosophy: From the Rediscovery of Aristotle to the Disintegration of Scholasticism, 1100–1600*. Edited by Norman Kretzmann, Anthony Kenny, and Jan Pinborg (Cambridge: Cambridge University Press, 1982), 706–719. As is well known, they were central to the way that the scholars of the School of Salamanca sought to address the claims of the Spanish monarchy and its competitors in this period. For a recent exploration of them in action in the thought of Vitoria and Soto, see Annabel Brett, *Changes of State: Nature and the Limits of the City in Early Modern Natural Law* (Princeton, NJ: Princeton University Press, 2011), ch. 1. On some of these ideas before this, see José Luis Egío and Christiane Birr, 'Before Vitoria: Expansion into Heathen, Empty, or Disputed Lands in Late-Mediaeval Salamanca Writings and Early 16th-Century Juridical Treatises'. In *A Companion to Early Modern Spanish Imperial Political and Social Thought*. Edited by Jörg Tellkamp, 53–77 (Leiden: Brill, 2020). Later, a new understanding of *ius gentium* as a part of the public law (a law of 'nations' in the more modern sense) became more common, in the work of scholars such as Grotius, but this is not the sense that concerns us here.

[150] For a discussion of this dimension of the *ius gentium* in the early modern period in contrast to more modern ideas of a 'law of nations', see Annabel Brett, 'Sources in the Scholastic Legacy: The (Re)Construction of the Ius Gentium in the Second Scholastic'. In *The Oxford Handbook of the Sources of International Law*. Edited by Samantha Besson and Jean d'Aspremont, 64–82 (Oxford: Oxford University Press, 2017).

[151] It was by appealing to these concepts, after all, that various medieval jurists and canonists had sought to get around constraints of the claims of universality of the Roman Empire (and its *ius civile*) and the Papacy. On this see Magnus Ryan, 'Bartolus of Sassoferrato and Free Cities: The Alexander Prize Lecture'. *Transactions of the Royal Historical Society* 10 (2000): 65–89; and Joseph Canning, 'Ideas of the State in Thirteenth and Fourteenth-Century Commentators on the Roman Law'. *Transactions of the Royal Historical Society* 33 (1983): 1–27, and *Conciliarism, Humanism and Law:*

Any deviation from this supposedly universal template tended instead to be understood to have been a later innovation, a product of more recent rulemaking: whether deliberately by some legislator or more organically through custom. Spaniards were to monitor these innovations closely, and if they found anything to have been 'imposed tyrannically against reason and justice', or 'without good title', they were to intervene to remove it. Equally, even if some norm had been introduced legitimately but was deemed excessive, Spanish authorities were obliged to moderate these excesses and restore good government.[152] As a result, when *Audiencia* officials sought to curb the supposed tyranny of Muisca leaders or the apparently excessive displays of obedience and submission that their subjects showed them, they were convinced that this could only – surely – serve to strengthen their authority, for they understood those features to contravene natural law or the *ius gentium* and therefore to put their power in jeopardy.[153] It was in this spirit that the authorities had sought to chip away at different aspects of the protocol and ceremony surrounding Indigenous rulers as early as the 1563 visitation of *oidor* Diego de Villafañe, who had ordered Indigenous commoners in each town he visited to stop 'bearing *caciques* and *principales* on their backs', as had been their custom, on pain of fines and penalties, and encouraged the latter to 'buy some horses, which are cheap' and less grievous to their subjects.[154] It was paternalistic and self-serving, but it was also a reflection of their understanding of Indigenous politics – or at least of their refusal to contemplate the possibility that they might work differently to their own.

In the same way, the authorities felt free to conscript and transform Indigenous rulers into intermediaries through which to govern, tax, and Christianise the people that they ruled. In 1569, for example, before his visitation of Tunja, Cepeda had issued legislation requiring Indigenous people to attend Christian instruction 'without excuse, on pain of their *cacique* or captain apprehending and punishing them, whipping them,

---

Justifications of Authority and Power, c. 1400–c. 1520 (Cambridge: Cambridge University Press, 2021), ch. 4. The quotations are from the rescript, 'That the rights of *caciques* be recognised and their excesses moderated', first issued in 1552 and reissued multiple times in the seventeenth century, compiled and published as *Recopilación* 6.7.8.

[152] As in Ibid.

[153] On these signs of submission in contemporary chronicles, see Jaime Humberto Borja Gómez, *Los indios medievales*, 118–123.

[154] This was part of the standard *plática* with which he began each visitation. See for example that of Suta and Tausa, at AGN VC 4 d. 11, 977v.

168   *The Failure of Colonial Governance*

with moderation, in front of the *encomendero* or the priest and cutting their hair or *mantas* depending on their offense', and instructing *caciques* to work to root out Indigenous ritual practices.[155] This was also how Zapata expected *caciques* to contribute to the project of Christianisation in his 1576 *Catechism*, in which their own instruction and discipline was a priority, so that they could serve as informants and assistants to the parish priest and Spanish authorities.[156] These were also the roles envisioned for these figures in innumerable petitions by the civil and ecclesiastical authorities of Spanish America to the king over the course of the sixteenth and seventeenth centuries, which crystallised into multiple royal rescripts eventually compiled as an entire title – 'On *caciques*' – of the *Recopilación* of 1688.[157] Across the monarchy, as is well known, these figures – and particularly their children – were also targeted for special religious instruction, from the very earliest missionary efforts in Mexico.[158] All of this, in light of these ideas, should surely only have had a positive effect: after all, grace, as per Aquinas's famous dictum, should only perfect nature, not destroy it.[159] And yet, this is exactly what these policies – and the violence of 1577–1578 – achieved in the highlands of the New Kingdom. In Ubaté in 1592 *cacique* don Pedro complained of how his authority over his subjects had collapsed entirely since inheriting the role, so that 'even though he is principal *cacique*, the Indians his subjects do not obey him, or do his planting, or pay him tribute, or respect him as they should', despite the fact that 'the *encomendero* and the parish priest have ordered them to do so many times'.[160] But was it not he who was supposed to be aiding them?

---

[155] Autos of *oidor* Juan López de Cepeda, 14 May 1569, AGI CI 70 d. 28, 616r.

[156] For example inspecting the town and the homes of their subjects, sending their children to special catechism classes, or being subject to particularly strict penalties in order to serve as examples to their people Zapata de Cárdenas, 'Catecismo', 149, 152, 214.

[157] *Recopilación* 6.7.1–17. For a survey of some of this legislation and associated jurisprudence, see Jorge Augusto Gamboa, 'Los caciques en la legislación indiana: una reflexión sobre la condición jurídica de las autoridades indígenas en el siglo XVI'. In *Juan de Solórzano y Pereira: pensar la colonia desde la colonia*. Edited by Diana Bonnett Vélez and Felipe Castañeda Salamanca, 153–190 (Bogotá: Universidad de los Andes, 2006).

[158] On New Spain, see Richard C. Trexler, 'From the Mouths of Babes: Christianization by Children in 16th Century New Spain'. In *Religious Organization and Religious Experience*. Edited by J. Davis (London: Academic Press, 1982), 115–135. On Peru, Estenssoro Fuchs, *Paganismo*, 42–43. For a recent study of the role of the resulting 'niños de monasterio' in Mexico, see Crewe, *The Mexican Mission*, 68–77.

[159] Aquinas, *Summa*, Ia q. 1 a. 8 ad 2 (= vol. 1, 13).

[160] Visitation of Ubaté by Bernardino de Albornoz, May 1592, AGN VC 5 d. 2, 212r.

'This Kingdom ... Is a Fiction' 169

This brings us full circle to the leader of Suba with whom this chapter began. Already in 1569 Suba and Tuna had been investigated by the *Audiencia* following reports of *xeques* and sorcerers, as discussed in Chapter 1, in the context of efforts to resettle these communities into a new planned town.[161] The following decade, in 1577, don Pedro of Suba's community was looted by their *encomendero*, Luis Cardoso, and then by cathedral treasurer Espejo and *oidor* Auncibay. The following year, in 1578, don Pedro had also been among the Indigenous authorities 'beset and punished by the most reverend archbishop', to quote a complaint he presented to the *Audiencia* of December of that year, 'as a result of which the Indians of his community have been abandoning it'. And a few months after Zapata left, the priest of nearby Usaquén had descended on the town to 'mistreat and imprison' two of his *capitanes*, don Juan and Martinico, whom he was apparently presently torturing. If the *Audiencia* did not intervene, he warned then, 'the Indians will not take any more suffering and will leave'.[162] A quarter century later, his authority over his people had broken down completely, and with it went his ability to serve as the intermediary that Spanish authorities needed him to be.

The decline of *caciques* threatened to deprive Spanish authorities of their principal interface with their Indigenous subjects, but it was also a manifestation of broader malaise. The structures that underpinned their authority were part of a wider nexus of bonds and relations that held their communities together, but which were breaking and collapsing too. The most visible sign of this was the growing emigration of Indigenous people to Spanish cities and other towns, or beyond the highlands altogether, abandoning their communities in order to escape the pressures and demands that were making their lives intolerable. This was the context for Cepeda's 1569 legislation, in which he also ordered Indigenous commoners to 'obey, follow, serve, and recognise their *caciques* and superiors in all that they command as their natural lords and *caciques*', which also involved 'living and residing in their lands' as they were supposed to. For this he also ordered *caciques* to track down and round up *émigrés* and bring them back to their towns.[163] He repeated all of this in each town he inspected on his visitation three years later, in which he also tried to identify immigrants from other communities and send them back.[164]

---

[161] Inquiry concerning Suba and Tuna, 1569, AGN C&I 27, doc. 23 652r–667v.
[162] Don Pedro of Suba to the *Audiencia*, 12 December 1578, AHSB L2, 117r–118v.
[163] Autos of *oidor* Juan López de Cepeda, 14 May 1569, AGI CI 70 d. 28, 616r, 620r.
[164] See for example his visitation of Motavita, AGN VB 2 d. 1, 2v–4v.

170   *The Failure of Colonial Governance*

This was made worse by the violence of 1577. Already that year, some *encomenderos* and other observers had tried to warn the authorities. Leonor Gómez, *encomendera* of Serrezuela (modern-day Madrid, Cundinamarca) alerted the *Audiencia* in September 1577 that Vilches and Bermúdez had apprehended 'seven Indians, telling them they will torture them if they do not hand over *santuario* gold', prompting everyone else in the town, including the *cacique*, to flee, 'and they have abandoned the community and fled to other towns and to the mountains', leaving her, in effect, without a functioning *encomienda*.[165] This was an extreme case, but throughout the two provinces Indigenous emigration gathered pace. When *oidor* Miguel de Ibarra visited the *encomiendas* of the province of Santafé in 1593–1595, Indigenous witnesses reported that at least 1,273 men of working age had abandoned their communities in the 53 *encomiendas* of the province – some 6.2 per cent of its remaining population of around 20,000 tributaries, and up to 28 per cent in some places – and this only gathered pace.[166] Before the end of the century, the *Audiencia* twice commissioned officials to track down and bring back *émigrés* belonging to *encomiendas* held by the crown.[167] But what could less well-resourced *encomenderos*, or, indeed, *caciques*, do?

By the beginning of the seventeenth century, the settlers of Santafé, Tunja, and other highland cities were fed up. At significant expense, they came together to fund one of their own to travel to the court of the king and present a long report on the desperate state of their provinces and a detailed petition seeking redress and proposing substantial reforms, which they had typeset and printed for distribution at court. It was in this way that their procurator, Juan Sanz Hurtado, finally appeared before Philip III in February 1603 to deliver a stark diagnosis of their problems, which by now were not just affecting Indigenous leaders or *encomenderos* like himself. Christianisation, in the form it had taken up to this point, was not working. Far from serving to consolidate colonial rule by transforming Indigenous people into Christian subjects, it was

---

[165] Leonor Gómez to the *Audiencia*, 28 September 1577, AHSB Libro 2, 85r.

[166] 'Report of the *encomenderos* and Indians of Santafé' by Miguel de Ibarra, 1595, AGI SF 164 n. 8, 1v. This document was also collated and published in Julián Bautista Ruiz Rivera, *Fuentes para la demografía histórica de Nueva Granada* (Seville: Escuela de Estudios Hispano-Americanos, 1972), 31–33, and discussed in Ruiz Rivera, *Encomienda y mita*, 31–32.

[167] On this, see Francis, 'The Muisca', 188–194. Michael Francis has also shown that at least one wealthy *encomendero*, Juan Zárate de Chacón, commissioned an inspection of this kind of his own. See Francis, 'Resguardo', 375–376.

threatening its very survival. Tribute collection was collapsing, Indigenous communities were fragmenting, people were leaving the region, and crops were going unplanted. In fact, this unravelling of Indigenous communities in the highlands was threatening the supply of food and resources to the gold and emerald mines of the lowlands, the beating heart of the region's extractive economy. 'This kingdom, Powerful Lord', Sanz explained, 'is a fiction' – an assumption, '*un supuesto*' – and it was wearing thinner than ever and coming close to falling apart.[168] It was time for a new approach.

[168] Juan Sanz Hurtado, *Supplica q[ue] haze Iuan Sanz Hurtado vezino y encomendero de la ciudad de Tunja a V. M. en nombre de nueuo reyno de Granada; para su restauracione spiritual y temporal* (Madrid, [1603]). The working copy of the Council of the Indies, with its marginal annotations, can be found at AGI SF 16, n. 44.

4

The Friends of Ceremony and the Introduction of Reform

In the middle of August 1606, Archbishop Bartolomé Lobo Guerrero and President Juan de Borja of Santafé sent a joint letter to the king that marked a watershed in the development of the New Kingdom of Granada and its missionary project. It began with a familiar litany of the kingdom's afflictions: Indigenous people 'as gentile and idolatrous as they were before the arrival of Spaniards'; priests, 'whether regular or secular', failing to perform their duties, 'lacking all zeal for the salvation of souls, having no doctrine, and living far from exemplary lives'; and a Spanish laity 'overburdened with the vices of carnality, greed, and lack of religion'.[1] After the catastrophic actions of their predecessors in the sixteenth century, however, the pair proposed a path to overcome these ills that differed from earlier approaches in two key ways. The first was that they announced an ambitious joint plan for the kingdom's reformation, a complete overhaul of its church and programme of Christianisation. This would be a renewed attempt to introduce Tridentine reform, based on a new and more comprehensive interpretation of what this should involve. The second, subtler, but no less fundamental change was that their initiative had the backing and support of the *encomenderos* and Spanish settlers of the highlands of the New Kingdom, for it was, in fact, their plan. What Lobo Guerrero and Borja were beginning to implement was a design that had first been proposed three years before by none other than the cabildos of Santafé, Tunja, and other highland cities through their procurator at court, Juan Sanz Hurtado. Having made its way

[1] Letter of Archbishop Lobo Guerrero and President Borja to the king, 17 August 1606, AGI SF 226, no. 103, 1r.

172

'The Good of the Republic'

through the machinery of the king's court and chancery, obtained the purchase and support of leading figures, and assumed its definitive shape in the minds of Lobo Guerrero, Borja, and other ambitious reformers, the settlers' own design for the overhaul of the kingdom had made it back across the Atlantic and was now beginning to take root.

This chapter focuses on the beginning of this ambitious experiment to reform the church of the New Kingdom of Granada. One aspect would be legislative, renewing the ecclesiastical legislation of the New Kingdom by adapting and translating the normativity of the centres of empire to suit a new interpretation of local conditions. This would involve, over the next few years, a better organised and comprehensive engagement with Indigenous languages, the production of systematic and uniform catechetical materials, and the introduction of new methods and priorities in religious instruction that reflected the most current ideas and practices of Catholicism at a global level. The other aspect would be practical: an ambitious experiment to hand over several Indigenous parishes to a newly arrived, radical cohort of Jesuits – effectively exiled from the Central Andes – to use as a testing ground for reform, with the aim of extending the lessons learned throughout the archdiocese and beyond.

Underpinning all these changes would be a reassessment of the functioning of conversion, rooted in a distinction between internal and external piety that was central to Jesuit spirituality, that prioritised everyday participation in a broad range of Christian devotions and institutions, and moved decisively away from the failed punitive policies of Zapata. The result would make room for Indigenous people to begin to interact with Christianity in new ways and set the development of the New Kingdom and its church on a distinctive course for decades to come. To understand how, we must start in the rubble of the crises of the late sixteenth century.

'THE GOOD OF THE REPUBLIC'

The monarchy's response after visitor-general Juan Prieto de Orellana uncovered the extent of the failures of governance of the *Audiencia* of Santafé of the late 1570s and early 1580s was to attempt, yet again, to overhaul the government of the kingdom. For this, at least, the slate was relatively clean. By the time Prieto left Santafé in May 1585 with the records of his inquiry, he had removed, arrested, charged, sentenced, or exiled practically everyone who had been in power during the *santuarios* scandal of the late 1570s, the disastrous coverup and assay scandal that followed, and the attempted sabotage of his and his predecessor's

174   *The Friends of Ceremony and the Introduction of Reform*

investigations.[2] Only Archbishop Zapata remained, until his death in January 1590 following a hunting accident. It would take until the end of the century for a new archbishop to arrive in Santafé, after two nominees died and a third was promoted away before taking office.[3] For the job of president, after much negotiation, the king appointed a reluctant trusted senior administrator, the Salamanca-educated lawyer Antonio González, a member of the Council of the Indies who had previously served as president of Guatemala and senior *oidor* in Granada, with instructions to 'reduce, quieten, comfort, and bring to conformity the disorders of the past', increased judicial and executive powers, a generous salary, and the promise that he could return to his old job once he sorted out the beleaguered kingdom.[4] González arrived in Santafé in early 1590.

His response to the crises of the 1570s and 1580s was to blame the settlers, particularly *encomenderos*, and to strengthen and broaden the reach of the very institutions that had caused the crises in the first place. For this he implemented a tripartite strategy, partly based on broader reforms introduced by his counterparts elsewhere. The first part was to clean house, carrying out *composiciones* – inspections and registrations of titles – of *encomiendas*, to tidy up after decades of haphazard grants by his predecessors to their clients and favourites, and to raise some much-needed cash for Philip II's ruinously expensive war with England. On his arrival, González thus set about identifying *encomiendas* that had been obtained or inherited irregularly and seizing them from their holders or, preferably, legalising their titles on payment of a fine, with comfortable payment plans made available if necessary. By González's own account this raised just shy of 42,000 gold pesos for the royal treasury in a few short years, affecting some 128 *encomiendas* in the lowlands, and ten in the provinces of Santafé and Tunja.[5]

---

[2] Gálvez Piñal, *La visita*, 124–135; Mayorga García, *La Audiencia*, 189–191.

[3] Treasurer Miguel de Espejo would follow in October 1591. See Pacheco, *La evangelización*, 236. Zapata's immediate replacement, Alonso López de Ávila, archbishop of Santo Domingo, died in December 1590 before setting off for Santafé. His replacement, Bartolomé Martínez, bishop of Panama, only made it as far as Cartagena, dying there in August 1594. The third, Andrés de Caso was appointed Bishop of León. Schäfer, *El Consejo*, vol. 2, 594.

[4] González's commission, issued 8 October 1587, can be found at AGI SF 535 L6, 236–238v. On González's career before his appointment, see Eugenio Martínez, *Tributo y trabajo*, 103–104, n. 119. On the terms of his appointment and additional powers, see Mayorga García, *La Audiencia*, 45–49.

[5] Eugenio Martínez, *Tributo y trabajo*, 106–107.

'The Good of the Republic'

The second, and more comprehensive, effort was the introduction of *corregidores*, middle-ranking royal justices answerable directly to the *Audiencia* and designed to extend its reach over *encomenderos* and Indigenous communities.[6] These had been a feature of the crown's efforts to turn back the clock on the growing autonomy of its subjects in different contexts since mid-fourteenth-century Iberia, and had been instituted in Mexico and the Central Andes decades before.[7] González introduced them to the provinces of Santafé and Tunja from 1593, with comprehensive legislation granting them broad powers.[8] *Corregidores* were to police and punish Indigenous people and their leaders for holding '*borracheras*' and other such practices, for theft and other crimes, and for engaging in illicit unions and sexual relations; to encourage Indigenous people to engage in the market economy by growing crops, raising animals, and producing commodities needed 'for the good of the republic' and selling them for cash, which they would help them manage; and to oversee their participation in the labour drafts.[9] They were also, crucially, to be first-instance magistrates, bearing the rod of justice, with civil and criminal jurisdiction over simple cases involving Indigenous people, over whom they were to administer 'brief and summary' justice, referring more

---

[6] For a recent study of this process in New Granada, with particular attention to their impact on Indigenous communities, see Muñoz Arbeláez, 'The New Kingdom', 289–299. Muñoz notes how other officials of the same name had been a feature of the New Kingdom in the past. These included the '*corregidores*' who managed royal *encomiendas*, and the '*corregidores*' or local magistrates of Spaniards (at 289–290, n. 19).

[7] For an overview of *corregidores* in Castile from the fourteenth century, see Benjamín González Alonso, *El corregidor castellano (1348–1808)* (Madrid: Instituto de Estudios Administrativos, 1970). On the afterlife of the medieval institution in the New World, Karen B. Graubart, 'Learning from the Qadi: The Jurisdiction of Local Rule in the Early Colonial Andes'. *Hispanic American Historical Review* 95, no. 2 (2015): 202. On *corregidores* in the Central Andes, introduced from 1565 by Governor García de Castro, see Guillermo Lohmann Villena, *El Corregidor de indios en el Perú bajo los Austrias* (Lima: Fondo Editorial PUCP, 2001), especially chs 2–4. On their Mexican counterparts, the *alcaldes mayores*, see Woodrow Borah, 'El gobernador novohispano (alcalde mayor/corregidor): consecución del puesto y aspectos económicos'. In *El gobierno provincial en la Nueva España, 1570–1787* (Mexico City: Universidad Nacional Autónoma de México, 2002), 39–53.

[8] The 'Ordinances for *corregidores*', 22 September 1593, survive in two copies: in full in AGN C&I 42 d 4, and in a partial copy at AHSB L3, 1r–4r. The latter contains multiple other items of legislation with instructions to *corregidores*, the latest of which date to the 1620s. Cf. equivalent legislation issued in Peru by García de Castro and later Viceroy Toledo, compiled in Lohmann Villena, *El Corregidor*, 563–643.

[9] 'Ordinances for *corregidores*', nos 7–10 and 28, AGN C&I 42 d 4, 84v–85v, 90v.

176 *The Friends of Ceremony and the Introduction of Reform*

complex ones to the *Audiencia*.[10] They were also to ensure that people obeyed their *caciques* and captains – for 'some Indians are so evil that they mistreat their *caciques* and do not obey them' – and that these authorities treated their subjects well and distributed tributary obligations fairly among them. *Corregidores* were also to ensure that everyone stayed in their communities, and that these relocated and remained in their new *reducción* towns, for which they were empowered to act 'with all rigour, burning their old houses and ranches if necessary'.[11]

Their main purpose, however, was to limit the role of *encomenderos* in the lives of Indigenous people. For this it would now be *corregidores*, and not *encomenderos*, who should collect the *demora*, or *encomienda* tribute, 'so that the *encomendero* should have nothing to do with the *caciques*'. For this *corregidores* were to keep copies of the latest tribute assessments and detailed records of all those liable for payments – specified to be males aged between seventeen and fifty-five – adjusting the amount collected as people aged or died.[12] This had an immediate effect on the revenues of *encomenderos*, as tribute rates began to be adjusted regularly by the new *corregidores*, instead of every few years (or every few decades) by *oidores* on visitation tours. The *encomendero* of Tupachoque in Tunja, Juan Sanz Hurtado, thus saw his income collapse from 216 gold pesos a year to just 74 in 1593, when *corregidor* Lope González de Piña adjusted it to reflect the 85 tributaries that remained in his *encomienda*, out of the 247 counted in the last general inspection decades before.[13] Once collected, *corregidores* were to pay the priest's stipend directly, retain any taxes, and only then pay the *encomendero* their share, keeping detailed accounts. They were also to ensure that 'no *encomendero*, his wife, children, or servants dare enter the repartimientos' of their Indians, and were given express powers to evict them. Their wages, in turn, were to be paid directly by Indigenous people, without having anything to do with the *encomenderos*, at the rate of one *tomín* (an eighth of a gold peso) per tribute payer, plus a bonus of 4 per cent of the yields of the community farms and cattle rearing that *corregidores* were supposed to introduce and foster – increased to 10 per cent in 1600 when it proved not to be

---

[10] Ibid., nos 25–27 (89r–90v). On 'justicia breve y sumaria', see Herzog, *Upholding Justice*, 31.

[11] 'Ordinances for *corregidores*', nos 21–23, and 35–36, AGN C&I 42 d 4, 88v, 92r–92v.

[12] Ibid., no. 23 (89r).

[13] Readjustment of the tributes of Ocavita and Tupachoque, 1593, AGN VB 10 d 3, 355r–363v.

'The Good of the Republic'   177

incentive enough.[14] Finally, *corregidores* were to be in charge of levying a new royal poll tax on Indigenous people – the *requinto*, or fifth of the fifth, equivalent to 20 per cent of the value of the *demora* – first introduced by Philip II in 1591 in aid of his dismal finances.[15]

The third and final dimension of González's reforms was the thornier question of landholding, drawing on recent legislation that ordered officials across Spanish America to carry out *composiciones* of land titles as well, particularly to help cover the cost of the Anglo-Spanish War.[16] This legislation asserted the king's ownership over all land in his American kingdoms, and ordered administrators to examine by what means different groups and individuals had come to possess theirs. All land found to be held without a proper title would revert to the crown, although – as with the *composición* of *encomiendas* – those with irregular titles had the option of legalising them for a price, depending on the circumstances. Just as in Mexico and Peru, this process then freed the crown to dispose of its newly recovered lands as needed, although the legislation urged officials to ensure that they assigned some 'to the Indians that lack them', for their sustenance.[17]

In addition to raising cash, González saw this as the perfect opportunity to complete the effort to resettle the Indigenous inhabitants of Santafé and Tunja into planned, gridded towns once and for all.[18] For this, he commissioned *oidores* Miguel de Ibarra and Andrés Egas de Guzmán to conduct thorough visitations of the provinces of Santafé and Tunja, respectively. It was these that revealed the extent of the collapse of the authority of Indigenous leaders considered in Chapter 3. The first, Ibarra's visitation of Santafé, completed between 1593 and 1595, was the most thorough, with the visitor reporting having 'personally visited every place in the province'.[19] Records for just 13 *encomiendas* survive,

---

[14] 'Ordinances for *corregidores*', nos 11, 13, 31, and 34, AGN C&I 42 d 4., 86v, 90v–92r. The rate was adjusted by decree of President Sande on 29 May 1600, AHSB L3, 9r–10r.

[15] Ruiz Rivera, *Encomienda y mita*, 231–235.

[16] These instructions came in three royal decrees of 1 November 1591, dispatched across Spanish America. These are compiled in Solano, *Cedulario de tierras*, 269–275.

[17] Royal decree (cédula) on *composiciones* of land, 1 November 1591, in Ibid., 271. On this process in Peru, see Luis Miguel Glave, 'Propiedad de la tierra, agricultura y comercio, 1570–1700: El gran despojo'. In *Compendio de historia económica del Perú, II: Economía del período colonial temprano*. Edited by Carlos Contreras (Lima: Banco Central de Reservas del Perú, Instituto de Estudios Peruanos, 2009), 353–357.

[18] Germán Colmenares, *Historia económica y social de Colombia, 1537–1719*. 3rd edition. (Bogotá: Editorial La Carrera, 1978), 203.

[19] Miguel de Ibarra to the Council of the Indies, 20 April 1595, AGI SF 17 n 120, 1r.

178   *The Friends of Ceremony and the Introduction of Reform*

although summaries of his findings across 103 towns in 52 *encomiendas* were sent to Spain that showed that the Indigenous population of the province had collapsed to 20,545 tributaries, and a total of 62,771 individuals.[20] This was a precipitous fall from the 35,482 tributaries counted by Tomás López 35 years before, and the total population of over 110,000 that historians have estimated on its basis, discussed in Chapter 2. Egas de Guzmán's visitation of Tunja began in 1595 but was interrupted the following year and never completed. Records survive for just six communities, and no summaries appear to have been sent to Spain.[21]

In addition to the familiar inspections, interrogation of Indigenous witnesses, and population counts, a key focus of these visitations was the overhaul of land titles. Ibarra's visitation was preceded by a general call for the settlers of Santafé to exhibit their land titles at the *Audiencia* within twenty days and to legalise them if irregular, or have them declared null and void.[22] This done, the visitation itself paid special attention to land tenure, in line with the 1591 legislation, serving as an opportunity to measure and inspect estates and landholdings in the province, and to use land redistribution to advance the effort of Indigenous resettlement.[23] It was in this way that Ibarra and Egas de Guzmán assigned each community they visited a *resguardo* – an inalienable holding of land – surrounding the new settlements to which they were relocated. The term 'resguardo' may have been rare outside the New Kingdom, but similar policies were of course introduced by administrators across Spanish America and are recognisable in other contexts too. The idea was to guarantee that Indigenous communities had enough land to sustain themselves, fulfil their tributary obligations, and – under the watchful eye of *corregidores* – produce surpluses with which to engage in the market economy. In practice, as elsewhere, it also legitimised formally stripping Indigenous communities of most of the lands, even if in practice these had already been taken from them long before.[24]

---

[20] 'Report of the *encomenderos* and Indians of Santafé' by Miguel de Ibarra, 1595, AGI SF 164 n 8, 1v. This document was also collated and published by Julián Bautista Ruiz Rivera in *Fuentes*, 31–33; and discussed in *Encomienda y mita*, 31–32.

[21] On his abortive visitation, see Colmenares, *La provincia*, 143–147.

[22] Santiago Muñoz explores the complex and contested processes through which colonial officials like Ibarra sought to convert landscapes to property by abstracting and translating it into paper, in 'The New Kingdom', 299–306. On the call for titles see p. 301.

[23] See Ibarra's letter and report to the king, 24 February 1594, AGI SF 17 nos. 80, at 1v.

[24] On this process in the New Kingdom, see Marta Herrera Ángel, 'Ordenamiento espacial de los pueblos de indios: dominación y resistencia en la sociedad colonial'. *Fronteras de la Historia* 2 (1998): 93–128; Francis, 'Resguardo', 396–406; and indeed Margarita

'The Good of the Republic'

One such town was Chocontá, where in July 1593 Ibarra determined that its 2,549 inhabitants would need a measure of land stretching out from their new planned town in a rough circle with a radius of between 4,300 and 5,000 paces. He had this measured out in each direction, and ordered the local *corregidor* to draw a boundary around it and distribute the land inside to different individuals and groups within the community 'according to their possibilities and quality', being careful to favour *caciques* and captains especially.[25] The idea, Ibarra explained, was to 'encourage them to live like Christians and in Spanish *policía*' by rewarding them with land, which was also why he took into account the devotion with which they had apparently endowed their church with an elaborate crucifix and established a confraternity devoted to the True Cross.[26] Conversely, as in other regions, this process of determining which lands were to belong to Indigenous communities – enough for their needs, in theory, but no more – freed up the rest of the region for new rounds of land grants and sales by the crown. Ibarra repeated the procedure through-out the province, and Egas de Guzmán followed suit in those towns in Tunja that he managed to inspect before his visitation was cut short. That task would be completed by his successor Luis Enríquez, on a new and more thorough visitation tour of Tunja at the turn of the century.

In the meantime, the secular church languished. Zapata's death in 1590 gave way to a long period of *sede vacante* during which the secular church lacked an effective leadership, despite the efforts of various members of the cathedral chapter that governed the archdiocese to con-tinue to pursue some of the policies of their late archbishop. From 1591, for example, Francisco de Porras Mejía, the *maestrescuela*, lobbied the crown for help in re-establishing the diocesan seminary that had been forced to close, but these designs came to nothing.[27] In the vacuum, it was the *Audiencia* that increasingly came to concern itself with religious affairs, much to the chapter's annoyance. It was thus that González's

---

González, *El resguardo en el Nuevo Reino de Granada* (Bogotá: Universidad Nacional de Colombia, 1970).

[25] These tended to be divided into different sectors: the bulk of the land was divided up into '*labranzas particulares*' and each assigned to one of the community's constituent groups (*parcialidades* or *capitanías*); a second section was set aside for '*labranzas de comunidad*', or communal farming, under the direction of *corregidores*; and other sections were assigned to important individuals or set aside for cattle and other animals. See González, *El resguardo*, 44–45.

[26] Visitation of Chocontá by Ibarra, AGN VC 11 d 1, 259r–264r.

[27] Letter of Francisco de Porras Mejía to the king, 7 May 1591, AGI SF 231, no. 27.

180 *The Friends of Ceremony and the Introduction of Reform*

new *corregidores* were instructed not only to cooperate with parish priests the running of parishes – 'that they may come to love the priests and fear the *corregidor*' – but also to watch and inform on them and their churches to the *Audiencia*, even keeping their own inventories of the property of each parish.[28] In the same way, Ibarra and Egas went further than any of their predecessors in investigating ecclesiastical affairs, instructing priests on how to conduct their duties and interrogating witnesses on the actions of their priests.[29] The ecclesiastical authorities soon began to complain of the *Audiencia*'s intrusions on their turf, particularly Ibarra's willingness to fill vacant positions in Indigenous parishes without involving the diocesan authorities.[30] Thus it was in 1597, when he divided each of the parishes of Machetá, Bosa, and Ubaté in two, and asked the Franciscans of Santafé, and not the cathedral chapter, to nominate candidates for the new positions.[31]

The religious orders, previously beaten back by Zapata, were delighted to oblige, and used this period to claw back the independence and influence of which the late archbishop had sought to deprive them. Complaints by diocesan authorities flooded the royal chancery throughout this period, complaining of the regulars' desire 'to attempt once again to take root in the towns of Indians', dusting off privileges granted in the 1560s to justify their actions; of their refusal to recognise the power of jurisdiction of the secular church, bypassing its courts and disciplinary mechanisms in favour of their own; and even of their attempt to excommunicate the cathedral chapter altogether by the end of the century, when it attempted to collect its appointed share of parish revenues.[32] Many of the *criollo* and *mestizo* priests ordained by Zapata, for their part, found themselves unemployed and displaced from their parishes.[33] All of this was exacerbated by the controversial Francisco de Sande, erstwhile governor and captain-general of the Philippines, failed conqueror of Borneo, and former president of Guatemala, who arrived in Santafé in

---

[28] Numbers 3, 4, 5, and 6 (AGN C&I 42 d 4, 83v–84r).

[29] See Ibarra's report to the king, 24 February 1594, AGI SF 17 n 80a, 3r–4v.

[30] Letter of Archbishop Lobo Guerrero to the king, 16 May 1599, AGI SF 226, no. 61, 3r.

[31] See the nomination papers, dated 9 December 1597, APSLB Parroquias Cundinamarca 2/ 5/35, 5r–7v.

[32] See the letter of the cathedral chapter of Santafé to the king, 23 May 1598, AGI SF 231, no. 37. The attempted excommunication, which involved initiating a legal process that involved appointing a '*juez conservador*' with the authority to do so, was reported by Archbishop Lobo Guerrero after his arrival, in his letter to the king of 16 May 1599, AGI SF 226, no. 61, at 2r.

[33] Letter of Archbishop Lobo Guerrero to the king, 16 May 1599, AGI SF 226, no. 61, 1r.

August 1597 as González's replacement and continued his efforts to extend the *Audiencia*'s control over the affairs of *encomenderos* and the church.

In this way, the situation that the third archbishop of Santafé, the former academic and inquisitor Bartolomé Lobo Guerrero, encountered on his arrival in Santafé in March 1599 was eerily similar to that faced by his predecessor Zapata a quarter century before. Once again, the new archbishop of Santafé, equipped with minimal resources, would have to find a way of asserting his power over the government of the church and its missionary programme, to work out what Tridentine reform might look like in this context, and to implement those reforms. The problem was that he shared this ambition with President Sande, who had his own designs and expected the archbishop to be little more than a rubber stamp.

'THE GREATEST BLIGHT'

It was essential not just for the reform of the church, but to its very functioning, that the civil and ecclesiastical authorities work in tandem. Both the archbishop and the president exercised power over ecclesiastical affairs within the framework of royal patronage, and with the same ostensible aim, so it is anachronistic and misleading to understand these struggles in terms of a binary opposition of church and 'state' in the modern sense, of independence and separation.[34] Instead, both had competence over aspects of the operation of the church, and both tried to pursue initiatives they believed would advance the missionary project. It was for this reason, and not just venal self-interest, that Sande, and González before him, had devoted significant efforts and resources to initiatives such as the resettlement of Indigenous communities or the configuration of parishes. The problem was duplication. Both authorities sought to do similar things, and this overlap created jurisdictional conflicts that frequently resulted in the failure of both efforts. Conflict resulting from the overlap of functions and responsibilities would only cause division, confusion, and discord, and it ran against contemporary notions of good government, frequently characterised through reference

---

[34] On this see Alejandro Cañeque, *The King's Living Image: The Culture and Politics of Viceregal Power in Colonial Mexico* (New York: Routledge, 2004), 73; and Jorge E. Traslosheros, *Iglesia, justicia y sociedad en la Nueva España: La audiencia del arzobispado de México, 1528–1668* (Mexico City: Editorial Porrúa; Universidad Iberoamericana, 2004), 71.

182   *The Friends of Ceremony and the Introduction of Reform*

to the image of a monstruous body with two heads.[35] A similar argument
applied in relation to the religious orders, who also had a share in these
powers because they had a share in the same responsibilities.[36]

The first years of Lobo Guerrero's time in office were mired in jurisdictional, institutional, and personal conflict with president Sande, in what
appears to have been just the latest chapter in a longer-running rivalry
between the two administrators, who had most recently overlapped in
Mexico City during the 1580s.[37] Most of the archbishop's correspondence with the crown in this period consisted of complaints about Sande
and his right-hand man, *oidor* Luis Enríquez. They clashed over matters
of ceremony and protocol, from the icy reception Sande gave the new
archbishop on his ceremonial entry into Santafé in 1599, to conflicts over
the order of precedence during the mass and processions – with Sande
presumptuously demanding to be afforded the privileges of a viceroy,
according to the archbishop, and Lobo Guerrero wilfully disrespecting
the president and through him the king's own dignity, according to
Sande.[38] So too over questions of jurisdiction, with Sande drafting

[35] Cañeque, *King's Living Image* 20–21, 82–93. This very language had been used by
Archbishop Zapata in his struggles with the *Audiencia* in his letter to the king of
21 December 1583, AGI SF 226, no. 41, 2r.

[36] José de Acosta warned against the issues of duplication that might arise from regulars not
being easily subjected to episcopal jurisdiction as a result of their many privileges in
similar terms: he compared it to a body ruled by two heads, to a cloth woven both of linen
and wool, and a field sown with two different seeds (the latter two explicit references to
Deuteronomy 22:11 and Leviticus 19:19). See José de Acosta, *De procuranda Indorum
salute*. Edited by Luciano Pereña (Madrid: Consejo Superior de Investigaciones
Científicas, 1984), book 5, ch. 16 (vol. 2, 300–309).

[37] Sande had been *oidor* in the *Audiencia* of Mexico (1572–1574, 1580–1593), eventually
serving as interim president of the *Audiencia* of Mexico between the death of viceroy
Suárez de Mendoza (1583) and the appointment of his successor Pedro Moya de
Contreras (in September 1584). This period overlapped with Lobo Guerrero's career in
the Mexican Inquisition (1580–1596). See Pedro Rubio Merino, 'El presidente Francisco
de Sande y don Bartolomé Lobo Guerrero, arzobispo de Santa Fe'. In *Andalucía y
América en el siglo XVI: actas de las II Jornadas de Andalucía y América. Vol. 2.*
Edited by Bibiano Torres Ramírez and José J Hernández (Seville: Escuela de Estudios
Hispanoamericanos, 1983), 67–114; and Alberto Miramón, *El doctor Sangre* (Bogotá:
Academia Colombiana de Historia/Editorial ABC, 1954). Previously, both had been
students at the University of Salamanca and then the Colegio Mayor de Santa María de
Jesús de Sevilla, but they do not seem to have overlapped. See Javier Barrientos Grandón,
'Estado moderno y judicatura letrada en las Indias: Colegiales del de Santa María de Jesús
de Sevilla en plazas togadas'. *Ius fugit: Revista interdisciplinar de estudios histórico-
jurídicos* no. 3 (1994): 286.

[38] There was more at stake here than 'quaint and apparently rather irrelevant disputes over
matters of precedence', to paraphrase Alejandro Cañeque, who reminds us that these
actions were 'charged with dense political meaning', in 'Imaging the Spanish Empire: The

'The Greatest Blight'   183

legislation on ecclesiastical matters and sending it to Lobo Guerrero to promulgate – 'usurping the ecclesiastical jurisdiction', as Lobo Guerrero bitterly complained.[39] Nowhere did the pair clash more bitterly, however, than in the conduct of visitations.

Just as González had relied on Egas de Guzmán and Ibarra, Sande commissioned Luis Enríquez to conduct two extensive circuits of visitation to implement his designs on the ground at the turn of the century. The first, from August 1599, was a thorough tour of Tunja, completing the visitation of Egas de Guzmán. The second, starting in June 1600, was a new inspection of some sections of the province of Santafé. Records survive for his inspection of sixty-four *repartimientos* across both provinces, together with three detailed reports with summaries of his actions dispatched to Spain.[40] In these he reported that the Indigenous population had collapsed further, to about '16,000 tributaries in the province of Santafé', down from the 20,545 counted in 1595, 'and in Tunja 20,000 tributaries', a dramatic collapse from the 52,564 tributaries that López had counted in 1560.[41] In response, in addition to the usual inspections and conversations with witnesses, a key focus for Enríquez's visitations was the consolidation of smaller communities into larger towns. In this way, in May 1601 he reported having visited 42 towns in the province of Tunja, and 'reduced them to 17 larger ones, each with a parish, so that their inhabitants could have a priest continuously', year-round. He repeated the process in Santafé, where 'he reduced 83 towns of Indians, large and small, into 23 large towns'.[42] The following year, in

---

Visual Construction of Imperial Authority in Habsburg New Spain'. *Colonial Latin American Review* 19, no. 1 (2010): 29. As Sande himself put it his letter to the king of 24 May 1599, 'nowhere should the royal pre-eminence shine more than in the Indies, where their kings are unlikely ever to be and which must always be governed by their ministers', AGI SF 17 n 157, 4r. For Lobo Guerrero's perspective on his reception see his letter to the king of 16 May 1599, AGI SF 226, no. 61, 1r; and on precedence during the Mass and processions, two of 9 June 1599, AGI SF 226, no. 64a and 64b, respectively. The king issued his ruling in a rescript of 4 May 1600, AGI SF 528, 193r–194r.

[39] In a third letter of 9 June 1599, AGI SF 226, n. 64, 1r.

[40] These were collated and published by Julián Bautista Ruiz Rivera in *Fuentes*, 35–108; and discussed in *Encomienda y mita*, 37–46.

[41] Report on the visitations of Luis Enríquez, 28 April 1602, AGI SF 18, n 11a, 2v. Based the actual surviving records of the population counts in these visitations, Germán Colmenares estimated that the population of tributaries of Tunja may have been closer to 16,348 and the total to 52,313. See *La provincia*, 52–53. These figures are discussed in Francis, 'Tribute Records', 300–301. On López's figures, see Chapter 2 of this book.

[42] Report on the visitations of Luis Enríquez, 15 May 1601, AGI SF 18, n 29, 6r, 10v–11r.

184 The Friends of Ceremony and the Introduction of Reform

March, he reported visiting and reducing a further 104 small communities in Tunja 'into 41 large ones'.[43]

One such town was the new settlement of Sátiva in Tunja, created by Enríquez in February 1602, which brought together the communities of Tupachoque, Ocavita, Chitagoto, and Sátiva on a new site located roughly between their old settlements, and whose people were ordered to move to the new town and assigned a new *resguardo,* while their *encomenderos,* including Juan Sanz Hurtado, were ordered to come together to pay the year-long stipend of the Franciscan Juan de Fuentes, the new parish's priest.[44] Sátiva was far from unique: many towns and villages of modern-day Cundinamarca and Boyacá, and often their parish churches, date to Enríquez's visitation. As Guadalupe Romero has shown, of his eighty-one new towns, records survive for the establishment and layout of twenty-eight, all commissioned according to a standard plan, radiating from a central square faced by the parish church, the priest's house, and plots allocated to Indigenous notables.[45] The process also generally involved commissioning the construction of new churches, as he found existing buildings to be almost universally inadequate. As he reported in April 1602, 'in the province of Santafé there are just 4 or 6 decent churches', with a further six or seven in Tunja. 'Among the rest a few are of poor-quality brick and thatch', he explained, 'but most of them are meagre houses of adobe and mud, worse than the houses of many Indians.'[46]

Much to Lobo Guerrero's annoyance, Enríquez did all of this and more without any input from the ecclesiastical authorities. As the archbishop reminded the king in May 1599, royal legislation required *oidores* on visitation to request from the archbishop 'a delegate to accompany him' to inspect and resolve ecclesiastical matters, but Enríquez instead intruded in ecclesiastical affairs without bothering with the diocesan authorities.[47] In the parish of Suta and Moniquirá, for example, Enríquez demanded

---

[43] Report on the visitations of Luis Enríquez, 20 March 1602, AGI SF 18, n 29, 6r, 19v.

[44] Decree for the resettlement of Tupachoque, Sátiva, Ocavita, and Chitagoto, AGN VB 10 d 3, 374r–376r.

[45] All of which were transcribed and collated in her monumentally detailed study of the construction of Indigenous towns and parish churches in the New Kingdom, Guadalupe Romero Sánchez, 'Los pueblo de indios en Nueva Granada: Trazas urbanas e iglesias doctrineras' (PhD dissertation, University of Granada, 2008). See particularly chs 7 and 8.

[46] Report on the visitations of Luis Enríquez, 28 April 1602, AGI SF 18, n 11a, 1r.

[47] Letter of Archbishop Lobo Guerrero to the king, 16 December 1599, AGI SF 226, no. 66, 1r. On the issue of clerical immunity, see Cañeque, *King's Living Image,* 73.

that the parish priest give him the keys to the church, so he could inspect the building and its ornaments himself.[48] As Chapter 6 discusses, this was a central task in the conduct of ecclesiastical visitations, governed by a clear procedure and ceremony that was supposed to express the absolute power of the archbishop as ordinary in the disciplinary affairs of his church and clergy.[49] When the priest of Suta refused, the *Audiencia* ordered Lobo Guerrero to remove him from the parish. 'They did not communicate with me', he later complained, 'except to charge me to execute what they had decided.' The archbishop had no choice but to comply, and all he could do was write to the king.[50]

At the same time, Lobo Guerrero attempted to conduct visitations of his own, whether directly or through his agents, but the civil authorities undermined their efforts. One area of contention was the power of ecclesiastical visitors to fine laypeople. These were usually applied to the expenses of the visitation and to the construction or maintenance of the parish in which they were levied, but the *Audiencia* disputed their legality. When Lobo Guerrero imposed these fines himself while visiting the lowland city of Mariquita, the *Audiencia* ordered him to stop, and its agents confiscated the documentation of his visitation and arrested his notary. Frustrated, Lobo Guerrero could only complain to the king that he had been forced to abandon his visitation altogether.[51] His agents fared worse still. One Alonso Domínguez de Medellin, a *corregidor* in the province of Tunja and a close associate of Enríquez, allegedly declared to the Indigenous authorities of the province that the ecclesiastical visitor that Lobo Guerrero had sent to inspect them 'was not their judge and had no

---

[48] Report of Archbishop Lobo Guerrero on Alonso Rodríguez Medellín and Luis Enríquez, 26 January 1600, AGI SF 226, no. 69, 1r.

[49] The power of the bishop was absolute in the sense that he recognised no superior in his diocese (while all others in it exercised power only as his deputies), and also in the context of the Tridentine definition of their disciplinary and legislative powers, according to which there was no recourse of appeal even to the Papacy concerning the disciplinary decisions of a bishop in his diocese. See Trent, Sess. XIII, de ref., canon 1 (Norman Tanner, ed., *Decrees of the Ecumenical Councils* (London: Sheed & Ward, 1990), vol. 2, 699) and Traslosheros, *Iglesia, justicia y sociedad*, 82–83. On ecclesiastical visitations, see Ramos, 'Pastoral Visitations'.

[50] Report of Archbishop Lobo Guerrero on Alonso Rodríguez Medellín and Luis Enríquez, 26 January 1600, AGI SF 226, no. 69, 1v. This sits in stark contrast with the power of Lobo Guerrero's counterparts in the centres of empire in the seventeenth century. In Mexico, for Alejandro Cañeque 'the capacity of the viceroys to impose their decisions without the archbishops' consent was practically zero'. See *King's Living Image*, 82.

[51] Letter of Archbishop Lobo Guerrero to the King, 4 February 1600, AGI SF 226, no. 70, 1r.

186   *The Friends of Ceremony and the Introduction of Reform*

power to punish them', and to resist him if he tried to punish them. 'If the visitor tries to apprehend anyone', Lobo claimed Domínguez had said, 'the Indians should get together and tie him up first, and their priest too', and take them to the *Audiencia* for trial.[52] Witnesses, mostly priests, presented by Lobo Guerrero predictably claimed to have overheard their parishioners celebrating after learning of Domínguez's instructions, saying that 'there is no need to believe in what our priest says and commands any more'. Others tried to draw parallels with what they had heard about Protestant Geneva and England, where this sort of thing apparently happened all the time.[53] Worse, when Lobo Guerrero summoned Domínguez to testify about these allegations, the *Audiencia* intervened to protect him.[54] When he summoned other witnesses to testify about his actions and those of Enríquez in order to report to the king, the *Audiencia* seized the documentation, and tracked down and arrested every witness, priests and all.[55] Lobo Guerrero tried again, and when he refused to hand over the resulting papers to the *Audiencia*, Sande and his men 'surrounded his house, barred the doors, and took it from him violently, with much scandal among the people'.[56]

Lobo Guerrero was not alone in flooding the royal chancery with complaints of Sande and Enríquez. So too did the *encomenderos* and other settlers of Santafé and Tunja, who found themselves on the receiving end of their policies and initiatives. These prompted the king to send a visitor to investigate Sande's conduct, Andrés Saldierna de Mariaca, who arrived in March 1602 and promptly suspended Sande and arrested and imprisoned Enríquez, pending investigation, only for both he and Sande to die unexpectedly in September 1602, after which Enríquez went free.[57] It in this context that Enríquez penned his final report on his visitations of the two provinces, in April 1602, in which he made his fiercest condemnation of the settlers and archbishop and proposed the most radical of solutions. *Encomenderos*, he wrote, were to blame for the problems of the kingdom: they were 'the greatest blight devouring the Indians', showing little concern

---

[52] Report of Archbishop Lobo Guerrero on Luis Enríquez's visitation of the province of Tunja, 8 December 1599, AGI SF 226, 68i, at 1r and 6v.

[53] Ibid., 6v–9v.

[54] Auto of the Audiencia of Santafé, 14 January 1600, AGI SF 226, no. 68l, 1r.

[55] Report of Archbishop Lobo Guerrero on his conflict with the Audiencia, 22 April 1600, AGI SF 226, no. 74a.

[56] Report of Cristóbal Guerrero on behalf of Archbishop Lobo Guerrero, 14 March 1601, AGI SF 226, no. 78, 1v.

[57] On his visitation, see Mayorga García, *La Audiencia*, 193.

for Christianisation, 'taking and occupying the best lands', abusing their labour, and 'telling the Indians that it is they who are their real lords: that the *corregidor*, *oidor*, or president might be replaced tomorrow, but that they will endure'. In response, he argued, the king should abolish *encomenderos* altogether, revert all *encomiendas* to the crown and assign all tributes directly to the royal treasury, so that if he wished to reward the service of any settlers in future, a portion of these revenues could be assigned to them 'in the manner of a pension' but 'without the title of *encomenderos*'.[58]

It is easy to see why historians since Orlando Fals Borda have characterised these efforts by the civil authorities at the turn of the seventeenth century as the 'triumph of the royal patron over the local power of the *encomenderos*'.[59] After all, it is from Enríquez that we see the sternest condemnation of the *encomienda* from a royal official in the New Kingdom yet, and the most radical proposal to address it. But this is all it was: paper and complaints, as so many times before. Even his ambitious resettlement campaigns, like those of Tomás López and Zapata before him, were easier to plan and commission than to execute. Land was abundant and records show that laying out the grids for the new settlements cost the royal treasury only between thirty and one hundred pesos in wages for a surveyor.[60] As before, however, getting people to actually move to the new sites and remain there was another matter entirely. The next visitations of Santafé and Tunja, in the 1630s, found that far from remaining in Enríquez's 81 consolidated towns, people were still living in over 200 settlements of different sizes, even as demographic collapse continued to gather pace.[61] In the same way, González and Sande's *composiciones* and other measures to reorganise tribute collection and land tenure were the boldest to date, but these had more to do with raising much needed cash for the Anglo-Spanish War than with the imposition of a new colonial relationship on the settlers. The 'local power of the *encomenderos*' continued to be, in practice, the foundation of the power of 'the royal patron' as much as it had been in the previous century. The latter could not function – let alone triumph – without the former.

Instead, the efforts of the civil authorities had a similar effect to those of Zapata a few decades before, making strange bedfellows of a broad

---

[58] Report of the visitations of Enríquez, 24 April 1602, AGN SF 18 11A, 2v–3r.

[59] Orlando Fals Borda, 'Indian Congregations in the New Kingdom of Granada: Land Tenure Aspects, 1595–1850'. *The Americas* 13, no. 4 (1957): 333.

[60] Romero Sánchez, *Los pueblos*, 209–210.

[61] These are discussed in Chapter 6. For now, see Ruiz Rivera, *Encomienda y mita*, 49, 56.

188   *The Friends of Ceremony and the Introduction of Reform*

coalition of local opposition to these measures that included not only the *encomenderos* of the interior of the kingdom and the cabildos of their cities, but also the beleaguered Archbishop Lobo Guerrero, who wrote enthusiastically in support of their proposals. This was the context for Juan Sanz Hurtado's mission to court, through which the *encomenderos* of Santafé and Tunja presented their own diagnosis of the kingdom's woes and counter-proposal to address them in early 1603 – alongside a letter of recommendation from Lobo Guerrero himself urging the king to listen to him, for he spoke 'with one voice' on behalf of the entire kingdom.[62]

The petition Sanz presented comprised two parts, concerning temporal and spiritual affairs in turn. The first described the bleak state of the kingdom, a familiar picture of precipitous demographic collapse, especially in the lowlands, where the population, by their estimation, had crashed by 80 per cent in twenty years; of shortages of provisions and labour, uncoupling the highlands from the lowlands, and threatening the tributary and mining economies; and of growing emigration of Indigenous people from their communities, and collapse of the authority of *caciques*.[63] But far from being caused by *encomenderos* and settlers – they argued – all these issues were to be blamed on the efforts of successive administrators to displace them, imposing further obligations on Indigenous people in the process. Demographic collapse – they alleged – was the result of 'pestilences of smallpox and measles', and from ever growing colonial pressures, particularly the introduction of the *requinto* tax ('a knife that has destroyed their lives') and of *corregidores* ('known here as *requinto* collectors'), which pushed Indigenous people to breaking point, resulting in growing emigration, lower birth rates, and even mass suicides. It was these innovations that should be rolled back, and not the *encomienda*. This, they argued, predictably, should instead be strengthened and made permanent, for no *encomendero* would run their subjects to the ground with no regard for sustainability if they knew that their position would be inherited by their children and grandchildren and be 'their own lifeblood, substance, and honour'.[64]

That *encomenderos* would rally to defend the *encomienda* and its privileges should surprise precisely no one, but what is more interesting

---

[62] Lobo Guerrero to the king, 5 June 1602, AGI SF 226, n. 84, 1r.

[63] Hurtado, *Supplica* (AGI SF 60, n 44), 1r–2v.

[64] Ibid., 9r. As for the crisis of the lowlands, they argued, this should be addressed by subsidising the importation of enslaved Africans to replace Indigenous labourers in mines and other occupations.

The Coming of the Jesuits 189

about their petition was the second part, their assessment of the religious affairs of the kingdom and their proposal for their reform. Here they painted a picture of negligible progress in Christianisation, resulting from mediocre instruction and the depredations of ill-educated, undisciplined, and venal priests and administrators, and from the failure of the authorities to discipline and rein them in. Far from fulfilling the monarchy's self-declared aim and justification for empire, in the form it had taken until now Christianisation was in fact undermining the kingdom. Quite simply, 'the principal cause for the consumption of the Indians has been and remains the preaching of the holy Gospel and our desire to make these idolaters into Christians'. This had made the missionary project entirely counter-productive. 'Its proponents, lacking what it takes for such ministry, have been and remain a blazing thunderbolt and powerful instrument for the will of Satan', rather than a force for good.[65]

In response, what was needed was a complete overhaul of the church and its missionary project. The effort to congregate Indigenous people into towns should be completed, but in consultation with Indigenous leaders, and only in sites where large groups were known to have already been able to make a living. Once settled in the new towns, their instruction should not be in the hands of the mendicants, who had disgraced themselves and should be sent back to their convents to reflect on their vows, but instead run by Neogranadian-born secular priests. Because these might need some help, owing to their imperfect educations – after all, they lamented, 'there have been few professors to teach in our wretched kingdom' – these should be assisted by members of one of the new discalced orders, 'or by fathers from the Society of Jesus, whose fruits are already known across the world'. These should also set up schools in Santafé and Tunja to teach Indigenous and Spanish children – perhaps fifty of each – who could then teach their elders, bringing Indigenous people into the faith and improving the behaviour of Spaniards.[66] Only this way could the kingdom be saved.

THE COMING OF THE JESUITS

In the historiography of Peru, Bartolomé Lobo Guerrero is generally regarded as a strong figure who initiated the first systematic, centrally organised campaign for the extirpation of idolatry in the archdiocese of

---

[65] Sanz Hurtado, *Supplica* (AGI SF 60, n 44), 10r–12r, 4v–5r.
[66] Ibid., 14v–16r.

190   *The Friends of Ceremony and the Introduction of Reform*

Lima, where he served as archbishop after leaving the New Kingdom (1609–1622).[67] Lobo Guerrero – the story goes – arrived from Santafé already armed with 'convictions and inclinations toward the forceful reform of Indian religiosity'.[68] This made him especially receptive to the ideas of a group of missionaries who favoured a similar approach, including Francisco de Ávila, whom he met within days of his arrival, and a group within the Society of Jesus that included Juan Sebastián de la Parra, Pablo José de Arriaga, and Diego Álvarez de Paz.[69] This Jesuit connection was crucial, given that 'during his time in New Granada (1599–1607), Lobo' – apparently – 'demonstrated a particular desire to work with the Society of Jesus in the investigation and destruction of Indian religious error'.[70] The result was that over the next few years, Lobo Guerrero, this group of Jesuits, and the viceroy, the Marquis of Montesclaros, were able to promote an approach to Christianisation that prioritised forceful means to promote the reform of the religious life of Indigenous peoples, transforming the 'personally motivated and regional initiative' of Ávila in Huarochirí into 'an intermittent archiepiscopal enterprise' that would assail Indigenous parishes over the next century. More broadly, it led to the emergence of a religious atmosphere that favoured extirpation.[71]

The shadow that Lobo Guerrero's career in Peru casts on his time in New Granada is problematic. For a start, the feeble figure of the first years of his time in Santafé stands in stark contrast to that of the powerful Peruvian extirpator, capable of asserting his will on the most important diocese in South America and reshaping it to fit his priorities and preoccupations. Lobo Guerrero would come to wield significant influence over the reform of the New Kingdom soon enough, but only with the support and collaboration of many others. More significantly, given his traditional portrayal in the historiography of Peru as a dyed-in-the-wool advocate of 'forced conversion as a means of eliminating the Indians' fidelity to the traditional divinities', it would be natural to expect him to put forwards similar policies in the New Kingdom as soon as he had the chance; and yet, no such campaign against Indigenous 'idolatry' developed in the region under Lobo Guerrero or his successors, and the

---

[67] For an outline of this aspect of Lobo Guerrero's archiepiscopate in Lima (1609–1622), and this 'First Campaign' according to the nomenclature and periodisation proposed by Pierre Duviols, see *La lutte*, 147–161.

[68] Mills, *Idolatry*, 27.   [69] Duviols, *La lutte*, 152–153.   [70] Mills, *Idolatry*, 27.

[71] Ibid., 26–36. For a more recent analysis of Ávila's 1609 meeting with Lobo Guerrero and its aftermath, see John Charles, *Allies at Odds: The Andean Church and Its Indigenous Agents, 1583–1671* (Albuquerque: University of New Mexico Press, 2010), 132–139.

The Coming of the Jesuits

191

strategies he sponsored in fact advocated the opposite.[72] His background, his relationship to the Jesuits, and the circumstances of his alliance with Borja all deserve closer attention.

Lobo Guerrero came from different circumstances to his Neogranadian predecessors. Barrios and Zapata had been Franciscan reformers, and the latter had spent considerable time in Peru introducing reforms through disciplinary methods. Once archbishop, Zapata sought to use his new powers – not least the power to ordain new priests – to full effect. Lobo Guerrero had different ideas. A doctor of canon law, he had been an academic in Salamanca and later Seville, where he had risen to the position of rector of the Colegio de Santa María de Jesús.[73] In 1580, he had had been sent to Mexico to serve as *fiscal*, or prosecutor, for the Mexican Inquisition, becoming inquisitor in 1593, and eventually the most senior official in the institution at the time of his appointment to the see of Santafé in 1596.[74] By then, he had developed close links to the Jesuits and to their provincial in New Spain, Esteban Páez. One of his first acts after his consecration as bishop, even before setting off for New Granada, was to ordain the Jesuit novice Francisco de Figueroa to the priesthood, at Páez's request.[75] Lobo Guerrero's close links to the Jesuits dated from Mexico, and he sought to take advantage of them in his new appointment. Rather than setting off for his new see immediately, Lobo Guerrero spent some time in Mexico preparing for his new mission and convincing Páez to allow two Jesuits to accompany him, and to petition his superiors in Rome to allow them to establish a permanent presence in Santafé.[76] It was only after this request was approved by Rome that Lobo

---

[72] Charles, *Allies at Odds*, 134.

[73] See Gil González Dávila, *Teatro eclesiástico de la primitiva iglesia de las Indias Occidentales, vidas de sus arzobispos y obispos, y cosas memorables de sus sedes* (Valladolid: Universidad de León, Junta de Castilla y León, Consejería de Educación y Cultura, 2001), vol. 2, 15; and Mills, *Idolatry*, 27.

[74] Lobo Guerrero was not the king's first choice. He had appointed the Dominican Andrés de Caso in 1595, also an Inquisitor in Mexico. Caso had originally accepted, but later declined the appointment, perhaps with something more illustrious in mind. In 1603 he was appointed bishop of León. See Juan Manuel Pacheco, *La consolidación de la iglesia, siglo XVII. Historia extensa de Colombia. Vol. 13, part 2* (Bogotá: Academia Colombiana de Historia, 1975), 29.

[75] On 20 September 1597. Ibid., 29. On Francisco Figueroa (1573–1623), see José del Rey Fajardo, *Biblioteca de escritores jesuitas neogranadinos* (Bogotá: Editorial Pontificia Universidad Javeriana, 2006), 236.

[76] This is described in an unsigned and undated 'Descripción del Nuevo Reino de Granada', a document probably written around 1600 by one or both of the two Jesuits, Medrano and Figueroa, who accompanied Lobo Guerrero to Santafé (ARSI NR&Q 14, 1r–20v).

192   *The Friends of Ceremony and the Introduction of Reform*

Guerrero set off for Santafé with Francisco de Figueroa and a second Jesuit, Alonso de Medrano, at the end of April 1598, almost two years after his appointment.[77]

Lobo Guerrero installed the two Jesuits in Santafé and began to rely on them for various tasks – even to the exclusion of the regular and secular clergy of the archdiocese. This bears a striking resemblance to the strategy of Viceroy Francisco de Toledo, who on his arrival in Peru fostered the Jesuits, installed them – not without controversy – in a couple of Indigenous parishes, and relied on them in his plans for reform, notably during the general visitation he soon conducted of his viceroyalty.[78] Lobo Guerrero would do much the same, starting by taking these Jesuits with him in his initial abortive visitation of the archdiocese of Santafé as secretaries and interpreters.[79] Although later abandoned in the fallout of the archbishop's row with the civil authorities, the visitation was nevertheless revealing of the state of Christianisation in the kingdom, the lack of a systematic language policy, the independence of the regular clergy, and the priorities of missionaries around the region, including their attitudes to admitting Indigenous people to the sacraments and participation in other aspects of everyday Christian devotion. The reports that emerged from these visitations were used by Lobo Guerrero to lobby the king, and by the two Jesuits their Roman superiors, to establish a permanent presence in the New Kingdom and to send reinforcements, arguing that 'no other remedy could morally be found' to the ills of the

This text has been attributed to Lobo Guerrero himself by J. Michael Francis (in '"La tierra clama por remedio": la conquista espiritual del territorio muisca'. *Fronteras de la Historia* 5 (2000): 99), but while it is difficult to be certain of its authorship, it is almost entirely certain that it was not Lobo Guerrero. The text refers to Lobo Guerrero in the third person, to Jesuits and the Society in the first, and has the style and forms of address that are characteristic of other Jesuit correspondence from the period. This is particularly clear in the latter portions of the text. Pacheco attributes it to both Medrano and Figueroa, which seems as close as we can get to its authorship. See Pacheco, *La consolidación*, 30.

[77] 'Descripción', c. 1600, ARSI NR&Q 14, 9r.

[78] Their relationship only began to cool after 1576, for reasons discussed later. See Aliocha Maldavsky, *Vocaciones inciertas: misión y misioneros en la provincia jesuita del Perú en los siglos XVI y XVII* (Seville; Lima: Consejo Superior de Investigaciones Científicas; Instituto Francés de Estudios Andinos; Universidad Antonio Ruiz de Montoya, 2012), 37–40. Also Xavier Albó, 'Jesuítas y culturas indígenas: su actitud, métodos y criterios de aculturación'. *América Indígena* 26 (1966), 258ff.

[79] As these Jesuits themselves reported in 'Descripción', c. 1600, ARSI NR&Q 14, 11v–12v.

The Coming of the Jesuits

New Kingdom of Granada 'than to bring the Society to this land', as the means to 'rescue it from its wretched darkness'.[80]

These requests initially fell on deaf ears, even after Figueroa crossed the Atlantic in 1601 to seek support for their initiative personally, with detailed reports and even a proof-of-concept grammar and catechism of the 'Muisca language', discussed in Chapter 5.[81] As late as September 1602, the king continued to dismiss the archbishop's requests, arguing that if he was concerned about 'how poorly taught and indoctrinated the natives of the Kingdom are' he should rely on the 'many orders and very respected people' already there.[82] What brought about the change was the petition of the *encomenderos* of the kingdom and the lobbying of Juan Sanz Hurtado, who took advantage of his time in court to present his ideas widely.

Among the people Sanz met was the influential aristocrat Juan de Borja y Armendía, who served as *mayordomo* to the king's grandmother, the dowager Holy Roman Empress Maria of Austria, and who was appointed the new president of the *Audiencia* of Santafé in August 1604.[83] Borja quickly became an enthusiastic supporter of their plans for reform, and – no doubt in part as a result of his family connections, as the grandson of Francis Borgia, third Jesuit superior general – not only shared the archbishop's conviction that the Jesuits should play a key role in these efforts, but also had the ear of the Jesuit authorities in Rome, who soon began to receive regular petitions from the new president for support of their plans.[84] This was how the first batch of six Jesuits – four priests and two brothers – was finally sent to the New Kingdom in 1604 with instructions to establish a new vice-province, to be led by one Diego de Torres Bollo, an experienced and ambitious reformer who would later go on to be one of the architects of the Jesuit missions of Paraguay, but who currently found himself effectively exiled from Peru by his opponents.

---

[80] They visited the towns of Fontibón, Bojacá, Cajicá, Chía, la Serrezuela, and Suba and Tuna. Ibid., 12r–14v (quotation at 12v).

[81] The recently rediscovered *Arte de la lengva mosca*. On Figueroa and his mission, see Rey Fajardo, *Biblioteca*, 236. On the arrival of this first crop of new Jesuits, the draft of the 1604–1605 *littera annua*, ARSI NR&Q 12 I, 32v.

[82] King to Lobo Guerrero, 9 September 1602, AGI SF 528, 197v–198r.

[83] See papers of Borja's appointment as president of the New Kingdom, 11 August 1604, AGI Indiferente 481, lib. 1, 296v. Borja would come to rely on Sanz Hurtado for various tasks during his long term in office. On this relationship, see Borja's letter to the king in his support of 10 June 1617, in AGI Escribanía 1020B, 11r–16r.

[84] Even if, as in March 1608, they had to deny his request owing to a dearth of available candidates. ARSI NR&Q 1–2, 3v.

194 *The Friends of Ceremony and the Introduction of Reform*

As Aliocha Maldavsky has shown, by the beginning of the seventeenth century the Jesuits of the province of Peru, which then covered most of Spanish South America, were deeply divided. The question at the root of the conflict concerned the role that the Society should play in the New World, particularly in relation to Indigenous people.[85] This was not a new debate. The Jesuits of Peru had long been divided on the roles and responsibilities they should take: whether they should actively hold cure of souls in Indigenous parishes; something less involved, such as concentrating on the education of the children of Indigenous elites; even less, limiting their involvement to occasional itinerant missions; or even minister primarily to Spaniards instead.[86] These old divisions, never resolved, rose to prominence once again at the turn of the century, when the Jesuits of Peru came together to deliberate on their affairs in their Provincial Congregation of 1600.[87] The debate there concerned the division of the province of Peru, separating the regions of Chile, Tucumán, and Paraguay from the province's Central Andean heartlands and establishing them as an independent province of their own. Because these regions had been the focus of much Jesuit missionary activity since the 1580s, spinning off these regions also meant shedding much of the province's missionary focus along with them, breathing new life into the old debate over the nature and shape of Jesuit involvement in missionary activity in South America.[88]

By now, two camps had emerged, broadly composed of those who believed that the Jesuits' priority in Peru should be missionary activity among Indigenous people – holding more Indigenous parishes and conducting itinerant missions – and those who favoured focusing on the Spanish.[89]

---

[85] Maldavsky, *Vocaciones inciertas*, 92–100, also Giuseppe Piras, 'El P. Diego de Torres Bollo: Su programa, su partido y sus repercusiones'. In *Sublevando el virreinato: documentos contestatarios a la historiografía tradicional del Perú Colonial*. Edited by Laura Laurencich Minelli and Paulina Numhauser (Quito: Abya-Yala, 2007), 125–156.

[86] These four options were had been accepted by the First Provincial Congregation of the Jesuits of Peru, held in 1576 under the leadership of José de Acosta. See Maldavsky, *Vocaciones inciertas*, 75. On these 'missions to the countryside', see John W. O'Malley, *The First Jesuits* (Cambridge, MA: Harvard University Press, 1993), 126ff; and Louis Châtellier, *The Religion of the Poor: Rural Missions in Europe and the Formation of Modern Catholicism, c.1500–c.1800* (Cambridge: Cambridge University Press, 1997), 9ff.

[87] Maldavsky, *Vocaciones inciertas*, 92.

[88] For Maldavsky, 'dividing the province and separating from the frontier missions meant reducing the range of missionary activities for the Jesuits of the province that would continue to call itself Peru'; it 'displaced its missionary identity'. *Vocaciones inciertas*, 72–73.

[89] Letter of Esteban Páez to General Acquaviva, 1 May 1601, compiled in Antonio de Egaña and Enrique Fernández, *Monumenta Peruana VII (1600–1602)* (Rome: Institutum historicum Societatis Iesu, 1981), 478–482, at 480. See Piras, 'Diego de Torres Bollo', 126ff.

The Coming of the Jesuits

The first was headed by Diego de Torres Bollo, who had arrived in Peru two decades earlier and spent much of his career ministering to Indigenous people, first in their Indigenous parish of Julí and later from the colleges of Cuzco, Quito, and Potosí. From as early as the 1580s, Torres had been a passionate advocate within the order for keeping their Indigenous parishes and even accepting more.[90] The second, by his rival Juan Sebastián de la Parra, who had taken a different path, serving as rector of the Jesuit colleges in Potosí and Lima before serving as head of the province.[91] After much disagreement, the Provincial Congregation of 1600 elected Torres procurator and entrusted him with the mission of travelling to Rome to lobby for the division of the province of Peru.

Torres crossed the Atlantic the following year and remained in Rome until 1604, developing links to influential reformers and gaining supporters for the Paraguayan project within and beyond his order.[92] The result was that the Jesuit authorities in Rome approved the division of the Province of Peru, appointed Torres as the new provincial of the Province of Paraguay, Chile, and Tucumán, and sent him back across the Atlantic to set up his new province as the head of fourteen Jesuits, including the phenomenally well connected reformer, Martín de Funes, former tutor to the queen, Margaret of Austria, and close correspondent of leading cardinals.[93] It was at this point that Torres's opponents in Peru, led by Sebastián de la Parra, decided to strike. They had not been able to prevent his election as procurator in 1600 or his trip to Rome, but when he passed through Lima they were able to convince Esteban Páez – Lobo Guerrero's old ally from Mexico, who had since become the head of the Peruvian province – to stop him from going to Paraguay and send him to the 'wretched darkness' of the New Kingdom instead.[94]

With this, Páez killed two birds with one stone: he answered the pleas for Jesuits from his old supporter Lobo Guerrero, and rid himself – at least temporarily – of the troublesome Torres Bollo and the Paraguayan

---

[90] On Diego de Torres Bollo (1551–1638), see Giuseppe Piras, *Martin de Funes S. I. (1560–1611) e gli inizi delle riduzioni dei gesuiti nel Paraguay* (Rome: Edizioni di Storia e letteratura, 1998), 41ff and 'Diego de Torres Bollo'. Also Rey Fajardo, *Biblioteca*, 689–690.

[91] Maldavsky, *Vocaciones inciertas*, 94–95.

[92] This included Cardinals Federico Borromeo and Cesare Baronio, confessor to Clement VIII. Piras, 'Diego de Torres Bollo', 126–127.

[93] The approval came on 9 February 1604. Ibid., 130–131. On Funes see Piras, *Martin de Funes*.

[94] Piras, *Martin de Funes*, 88.

196   *The Friends of Ceremony and the Introduction of Reform*

project that was causing such division in Peru.[95] Torres's opponents would remain entrenched in Lima, and it was precisely this faction of Jesuits that would receive Lobo Guerrero there towards the end of the decade: Torres's old rival Juan Sebastián de la Parra, who by then had been elected provincial for the second time, Diego Álvarez de Paz, and their ally Pablo José de Arriaga.[96] That alliance would result in the development of idolatry visitations as a centrally organised archiepiscopal venture and key feature of ecclesiastical politics in that region.[97]

For the New Kingdom of Granada, however, the result of these machinations was that in 1605 two immensely influential Jesuits – Torres Bollo and Funes – arrived in Santafé with a very particular vision of how evangelisation should be conducted, a desire to work among Indigenous people in the parishes even on a permanent basis, and broad experience in missionary theatres around the New World and the Old.[98] This brings us full circle to the joint letter that Borja and Lobo Guerrero sent the king in mid August 1606: a proposal that outlined a vision for the reformation of the New Kingdom of Granada first articulated by the *encomenderos* and settlers of Santafé and Tunja, given shape by the archbishop and the president, and fully articulated and developed in collaboration with Diego de Torres Bollo, Martín de Funes, and the other Jesuits. Their plan deserves a closer look.

THE PLAN FOR REFORM

In their proposal of 1606, Lobo Guerrero and Borja identified three areas in need of remedy: the lack of education and lax behaviour of the clergy, the corruption of the Spanish laity, and the dismal state of the

---

[95] It would take another two years for Torres Bollo to obtain permission to continue to Paraguay, where he travelled in 1607. Rey Fajardo, *Biblioteca*, 690; Piras, 'Diego de Torres Bollo', 131.

[96] Duviols, *La lutte*, 153.

[97] For Aliocha Maldavsky, the division of the Jesuit province of Peru 'represents a real watershed ... by dividing into two provinces the frontier missions that gave rise to the reducciones of Paraguay [in the first, and in the second] the activities of evangelisation of the Indians already considered Christians, which led to the participation of the Jesuits in the visitations for the extirpation of idolatry' in Peru. *Vocaciones inciertas*, 69. Analyses such as this, of course, neglect the third province that was carved out of the early Jesuit province of Peru in the early seventeenth century: New Granada and Quito.

[98] I am indebted to Guillermo Wilde and Andrés Castro Roldan for highlighting the centrality of Martín de Funes and Diego de Torres Bollo to the establishment of the Jesuit missions in Paraguay and the Congregation of Propaganda Fide.

The Plan for Reform
197

Christianisation of Indigenous people. The first they could begin to remedy easily enough. They had already reopened a diocesan seminary a few months before, and now the pair proposed placing it 'under the discipline and government of the fathers of the Society' to foster a new generation of properly trained and disciplined priests. Their general 'lack of doctrine', moreover, could be addressed by establishing chairs to teach seminarians and priests not just Indigenous languages, as had been the case since the 1580s, but also Latin, arts, and theology – all of which were absent in the region. For this purpose, they asked the crown for 3,000 pesos to establish a Jesuit college in the city.[99] The other two problems were more complex. To begin to deal with them, the pair proposed overhauling the ecclesiastical legislation of the kingdom, to serve as a 'general remedy' and foundation for reforms. For this they planned to hold the first diocesan synod for half a century, in which they would 'receive' the legislation of the Third Provincial Council of Lima, of 1582–1583, which the Jesuits had brought with them, and which had been 'approved by the Holy See, Your Majesty, and 23 years of experience'.[100] This would avoid the difficulties of holding a provincial council in Santafé for some time, and allow the reform of the church to begin at once.

In what concerned Indigenous people more specifically, the reformers proposed implementing three strategies advanced by Lima III. First, they would round up all the 'priests of idols and sorcerers that are here known as *xeques* and *mohanes*', and enclose them in a building in the city of Santafé where they could live for the rest of their lives, out of harm's way.[101] They also advocated for a renewed emphasis on the use of Indigenous languages for religious instruction and the production of standardised translations of catechetical texts – explored in greater detail in Chapter 5 – which the Jesuits had already started to prepare. Third, recalling the request of Sanz Hurtado and the *encomenderos* of the

---

[99] Letter of Archbishop Lobo Guerrero and President Borja to the king, 17 August 1606, AGI SF 226, no. 103, 1r.

[100] Ibid., 2r–2v.

[101] This separation of 'sorcerers' from the rest of the laity, and their permanent isolation, had been ordered by Lima III 'so that they could not with their contact and communication infect the rest of the Indians'. See Constitutions of Lima III, actio 2a, ch. 42, compiled in Rubén Vargas Ugarte, 'Tercer concilio provincial limense'. In *Concilios Limenses (1551–1772)* (Lima: Tipografía Peruana, 1951), vol. 1, 340. This requirement had first been introduced by the Second Provincial Council of Lima in 1567 (Sess. 3, cap. 107, compiled in Ibid., 254), but by Lima III's own admission never implemented.

198   *The Friends of Ceremony and the Introduction of Reform*

kingdom, they called for the successors of *caciques* be educated in a school run by the Jesuits, 'where they can grow as new plants in the faith and Christian devotion, and forget their superstitions', so that they could later set a good example to their subjects, and serve as allies and agents of reform.[102] If these policies seem like a straightforward implementation of a Peruvian template in a new context that is, in large part, deliberate. In presenting their proposals, the reformers minimised the complexity and innovation of their designs. Instead, they highlighted the continuities with existing precedent to neutralise potential opposition to their more contentious initiatives. Nowhere is this clearer than in their final and most controversial proposal: to use the Jesuits to overhaul the administration of Indigenous parishes.

In their letter, the president and the archbishop petitioned the crown for as many Jesuits as possible to be sent to New Granada, who, on arrival, were 'to be divided in pairs or in trios, and deployed in Indigenous towns', where they could master Indigenous languages. In doing so they would 'perform the office of priests', but only temporarily – 'until they have instructed [the Indians] well in the faith and Christian customs' – before leaving the parishes in capable hands and repeating the process elsewhere, 'returning them after they have been reformed'.[103] In reality, what the reformers had in mind was for the Jesuits to hold a number of parishes indefinitely, to serve as laboratories for new missionary methods and initiatives, which would then be extended and introduced across the archdiocese through legislation, frequent rounds of ecclesiastical visitations, and the support of the civil authorities and *encomenderos*. These would also serve as sites for the Jesuits to engage with Indigenous languages, and to train their own members in the sorts of missionary

---

[102] AGI SF 226, no. 103, 1v. This third proposal also had Torres's fingerprints all over it. Whilst on his mission to the Holy See at the beginning of the decade, Torres had been approached by the head of the Council of the Indies, the Count of Lemos, to voice his thoughts on how best to proceed with the evangelisation of the Indigenous peoples of the New World. The proposal included precisely the idea of 'founding in the seat of each diocese a seminary school for the education of the sons of caciques who are to succeed them', where they were to be taught 'the things of our faith and Christian *policía*'. See his 'Memorial sobre el recto gobierno de las Indias', c. 1603, compiled in Enrique Fernández, ed., *Monumenta Peruana VIII (1603–1604)* (Rome: Institutum Historicum Societatis Iesu, 1986), 458–482, at 466. On this text, see Juan Carlos Zuretti, 'Un precursor de los derechos humanos en el Tucumán del siglo XVI: El padre Diego de Torres Bollo SJ'. *Teología: revista de la Facultad de Teología de la Pontificia Universidad Católica Argentina* 57 (1991): 16 and Piras, 'Diego de Torres Bollo', 128ff.

[103] Letter of Archbishop Lobo Guerrero and President Borja to the king, 17 August 1606, AGI SF 226, no. 103, 2r.

The Plan for Reform

activity that Torres Bollo and his allies wanted to foster among their order. The experiment was, in fact, already under way: Lobo Guerrero and Borja had given the Jesuits the parish of Cajicá, near Santafé, in 1605 and they had been running it ever since.

The reformers also had to convince the Jesuit authorities in Rome, which meant wading into the old controversy over the kind of missionary activity that was desirable, or indeed permissible, to the Jesuits in the New World. In the 1570s, the Jesuits of Peru had reluctantly agreed to accept a small number of parishes in Peru under pressure from viceroy Toledo, but many in the order were opposed to the decision. These included the influential José de Acosta, then provincial, who was uneasy with regulars of any sort holding parishes, least of all the Jesuits.[104] Holding the cure of souls was expressly forbidden by the constitutions that governed the society.[105] This had not, however, deterred Torres Bollo, who had not only supported taking on additional parishes in Peru since the 1580s, but had also spent much of the 1590s lobbying for the establishment of an even more permanent and ambitious cure of souls – what would become the famous Jesuit missions of Paraguay.[106] Now it fell to him to convince their Roman superiors to go along with the plan for Santafé. In a draft of their earliest annual report – *littera annua* – for 1605, Torres mentioned that two Jesuits number had been sent 'on a mission to a large Indian town belonging to the crown, called Cajicá, holding the office of priests for the period of the mission', and that two more had joined them later,

---

[104] Acosta discussed the issue of regulars first, arguing that jurisdictional confusion might cause problematic duplication and disorder, and that it went against the rules of the mendicants. He also identified additional issues specific to the Jesuit constitutions. In the end, he had accepted the limited concession of holding two parishes, but asserted that 'in holding parishes we do little for the salvation of the Indians' – a policy he contrasted with his preferred method of short-term missions. See *De procuranda*, book 5, ch. 16 on regulars, chs 17–20 on Jesuits, and ch. 21 on missions (= vol. 2, 300–335). On this see Maldavsky, *Vocaciones inciertas*, 59ff. Others have highlighted how Acosta's position was in practice more nuanced, e.g. Alexandre Coello de la Rosa, 'La doctrina de Juli a debate (1575–1585)'. *Revista de Estudios Extremeños* 63, no. ii (2007): 951–990.

[105] The constitutions of the order strictly forbade holding the cure of souls. *The Constitutions of the Society of Jesus and Their Complementary Norms: A Complete English Translation of the Official Latin Texts*. Edited by John W. Padberg (St Louis, MO: The Institute of Jesuit Sources, 1996), part 6, ch. 3, §588 (p. 259). On this issue in Peru, see Maldavsky, *Vocaciones inciertas*, 61; and Norman Meiklejohn, *La iglesia y los Lupaqas de Chucuito durante la colonia* (Cuzco: Centro de Estudios Rurales Andinos "Bartolomé de las Casas", Instituto de Estudios Aymaras, 1988), 194ff.

[106] On these, see Guillermo Wilde, *Religión y poder en las misiones de guaraníes* (Buenos Aires: Editorial SB, 2009).

200 *The Friends of Ceremony and the Introduction of Reform*

'to help them and learn the language in that town'.[107] By the time he composed the final version, Torres leaned more heavily still on the language argument: they had 'taken charge of a town of the king', he explained, 'mainly because we have found no other means for our own to know the language, which is the most difficult one known in the Indies'.[108]

Claudio Acquaviva, the superior general, was not keen, reminding the Jesuits of Santafé 'that it is not in accordance with the Institute of the Society to take charge of *doctrinas* permanently' – but, in the end, as in Peru, the archbishop and civil authority were able to convince the superior general to concede a compromise. In June 1608, Acquaviva agreed to allow the Jesuits of Santafé to keep their parishes temporarily, in the manner of a mission, until the laity was 'informed in the faith and Christian life' – for which he provided a series of instructions and requirements. Then, when a replacement was appointed, they were to 'move to another town and parish which has the same needs as the first'.[109] The compromise would, in fact, be the thin end of a wedge and the beginning of a much more permanent arrangement. That same year, in 1608, the Jesuits of Santafé had in fact obtained a second parish, the larger town of Fontibón. Further negotiations capped the number of parishes they could take on to two, and in 1615 when they obtained the parish of Duitama in Tunja they returned that of Cajicá. They would later exchange that for Tópaga and eventually obtain Tunjuelo, holding their parishes for years and even decades at a time.[110]

[107] Only a fragment of this document survives, and it is not signed, but it seems to have a draft of the annual letter that was eventually sent by Torres in September 1605. ARSI NR&Q 12 I, 35r.

[108] Jesuit *littera annua* for 1604–1605, dated 6 September 1605, ARSI NR&Q 12 I, 22r. Notably, to highlight the importance of this work, Torres neglected to mention the progress that had been made in learning Indigenous languages in New Granada until this point, deliberately. This is discussed in greater detail in Chapter 5.

[109] Instructions of Acquaviva concerning Indigenous parishes in Santafé, 10 June 1608, ARSI NR&Q 1–2, 6r–6v, at 6r.

[110] Torres Bollo had been behind a similar strategy in Peru. There the Jesuits had grudgingly accepted the parish of Juli in Chucuito in 1576 as a personal arrangement, which Torres Bollo seems to have been instrumental in turning into a more permanent one by appealing to the need for a base from which to learn Indigenous languages. See Meiklejohn, *La iglesia y los Lupaqas*, 207. In Santafé, the Jesuits held the parish of Cajicá until 1615, when they gave it up for that of Duitama in the province of Tunja. See their *littera annua* for 1615 (ARSI NR&Q 12 II, 218v). They held Duitama until 1636, when they exchanged it for that of Tópaga. Around 1617 they obtained Tunjuelo (Suit concerning Duitama, 1619, AGN C&O 20 d 21, 24r), which they retained until 1649, when they abandoned it as a result of a dearth of both parishioners and priests.

'LITTLE ELSE TO ADD'

There was a similar strategy of emphasising continuity and downplaying complexity in the legislation of the Second Synod of Santafé, the cornerstone of the new programme of religious reform, which concluded after a brisk two weeks of sessions on 2 September 1606. In broad terms, the legislation adapted the constitutions of Lima III, as the text itself claimed – 'with little else to add'.[111] But this concealed a more subtle reality. The synod in fact emphasised those aspects of the Lima council that reflected the concerns and priorities of its principal architects – Lobo Guerrero, Borja, and their Jesuit allies – and left the rest behind. The Third Provincial Council of Lima, held over a number of sessions between August 1582 and October 1583, and marked by the development of a number of conflicts among those convened, had produced a sprawling and generally unstructured collection of constitutions discussing a variety of issues pertaining to the church of the region.[112] The constitutions of Santafé, in contrast, were composed in a little over ten days, structured in a more systematic fashion, and covered far fewer subjects.[113] In other words, the synod was an opportunity to adapt select aspects of Lima III for use in Santafé, but given the constraints of time and the clear agenda of the ecclesiastical elite that convened it, not much of a forum for discussion or the voicing of concerns by the rest of the clergy. The choice of material imported from Lima is revealing.

For a start, both Spaniards and Indians were to be required to learn the basic prayers, the sacraments, the principal mysteries of the Christian faith, 'and that all other things worshipped by other people are not God, but are lies and demons'.[114] For this purpose, the synod introduced

---

[111] 'Constituciones sinodales 1556', 226.

[112] On this structure, its causes, and its differences with the First and Second Provincial Councils of Lima, see Francesco Leonardo Lisi, *El tercer concilio limense y la aculturación de los indígenas sudamericanos: estudio crítico con edición, traducción y comentario de las actas del Concilio Provincial celebrado en Lima entre 1582 y 1583* (Salamanca: Universidad de Salamanca, 1990), 46–52, and 60ff.

[113] Lima III produced eighty-nine chapters of constitutions, distributed among the last four of five *actiones*. See Ibid., 384–388; and Vargas Ugarte, *Concilios*, vol. 1, 416–419. The synod of Santafé almost two-thirds fewer, at thirty-one chapters, in a meeting that took less than two weeks: from 21 August to 2 September 1606.

[114] 'Constituciones sinodales celebradas en la ciudad de Santafé del Nuevo Reino de Granada por el señor doctor don Bartolomé Lobo Guerrero, arzobispo del dicho Nuevo Reino, acabadas de promulgar a 2 de septiembre de 1606 años', ch. 2. In *La legislación*, 230. These requirements were copied verbatim from the constitutions of Lima, where the original text refers to '*figmenta*'. Cf. Lima III, acción 2, cap. 4 (Vargas Ugarte, 'Tercer concilio', 267).

202 The Friends of Ceremony and the Introduction of Reform

the key texts of the council of Lima for use in New Granada: the *Catecismo mayor*, the Brief catechism for Indians, and the Confessionary.[115] The latter two were to be translated into Muisca, as Chapter 5 examines, and the first was to be adapted into sermons composed in Muisca for use among Indigenous people. Every Sunday and feast day, the parish priest was to preach an explanation of doctrine, in Spanish to Spaniards and in Indigenous languages in *doctrinas*. Spaniards were to receive daily catechism during Lent, while adults in Indigenous parishes were to be catechised every Tuesday and Thursday – until the priest was satisfied – and children and the elderly daily.[116]

The text devoted an entire chapter to the reformation of the clergy.[117] Following Lima III, it banned priests from being involved in business transactions, on pain of excommunication. They were not to take part in campaigns of war against Indigenous groups, comedies and indecent plays, gambling, or close relations with women. The synod even issued regulations on appropriate dress, the length of beards, the bearing of arms, and the size of ruffs and collars. Such legislation might seem trifling, but underpinning it was a concern with discipline and the imposition of the authority of diocesan authorities over the clergy. It addressed more fundamental concerns in the same spirit. For example, the synod introduced a clear prohibition on non-residency. Secular priests were forbidden from leaving the archdiocese without the express permission of the archbishop.[118] Indeed, they were not to absent themselves from their benefices at all, except under a limited number of circumstances – to confess, or in the case of urgency; and even then, it was to require the consent of the ordinary, and the appointment of a replacement during

---

On contemporary ideas concerning sense perception and the workings of such phantasms, see MacCormack, *Religion in the Andes*, 7ff and 15–35.

[115] Lima III's 'Brief catechism for Indians' was reproduced as 'Constituciones sinodales 1606', ch. 30, 268–275. A near-contemporary translation of this text is among the anonymous Muisca materials known as Manuscript 158 of the Colombian National Library, published as María Stella González de Pérez, '*Diccionario y gramática chibcha*': *manuscrito anónimo de la Biblioteca Nacional de Colombia* (Bogotá: Instituto Caro y Cuervo, 1987).

[116] 'Constituciones sinodales 1606', ch. 2, 229–230. The exact wording of the requirement, and the confusion it has generated among historians, is discussed in detail in Chapter 5.

[117] Ibid., ch. 14, 245–249.

[118] Ibid., 246. This issue of priests leaving New Granada had long been an issue in the region, as priests left in search of better opportunities for advancement in Peru and elsewhere. This requirement is absent from the constitutions of Lima, except in what concerns those holding prebends in cathedral chapters, and provincial parish priests absenting themselves to attend celebrations in cities. See Constitutions of Lima III, actio 3a, ch. 28 and actio 4a, ch. 18, compiled in Vargas Ugarte, 'Tercer concilio' 355–356, and 369, respectively.

'*Little Else to Add*'

their absence – requirements that went beyond those of the Peruvian legislation the synod took as its model.[119] Turning to their education, the archbishop's deputies in the provinces, his vicars, were to appoint examiners to assess the training and conduct of the priests, paying special attention to their knowledge of ceremonies – another aspect that the legislation of Lima did not see the need to address.[120]

None of this, of course, was strictly innovative. It was, at face value, just the application of the requirements of Trent and Lima III, with a few adjustments. But these changes, and the careful selection of what to include, what to emphasise, and what to leave behind, fundamentally adapted the legislation to the reformers' reading of local conditions in Santafé – making this, in effect, an innovative legal translation.[121] Other adaptations are even clearer. For example, the legislation firmly subordinated the regular clergy involved in the cure of souls to the jurisdiction of the diocesan authorities. After years of jurisdictional conflict – the result of the confusion over the validity of the privileges and exemptions of the religious orders after the Council of Trent, the upheaval of the years after Zapata's death, and the chaos of the period of Lobo Guerrero's feud with President Sande – the synod devoted a whole chapter to the male religious orders, which made the new position abundantly clear. 'The said religious,' the text ordered, 'shall not say mass, preach, or hear confessions without our licence'.[122] The synod urged the regular authorities to cooperate in the programme of reform, and sought to avoid engendering a new wave of antagonism, but it was clear who was to be in charge of the missionary project. In contrast, the equivalent legislation in the constitutions of Lima is far less forceful, simply reminding regulars not to

---

[119] 'Constituciones sinodales 1606', 251. These strict requirements are absent from the Lima texts cited earlier.

[120] Ibid., ch. 12, 243. The emphasis in Lima, in contrast, was on knowledge of the catechism and Indigenous languages. Constitutions of Lima III, actio 4a, ch. 17, compiled in Vargas Ugarte, 'Tercer concilio'.

[121] Indeed, Thomas Duve encourages us to consider legal history as the history of the translation of knowledge of normativity, in which efforts of epitomisation such as this also played key roles. For a recent introduction to these ideas in English, see Thomas Duve, 'Legal History as a History of the Translation of Knowledge of Normativity'. *Max Planck Institute for Legal History and Legal Theory Research Paper Series 2022*, no. 16 (19 September 2022) and 'Pragmatic Normative Literature and the Production of Normative Knowledge in the Early Modern Iberian Empires (16th–17th Centuries)'. In *Knowledge of the Pragmatici: Legal and Moral Theological Literature and the Formation of Early Modern Ibero-America*. Edited by Thomas Duve and Otto Danwerth (Leiden: Brill, 2020), 1–39.

[122] 'Constituciones sinodales 1606', ch. 16, 253.

204 *The Friends of Ceremony and the Introduction of Reform*

perform the sacraments of baptism or marriage except when they held the office of parish priest.[123] There, an explicit assertion of the monopoly of the ordinary and the secular clergy over the cure of souls of the laity of the archdiocese seemed unnecessary.

The legislation concerning Indigenous people was also an abbreviated selection of the comprehensive legislation of Lima, that gave priority to those aspects that reflected the priorities of the reformers. The starting point, as in so much legislation of this period, was the characterisation of Indigenous people as 'new to the faith and of very limited capacity, poor, oppressed, and afflicted', and therefore in need of special protection.[124] Their faith was to be fostered and their faults corrected by instilling Christian civility and the qualities of political life – the broad range of ideas encapsulated by the contemporaneous concept of *policía*. This idea can be found in broad terms in much of the legislation of Lima III, and indeed this section of the Santafé legislation was based on a constitution from the Lima council that dealt with it more explicitly.[125] The difference is that in the latter this appeared in the very last session of the council and seems almost an afterthought, whereas in Santafé it was the very foundation of the synod's strategy. This clear, the synod then summarised several other constitutions from Lima concerning Indigenous people into four concise chapters with the same emphasis. These began by ordering parish priests to 'have great vigilance and take great care to teach them how to live politically' as a precondition for their spiritual development, and moved on to legislating on how they were to care for themselves, sleep on beds or hammocks and not the floor, how they should dress (even inside their homes), and how they should raise their children. Those found to be drunk were to be shorn, and if they were *caciques* they were to be reported to the civil authorities to receive exemplary punishment. Some of this is reminiscent of the legislation of Archbishop Zapata the previous century, but the difference is that among these hackneyed

---

[123] Constitutions of Lima III, actio 2a, ch. 12. Vargas's Spanish translation of the published text of Lima III is not entirely clear on this point, but it is much clearer in Lisi's translation of the manuscript version: Lisi, *El tercer concilio*, 132–133.

[124] 'Constituciones sinodales 1556', ch. 26, 265. On the characterisation of Indigenous people as *miserabilis* or wretched, see Thomas Duve, 'La condición jurídica del indio y su consideración como persona miserabilis en el derecho indiano'. In *Un giudice e due leggi: pluralismo normativo e conflitti agrari in Sud America*. Edited by Mario G. Losano (Milan: Dipartamento Giuridico-Politico dell'Università deglo Studi di Milano, 2004), 3–33; Estenssoro Fuchs, 'Simio de Dios'; and Cañeque, *King's Living Image*, ch. 6.

[125] 'That the Indians be taught to live politically', Lima III, actio 5, cap. 4, (Vargas Ugarte, 'Tercer concilio', 373).

'Little Else to Add' 205

markers of civility were others that reflected the new priorities of the reformers. In this way, when the synod explained that Indigenous people should be taught the habits of a Christian life, 'things pertaining to good Christians', much of it was new in the context of the New Kingdom: that Indigenous people should be taught to pray on waking and before going to sleep, to visit their parish churches to pray before work, to keep images and crosses in their houses for their private devotions, and to have rosaries and use them to pray.[126]

Indeed, a recurring emphasis of the reformers was on the importance of frequent participation in devotional activities private and public, and most significantly in the sacraments. The synod began by emphasising the importance of regular confession. The annual obligation to confess during Lent had been in place since it was introduced at the Fourth Lateran Council in 1215, but in the New Kingdom it had been largely impossible to meet for Indigenous people. This was beginning to change with a greater emphasis on Indigenous language education for priests, as Chapter 5 explores, and with growing numbers of them working in Indigenous parishes. Their task was also about to get easier, with the introduction of new translations of the Lima III confessionary a few months later. Building on this, the synod now underscored the obligation of confessors 'to understand the whole conscience of the Indians when they confess', and not to be satisfied with less 'for lack of language, or out of laziness and tiredness'. For this, the synod also revoked the licences of all confessors, pending a new examination, with which the authorities intended to check that they met these new requirements.[127] Beyond its sacramental function, confession was to also serve a more practical purpose, typical of the reconfiguration of the sacrament after Trent, as an opportunity to evaluate the progress of religious instruction.[128]

---

[126] 'Constituciones sinodales 1606', ch. 26, 265–266.

[127] Ibid., ch. 6, 234–236. This strategy was also utilised by reforming archbishops elsewhere. On Mexico see Traslosheros, *Iglesia, justicia y sociedad*, 32. Especially influential was the use of these powers by Carlo Borromeo for his reformation of Milan. See Wietse de Boer, 'The Politics of the Soul: Confession in Counter-Reformation Milan'. In *Penitence in the Age of Reformations*. Edited by Katharine Jackson Lualdi, Anne T. Thayer, and Wietse de Boer (Aldershot: Ashgate, 2000), 116–133.

[128] For Wietse de Boer, the leaders of the post-Tridentine Church 'adapted a procedure designed primarily for the redemption of the individual soul to serve what they considered the public good'. Boer, 'Politics of the Soul', 119. On the Jesuit use of the sacrament, see Michael Majer, 'Confession and Consolation: The Society of Jesus and Its Promotion of the General Confession'. In *Penitence in the Age of Reformations*. Edited by Katharine Jackson Lualdi and Anne T. Thayer (Aldershot: Ashgate, 2000),

206   *The Friends of Ceremony and the Introduction of Reform*

Confessors, 'at the beginning of confession', were to require penitents to recite 'the Creed, the Our Father, and the commandments, and at least instruct them in the principal mysteries of our holy faith'.[129]

The synod also allowed Indigenous people greater access to the Eucharist, the central sacrament of the Tridentine church. This had been expressly forbidden by the previous synod, in 1556, which had ruled it was 'not to be administered under any circumstance, except to a woman married to a Spaniard' and even then only with great care and preparation.[130] Zapata, for his part, had maintained this prohibition in 1576, 'because these Indians are most imperfect in knowing and appreciating the good that there is in this sacrament', except in the most exceptional circumstances, with the explicit approval of the archbishop himself, 'and in no other way'.[131] Hostility to administering the Eucharist to Indigenous people was by no means unique to New Granada. It remained controversial in Mexico and Peru, where it had been allowed by the legislation of its provincial councils since the 1550s and 1560s, respectively.[132] At the time, much of the controversy hinged on the question of whether the person receiving the sacrament was worthy of doing so. This required, as it did everywhere else, that communicant was in a state of grace, having said a full confession and received absolution, the essential precondition, and also that they had sufficient understanding of the significance of the sacrament and an adequate disposition to receive it.[133] But in this colonial context, it inevitably raised a more fundamental question, whether Indigenous people were capable of meeting these requirements at all. The framers of Lima III were inclined to think that Indigenous people could one day be capable but determined that they had not yet met the necessary requirements, explaining that the Eucharist had

---

184–200. On the history of individual confession from seventh-century Ireland to its Tridentine reconfiguration, see Groupe de La Bussière, *Pratiques de la confession. Des Pères du désert à Vatican II. Quinze études d'histoire* (Paris: Cerf, 1983). On the latter, also Henry Kamen, *The Phoenix and the Flame: Catalonia and the Counter Reformation* (New Haven, CT: Yale University Press, 1993), 123.

[129] 'Constituciones sinodales 1606', ch. 6, 235.

[130] 'Constituciones sinodales 1556', 26.   [131] Zapata de Cárdenas, 'Catecismo', 176.

[132] Pardo, *Mexican Catholicism* 136–137, and 145–147.

[133] It was for this reason, for example, that when Lima II relaxed the prohibition on Indigenous communion of Lima I, it specifically required priests to ascertain whether communicants 'understand the difference between this life-giving food' and ordinary bread 'as we from the faith understand'. Constitutions of Lima II, cons. 58, in Rubén Vargas Ugarte, 'Segundo concilio provincial limense, 1567–1568'. In *Concilios Limenses (1551–1772)* (Lima: Tipografía Peruana, 1951), vol. 1, 186.

'Little Else to Add'   207

not been widely administered to Indigenous people because of the 'obstacle of *borracheras*, concubinage, and especially superstitions and idolatry'.[134]

Many Jesuits took a different view.[135] For them, the question of whether to admit Indigenous people to the Eucharist was not just a matter of preparation, but also hinged on a subtler theological understanding of the sacrament. In this view, encapsulated by the influential Jesuit theologian José de Acosta, the Eucharist could play an active role in the moral improvement of Indigenous people. For a start, it could be presented to the new converts as a reward to which they should aspire, serving to incentivise them to embrace Christianity and reform their lives. More subtly and significantly, however, for Acosta and other Jesuits, receiving the sacrament would in itself have a salutary and improving effect, which would strengthen the fledgling faith of the new converts.[136] This same perspective was brought to the New Kingdom by Torres Bollo and his fellows, and is reflected in the 1606 synod, which echoed the Jesuit emphasis on the sacrament as a key pillar of missionary strategy. It was for this reason that the synod relaxed the barriers to access, allowing Indigenous people to receive it with just the approval of the archbishop's vicars – deputies, often the priests of the larger parishes, appointed by Lobo Guerrero across the archdiocese in greater numbers to help implement his reforms.[137] It also ordered priests to take special care to administer it to the dying as viaticum, and required the display of the consecrated host – the Blessed Sacrament – on the altar of every parish church so that, in its words, 'with its presence, we hope idolatry will be banished', a statement, as we will see, drawn directly from Jesuit practice.[138]

The idea of eliminating influences counter to Christianisation – to be clear – was not absent from the legislation, or indeed from the broader project of reform. It was implicit in the sections that aimed to reform the way that Indigenous people lived and behaved. Introducing *policía*, after all, was also a means to isolate people from the supposedly malign

---

[134] Lima III, actio 2a, ch. 20, in Vargas Ugarte, 'Tercer concilio', 331. See also Pardo, *Mexican Catholicism*, 146.

[135] On the Jesuit emphasis on frequent Communion, see O'Malley, *First Jesuits*, 152–157. On its integration into their missionary practice from 1540, in Châtellier, *The Religion of the Poor*, 11. On their critics in Spain, Kamen, *The Phoenix and the Flame*, 121–123.

[136] Acosta discussed the issue in *De procuranda*, book 6, chs 7–10, especially at 417–419. For a discussion of Acosta's view, see Pardo, *Mexican Catholicism*, 147–150.

[137] 'Constituciones sinodales 1606', ch. 12, 243.   [138] Ibid., ch. 8, 237–238.

208   The Friends of Ceremony and the Introduction of Reform

influences of their former environments and ways of life.[139] It was also explicit in the reformers' proposal for the removal of *xeques* and their confinement in the sort of perpetual re-education institution that had also been envisioned by Lima III. Indeed, Lobo Guerrero and the Jesuits also reported seizing and destroying Indigenous ritual objects they encountered in the course of visitations.[140] None of this, however, was at the centre of their efforts. Instead, the reformers proposed that the introduction and promotion of new practices, routines, and rituals among Indigenous people would lead them to abandon these practices and embrace Christianity without the need for this direct, punitive intervention. It was initiatives such as the display of the Blessed Sacrament in parish churches, and not campaigns of extirpation, that would become central to the development of the missionary project in the New Kingdom for decades.[141] To understand how, we must look more closely at these Jesuit parishes to see reform in practice.

THE JESUIT EXPERIMENT

The Jesuit experiment in overhauling Christianisation in the New Kingdom began in the parishes of Cajicá and Fontibón, in the province of Santafé. These were ideal sites for their purposes. They were both located near the city; both were royal *encomiendas*, which meant that there was no lay authority to contend with aside from President Borja and the towns' *caciques*, don Juan Sachigua of Cajicá and don Diego of Fontibón; and they were of a reasonable size.[142] Cajicá had a population roughly the size of a standard *reducción* town – '776 men and women, old

---

[139] It is for this reason that in his classification, Pierre Duviols classed these policies as 'preventative' measures against Indigenous heterodoxy. Duviols, *La lutte*, 248–263.

[140] The confinement of perceived corrupters of the flock had been a feature of Viceroy Toledo's approach in his general visitation of Peru in the 1570s. The Neogranadian reformers explicitly referred to the policy promoted by Lima III, which they claimed was already proving to be a great success. 'Constituciones sinodales 1556', ch. 29, 268. On the Peruvian case, see *La lutte*, 192ff. The same chapter of the synod recommended confiscating feathers, 'which are known to be a thing of superstition and of idolatry', and forbade the sale of parrots along with substances such as tobacco and *moque* 'and other superstitious things'.

[141] This is very much in line with José de Acosta's exhortation that 'although we must also seek to remove the idols from their eyes and ways of life' to 'remove the idols from their hearts ... the best means are teaching and exhortation'. Acosta, *De procuranda*, book 5, ch. 11 (vol. 2, 271).

[142] See the records of the visitations of Cajicá, 20 February 1603 (AGN VC 8 d 5, 603r), and of Fontibón, 26 July 1608, (AGN VC 12 d 10, 1021r–1022v) by Diego Gómez de Mena.

The Jesuit Experiment

and young', as per a 1603 visitation – while Fontibón had perhaps double that.[143] They also, of course, had a difficult recent history. The two towns had been at the centre of Zapata's campaign to confiscate *santuario* offerings in the 1570s, and subsequent visitors had found and confiscated further objects in the years since, including Lobo Guerrero himself, at the beginning of his time in Santafé, with the two Jesuits who had come with him from Mexico.[144] Now the two parishes would be the epicentre of the new approach.

While there would be several refinements to the Jesuit approach to managing their parishes, the broad features can already be identified in Cajicá from their arrival in 1605. One aspect was to bring their parishes up to the standards required by existing legislation, a task made easier by the fact that, unlike every other parish, the Jesuits tended to staff theirs with three priests and a novice each and could fund them independently. Their earliest reports from Cajicá claimed that they had found a parish in disarray: the roof of the church had collapsed a year earlier and lay in disrepair; the church lacked the necessary ornaments and objects required for worship; and there was no programme of religious instruction.[145] The new arrivals repaired the church, purchased the necessary equipment – standard practice, at least in theory, for any new incumbent arriving in a new parish – and established a systematic programme of catechisation.[146] For this, they ordered children and the elderly to come together in the mornings and afternoons to learn the catechism. 'In less

---

Don Diego of Fontibón was the successor of don Juan, whom we met in Chapter 3, who in turn had been heir to his uncle, don Alonso, from Chapter 1.

[143] Visitation of Cajicá by Diego Gómez de Mena, 20 February 1603, AGN VC 8 d 5, 664v. We have no contemporaneous figures for Fontibón, but Miguel de Ibarra counted a total of 1,831 inhabitants in the mid 1590s (as per Ruiz Rivera, *Fuentes*, 23) and Gabriel de Carvajal 1,092 in his visitation of July 1539 (AGN VC 12 d 10, 993v). Standard *reducción* towns were supposed to have around 800 inhabitants. See, for example, Sanz Hurtado, *Supplica* (AGI SF 60, n 44), 14v.

[144] As reported in the 'Descripción de el Nuevo Reino de Granada', c. 1600, ARSI NR&Q 14, 14v.

[145] This according to the draft of the 1604–1605 Jesuit *littera annua*, c. 1605, ARSI NR&Q 12 I, 35r, and following.

[146] The notion of the 'decorum and decency' of churches was, notably, a priority at Trent and in the instructions and legislation of Carlo Borromeo in Milan that served as a model for the legislation of the third provincial councils of Lima and Mexico. As a result, it was also a common trope in reports such as these. See Elena Isabel Estrada de Gerlero, 'Nota preliminar'. In *Instrucciones de la fábrica y del ajuar eclesiásticos [Instructiones fabricae et supellectilis ecclesiasticae Caroli S. R. E. Cardinalis Tituli S. Praxedis]*. Edited by Bulmaro Reyes Coria (Mexico City: Universidad Nacional Autónoma de México, Impr. Universitaria, 1985), XIX–XX. In Cajicá, the reforms cost a total of 1,000 ducats,

210 *The Friends of Ceremony and the Introduction of Reform*

than a month', they claimed, 'over 300 children learnt it, as did many older people who, anxious to learn, came at the times designated for children'.[147] So too in Fontibón, where 'some of the mysteries of the faith have seemed so new', as they reported in 1609, 'that they had never heard such things, especially of the resurrection of the flesh, which they find very novel'.[148]

Examining the work carried out by the Society of Jesus in Indigenous parishes necessarily involves examining the writings and reports of the Jesuit themselves, which poses methodological challenges. These require a particularly careful reading, not simply because of their immediate context of the polemic concerning obtaining and retaining these Neogranadian parishes, which frequently led the Jesuits to denigrate the efforts of previous holders and to idealise their own progress, as in the earlier quotations, or because the Jesuits – like their contemporaries – made sense of their experiences and the lives of Indigenous people through European interpretative frameworks. Rather, because there are issues specific to Jesuit materials, and particularly, as Marcus Friedrich explains, to the 'edifying correspondence': the *relationes*, or missionary reports, often meant to be widely disseminated, and the *litterae annuae*, annual letters sent to Rome that brought together reports from across each province and which were then edited, translated, compiled, published, and circulated within the society.[149]

Although these materials aimed to present factual information about their work, their principal aim was to edify, console, and encourage their readers, whether within or beyond the society, to emulate them.[150] Their

---

which were provided by the crown, through Borja. See the Jesuit *littera annua* for 1604–1605, dated 1605-09-06, ARSI NR&Q 12 I, 35r.

[147] Jesuit *littera annua* for 1604–1605, dated 6 September 1605, ARSI NR&Q 12 I, 35r, 35v.

[148] Jesuit *littera annua* for 1608–1609, dated 10 September 1609, ARSI NR&Q 12 I, 52v.

[149] On the production of the *litterae annuae*, and their place within the Jesuit system of communication, see Markus Friedrich, 'Circulating and Compiling the Litterae Annuae. Towards a History of the Jesuit System of Communication'. *Archivum Historicum Societas Iesu* 77 (2008): 3–39, who also notes how after about 1600 *litterae annuae*, as opposed to the *relationes*, came to be intended primarily for a public within the society (6–7). On Jesuit communication more broadly, see Markus Friedrich, 'Communication and Bureaucracy in the Early Modern Society of Jesus'. *Schweizerische Zeitschrift für Religions- und Kulturgeschichte* 101 (2007): 49–75.

[150] Friedrich, 'Circulating and Compiling the Litterae Annuae', 10. On the purpose of these Jesuit reports, see also Daniel T. Reff, *Plagues, Priests, and Demons: Sacred Narratives and the Rise of Christianity in the Old World and the New* (Cambridge: Cambridge University Press, 2005), 133, 215–235, and O'Malley, *First Jesuits*, 239 and 375.

The Jesuit Experiment

content and narrative structure were powerfully shaped by the rhetoric, conventions, and type scenes of the early Christian literature in which their own training, meditations, and writing were steeped: the writings of church fathers, early Christian histories, the lives of saints, and accounts of the Christianisation of Europe in late Antiquity and the early Middle Ages.[151] The time of the great miracles may have been long past, in the well-known words of José de Acosta, but edifying accounts of more quotidian miracles – from scenes of miraculous conversions and healing, to battles with demons and the destruction of ancient cairns and idols – were ubiquitous in Jesuit edifying correspondence, all carefully recounted in short, accessible, and easily excerpted narratives known as *exempla*.[152] And yet, for all their issues, it is these sources that provide the most detailed insights into the conduct of Jesuit missionary in the parishes of the New Kingdom, and the changes they introduced to Christianisation in the early decades of the seventeenth century.

Miracles aside, these show a shift in practice in three interconnected directions: a reassessment of the capacity of Indigenous people, a greater inclusion of Indigenous people in the running of their parishes, and a new emphasis on the everyday practice of Christian devotions. The first of these changes was most visible in a renewed emphasis on education – not just religious instruction, but a broader complement involving the teaching of alphabetic and pictorial literacy, music, and the introduction of parish offices and institutions as new makers of *policía* and of spiritual potential.[153] While earlier efforts had long emphasised the importance of educating Indigenous children, the amount of teaching involved was always remarkably limited. The Laws of Burgos-Valladolid of 1512–1513, for example, had only required *encomenderos* in command of fifty or more Indigenous people to teach a single young man to read, so

---

[151] This is not to say that this was not the case for other religious orders, but that they enjoyed an especially pre-eminent and influential position in the training and perspective of the Jesuits. Texts such as these had played a key role in the conversion of Ignatius Loyola himself, and they featured prominently in the *Ratio Studiorum* that formed the bedrock of Jesuit education. See O'Malley, *First Jesuits*, 313–315, 37–50, and Reff, *Plagues*, 212, 132.

[152] On miracles in Acosta, see *De procuranda*, book 2, chs 9 and 10, vol. 1, 312–330 (quotations at 327–329). *Exempla* were by no means exclusive to Jesuit writing. On the genre and their use in Mexico, see Danièle Dehouve, *Relatos de pecados en la evangelización de los indios de México (siglos XVI–XVIII)* (Mexico City: Centro de Estudios Mexicanos y Centroamericanos, 2010).

[153] Guillermo Wilde explores the introduction of a similar nexus of educational elements in the Guaraní missions, in *Religión y poder*, 51.

212   *The Friends of Ceremony and the Introduction of Reform*

that he could then teach others and help friars with evangelisation.[154] The legislation of the synod of 1556 had encouraged priests to teach the Indigenous inhabitants of 'major towns' to 'read and write, count, [and] sing' on feast days, along with learning the Spanish language, but with barely any missionary activity in the archdiocese this was hopelessly overoptimistic.[155] Zapata moderated this, ordering priests to teach just twenty or so children to read and write in every parish.[156] In contrast, Lima III ordered that more comprehensive schools be established in each Indigenous parish, a requirement also incorporated into the synod of Santafé, and the Jesuits set about demonstrating how this should be put into practice on the ground in their parishes.[157]

In Cajicá they had already followed these instructions to the letter, establishing a 'school for the children of the most notable Indians, to read and write'.[158] These were not just the children of Indigenous leaders, but a broader slice of the parish's population. In Cajicá they reported selecting '50 children, the most able', in 1605, and in 1613 they reported that the school for children in Fontibón had over one hundred pupils, 'taught to read, and write, and sing, and play flutes and viols'.[159] This sort of education was integral to the Jesuit conception of mission, but it also represented an incentive for Indigenous people to participate in Jesuit initiatives. Jesuit accounts provide glimpses of the fact that these benefits were recognised by Indigenous people even in towns not under their care. An *exemplum* from their 1611–1612 *littera annua*, for example, which described how the inhabitants of neighbouring towns had visited Cajicá on a certain feast day, and apparently been so impressed by what the Jesuits were doing in the parish that clamoured for their own parish to be run by the society – a common trope in reports of this kind – mentioned,

---

[154] 'Ordenanzas para el tratamiento de los indios', law 9, 23 January 1513, AGI Indiferente 419 lib. 4, 83r–96v, at 87v–88r.

[155] 'Constituciones sinodales 1556', 41.   [156] Zapata de Cárdenas, 'Catecismo', 152.

[157] See the Constitutions of Lima III, actio 2a, ch. 43 (Vargas Ugarte, 'Tercer concilio', 340–341), and its Neogranadian counterpart, 'Constituciones sinodales 1556', 252. This was also in keeping with Acquaviva's 1608 conditions for their involvement in Indigenous parishes, that they imitate the efforts of their fellows in 'Peru, Mexico, and the Philippines' by 'teaching the sons of the most capable Indians to read and write and sing and play diverse instruments' (ARSI NR&Q 1–2, 6r). On the use of literacy in missions in Peru, see Charles, *Allies at Odds*, 21–24.

[158] Jesuit *littera annua* for 1608–1609, dated 10 September 1609, ARSI NR&Q 12 I, 36r–60v, at 50r.

[159] On the first, see the draft of the 1604–1605 Jesuit *littera annua*, c. 1605, ARSI NR&Q 12 I, 24r–35v, at 35v. On Fontibón, Jesuit *littera annua* for 1611–1612, dated 6 June 1613, ARSI NR&Q 12 I, 61v–108v, at 79v.

The Jesuit Experiment   213

amid the self-aggrandising remarks of a Jesuit keen to impress his superiors, the request that the group made when they asked 'if they could send their children here, to be taught how to read and sing'.[160]

Jesuit education in literacy was not limited to the alphabetic, but also involved the transmission of broader visual systems of referentiality.[161] The Jesuits were key to introducing, for the first time in some parishes, devotional images for use in catechisation and the liturgy. When the Jesuits arrived in Duitama in 1615, for example, they soon set about raising funds for the purchase of votive images, importing three Spanish sculptures of the Christ Child, the Virgin of the Immaculate Conception, and St Lawrence, the patron of the parish.[162] In Tópaga, the new church was 'adorned by beautiful busts of cherubim of great stature' around the tabernacle. The main altar was adorned with a reredos with 'elaborate images in the niches, especially a beautiful one of the Our Lady the Virgin of the Immaculate Conception', while a side altar was dedicated to St Peter, and decorated with a bust of the saint.[163] Not all images were as elaborate. In 1610 the Jesuit Joseph Dadey petitioned Acquaviva from Fontibón for a 'set of the prints of Father Nadal', which 'were well known for the fruit they provide' in catechisation.[164] These were the *Evangelicae Historiae Imagines* – Images of the Gospel Story – of Jerónimo Nadal, one of the founding members of the Society of Jesus, engraved by the Wierix brothers in Antwerp in 1593, and widely used and reproduced in Jesuit missions around the world.[165] Through these images the Jesuits sought

---

[160] Jesuit *littera annua* for 1611–1612, dated 6 June 1613, ARSI NR&Q 12 I, 61v–108v, at 77r.

[161] Joanne Rappaport and Thomas Cummins remind us of the importance of considering a more capacious understanding of literacy contexts such as these, including learning to read images 'within the paradigms of European visual culture'. *Beyond the Lettered City*, 5–6. For an excellent study of visual literacy education and practices in the Guaraní missions, see Guillermo Wilde, 'Regímenes de memoria misional: Formas visuales emergentes en las reducciones jesuíticas de América del Sur'. *Colonial Latin American Review* 28, no. 1 (2019): 10–36.

[162] Suit of the Jesuits of Duitama, 10 October 1619, AGN C&O 20, doc. 21, 118v.

[163] Jesuit *littera annua* for 1642–1652, dated 23 October 1652, ARSI NR&Q 12 I, 200v.

[164] Letter of Joseph Dadey to Acquaviva, Fontibón, 24 April 1610, ARSI NR&Q 14, 74v.

[165] On this see Jean Michel Massing, 'Jerome Nadal's *Evangelicae Historiae Imagines* and the Birth of Global Imagery'. *Journal of the Warburg and Courtauld Institutes* 80, no. 1 (2017): 161–220, who argues that Nada's *Imagines* were perhaps the first images to have been reproduced on four continents, and traces their adaptations around the world. On a famous 1638 version produced in China, see José Eugenio Borao Mateo, 'La versión china de la obra ilustrada de Jerónimo Nadal *Evangelicae Historiae Imagines*'. *Goya: Revista de Arte* no. 330 (2010): 16–33. Dadey's request was granted in 1611 (letter of Acquaviva to Dadey, 19 July 1611, ARSI NR&Q 1–2, 20v).

214   *The Friends of Ceremony and the Introduction of Reform*

not only to reach a broader share of their parishioners, beyond those they could teach to read and write, but also to transmit a new visual literacy to Indigenous people, an ability to understand Christian imagery. This too became a priority for the archdiocese, which began to concern itself with systematically promoting the introduction of devotional images in Indigenous churches and homes.[166]

Musical education was another innovation, promoted in Peru by Lima III and included by the reformers in the synod of 1606.[167] Children in Jesuit schools were taught to sing and play instruments in the church.[168] By 1612 the students of the Jesuit school for children in Cajicá were taught to sing in 'plainchant [and] accompanying an organ, and [to play] music with instruments (flutes, *chirimías*, and viols), with which they performed in the mass and other divine offices'.[169] Their musical training served a range of purposes, responding to the Tridentine desire to exalt the mass and divine offices through art and music, and promoting the Jesuit model of parish management: the music of Cajicá, the Jesuits reported, 'was the envy of surrounding towns, so that they all wanted to have us as their parish priests'.[170] The Jesuits were not subtle about the success of their efforts to train choristers and musicians. They deliberately invited priests in nearby parishes to visit them for celebrations on feast days and recorded their reactions. On the feast of the Immaculate Conception in 1611 or 1612, for example, a friar who held a nearby parish was so impressed by what he witnessed – or so they claimed – that he confessed that 'he thought it was a miracle to have achieved such a great thing, and I would not have believed it if I had not seen and heard it'.[171] Most significantly, the

---

[166] This is not to say, of course, that earlier missionary strategies did not incorporate images. But the new Jesuit emphasis on devotional images gave their use and spread in New Granada a new impetus. Indeed, two sets of catechetical murals from this period that have discovered in Indigenous towns in the late 1980s and 1990s are discussed in Chapter 6.

[167] On musical education in Indigenous parishes in the New Kingdom, see Diana Farley Rodríguez, "'Y Dios se hizo música": la conquista musical del Nuevo Reino de Granada. El caso de los pueblos de indios de las provincias de Tunja y Santafé durante el siglo XVII'. *Fronteras de la Historia* 15 (2010): 13–38.

[168] Draft of the 1604–1605 Jesuit littera annua, c. 1605, ARSI NR&Q 12 I, 35v.

[169] A *chirimía* is a kind of oboe. Jesuit *littera annua* for 1611–1612, dated 6 June 1613, ARSI NR&Q 12 I, 76v–77r.

[170] Ibid., 77r.

[171] Ibid., 77r. On the devotion to the Immaculate Conception, and its promotion by the Spanish crown, see Anthony M. Stevens-Arroyo, 'The Evolution of Marian Devotionalism within Christianity and the Ibero-Mediterranean Polity'. *Journal for the Scientific Study of Religion* 37, no. 1 (1998), 50–73, 64–67. On the adoption of the

The Jesuit Experiment

initiative embodied a new conception of the capacity of their Indigenous parishioners. For the Jesuits, earlier efforts to evangelise Indigenous people, in short, had underestimated them.

Earlier efforts had also underutilised them. The second shift in practice, derived from the first, was a greater inclusion of Indigenous people in the running of their parishes and the conduct of their own Christianisation. This involvement ranged from the traditional – employing Indigenous agents in catechisation, as had long been the case in other regions – to other roles more novel for this context.[172] This included employing children, who received daily instruction and learned how to read and write, to aid in the catechisation of the adults of their *parcialidades* when these came for instruction on Sundays and feast days. As their *littera annua* for 1609 explained, in Cajicá the adults would gather in the main square and arrange themselves into a circle with children in the middle, holding a long cross, leading the rest in the recitation of prayers and the catechism. Only after this preparation would they be instructed by the priest, before moving to the interior of the church for a sermon and sung mass, in which the children and other Indigenous people would also feature.[173] After all, a central purpose of literate and musical education was to support the celebration of the liturgy. This extended into other arenas as well. Scholars of other regions have highlighted how Jesuits invested considerable efforts in the training of Indigenous assistants in different missionary contexts, who could act with some degree of independence – a practice not without controversy.[174] The New Kingdom was

---

devotion by Spain for propagandistic purposes, see, for example, Christopher F. Black, 'The Public Face of Post-Tridentine Italian Confraternities'. *Journal of Religious History* 28, no. 1 (2004): 99.

[172] Indigenous assistants had long been used formally and informally around the New World for a variety of tasks – starting with the infamous *niños de monasterio* of New Spain – and were included in the earliest corpora of legislation issued to govern Christianisation in the New World. On these see Trexler, 'From the Mouths of Babes', and more recently Crewe, *The Mexican Mission*, 68–77. A limited provision for Indigenous agents was made in the constitutions of the synod of 1556, drawing on the legislation of Lima I and Mexico I. The role of Indigenous agents in the development of Christianisation in Peru is the focus of Charles, *Allies at Odds*.

[173] Jesuit *littera annua* for 1608–1609, dated 10 September 1609, ARSI NR&Q 12 I, 50r. This performative aspect of catechisation has been well documented and examined in the context of Peru. See for example Alan Durston, *Pastoral Quechua: The History of Christian Translation in Colonial Peru, 1550–1650* (Notre Dame, IN: University of Notre Dame Press, 2007), 273ff.

[174] For example in Peru, Ibid., 83; in Northern Mexico, Reff, *Plagues*, 165; and in Japan, J. F. Moran, *The Japanese and the Jesuits: Alessandro Valignano in Sixteenth-Century Japan* (London: Routledge, 1993), 167ff.

216   *The Friends of Ceremony and the Introduction of Reform*

no different: here their roles ranged from administering baptism in cases of emergency, helping to establish and manage parish hospitals for the care of the dying, preparing their fellows to receive various sacraments, and assisting with the organisation and running of public celebrations.[175] By the time of their 1613 *annua* the Jesuits explained how priests in Cajicá had come to rely on 'the more advantaged Indians, who help to catechise and die well', to the point 'that we are not needed where they attend'.[176]

The third and final departure in their missionary methods involved a new emphasis on the everyday practice of Christianity, including regular participation in the sacraments, private devotions, and public celebrations. Frequent participation in Penance and the Eucharist, as we saw, was a pillar of the Jesuit mission strategy, to the point of being a favourite measure of the success of their endeavours in their edifying correspondence and in their letters to the king. In the *annua* for 1609, for example, Francisco Vargas, a Jesuit attached to the college of Santafé, boasted of the great number of confessions he heard from Indigenous people. In Cajicá he granted certificates of confession to 200 people, so that they could take communion, of whom one hundred had made the longer, general confessions favoured by the Jesuits.[177] During Lent in 1608, he had 'spent 11 or 12 hours every day confessing the Indians' in Santafé, well into the evening, estimating that 'over 4,000 people have confessed with me in this school, many of them general confessions'.[178] In their *annua* for 1652 the Jesuits of Santafé reminisced about their arrival in Fontibón, writing of how 'in the town there was not one person who took communion' then, but that it had now 'been many years since even one person has failed to take it' – an exaggeration, perhaps, but revealing of how they assessed their success. They could be proud, he added, 'that such a holy custom and unavoidable obligation, previously unknown in this Kingdom, has spread in its observance to the rest of the towns' of the

---

[175] The practice of training Indigenous laymen in the formula for baptism in cases of emergency was quickly adopted elsewhere in the archdiocese. This is clear, for example, from Archbishop Arias de Ugarte's visitation a few years later, when parishioners were specifically asked to declare whether anyone had received this training. See for example the records of his visitation of the parish of Fúquene, 1619-10-16, AHSB Caja 1, 175r–187v, at 179r.

[176] Jesuit *littera annua* for 1611–1612, dated 6 June 1613, ARSI NR&Q 12 I, 79v.

[177] Letter of Francisco Vargas to Gonzalo de Lyra, 2 October 1609, quoted in the Jesuit *littera annua* for 1608–1609, dated 10 September 1609, ARSI NR&Q 12 I, at 46r.

[178] This he reported shortly after Easter, which fell on 6 April 1608. Ibid., 46r.

The Jesuit Experiment 217

archdiocese.[179] Indeed, this new approach, as Chapter 6 shows, would eventually be enshrined in legislation, and spread around the archdiocese by reforming prelates through systematic ecclesiastical visitations.

Another practice that would soon spread and take root was the devotion to the Blessed Sacrament, the display of the consecrated host on the altar in the parish church for its adoration by the faithful.[180] Devotion to the Blessed Sacrament, and participation in the associated feast of Corpus Christi – both celebrations of the doctrine of the real presence of Christ in the consecrated Eucharist – were both reinforced by the Council of Trent in the face of Protestant challenges.[181] Trent had made clear the duty of all Christians to pay the consecrated host 'the cult of *latria* that is owed to the true God', but the practice had been rare in Indigenous parishes in the New Kingdom before the Jesuits began to introduce it to Indigenous parishes under their care, starting with Cajicá.[182] So too with Corpus Christi celebrations, which centred around the triumphal procession of the Eucharist, under a dossel, along a decorated route, and which had acquired a new significance by middle of the sixteenth century.[183] These

[179] Jesuit *littera annua* for 1642–1652, dated 23 October 1652, ARSI NR&Q 12 I, 198r–198v.

[180] The practice was then introduced in the synod of 1606, which followed a similar requirement present in the constitutions of Lima III. See, 237–238. Revealingly, this legislation used practically the same language as the Jesuits had used in their reports to their superiors, rather than that of the text of Lima III that was reproduced almost verbatim in so many other instances. Cf. Lima III, actio 2a, ch. 21 (Vargas Ugarte, 'Tercer concilio', 331).

[181] As the Council of Trent proclaimed in 1551, these devotions would cause the enemies of the faith, 'faced with such splendour and witnessing the great rejoicing of the universal Church, weakened and broken are consumed with envy, or ashamed and confused change their ways' – language frequently repeated by the Jesuits. See Trent, Sess. XIII, ch. 5 (Tanner, *Decrees*, vol. 2, 695–696). On the broader history of the display and veneration of the Blessed Sacrament, see Miri Rubin, *Corpus Christi: The Eucharist in Late Medieval Culture* (Cambridge: Cambridge University Press, 1991), 181–185, 290–291.

[182] The Jesuits went as far as to suggest that Cajicá, was 'the first church in this entire kingdom that had the Blessed Sacrament' on display, a claim that is difficult to verify. See the draft of the 1604–1605 Jesuit *littera annua*, c. 1605, ARSI NR&Q 12 I, 35r.

[183] Corpus Christi had a long history since its introduction in the thirteenth century to affirm the doctrine of the real presence – a task all the more significant after the Reformation. In this way, Trent Sess. XIII ch. 5 urged Christians to participate in Corpus celebrations, which represented not only the triumph of Christ, 'His victory over death', but also 'the victory of religious truth in the same way over lies and heresy' (Tanner, *Decrees*, vol. 2, 695–696). As Carolyn Dean highlights, as a non-penitential Christian procession it employed the vocabulary 'derived from Roman imperial ceremonies that themselves were based on a variety of earlier, circum-Mediterranean celebratory practices'. These include triumphal arches and adorned processional paths, used

218 The Friends of Ceremony and the Introduction of Reform

had been common in Spanish cities for some time – we saw in Chapter 3 how in 1577 Corpus Christi celebrations in Santafé had drawn the leaders of neighbouring communities to the city to watch – but rare in Indigenous parishes before the coming of the Jesuits. Under their direction, these became momentous occasions, serving as theatrical statements of the Jesuits' emphasis on the value of the devotion, but also tangible demonstrations of the effects of all their policies to transform the Christianisation of Indigenous people.[184]

When the Jesuits first installed the Blessed Sacrament in Fontibón on the feast of Corpus Christi, they organised an elaborate two-day celebration, inviting not only President Borja and the *oidores*, Spanish notables, and a number of priests, but also *caciques* of neighbouring towns with their subjects. The first day featured 'many Indians with banners and trumpets, and other sorts of music', lavish decorations, an elaborate mass in the parish church, and, in the evening, plays performed by Indigenous actors, complete with parades on horseback and dances performed in ingenious costume, before 'many fireworks, and [the lights of] many lamps on the church, and a castle made of straw and flowers in the middle of the square, with three sets of *chirimía* players, and people dressed as soldiers, firing blanks'. The next day, the square was decorated with flowers and three altars were placed around it. Celebrations began with another mass, a sermon explaining the purpose of the celebration, and then a procession started, 'with great ecclesiastical spectacle, the priests dressed in rich vestments, carrying the float of the Blessed Sacrament on their shoulders', processing 'under a dossel, and behind them floats of other saints, and many banners, and much music of trumpets, three sets of *chirimías*, [and] the firing of muskets and arquebuses'.[185]

In case the role of the devotion in the Jesuit mission was not abundantly clear by now, a short play was put on with Indigenous actors before the three altars positioned around the central square. In the first, an actor dressed as an angel appeared with a representation of drunkenness,

---

to herald a victor. See Carolyn Dean, *Inka Bodies and the Body of Christ: Corpus Christi in Colonial Cuzco, Peru* (Durham, NC: Duke University Press, 1999), 9. For a recent exploration of such celebrations, see Mary Beard, *The Roman Triumph* (Cambridge, MA: Belknap Press of Harvard University Press, 2007). These military associations, amid people dressed as soldiers and the sound of arquebuses, could scarcely be clearer.

[184] On the Jesuit embrace and development of the Corpus Christi devotion, and their theatrical processions in different contexts, see O'Malley, *First Jesuits*, 156–157.

[185] Jesuit *littera annua* for 1611–1612, dated 6 June 1613, ARSI NR&Q 12 I, 83r–83v.

'carrying many of the insignia of intoxication with which the Indians celebrate their *borracheras*' but bound in ropes, which then 'collapsed before the Blessed Sacrament, so that there would never again be that vice in the town, now that the Blessed Sacrament was present'. The process was repeated at the other two altars as the procession moved through the square, 'where another angel destroyed in the same way dishonesty, and in the third platform ... idolatry'. These celebrations were an advertisement of their model of evangelisation to the elite of Santafé, and through them to the rest of the clergy; and central to this was asserting their understanding of the capacity and potential of Indigenous people. In this way, the highlight of a banquet to which visiting dignitaries were invited afterwards was a recitation by a young Indigenous boy from the parish 'of rare ability' from the pulpit of the church, dressed in the garb of a priest, 'in all the languages: Latin, Castilian, Greek, Italian, Muisca, Quechua, Valencian, [and] Portuguese'.[186]

'FRIENDS OF CEREMONY'

The installation of the Blessed Sacrament in Fontibón in many ways encapsulated the experiment in the reform of the church and Christianisation called for by the *encomenderos* of Santafé and Tunja, initiated by Archbishop Lobo Guerrero and Borja, and given shape by Diego de Torres Bollo and his fellow Jesuit exiles. Their plan was to reform the church and reset its missionary project along new lines, departing from the punitive policies of their sixteenth-century predecessors, and offering a new interpretation, tailored to the Neogranadian context, of how Tridentine reform could work. In doing so they drew on the legislation of Lima III, which had itself sought to reform the Peruvian church along Tridentine lines, but subtly and carefully translated to suit local conditions and their own priorities, and on Jesuit experience in managing Indigenous parishes in Peru and their broader missionary enterprise in theatres around the world. In doing this, the reformers may have emphasised continuity and precedent, but their approach in the New Kingdom was nothing short of revolutionary. In their parishes, the Jesuits introduced a more systematic programme of religious instruction, employed new methods, and introduced new practices and standards of behaviour among their parishioners. They

[186] Ibid., 83v.

220 *The Friends of Ceremony and the Introduction of Reform*

encouraged active participation in the sacraments, redoubled efforts to catechise in Indigenous languages, and imported the pageantry and ceremony of some of the central devotions of the Tridentine church.

These policies contrasted sharply with those of their sixteenth-century predecessors, whether in the religious orders, the secular church, or the civil authorities, and also with the approach that Torres Bollo's rivals would promote in Peru over the following decades, and which would culminate with the campaigns for the extirpation of idolatry of the archdiocese of Lima. Instead of withholding features that were central to the everyday practice of Catholicism in Europe and other regions, such as private devotions, public celebrations, participation in the sacraments, the use of devotional images, and other aspects of the cult of saints and – as we will see – religious confraternities, owing to concerns that Indigenous people might misuse them as a result of the imperfection of their Christianity, the idea instead became to use these practices to cultivate it. As the Jesuit Vice-Provincial Gonzalo de Lyra reported in 1613, even if Indigenous people lacked a real 'interior piety', acquiring and maintaining 'the appearance of Christians' through frequent participation in the sacraments, devotional practices, and pious institutions would engender and foster this piety, so that with time 'they will be as Christian on the inside as they appear to be' on the outside.[187]

This logic was based, on one hand, on a distinction between 'internal' and 'external' piety that was central to Jesuit spirituality, as can be seen, for example, in their *Spiritual Exercises*.[188] And on the other, on the idea, by now widely established, that Indigenous people were particularly easily influenced by 'external things'.[189] As Lyra explained in 1613, 'the cleanliness and adornment of the Church, elaborate processions, divine services with music of voices and instruments: all of this moves them greatly' because 'their understanding has been obfuscated by the barbarous lives that they and their ancestors lived'. What is more, because he

---

[187] Ibid., 79r.

[188] On this see O'Malley, *First Jesuits*, 196. It was by no means a new distinction, but was in fact clear in the work of Augustine (e.g. in *On the City of God*, book 10, ch. 19, 421), and Aquinas, as in his influential definition of the characteristics of idolatry (*Summae theologiae*, IIaIIae 94.3 = vol. 40, p. 29).

[189] On this issue, already common among the writings of some of the earliest missionaries in Mexico, see Louise M. Burkhart, 'Pious Performances: Christian Pageantry and Native Identity in Early Colonial Mexico'. In *Native Traditions in the Postconquest World.* Edited by Elizabeth Hill Boone and Thomas Cummins (Washington, DC: Dumbarton Oaks, 1997), 361–382.

and his fellows assumed that Indigenous religious practices were functionally equivalent – if the inverse – of Christian ones, they assumed that the introduction of Christianity would involve simply displacing one set of practices with another. 'They are such friends of ceremony in the offerings and sacrifices to their idols', Lyra concluded, that this fondness could be exploited by 'swapping them for the cult and adoration of the true God'. All that was needed was to 'introduce ecclesiastical things with the greatest pomp possible: this is how they will forget their idolatries'.[190]

In their concern for fostering 'external devotions', the Jesuits had stumbled – quite unintentionally – on a solution to overcome the fundamental failing of the earlier model of evangelisation. They understood public ceremonies, the cult of saints, religious confraternities, hospitals and visits to the sick, the promotion of visual and alphabetic literacy, and the inclusion of Indigenous agents in the running of some aspects of the life of the parish in terms of contributing to foster an inner spirituality. Perhaps it did. But for the Indigenous peoples of Santafé and Tunja, the new approach of these Jesuit 'friends of ceremony' opened new avenues for them to interact with Christianity and new opportunities to pursue their interests in different ways. This was not because these practices were equivalent to Indigenous ones, as the Jesuits assumed, but because they provided individuals and communities new ways of satisfying their personal and collective, political and social, and material and spiritual needs and concerns in a period of intense change. The experience of the many Indigenous immigrants in the Spanish cities of Santafé and Tunja who had for years been embracing many of these practices on their own, as evidenced in their wills and other documents considered in Chapter 6, suggest there was more that was attractive about the new approach than just the respite it provided from the terror and dispossession of the previous century. It made space, in other words, for Indigenous people to interact with what Christianity had to offer them.

Celebrations as elaborate as that first introduction of the Blessed Sacrament to Fontibón, to be sure, would be rare even in Jesuit parishes, but over the next few years, public celebrations, private devotions, images, and pious institutions of the sort introduced by the Jesuits became a regular feature of everyday life in Indigenous parishes, organised by Indigenous people themselves. These may not have involved banquets for the kingdom's leading dignitaries or displays of expensive imported

---

[190] Jesuit *littera annua* for 1611–1612, 6 June 1613, ARSI NR&Q 12 I, 76v.

222 *The Friends of Ceremony and the Introduction of Reform*

fireworks, but they were no less important to the people who made them possible. Many, in fact, were a consequence of a final innovation, the promotion of confraternities in Indigenous towns, a focus of Chapter 6, which would soon become fundamental to the very functioning and financing of the church at a local level. To understand how these changes spread and took root around the archdiocese, however, we must first turn to the thorny question of language, the subject of Chapter 5.

5

Language Policy and Legal Fiction

The Jesuit Jerónimo Navarro was shocked when he arrived in the parish of Duitama in April 1615. The town, some one hundred miles north-east of the city of Santafé, had recently been placed under the care of his order, and Navarro was among the first Jesuits sent there to preach, catechise, and administer the sacraments. Duitama was not far from the city of Tunja, the provincial capital. But something was not right. 'I began to preach in the language of the Indians,' he explained to his Provincial, but this 'was something new and that they had never heard'.[1] Navarro was not referring to the Gospel. The problem, he admitted, was that his new parishioners could not understand him. He had taken with him the archdiocese's standardised translation of catechetical materials in 'the language of the Indians' ('*la lingua de gl'Indiani*'), produced in response to far-reaching empire-wide legislation and as a core part of the reforms of Lobo Guerrero, Borja, and his own fellow Jesuits. But it was of no use. Instead, Navarro was forced to learn the language of his new parishioners and produce a new bespoke translation of key texts, starting with the confessionary, in order to perform his duties. What was going on?

Navarro was not alone in his predicament. Linguistic diversity posed a fundamental problem to priests and administrators around Spanish America and the Philippines who sought to evangelise Indigenous peoples, just as it did to their fellows in other missionary theatres around the world. It was also a challenge for the Spanish crown, which twice in the sixteenth century sought to put in place a systematic language policy

---

[1] Jerónimo Navarro to Manuel de Arceo, quoted in the Jesuit *littera annua* for 1615, dated 22 July 1616, ARSI NR&Q 12 II, 159v.

224   *Language Policy and Legal Fiction*

for all of its territories in the New World, based on experiments and feedback it received primarily from the two centres of empire, Mexico and Peru. The latest of these, which sought to incorporate Indigenous 'general languages' into religious instruction, was how Navarro had come to be equipped with standardised linguistic materials in 'the language of the Indians' of the New Kingdom of Granada. Both royal efforts to institute a universal solution to the problems of language, however, failed in the New Kingdom because they were wholly unsuited to the region's linguistic conditions, and local actors like Navarro eventually had to produce their own solutions.

This episode, and others like it, are revealing of the complexity of the linguistic landscape of the New Kingdom of Granada, of how linguistically heterogeneous even the region closest to the centres of Spanish colonial power remained decades after the European invasion. But it also reveals something more fundamental: the distance that existed between the expectations and pretentions of authorities at the centre of the monarchy and realities on the ground, between empire-wide legislation and local initiatives, and between the different registers of writing – as well as the images of Indigenous peoples that they painted – that emerged alongside the colonial regime of the New Kingdom of Granada. As such, the history of language policy in the first century after the arrival of the secular church in the region – the subject of this chapter – throws valuable light not only on the development of the Spanish colonial project and the changing priorities and concerns of religious reformers, but invites us to reflect on the complexity of translating normativity into local contexts, the role and initiative of Indigenous actors, and the limitations of the colonial archive.

The role of language as both an instrument and a theatre of interaction between colonial powers and their subjects has been an important focal point for modern historians of colonialism, of Spanish America and elsewhere, and the subject of much theoretical discussion.[2] In contrast,

---

[2] The historiography of language policy in colonial contexts is considerable, from foundational texts such as Johannes Fabian, *Language and Colonial Power: The Appropriation of Swahili in the Former Belgian Congo, 1880–1938* (Cambridge: Cambridge University Press, 1986); and Vicente L. Rafael, *Contracting Colonialism: Translation and Christian Conversion in Tagalog Society under Early Spanish Rule.* 2nd edition (Durham, NC: Duke University Press, 1993), to more recent surveys such as Joseph Errington, *Linguistics in a Colonial World: A Story of Language, Meaning, and Power* (Oxford: Blackwell, 2008). In the Spanish American context, key recent works include Durston, *Pastoral Quechua*; Nancy Farriss, *Tongues of Fire: Language and Evangelization in Colonial Mexico*

Language Policy and Legal Fiction

comparatively little has been written about the New Kingdom of Granada, and less still about the sixteenth and seventeenth centuries. Lacking the Indigenous-language archives of many regions of Mesoamerica, and faced with a paucity of colonial texts in and on Indigenous languages compared with other regions of South America, an underlying concern of many studies on New Granada has been loss. Even though in recent decades the Colombian state has finally sought to safeguard and promote surviving Indigenous languages, not least granting them co-equal status with Castilian in the landmark 1991 constitution, an incalculable number of Indigenous languages formerly spoken in the territory of modern-day Colombia have disappeared.[3] These included the Muisca languages, which largely ceased to be spoken by the mid eighteenth century, at least until modern efforts of linguistic revival.[4] Because the Spanish crown issued legislation in the 1770s to 'banish' or suppress Indigenous languages across Spanish America, it is common to ascribe the disappearance of Indigenous languages to deliberate colonial policy, and to assume similar policies were implemented throughout the colonial period.[5] Indeed, much of the historiography has focused on how – to quote what remains the most comprehensive survey of colonial language policy, by Humberto Triana y Antorveza – 'in colonisation, Spain imposed the Castilian language, destroying without consideration

(Oxford: Oxford University Press, 2018); and Daniel I. Wasserman-Soler, *Truth in Many Tongues: Religious Conversion and the Languages of the Early Spanish Empire* (University Park: Penn State University Press, 2020).

[3] On the loss of Indigenous languages in Colombia, see Ximena Pachón and François Correa, *Lenguas amerindias: Condiciones sociolingüísticas en Colombia* (Santafé de Bogotá: Instituto Colombiano de Antropología, 1997), 17–19; and Departamento Administrativo Nacional de Estadistica, 'Lenguas y dialectos indígenas'. In *Ayer y hoy de los indígenas colombianos* (Bogotá: Departamento Administrativo Nacional de Estadistica, 1971), 45–49. For an overview of contemporary language policy, including in the 1991 Constitution, see Javier García León and David García León, 'Políticas lingüísticas en Colombia: tensiones entre políticas para lenguas mayoritarias y lenguas minoritarias'. *Boletín de filología* 47, no. 2 (2012): 47–70.

[4] On the disappearance of Muisca, see Nicholas Ostler, 'Fray Bernardo de Lugo: Two Sonnets in Muisca'. *Amerindia: Revue d'ethnolinguistique Amérindienne* 19–20 (1995): 129. And on modern revival efforts, Richard Alberto Cardozo Sarmiento and Jose Fernando Páez Jaramillo, 'Proceso de revitalización lingüística de la lengua muisca de la comunidad de Cota'. BA dissertation, Facultad de Comunicación y Lenguaje, Pontificia Universidad Javeriana, 2008.

[5] The decree in question is compiled in Richard Konetzke, *Colección de documentos para la historia de la formación social de Hispanoamerica, 1493–1810* (Madrid: Consejo Superior de Investigaciones Científicas, 1953), vol. 3, 364–368.

226   *Language Policy and Legal Fiction*

our Indigenous languages'.[6] As a result, most historians have tended to focus on the view from the top, and especially on royal legislation.[7]

These perspectives, although understandable, are problematic, in part because they gloss over a much more complicated reality on the ground, leaving fundamental questions unanswered. On a basic level, we know little of how communication in religious instruction actually worked in practice. We know that the Indigenous inhabitants of New Granada spoke a multitude of languages, and we know that they were (eventually) catechised, but little has been written about how this was actually done, beyond speculation. There are very few surviving texts in Indigenous languages, whether simple '*vocabularios*' – word lists – or more sophisticated dictionaries and catechetical texts.[8] And yet we know that Indigenous languages must have been used because even though we have evidence of the spread of Spanish among Indigenous people throughout this period, we also know that many groups and individuals did not speak it – as evidenced, for example, by the continued presence of interpreters in the interactions of Indigenous people with colonial officials, whether at court in Santafé or visitations.[9] More fundamentally, these perspectives have tended to take the claims and pretentions of royal authority at face value. In fact, owing to the peculiar position occupied by the New Kingdom of Granada, local authorities took advantage of royal

[6] Humberto Triana y Antorveza, *Las lenguas indígenas en la historia social del Nuevo Reino de Granada* (Bogotá: Instituto Caro y Cuervo, 1987), xv.

[7] Javier Real Cuesta, 'Política lingüística en el Nuevo Reino de Granada durante los siglos XVI y XVII'. In *Estudios sobre política indigenista española en América* (Valladolid: Seminario de Historia de América, Universidad de Valladolid, 1975), vol. 1, 279–302; Triana y Antorveza, *Las lenguas indígenas en la historia social* and also his other works, *Las lenguas indígenas en el ocaso del imperio español* (Santafé de Bogotá: Instituto Colombiano de Antropologia, 1993) and 'Factores políticos y sociales que contribuyeron a la desparición de lenguas indígenas (Colonia y Siglo XIX)'. In *Lenguas amerindias: condiciones sociolingüísticas en Colombia*. Edited by Ximena Pachón and François Correa (Santafé de Bogotá: Instituto Colombiano Antropología, 1997), 85–154.

[8] Christiane Dümmler identified eight texts in 'Chibcha' for the entire colonial period, in 'La Nueva Granada como campo de labor lingüístico-misionera: presentación y análisis de varias obras de la época colonial'. In *La descripción de las lenguas amerindias en la época colonial*. Edited by Klaus Zimmermann (Frankfurt; Madrid: Vervuert Iberoamericana, 1997), 429–439. A further text, discussed later, was identified by Santiago Muñoz in 2015. A number of these have been digitised and compiled online by the Grupo de Investigación Muysccubun (at http://muysca.cubun.org).

[9] Jorge Augusto Gamboa, 'Presentación'. In *Gramática en la lengua general del Nuevo Reino, llamada mosca* (Bogotá: Instituto Colombiano de Antropología e Historia, 2010), 15–19.

'GREAT DISSONANCE AND IMPERFECTION'

legislation on language to implement policies that directly contradicted the original intentions of this legislation, but which served their interests and reflected local priorities and concerns. To understand how this worked, we need to start at the centre and at the beginning.

'GREAT DISSONANCE AND IMPERFECTION'

Early royal legislation on the issue of language had left most of the responsibility for evangelisation and language teaching to people on the ground: missionaries from the religious orders and *encomenderos*. The Laws of Burgos-Valladolid of 1512–1513, for example, included a small number of instructions regarding language, most significantly a provision (law 9) ordering all *encomenderos* in charge of fifty or more people to teach a young man to read, so that he could then teach others and help the friars with religious instruction.[10] As in so many other areas the crown was by no means taking the initiative. Instead, early missionaries and settlers responded to the challenges posed by Indigenous languages with a two-pronged policy that would come to characterise the Spanish response to the problems posed by language throughout Spanish America and the Philippines: learning the languages of the inhabitants of the areas in which they were active while teaching them how to speak Castilian as well. Unsurprisingly, this began in the Antilles, New Spain, and Peru, areas that had been settled by Europeans long before their invasion and settlement of the interior of New Granada in the late 1530s and 1540s.

Eventually, however, the crown sought to take a more active role, and decided to institute the first systematic language policy for all of its American territories in 1550. This first empire-wide policy was to throw its weight behind one of the two strategies pioneered by people on the ground, favouring the teaching of Spanish. In this way, in June 1550, Charles V decreed that in order to evangelise Indigenous peoples what was necessary was 'to ensure that these peoples are taught our Castilian tongue, and that they adopt our manners and customs'. Only in this way, he proposed, 'can [they] be instructed in doctrine and will understand the things of our Christian religion'.[11] In these instructions, then, the teaching of Spanish was fundamental not only to catechesis, but also of the

---

[10] 'Ordenanzas para el tratamiento de los indios', or Laws of Burgos-Valladolid, 23 January 1513, AGI Indiferente 419, lib. 4 83r–96v, at law 9 (87v).

[11] Royal decree (*cédula*) on teaching the Indians the Spanish language, 7 June 1550, compiled in *Recopilación* 6.1.18.

228 *Language Policy and Legal Fiction*

assimilation of Indigenous people into colonial rule more generally. Language, in other words, was a powerful tool to be deployed alongside measures to improve the 'manners and customs' of Indigenous people. It was a tool for the promotion of Spanish *policía*.

The legislation of 1550 responded to the preoccupations of three interrelated trends. The first, as we have seen, was the ongoing emergence of an identity of 'Spain' and Spanishness increasingly characterised by ideas of cultural unity, expressed in increasingly religious terms, that saw religious heterogeneity as an obstacle to political stability.[12] The second was the justification of the conquest and possession of the New World based on the need for evangelisation and eventually on the preservation of orthodoxy.[13] But a third trend concerned language specifically. This was the growth in importance of vernacular Spanish and the concomitant development of ideas about language and its role in early modern Europe.[14] Of course, this increasing vernacularisation was not limited to the Iberian Peninsula, but it was nevertheless well suited to become one of the markers of the developing identity of a united Spain, and one that would be exported to the New World.[15]

---

[12] On 'Spanishness', see Albert A. Sicroff, *Los estatutos de limpieza de sangre: controversias entre los siglos XV y XVII* (Madrid: Taurus, 1985); M. J. Rodríguez-Salgado, 'Christians, Civilised and Spanish: Multiple Identities in Sixteenth-Century Spain'. *Transactions of the Royal Historical Society* 8 (1998): 233–251; Margaret Rich Greer, Walter Mignolo, and Maureen Quilligan, eds, *Rereading the Black Legend: The Discourses of Religious and Racial Difference in the Renaissance Empires* (Chicago: University of Chicago Press, 2007); María Elena Martínez, *Genealogical Fictions: Limpieza de Sangre, Religion, and Gender in Colonial Mexico* (Stanford, CA: Stanford University Press, 2008).

[13] On the justification for the conquest, see Enrique Dussel, *El episcopado latinoamericano y la liberación de los pobres, 1504–1620* (Mexico City: Centro de Reflexión Teológica, 1979), 57ff; M. J. Rodríguez-Salgado, 'How Oppression Thrives Where Truth Is Not Allowed a Voice": The Spanish Polemic about the American Indians'. In *Silencing Human Rights: Critical Engagements with a Contested Project.* Edited by Gurminder K. Bhambra and Robbie Shilliam (Basingstoke: Palgrave Macmillan, 2009), 19–42; and Gonzalo Lamana, 'Of Books, Popes and Huacas; or, the Dilemmas of Being Christian'. In *Rereading the Black Legend: The Discourses of Religious and Racial Difference in the Renaissance Empires.* Edited by Margaret Rich Greer, Walter Mignolo, and Maureen Quilligan (Chicago: University of Chicago Press, 2007), 117–149.

[14] Peter Burke, *Languages and Communities in Early Modern Europe* (Cambridge: Cambridge University Press, 2004).

[15] For Penelope Harvey, 'the abstraction of spoken language into stable rule-governed forms began to lend language a timeless form and facilitate the emergent association of language with singular, person-specific identities or ethnicity'. See Penelope Harvey, 'Language States'. In *A Companion to Latin American Anthropology.* Edited by Deborah Poole (Malden, MA: Blackwell, 2008), 197. Also Durston, *Pastoral Quechua*, 34; and Sheldon Pollock, 'Cosmopolitan and Vernacular in History'. *Public Culture* 12, no. 3 (2000): 592.

'Great Dissonance and Imperfection' 229

Vernacularisation was problematic, and especially in a religious context. A clear illustration of this can be seen in the ambiguous treatment of vernacular languages later in the century at the Council of Trent. On one hand, one of the principal means through which reformers sought to further involve the laity in ecclesiastical life was through the use of vernacular languages. Session XXII required priests to preach in the vernacular, and during the mass explain 'some of what is recited', to give some explanation – a departure from the almost theatrical form of late medieval Catholicism, in an attempt to turn congregations in many senses from spectators into active participants. But at the same time, the same concerns of religious orthodoxy made it much more cautious about the use of the vernacular for the liturgy, explaining that 'council fathers did not think it advantageous that it should everywhere [*passim*] be celebrated in the vernacular' – and, later, anathemised the opinion 'that mass should be celebrated only in the vernacular'.[16] So while these developments led to a boom in the publication of vernacular pastoral texts and religious literature in the peninsula, not only in Castilian but also in other peninsular languages, this literature was also a source of anxiety and the subject of great scrutiny, not least since the Inquisition had banned translations of Scripture in Spain from 1551.[17] These ambiguous experiences formed the context that framed the ideas about language of the people at the centre of the monarchy who determined language policy in the Spanish America: men who recognised the fundamental importance of communication for conversion but who were uneasy with the use of even their own language to achieve it.

This anxiety about language can be seen in the legislation of 1550. The central problem lay with the languages themselves: 'having particularly examined whether even in the most perfect Indian language the Mysteries

---

On the standardisation of language around Europe, see Burke, *Languages and Communities*, 89–110.

[16] Trent, Sess. XXII, 'Teaching and canons on the most holy sacrifice of the mass', ch. 8, and 'Canons on the most holy sacrifice of the mass', can. 9, in Tanner, *Decrees*, vol. 2, 735–736. John O'Malley noted that this was 'a far cry from forbidding the vernacular', although, oddly, he translated '*passim*' ('everywhere') in the second quotation as 'elsewhere' ('*alibi*'). See O'Malley, 'Trent: Myths', 220.

[17] This prohibition was preceded by another banning all books on doctrine printed outside of Spain the previous year. On these restrictions, and the broader context of the controversy over the prosecution of the archbishop of Toledo, Bartolomé de Carranza by the Inquisition, see Wasserman-Soler, *Truth in Many Tongues*, ch. 1; and Marcel Bataillon, *Erasmo y España: estudios sobre la historia espiritual del siglo XVI* (Mexico City: Fondo de Cultura Económica, 1966), 549–557.

230   Language Policy and Legal Fiction

of our Holy Catholic Faith can be well and properly explained', the decree read, 'it has been recognised that it is not possible to do so *without great dissonance and imperfection*.'[18] Indigenous languages, the logic went, were just not up to the task. The issue was maintaining and policing the orthodoxy of what was taught, and the simplest solution was to avoid the problem altogether and discount Indigenous languages as means to transmit the tenets of Christian doctrine, and with it Spanish *policía*. Reality, however, would not disappear at the stroke of a pen.

When the legislation of 1550 reached Santafé, the civil and ecclesiastical authorities of New Granada charged with putting the king's dispositions into practice soon became aware of the difficulty of doing so. For a start, both the church and the civil administration of New Granada were in their infancy, and the resources available to them were negligible. All that the first bishop of Santafé, Juan de los Barrios, could do was to echo this official policy in his Synod of 1556. In this way, his constitutions began by emphasising the necessity of teaching doctrine in Spanish, and of doing so uniformly, before laying out a method for teaching children, who were to take lessons every day for two hours. All teaching, including prayers, were to be taught in Spanish, alongside 'reading, writing, singing, and counting'.[19] In Chapter 2 we saw how the constitutions of synod of 1556 were divorced from local realities and incapable of effecting change. But even here, in what was predominantly an aspirational text, the cracks in the royal policy of 1550 were already beginning to show. After outlining this programme of religious instruction in Spanish, the same synod, in a rare moment of perspicacity, required that adult converts seeking baptism be examined on their knowledge of the catechism 'in a language they understand'.[20] How else, after all, could one be sure that everything had been transmitted reliably?

Although the policy of 1550 gave priority to the teaching of Spanish, missionaries active in Mexico and Peru had not abandoned their study of Indigenous languages and were ready to provide an alternative when the shortcomings of the crown's policy began to become obvious. There, missionaries and scholars had been debating the merits and usefulness of Indigenous languages for decades, and many had been petitioning the crown for a change of policy. This is the context, for example, of the prologue to the famous 1560 Quechua grammar of Domingo de Santo

---

[18] Royal decree on teaching the Spanish language, 7 June 1550, in *Recopilación* 6.1.18, my italics.
[19] 'Constituciones sinodales 1556', 19, 41.   [20] Ibid., 22.

'Great Dissonance and Imperfection'

Tomás, in which he directly responded to the language of the legislation of 1550, praising 'the great *policía* of this language, its abundance of vocabulary', comparing it favourably to Latin and Castilian in its elegance and virtues.[21] By the end of the decade they came to be joined by the civil authorities, first in New Spain, under viceroy Luis de Velasco, and then in Peru, under Francisco de Toledo. In 1558, for example, Velasco had started to petition for the establishment of a school in Guadalajara for the teaching of Nahuatl to Indigenous children.[22] Toledo, for his part, attempted over the course of four letters in 1570 to convince the king of the necessity of using Indigenous languages.[23] Within a few years, the result was a fundamentally different policy at the centre of the monarchy, a shift towards a strategy that sought to incorporate Indigenous languages into the program of evangelising the Indigenous peoples of the New World.

The change began with the *Cédula magna* of royal patronage of 1574, discussed in Chapter 3, that was so central to the crown's effort to assert its control over ecclesiastical institutions and the missionary project, dispatched to civil and ecclesiastical authorities throughout Spanish America. For the purposes of this chapter, however, one thing stands out among the sections to do with the appointment of candidates to ecclesiastical positions. Hoping that in 'the presentation and provision to all prelacies, dignities, offices and ecclesiastical benefices, the most meritorious be presented and provided', article 19 ordered that local civil and ecclesiastical authorities were to prefer candidates 'who know the language in which they are to indoctrinate'.[24] These instructions about language were reiterated in 1578, when Archbishop Zapata de Cárdenas was ordered not to appoint any candidate ignorant of the local language to an Indigenous parish.[25] The same year, the king wrote to the archbishop of Lima compelling him to do the same.[26] In December, he decreed that all priests travelling to Spanish America from the peninsula or

---

[21] Santo Tomás, *Grammatica, o Arte de la lengua general de los Indios de los reynos del Peru* (Valladolid: por Francisco Fernandez de Cordoua, impressor de la M. R, 1560), [7–8]. On this see Juan Carlos Estenssoro Fuchs, 'Las vías indígenas de la occidentalización. Lenguas generales y lenguas maternas en el ámbito colonial americano (1492–1650)'. *Mélanges de la Casa de Velázquez* 45, no. 1 (2015): 15–36.

[22] Rosenblat, 'La hispanización de América', 91; Pardo, *Mexican Catholicism*, 108ff.

[23] Triana y Antorveza, *Las lenguas indígenas en la historia social*, 163–164.

[24] *Cédula magna del patronato*, AGI Indiferente 427, lib. 30, 258r.

[25] Alberto Lee López, 'Gonzalo Bermúdez, primer catedrático de la lengua general de los Chibchas'. *Boletín de Historia y Antigüedades* 51, nos 594–597 (1964): 186.

[26] Real Cuesta, 'Política lingüística', 299.

232   *Language Policy and Legal Fiction*

elsewhere would be required to demonstrate a knowledge of local languages in order to be admitted to Indigenous benefices and parishes.[27]

The new legislation concluded with two decrees of 1580, which now
also affected those already in possession of Indigenous parishes. The first
decree, issued by Philip II in August 1580, once again required priests
working in Indigenous parishes to know the language of their parishioners, forbidding the installation of those who did not.[28] The second, issued
a month later, ordered the establishment of a chair or professorship, a
cátedra, in each diocese for an expert in its 'general language' to teach it to
those who required it and to examine them.[29] It also forbade even the
ordination of 'anyone lacking a knowledge of the general language of the
said Indians'. Such knowledge would be assessed and certified by the
holder of the chair, and candidates would be required to study under
him for at least a year. This was to be obligatory 'even if the said ordinand
possessed the ability and sufficiency in the faculties that the Church and
sacred canons require' because, 'for the teaching and indoctrination of the
said Indians what is most important is knowing the said language'. Only
in this way would 'the spiritual good of the said Indians [be] achieved'.
Priests already in possession of parishes were not exempt: they were all to
be examined in the language within the year, or lose their parishes.[30] This
new strategy represented a fundamental change from the policy that the
crown had favoured in the mid sixteenth century. But it relied on a
problematic idea.

WHAT IS A 'GENERAL LANGUAGE'?

The language policy implemented between 1574 and 1580 depended on
the use of 'general languages'. But what were they? In a recent study of the
'general language' of colonial Peru, César Itier highlighted a fundamental
problem: 'In historical sources, the term *lengua general* is applied to what
in reality are several different concepts.' In the case of Peru, it is applied in

---

[27] Royal decree 'Que los clérigos y religiosos no sean admitidos a doctrinas sin saber la
lengua general de los Indios que han de administrar', 2 December 1578, in *Recopilación*
1.6.30.

[28] Royal decree 'Que los Religiosos doctrineros sean examinados por los prelados diocesanos en la suficiencia y lengua de los Indios de sus doctrinas', 5 August 1580, in
Recopilación 1.15.6.

[29] The copy dispatched to New Granada can be found in AGN C&O 9, 226r–227v.

[30] Royal decree for the establishment of a professorship in the general language,
22 September 1580, AGN C&O 9, 226v–227r.

What Is a 'General Language'?

some sources to 'the entire Quechua language family; in others, to the specific dialect that served as the lingua franca of Tawantinsuyu; in others still, to a collection of dialects that seems to coincide with what modern classifications call "Quechua IIc"'.[31] This ambiguity is problematic, and has led to a great deal of confusion about the linguistic reality of areas such as the New Kingdom of Granada. What the legislation of 1580 referred to was a single Indigenous language that could be used widely within a territory for the purpose of evangelisation, an Indigenous lingua franca that could be appropriated by colonial officials for their purposes. The idea was simple and the advantages were obvious: instead of trying to learn and use all the languages of a particular region for the purposes of indoctrination, efforts were focused on what was seen as the dominant language. This idea was attractive because it provided a means to overcome the most difficult aspect of the problem of language in the New World: the heterogeneity of the linguistic landscape.

It had first arisen in New Spain and Peru, where friars had been learning Indigenous languages for decades with varying degrees of success. There, missionaries had sought to best employ their resources by focusing their efforts on what seemed to be the most predominant language in the regions where they operated.[32] Their decision was facilitated by the fact that these were regions where certain languages had become widespread before European contact, as a consequence not only of the military and economic expansion of the Mexica and the Inca, but also of deliberate language policies that they implemented.[33] In contrast, no such processes had occurred before the European invasion in the region that became the New Kingdom: for all the claims and embellishments of explorers and chroniclers, Muisca groups lacked political unity, and no single group had imposed its control over all others. Indeed, research into the social and political organisation of the Muisca at the moment of contact with Spaniards over the past few decades, as Chapter 1 discussed,

---

[31] César Itier, 'What Was the "Lengua General" of Colonial Peru?' In *History and Language in the Andes*. Edited by Adrian J. Pearce and Paul Heggarty (Basingstoke: Palgrave Macmillan, 2011), 63.

[32] As Juan Carlos Estenssoro explains in his survey of the emergence of the term 'general language', it was a matter of 'linguistic economy'. Estenssoro Fuchs, 'Las vías indígenas'.

[33] Harvey, 'Language States', 194. In the words of Santo Tomás – whom Estenssoro suggests coined the term 'general language' in his 1560 grammar – Quechua 'was the language that was used throughout the domain of great lord Huayna Capac', explaining that 'it was used generally by lords and *principales* of that land, and the greater part of the commoners'. See Estenssoro Fuchs, 'Las vías indígenas', 21, citing Santo Tomás, *Grammatica*, [9].

234   *Language Policy and Legal Fiction*

has generally questioned received wisdom about the cultural, political, and social homogeneity of these groups. As a result, no Indigenous lingua franca had emerged.

In New Spain and Peru, Spaniards soon began to appropriate and spread apparently dominant languages among Indigenous peoples under their rule – the next logical step – often far beyond the areas where they had been dominant before European contact.[34] Moreover, missionaries had devoted a great deal of effort to codifying and employing certain Indigenous languages for their purposes from an early date, a fact that is evident from the volume of surviving works in Indigenous languages and from their dates of publication.[35] The printing press was introduced to New Spain by Bishop Fray Juan de Zumárraga, in 1539, and it seems that its first publication was a bilingual Nahuatl-Castilian catechism, his *Breve y más compendiosa doctrina christiana en lengua mexicana y castellana.*[36] Similarly, the first publication of the press in Lima was a 1583 trilingual doctrinal work, in Spanish, Quechua, and Aymara, while Santo Tomás's Quechua grammar and vocabulary, the *Grammatica o Arte de la lengua general de los indios de los reynos del Perú* – featuring the first appearance of the term 'general language' – had been published in Valladolid in 1560.[37]

Of course, references to 'the Mexican language' or 'the general language of the Indians of the kingdoms of Peru' gloss over what were in fact complicated linguistic realities, ignoring the prevalence of dialects, geographical variation, and a whole host of other important considerations.[38] In the case of Peru, for example, significant debate remains about the connection between the lingua franca of Tawantinsuyu and the 'general language' Quechua of colonial sources and pastoral

---

[34] Rosenblat, 'La hispanización de América', 91; Harvey, 'Language States', 197; Durston, *Pastoral Quechua.*

[35] Resines, *Catecismos americanos*, vol. 2, 725–727.

[36] Rosenblat, 'La hispanización de América', 89; Joaquín García Icazbalceta, *Bibliografía mexicana del siglo XVI; primera parte: catálogo razonado de libros impresos en México de 1539 a 1600 con biografías de autores y otras ilustraciones, precedido de una noticia acerca de la introducción de la imprenta en México* (México: Librería de Andrade y Morales, 1886), 1; and Resines, *Catecismos americanos*, vol. 2, 236–237.

[37] On the former, see Durston, *Pastoral Quechua*, 49–55. On the latter, Estenssoro Fuchs, *Paganismo*, 33–34, 84, and 'Las vías indígenas'. In contrast, the New Kingdom would have to wait until the seventeenth century for a work concerning one of its Indigenous languages to be printed, and until the eighteenth for its own printing press. On the latter See Medina, *La imprenta en Bogotá.*

[38] Itier, 'What Was the "Lengua General"', 73.

What Is a 'General Language'?

literature: whether the latter was an artificial construct produced after the former had disappeared (as argued by Cerrón-Palomino), whether it reflected the language that Indigenous people actually spoke (as argued by Durston), or whether it was indeed a lingua franca widely spoken by Indigenous people (as proposed by Taylor and Itier).[39] These debates continue, but what is crucial is that a lingua franca could be, and was, used in evangelisation in these centres of empire, and that this cemented the idea that the same would be the case elsewhere. The legislation of 1580 accepts this as a given, assuming that an equivalent lingua franca existed in each individual realm, and that it was widespread enough to justify constructing an educational framework for missionaries to be trained in it and for standardised translations of a pastoral and catechetical corpus to be produced. Characteristically, the crown was attempting to extend what seemed to be working in one region across the rest of Spanish America. Indeed, the second decree of 1580, which called for the establishment of a *cátedra* in the general language of each region, explicitly referred to the successful experience of the Quechua *cátedra* in Lima.[40]

Crucially, what the legislation of 1580 did by introducing the expectation that an Indigenous lingua franca existed and should be employed was to open the way for the authorities in charge of areas where no language had been identified as 'the *general* language' to choose any language and label it as such, as long as they were under the impression that it was or could be used in a similar manner to what the legislation described was the case elsewhere. In other words, the concept was ambiguous, and while a 'general language' could be an Indigenous lingua franca in Mexico or Peru, elsewhere it could easily be little more than an optimistic fiction. When these instructions reached the New Kingdom in 1581, where languages were as overwhelmingly heterogeneous as they were uncharted, manpower was scarce, political will was negligible, and

---

[39] Gerald Taylor, 'Un documento quechua de Huarochirí-1607'. *Revista andina* 5, no. 1 (1985): 157–185; Rodolfo Cerrón Palomino, 'Unidad y diferencia lingüística en el mundo andino'. *Lexis: Revista de lingüística y literatura* 11, no. 1 (1987): 71–104; Durston, *Pastoral Quechua*; and César Itier, 'Lengua general y quechua cuzqueño en los siglos XVI y XVII'. In *Desde afuera y desde adentro: ensayos de etnografía e historia del Cuzco y Apurímac*. Edited by Luis Millones Figueroa, Hiroyasu Tomoeda, and Tatsuhiko Fujii (Osaka: National Museum of Ethnology, 2000), 47–59 and 'What Was the "Lengua General"'.

[40] Royal decree for the establishment of a professorship in the General Language, 22 September 1580, AGI SF 234 n. 47, 1r.

236   *Language Policy and Legal Fiction*

little progress had been made in studying and codifying the languages that were known, it would turn out to be the latter.

'THERE IS NO GENERAL LANGUAGE IN THIS KINGDOM'

The second decree of 1580, which arrived in Santafé on 2 July 1581, required the *Audiencia* to make a difficult decision. After all, in order to establish a *cátedra* in the 'general language', it was first necessary to decide which language that might be. The following December, the *Audiencia* published edicts calling for candidates to present themselves to the newly created chair in 'the general language', explaining that the *Audiencia* 'declared it to be that of this valley of Bogotá and Tunja'.[41] This decision involved two important assumptions: that a single language – described as 'Mosca' in most contemporary sources and 'Chibcha' and Muisca in modern literature – was present throughout this region, and that it was widespread enough to be useful as a lingua franca.[42] But the reality was very different. For a start, there was no single, homogenous Muisca that was spoken throughout the 'valley of Bogotá and Tunja'. This became clear as soon as people with a knowledge of local languages were consulted and when the new legislation was first criticised, after which the reference to Tunja, which is in fact located several valleys away (see Map 2 in the Prelims), was generally dropped.[43] Instead, the language the *Audiencia* selected was the language of the region immediately surrounding the city of Santafé.

It is difficult to reconstruct the details of the process through which the *Audiencia* settled on this variant of Muisca, owing to a dearth of documentation, but the rationale was straightforward enough. They chose the language spoken by the people with whom they had the greatest contact,

---

[41] Edict advertising for the position of *catedrático*, 23 December 1581, AGI SF 234, no. 47, 4v.

[42] Even though in an earlier literature the terms 'Muisca' and 'Chibcha' were often used interchangeably, the term 'Chibcha' is primarily used by linguists to refer to the broader linguistic family of Chibchan languages of which the Muisca languages were part, historically spoken in parts of northern South America and in Central America as far north as Nicaragua. To avoid confusion, throughout this book I prefer the term 'Muisca'. See Departamento Administrativo Nacional de Estadistica, 'Lenguas y dialectos indígenas', 45.

[43] For example, by witnesses called to support the legislation in 1582 (Proceedings on the case of the salary of Gonzalo Bermúdez, AGI SF 234, no. 47, 33v, 36v, 39r, 44r). As one explained, 'there is a general language in this valley of Bogotá, except in the valleys of Guatavita and Ubaque and Tunja' (at 46r).

'There Is No General Language in This Kingdom'   237

who inhabited the towns nearest the city, and assumed it would be good enough for the rest of the highlands of the eastern *cordillera*. As supporters of using this Indigenous vernacular later argued, people from around the region went to the *Audiencia* for redress of their 'suits and grievances', as well as to a market frequently held in the city, 'to contract, to sell and to shop, and in doing so' – they deduced – 'they *must* be able to understand each other in this general language of the valley of Santafé'.[44] From this uninformed perspective, unaware of the extent of linguistic heterogeneity but optimistic about the potential of the new legislation, Santafé Muisca would do just fine.

Unfortunately for them, this Muisca of Santafé was not widely understood within most Muisca-speaking territories. As the linguist María Stella González de Pérez affirmed in her survey of studies of the language, 'it can be unequivocally said that, before the arrival of Spaniards, the aborigines of the Chibcha territory did not constitute a unilingual mass'.[45] And in any case this language bore little relation to the overwhelming majority of Indigenous languages in the rest of the New Kingdom of Granada, outside the Muisca highlands. The problem was not going to go away: almost forty years later, in 1618, the then archbishop of Santafé, Hernando Arias de Ugarte, still bemoaned how, unlike in Peru, '*there is no general language in this kingdom*, but many particular ones'.[46]

These issues were further complicated by the fact that, as earlier chapters have discussed, this was a tumultuous period for the New Kingdom. On one hand, Indigenous communities were coming under unprecedented pressure as a result of demographic collapse and colonial impositions, most recently the violence unleashed by the scramble for *santuarios*. What was left of the civil authorities spent the early 1580s, as we saw, trying to cover up their tracks, while the secular church, for its, part, was in the throes of Archbishop Zapata de Cárdenas's reform programme. In Peru and Mexico, the implementation of the new language policy advanced significantly with the influential provincial councils that were held there in the 1580s. Both councils published not only sophisticated guidelines to govern and homogenise the conduct of evangelisation,

---

[44] Proceedings on the case of Gonzalo Bermúdez, AGI SF 234, no. 47, 39r, my italics.

[45] María Stella González de Pérez, *Trayectoria de los estudios sobre la lengua chibcha o muisca* (Bogotá: Instituto Caro y Cuervo, 1980), 60.

[46] Letter of Archbishop Arias de Ugarte to the king, 11 June 1618, AGI SF 226, no. 142, 1r–1v. My italics.

238 *Language Policy and Legal Fiction*

but also sought – with varying success – to produce catechetical corpora that embraced the new language policy and took advantage of the opportunities provided by the existence of dominant Indigenous languages.[47] Things would be more difficult in Santafé, where Zapata had already been struggling against the limits of his resources and authority – even before his efforts to hold a provincial council and establish a seminary, which occupied him for much of the 1580s, both failed by the middle of the decade. Priests in his archdiocese would have to make do with his 1576 *Catechism* instead of the catechetical materials translated into Indigenous languages or the sophisticated legislation available to their contemporaries in the centres of empire.

In this context, the language provisions of the *Cédula magna* of 1574 provided a lifeline for Zapata. Language became central to his justification for his most controversial policies, the ordination of at least 124 men to the priesthood before his death in 1590 – including 22 *mestizos* – and his ruthless efforts to place them in Indigenous parishes to the exclusion of the religious orders. As early as 1575, Zapata pointed to the ability and fluency in Indigenous languages of his candidates to justify admitting them to the priesthood and using them to displace regulars from Indigenous parishes, reiterating this in letter after letter – especially as his ordination of *mestizos* became the focus of the antagonism of the religious orders, and a huge controversy in its own right.[48] Owing to political conditions in the New Kingdom, then, evangelisation in Indigenous languages quickly became an especially thorny question, and when the legislation of 1580 arrived it soon become a focal point in this broader conflict.

By 23 December 1581 the *Audiencia* had published edicts declaring the general language to be Santafé Muisca, advertising the professorship, and offering a salary of 400 pesos of twenty-karat gold. Applicants were informed of the requirements for office, that the successful candidate was to examine all those who presented themselves, teach every working

---

[47] Rosenblat, 'La hispanización de América', 89; Estenssoro Fuchs, *Paganismo*, 32ff; Durston, *Pastoral Quechua*, 28–29; Resines, *Catecismos americanos*, vol. 2, 236–237. However, as Poole shows (in *Pedro Moya de Contreras*, 160–162), the publication of catechetical texts in Mexico was not straightforward either.

[48] He defended his actions in these terms in his letters to the king of 22 April 1575 (AGI SF 226, no. 7), 8 August 1577 (AGI SF 226, no. 12), 30 March 1580 (AGI SF 226, no. 31), and 26 March 1583 (AGI SF 226, no. 44). This controversy, and what it reveals about emerging ideas about race and difference, was the subject of my first book, *Mestizos heraldos de Dios*.

'There Is No General Language in This Kingdom'   239

day, and compose a grammar and a vocabulary of the language so that students could make copies. He would also be required to say mass every Sunday, preaching and catechising in the language. Gonzalo Bermúdez, whom we met in Chapter 3, a secular priest from Santafé with experience working in the language preaching, teaching, and – as we saw – interrogating Indigenous leaders and seizing their valuables, applied shortly after. He was examined, selected, and appointed in early March 1582.[49] After a few months, the archbishop declared all Indigenous parishes vacant so that they could be filled in line with royal instructions.[50] Everything seemed to be running smoothly, until Bermúdez collected his first wages on 4 July 1582.

Five days later the Franciscan and Dominican provincials petitioned the *Audiencia* to suspend the general languages policy, arguing that it was pointless, not least because many Indigenous people already knew Spanish. They also argued that these languages could not be reduced to writing, much less to a grammar; and that they had poor vocabularies, lacking the words necessary to describe the mysteries of the faith, or properly and honestly translate concepts such as 'Christ', 'charity', 'grace', 'contrition', or 'penance', so that it was far more fruitful to make the Indigenous speak Castilian.[51] Such arguments were, of course, not new, and had been prominent in discussions about the validity of these languages at court and in other dioceses around Spanish America, especially in New Spain and Peru. Proposed solutions there had included the extensive use of loan words, the appropriation not just of Indigenous vocabulary but also rhetorical devices (with important consequences for the translation of concepts themselves), and other methods to bridge the linguistic and conceptual gap. But translation inevitably remained slippery and full of problems, and the use of Indigenous languages was a great source of anxiety at a time when even the Castilian language of which contemporary grammarians spoke so highly was not free from suspicion as a vehicle of evangelisation.[52]

---

[49] Proceedings on the case of Gonzalo Bermúdez, AGI SF 234, no. 47, 7r–8v. On Bermúdez, see his petitions for promotion of 19 April 1596 (AGI SF 238, no. 10), and 12 March 1613 (AGI SF 242); and the documentation of the suit over his wages as *catedrático* (AGI SF 234, no. 47). For a discussion of the latter document, see Lee López, 'Gonzalo Bermúdez'.

[50] Ibid., 197.

[51] Proceedings on the case of Gonzalo Bermúdez, AGI SF 234, no. 47, 21r.

[52] Louise M. Burkhart, *The Slippery Earth: Nahua-Christian Moral Dialogue in Sixteenth-Century Mexico* (Tucson: University of Arizona Press, 1989), 11–14; Estenssoro Fuchs, *Paganismo*, 43ff.

240   *Language Policy and Legal Fiction*

At the same time, the friars argued that the main requirement for religious instruction was a knowledge of Latin and theology, not a familiarity with the 'language of the Indians'. Few people actually knew the language, they argued, and they lacked the experience of those who had spent years working in evangelisation. Last but not least, they argued that if priests with no knowledge of the language were excluded, most of the regulars of the New Kingdom would have to return to the peninsula, at great cost to the colonial administration, which would not only have to subsidise their travel expenses but take over the funding of missions, church building, and even the procurement of oil and wine for consecration.[53] This financial argument may have been particularly attractive to an administration afflicted by insufficient resources.

The secular clergy, led by Alonso Romero de Aguilar and his fellows, presented their case three days later, arguing that the last forty years of missionary activity in New Granada had achieved little progress. Priests, they argued, had been forced to rely on Indigenous or African interpreters who were incapable of translating the basic tenets of Christian doctrine accurately, and who were difficult to police.[54] In doing so they were echoing the criticism of the use of interpreters that had been common in the first decades of Spanish colonisation of the New World, and – like the legislation of 1580 – they invoked the success of the *cátedras* of New Spain and Peru as proof of the viability of the policy.[55] They proposed that it was certainly possible to learn the language, as the first Dominicans and Franciscans, they claimed, had apparently done so fruitfully, and all the more now that the legislation of 1580 included the provision that Bermúdez compose a clear grammar, which he was already drafting. They recognised that it was not easy to translate the mysteries of the Christian faith, but that it had been a problem throughout the history of the church: similar problems had come up when translating the tenets of Christian theology from Greek to Latin, but they had been overcome, as Bermúdez was now doing. Even though few priests knew the language, very few Indigenous people knew Spanish, and it was ridiculous to demand that the thousands of inhabitants of the provinces of Bogotá and Tunja learn it when the majority of them were adults who had to work for a living, and even the young found it difficult. Instead, thirty or forty learned priests with time to devote to the study of Muisca could learn it easily, especially

---

[53] Proceedings on the case of Gonzalo Bermúdez, AGI SF 234, no. 47, 20v–22r.

[54] Ibid., 22r–27v.

[55] On the former, see Harvey, 'Language States', 196; Durston, *Pastoral Quechua*, 314.

'There Is No General Language in This Kingdom' 241

now that they were to have access to linguistic resources and catechetical texts in translation.

In response to the argument that they lacked the necessary experience, they reminded the *Audiencia* of petitions from local *caciques* during Lent, when they were apparently asked to provide Muisca-speaking priests to hear confessions from the Indigenous people. They even pointed to the discovery of *santuarios* by Zapata, Bermúdez, and others the previous decade, claiming these survived because Indigenous people had never been catechised properly, with friars content to teach them to recite the *Paternoster* and *Ave Maria* in Spanish, unable to explain what they meant. When called to administer Extreme Unction, they continued, ignorant friars unable to understand their parishioners would simply give them a blessing, saying 'may your faith and contrition save you, because I do not understand you'.[56]

The controversy raged on. The archbishop's opponents later focused their efforts on Bermúdez, convincing their allies in the *Audiencia* to withhold his wages and later suppress the chair. They even used Zapata's argument for ordaining *criollos* and *mestizos* against him: since these men already knew the language, no chair was necessary, especially as no peninsular priest had managed to learn the language – although no doubt in part as a result of the fact that the regulars had been ordered to boycott Bermúdez's lessons.[57] A smallpox epidemic that ravaged the region in the late 1580s inflamed things further, encouraging Zapata to strip the friars of their parishes with greater enthusiasm because their priests were 'unqualified by their lack of knowledge of the language of the Indians to whom they are to administer the holy sacraments', so that 'a great number of Indians have died without confession'. The friars claimed this was untrue, since 'the Indians know the Spanish language, because the said friars have taught it to them, and if some of them fail to learn it, it is because they are so old and decrepit, that language or no language, they do not want to be catechised or disciplined'.[58]

The policy was there to stay, and the crown reiterated this repeatedly in the face of petitions to the contrary, reissuing, whenever it seemed necessary, the provision that friars were to be examined in the language by diocesan authorities before they could be appointed to any Indigenous

---

[56] Proceedings on the case of Gonzalo Bermúdez, AGI SF 234, no. 47, 27r.

[57] Lee López, 'Gonzalo Bermúdez', 203–204.

[58] Proceedings concerning Zapata's seizure of Franciscan parishes, 19 January 1588, AGN C&O 9, 221r, 22v.

benefice.[59] At the same time, however, the crown sought to avoid alienating the religious orders by restoring some of their parishes and reining in successive archbishops. It even made sure that Bermúdez's wages were paid, and he remained in office until his death in 1625.[60] For their part, the religious orders would continue to oppose the requirements to learn Indigenous languages until the early seventeenth century, when Lobo Guerrero, Borja, and the Jesuits were able to establish a consensus around the use of Indigenous languages as part of their project to reform evangelisation, at least as far as the regular authorities of New Granada were concerned. The result was that the religious orders, who had been so strongly opposed to the use of Indigenous languages, produced their own linguistic texts and translations into Indigenous languages – most notably fray Bernardo de Lugo's famous Muisca grammar – even if individual friars continued to criticise the policy.

It is tempting to focus on the controversy over the use of Indigenous languages at this top level, as a number of scholars have done. After all, the arguments used by the supporters and opponents of the policy are revealing, not just of the politics and tensions that affected the church of the New Kingdom in this period, the relationship between the secular clergy and the religious orders, or competing perspectives on how best to evangelise Indigenous people, but also of more fundamental ideas and prejudices about language and its role. To do this, however, would be to leave crucial questions unanswered.

The most basic problem that the linguistic landscape of the New Kingdom of Granada posed to implementing the legislation of 1574–1580 was its heterogeneity. The legislation relied on the use of an Indigenous lingua franca, but everyone involved in the controversy of the 1580s was aware that the New Kingdom did not have one. Even Zapata, who had been an enthusiastic supporter of the idea of using Indigenous languages in evangelisation even before the landmark legislation of 1580, was well aware of the linguistic heterogeneity of the region. This was clear as early as 1577, when he proposed that 'the best method for it [evangelisation] is to preach and declare the Holy Gospel to them in their own languages', adding the caveat:

---

[59] The decree of 1580 that ordered friars be examined was reissued for different jurisdictions in 1603, 1618, 1622, 1624, and 1637. Royal decree 'Que los Religiosos doctrineros sean examinados por los prelados diocesanos en la suficiencia y lengua de los Indios de sus doctrinas', originally issued 5 August 1580, in *Recopilación* 1.15.6.

[60] Lee López, 'Gonzalo Bermúdez', 209.

'There Is No General Language in This Kingdom'   243

and I say *languages*, because in this Kingdom every valley or province has a different one, and it is not like Peru and New Spain, where there are different languages but one general language, which is used throughout the land. But in this land a friar goes to his catechumens and preaches the catechism in a language that is as if he did not preach it at all.[61]

The Jesuit Navarro, after all, would experience this first-hand a few decades later. It is not surprising that Zapata supported the policy of 1574–1580, for all its flaws. The 'general language' of Santafé might have been part misconception and part legal fiction, but it allowed him to use the legislation of 1574–1580 to support his attempts to reorganise the church.

His opponents were also well aware of this reality, and repeatedly highlighted the fact that there was no such thing as an Indigenous lingua franca in the New Kingdom of Granada in their campaign against the policy. As Diego Malo de Molina, Franciscan *comisario general*, argued in 1588, 'in a single valley there are usually two or three languages, and the same in other valleys, so that if a priest somehow manages to learn some of the language of Bogotá, he does not know that of Suesca or Nemocón' or of other places, so that Zapata's *criollo* and *mestizo* priests were hardly a solution.[62] The policy could only work in the long term if there was a steady supply of priests from the various parts of the highlands, and if care was taken to ensure they remained in the areas where they were from.[63] Using *mestizo* priests would be difficult, after the huge backlash against Zapata's ordinations. As time would show, his successors would not share his stubborn enthusiasm for ordaining them in such large numbers. Indeed, the long period of vacancy that followed his death resulted in a dearth of new ordinations. At least according to the Jesuit vice-provincial, Gonzalo de Lyra, *criollos* would not do either. As he claimed in a letter to his superiors of 1609, unlike in other parts of the New World, the New Kingdom by this point lacked 'the custom that

---

[61] Letter of Archbishop Zapata to the king, 8 February 1577, AGI SF 226, no. 12, 1r (my italics).

[62] Proceedings concerning Zapata's seizure of Franciscan parishes, 19 January 1588, AGN C&O 9, 222.

[63] Aside from some more specific temporary missions, such as hearing confessions in Lent, or serving as interpreters. This was the experience of the mestizo priest Alonso Romero de Aguilar, which he described in his *información de méritos* of 20 December 1588, at AGI SF 236, no. 14, 1r–16r. A similar experience was reported by Gonzalo Bermúdez in his petitions for a canonry in 1596: he was ordinarily the Muisca *catedrático* but also the priest of the parish of Santa Bárbara in the city of Santafé and occasionally served the archbishop as an interpreter and a preacher, including visitations (AGI SF 238, no. 10).

244 *Language Policy and Legal Fiction*

Indigenous women raise the children of Spaniards born in this land', so that new generations of *criollos* were raised with no knowledge of local languages – although, as we will see, this was no small exaggeration.[64]

Moreover, Zapata's efforts had focused on the training of priests, fostering and protecting the new Muisca chair and its incumbent. Bermúdez's task was to teach the 'general language' to the clergy, but it was not to produce a standardised translation of catechetical texts for use in the parishes. It is entirely possible that he produced a translation of catechetical material as a teaching aid, as some historians have suggested.[65] No such text has survived, and in any case there was no effort to issue standardised Muisca catechetical material in this period. The closest the archdiocese came to having a standard catechetical corpus was Zapata's 1576 manuscript *Catechism*, written in Spanish and designed more to be an aid to evangelisation rather than a single, systematic corpus for the obligatory use of everyone in the archdiocese, like the texts of Lima III.[66] In other words, a knowledge of Indigenous languages was required, and the means to learn them provided, but beyond this priests working in Indigenous parishes were to be left to their own devices.

Zapata's approach to the problem of language was pragmatic and ambitious, and very much in line with his broader desire to introduce greater homogeneity and order to Christianisation across the archdiocese, but it was still haphazard and unsustainable in the long term. Of course, Spanish had continued to spread among Indigenous people, as some of Zapata's opponents were eager to highlight, and bilingualism became even more prevalent from the 1580s.[67] But it was by no means universal. When his successor, Bartolomé Lobo Guerrero, arrived in Santafé in 1598 the problem had not gone away. In this area too Lobo Guerrero and his allies would need a new strategy, and they found one.

---

[64] Gonzalo de Lyra to Claudio Acquaviva, 1609, ARSI NR&Q 1–2, 15r.

[65] Gamboa, 'Introducción', 27.

[66] Fernando Campo argues that this text was translated into Indigenous languages and used around the archdiocese, citing the chronicler Zamora (who wrote in the 1690s). This may well have been the case, although it was by no means an official text of obligatory use, and no such translations have been found. See Fernando Campo del Pozo, 'Catecismos agustinianos utilizados en Hispanoamérica'. In *Provincia Agustiniana de Nuestra Señora de Gracia en Colombia: escritos varios. Vol. 4.* Edited by José Pérez Gómez OSA (Bogotá: Provincia Agustiniana de Nuestra Señora de Gracia en Colombia, 1993), 321–369.

[67] Gamboa, 'Introducción', 17–19.

NEW TEXTS FOR NEW PRIORITIES

By the time Archbishop Lobo Guerrero arrived in Santafé almost twenty years had passed since the general languages policy had been introduced in the region, and yet a large number of parishes remained in the hands of regulars with no knowledge of Indigenous languages. Even when friars did know them, their authorities were so unconcerned with the issue of language that they failed to send them to parishes where they could use them. Legislation to remove those failing to meet the linguistic requirements, as he put it, had been 'promulgated but not executed'. And the friars had used the vacuum left by the death of his predecessor eight years earlier to entrench their privileges and exemptions, turning back the clock on Zapata's reforms. Lobo Guerrero set to work, and shortly after his arrival announced his intention to force the holders of Indigenous parishes to be examined in their proficiency in Indigenous languages, in his presence, even if it meant enlisting the support of Rome.[68] Two years later he reported that his investigation had revealed that only seven or eight Franciscans knew the languages, three or four Dominicans, and three Augustinians.[69] Nevertheless, even though he had been able to compel all holders of parishes to be examined, the *Audiencia* under President Sande had taken over the examinations and was allowing a number of incompetent priests to keep their parishes.[70] This was going to be an uphill struggle. But here too he could rely on the Jesuits he had brought with him.

The Jesuits had become aware of the challenges posed by the region's linguistic heterogeneity early on, but also realised that it provided them with an opportunity. The first task facing Alonso de Medrano and Francisco de Figueroa, the two Jesuits that arrived with Lobo Guerrero in 1598, was convincing their superiors to establish a permanent presence in the New Kingdom. This involved treading a fine line: on one hand highlighting the failures of evangelisation, even if it meant mischaracterising the efforts of their peers in the other religious orders and the secular clergy, but, on the other, still making clear that the region constituted a viable missionary theatre where their order's resources would not be squandered. The New Kingdom's complex linguistic landscape – or at least their characterisation of it – was central to both arguments.

---

[68] Lobo Guerrero to the king, 16 May 1599, AGI SF 226, no. 61a, 1v.
[69] Lobo Guerrero to the king, 20 May 1603, AGI SF 226 no. 87, 3v.   [70] Ibid., 3v–4r.

246 *Language Policy and Legal Fiction*

To make their case, Medrano and Figueroa sent their superiors a detailed report on the New Kingdom of Granada around the turn of the century, containing detailed descriptions of the conditions of the kingdom, its size, its Spanish cities, its Indigenous inhabitants, the Spanish authorities, the needs of the church, and the state of evangelisation.[71] A central concern was language. The Jesuits explained that the largest 'Indigenous nation' was 'the province of the Muisca Indians, which comprises Santafé and Tunja', and 'whose language is general in the whole Kingdom', only to then claim that it was in fact 'so horrible and difficult to pronounce and lacking in vocabulary' that no one had been able to codify or translate prayers and the catechism into it – at least until they had arrived on the scene. Neglecting to inform their superiors of the work of Gonzalo Bermúdez and other linguists and interpreters over the previous half century, the pair proceeded to claim they had cracked the issue of language for the first time and produced the very first translation of the catechism and a basic grammar of the language, which they enclosed for publication, 'to the astonishment of the entire land'.[72]

This Jesuit grammar and catechism, long thought lost, or perhaps even fictitious, was recently located by Santiago Muñoz and appears to have been printed in Seville in 1603, alongside a much better known Quechua grammar by Diego de Torres Rubio, on which it is closely modelled.[73] This *Grammar of the Muisca Language of the Indians of the New Kingdom of Granada* takes the linguistic homogeneity of Muisca groups for granted, and served to underscore both the viability of organising a

---

[71] 'Descripción del Nuevo Reino de Granada de las Indias Occidentales en orden a la fundación que el mismo Reino pretende y pide se haga en él de casas y colegios de la Compañía de Jesús', ARSI NR&Q 14, 15r–15v.

[72] Ibid., 2v, 15r–15v.

[73] *Arte de la lengua mosca de los Indios del nueuo Reyno de Granada, en las Indias Occidentales*, which Muñoz and I attribute to Alonso de Medrano and Francisco Figueroa and which was likely printed in Seville in 1603 by Clemente Hidalgo. This extraordinary book, of which the only known copy is held at the Bodleian Library of the University of Oxford, comprises twenty-five printed pages containing a basic grammar with the most basic structures of the language and the conjugation of two types of verbs, followed by a 'doctrina cristiana' with translations of religious terms and expressions, and Muisca translations of the Creed and the Ten Commandments. The book is undated and unsigned, but through a careful analysis of the paper, typography, and other characteristics we have been able to determine that it was printed at the same time as Diego de Torres Rubio's better known *Grammatica y vocabolario en la lengva general del Perv llamada Quichya, y en la lengua Española: El mas copioso y elegante que hasta agora se ha impresso* (Impresso en Seuilla: en casa de Clemente Hidalgo, 1603), with which the Bodleian copy is bound. If this is correct, it is the earliest text in Muisca to have been discovered to date.

New Texts for New Priorities

247

permanent Jesuit presence in the region, and the applicability of the missionary methods they had been implementing in regions such as Mexico and Peru, whilst emphasising that without them the enterprise would never succeed.

This was a claim that the Jesuits of Santafé continued to push in their correspondence with their Roman superiors for years, even after a vice-province was established with the arrival of Torres Bollo and greater numbers of Jesuits arrived in the region. In this vein, their very first *littera annua*, in 1605, described how the Jesuits had begun their work by preaching to the Indigenous inhabitants of the city of Santafé on Sundays and market days, only to realise that 'little fruit was reaped from this work' because 'few Indians understand the Spanish language' and the Jesuits 'did not know that of the Indians'.[74] It was as if the history of the Spanish encounter with Indigenous languages was repeating itself. Behind these stories for external consumption, of course, the Jesuits were availing themselves of Zapata's legacy. For all their claims that they had learned Muisca without assistance, the Jesuit vice-provincial Gonzalo de Lyra himself acknowledged the Jesuits' debt to Gonzalo Bermúdez in 1611, 'for having taught [them] the language', and advocated for his promotion and reward by the authorities.[75]

What is more significant about the involvement of the Jesuits in language policy is that they were at the centre of the production of a new consensus on language policy at a local level. In the 1580s Bermúdez had been appointed to enable priests to learn Indigenous languages, producing a Muisca grammar and vocabulary, and using them to teach priests who wanted to retain or to be appointed to Indigenous parishes. Now Lobo Guerrero and the Jesuits went much further: they wanted to produce a standardised translation of catechetical texts in the general language, thereby homogenising the contents and practice of catechisation.

Just as Torres Bollo had envisioned the Peruvian parishes under the care of his order in Chucuito to serve as language school for Jesuit missionaries, their Neogranadian parishes became centres of translation and language teaching.[76] Only months after their arrival in the

---

[74] Draft 1604–1605 Jesuit *littera annua*, c. 1605, ARSI NR&Q 12-I, 34r–34v.

[75] This was in a letter supporting Gonzalo Bermúdez's petition for the position of dean or archdeacon in the cathedral of Santafé in the 1610s, at AGI SF 242, not numbered, dated 6 May 1611, fol. 1r.

[76] Even though, as Aliocha Maldavsky has shown, few Jesuits in the Peruvian province were enthusiastic about actually having to learn Indigenous languages and considered this a menial skill better left to less distinguished members of their order, in particular *criollos*

248   *Language Policy and Legal Fiction*

Indigenous parish of Cajicá, Lobo Guerrero reported how 'with their help the catechism [*doctrina cristiana*] and prayers were translated into their language', and that he had ordered that catechisation and prayers be conducted in it 'as is done in New Spain and Peru'.[77] The text in question was the translation of the *Catecismo breve* of Lima III.[78] Moreover, an unnamed Jesuit described how he had been given a copy of the confessionary used in the diocese of Lima, 'which [he] translated' as well.[79] Nevertheless, while Lobo Guerrero praised the success of these translations in June 1606, they had been the subject of great criticism. As a Jesuit source of the same period put it, 'when our priests began to try it out, there were many contradictions'. This time, however, the criticism was constructive, and the result was a concerted collaborative effort to improve the Jesuit translation of the text, with 'the twelve best linguists of the kingdom coming together, in the presence of the lord archbishop, an *oidor* of the *Audiencia*, and our father Rector'. After 'many months of meetings', the result was 'a most perfect translation of Christian doctrine, catechism, and confessionary', which was completed a year later, in August 1606.[80]

A decree of President Borja of 15 August provides further details about how this worked. He explained that the text comprised 'the Creed, the *Paternoster*, the *Ave Maria* and *Salve Regina*, the Ten Commandments of the law of God, the Works of Mercy, and a brief catechism in the form of questions and answers containing the articles of our faith'. That the Jesuits, with the input of Gonzalo Bermúdez and other unnamed experts, under the supervision of Lobo Guerrero, had translated it 'from the Castilian language to the general language of the Indians of this province of Santafé de Bogotá that they call Chibcha', only for it to be criticised, and that he had therefore intervened, and brought together a committee that included the Franciscan, Dominican, Augustinian, and Jesuit provincials, Gonzalo Bermúdez, a number of other secular priests and friars, an

---

and *mestizos*. Aliocha Maldavsky, 'The Problematic Acquisition of Indigenous Languages: Practices and Contentions in Missionary Specialization in the Jesuit Province of Peru (1568–1640)'. In *The Jesuits II: Cultures, Sciences, and the Arts, 1540–1773*. Edited by John W. O'Malley, Gauvin Alexander Bailey, Steven J. Harris, and T. Frank Kennedy (Toronto: University of Toronto Press, 2006), 602–615. On Torres Bollo in Chucuito, see Meiklejohn, *La iglesia y los Lupaqas*, 207.

[77] Letter of Archbishop Lobo Guerrero to the king, 6 October 1606, AGI SF 226, no. 101, 1v.

[78] Gamboa, 'Introducción', 28.

[79] Jesuit *littera annua* for 1608–1609, dated 20 September 1609, NR&Q 12-I, 46r.

[80] Draft 1604–1605 Jesuit *littera annua*, c. 1605, ARSI NR&Q 12-I, 34r.

New Texts for New Priorities

encomendero expert in the language, and the *Audiencia's* own official interpreters. The Jesuit Joseph Dadey then read the earlier translation clause by clause, and each was considered and modified by the committee until all were satisfied and the translation was so authoritative that 'it could not be improved further'. This done, a further meeting was called, this time also including the municipal council of Santafé and other local notables, who all swore that it was an accurate translation.[81]

Since the translation had been the result of a communal effort and approved with such broad consensus, it had a legitimacy that no previous text had enjoyed. The Jesuit source was not exaggerating in praising the skills and experience of the members of the committee: some, such as the Augustinian Provincial Vicente Mallol, and the Dominican Bernardo de Lugo, were themselves the authors of other translations of catechetical and linguistic material.[82] Indeed, Borja even highlighted the fact that because the committee included not only experts in the language but eminent theologians (the Jesuits), it was more faithful than any previous translation could have hoped to be. The result was that the controversy over the validity of using Indigenous languages for evangelisation that had been raging since the 1570s was finally laid to rest, at least at the level of the authorities. Finally, Borja ordered that this text be published, and that 'by it and by no other' the Indians were 'to be taught and instructed from today on in the things of our holy Catholic faith', establishing harsh penalties – 200 pesos, one year's exile, and potentially 200 lashes – for those who questioned its accuracy, and decreeing that the stipends of parish priests who refused to use it were to be withheld.[83]

---

[81] Decree of President Borja on the official translation of the catechism to the General Language of Santafé, 25 August 1606, ARSI NR&Q 14, 48r–49r. The *encomendero* was none other than Diego Romero de Aguilar, the brother of *mestizo* priests Andrés and Alonso.

[82] Vicente Mallol had explained to the king in July 1603 that he had produced his own catechism in Muisca, which has not survived (AGI SF 240, not numbered, letter dated 2 July 1603, 1r). On this missing text, Fernando Campo del Pozo, 'El P. Vicente Mallol, OSA, su actuación y catecismo en la lengua chibcha'. In *Provincia Agustiniana de Nuestra Señora de Gracia en Colombia: escritos varios. Vol. 4*. Edited by José Pérez Gómez OSA (Bogotá: Provincia Agustiniana de Nuestra Señora de Gracia en Colombia, 1993), 11–34. Lugo's grammar and confessionary, until recently thought to have been the only text in Muisca ever actually published in the colonial period, is better known. Bernardo de Lugo, *Gramatica en la lengua general del Nuevo Reyno, llamada Mosca* (Madrid: Bernardino de Guzmán, 1619).

[83] Decree of President Borja on the official translation of the catechism to the General Language of Santafé, 25 August 1606, ARSI NR&Q 14, 49v.

250   *Language Policy and Legal Fiction*

A few days later, in September 1606, Lobo Guerrero and the other reformers held the second synod of the archdiocese of Santafé, and the first since 1566. Aware of the archdiocese's limitations and of the urgency of its situation, rather than delve into the complicated process of producing its own catechetical corpus, the synod effectively sought to buy some time by temporarily introducing the material produced by Lima III that had just been translated, which it reproduced in Spanish.[84] A few years later, in 1625, the first Provincial Council of Santafé was finally called, and the archdiocese issued its own catechetical materials at last.[85] Nevertheless, the real change in the use of Indigenous languages for evangelisation had come not in 1625 but in 1606, with the production of this official translation. And yet, the biggest problem of all had still not gone away.

LOCAL CONDITIONS AND LOCAL SOLUTIONS

Despite the innovations of the early decades of the seventeenth century, nothing had been done to overcome the problem of linguistic heterogeneity, the crucial weakness in any argument in favour of using an Indigenous lingua franca for evangelisation in the New Kingdom of Granada. After all, what use was an official translation of catechetical material into the 'general language' if there was no such thing?

Historians have tended to propose that the solution to the problem of the linguistic heterogeneity of New Granada was to use more than one 'general' language, in the sense of lingua franca. For Ortega Ricaurte, for example, in addition to Muisca, Quechua was used in the diocese of Popayán, as it was spoken by a number of groups in the south and south-west of the New Kingdom of Granada, and 'those in the south [used], Siona ... and because it seemed that *Tupí-rupí* or *Yeral* was common in Brazil and the Amazon, this was to be used there'.[86] This idea seems to arise at least in part from a misreading of the legislation of the synod of 1606, which declared that the texts of Lima III had been translated into 'the general language' – that is Santafé Muisca – 'with great care and diligence by the most intelligent and able people that have been found'. Like Borja, the synod declared this was to be the only

---

[84] 'Constituciones sinodales 1606', 226, 268–275.
[85] 'Concilio provincial 1625', 336–339.
[86] Carmen Ortega Ricaurte, *Los estudios sobre lenguas indígenas de Colombia: notas históricas y bibliografía* (Bogotá: Instituto Caro y Cuervo, 1978), 32.

Local Conditions and Local Solutions

translation and the only catechetical text in this language that was to be used, and also established penalties for non-compliance – in its case, excommunication. This did not mean, however, that the synod was ignoring the uncomfortable reality of the archdiocese's linguistic hetero-geneity. It ordered priests active in 'the other districts [*partidos*] ... bring-ing together the best linguists in these villages, [to] translate the same doctrine and catechism of Lima into the language used in the said districts [*partidos*]'.[87]

How historians interpret these requirements rests on their interpret-ation not only of the ambiguous term 'general language', but also of what they understand to be a 'district' or '*partido*'. In light of the experience of New Spain and Peru, it is easy to see how some scholars have tended to assume that these districts were vast areas, even corresponding to entire dioceses, so that 'the language' referred to a lingua franca spoken across a large geography. This impression is reinforced by the legislation of the First Provincial Council of Santafé, in 1625, which produced standard-ised, official catechetical materials for the entire archdiocese – including the dioceses of Cartagena, Popayán, and Santa Marta – and banned the use of all other versions, while also legislating on the question of translations. The council had been called by Archbishop Hernando Arias de Ugarte, after a long visitation of a great deal of the metropolitan archdiocese, and the council referred to this visitation in its constitutions concerning the languages that were to be used for evangelisation.[88] The text explained that over the course of the visitation, 'in the Provinces [*Provinciis*] of Tunja, of Merida, of Muzo, and of La Palma', the Jesuit Miguel Jerónimo de Tolosa 'produced a version of the catechism in the language of the same Indians'.[89] The text referred to '*Indorum linguam*' in the singular, but does this mean that the inhabitants of these provinces (which cover most of the northern section of the eastern range of the Andes) all spoke a single language?

Historians have tended to assume so, even if they are also aware of, and indeed cite, the various sources that complain about linguistic heterogen-eity. Looking at this problem from the top it is easy to get this impression. Even so, the idea that a handful of general languages – Muisca, Quechua,

---

[87] 'Constituciones sinodales 1606', 229–230.
[88] Arias de Ugarte's visitation is scrutinised in Chapter 6. For now see Pedro Antonio Ospina Suárez, *Hernando Arias de Ugarte (1561–1638): El criollo arzobispo de las tres sedes sudamericanas* (Rome: Pontificia Universitas Gregoriana, 2004).
[89] 'Concilio provincial 1625', 338–339.

252 *Language Policy and Legal Fiction*

Siona, Tupí-rupí – were used, rather than just one, hardly explains how the issue of linguistic heterogeneity was addressed, given the size of the New Kingdom of Granada. This is why it is important to examine what actually happened within one of these allegedly homogenous blocks, through local sources that describe the situation inside the Muisca heartlands of the 'valley of Bogotá and Tunja' to which the *Audiencia* referred in 1581, and even the 'province of Tunja' of the 1625 legislation – which may scholars have assumed constituted a homogenous linguistic block. These local sources paint a very different picture.

In February 1608 Archbishop Lobo Guerrero presented the priest Diego de Sanabria to fill the Indigenous parish of Paipa, vacant after the death of its previous incumbent. The town is located some twenty-five miles north-east of Tunja, in the north-eastern highlands of the archdiocese. It was part of the province of Tunja, and firmly in the region that all the legislation described as being inhabited by speakers of Muisca. Of course, the legislation of the 1580s required Sanabria to be fluent in the 'general language' of the New Kingdom of Granada – that is Santafé Muisca – to have studied it under the *catedrático*, Gonzalo Bermúdez, and to have passed his examination. Naturally, this came up in the documentation surrounding his appointment. Indeed, the archbishop described how 'father Diego de Sanabria, priest, said that he knows and understands and is fluent in the language of those Indians *of the said parish*'. But the archbishop was not referring to the general language of the New Kingdom of Granada: President Borja accepted Sanabria, 'since he knows the general language, *and that of Sogamoso, and that of the said town of Paipa*'.[90] Paipa is about 120 miles away from Santafé, but it is only twenty miles away from Sogamoso, and yet the languages spoken are listed separately. Here we have further indication of the linguistic heterogeneity of New Granada.

Records such as this are rare. Most of the documentation surrounding the appointment of priests to Indigenous parishes contains no details about the linguistic qualifications of the people concerned, or indeed anything else, since they tend to be short and formulaic texts. When the Dominican Francisco de León was nominated to the parish of Siachoque, in 1615, all that was mentioned was that his ability in the language had been 'examined and approved by our lord archbishop'.[91] Alonso Macías,

---

[90] Language examination of Diego de Sanabria, 1608–1610, APSLB Parroquias Boyacá 4/2/7, 13r, my italics.

[91] Appointment of Francisco de León to the parish of Siachoque, 1615, AGN C&O 28, doc. 88, 125r.

Local Conditions and Local Solutions 253

elected to the parish of Tabio in the same year, 'was examined in his Christianity and cases of conscience and in the general language of the natives by the *catedrático* Gonzalo Bermúdez'.[92] Hernando Vásquez got little more in 1625, when he was admitted to the parish of Monguí in 1625: his sufficiency 'in the exam both of the language and of cases of conscience' was 'moderate' ('*mediana*'), but, still, off he went to his new parish.[93] No information about these exams, what they contained, or even what made Vásquez's effort unimpressive, seems to have survived. But in this regard Sanabria's records are once again unusual.

Two years after his appointment, the cathedral chapter issued an edict requiring all priests holding Indian parishes in the region to be tested in their ability with the languages of their parishioners, even if they had already been examined in the past. Sanabria duly appeared before the chapter in September 1610, stating that he had received news of edict, which required parish priests 'to be examined *in the general language of the Indians of the district of Tunja*'. The chapter explained that he was to be examined not just 'in the language of the district of Tunja', but also 'particularly in the language of the Indians of the *repartimiento* of Paipa and its surroundings'.[94]

As might be expected, the chapter summoned 'Gonzalo Bermúdez, priest, *catedrático* of the general language of the district of this kingdom', but also 'Juan de Sepúlveda, linguist and interpreter of the *Real Audiencia*', and 'Alonso Sanz, native of the said city of Tunja'. Different specialists, different languages. First, Sanz was ordered 'to ask the said Diego de Sanabria in the general language of the Indians of Tunja, and in that of the Indians of the said town of Paipa, some questions ... touching the administration of the Holy Sacraments' and his pastoral duties. Sanabria passed. Sanz was then taken aside and told to ask Sanabria some more questions in the language of Paipa, 'related to his office of priest and the teaching of his parishioners'. Sanabria was asked to answer them 'in our Castilian language', which he did. Sanabria was then asked to step outside, and the specialists were required to confirm whether he 'knew and understood the said languages' (plural): 'that of the Indians of the district of Tunja, of the said town of Paipa, and of the valley of

---

[92] Appointment of Alonso Macías to the parish of Tabio, 1615, AGN C&O 28, doc. 91, 129r.

[93] Appointment of Hernando Vásquez to the parish of Monguí, 1625, AGN C&O 28, doc. 234, 314v.

[94] Proceedings of the language examination of Diego de Sanabria, 24 September 1610, APSLB Parroquias Boyacá 4/2/7, 14r.

254   *Language Policy and Legal Fiction*

Sogamoso'.[95] They agreed that he did, and Sanabria was allowed to return to his parish.

Unfortunately, these documents do not record further details of what was asked, let alone the questions presented to him in the original language, so it is not possible to reconstruct even a glimpse of these different languages, or of concrete differences between them. There is also some ambiguity as to whether the languages of Sogamoso and Paipa were one, as president Borja suggested when he confirmed Lobo Guerrero's appointment of Sanabria in 1608, or whether they were different. What is clear, at least, is that even the experts identified a language of Tunja that was distinct from that of Santafé, and a language of Paipa that was distinct from these two, and this makes the text clear evidence of the linguistic heterogeneity of even this small corner of the archdiocese.

The documentation surrounding the presentation of Sanabria is unusually detailed, but fortunately not unique. A fellow Dominican, Tomás Benítez, appeared before the cathedral chapter at around the same time as Sanabria, in response to the same edict.[96] Benítez was the parish priest of Lenguazaque, which was located in the province of Santafé rather than that of Tunja, but still some seventy miles north-east of the seat of the archdiocese. Benítez was to be examined 'in the general language of the Indians of this kingdom, and in particular in the language of the Indians of Lenguazaque'.[97] Bermúdez and Sepúlveda were summoned and given the same instructions. But they replied that he should only be examined in the general language of Santafé, since 'the Indians of the district of this city can make themselves understood very well in the language of the Indians of the said town of Lenguazaque'.[98] Once again, there is no concrete information about the similarities, but what is striking is that the authorities assumed that the languages were different and that this necessitated two separate exams. It was only when the experts arrived that they learned that the languages were similar enough, and that only one exam was therefore necessary.

What these records demonstrate was that the linguistic landscape was indeed heterogeneous, even within an area traditionally assumed to have been largely homogenous. It also demonstrates that the idea of using one lingua franca could not work in New Granada, and that the authorities

---

[95] Ibid., 14v.

[96] Proceedings of the language examination of Tomás Benitez, 22 September 1610, AGN C&O 28, 153r–161v.

[97] Ibid., 154r.   [98] Ibid., 155r.

Solutions on the Ground

were aware of the situation. But how could this be combined with the drive to homogenise the conduct of religious instruction? After all, the standard catechetical literature that was issued in the general language might have been good for Lenguazaque, but not for Paipa and elsewhere. The answer the New Kingdom's authorities came up with was remarkably simple.

SOLUTIONS ON THE GROUND

Chapter 6 examines surviving records of the exhaustive visitation of the Indigenous parishes of the archdiocese that was conducted over six years by Archbishop Arias de Ugarte before he called the First Provincial Council of Santafé in 1625. For now, what is key is that surviving documentation provides a glimpse of how linguistic issues were being overcome at a local level by the 1620s.[99] Priests examined by the archbishop were required, among other things, to produce a number of items and texts integral to the performance of their duties. Andrés de Córdoba, parish priest of Soracá (some five miles east of Tunja), was thus asked in November 1621 to produce the documentation of his ordination and appointment to his benefice, adequate parish records, a breviary, and other documents. Crucially, he was also asked to produce copies of 'the Christian doctrine and catechism *in the language*' and 'the Confessionary *in the language*'.[100]

Córdoba had a copy of the constitutions of the Council of Trent, the decrees of the synod of 1606, some parish records, and the documents of his ordination and installation, but he failed to produce most of the others.[101] Since the archdiocese still lacked its own catechetical corpus, priests like Córdoba were required to use the catechetical material produced by Lima III, specifically its Catechism for Indians, which the synod had introduced to the archdiocese in Spanish. He lacked this text, and also the catechism and confessionary 'in the language'. The archbishop admonished him, and recorded how despite, 'being so able in the language he has not made [*hecho*] the catechism, prayers, and confessionary

---

[99] Little of the documentation of the visitation has survived, not least because much of it was lost during the arduous progress of the visitation itself, during which Arias de Ugarte almost drowned. Pacheco, *La consolidación*, 67–79; and Ospina Suárez, *Hernando Arias de Ugarte*.

[100] Visitation of the parish of Soracá by Archbishop Arias de Ugarte, 24 November 1620, AHSB Libro 6, 13r (my italics).

[101] Ibid., 13v.

256 *Language Policy and Legal Fiction*

in the language, nor has he taught the Indians the said catechism in it, as he should do'.[102] 'The language' was not the 'general language' of the archdiocese, but the language of the people of the town. This was even more explicit when, in June 1623, still on his visitation, Arias de Ugarte made similar charges to Fernando de Gordillo, parish priest of San José de Pare, some fifty miles north-west of Tunja. Gordillo too failed to produce 'the catechism and confessionary *in the language of the Indians of this parish*', and he could not even speak it.[103]

To the charge, of 'not having made the catechism and prayers and confessionary in the language' ('*no tener hecho*'), Córdoba gave a revealing answer: 'I have not yet made it before seeing how I was commanded to do it in this visitation, which I will now do in light of what has been commanded to me.'[104] A mediocre excuse, but a revealing one: priests in the archdiocese of Santafé were required to produce their own translations or adaptations of catechetical and pastoral literature in the language of their parishioners.[105] The archbishop ordered both priests to produce their translations and to send them to Santafé for approval – Córdoba within six months, Gordillo within four.[106] Moreover, when the archbishop had cause to doubt the ability of a priest to produce an adequate translation for his parish, he still had a solution. In July 1623, when he charged Rodrigo Alonso, the parish priest of Saboyá, of 'not having produced the catechism and confessionary in the language of the Indians', he ordered him to produce one within four months, or 'someone will be sent at his cost to do so' for him.[107] The same choice had been given to Juan de Guevara, priest of Moniquirá, in June.[108]

Arias de Ugarte was aware of the spread of Spanish among Indigenous people, but this was no reason to abandon the use of Indigenous

---

[102] Ibid., 14r (my italics).

[103] Visitation of the parish of San José de Pare by Archbishop Arias de Ugarte, 8 June 1623, AHSB Libro 6, 98v (my italics).

[104] Ibid., 15r.

[105] This may be why there is such a dearth of surviving catechetical texts in Indigenous languages for New Granada. Indeed, comparatively few parish documents of any sort survive for the sixteenth and early seventeenth centuries in most parishes in Cundinamarca and Boyacá.

[106] Visitation of the parish of San José de Pare by Archbishop Arias de Ugarte, 8 June 1623, AHSB Libro 6, 16r, 98v.

[107] Visitation of the parish of Saboyá by Archbishop Arias de Ugarte, 18 July 1623, AHSB Libro 6, 125v.

[108] Visitation of the parish of Moniquirá by Archbishop Arias de Ugarte, 10 June 1623, AHSB Libro 6, 105v.

languages. When Gerónimo García Vásquez, the parish priest of Fúquene, a town some forty-five miles south-west of Tunja, had tried to argue that the majority of his parishioners could speak Spanish in October 1619, Arias de Ugarte ordered him to also catechise in Indigenous languages regardless, and to produce the required translations.[109] In March 1621 Arias de Ugarte had encountered Cristóbal de Cifuentes, another reprobate who made a similar argument for teaching only in Spanish.[110] Cifuentes was the priest of Guacamayas, a more remote town – located around 140 miles north-east of Tunja, 240 miles away from Santafé – but distance was no excuse, and when he failed to produce the texts, he was duly charged, for 'despite being required to have produced a confessionary and catechism in the language of the Indians ... he has not done so in the 27 years that he has been parish priest'.[111] The policy would remain in place, despite the fact that the adoption of Spanish among Indigenous people only grew, and even when the authorities introduced policies to bolster the use of Spanish. In 1641, for example, when a rescript was promulgated across the Indigenous parishes of the region that ordered that 'all young Indians who can learn the Castilian language be taught it' – for reasons similar to those quoted by the legislation of 1550 – three years later it was suspended because it seemed to be resulting in the abandonment of evangelisation in Indigenous languages altogether.[112]

Perhaps the discovery of new sources in the future might make possible an exhaustive linguistic analysis that can explore the extent of the heterogeneity of the different varieties of Muisca, but for now one thing is clear: what these sources reveal is that the authorities of the New Kingdom of Granada had abandoned the idea of using a single Indigenous lingua franca in evangelisation, and instead required that bespoke catechetical material tailored to the languages of the localities be produced as a matter of course.

---

[109] Visitation of the parish of Fúquene by Archbishop Arias de Ugarte, 16 October 1619, AHSB Caja 1, 184v.

[110] Visitation of the parish of Guacamayas by Archbishop Arias de Ugarte, 9 March 1621, AHSB Libro 6, 19r–38v.

[111] Ibid., 31r.

[112] A copy of this decree and its subsequent retraction survives in the book of baptisms of the parish of Oicatá (AGN PB, Oicatá, Libro 1, at 121v–123r and 130r, respectively). The decree was promulgated around the empire, and its reasoning seems familiar: that with a knowledge of Spanish would be beneficial to the salvation and *policía* of Indigenous people, and even that it did not seem very difficult (*'muy dificultoso'*) given how the Inca had managed to impose Quechua.

258   *Language Policy and Legal Fiction*

When the provinces of Santafé and Tunja were inspected in the second half of the 1630s by the *oidores* Gabriel de Carvajal and Juan de Valcárcel, respectively, in the last such inspections the *Audiencia* would carry out until the end of the century, their conversations with Indigenous witnesses reveal that the usage of Indigenous languages in catechisation at a local level was by now well entrenched and that Arias de Ugarte's *ad hoc* solution was working. Records for the twenty-eight parishes for which records survive – explored in greater detail in Chapter 6 – show that in each and every town the priest was deemed by Indigenous people to be competent in their language, even though most witnesses also reported large numbers of Spanish speakers in their towns. These were often perfunctory statements confirming the priest knew the language, but occasionally give us a little more. So it was in Tibaguyas, where Indigenous governor Pedro Cabra explained that their priest, Francisco Delgado, 'teaches them the prayers of Christian doctrine and preaches sermons in their language, explaining the things of God with much Christian zeal, and the Indians are *ladinos* and understand him in their Muisca language and in Spanish, and he confesses and marries them and baptises their children and buries their dead'.[113] By then, the overwhelming majority of priests in Indigenous parishes – regulars as well as seculars – were *criollos*, so that many had grown up in the multilingual environments that were the cities of Santafé, Tunja, and smaller towns, regardless of whether or not, as Lyra claimed in 1609, they had been raised by Indigenous nannies. So explained Juan de Betancur y Velosa, parish priest of Samacá, who matter-of-factly told visitor Valcárcel that of course 'he knows and understand the language' and had met all the requirements, for he was 'a native person [*persona natural*] and patrimonial son of the city of Tunja'.[114]

LANGUAGE AS LEGAL FICTION

The linguistic heterogeneity of the Muisca territories meant that colonial authorities lacked a lingua franca that they could take advantage of for their purposes. Attempts to use the variant of Muisca spoken in the region around Santafé as a lingua franca were unsuccessful, and recognised as such by the authorities of New Granada. This was evidenced by the adoption of multiple variants of Muisca for catechetical purposes, and

---

[113] Visitation of Tibaguyas by Gabriel de Carvajal, 22 March 1638, AGN VC 12 d. 2, 299v.
[114] Visitation of Samacá by Juan de Valcárcel, 2 August 1636, AGN VB 12 d 6, 560v.

Language as Legal Fiction 259

the creation of a formal and standardised procedure for ensuring the production of bespoke translations of catechetical material. The legal and disciplinary mechanisms that underpinned these procedures relied on the legislation of 1574–1580, in which the ambiguous idea of 'general languages' was at the centre. In this sense, the impression – or fiction – that New Granada did have an Indigenous lingua franca was essential, even if the policies that the legislation made possible were very different. In other words the New Kingdom of Granada did have a 'general language' (in the sense of general misconception among those unversed in local languages, and, crucially, as a legal fiction), and this was essential to the implementation of a language policy by local authorities to overcome the fact that, unlike other regions of Spanish America, it did not have a 'general language' in the sense of Indigenous lingua franca.

One consequence of the language policy ultimately implemented at a local level was that 'general Muisca' never became a lingua franca. Some scholars of 'general Quechua' in Peru propose the language was an artificial construct that fulfilled this role, and as a result influenced other variants of Quechua spoken around Peru, a thesis that continues to be the subject of debate.[115] In the case of New Granada it is clear is that there could be no equivalent process: the linguistic heterogeneity of the Muisca territories and the dearth of manpower available to Spanish authorities guaranteed this. The use of Indigenous languages in catechisation in New Granada instead reinforced linguistic particularism, contributing to the linguistic isolation of the localities and its inhabitants. The 'Muisca language' (singular) existed only on paper, in colonial texts, as a paper reality: a fiction born of the peculiar conditions of the region, and designed precisely to give the impression that the New Kingdom of Granada conformed to the expectations and models set by other regions – whether for the purposes of justifying Zapata's controversial reforms, the efforts of Jesuits to establish themselves in Santafé, or the attempts of successive civil and ecclesiastical authorities to make material their authority over the local clergy. Significantly, it was a paper reality that existed only in the register of writing on the New Kingdom of Granada and its inhabitants that was produced for export, for foreign audiences – whether the papacy, the crown, the Jesuit curia, or other readers – and contrasted sharply with the picture of linguistic heterogeneity seen so clearly in the more mundane bureaucratic archive of local

---

[115] Cerrón Palomino, 'Unidad y diferencia lingüística'; Durston, *Pastoral Quechua*.

260   *Language Policy and Legal Fiction*

colonial institutions. But it is a powerful fiction that has contributed to cementing the idea that the disparate inhabitants of the highlands constituted a single, homogenous 'nation' before the European invasion.

These conclusions also challenge those of scholars who have examined the question of language in the New Kingdom in the past and has important consequences for understanding of the experience of the Muisca in the colonial period. Schwartz and Salomon, for example, argue that the imposition of general languages contributed to the cultural homogenisation and creation of new, homogenous identities among the Indigenous groups on which they were imposed, a suggestion repeated, if not elaborated, by Jorge Gamboa in his discussion of the Muisca.[116] Such an idea seems straightforward, except that in reality, at a local level, there was no such imposition. Policies such as the forced resettlement of disparate Muisca communities into *reducciones* that gathered pace towards the end of the sixteenth century, increased internal movement from Indigenous migration and labour drafts, and the reconfiguration of patterns of trade and exchange all undoubtedly represented new pressures towards cultural and linguistic homogeneity. But because the linguistic strategy implemented by local agents did not favour linguistic homogenisation around an Indigenous vernacular, it may have been responsible for these processes to bypass Muisca languages altogether, since the only practical lingua franca was increasingly Spanish, which had been spreading among Indigenous people, and offered those who could speak it advantages in pursuing their interests. Indeed, the resulting situation encourages speculation in an entirely different direction, suggesting that the language policy eventually implemented in the localities may in fact help to account for the eventual disappearance of Muisca from the region and increasing Hispanisation – all of which ensured that the 'general language' of the New Kingdom of Granada, in the sense of lingua franca, could only ever be Castilian. These are, however, questions for future scholarship. For now, the story of language policy clearly illustrates how

---

[116] Frank Salomon and Stuart B. Schwartz, 'New Peoples and a New Kind of People: Adaptation, Readjustment and Ethnogenesis in South American Indigenous Societies (Colonial Era)'. In *The Cambridge History of the Native Peoples of the Americas. Vol. 3: South America, part 2*, 443–501 (Cambridge: Cambridge University Press, 1999); and Gamboa, *El cacicazgo*, 14, 458. Similarly, the creation of a lingua franca, for James Sidbury and Jorge Cañizares-Esguerra, was one way in which 'the church contributed mightily to the homogeneisation' of Indigenous communities. See 'Mapping Ethnogenesis in the Early Modern Atlantic'. *The William and Mary Quarterly 68*, no. 2 (2011): 195.

Language as Legal Fiction 261

local conditions fundamentally shaped and altered the application of imperial policy in the New Kingdom Granada, even beyond recognition. A policy that had the ostensible aim of advancing linguistic homogeneity could be transformed by local contingencies into one that reinforced heterogeneity.

Ultimately, however, this is also the story of how the authorities of the New Kingdom found creative solutions to ensure that religious instruction across the parishes of the provinces of Santafé and Tunja took place in languages that Indigenous people could understand, whether these were Indigenous languages, Spanish, or a combination, and that in doing so priests adhered, as much as practically possible, to a uniform and homogenous methodology. The alignment of Lobo Guerrero, the Jesuits, and Borja was central to this process, laying to rest the long-running controversy over whether or not to use Indigenous languages in evangelisation at all, and reaching a general consensus with the input of as broad a coalition of lay and religious authorities as possible. Indigenous language teaching thus became central to the reform movement they initiated in 1606, allowing their new approach to Christianisation to actually reach Indigenous people on the ground, and making it possible for them to interact with Christianity in new and transformative ways.

6

Indigenous Confraternities and the Stakeholder Church

In early March 1617 Juan Guabatiba presented a petition before the *Audiencia* on behalf of eight of his brothers and their families. Recently, Francisco Maldonado, a wealthy landowner and *encomendero* of the Indigenous town of Bogotá (modern-day Funza), frustrated with dwindling tributes as a result of continued demographic decline, had secured a rescript from the *Audiencia* empowering him to round up émigrés from his *encomienda* town who had made their homes in Indigenous towns and Spanish cities across the highlands. Guabatiba and several of his brothers had left Bogotá decades before and settled in the city of Santafé, while the rest had been born there to parents from the town, but now Maldonado wanted them all to return to Bogotá. In response they petitioned the authorities to exempt them from the rescript and to let them stay in Santafé, where they had built their lives, for which they provided a detailed report of the connections they had made and roots they had put down. They were all experienced and skilled in their trades – Guabatiba and two others were hatmakers, two were cobblers, two were tailors, and two were builders – so that removing them, they argued, 'would deprive the republic of this city of its craftsmen'. Despite living in Santafé, they always paid Maldonado his *demora* and the king his *requinto*, 'punctually, from what we earn', and most of them had wives and children who relied on them. Most importantly, as was 'public and notorious', they were all members of the Confraternity of St Lucy of the cathedral church of Santafé, in which they participated diligently, looking after each other and processing proudly with their banners 'in the processions of Corpus Christi and other solemn feasts', contributing to the religious life of the city. It was in this way that they were brothers: they

Indigenous Confraternities and the Stakeholder Church   263

were not blood relatives, but instead had formed bonds of *ritual* kinship through their membership of their confraternity and their support of one another in their lives in Santafé. For these reasons, they argued, they should be considered citizens (*vecinos*) of the city and left in peace – especially given that a recent royal decree sent to New Spain, Peru, and the Kingdom of Quito had apparently awarded such status to Indigenous migrants 'resident in a given place for ten years, provided they still paid their obligations', or so they had heard.[1]

The petition of Juan Guabatiba and his fellows is a powerful reminder that the Spanish cities of the New Kingdom of Granada, like so many others across Spanish America, were also Indigenous spaces, home to diverse populations of Indigenous people who not only built their lives in them but through their labour made it possible for countless others to do the same. For decades Indigenous men and women, rich and poor, young and old, had been leaving their settlements and towns across the provinces of Santafé and Tunja in search of better opportunities in a rapidly changing world. Some, as we have seen, left the highlands entirely, others migrated to other Indigenous towns, and others still went to Spanish cities like Santafé – there joining a diverse community of Indigenous immigrants from across the New Kingdom and as far afield as Quito and Peru.[2] While legislation and the observations of colonial officials often characterised these immigrants as interlopers – likely 'lay-abouts and vagrants', antithetical to good order – they quietly navigated this period of intense change, putting down roots, overcoming linguistic barriers, acquiring skills and trades, creating new communities, and

---

[1] Petition of Juan Guatiba and his brothers, 4 March 1617, AGN Miscelánea 132 d 54, 617r–672v. On 'vecindad' and in colonial Spanish America, which in many places tended to exclude Indigenous people, see Tamar Herzog, *Defining Nations: Immigrants and Citizens in Early Modern Spain and Spanish America* (New Haven, CT: Yale University Press, 2008), 6–12, and especially ch. 3.

[2] As shown by surviving wills they drew up before Santafé's notaries. An invaluable collection of these was edited and published as Pablo Rodríguez Jiménez, *Testamentos indígenas de Santafé de Bogotá, siglos XVI–XVII* (Bogotá: Alcaldía Mayor de Bogotá, 2002), which has made possible a variety of studies of Indigenous immigrants in the city, such as Monika Therrien and Lina Jaramillo Pacheco, *Mi casa no es tu casa: procesos de diferenciación en la construcción de Santa Fe, siglos XVI y XVII* (Bogotá: Alcaldía Mayor de Bogotá, Instituto Distrital de Cultura y Turismo, 2004), and Sandra Turbay Ceballos, 'Las familias indígenas de Santafé, Nuevo Reino de Granada, según los testamentos de los siglos XVI y XVII'. *Anuario Colombiano de Historia Social y de la Cultura* 39, no. 1 (2012): 49–80.

264 Indigenous Confraternities and the Stakeholder Church

renegotiating old communal bonds.[3] Their wills, petitions, and litigation show how, for many, Christianity – and particularly participation in Christian social institutions such as confraternities – was central to these processes. So it was with the Confraternity of St Lucy, which appears in Indigenous wills as early as 1567, when, as we saw, Christianisation in Indigenous communities in rural settings had barely started.[4] Through their membership in this and other confraternities in Santafé, generations of Indigenous immigrants offered each other support in life and in death, negotiated their places in the city, pursued their interests, and survived. After the reforms inaugurated in 1606, this engagement with confraternities also became possible for ever-growing numbers of people in rural towns and settlements across the region.

This chapter explores the aftermath of the reforms of the early seventeenth century. One part of the story was institutional: by the middle of the seventeenth century the Neogranadian church came to be better staffed, organised, and equipped than ever before. It could rely on ever growing numbers of secular and regular priests able to preach and teach in Indigenous languages, trained in increasingly advanced educational institutions, governed by comprehensive ecclesiastical legislation that drew from the most up-to-date and relevant contexts worldwide, and equipped with standardised texts and translations of catechetical materials. Another part was ideological, as the lessons of the Jesuit-led experiment of the early seventeenth century were applied around the archdiocese of Santafé in the decades that followed. While earlier evangelisation had been limited to the transmission of basic prayers and tenets of Christian doctrine, now the Catholicism of everyday practice, of private devotions, of public celebrations, of regular participation in the sacraments, and of social institutions came to be seen as the key to Christianisation. Underpinning these changes was a new vision of Indigenous peoples and their religiosity, new ambitions, and new priorities, which set the New Kingdom of Granada on a distinctive course.

---

[3] 'Ociosos y vagabundos', to quote the language of the 1594 instructions issued by President Antonio González when he created the position of 'Administrator for Indians, *mestizos*, and *mulatos*' of Santafé to deal with them. See Santiago Muñoz Arbeláez, 'Vagabundos urbanos. Las instrucciones para administrar indios, mestizos y mulatos en Santafé de Bogotá a fines del siglo XVI'. *Anuario de Historia Regional y de las Fronteras* 22, no. 1 (2017): 230.

[4] As early as in the will of Juan Navarro of Tunja, who recorded his will on 19 August 1567, AGN Notaría 1a de Santafé 4, 215r–216v (also Rodríguez Jiménez, *Testamentos*, no. 1).

The third and most important dimension of these changes, however, was Indigenous. The shift in emphasis and concern of the kingdom's authorities away from punitive policies and towards a more inclusive interpretation of Tridentine reform, coupled with the implementation of a language policy actually tailored to the needs of the enormous linguistic diversity of the New Kingdom, created space and opportunities for people in Indigenous towns in rural areas to interact with Christianity in new ways. As a result the inhabitants of small towns across the provinces of Santafé and Tunja were able to begin to participate in the sorts of practices, devotions, and institutions that had long been central to the lives of Indigenous people in urban settings, like Juan Guabatiba, and to countless others across the Catholic world in this period. Many Indigenous authorities who survived the crises of the sixteenth century thus came to use participation in institutions such as religious confraternities, or the sponsorship of Christian art and devotional objects, to find new ways to maintain their positions of leadership in their communities and to offer support to their subjects. In other places, where traditional Indigenous leadership had collapsed, these same mechanisms allowed commoners to rise to positions of influence and responsibility, when new leadership was needed the most.

All around the region religious confraternities and other everyday devotions, in particular those related to poor relief and social assistance, came to be crucial sites for the transformation and reconfiguration not only of Indigenous communities but of the Neogranadian church itself. By the middle of the century, the fees, donations, and alms paid by Indigenous people engaged in these voluntary activities came to constitute a key portion of the funding of Indigenous parish churches and the salaries of their priests, fundamentally altering the relationship between the church, at a local level, and its Indigenous stakeholders. This went much further than the *Audiencia* and archdiocesan authorities had intended, as they learned when they sought to rein in and control the activities of Indigenous confraternities towards the middle of the century, only to discover that these changes had long since outrun them. To understand these shifts, we need to return to the first decades of the century and explore each of these three dimensions in turn.

THE INSTITUTIONAL DEVELOPMENT OF THE CHURCH

Towards the end of his life, in March 1663, the scribe Rodrigo Zapata de Lobera compiled a detailed report of the state of the Indigenous parishes

266   *Indigenous Confraternities and the Stakeholder Church*

of the archdiocese of Santafé according to the most recent visitation records available. Zapata de Lobera had been the principal scribe for the visitations carried out by *Audiencia* officials since setting off with Luis Enríquez on his visitation of the province of Tunja in 1599, and had participated in practically every visitation since – not only in Santafé and Tunja, which after Enríquez had only been inspected thoroughly once more in the late 1630s by the *oidores* Gabriel de Carvajal and Juan de Valcárcel, respectively – but also in those of other provinces carried out by command of President Juan de Borja and his successors.[5] His report provides perhaps the first birds-eye view of the configuration of the archdiocese, allowing us to piece together the location of at least 118 Indigenous parishes in Santafé and Tunja, serving 247 Indigenous towns, villages, and other inhabited places (see Maps 2 and 3 in the Prelims), and is an excellent vantage point from which to examine the institutional development of the church of the New Kingdom by the middle of the seventeenth century.[6]

For a start each of these parishes had its own priest. This was a dramatic contrast to the sixteenth century, when one of the greatest obstacles successive reformers faced had been the lack of clerical manpower. In the 1550s, as discussed in Chapter 2, the ambitious claims of the first synod of Santafé had contrasted sharply with the small handful of priests actually present, even temporarily, in Indigenous settlements and communities. This changed only slowly, initially through the arrival of further cohorts of regulars, at least to Spanish cities. Their Atlantic crossings peaked in the 1560s, when 190 Dominicans and Franciscans were sent to the New Kingdom, and began a steady decline thereafter, in part as a result of Archbishop Zapata de Cárdenas's animosity towards them: from 131 dispatched in the 1570s (including the first cohorts of Augustinians), through ninety-one in 1580s, to seventy-five in the 1590s. In the seventeenth century new arrivals of mendicants continued to dwindle, with just seventy-one travelling to destinations in the New Kingdom in the entire century, even if the decline was partly made up by the arrival, in response to the enthusiastic requests of their supporters, of 279 Jesuits between 1604 and 1694 – of whom 112 arrived before 1650.[7]

---

[5] On these visitations, see Ruiz Rivera, *Encomienda y mita*, 63–88.

[6] If we include the glaring omission of Fontibón and nearby Techo, whose visitation by Gabriel de Carvajal in July 1639 he dutifully recorded (AGN VC 12 d 10). Zapata's report also contains information for the other provinces of the archdiocese, which brings the total of parishes up to 171. Report of the parishes of the archdiocese of Santafé, 10 March 1663, AHSB Caja 6A, 376r–492v.

[7] Borges Morán, *El envío de misioneros*, 477–540.

The Institutional Development of the Church   267

These numbers, drawn once again from *Casa de Contratación* records of royally subsidised passages across the Atlantic to Neogranadian destinations, are necessarily inexact. They do not provide an indication of how many people actually reached the highlands or remained there, nor do they account for the ever-growing number of people joining the religious orders in different capacities in the New Kingdom. Reports from local authorities, although also patchy, offer some additional clues. In May 1609, for example, four months after Archbishop Lobo Guerrero left to take up his new position as Archbishop of Lima, the cathedral chapter of Santafé submitted a report to the crown describing the state of the regular church in the archdiocese, with details on the number of convents, their affiliation, and the number of friars attached to each one.[8] The Dominicans, they reported, had by now eight convents, and a total of 107 friars, of whom seventy, they explained, were active in the provinces of Santafé and Tunja, although without specifying how. The Franciscans, for their part, had seven convents, with a total of seventy-three friars, of whom sixty were active in Santafé and Tunja. The Augustinians had another six, with fifty-one friars, of whom twenty-six were active in the highlands, nine as parish priests, while the Augustinian Recollects had set up an additional convent near Villa de Leyva that was home to ten friars.[9] Still, to put things in perspective, while in 1609 there were 241 mendicants active in the entire archdiocese of Santafé, in the 1590s there were some 500 in the city of Lima alone, and some 4,500 regulars in monasteries in New Castile in the 1570s and 1580s.[10] Over time these friars became less and less involved in the running of Indigenous parishes. In a letter of June 1620 the fifth archbishop of Santafé, Hernando Arias de Ugarte (in office 1616–1625), reported that the mendicant orders were in control of sixty-five Indigenous parishes: the Dominicans held twenty-eight, Franciscans twenty-four, Augustinians ten, and the Jesuits three.[11] By 1639 according to Zapata de Lobera's reports, this had dropped to fifty: nineteen held by

---

[8] Cathedral chapter of Santafé to the king, 18 May 1609, AGI SF 231, no. 60.

[9] Report by the cathedral chapter of Santafé on the houses and convents of the religious orders, 18 May 1609, AGI SF 231, no. 60a, 1r–1v.

[10] See Juan Bautista Olaechea Labayen, 'Las instituciones religiosas de Indias y los mestizos'. *Cuadernos de investigación histórica* 16 (1995): 234. On New Castile, William A. Christian, *Local Religion in Sixteenth-Century Spain* (Princeton, NJ: Princeton University Press, 1981), 15.

[11] In his letter to the king of 3 June 1620, AGI SF 226, no. 146, 1r.

268 *Indigenous Confraternities and the Stakeholder Church*

Dominicans, eighteen by Franciscans, eleven by Augustinians, and two by Jesuits. The remaining sixty-eight were held by secular priests.[12]

By then the secular clergy had also seen dramatic growth, from numbering a handful under Barrios, growing with the 124 men that Archbishop Zapata ordained to the priesthood over his 17 years in office, and continuing to expand under their successors. By the time of Arias de Ugarte's letter of June 1620, the archdiocese could boast 240 secular priests: 170 employed in benefices, sacristies, and other tasks, and seventy unemployed.[13] Eight years later his successor Julián de Cortázar (in office 1627–1630) reported that the number of unemployed secular priests had risen to 118, most of whom were 'sons and grandsons of conquistadors, and graduates in the faculty of arts and theology' and which he had ordained himself.[14] In another letter of 1628 the cathedral chapter provided details for all of these men, of whom fifty-eight were resident in the province of Santafé and forty-two in Tunja, not including ordinands 'studying Latin and arts, who might number 300, give or take'.[15] Even if we assume that the number of benefices and positions available to secular priests had remained constant in the eight years between the reports of Arias de Ugarte and Cortázar, then the total number of secular priests in the archdiocese of Santafé in 1628 was somewhere in the region of 278, and set to increase much further when the current crop of seminarians became ordained. This also meant that the clergy of the New Kingdom came increasingly to be composed of Neogranadian *criollos*, as envisioned by the *Cédula magna* of 1574. One of these *criollos*, born and raised in Santafé and ordained to minor orders by Archbishop Zapata, was Hernando Arias de Ugarte himself. The son of treasury official Hernando Arias Torero, Arias had left the New Kingdom in 1577 to study law at Salamanca and Lérida, before pursuing a career in the imperial administration, serving as *oidor* in the *audiencias* of Panamá, Charcas, and Lima, and later receiving major orders and rising through the ranks of the ecclesiastical administration.[16]

---

[12] Report of the parishes of the archdiocese of Santafé, 10 March 1663, AHSB Caja 6A, 376r–492v.

[13] Archbishop Arias de Ugarte to the king, 3 June 1620, AGI SF 226, no. 146, 1v.

[14] Archbishop Julián de Cortázar to the king, AGI SF 245 (unnumbered, dated 24 June 1628), 1r.

[15] Report by the cathedral chapter of Santafé on the unemployment of the secular clergy, AGI SF 245 (unnumbered, dated 5 January 1628), 3r–3v. The remaining eighteen were resident in the other provinces under the jurisdiction of the archdiocese.

[16] For a biography, see Ospina Suárez, *Hernando Arias de Ugarte*.

The Institutional Development of the Church 269

The re-establishment of a diocesan seminary, and the introduction of new educational institutions, was another key component in the new strategy to reform the church. Archbishop Zapata's first attempt at a seminary had opened in 1582, as a central part of his own designs, but struggled with financing from the start.[17] Zapata had even sent a procurator to petition Madrid and Rome for this purpose in 1583, but funds were not forthcoming, not least because of growing opposition to Zapata's controversial ordinations.[18] When in 1586 the archbishop placed additional duties on the seminarians, ordering them to serve and sing at the cathedral with no additional pay, the seminarians walked out, and the seminary was disbanded.[19] It took nearly two decades for it to reopen, in 1605, when it was re-established by Lobo Guerrero with the support of the Jesuits as a key 'remedy for the idiocy and ruinous customs of the clergy of this archdiocese' – as Diego de Torres Bollo, its first rector, put it in a letter to the king of 1606.[20] For this the archbishop donated a house and used the synod of 1606 to require all holders of Indigenous parishes to pay eight pesos each to provide it with an endowment.[21] In 1619 Arias de Ugarte issued the seminary with a new set of constitutions, and sought to bolster its financial security by requiring the holders of every benefice in the archdiocese, excluding Indigenous parishes, to contribute 'two percent of the real value of each benefice' – that is, of their endowments – plus 2 per cent of their income every year.[22] To enforce it he compiled declarations of the endowments and rents of dozens of benefices in the archdiocese, which he remarkably managed to compel their holders to provide.[23] Moreover, after Gregory XV issued *In Supereminenti* in 1621, empowering Jesuit colleges in the New World to

---

[17] Letter of Archbishop Zapata to the king, 12 April 1582, AGI SF 226, no. 40.

[18] Instructions of Archbishop Zapata to Alonso Cortés, 2 April 1583, AGI SF 226, no. 46.

[19] Report concerning the closure of the seminary, 21 January 1586, AGI SF 226, no. 57.

[20] Letter of Diego de Torres Bollo to the king, AGI SF 242 (unnumbered, dated 8 January 1606), 1r. The seminary's successor institution, the Colegio de San Bartolomé, traces its foundation back to 1604. Nevertheless, the date of its official establishment in the documentation of the diocesan authorities, including the constitutions issued for the seminary by Arias de Ugarte in 1619, date it to 1605 ('Constituciones originales', 7 January 1619, AHSB Caja 1, unnumbered, 11r).

[21] 'Constituciones sinodales 1606', ch. 15, 251.

[22] 'Constituciones originales', AHSB Caja 1, unnumbered, 11r.

[23] A large number of these, starting with those of the members of the cathedral chapter and continuing through to the beneficiaries of small chapels, have survived among the documents concerning the foundation and endowment of the school in AHSB Caja 1. Some inevitably failed to pay the requisite amount, and even in 1639 the then Archbishop Cristóbal de Torres had to issue legislation to compel reprobates to contribute their share,

270   *Indigenous Confraternities and the Stakeholder Church*

grant degrees, their college in Bogotá began to supplement the diocesan seminary in the education of the clergy, offering teaching in moral theology, philosophy, rhetoric, grammar, and arts.[24]

These developments also had a legislative component. In 1606 the effort by Lobo Guerrero and his allies to introduce the legislation of the Third Provincial Council of Lima, and with it its catechetical and pastoral materials, had been meant as a temporary measure, a pragmatic solution to the urgent need they identified to introduce reforms and the few resources that they had at their disposal. The need to hold a proper provincial council, to legislate on a much broader range of issues than the reformers had been able to get to in 1606, but also to consolidate and extend reforms to the suffragan dioceses of Cartagena, Popayán, and Santa Marta, did not, however, go away. It was inherited by Lobo Guerrero's short-lived successor, Pedro Ordóñez y Flórez, who arrived in Santafé in March 1613 but died in June of the following year before being able to do very much. The task then fell to Hernando Arias de Ugarte, fifth archbishop of Santafé, who on his arrival in 1618 began to make preparations – which for him meant conducting a marathon five-year visitation of his archdiocese, the first systematic pastoral visitation in the region's history.[25] This done, the First Provincial Council of Santafé was finally called in June 1624.[26] The diocese of Cartagena was vacant at the time and sent a representative, as did the bishop of Popayán, who excused himself owing to ill health, but the bishop of Santa Marta travelled to Santafé to participate, as did delegates from each and every city and province in the New Kingdom, in sharp contrast to the failed efforts of Archbishop Zapata half a century before. So too did President Juan de Borja, who was still in office. The Provincial Council began on 13 April 1625 and concluded on 25 May.

---

but the seminary was established and prospered. See the decree of Archbishop Torres, dated 21 June 1639, in AHSB Caja 1, 160r.

[24] On this Jesuit initiative, which would become the Universidad Javeriana, and on the Dominican Colegio Mayor de Santo Tomás, see Germán Pinilla Monroy and Juan Carlos Lara Acosta, 'El aporte de la Arquidiócesis de Santafé a la educación, siglos XVI, XVII y XVIII'. In *Arquidiócesis de Bogotá, 450 años: miradas sobre su historia*. Edited by Jaime Alberto Mancera Casas, Carlos Mario Alzate Montes OP, and Fabián Leonardo Benavides Silva (Bogotá: Universidad Santo Tomás, Arquidiócesis de Bogotá, 2015), 133–162. On *In Supereminenti*, see the Jesuit *littera annua* for 1642–1652, ARSI NR&Q 12 I, 191r–238v, at 192r.

[25] Arias Ugarte to the king, 11 June 1618, AGI SF 226, n. 142, 7r. This was granted, for five years, by Paul V in the brief *Exponi nobis nuper fecit*, 7 August 1620, Ibid., n. 154a.

[26] On its convocation, see Arias Ugarte to the king, 30 June 1624, AGI SF 226 n. 162.

The Institutional Development of the Church

The result was very different to the synod of 1606. The text of its constitutions is by comparison vast and comprehensive, made up of 362 detailed chapters touching on a much broader range of issues to earlier ecclesiastical legislation.[27] These incorporated many of the key reforms of successive archbishops of Santafé over the previous fifty years, extending them to regions beyond the highlands of Santafé and Tunja. It thus legislated on the production of standardised translations of catechetical materials and the use of Indigenous languages, as we saw in Chapter 5; on the importance of fostering Christian *policía* and eliminating impediments to catechisation, such as drunkenness, gambling, and clandestine celebrations; and on continuing the policy of resettling Indigenous people into gridded towns.[28] Much of this follows closely the legislation of the synod of 1606 and even the *Catechism* of Zapata de Cárdenas, if in a much more elaborate form. The same is the case with the constitutions related to the sacraments, which reflected the emphases and priorities of the reforms inaugurated by Lobo Guerrero and his allies and took them further. Reflecting their concern for frequent participation in the sacraments, and particularly in the Eucharist, the council ordered all priests of Indigenous parishes to make preparation for the sacrament a 'frequent and important' part of their teaching. It also further relaxed the requirements for admission to the Eucharist, doing away even with the watered-down 1606 requirement that Indigenous people obtain permission from one of the archbishop's deputies, leaving it instead to the discretion of each parish priest.[29] Other constitutions concerned the sorts of everyday devotions and practices that the reformers had centred in their approach to Christianisation. It thus required priests to place the Blessed Sacrament on the altars of their churches, in properly appointed tabernacles, in every town and settlement with over twenty inhabitants, including Indigenous churches that were up to standard.[30]

The council also legislated extensively about the ordination of candidates to the priesthood, defining every aspect and requirement clearly, and urging prelates to approach with 'the greatest caution', but, crucially,

---

[27] Reflecting the scope of its ambitions, these are arranged into five books following the structure of classical canon law (and, indeed, of Mexico III) – *iudex, iudicium, clerus, connubia, crimen.* On this see James A. Brundage, *Medieval Canon Law* (London: Routledge, 1995), 194–200.

[28] 'Concilio provincial 1625', 3.2.28 and 1.1.2 (560–561 and 337–339); 1.1.13 (350–351); 1.1.15 (354–355); and 1.1.14 (352–353).

[29] Ibid., 1.3.21 (388–389).

[30] Which was left to the discretion of each bishop to determine. Ibid., 1.3.17–18 (388–389).

272   *Indigenous Confraternities and the Stakeholder Church*

allowing the ordination of people of mixed European and Indigenous or African descent.[31] This same thoroughness can be seen in the detailed constitutions that described and regulated the functions of a broad range of ecclesiastical officials, from bishops themselves, through vicars and judges, down to notaries and the lowest-ranking officials.[32] Overall, it had a much greater institutional emphasis than earlier legislation, touching on a broad range of matters entirely absent in earlier texts. In this way the vast majority of its legislation was concerned with matters beyond the missionary project or Indigenous people, and instead with the minutiae of the ecclesiastical bureaucracy, the religious lives of Spaniards, and the behaviour of priests and nuns. To do this Arias de Ugarte and his collaborators drew on a much broader range of sources than their predecessors. The legislation of the provincial councils of the centres of the empire remained paramount but were now by no means alone. An exhaustive analysis of the sources of each of its 362 constitutions revealed that 93 were closely based on the legislation of Lima III, often materials already incorporated into the context of Santafé by the synod of 1606. But the bulk of its constitutions – 253 chapters – were in fact drawn from the Third Provincial Council of Mexico of 1585. And, through these texts, Santafé I also drew from a broad range of normative sources, ranging from classical canon law through to the influential legislation of Carlo Borromeo in Milan.[33]

Like all other legislation of this kind there is much here that is undoubtedly aspirational. We have no sense, for example, of whether the dozens of chapters regulating every aspect of the archdiocese's judicial apparatus, dutifully adapted from its Mexican template, bore any relation to reality, and we do know, from the way subsequent archbishops saw the need to reiterate different decrees in the decades that followed, that nothing was accomplished at the stroke of a pen. The provincial council, in an important sense, laid out a series of goals and objectives to aim for over the following decades – but this in itself was a significant change, inaugurating a new phase of institutional development. Indeed Arias de Ugarte's successors would not see the need to hold another provincial council to replace these constitutions until the 1770s, and they remained

---

[31] Ibid., 1.5.1–10 (401–415). The ordination of candidates of mixed descent is discussed in 1.5.5 (408–409)

[32] Ibid., 1.6.1–20 (416–437).

[33] See Cobo Betancourt and Cobo, *La legislación*, which contains a paragraph-by-paragraph analysis of each of its constitutions and their sources.

'To Know and Understand'

in place until well after Colombian independence.[34] By the same token, the breadth and scope of this legislative project also marked the conclusion of a long phase of haphazard institutional development of the archdiocese of Santafé that had started in the days of Juan de los Barrios, with stop-gap legislation of limited scope quickly introduced in reaction to specific issues. Subsequent archbishops would continue to issue decrees and requirements in the future, to be sure, and to reiterate requirements of the provincial council or to modify or extend its norms as needed, but they had a firm legislative foundation on which to build. To see this more clearly, we must turn to another key institutional development, the introduction of regular, comprehensive pastoral visitations.

'TO KNOW AND UNDERSTAND'

Pastoral visitations, as we have seen, were by no means new even for the New Kingdom. They had been promoted by the Council of Trent precisely as a key instrument for the introduction of reform and were used everywhere as a key instrument of episcopal government, not least as a visible manifestation of the jurisdictional power of the bishop.[35] In the New Kingdom, given the dearth of other instruments at the disposal of the bishop, they took on an additional significance. This was still a manuscript culture in an age of print, and there were few methods more effective to propagate legislation or ensure that their instructions were carried out than to do so directly. Because it involved an assertion of authority, the frequency with which they were carried out is also one measure of the growing ability of successive archbishops to bring their ambitions to bear onto the parishes.

Archbishop Zapata, as we saw, conducted a limited number of visitations over the course of his archiepiscopate, most notably in the late 1570s when his investigations in Fontibón and Cajicá ignited the violence,

---

[34] Under Archbishop Manuel Camacho y Rojas in 1773. See Ibid., xlvi. This effort was nevertheless unsuccessful, and a new provincial council did not take place until 1868. On this, John Jairo Marín Tamayo, 'La convocatoria del primer Concilio neogranadino (1868): Un esfuerzo de la jerarquía católica para restablecer la disciplina eclesiástica'. *Historia Crítica* 36 (2008): 174–193.

[35] Hsia, *The World of Catholic Renewal*, 23; Juan Villegas, *Aplicación del Concilio de Trento en Hispanoamérica, 1564–1600: Provincia eclesiástica del Perú* (Montevideo: Instituto Teológico del Uruguay, 1975), 72; Traslosheros, *Iglesia, justicia y sociedad*, 38. Recently Gabriela Ramos explored pastoral visitations in the Central Andes as spaces of interaction and negotiation between Andeans and ecclesiastical institutions in 'Pastoral Visitations'.

274   *Indigenous Confraternities and the Stakeholder Church*

terror, and dispossession explored in Chapter 3. His successor Lobo Guerrero conducted more extensive visitations, but he was forced to abandon them during his conflict with President Sande. Nevertheless, these resumed through representatives later in the decade, and a set of instructions issued to visitors in 1608 provides some evidence of his priorities. These instructions issued by Lobo Guerrero reflected the concerns of the constitutions of the synod of 1606, which the visitors were required to carry with them. The synod had made frequent mention of them, and it is not unlikely that this was one of the principal means through which the instructions propagated to the localities at a time when they could not be distributed in print. Visitors were instructed to examine the interior of churches, their baptismal fonts, the parish's record books, and other objects. They were to inspect parish accounts, and they were to hear complaints made against priests by their parishioners. If necessary, they were also to examine parish priests on their ability to hear confessions, and issue licences.[36] The documentation of these visitations has either been lost or it is held in archives inaccessible to researchers, but because Lobo Guerrero employed Jesuits to accompany him or his visitors, some information about what they encountered has survived in their letters to their Roman superiors. These are so full of complaints about the scandalous ignorance and illiteracy of local priests, of consecrated hosts being cut with scissors to fit monstrances, and of other shocking practices that they perhaps have more to do with Jesuit narrative models than with their first-hand observations.[37]

Lobo Guerrero's successor, Ordóñez y Flórez, does not seem to have conducted visitations, and his time in office was cut short by his death in June 1614, after a mere fifteen months in office. But his successor, Hernando Arias de Ugarte, conducted the most extensive pastoral visitations of any archbishop of Santafé in the seventeenth century, in order 'to know and understand' the state of Indigenous parishes.[38] These took place in three rounds, setting off shortly after his arrival in the

---

[36] These instructions were sent to the crown in response to a controversy over the legality of the practice by ecclesiastical agents of levying of pecuniary fines. Instructions to ecclesiastical visitors issued by Archbishop Lobo Guerrero, sent to the king on 26 February 1608, AGI SF 226, no. 123b, 1v–2r.

[37] For example, the Jesuit *littera annua* for 1608–1609, dated 20 September 1609, ARSI NR&Q 12 I, 36r–60v, at 43v.

[38] The most thorough study of these is Ospina Suárez, *Hernando Arias de Ugarte*, 22. The quotation is from Arias de Ugarte's standard *plática* at the beginning of each visitation, e.g. of Suta and Tausa, AHSB Caja 1, 172r.

'To Know and Understand'   275

archdiocese.[39] In the provinces of Santafé and Tunja, Arias de Ugarte visited Zipaquirá, Ubaté, Fúquene, Suta and Tausa, Ciénaga, Bogotá, Guateque, and Choachí between May 1619 and April 1620, before returning to the city for Holy Week.[40] After Easter he headed to the province of Tunja, visiting Soracá, Chivatá, Cocuy, and Chita, before heading down to the lowlands of the Llanos Orientales, and returning to Santafé.[41] And in September 1621 he set out on a third round, visiting the towns of Fosca, Paipa, Monguí, and Tópaga, before entering the province of Pamplona, and then visiting the town of Chiquinquirá on his way back to Santafé in July or August of 1623.[42] He was accompanied by the Jesuit Miguel de Tolosa, who also served as an interpreter.[43] Much of the resulting documentation has been lost, not least during the arduous progress of the visitation itself, during which the archbishop almost drowned, but detailed visitation records survive for ten parishes in the highlands, which provided valuable insights into questions of language in Chapter 5, and which we will examine again in a moment.[44]

Apart from the documentation arising from the visitation themselves, which were kept by the diocesan authorities, records of visitations survive in the books that parish priests were required to keep in order to record births, deaths, access to the sacraments, parish accounts, and inventories of parish property, since these were examined in each round of visitations. Very few of these books have survived for the first half of the seventeenth century, at least in archives accessible to researchers.[45] One is a book for the parish of Oicatá for the years 1608–1649, which shows that the parish was visited nine times in this period. The town is located a mere eight miles from Tunja, so the frequency of the visitations is likely to be greater than that of more remote parishes, but surviving documentation makes clear that systematic programmes of visitation became a feature of the government of the church in the first half of the seventeenth century,

---

[39] On his visitations, see Pacheco, *La consolidación*, 67–79.
[40] Ospina Suárez, *Hernando Arias de Ugarte*, 32–71.
[41] He described this part of his visitation in his letter to the king of 6 May 1622, AGI SF 226, no. 155, 1v. Ospina Suárez, *Hernando Arias de Ugarte*, 76–97.
[42] Ibid., 99–168.
[43] Letter of Arias de Ugarte to the king, 6 May 1622, AGI SF 226, no. 155, 1v.
[44] Pacheco, *La consolidación*, 75.
[45] Only one, from the parish of Suta (Sutatenza) in Tunja, dating to 1653, is available in manuscript form, at the Dominican archive in Bogotá (APSLB Parroquias Boyacá, 6/6/207/1-197). The AGN holds microfilms of a handful of others from parishes in the province of Tunja, cited later. It is unclear how many of these still survive, and how many others remain in parish churches elsewhere in the region.

276   *Indigenous Confraternities and the Stakeholder Church*

becoming a biennial event in some parishes by the time of Archbishop Cristóbal de Torres (in office 1635–1654), conducted by carefully organised agents.[46] These visitations were occasions to examine priests in the conduct of their duties, to assess the implementation of the directives of diocesan authorities, to address the grievances of the laity, and to implement reforms.

The well-documented visitations of Hernando Arias de Ugarte provide the clearest illustration of how they worked. They adhered to a carefully choreographed model that was designed to highlight the significance of the occasion and the power of the bishop.[47] The entire town was called together and assembled to witness the archbishop arriving in splendour. He was received solemnly at the door of the parish church by the priest in vestments, his assistants singing, and bearing incense and holy water. The ceremony was calculated to be spectacular, not least because a visitation such as this was often the first time that most of the inhabitants of a town were likely to have seen their ordinary. Once inside prayers were said and the archbishop blessed the church and the town. The congregation followed him inside, and an edict was read in Spanish and through interpreters to convey the purpose of the visitation. This began by appealing to the authority of church councils and explaining that this was one of the functions of the ordinary, that the priest was to be examined, and that the purpose of the visit was to ensure that he was fulfilling his obligations properly, especially in what concerned the administration of the sacraments, his personal conduct, and his treatment of the laity. They were also told that the archbishop would also enquire about the public sins of the inhabitants of the town. A standard ceremony followed: the archbishop would change his vestments in the sacristy, and process around the church to inspect it, stopping to check the baptismal font, the holy oils, and the cemetery, where prayers were said for the dead. A more detailed visitation of the objects and ornaments of the parish was then conducted, checking everything against the records left in the parish book by the previous visitation, noting down any changes and additions. Often the archbishop said mass, and then administered confirmation to those among the laity who were able and eligible. The priest was then sent away, and the congregation was instructed to come

---

[46] In this case, in 1610, 1621, 1625, 1628, 1634, 1638, 1640, 1642, and 1644. See AGN PB, Oicatá, Libro 1, 86r, 14r, 92v, 94v, 48r, 107r, 115r, 122r, and 131r, respectively.
[47] A typical model is provided by Arias de Ugarte's visitation of the parish of Soracá on 24 November 1620 (AHSB, Libro 6, 5r–18v).

'To Know and Understand'   277

forward to make their complaints or present their petitions, over a longer
period. Local notables and the elderly were also called and interviewed.

The text of the questionnaire that Archbishop Arias de Ugarte used in
his interviews with witnesses is lost, but the answers that survive reveal it
was a long and detailed list of at least sixty-one questions, touching all
aspects of the administration of the parish and of the life of the town. It is
revealing of the priorities of the archdiocese at the time that none of the
questions were concerned with Indigenous heterodoxy. In his interviews
with priests and witnesses Arias was far more interested in public sins,
such as extramarital or incestuous sexual relations, usury, sacrilege, or
other matters 'that have scandalised the inhabitants and people of the
parish' – the sorts of concerns that will be familiar to scholars of a broad
range of Christian contexts, across confessional divides, in early modern
Europe and beyond, generally described under the rubric of social or
church discipline.[48] So it was that Arias de Ugarte heard that Sebastián
Duarte, a wealthy Indigenous man in Fúquene, had several illegitimate
daughters with his servant Catalina, or that four Indigenous nobles in
Saboyá were in incestuous relationships.[49]

The principal focus, however, was to investigate parish priests themselves: whether they administered the sacraments properly, placed any
illegal burdens or levies on Indigenous people, and indeed whether they
fulfilled the language requirements and other legislation of the archdiocese.[50] Questions also concerned Indigenous assistants to the priest, the
local *encomendero*, and other authorities. These served as opportunities
to discipline miscreants – such as Gerónimo García, the parish priest of
Fúquene, whom he found had often abandoned his post in the parish
without leave.[51] He also investigated local conditions, such as whether
parish priests had copies of the texts required by the archdiocese, and
tried to identify potential problems. In Moniquirá, for example, the

---

[48] To quote his *plática* in the visitation of Suta and Tausa, 22 November 1619, AHSB Caja
1, 172r. On social discipline, see Ute Lotz-Heumann, 'Imposing Church and Social
Discipline'. In *The Cambridge History of Christianity. Vol. VI: Reform and Expansion,
1500–1660*. Edited by R. Po-Chia Hsia (Cambridge: Cambridge University Press, 2007),
244–260.

[49] See the visitations of Fúquene, 16 October 1619 (AHSB Caja 1, 179v) and Saboyá by
Arias de Ugarte, 18 July 1623 (AHSB L6, 123v).

[50] A detailed example of answers to the questionnaire can be found in the documents
pertaining to the visitation of Tópaga, AHSB, Lib. 6, 39r–60v, at 42r–47v.

[51] Visitation of Fúquene by Arias de Ugarte, AHSB Caja 1, 178v.

278   *Indigenous Confraternities and the Stakeholder Church*

archbishop learned that the priest was unable to obtain a copy of the Roman Catechism and a pastoral manual, owing to a shortage of these books in the archdiocese.[52] Finally, as with their civil counterparts, these visitations concluded with the archbishop or his agent drawing up a list of charges against the priest or other people, who had a chance to answer them, before the issuing a sentence to condemn the guilty and to rectify whatever was wrong. The visitation ended with the production of a census of the inhabitants of the town and the settling of accounts before the archbishop or his representative moved to the next town.

As a result of their thoroughness, even the limited sample of the documentation of the visitations of Arias de Ugarte that survives provides a valuable glimpse of the state of the parishes of New Granada, and of the religious life of their Indigenous inhabitants. Chapter 5 considered some of the findings of this visitation concerning the knowledge of Indigenous languages. Other questions sought to establish, for instance, whether the priest provided adequate and regular religious instruction, or classes to teach parishioners how to read and write. In Soracá, for example, Archbishop Arias de Ugarte found the latter lacking.[53] Reflecting the new emphasis on the centrality of the sacraments, a crucial concern was whether the priest heard confessions and whether he prepared and admitted parishioners to communion. Most priests were found wanting on both counts, with a few questionable exceptions, such as the priest of Fúquene, Gerónimo García, who claimed to routinely hear the confessions of his parishioners, despite also admitting that he did not bother preaching to them because he did not know the local language.[54]

Encounters of this kind shaped the production of norms and policies for use across the archdiocese, great and small. The visitation of Arias de Ugarte, for example, was designed to inform the archbishop of conditions in the parishes in preparation for the Provincial Council of 1625. His interviews with witnesses during the visitation revealed, for example, that the new policy of encouraging priests to admit their Indigenous parishioners to the Eucharist – after fifty years of forbidding it – was very slow to gain traction.[55] In Tópaga, for example, the parish priest, excused himself by saying that he had not yet catechised them sufficiently, because

---

[52] Visitation of Moniquirá by Arias de Ugarte, AHSB Libro 6, 100r–107v, at 104r.
[53] Visitation of Soracá by Archbishop Arias de Ugarte, AHSB, Libro 6, 8v.
[54] Ibid., 182v.
[55] He found that it was not administered in the parishes of Guacamayas, Tópaga, San José de Pare, and Saboyá. See AHSB, Libro 6, 19r–38v, at 234, 245, and 25v; Libro 6, 43r, 44v; Libro 6, 94r–99v, at 97v–98v; and Libro 6, 126, respectively.

'To Know and Understand'

he had not been in office for long.[56] In San José de Pare parish priest Fernando de Gordillo explained that he thought Indigenous people were incapable of the sacrament – a reminder that the controversies surrounding their admission were not limited to the highest echelons of the church.[57] Most priests also failed to administer the last rites, and the archbishop instructed several on how they were to go about taking the sacrament to the sick, down to providing guidelines for the production of special decorated bags to carry the consecrated host across difficult terrain to the homes of the dying.[58] These experiences were then reflected in the legislation of Santafé I – from stricter admonitions to admit Indigenous people to the sacraments to the design for these special bags.[59]

Conversely these inspections were also opportunities to promulgate and implement legislation on the ground, giving us a glimpse of the continued development of the archdiocese's missionary strategy in the years after Santafé I. So it was in November 1636 when Archbishop Torres issued legislation to further reiterate the archdiocese's policy of fostering frequent participation in the Eucharist among Indigenous people – 'for these Indians will not finish becoming fully Christian if they are denied holy communion' – and chastising priests who continued to withhold it from them.[60] Not content with simply publishing the edict in Santafé, Torres ordered that it be taken by his visitors on their rounds 'and a copy stuck in a public place in the sacristy of every parish and *doctrina*', and announced that this was henceforth to be 'the most substantial point' that his agents were to investigate in pastoral visitations. While Torres's contemporaries in Lima and Mexico could distribute printed copies of their decrees and admonitions, Torres instead relied on what had by then become biennial systematic visitations of the archdiocese. When a few years later, in 1640, Torres issued legislation to foster a number of devotional practices in the archdiocese, this very quickly reached the parishes through what was by now an established system. Surviving parish books across the region show how his visitors required

---

[56] Visitation of Tópaga by Archbishop Arias de Ugarte, AHSB Libro 6, 52r.

[57] Visitation of San José de Pare by Arias de Ugarte, AHSB Libro 6, 97v.

[58] A typical example is Saboyá, where the archbishop gave instructions even on how this bag was to be made to carry the consecrated hosts, and how precautions were to be taken to ensure the homes of parishioners were clean and decent enough to receive it. Visitation of Saboyá by Arias de Ugarte, AHSB Libro 6, 126r.

[59] The latter in 'Concilio provincial 1625', 1.5.20 (386–387).

[60] Edict of Archbishop Torres concerning the sacraments, 28 November 1636, AGI SF 227, no. 17, 1r–3v, at 1r.

280 *Indigenous Confraternities and the Stakeholder Church*

individual priests to copy the decrees they carried into their parish books and to read them to the laity before the visitor, dealing with the problem of dissemination, ensuring copies were accurate, and leaving a clear paper trail. Copies of Torres's 1640 edict can thus be found in the parish books for Oicatá, Pánqueba, and other parishes, alongside multiple others in the years and decades that followed, testament to how closely successive archbishops of Santafé came to involve themselves and supervise the affairs of Indigenous parishes and their priests, even despite the very material limitations of the resources at their disposal.[61]

It is tempting to focus on centrally directed efforts of this kind to explore the development of the reform movement that had been initiated by Lobo Guerrero and his allies in 1606. Legislation of this sort was, after all, a key way in which the new approach to Christianisation that centred quotidian devotions took root and expanded across the New Kingdom in the first half of the seventeenth century. Torres's legislation of 1640, for example, required the priests of Indigenous parishes to encourage their parishioners to adopt the devotion to the rosary, incorporating its mysteries and miracles into their teaching and preaching, and establishing confraternities dedicated to the Virgin of the Rosary in every parish, 'so that the faithful can enjoy her innumerable and assured indulgences' by holding processions on the first Sunday of every month and other celebrations. The same decree also ordered priests to require Indigenous people to keep Christian images in their homes for their private devotions – 'at least a cross and an image' each – or face a two peso fine, to be applied to their purchase. Each priest was to answer to the archbishop's visitors on the edict's execution, and for this they were to visit their parishioners' homes every four months to check for images, in effect extending the reach of the archdiocese's policies – and of the inspection system – from sacristy to hearth.[62] But legislation only tells one part of the story. Far more significant is what these and other contemporary records reveal of what Indigenous people themselves were doing with Christianity in this period; how they took advantage of the space afforded to them by the reforms. This brings us back to the Confraternity of St Lucy of Santafé, and to others like it that took root among Indigenous communities in urban and rural settings across the archdiocese of Santafé.

---

[61] E.g. AGN PB, Oicatá, Libro 1, 115v–117r; AGN PB Pánqueba, Bautismos 1, [73r].
[62] Edict of Archbishop Torres concerning the sacraments, copied 29 May 1640, AGN PB Oicatá, lib. 1, 116v.

'THE USAGE AND CUSTOM OF THE NATIVES OF THIS KINGDOM'

Religious confraternities or sodalities – variously known as *cofradías*, *hermandades*, *congregaciones* – were usually voluntary associations of laypeople structured around the promotion of a particular devotion, such as the cult of a saint, advocation of the Virgin Mary, or a feast such as Corpus Christi, through works of piety. They tended to provide specific functions of care for their members, and none more important than commemorating the dead and pleading for their salvation through the periodic celebration of masses and the performance of works of charity on their behalf – something that took on an additional significance in missionary contexts such as this, in which they contributed to the Christianisation of practices surrounding death.[63] They also provided aid in times of need, helped the sick prepare for death, organised funerary rituals and associated ceremonies, aided impoverished dependents, and often also offered some element of charity to the wider community in which they were set. They were ostensibly self-governing, electing leaders for limited terms, and running their own affairs – at different times a source of considerable anxiety for the authorities of the New Kingdom. In most membership involved the payment of dues, whether on joining, regularly, or both, and many confraternities acquired endowments, lands, and other property as people gave them gifts and bequests. Because many of these funds were spent on the maintenance and provision of the images, altars, and churches associated with their activities, and particularly on hiring priests and the religious to officiate in their celebrations, say masses for their dead, and other activities, they frequently became key to the funding and upkeep of their churches and their priests, and some even major economic players in local contexts, holding property for their broader communities, providing loans, and distributing aid, as we will see.

These institutions have long been a focus of study by scholars of early modern Catholic societies in Europe and around the world in a variety of contexts.[64] Their broad features remained constant – 'a common

---

[63] On this in the Central Andes, see Ramos, *Death and Conversion*; in Spain, Maureen Flynn, *Sacred Charity: Confraternities and Social Welfare in Spain, 1400–1700* (Basingstoke: Macmillan, 1989), 64–74.

[64] For an outline of the field since the 1960s, see Christopher F. Black, 'The Development of Confraternity Studies over the past 30 Years'. In *The Politics of Ritual Kinship: Confraternities and Social Order in Early Modern Italy*. Edited by Nicholas Terpstra (Cambridge: Cambridge University Press, 2000), 9–29; and Nicholas Terpstra, *Lay Confraternities and Civic Religion in Renaissance Bologna* (Cambridge: Cambridge

282   Indigenous Confraternities and the Stakeholder Church

vocabulary of rituals structured by a common grammar of conditions, expectations and relations' – from medieval Europe to early-modern Spanish America, even as local conditions resulted in significant variations, so that this common vocabulary and grammar, to paraphrase Nicholas Terpstra, 'was always spoken in dialect', making them fertile ground for comparative study.[65] Spanish America has been no exception: scholars of different areas have long explored how confraternities were productive sites for the development and maintenance of new community identities and politics – not only among Indigenous groups, but particularly among people of African descent, enslaved and free, whose confraternities in different contexts have been the subject of important recent studies.[66] Perhaps owing to a comparative dearth of sources, however, the confraternities of the New Kingdom of Granada have received relatively

University Press, 1995). On Spain, see Maureen Flynn, 'Charitable Ritual in Late Medieval and Early Modern Spain'. *The Sixteenth Century Journal* 16, no. 3 (1985): 335–348. Confraternities also featured prominently in discussions of religious reform and renewal in New Castile and the diocese of Cuenca, Christian, *Local Religion*, and Sara Tilghman Nalle, *God in La Mancha: Religious Reform and the People of Cuenca, 1500–1650* (Baltimore: Johns Hopkins University Press, 1992).

[65] Terpstra, *Lay Confraternities*, xviii.

[66] Most recently, Javiera Jaque Hidalgo and Miguel A. Valeiro, *Indigenous and Black Confraternities in Colonial Latin America* (Amsterdam: Amsterdam University Press, 2022). In the Central Andes, Gabriela Ramos explored the role of confraternities in the urban centres of Lima and Cuzco in *Death and Conversion*. More recently, Elizabeth Penry examined their part in the reconfiguration of Indigenous politics and community identity in rural contexts, in particular to contest and negotiate resettlement. See Penry, *The People Are King*. In New Spain, Laura Dierksmeier recently studied how Indigenous confraternities introduced by Franciscans served as a means to protect and reconfigure Indigenous governance, in *Charity for and by the Poor: Franciscan and Indigenous Confraternities in Mexico, 1527–1700* (Norman: University of Oklahoma Press, American Academy of Franciscan History, 2020). Laura E. Matthew reviews their role in the definition and development of group identities among the descendants of Mexican participants in invasion of Guatemala, in *Memories of Conquest: Becoming Mexicano in Colonial Guatemala* (Chapel Hill: University of North Carolina Press, 2012). For a recent survey of these institutions in New Spain, see Murdo J. MacLeod, 'Confraternities in Colonial New Spain: Mexico and Central America'. In *A Companion to Medieval and Early Modern Confraternities*. Edited by Konrad Eisenbichler (Leiden: Brill, 2019), 280–306. An older overview of literature from both contexts is Susan Verdi Webster, 'Research on Confraternities in the Colonial Americas'. *Confraternitas* 9, no. 1 (1998): 13–24. On Afro-Mexican confraternities, see Nicole von Germeten, *Black Blood Brothers: Confraternities and Social Mobility for Afro-Mexicans* (Gainesville: University Press of Florida, 2006). In Peru, Karen B. Graubart, '"So Color de Una Cofradía": Catholic Confraternities and the Development of Afro-Peruvian Ethnicities in Early Colonial Peru'. *Slavery & Abolition* 33, no. 1 (2012): 43–64.

'The Usage and Custom of the Natives of This Kingdom' 283

little scholarly attention, and its Indigenous confraternities, at least before the eighteenth century, when they become better documented, even less.[67]

The first confraternities established in the New Kingdom, from the 1540s, initially catered primarily to the city's most prominent Spanish citizens but broadened their membership over time. One was the Confraternity of the True Cross, established as early as 1543 in the cathedral church of Santafé, which came to admit at least one Indigenous member – Francisca Robles, a wealthy Indigenous woman – by the 1590s.[68] When Dominicans arrived in the city in the 1550s they too established confraternities in their convent, dedicated to the Virgin of the Rosary. The Franciscans, for their part, tried to take the Confraternity of the True Cross to their church – as a disgruntled *Audiencia* complained to the incoming Archbishop Zapata in 1571 – along with a second, dedicated to the Blessed Sacrament, that had been established by then too. The Franciscans later had to make do with establishing their own confraternity, dedicated to the Immaculate Conception, in 1584 instead.[69] So did the Jesuits, first for students at their college, then for Spaniards, and eventually also for enslaved people, 'Indigenous men and women, *morenos*, and *mestizos* in Indian dress'.[70] This final confraternity was dedicated to the Christ Child, and met every Sunday for catechism and preaching. Members participated in confession regularly, said the

---

[67] One exception is Juan Francisco González Acero, 'La cofradía de las Benditas Ánimas del Purgatorio en Fontibón 1683–1693' (MA dissertation, Pontificia Universidad Javeriana, 2013), which considers confraternities in Fontibón in the 1680s and 1690s. Religious confraternities in the New Kingdom were the subject of a 1973 doctoral dissertation, Gary Wendell Graff, 'Cofradias in the New Kingdom of Granada; Lay Fraternities in a Spanish–American Frontier Society, 1600–1755' (PhD dissertation, University of Wisconsin, 1973), which nevertheless paid little attention to their foundation, role, and development among Indigenous people. The most comprehensive study of Indigenous confraternities in rural spaces remains María Lucía Sotomayor, *Cofradías, caciques y mayordomos: Reconstrucción social y reorganización política en los pueblos indios, siglo XVIII* (Bogotá: Instituto Colombiano de Antropología e Historia, 2004), which focuses on the eighteenth century. For a recent outline of confraternity studies in Colombia, see Jerson Fidel Jaimes Rodríguez and Santiago Mendieta Afanador, 'Devociones católicas, prácticas religiosas, y cofradías – hermandades en Colombia (siglos XVI–XIX): Una aproximación bibliográfica'. *Anuario de Historia Regional y de las Fronteras* 25, no. 1 (June 2020): 173–203.

[68] According to her will of 20 October 1591, at AGN Notaría 2a de Santafé 8, 910v. On the confraternity, Graff, 'Cofradias in the New Kingdom of Granada', 40–44.

[69] Audiencia of Santafé to Zapata, 1 May 1571, AGI SF 16 n. 31, 1v. Ibid., 40–44.

[70] That is people of mixed descent living among their Indigenous, and not their Spanish, families. This they began to report in the Jesuit *littera annua* for 1608–1609, dated 10 September 1609, ARSI NR&Q 12 I, 44r–45r, 64v.

284 *Indigenous Confraternities and the Stakeholder Church*

rosary together, pooled their resources to aid each other when they fell ill or their dependents when they died, and remembered and prayed for their dead. The confraternity was not limited to men, and most of its members by 1613 were women.[71]

Other urban confraternities, especially those of Indigenous people, are more difficult to trace, but here surviving Indigenous wills provide some light. Those published in Pablo Rodríguez's exhaustive compilation of wills from Santafé's notarial records document the participation and patronage of Indigenous people in twenty-nine separate confraternities in the city by 1640 through their bequests and funeral arrangements. These ranged from the bequests of Juan Navarro, an immigrant from Tunja who in 1567 left a little money to the confraternities of St Lucy and of the Virgin of the Rosary; through donations to Franciscan and Augustinian confraternities as these were established in the 1570s and 1580s, and later to Jesuit confraternities at the turn of the century; to a real flourishing of confraternities dedicated to dozens of other devotions across the city. By 1640 the city's four parishes – the cathedral and the churches of Santa Bárbara, San Victorino, and Las Nieves – were each home to multiple vibrant sodalities, involving broad swathes of the city's Indigenous inhabitants.[72]

In addition to their central role in connection to preparations for death, funerary arrangements, and remembrance and intercession for the dead that their wills document, petitions and litigation by their members – such as that of Juan Guabatiba with which this chapter began – also speak to their centrality as spaces for sociability, solidarity, and celebration, often to the authorities' suspicion. So it was when Domingo de Guamanga, *mayordomo* of the Confraternity of the Virgin of Solitude of the cathedral church of Santafé complained of a civil official disrupting the preparations for one of their celebrations in 1640. In order to bring people together and raise some funds for a new mantle and silver band for their image of the Virgin, they had decided to organise 'a party, as is the usage and custom of the natives of this kingdom', for which they had ordered fifty vessels of *chicha* and mead 'so that our brothers would come and to share with them', explaining that 'otherwise no one would come'. Before the party, however, the overzealous official had come upon their preparations and spilled the drink and smashed the pots, ruining their

---

[71] Ibid., 65r–66r. I am grateful to Larissa Brewer-García for a stimulating exchange about this early Jesuit confraternity in Santafé.
[72] Rodríguez Jiménez, *Testamentos*.

'The Usage and Custom of the Natives of This Kingdom'   285

celebration and leaving them liable to replace the vessels they had borrowed from the brewers.[73]

Records for Tunja, which are scarcer, still reveal Indigenous patronage of at least three confraternities in its parish church of Santiago by the 1590s, dedicated to the True Cross, the Virgin of Solitude, and Santiago.[74] We know little of their activities in this period, except that by the early seventeenth century they seem to have become central to the financing of the churches of the city. When in 1620 the *cabildo* petitioned Archbishop Arias de Ugarte to create two additional parishes, Las Nieves and Santa Bárbara, to make proper provision for the growing populations of Indigenous migrants living in the periphery of the city, opponents of the proposal argued that this might lead to the ruin of the existing parish church and financial difficulties for the churches of the religious orders, 'for parishioners will cease to fund their confraternities', establishing new ones in the new parishes instead.[75]

The visitation of Miguel de Ibarra to Chocontá in 1593 provides the earliest glimpse so far of a confraternity established in an Indigenous town in the New Kingdom. There, as we saw in Chapter 4, Ibarra found that the people of the town had 'already constituted among them a Confraternity of the Holy True Cross in the church of the town, and placed in it a very devout image of a Holy Crucifixion', which he rewarded when he allocated their *resguardo*.[76] Records of papal approval granted to Indigenous confraternities also suggest that two more were well established around the turn of the century – the Confraternity of the Souls of Purgatory of Ubaque, which was approved in October 1600, and that of St Agatha in Cocuy, approved in February 1603.[77] Unfortunately we know little else about these three or what they did. Better documented are the confraternities that the Jesuits began to introduce in their parishes after 1605, in the model of those they set up on their arrival in Santafé.

---

[73] Petition of Domingo de Guamanga, 15 July 1640, AGI SF 227, n 25g.

[74] See for example the wills of Gaspar, *cacique* of Soatá, or 5 April 1596 (AHRB AHT 30 d 10) and Gaspar, *cacique* of Chita, of 6 May 1596 (AHRB AHT 27 d 7), both of whom left bequests to all three. On these, and confraternities for Spaniards, see Abel Fernando Martínez Martin and Andrés Ricardo Otálora Cascante, 'Una tradición de larga duración: la Semana Santa en Tunja'. *Historia y Espacio* 17, no. 57 (2021): 75–114.

[75] So argued parish priest Sancho Ramírez de Figueredo in his letter to Arias de Ugarte, 25 August 1620 (AHRB E 1, n. 2, 31r).

[76] Visitation of Chocontá by Ibarra, 23 July 1593, AGN VB 11 d 11 295v.

[77] Josef Metzler and Giuseppina Roselli, *America Pontificia III: documenti pontifici nell'archivio segreto vaticano reiguardanti l'evangelizzazione dell'America: 1592–1644* (Vatican: Libreria editrice vaticana, 1995), 773, 800.

286   *Indigenous Confraternities and the Stakeholder Church*

The first of these they founded in Cajicá soon after their arrival, to promote frequent communion and devotion to the Blessed Sacrament.[78] They would later do the same in Fontibón and in Duitama. Few documents related to the inner workings of these organisations survive, and most of what we have comes from the reports the Jesuits submitted to their superiors in Rome. But the first confraternity they established in Fontibón, dedicated to the Christ Child, is an exception, for some of its internal documentation has survived, providing crucial insights into the purpose, social functions, and activities of these organisations in the parishes.[79]

THE CHRIST CHILD OF FONTIBÓN

Even though in many contexts confraternities were largely self-governing and independent of the clergy, in the New Kingdom of Granada, as in other regions of Spanish America, this was a recurring cause of concern and anxiety among ecclesiastical authorities and reformers, who sought to limit their autonomy and to place them firmly under their supervision. For the Jesuits, the risks were worth taking, and the additional effort of closely monitoring the activities of the confraternities was a valuable investment, since in order to introduce reforms into their parishes they needed the support of influential members of the Indigenous laity. Despite these limitations and scrutiny, the institutions proved attractive to a broad range of Indigenous people, for a variety of reasons. This is abundantly clear from the experience of the Confraternity of the Christ Child of Fontibón, which served as a powerful vehicle for social mobility and political reconfiguration in the aftermath of enormous disruption.

It might be assumed that the most obvious constituency for the Jesuits to target with their new confraternity in Fontibón would have been the Indigenous nobility, particularly the *cacique* and his family. But by this point the Indigenous nobility of Fontibón had largely collapsed. The town was at the epicentre of many of the most significant developments wrought on Indigenous communities in the New Kingdom since the days of Archbishop Zapata. It was here, and in nearby Cajicá, that the violent seizures of *santuario* gold had begun in 1577, after all. A few years later, in the early 1580s, the community was consolidated into a gridded town

---

[78] Jesuit *littera annua* for 1608–1609, dated 10 September 1609, ARSI NR&Q 12 I, 51v.
[79] Documents of the Confraternity of the Christ Child, Fontibón, AHSB Caja 1, 373r–382v.

The Christ Child of Fontibón

after its church was built.[80] The following decade, during González's *composiciones*, much of the land previously controlled by the inhabitants of the town was redistributed to its Spanish neighbours. Ample documentation survives of Indigenous authorities in the town who tried, unsuccessfully, to recover some of it. The *cacique*, don Alonso, attempted to do so on various occasions, even purchasing several tracts, only to lose them again in the years that followed or see the crops planted on them destroyed by the cattle of his Spanish neighbours.[81]

As with so many other Indigenous rulers, don Alonso's authority began to crumble under these pressures, while the balance of power and wealth in the town shifted rapidly as these changes affected different members of the community unevenly.[82] The redistributive cycle of the town's Indigenous ritual economy that had kept the *cacique* at the head of the community began to collapse, and by 1590 several of Fontibón's inhabitants sued him before the *Audiencia* to demand that he pay them in currency for their work in his fields, which had traditionally been remunerated through the traditional means discussed in Chapter 1. Soon after don Alonso complained that many of his subjects had ceased to recognise him as their ruler and had instead installed one Alonso Saqueypaba, formerly one of his captains, as *cacique*, paying him tributes instead. Several of his subjects even accused don Alonso before the *Audiencia* of having poisoned one of the people involved, in a desperate attempt to cling on to his position of pre-eminence.[83]

Things were worse for his successor, don Juan, who in November 1595 petitioned the *Audiencia*, as detailed in Chapter 3, to force his subjects to obey him, to little avail.[84] Three years later, as we saw, Lobo Guerrero's first visitation once again resulted in the confiscation and destruction of ritual objects in Fontibón, belonging to a broad section of the town's population. The Jesuits Medrano and Figueroa, who accompanied the archbishop, reported that 'there was hardly a single house where we did not find some idols', which they located 'hidden under ground and in the ceilings and walls of their houses', and that they punished more than eighty 'priests of the sun' who maintained them.[85] Whatever authority

---

[80] Report on the building of Fontibón, AGN FI 21, 880r–880v.
[81] Suit over lands of Fontibón, 5 September 1590, AGN Miscelánea 6, n. 8, 254r–254v.
[82] Visitation of Fontibón by Gabriel de Carvajal, 11 July 1639, AGN VC 19.
[83] As several witnesses reported in the suit of Lucía, India, vs. Alonso, *cacique* of Fontibón, 10 May 1591, AGN CJ 82 n. 33.
[84] Suit of Juan, *cacique* of Fontibón vs. his subjects, AGN C&I 9 n. 13, 451r–501v.
[85] 'Descripción del Nuevo Reino de Granada', c. 1600, ARSI NR&Q 14, 11r.

288   *Indigenous Confraternities and the Stakeholder Church*

and support don Juan of Fontibón still derived from the sponsorship and direction of the town's Indigenous ritual economy finally collapsed. By 1613 political power in Fontibón had come to be exercised by a succession of Indigenous governors, reducing the role of the *cacique* further.[86] When the Confraternity of the Christ Child was introduced by the Jesuits, then, the people who joined it and rose to leadership positions were not members of the Indigenous nobility. The names of several members – *Pescador, Curtidor* – even hint at some of the humblest origins.[87] The Jesuits who administered the parish knew of Fontibón's recent history, but it is unclear whether they excluded the nobility from the confraternity deliberately or if it simply attracted a different section of the town's population.

For the Jesuits, the confraternity served to refocus Christianisation on the promotion of everyday devotional practices. Most immediately, it served to cultivate the Christianity of the confraternity's members, who were required to adhere to a strict code of behaviour that reflected Jesuit priorities. Confraternity records show, for example, how members were required to confess frequently, to take communion at least three times a year, and to come together regularly to hear sermons and participate in meditations. All were required to lead exemplary lives, according to the standards of the Jesuits, and the constitutions envisioned that they would supervise one another, aware that the penalty for breaking the rules was expulsion. The Jesuits, for their part, ensured that the men and women who made up the confraternity enjoyed special privileges that all could see. Their exalted status was visible each time anyone went to the church – where the Jesuits had hung big boards with the confraternity's constitutions and the names 'of confraternity officials and the indulgences they had earned, in both languages' – and in every celebration held inside, where the confraternity members sat in their own special pews.[88] The idea, for them, was to contribute to the creation of a Christian elite in the town who could aid the Jesuits in pursuit of their reforms, partly by serving as intermediaries – helping to prepare other people in the town for confession during Lent, for example – and partly as part of a

---

[86] Documents of the *protector de naturales*, 14 November 1613, AGN Miscelánea 132 d. 64, 791r.

[87] The only exception was one Hernando Capitán, who in 1614 was appointed as one of the alféreces. AHSB Caja 1, 373r–382v.

[88] Ibid., 373r–373v, 379v.

The Christ Child of Fontibón

promotional strategy to showcase the success of their approach to Christianisation.[89]

Exploring the motivation of the confraternity's Indigenous members is more difficult. These people were the object of observations, stories, and reports in Jesuit correspondence, but rarely speak for themselves, and, as commoners, have left few other marks in the colonial archive. We can only assume that participation in the confraternity served to satisfy their material and spiritual needs as individuals in important ways, given the great investment of time and resources they chose to make in the institution. We can, nevertheless, ascertain some aspects of their collective motivations. One, at least here, no doubt had to do with the opportunities the confraternity offered people outside of the Indigenous nobility to play central roles in the religious and ceremonial life of the town. This was especially the case for people from backgrounds traditionally excluded from the organisation of traditional celebrations that had earlier underpinned the positions of Indigenous elites. The constitutions may have focused primarily on the private activities of the confraternity and on policies directed at its members, but the real impact of institutions such as this is actually to be found in their public presence and activities.[90] This is clear from the roles they played in parish celebrations, not only those that were central to the confraternity itself – Christmas and Corpus Christi – which tended to be sumptuous occasions to which the Jesuits invited the inhabitants of neighbouring towns and even influential members of the diocesan hierarchy, but even on more everyday occasions. When the confraternity came together to say the rosary, for example, it did so by processing through the town, carrying a large gold cross, singing, and accompanied by a priest in full vestments.[91] It was, in other words, impossible to live in Fontibón and ignore these people.

The confraternity offered its members a means of advancement and recognition within their communities. This included people who had been benefitting from the town's economic reconfiguration, but who had little claim to status or position. One such person was Juan de Bohorques, who served as *mayordomo* of the confraternity in the early 1610s. Documentation from Ibarra's visitation of 1594 showed that he was not one of the *principales* of the town, and that of Gabriel de Carvajal in the

---

[89] On the former, Ibid., 376r.

[90] In common with confraternities in urban contexts, where these public functions took on a key role after Trent. See Black, 'The Public Face', 87–89.

[91] Documents of the Confraternity of the Christ Child of Fontibón, AHSB Caja 1, 376r.

290   *Indigenous Confraternities and the Stakeholder Church*

1630s showed his widow and children were merely members of one of the ten *capitanías* that made up the community.[92] And yet, having left the confraternity a significant bequest, the anniversary of his death in 1614 was commemorated with two days of impressive celebrations to rival those of any Indigenous noble. They started with a solemn procession from his home to the church the previous evening, in which all members of the confraternity, and even visiting dignitaries from Indigenous confraternities in Santafé, accompanied his widow and his relatives to the church, for nocturns and responsories. The next day they reconvened for an elaborate mass in the packed church, featuring the music of choirs and instruments, all paid for by the confraternity, which also made a generous donation to the parish in his name.[93]

Through their participation in the confraternity – and alliance with the Jesuits who oversaw it – commoners like Bohorques could come to play central roles in the life of their town from which they had previously been excluded. Within this it is worth noting that the confraternity also offered opportunities for participation and leadership to women, even if in subordinate roles limited by European and Christian gender roles. The confraternity's members included multiple women, presided by a '*priosta* of the sisters'.[94] Together these innovations could subvert traditional social and political hierarchies in the town, allowing for the consolidation of new structures of ritual kinship and opening new avenues for social mobility – in common with many other confraternities around the Catholic world in this period, and particularly welcome in Fontibón in the middle of this period of upheaval.[95] This is because the confraternity also offered its members the means to perform much needed charitable work, especially as new waves of epidemics reached the highlands and continued to devastate Indigenous communities, the worse of which hit the region in 1618 and 1633.[96] Confraternity officials included two whose job it was to visit and monitor the sick, and two nurses – in 1614, Juana Bautista and Francisca Mendoza – while the documentation

---

[92] Visitation of Fontibón by Ibarra, 21 May 1594, AGI SF 17 n. 92b. Carvajal's visitation of 11 July 1639 confirms that his widow, Ana de Bohorques, and their descendants were all members of the *capitanía* of Tibasuso. AGN VB 12 d 10, 988r.

[93] Documents of the Confraternity of the Christ Child, Fontibón, AHSB Caja 1, 378 r.

[94] Ibid., AHSB Caja 1, 375v.

[95] On confraternities and 'ritual kinship', see Nicholas Terpstra, *The Politics of Ritual Kinship: Confraternities and Social Order in Early Modern Italy* (Cambridge: Cambridge University Press, 2000), 8.

[96] Measles and typhus, respectively. See Ruiz Rivera, *Encomienda y mita*, 104–105.

of the confraternity and the reports the Jesuits sent their superiors describe their role offering support and assistance to the inhabitants of the town.[97] As before this served a variety of purposes: it advanced the Jesuit missionary project, by aiding the Jesuits to prepare the dying for a Christian death, helping the dying ready their confessions, and dissuading them from turning to the sorts of Indigenous medicinal and healing practices that the Jesuits sought to remove, but it also provided much needed support and relief for the elderly and sick, contributing to the survival of their community and reinforcing their leadership within it.[98]

This mutually beneficial arrangement was central to the success of the reform movement initiated in 1606, and not just in Fontibón. By providing new avenues for different Indigenous actors to interact with Christianity, the reformers made it easier for them to become stakeholders in the missionary project. This is very clear from the rapid proliferation of confraternities across the archdiocese in the years that followed.

'JUNTAS Y CONVITES'

In the years that followed, the archdiocese's authorities actively founded dozens of confraternities across the Indigenous towns of Santafé and Tunja. Some were founded by the archbishops themselves, on their visitations. In Cajicá priest Diego de Rojas reported in 1639 that in addition to the Confraternity of the Blessed Sacrament that had been established by the Jesuits, one had been established by Lobo Guerrero, two by Arias de Ugarte, and another by his successor, Julián de Cortázar (in office 1627–1630), bringing the total to five.[99]

Another driver of this expansion was their adoption by Indigenous leaders, who came increasingly to sponsor Christian institutions and celebrations in communities where they still retained positions of authority. So it was in the town of Pesca where, in 1607, the new *cacique*, don Pedro Pirascosba, petitioned the ecclesiastical visitor Nuño Fernández de Villavicencio, inspecting the parish on behalf of Lobo Guerrero, to allow him to establish a devotion to St Peter in the town, for which he requested permission to place an image of the saint in the parish church, to celebrate his feast day with 'a sung mass, with vespers and a procession', and to say a low mass for the devotion 'every two weeks'. The visitor granted the

---

[97] Documents of the Confraternity of the Christ Child, Fontibón, AHSB Caja 1, 376r.
[98] Jesuit *littera annua* for 1611–1612, dated 6 June 1613, ARSI, NR&Q, leg. 12-I, 79v.
[99] Declaration of Diego de Rojas, 12 December 1639, AGI SF 227 25i, 8v.

292   *Indigenous Confraternities and the Stakeholder Church*

request, 'provided there are no *borracheras*, dances, parties, or disturbances', and the *cacique* agreed to pay three gold pesos in alms for the main celebration and half a peso for each low mass, for a total of sixteen pesos a year.[100] Don Pedro had recently taken over the *cacicazgo*, after a legal challenge to remove an Indigenous governor who had ruled instead of his late predecessor.[101] Around the same time, in 1605, Pesca had been amalgamated with the communities of Soacá and Tupia, and moved to their current site, where a church had recently been built.[102] In addition to whatever personal relationship don Pedro had to the saint whose name – likely not coincidentally – he shared, through the sponsorship of this devotion the *cacique* also staked a claim to part of the new church and the ritual calendar of the town, for himself and his community. After all the same 1607 visitation noted that the communities of Soacá and Tupia had brought with them their confraternities of San Jacinto and the Virgin of the Snows, respectively. By 1620 when the parish was inspected by Arias de Ugarte, the devotion to St Peter had grown into a full-blown confraternity, headed by don Pedro's successor don Cristóbal.[103]

Many other towns that were also the result of the consolidation of disparate communities often adopted separate confraternities that served to maintain their individual identities and to stake a claim on the ritual and religious life of the new settlements. So it was, for example, in the town of Tópaga, which in 1601 had been created by amalgamating four communities.[104] By 1620, when the town was inspected by Archbishop Arias de Ugarte, even though one confraternity dedicated to Corpus Christi brought together the whole town, the three largest communities, Gótamo, Chipatá, and Tópaga, each had their own competing confraternities as well, dedicated to St Peter, the Immaculate Conception, and the True Cross, respectively.[105] This continued for decades after resettlement. A well-known example is that of the Confraternity of the Souls of Purgatory of the parish of Cómbita, with which this book began, created in 1601 by forcibly bringing together the people of Cómbita, Motavita, and Suta, and which was particularly associated with the

---

[100] AGN PB Pesca L1, 37v.
[101] On this, see the petition of don Cristóbal, governor of Pesca, 19 March 1605, AGN, Archivos Privados, Enrique Ortega Ricaurte, Caciques e Indios 9, cr. 2, d. 11, 13r.
[102] Decree for the resettlement of Pesca, Tupia and Soacá, 13 April 1605, AGN VB 4, 205r.
[103] AGN PB Pesca L1, 38v, 55v.
[104] See the decree for the resettlement of Gótamo, Chiaptá, Satova, and Tópaga, 30 December 1606, AGN VB 13, 255r–256v.
[105] Visitation of Tópaga by Arias de Ugarte, 10 December 1621, AHSB lib. 6, 43v.

'Juntas y Convites' 293

people of the first.[106] As Mercedes López has shown in her study of the famous painting of St Nicholas of Tolentino and the Souls of Purgatory by Gaspar de Figueroa that it commissioned (Figure I.1), the confraternity's leader and *cacique* of Cómbita, don Pedro Tabaco, used the confraternity and its sponsorship of religious art to assert the importance of the community of Cómbita in the life of the town, and through it his own, well into the 1650s.[107]

The role of confraternities as spaces of sociability was not limited to religious celebrations. As early as 1604, for example, Lobo Guerrero had complained that the confraternities he had seen there were little more than covers for revelries and drunkenness, holding ruinously expensive parties 'lasting 8 or 15 days each time', allegedly bankrupting entire communities and serving as occasions for grievous sin, so that they should carefully scrutinised and limited – a requirement he also put the synod of 1606.[108] This was a dramatic exaggeration, but confraternity celebrations often did include gatherings in which a confraternity official – usually the *alférez*, or standard bearer – took the confraternity's banner to his home or another place and there provided confraternity members and their guests food, drink, and entertainment. It was for this reason that the Jesuits watched their confraternities so closely, why visitor Nuño Fernández de Villavicencio had felt the need to insert those caveats into his approval for the devotion to St Peter in Pesca, and why successive archbishops of Santafé made a point of legislating to forbid confraternities from having banquets and even *alféreces* altogether. The parish books for Oicatá and Pesca record a decree to this effect, dutifully copied into them in during a visitation of 1614–1615, ordering the priest to keep hold of the confraternity's banner.[109] Arias de Ugarte, who also used his visitation to promote the introduction of confraternities as part of the archdiocese's Christianisation strategy, even produced model constitutions to be used as a template for new foundations, such as for the Confraternity of the Immaculate Conception he established in Tibaguyas in July 1619, which expressly declared that 'in no way shall an *alférez* be appointed', and instead required members to draw lots to

[106] On creation of the town, see the decree for the resettlement of Cómbita, Motavita, and Suta, 9 October 1600 (AGN VB 14 d. 11, 749r–750r). On the number of confraternities in Cómbita, see the report of Bartolome del Río of July 1640 (AGI SF 227, no. 25h, 2v).

[107] See López Rodríguez, 'La memoria'.

[108] Lobo Guerrero to the king, 4 May 1604, AGI SF 226 n. 91, 2r–2v; 'Constituciones sinodales 1606', ch. 18, 254.

[109] AGN PB, Oicatá, L1, 90r; AGN PB Pesca, L1, 42v.

294   *Indigenous Confraternities and the Stakeholder Church*

determine who was carry the banner, and then promptly return it to the priest for safekeeping after the end of the procession.[110]

The practice did not go away. Arias de Ugarte included a question about these arrangements in the questionnaire of his visitation, which showed the practice was widespread. In Tópaga, for instance, Arias de Ugarte found that all four confraternities celebrated their principal feast day lavishly with '*juntas y convites*', gatherings and parties. Each celebration involved the appointment of an *alférez* to lead the procession with the confraternity's standard. The *alférez*, as witness Juan Banesta reported to the archbishop, funded the whole thing: 'he pays six pesos for the vespers, sung mass, and procession, and then takes the standard home and invites some of the Indians to a banquet, after which they drink and play'.[111] In other towns the *alférez* raised money for the celebration – in some across the whole the town, in others only from specific groups – and then hosted the party. Among the beneficiaries of this largesse were often the parish priests themselves. In Fúquene *cacique* don Juan explained the *alférez* there sent the priest a nice lamb and four chickens each time.[112] In Soracá the priest received 'roast chickens and venison and other little things, and a jar of wine' – *cacique* don Luis explained – 'for the honour of the celebration'.[113] For the ecclesiastical authorities, at least in the early decades of the century, these festivities undermined the sacred and solemn character of the religious celebration and struck them as likely a continuation of some pre-Hispanic practice. Lobo Guerrero, in 1604, had gone as far as to speculate about whether, having lost their featherworks and other objects, 'they turned to making silk banners with which to adore their gods under the holy pretext of founding confraternities', as if these were functionally equivalent.[114]

Within a few decades, however, the ecclesiastical authorities had come to understand that these banquets and celebrations played central roles in these communities, or at least that trying to suppress them only served to make confraternities poorer – 'for without the *juntas* the alms they collect are reduced' as visitor Bartolomé del Río explained in 1640.[115] It was thus that Archbishop Torres instead ordered that confraternities each

---

[110] Constitutions of the Confraternity of the Immaculate Conception of Tibaguyas, 12 July 1619, AGI SF 227, n. 25d.

[111] Visitation of Tópaga by Arias de Ugarte, 10 December 1621, AHSB lib. 6, 43v.

[112] Visitation of Fúquene by Arias de Ugarte, 16 October 1619, AHSB Caja 1, 178v.

[113] Visitation of Soracá by Arias de Ugarte, 24 November 1620, AHSB L6, 8v–9r.

[114] Lobo Guerrero to the king, 4 May 1604, AGI SF 226 n. 91, 2r.

[115] Bartolomé del Río to Archbishop Torres, 10 July 1640, AGI SF 227, 25a, 3r.

'Juntas y Convites'

hold three such celebrations per year, with the priest in attendance, effectively bringing legislation in line with what was already common practice, and recognising that it was impossible, as well as undesirable, to turn back the clock.[116] It was in this way that when Torres later sought to foster the devotion the rosary across Indigenous parishes, he turned to the establishment of even more confraternities to ensure it took root.[117] It was easier, he decided, to ride the wave than to try to hold back the tide. What is clear, in any case, is that by the early decades of the seventeenth century confraternities had become key means through which people in Indigenous towns organised and held communal celebrations in which resources were redistributed within the community. Local elites – whether old or new – distributed their patronage and formed or reinforced bonds of reciprocity and obligation during these celebrations, and these came to be central to the consolidation and maintenance of group identities, reinforcing pre-existing ones or engendering new ones.

Tempting though it is to focus on this aspect, which so concerned the authorities, it is also worth reflecting on the important role that confraternities came to play in these communities as economic corporations that held and administered community resources. There are few sources that allow us to explore the internal finances of these institutions in the first half of the seventeenth century, but one exception is the account book for the Confraternity of the Blessed Sacrament of Sutatenza, in the province of Tunja, which records the multitude of small donations contributed to by its members to fund its activities. In 1636, for instance, the confraternity paid for at least thirty-three masses for the souls of its dead, each recorded with its individual benefactors – from the *caciques* and captains who funded many, to commoners Leonor, Miguel, and Pedro who each paid for one or two, and others still who gave just a few candles.[118] These quotidian donations could be topped up by generous bequests by wealthier patrons, for multiple reasons. Surviving wills belonging to Indigenous leaders in the seventeenth century often include generous donations to confraternities that suggest that these had even become means to keep certain lands and resources in their communities, separate from the property they transmitted to their children and other heirs as per Spanish

---

[116] As Archbishop Torres explained to Jorge de Herrera, 10 July 1640, AGI SF 227, n. 25a, 1r–1v.

[117] As recorded, as we saw, in the parish book of Oicatá in May of 1640. AGN PB Oicatá, L1, 116v–117r.

[118] Fourth Parish Book of Sutatenza, AGN PB Sutatenza, L4, 7r.

296   *Indigenous Confraternities and the Stakeholder Church*

inheritance practices. So it was with don Andrés, *cacique* of Machetá and Tibirita, who had made his life in Santafé, and whose 1633 will ordered that his remains be buried in the Franciscan convent in the city, 'even if I die in my town'. He nevertheless left generous landholdings to the parish church and confraternities of the two towns: two plots in Tibirita to the confraternities of St Anne, St Barbara, and St Lucy of its church, and another plot in Machetá to the Confraternity of St Lucy of that town. To the church itself he left a large cattle ranch, 'to hold and keep and work and cultivate forever'.[119] A few days later, in a codicil, he added a number of images, including a statue of St Lucy that was housed in the church, which had cost him fifty pesos – ensuring these resources stayed in the hands of the people of Machetá and Tibirita, even as his own descendants made new lives in Santafé.[120]

In different towns, through subscriptions, membership fees, alms, and bequests, confraternities acquired significant capital and resources that served to meet some of the collective needs of their members, which increasingly also included elements of Christian practice. None was more significant than the operations of their parish churches themselves, which by the late 1630s had come to depend on the voluntary donations of Indigenous people, through their confraternities, for their very functioning.

'WHERE THERE ARE NO CONFRATERNITIES EVERYTHING IS IN TATTERS'

In addition to noting the location of the parish churches of the archdiocese, the affiliation of their parish priests, and the sizes and characteristics of the communities that they served, Rodrigo Zapata de Lobera's account of the state of the parishes of the archdiocese of Santafé paid special attention to the perennial problem of parish finance. By the time of the visitations of Santafé and Tunja of Carvajal and Valcárcel, the standard stipend for a parish priest in an Indigenous parish was set at just over 344 *patacones*, silver pesos of 8 *reales*.[121] Of the 106 parishes for which

---

[119] Will of don Andrés, *cacique* of Machetá and Tibirita, 25 May 1633, AGN Notaría 3a de Santafé 38, 90r, 91r (Rodríguez Jiménez, *Testamentos*, no. 74).

[120] Codicil of don Andrés, *cacique* of Machetá and Tibirita, 27 May 1633, AGN Notaría 3a de Santafé 38, 97r (also Ibid., no. 68).

[121] These were actually recorded, in Zapata de Lobera's calculations, as 306 pesos *corrientes* of 9 reales, an accounting unit. These are equivalent to 344.25 actual physical silver peso coins – *patacones* – of 8 *reales*. For a recent study of bimetallism in New Granada, see James Vladimir Torres Moreno, *Minería y moneda en el Nuevo Reino de*

Without Confraternities, Everything Is in Tatters 297

records of stipends survive, however, only in thirty-five did the priest receive the full payment – usually in the parishes of royal *encomiendas* or places with large populations of tribute payers, like Ubaté and Ubaque.[122] In the remaining seventy-one, priests were paid a fraction of the total expressed in terms of months. In Pesca, for instance, the priest received nine months' wages for a full year's work; in Cómbita, ten months; in Oicatá, eight; and in Gámeza, just six.[123] The average was 8.7, or about 250 *patacones* per year.

Shortly after these visitations, in 1640, Archbishop Torres ordered one of his visitors, Bartolomé del Río, to collate a report on the number of confraternities he had seen in the towns he inspected. In 45 towns, Río reported counting 125 confraternities, including one he had set up in Suta, 'at the request of the Indians, with some *fanegas* of farmland for an endowment'. These ranged from 8 confraternities in Siachoque and 6 in Turmequé, to a single confraternity in small towns like Tuta and Sotaquirá, with most having at least 2 and the average around 2.8. Only one, Oicatá, whose church was in terrible shape, lacked a single one, proving – in Río's words – 'that where there are no confraternities everything is in tatters'.[124] Each of these confraternities paid an annual fee to the parish priest for the celebration of the feast of its devotion, plus additional fees for masses said over the course of the year for various purposes, particularly for the funerals and anniversary masses of its members.

The amounts could be substantial, even in parishes with just one or two confraternities. So it was in Bojacá, a town composed of three communities, Cubia, Bobasé, and Bojacá, which had two confraternities between them. In 1639 its parish priest, Andrés Millán, explained how the Confraternity of St Lucy – associated with Cubia and Bobasé – hired him to say '24 low masses a year, giving a *patacón* in alms for each, plus 6 for the sung mass, procession, and vespers for the day of the feast', in addition to the funeral masses they paid for when their members died, at a peso each. He also noted how 'the mayordomos are quick to disburse aid to the sick, without which they would be in terrible shape'. The Confraternity of John the Baptist – associated with the community of

---

Granada: el desempeño económico en la segunda mitad del siglo XVIII (Bogotá: Instituto Colombiano de Antropología e Historia, 2013), ch. 3.

[122] Report of the parishes of the archdiocese of Santafé, 10 March 1663, AHSB Caja 6A, 376r–492v.

[123] Ibid., 466r, 485v, 386r–386v, 384v.

[124] Bartolomé del Río to Archbishop Torres, 10 July 1640, AGI SF 227, 25a, 1v–2v.

298   *Indigenous Confraternities and the Stakeholder Church*

Bojacá – paid him a further 30 pesos for 24 low masses and a sung mass each year, bringing his 9-month stipend of about 258 *patacones* up to nearly the full amount. Both, crucially, offered much needed poor relief from the income of two herds of 400 sheep, whose income provided 'for the many needs of that some Indians suffer for their poverty'.[125] Even in the town of Chocontá, whose parish priest enjoyed a full stipend, the payments of confraternities represented a substantial portion of his income. As don Marcos, brother of the town's *cacique*, reported to crown prosecutor Jorge de Herrera in 1640, his town had ten active confraternities. 'From each of these the *doctrinero* receives 6 *patacones* per year, plus another 6 *reales* each month for the mass he says for each confraternity', for a total of 150 pesos. In addition, the Confraternity of the Blessed Sacrament paid a further 2 pesos each month in alms, and those of the Virgin of the Rosary and the Souls of Purgatory 1 peso each – bringing the total to 198 *patacones* of additional income, increasing the priest's pay by almost 60 per cent – not counting the fees the confraternities paid ecclesiastical visitors and other officials for inspections, or the candles and other small items they gave throughout the year.[126]

One reason why there are such detailed figures for this period is that the diocesan authorities compiled a number of reports on confraternities across the archdiocese in the early 1640s in response to a renewed challenge against these institutions, this time led by the *fiscal* of the *Audiencia*, Jorge de Herrera, who wrote long complaints to the crown about the apparent evils of these institutions – likely covers, in his view, for 'terrible crimes, sins, and incest'.[127] By now, as with their gatherings and celebrations, Archbishop Torres had come to realise that trying to limit confraternities was counterproductive, and that it was better to take advantage 'of the great utility that these confraternities bring to their churches'. And not just to the parish churches: as multiple witnesses explained, and Torres certified, confraternities were integral to the financing of his biennial visitation programme. Each confraternity paid the visitor 6 pesos each time it was inspected – 'as per the immemorial custom of this archdiocese'.[128]

---

[125] Declaration of Andrés Millán, *doctrinero* of Bojacá, 17 December 1639, AGI SF 227 25i, 5v–7r.
[126] Don Marcos of Chocontá to Jorge de Herrera, 6 July 1640, AGI SF 227 25c.
[127] Herrera to the King, 30 June 1640, AGI SF 227 23a, 1r.
[128] Torres to the Herrera, 10 July 1640, AGI SF 227, n. 25a, 1v, 1r.

Without Confraternities, Everything Is in Tatters 299

In addition to providing much-needed additional income from their voluntary donations, confraternities were also key to the provision of parish churches with the objects, ornaments, and art they required. In his defence of the archdiocese's confraternities in 1640 Archbishop Torres forwarded examples of the inventories of several of these across the two provinces, testament to the enormous investment of their members in the decoration and appointment of their churches. The inventories are replete with expensive textiles, such as vestments of Chinese silk damask of the Confraternity of St Peter in Tenjo; processional objects and instruments, like the new scarlet banner, complete with silver cross, that the Confraternity of the Blessed Sacrament of Cajicá had recently purchased, or the 18-peso trumpet of the Confraternity of the Virgin of the Rosary of Tabio; or devotional objects like the silver lamp that the Confraternity of St Lucy of Bojacá had provided to illuminate the Blessed Sacrament at the cost of 137 *patacones* 'provided by all of the brothers', or that which its counterpart in Sopó had commissioned at similar expense.[129] The sums involved could be staggering. In Susa, near lake Fúquene, in December 1638 priest Diego de Sanabria showed visitor Gabriel de Carvajal around their church, pointing out all the things 'provided by the Indians with their own money': in the sacristy were expensive vestments made of imported silks and other materials, impressive silver plate and gold ornaments, multiple paintings, including of new devotions, such as the Virgin of Chiquinquirá, and even a set of three *chirimías* worth 300 *patacones*. Around the church Sanabria showed the visitor altars dedicated to the devotions of each of the confraternities of the town, decorated with images 'which cost them over 1,500 *patacones*', and on the walls murals 'painted in the atrium and inside the church, which cost over 300 *patacones*', depicting scenes from the life of Christ and scripture.[130]

The murals of Susa may be lost, but fragments of contemporaneous murals were rediscovered in from the late 1980s in the parish churches of Turmequé and Sutatausa. The first, which Eduardo Valenzuela and Laura Vargas date to the turn of the seventeenth century, much like the description of the murals of Susa, features a cycle of images of the Gospel interspersed with images of Old Testament scenes and portraits of saints

---

[129] Torres to the King, 14 August 1643, AGI SF 227, n. 25i, 6r, 9r.

[130] Visitation of Susa by Carvajal, 14 December 1638, 85r, 87r–88v. This Susa is not to be confused with the settlement of the same name located in the Valley of Ubaque and discussed in Chapter 1.

300 *Indigenous Confraternities and the Stakeholder Church*

of the congregation's devotions.[131] The second, in the town into which the communities of Suta and Tausa were resettled in the 1590s, is a much better preserved cycle of murals depicting scenes from the Passion, as well as the remains of a vast scene of the Last Judgement on the Gospel side, likely dating to the 1630s.[132] Underneath it an inscription still declares that 'this Judgement was painted at the devotion of the people of Suta' – and not, interestingly, Tausa – 'under *cacique* don Domingo and captains don Lázaro, don Juan Neaetariguia, don Juan Coruta and don And[rés]'. Some of these men are perhaps pictured, in Spanish dress, in the portraits that once surrounded the scene, and which still adorn the chancel arch. Most striking of all is the famous figure of a woman, holding a rosary, dressed in a beautiful *manta* decorated with geometric designs – reminiscent of those that had been so central in another ritual context – at the very front of the nave, for all to see (Figure 6.1).

A CHURCH OF STAKEHOLDERS

The parishes of the archdiocese of Santafé had undergone a dramatic transformation by the end of the 1630s, as a result of the participation, patronage, and involvement of their Indigenous parishioners. The civil visitations of Gabriel de Carvajal and Juan de Valcárcel – the last the *Audiencia* would carry out until the 1690s – are testament to how much had changed even in the seventeenth century. Detailed records survive for seventeen parishes in Santafé and eleven in Tunja, revealing, in most towns, thoroughly equipped and well-appointed churches, all staffed by resident parish priests conversant in Indigenous languages, in which Indigenous people played central roles.[133] All had programmes of

---

[131] Laura Liliana Vargas Murcia and Eduardo Valenzuela, 'Kerigma en imágenes: El programa iconográfico de los muros de la iglesia de Turmequé en el Nuevo Reino de Granada (Colombia)'. *Artefacto Visual: Revista de Estudios Visuales Latinoamericanos* 3, no. 4 (2018): 81–109.

[132] On these murals and their possible sources, see José Manuel Almansa Moreno, 'Un arte para la evangelización: Las pinturas murales del templo doctrinero de Sutatausa'. *Atrio: Revista de historia del arte* nos 13–14 (2008): 15–28; and Alessia Frassani and Patricia Zalamea, 'El templo doctrinero de Sutatausa y su pintura mural'. In *El patrimonio artístico en Cundinamarca. Casos y reflexiones*, 72–87 (Bogotá: Gobernación de Cundinamarca, Universidad de los Andes, 2014). The Last Judgement inscription includes the text 'Año 163', with the final digit cut off.

[133] The exceptions were towns like Bogotá, where the church was unfinished (AGN VC 8 d 2, 212v), or Tuta, where the church operated out of a temporary building after the old one had collapsed (AGN VB 4 d 7, 595r).

A *Church of Stakeholders* 301

FIGURE 6.1 Anonymous, mural portrait of Indigenous donor, Church of San Juan Bautista, Sutatausa, Colombia, c. 1630. Photograph by the author

religious instruction, and in almost every town witnesses declared that 'no Indians have died without confession or children without baptism' – as they did even in dilapidated Oicatá.[134] In many parishes, as Pedro Cabra, governor of Tibaguyas declared in 1639, 'many Indigenous men and

---

[134] Visitation of Oicatá by Gabriel de Carvajal, 3 July 1636, 425v.

302 Indigenous Confraternities and the Stakeholder Church

women take communion'.[135] By now some of the devotions of the inhabitants of a number of Indigenous were also becoming regional devotions, adopted more widely across the archdiocese. The best known, of course, is the devotion of the Virgin of the Rosary of Chiquinquirá, which became particularly well known across the archdiocese during the epidemic of 1633, and would, after independence, be proclaimed patroness of Colombia.[136] Less well known, but to its devotees no less significant, was the cult of another miraculous image, of the Virgin of Perpetual Succour, in the small town of Monguí, near Sogamoso, which by the time of its visitation by Valcárcel in 1636 was emerging as a regional pilgrimage centre, with richly painted murals and a complement of ornaments and images, complete with indulgences granted to pilgrims established by Torres's immediate predecessor, Archbishop Bernardino de Almansa, who had made several gifts to the parish during his own visitation a few years before.[137]

These inventories of parish property contrast sharply with the penury of earlier visitations, and it is striking just how much was donated by Indigenous people themselves, whether through confraternities, as we saw, or individually, through gifts and bequests of different kinds. The sponsorship of the sacred by a broad variety of Indigenous actors – traditional leaders, new elites, commoners, and others – served to transform their relationship to the Christian institutions in their midst. To be clear, the entire ecclesiastical apparatus had always depended on Indigenous labour: their *encomienda* tributes had paid for the wages of priests (or their lay substitutes) even before there were parishes; provided the wealth that allowed *encomenderos* to meet their obligations to contribute to fund the building, maintenance, and appointment of churches; and formed the basis of the tributary system that allowed the monarch's officials to oversee it all. Their churches, moreover, had been built by their hands, even if it is the names of Spanish master builders and other craftsmen that

---

[135] Visitation of Tibaguyas by Carvajal, 22 March 1639, AGN VC 1 d 2, 299v.

[136] Scholarship on the Virgin of Chiquinquirá is considerable, but three recent studies that reflect on its place in Indigenous religiosity are Karen Cousins, 'Shapes of Love in the Miracle Testimonies of the Virgin of Chiquinquirá, New Kingdom of Granada, 1587 to 1694'. *Colonial Latin American Review* 28, no. 3 (2019): 396–423; Max Deardorff, 'The Politics of Devotion: Indigenous Spirituality and the Virgin of Chiquinquirá in the New Kingdom of Granada'. *Ethnohistory* 65, no. 3 (2018): 465–488; and Alessia Frassani, 'La Virgen de Chiquinquirá y la religión muisca'. *Historia y sociedad* no. 35 (2018): 61–86.

[137] Visitation of Monguí by Valcárcel, 15 April 1636, AGN VB 8 d 2, 402r, 246r–246v.

A Church of Stakeholders

appear in the deeds and contracts that survive in the bureaucratic archive. What we see by this period, however, is an ever-increasing voluntary sponsorship of the church and its activities, on top of, and in addition to, any required tributary obligation. This was much more than a quantitative change. Indigenous people had long been required to fund the kingdom's missionary project – but what they funded now were their own churches, local institutions firmly ensconced in their lives, in which they were active and central stakeholders.

This is all the more remarkable given the unrelenting catastrophe of demographic collapse and new waves of epidemics, which in addition to causing vast disruption also meant that tributary obligations had to be shouldered by ever smaller numbers of people, even as *corregidores* scrambled to keep their population figures up to date. In 1602 Luis Enríquez had estimated that there had been some 20,000 tributaries in Tunja, and a total population of about 80,000 – already a dramatic collapse from the 52,564 tributaries that López had counted in 1560. The records for Valcárcel's visitation of 1635–1636 show the collapse had only intensified, for he counted a mere 10,144 tributaries and a total population of just 20,545 people – a collapse, as Michael Francis notes, of over 80 per cent.[138] Figures for Santafé, although less complete, are no less dramatic. Figures survive for Carvajal's visitation of 1638–1639 for only forty-three parishes in the province, excluding key sites like Fontibón, preventing us from comparing them wholesale to those of the visitation of Miguel de Ibarra in 1593–1595.[139] At the level of individual towns, however, the collapse is still precipitous: Ubaté collapsed from 938 tributaries to just 440, Chocontá from 765 to 345, Bogotá from 673 to 292, and Cajicá from 201 to 130.[140]

The tone and emphasis of the visitors had changed too. Civil questionnaires still included a question on so-called idolatry, answered perfunctorily by Indigenous witnesses who in every case, bar one, were keener to discuss more relevant matters, like disputes over land or the repair of a church roof. The one exception was the town of Oicatá, where they denounced an elderly couple, Isabel Toisaga and Andrés Cuchitamga,

---

[138] Francis, 'Tribute Records', 309.
[139] Report of the parishes of the archdiocese of Santafé, 10 March 1663, AHSB Caja 6A, 376r–492v.
[140] Cf. 'Report of the encomenderos and Indians of Santafé' by Miguel de Ibarra, 1595, AGI SF 164 n 8.

304   *Indigenous Confraternities and the Stakeholder Church*

who still maintained an old *santuario* in their fields.[141] Ecclesiastical visitors, for their part, were far more interested in pursuing reports of public sins, such as incest and concubinage, than anything to do with Indigenous heterodoxy. In 1643, for instance, Bartolomé del Río compiled a report of the sentences he had issued in his visitations, showing he had disciplined 298 couples across 55 Indigenous towns – admonishing those eligible to marry to do so and separating the rest. Revealingly this is also what he did in the cities of Spaniards, disciplining thirty-nine couples in Tunja alone – including some of the city's most prominent Spanish citizens.[142] These are ripe for further study, no doubt, but they are part of a new chapter – with new concerns, dynamics, and priorities – in the story of the kingdom.

For now the visitations of the late 1630s speak of endings of a different sort too. Among the new kinds of business pursued by the authorities on visitation were testamentary disputes, involving the distribution of estates. These provide a handful of those rarest of texts, the wills of rural Indigenous people, who made arrangements for disposing of their property and their remains not before the notaries and officials of Spanish cities, but before their priests and local notables. So it was with don Juan, *cacique* of Guasca, who, on his deathbed made arrangements for the disbursement of his possessions to his family and neighbours, settled his debts – including eight pesos 'owed to the Confraternity of Our Lady of the Rosary', which he had borrowed 'to make up the *demoras* and *requintos*' – and dictated detailed instructions for his funerary procession, vespers, prayers, and mass, and for anniversary commemorations. To each of the confraternities of the town he left two silver pesos, plus a little more to the church for the souls of people he had known and ruled over.[143] And how, after all of this, could it be otherwise?

---

[141] Visitation of Oicatá by Valcárcel, AGN VB 2 d 2, 428r. This case is cited in Colmenares, *La provincia*, 13.
[142] Reports on the visitations of Bartolomé del Río, 1 July 1643, AGI SF 246, unnumbered, 1r–8v.
[143] Will and codicil of don Juan, *cacique* of Guasca, 15 April–24 July 1625, AGN VC 7 d 17, 921r–923v.

Conclusion

The Coming of the Kingdom

In his influential *General History* of the New Kingdom of Granada, published in 1688, the chronicler Lucas Fernández de Piedrahita recalls a telling anecdote. Once upon a time, in the early 1560s, the *cacique* of Ubaque had appeared before the *Audiencia* of Santafé to request permission to hold a great celebration in his town. 'Arguing that if Spaniards were allowed to hold bullfights, jousting, masques, and carnival', the *cacique* requested that his people too be allowed the 'pastimes and pleasures that they used to vent their troubles and relieve the commoners of their work'. Given that the request 'had nothing that smelled of past idolatry' – something the *Audiencia* apparently confirmed by checking with 'interpreters of their language and other people' – they gave him permission and also sent a delegation to the town, headed by the *oidor* Melchor Pérez de Arteaga. The celebrations had been delightful, and the delegation returned 'full of admiration for the great things and curiosities they had witnessed', not least 'the great quantities of gold jewels and headdresses' on display in the procession. The events of Ubaque had been the talk of Santafé, and an account 'of all the circumstances, and the number of people present in the celebration' had been recorded for posterity and circulated widely. Writing over a century later, in the 1660s, Piedrahita wondered how much more impressive celebrations like these would have been in the old days 'of the Kings of Bogotá, or the *caciques* of Tunja and Sogamoso', whose histories he proceeded to recount.[1]

---

[1] Fernández de Piedrahita, *Historia general*, 25.

306   Conclusion: The Coming of the Kingdom

If this story seems familiar, it is because Piedrahita is retelling the story of the celebrations held at Ubaque in December 1563, that had so shaken Santafé, shocked the authorities, and which Pérez de Arteaga had been sent to stop. Instead of being dazzled in admiration, the *oidor* had scrambled to stop the proceedings, fully convinced that the feasting, dancing, and celebrations that he witnessed were – as he had in fact reported – for 'the cult and veneration of the devil'. Instead of recording what he saw for posterity out of curiosity and wonder, these events were documented as part of a criminal investigation against those involved.[2] It was not that Piedrahita was ignorant of the New Kingdom. Having been born in Santafé, of Spanish and Indigenous ancestry, Piedrahita (1624–1688) had in fact devoted much of his life to the service of its church and colonial administration. He had been educated at its Jesuit-run diocesan seminary, been among the first to obtain a doctorate from its Dominican university, and begun his work as a priest in the Indigenous parishes of Fusagasugá and Paipa, before obtaining a succession of positions in Santafé's cathedral chapter, and eventually appointments as bishop of Santa Marta and later Panama.[3] Instead his account is testament to how, by the second half of the seventeenth century, successive authors felt free to reimagine, embellish, and decorate the accounts they read and the stories they heard about the pre-Hispanic and early colonial past, because these were now free from taboo or suspicion. The Muisca and their ritual practices, in other words, had by now ceased to be a source of anxiety – they had become the stuff of legend.

This shift is a reflection of the distinctive direction that the New Kingdom of Granada and its missionary project had taken over the preceding decades. It was not just that the authorities of the New Kingdom, in contrast to their fellows elsewhere, had long since ceased to centre the removal, or even the investigation, of indigenous heterodoxy as a strategy of Christianisation – whether this heterodoxy was

---

[2] Documents pertaining to the case of Ubaque, 1563, AGI Justicia 618, 1396r–1397r.

[3] For an excellent recent study of Piedrahita's life and work, see Luis Fernando Restrepo, 'The Ambivalent Nativism of Lucas Fernández de Piedrahita's Historia general de las conquistas del Nuevo Reyno de Granada'. In *Creole Subjects in the Colonial Americas: Empires, Texts, Identities*. Edited by Ralph Bauer and José Antonio Mazzotti, 334–354 (Chapel Hill: UNC Press Books, 2012). Through his mother Piedrahita was the great-great-grandson of the Inca Huayna Capac, through his daughter Francisca Coya, but was nevertheless born in relatively humble conditions, as his father was apparently a carpenter. Restrepo situates the composition of the *Historia general* in the context of a suit involving his parentage.

Conclusion: The Coming of the Kingdom 307

understood as the survival of pre-Hispanic practice or as more recent innovation. Instead, in Piedrahita's account, the events of Ubaque in 1563 were transformed – gold headdresses aside – into an elaborate confraternity procession of the sort that he would have seen countless times over the course of his career, in Santafé and in Indigenous parishes across the two central provinces of the highlands. What is more, in his *History*, this idealised and reimagined vision of the early colonial period served, in turn, to make sense of the pre-Hispanic past: this section of his text concludes a description of the religious and cultural practices of the Muisca before the invasion, featuring a description of an imagined procession, led by high priests, in honour of the pantheon of deities of the solar religion that he had, in the preceding pages, so vividly described. Piedrahita projected, in other words, what were by then distinctive elements of the customs and ways of life of the Muisca of his colonial present to make sense of their pre-Hispanic past – a present in which the sixteenth-century obsession with 'past idolatry' was, overwhelmingly, fading, and in which authors like him instead took for granted the effectiveness of colonial institutions and the rootedness of Christianity, which in his account unfold over the Muisca with startling speed. The people of Ubaque in Piedrahita's account are, after all, already Christians by 1560, and the *Audiencia* of Santafé has the means to enforce its claims of power and jurisdiction to the point that Indigenous rulers turn to it for permission to run their internal affairs.

These characterisations of the pre-Hispanic past and the first decades after the European invasion, and those that followed, are powerful fictions that long shaped our understanding of the early colonial history of the New Kingdom of Granada and its missionary project. Instead of the common, unified, transcendental religion of accounts like these, a detailed examination of a broader range of bureaucratic writing revealed a series of highly localised immanentist practices centred on the maintenance of lineage deities and of a sophisticated ritual economy of reciprocal exchange central to the political and economic organisation of Muisca groups. This is important not because we should understand Christianisation as the progressive replacement of these practices with their Christian functional equivalents, but rather because identifying and exploring these features is key to understanding the profound, multidimensional challenge that the efforts of colonial authorities to introduce Christianity represented to the social organisation, political economy, and cultural life of Muisca communities – to the very foundations, in other words, on which these same colonial authorities sought to build their colonial project.

308 *Conclusion: The Coming of the Kingdom*

At the same time, instead of effective and powerful colonial officials and institutions, a careful re-reading of surviving early colonial visitations and other records, set against a reassessment of the workings and limitations of early colonial governance, revealed the vast distance that existed between the claims and aspirations of officials and missionaries, and the realities on the ground. From the vantage point of the late seventeenth century, or of the assumptions of later periods still, this large gap is all too easily ignored and glossed over, to the point that the late sixteenth century has often been read as the beginning of a period of stability and prosperity – a 'golden age' of colonial rule. In reality this was the period when colonial institutions were at their weakest. This is clearest in the catastrophic campaign of violence and dispossession that the venality, self-interest, and incomprehension of local conditions of civil and ecclesiastical officials unleashed on Indigenous people across the provinces of Santafé and Tunja. This dealt a deadly blow to the ability of many Indigenous rulers to keep their positions of leadership and authority, at a time when these same colonial authorities needed them the most. The late sixteenth century was not a period of the triumphal unfolding of colonial rule. It was, instead, a time of its overwhelming, profound, and multi-layered crises. The kingdom, its claims laid bare, was revealed to be – to paraphrase Augustine – little more than a great band of robbers.

It is this context that the settlers of Santafé, Tunja, and other highland cities came together, as they had in other occasions, to petition and lobby for change. Their efforts laid the ground for the ambitious initiative for the reform of the missionary project that was first implemented under the leadership of Archbishop Lobo Guerrero and President Juan de Borja, in close collaboration with their Jesuit allies. The initiative involved a number of institutional reforms, from the translation of influential legislation from other contexts to the establishment of educational institutions and systems of oversight, all of which would form the coordinates of Lucas Fernández de Piedrahita's own career later in the century. More significant still was the ideological shift that underpinned the reforms. Efforts to Christianise Indigenous people shifted to centre the introduction and fostering of what the reformers understood as 'external' manifestations of piety: popular devotions, public celebrations, and social institutions. This shift opened the way for many Indigenous groups and individuals to interact with Christianity in new and different ways. They adapted and appropriated Christian institutions and practices to pursue their interests, navigate colonial pressures, and survive a changing world.

Conclusion: The Coming of the Kingdom 309

It is tempting to imagine that this state of affairs was the result of the fulfilment of a predetermined plan, whether for the unfolding of a fully formed institutional church or even of a discrete programme of Tridentine reform, over the Indigenous peoples of this region. But there was no such linear trajectory. There was no single, coherent design. There were instead, many faltering, meandering, contested, and contingent trends driven by diverse actors. Even the reforms inaugurated by Lobo Guerrero, Borja, and their allies were subject to changes, reassessments, and reversals even among the authorities themselves, as the story of their acceptance of Indigenous *alféreces* holding banquets and celebrations shows so clearly.

Trent provided an impetus for reform, but no practical template. How successive archbishops and officials interpreted what Tridentine reform should involve varied widely according to their interests and circumstances. Zapata's efforts to reform the church in the 1570s were for him no less 'Tridentine' than those of the reformers of 1606 were for them. Only with time, and through the consolidation and circulation of models such as those articulated by Carlo Borromeo in Milan, or by the framers of the provincial councils of Mexico and Lima, did anything approaching a coherent template emerge. Even then, these templates were subject to significant shifts in emphasis and direction as they were translated and retranslated to suit the ever-changing understandings of dynamic local conditions of diverse actors who drew on, contested, and in turn contributed to the broad patchwork of methods, priorities, and practices that characterised early modern Catholicism.

Most significantly, and at every stage, Indigenous people shaped the introduction of Christianity in the New Kingdom, just as it shaped them. Their incorporation into Christianity, and of Christianity into their lives, was an effect of the coming together of a series of conditions that allowed them to interact with it in different ways, adapting and adopting what it had to offer them, and including many of its features into their lives. They did this for multiple reasons and purposes, some of which this book has traced, some yet to be uncovered, and some that will remain theirs alone. These interactions took place on uneven terrain, backed by the coercive power, however faltering and at times ineffective, of colonial rule, and in circumstances of profound inequality. But this was a collective story nonetheless, and one that we simply cannot understand if we do not centre the experiences of Indigenous people, however challenging this might be. The old fixation on missionary success or failure simply cannot capture its complexity.

Christianisation, to be sure, provided the justification for successive efforts and initiatives of colonial institutions, royal officials, ecclesiastical authorities, priests, and settlers to shatter many of the religious features, political structures, patterns of exchange, social relations, hierarchies, and cultural features of Muisca communities. They oversaw this destruction at times deliberately, at times accidentally, at times out of ignorance. At different moments and in different ways they did so at the expense of their own colonial project. And yet Indigenous individuals and communities also found in Christianity ways to navigate and survive profound upheaval, demographic collapse, and dispossession. They used it to shore up and preserve existing bonds and relations, to dissolve and shed old ones that were no longer relevant, and to create and foster new ones. Indigenous people had been doing this work all along, when they had the chance, sometimes under the gaze of colonial officials, and more often beyond it, in immigrant communities in Spanish cities and other settings, individually and in groups, in ways large and small. With time they came to do this more and more, especially in their towns and rural parishes, and in ways increasingly visible to us. Gradually, collectively, and with just a little fanfare, a new kingdom had taken shape in their midst.

References

ARCHIVES

Archivo General de Indias, Seville, Spain (AGI)
Archivo General de la Nación, Bogotá, Colombia (AGN)
Archivo Histórico Javeriano Juan Manuel Pacheco, SJ, Pontificia Universidad Javeriana, Bogotá, Colombia (AHJ)
Archivo Histórico Regional de Boyacá, Tunja, Colombia (AHRB)
Archivo Histórico, Fundación Colegio Mayor de San Bartolomé, Bogotá, Colombia (AHSB)
Archivo Histórico, Provincia de San Luis Beltrán de Colombia, Bogotá, Colombia (APSLB)
Archivum Romanum Societatis Iesu, Rome, Italy (ARSI)

PUBLISHED PRIMARY SOURCES

Acosta, José de. *De procuranda Indorum salute*. Edited by Luciano Pereña. 2 vols. Madrid: Consejo Superior de Investigaciones Científicas, 1984.

Aguado, Pedro de. *Recopilación historial*. Edited by Juan Friede. Bogotá: Empresa Nacional de Publicaciones, 1956.

Anonymous. 'Epítome de la conquista del Nuebo Reino de Gra(na)da [ca. 1544]'. In *Relaciones y visitas a los Andes, s. XVI. Vol. III: Región Centro-Oriental*. Edited by Hermes Tovar Pinzón, 121–143. Bogotá: Colcultura, Instituto de Cultura Hispánica, 1993.

Aquinas, Thomas. *Summa Theologiae: Latin Text and English Translation, Introductions, Notes, Appendices and Glossaries*. Edited by Thomas Gilby. Translated by the Fathers of the English Dominican Province. London: Blackfriars; Eyre and Spottiswoode, 1964–1981.

Arriaga, Pablo José de. *Extirpacion de la idolatria del Piru. Dirigido al Rey N. S. en su Real Consejo de Indias*. Lima: Gerónimo de Contreras, Impresor de libros, 1621.

311

References

Arte de la lengva mosca de los Indios del nueuo Reyno de Granada, en las Indias Occidentales. Attrib. to Alonso de Medrano and Francisco Figueroa. Seville: Clemente Hidalgo, 1603.

Asensio, Esteban de. *Memorial de la fundación de la provincia de Santa Fe del Nuevo Reino de Granada del orden de San Francisco 1550–1585.* Madrid: Librería General de Victoriano Suárez, 1921.

Augustine. *The City of God against the Pagans.* Edited and translated by R. W. Dyson. Cambridge: Cambridge University Press, 1998.

Cieza de León, Pedro de. *Crónica del Perú: El señorío de los incas.* Edited by Franklin Pease. Caracas: Fundación Biblioteca Ayacucho, 2005.

'Concilio provincial de Santafé, celebrado en el año de 1625 [Concilium provinciale sanctafidense celebratum anno 1625]'. In *La legislación de la arquidiócesis de Santafé en el periodo colonial.* Edited by Juan Fernando Cobo Betancourt and Natalie Cobo, 289–791. Bogotá: Instituto Colombiano de Antropología e Historia, 2018.

'Constituciones sinodales celebradas en la ciudad de Santafé del Nuevo Reino de Granada por el señor doctor don Bartolomé Lobo Guerrero, arzobispo del dicho Nuevo Reino, acabadas de promulgar a 2 de septiembre de 1606 años'. In *La legislación de la arquidiócesis de Santafé en el periodo colonial.* Edited by Juan Fernando Cobo Betancourt and Natalie Cobo, 221–288. Bogotá: Instituto Colombiano de Antropología e Historia, 2018.

'Constituciones sinodales hechas en esta ciudad de Santafé por el señor don fray Juan de los Barrios, primer arzobispo de este Nuevo Reino de Granada, que las acabó de promulgar a 3 de junio de 1556'. In *La legislación de la arquidiócesis de Santafé en el periodo colonial.* Edited by Juan Fernando Cobo Betancourt and Natalie Cobo, 1–137. Bogotá: Instituto Colombiano de Antropología e Historia, 2018.

The Constitutions of the Society of Jesus and Their Complementary Norms: A Complete English Translation of the Official Latin Texts. Edited by John W. Padberg. St Louis, MO: The Institute of Jesuit Sources, 1996.

Covarrubias, Sebastián de. *Tesoro de la lengua Castellana o Española.* Madrid: Luis Sánchez, impressor del Rey N. S., 1611.

Egaña, Antonio de, and Enrique Fernández, ed. *Monumenta Peruana VII (1600–1602).* Rome: Institutum historicum Societatis Iesu, 1981.

Encinas, Diego de. *Cedulario indiano Recopilado por Diego de Encinas. Reproduccion facsimil de la edicion única de 1596.* Edited by Alfonso García Gallo. 4 vols. Madrid: Ediciones Cultura Hispánica, 1945.

Equivalencias entre las pesas y medidas usadas antiguamente en las diversas provincias de España y las legales del sistéma métrico-decimal. Madrid: Imprenta de la Dirección General del Instituto Geográfico y Estadístico, 1886.

Fernández, Enrique, ed. *Monumenta Peruana VIII (1603–1604).* Rome: Institutum Historicum Societatis Iesu, 1986.

Fernández de Oviedo y Valdés, Gonzalo. *Historia general y natural de las Indias, islas y tierra-firme del mar Océano.* Madrid: Real Academia de la Historia, 1851.

Fernández de Piedrahita, Lucas. *Historia general de las conquistas del nuevo reyno de Granada: A la S. C. R. M. de D. Carlos Segundo, Rey de las Españas, y de las Indias. Por el doctor d. Lvcas Fernandez Piedrahita,*

References

313

Chantre de la Iglesia Metropolitana de Santa Fé de Bogotá, Calificador del Santo Oficio por la Suprema y General Inquisición y Obispo electo de Santa Marta. Madrid and Antwerp: Por Juan Baptista Verdussen, 1688.

Herrera y Tordesillas, Antonio de. *Historia general de los hechos de los castellanos en las islas i Tierra Firme del Mar Oceano.* Madrid: En la Emplenta Real, 1601.

Konetzke, Richard, ed. *Colección de documentos para la historia de la formación social de Hispanoamerica, 1493–1810.* Madrid: Consejo Superior de Investigaciones Científicas, 1953.

Levillier, Roberto, ed. *Gobernantes del Perú, cartas y papeles, siglo XVI: documentos del Archivo de Indias.* Madrid: Sucesores de Rivadeneyra, 1921.

Leyes y ordenanças nueuame[n]te hechas por Su Magestad, p[ar]a la gouernacion de las Indias y buen tratamiento y conseruacion de los indios: Que se han de guardar en el consejo y audie[n]cias reales q[ue] en ellas residen: Y por todos los otros gouernadores, juezes y personas particulares dellas. Fueron impressas ... en la villa de Alcala de Henares: En casa de Joan de Brocar, 1543.

Lisi, Francesco Leonardo. *El tercer concilio limense y la aculturación de los indígenas sudamericanos: estudio crítico con edición, traducción y comentario de las actas del Concilio Provincial celebrado en Lima entre 1582 y 1583.* Salamanca: Universidad de Salamanca, 1990.

López de Ayala, Ignacio. *El sacrosanto y ecuménico Concilio de Trento.* Madrid: La Imprenta Real, 1785.

López Medel, Tomás. *De los tres elementos: Tratado sobre la naturaleza y el hombre del Nuevo Mundo.* Edited by Berta Ares Queija. Madrid: Quinto Centenario: Alianza, 1990.

Lugo, Bernardo de. *Gramatica en la lengua general del Nuevo Reyno, llamada Mosca.* Madrid: Bernardino de Guzmán, 1619.

Metzler, Josef, ed. *America Pontificia: Primi saeculi evangelizationis, 1493–1592. Documenta Pontificia ex registris et minutis praesertim in Archivo Secreto Vaticano existentibus.* 2 vols. Vatican: Libreria editrice vaticana, 1991.

Metzler, Josef, and Giuseppina Roselli, eds. *America Pontificia III: documenti pontifici nell'archivio segreto vaticano reiguardanti l'evangelizzazione dell'America: 1592–1644.* Vatican: Libreria editrice vaticana, 1995.

Muñoz Arbeláez, Santiago. 'Vagabundos urbanos. Las instrucciones para administrar indios, mestizos y mulatos en Santafé de Bogotá a fines del siglo XVI'. *Anuario de Historia Regional y de las Fronteras* 22, no. 1 (2017): 225–233.

Remesal, Antonio de. *Historia de la provincia de S. Vicente de Chyapa y Guatemala de la orden de nuestro glorioso padre sancto Domingo.* Madrid: F. de Angulo, 1619.

Rodríguez Freyle, Juan. *El carnero.* Edited by Darío Achury Valenzuela. Caracas: Biblioteca Ayacucho, 1979.

Rodríguez Jiménez, Pablo. *Testamentos indígenas de Santafé de Bogotá, siglos XVI–XVII.* Bogotá: Alcaldía Mayor de Bogotá, 2002.

Ruiz Rivera, Julián Bautista. *Fuentes para la demografía histórica de Nueva Granada.* Seville: Escuela de Estudios Hispano-Americanos, 1972.

San Martín, Juan de, and Antonio de Lebrija. 'Relación del Nuevo Reyno: Carta y relación para su magestad que escriben los oficiales de v(uest)ra m(ages)t(ad) de la provincia de Santa Marta [1539]'. In *Relaciones y visitas a los Andes,*

314 *References*

s. *XVI. Vol. III: Región Centro-Oriental.* Edited by Hermes Tovar Pinzón, 91–117. Bogotá: Colcultura, Instituto de Cultura Hispánica, 1993.

Santo Tomás. *Grammatica, o Arte de la lengua general de los Indios de los reynos del Peru.* Valladolid: por Francisco Fernandez de Cordoua, impressor de la M. R, 1560.

Sanz Hurtado, Juan. *Supplica q[ue] haze Iuan Sanz Hurtado vezino y encomendero de la ciudad de Tunja a V. M. en nombre de nueuo reyno de Granada; para su restauracione spiritual y temporal.* Madrid, [1603].

Simón, Pedro. *Noticias historiales de las conquistas de tierra firme en las Indias occidentales.* Bogotá: Casa editorial de Medardo Rivas, 1892.

Tanner, Norman, ed. *Decrees of the Ecumenical Councils.* 2 vols. London: Sheed & Ward, 1990.

Torres Rubio, Diego. *Grammatica y vocabolario en la lengva general del Perv llamada Quichya, y en la lengua Española. El mas copioso y elegante que hasta agora se ha impresso.* Impresso en Seuilla: en casa de Clemente Hidalgo, 1603.

Tovar Pinzón, Hermes, ed. *Relaciones y visitas a los Andes, s. XVI. Vol. III: Región Centro-Oriental.* Bogotá: Colcultura, Instituto de Cultura Hispánica, 1993.

'Visita de 1560'. In *No hay caciques ni señores,* 21–120. Barcelona: Sendai Ediciones, 1988.

Solano, Francisco de, ed. *Cedulario de tierras: compilación de legislación agraria colonial, 1497–1820.* Mexico City: Universidad Nacional Autónoma de México, Instituto de Investigaciones Jurídicas, 1991.

Vargas Ugarte, Rubén, ed. *Biblioteca peruana: Manuscritos peruanos del Archivo de Indias. Vol. II.* Lima: Tall. Tip. de la Empresa Periodística La Prensa, 1938.

Concilios Limenses (1551–1772). Lima: Tipografía Peruana, 1951.

'Segundo concilio provincial limense, 1567–1568'. In *Concilios Limenses (1551–1772). Vol. 1.* Lima: Tipografía Peruana, 1951.

'Tercer concilio provincial limense'. In *Concilios Limenses (1551–1772). Vol. 1,* 313–375. Lima: Tipografía Peruana, 1951.

Villagómez, Pedro de. *Carta pastoral de exortacion e instruccion contra las idolatrias de los indios del arçobispado de Lima.* Lima: Por Jorge Lopez de Herrera, impressor de libros, en la calle de la carcel de Corte, 1649.

Zamora, Alonso de. *Historia de la provincia de San Antonino del Nuevo Reino de Granada.* Edited by Caracciolo Parra and Andrés Mesanza. Bogotá: Editorial ABC, 1945.

Zapata de Cárdenas, Luis. 'Catecismo, en que se contienen reglas y documentos para que los curas de indios les administren los santos sacramentos, con advertencias para mejor atraerlos al conocimiento de nuestra santa fe católica [1576]'. In *La legislación de la arquidiócesis de Santafé en el periodo colonial.* Edited by Juan Fernando Cobo Betancourt and Natalie Cobo, 139–219. Bogotá: Instituto Colombiano de Antropología e Historia, 2018.

SECONDARY SOURCES

Alba, Guillermo. 'Primicia documental del archivo de la ciudad de Bogotá'. *Boletín Cultural y Bibliográfico* 11, no. 10 (1968): 51–70.

References

Albó, Xavier. 'Jesuítas y culturas indígenas: su actitud, métodos y criterios de aculturación'. *América Indígena* 26 (1966): 249–308.

Almansa Moreno, José Manuel. 'Un arte para la evangelización: Las pinturas murales del templo doctrinero de Sutatausa'. *Atrio: Revista de historia del arte* nos 13–14 (2008): 15–28.

Arendt, Hannah. *On Violence*. New York: Harcourt, Brace & World, 1970.

Ares Queija, Berta. *Tomás López Medel: trayectoria de un clérigo-oidor ante el Nuevo Mundo*. Guadalajara: Institución Provincial de Cultura 'Marqués de Santillana', 1993.

Arroyo, Luis. *Comisarios generales del Perú*. Madrid: Consejo Superior de Investigaciones Científicas, Instituto Santo Toribio de Mogrovejo, 1950.

Asad, Talal. *Genealogies of Religion: Discipline and Reasons of Power in Christianity and Islam*. Baltimore: Johns Hopkins University Press, 2009.

Avellaneda Navas, José Ignacio. *La expedición de Gonzalo Jiménez de Quesada al mar del sur y la creación del Nuevo Reino de Granada*. Bogotá: Banco de la República, 1995.

    La jornada de Jerónimo Lebrón al Nuevo Reino de Granada. Bogotá: Banco de la República, 1993.

    The Conquerors of the New Kingdom of Granada. Albuquerque: University of New Mexico Press, 1995.

    'The Conquerors of the New Kingdom of Granada'. PhD dissertation, University of Florida, 1990.

Bakewell, Peter. 'Conquest after the Conquest: The Rise of Spanish Domination in America'. In *Spain, Europe, and the Atlantic World: Essays in Honour of John H. Elliott*. Edited by Richard L. Kagan and Geoffrey Parker, 296–315. Cambridge: Cambridge University Press, 1995.

Barrientos Grandón, Javier. 'Estado moderno y judicatura letrada en las Indias: Colegiales del de Santa María de Jesús de Sevilla en plazas togadas'. *Ius fugit: Revista interdisciplinar de estudios histórico-jurídicos*, no. 3 (1994): 247–308.

Bataillon, Marcel. *Erasmo y España: estudios sobre la historia espiritual del siglo XVI*. Mexico City: Fondo de Cultura Económica, 1966.

Beard, Mary. *The Roman Triumph*. Cambridge, MA: Belknap Press of Harvard University Press, 2007.

Bellah, Robert Neelly. *Religion in Human Evolution: From the Paleolithic to the Axial Age*. Cambridge, MA: Harvard University Press, 2011.

Bernand, Carmen, and Serge Gruzinski. *De la idolatría: Una arqueología de las ciencias religiosas*. Mexico City: Fondo de Cultura Económica, 1992.

Black, Christopher F. 'The Development of Confraternity Studies over the past 30 Years'. In *The Politics of Ritual Kinship: Confraternities and Social Order in Early Modern Italy*. Edited by Nicholas Terpstra, 9–29. Cambridge: Cambridge University Press, 2000.

    'The Public Face of Post-Tridentine Italian Confraternities'. *Journal of Religious History* 28, no. 1 (2004): 87–101.

Boada Rivas, Ana María. 'Organización social y económica en la aldea muisca de El Venado (Valle de Samacá, Boyacá)'. *Revista Colombiana de Antropología* 35 (1999): 118–145.

316

References

Patrones de asentamiento regional y sistemas de agricultura intensiva en Cota y Suba, Sabana de Bogotá (Colombia). Bogotá: Fundación de Investigaciones Arqueológicas Nacionales, Banco de la República, 2006.

The Evolution of Social Hierarchy in a Muisca Chiefdom of the Northern Andes of Colombia [La evolucíon de jerarquía social en un cacicazgo muisca de los Andes septentrionales de Colombia]. Pittsburgh: University of Pittsburgh, Department of Anthropology; Bogotá: Instituto Colombiano de Antropología e Historia, 2007.

Boer, Wietse de. 'The Politics of the Soul: Confession in Counter-Reformation Milan'. In *Penitence in the Age of Reformations.* Edited by Katharine Jackson Lualdi, Anne T. Thayer, and Wietse de Boer, 116–133. Aldershot: Ashgate, 2000.

Borah, Woodrow. 'El gobernador novohispano (alcalde mayor/corregidor): consecución del puesto y aspectos económicos'. In *El gobierno provincial en la Nueva España, 1570–1787,* 39–53. Mexico City: Universidad Nacional Autónoma de México, 2002.

Borao Mateo, José Eugenio. 'La versión china de la obra ilustrada de Jerónimo Nadal *Evangelicae Historiae Imagines*'. *Goya: Revista de Arte* no. 330 (2010): 16–33.

Borges Morán, Pedro. *El envío de misioneros a América durante la época española.* Salamanca: Universidad Pontificia, 1977.

Borja Gómez, Jaime Humberto. *Los indios medievales de fray Pedro de Aguado: Construcción del idólatra y escritura de la historia en una crónica del siglo XVI.* Bogotá: Centro Editorial Javeriano, 2002.

Boyer, Richard, and Geoffrey Spurling. *Colonial Lives: Documents on Latin American History, 1550–1850.* Oxford: Oxford University Press, 2000.

Brading, D. A. *The First America: The Spanish Monarchy, Creole Patriots, and the Liberal State, 1492–1867.* Cambridge: Cambridge University Press, 1991.

Brendecke, Arndt. *Imperio e información: funciones del saber en el dominio colonial español.* 2nd edition. Madrid: Iberoamericana, 2016.

'Informing the Council: Central Institutions and Local Knowledge in the Spanish Empire'. In *Empowering Interactions: Political Cultures and the Emergence of the State in Europe 1300–1900.* Edited by Wim Blockmans, André Holenstein, and Jon Mathieu, 235–252. Farnham: Routledge, 2017.

Brett, Annabel. *Changes of State: Nature and the Limits of the City in Early Modern Natural Law.* Princeton, NJ: Princeton University Press, 2011.

'Sources in the Scholastic Legacy: The (Re)Construction of the Ius Gentium in the Second Scholastic'. In *The Oxford Handbook of the Sources of International Law.* Edited by Samantha Besson and Jean d'Aspremont, 64–82. Oxford: Oxford University Press, 2017.

Broadbent, Sylvia Marguerite. *Los chibchas. Organización socio-política.* Bogotá: Universidad Nacional de Colombia, Facultad de Sociología, 1964.

Brundage, James A. *Medieval Canon Law.* London: Routledge, 1995.

Burke, Peter. *Languages and Communities in Early Modern Europe.* Cambridge: Cambridge University Press, 2004.

Burkhart, Louise M. 'Pious Performances: Christian Pageantry and Native Identity in Early Colonial Mexico'. In *Native Traditions in the*

Postconquest World. Edited by Elizabeth Hill Boone and Thomas Cummins, 361–382. Washington, DC: Dumbarton Oaks, 1997.

The Slippery Earth: Nahua-Christian Moral Dialogue in Sixteenth-Century Mexico. Tucson: University of Arizona Press, 1989.

Burns, Kathryn. *Into the Archive: Writing and Power in Colonial Peru*. Durham, NC: Duke University Press, 2010.

Campo del Pozo, Fernando. 'Catecismos agustinianos utilizados en Hispanoamérica'. In *Provincia Agustiniana de Nuestra Señora de Gracia en Colombia: escritos varios. Vol. 4*. Edited by José Pérez Gómez OSA, 321–369. Bogotá: Provincia Agustiniana de Nuestra Señora de Gracia en Colombia, 1993.

'El P. Vicente Mallol, OSA, su actuación y catecismo en la lengua chibcha'. In *Provincia Agustiniana de Nuestra Señora de Gracia en Colombia: escritos varios. Vol. 4*. Edited by José Pérez Gómez OSA, 11–34. Bogotá: Provincia Agustiniana de Nuestra Señora de Gracia en Colombia, 1993.

Fray Vicente de Requejada: Biografía y mito de un agustino quijotesco. Tunja: Academia Boyacense de Historia, 2012.

'Los agustinos en la evangelización del Nuevo Reino de Granada'. In *Provincia Agustiniana de Nuestra Señora de Gracia en Colombia: Escritos varios. Vol. 3*. Edited by José Pérez Gómez OSA, 399–422. Bogotá: Provincia Agustiniana de Nuestra Señora de Gracia en Colombia, 2000.

Cañeque, Alejandro. 'Imaging the Spanish Empire: The Visual Construction of Imperial Authority in Habsburg New Spain'. *Colonial Latin American Review* 19, no. 1 (2010): 29–68.

The King's Living Image: The Culture and Politics of Viceregal Power in Colonial Mexico. New York: Routledge, 2004.

Canning, Joseph. *Conciliarism, Humanism and Law: Justifications of Authority and Power, c. 1400–c. 1520*. Cambridge: Cambridge University Press, 2021.

'Ideas of the State in Thirteenth and Fourteenth-Century Commentators on the Roman Law'. *Transactions of the Royal Historical Society* 33 (1983): 1–27.

Cárdenas Arroyo, Felipe. 'La momia de Pisba Boyacá'. *Boletín del Museo del Oro* no. 27 (1990): 3–13.

'Moque, momias y santuarios: Una planta en contexto ritual'. *Revista de Antropología y Arqueología* 6, no. 2 (1990): 37–59.

Cardozo Sarmiento, Richard Alberto and Jose Fernando Páez Jaramillo. 'Proceso de revitalización lingüística de la lengua muisca de la comunidad de Cota'. BA dissertation, Facultad de Comunicación y Lenguaje, Pontificia Universidad Javeriana, 2008.

Casilimas Rojas, Clara Inés. 'Juntas, borracheras y obsequias en el cercado de Ubaque'. *Boletín del Museo del Oro* no. 49 (2001): 13–48.

Casilimas Rojas, Clara Inés, and Eduardo Londoño, eds. 'El proceso contra el cacique de Ubaque en 1563'. *Boletín del Museo del Oro* no. 49 (2001): 49–101.

Casilimas Rojas, Clara Inés, and María Imelda López Ávila. 'El templo muisca'. *Maguaré* 5 (1987): 127–150.

Cerrón Palomino, Rodolfo. 'Unidad y diferencia lingüística en el mundo andino'. *Lexis: Revista de lingüística y literatura* 11, no. 1 (1987): 71–104.

Charles, John. *Allies at Odds: The Andean Church and Its Indigenous Agents, 1583–1671*. Albuquerque: University of New Mexico Press, 2010.

Châtellier, Louis. *The Religion of the Poor: Rural Missions in Europe and the Formation of Modern Catholicism, c.1500–c.1800*. Cambridge: Cambridge University Press, 1997.

Christian, William A. *Local Religion in Sixteenth-Century Spain*. Princeton, NJ: Princeton University Press, 1981.

Clark, John E., and Michael Blake. 'The Power of Prestige: Competitive Generosity and the Emergence of Rank Societies in Lowland Mesoamerica'. In *Factional Competition and Political Development in the New World*. Edited by Elizabeth M. Brumfiel and John W. Fox, 17–30. New Directions in Archaeology. Cambridge: Cambridge University Press, 1994.

Cobo, Natalie. 'Creating Authority and Promoting Normative Behaviour'. In *The School of Salamanca: A Case of Global Knowledge Production*. Edited by Thomas Duve, José Luis Egío, and Christiane Birr, 210–244. Leiden: Brill, 2021.

Cobo Betancourt, Juan Fernando. *Mestizos heraldos de Dios: La ordenación de sacerdotes descendientes de españoles e indígenas en el Nuevo Reino de Granada y la racialización de la diferencia, 1573–1590*. Bogotá: Instituto Colombiano de Antropología e Historia, 2012.

Cobo Betancourt, Juan Fernando, and Natalie Cobo, eds. *La legislación de la arquidiócesis de Santafé en el periodo colonial*. Bogotá: Instituto Colombiano de Antropología e Historia, 2018.

Coello de la Rosa, Alexandre. 'La doctrina de Juli a debate (1575–1585)'. *Revista de Estudios Extremeños* 63, no. ii (2007): 951–990.

Colmenares, Germán. *Historia económica y social de Colombia, 1537–1719*. 3rd edition. Bogotá: Editorial La Carreta, 1978.

La provincia de Tunja en el Nuevo Reino de Granada; ensayo de historia social, 1539–1800. Bogotá: Universidad de los Andes, Facultad de Artes y Ciencias, Departamento de Historia, 1997.

Correa, François. *El sol del poder: Simbología y política entre los Muiscas del norte de los Andes*. Bogotá: Universidad Nacional de Colombia, Facultad de Ciencias Humanas, 2004.

'Fundamentos de la organización social muisca'. In *Los chibchas: adaptación y diversidad en los Andes Orientales de Colombia*. Edited by José Vicente Rodríguez Cuenca, 25–48. Bogotá: Universidad Nacional de Colombia, 2001.

Cortés Alonso, Vicenta. 'Visita a los santuarios indígenas de Boyaca en 1577'. *Revista Colombiana de Antropología* 9 (1960): 199–273.

Cousins, Karen. 'Shapes of Love in the Miracle Testimonies of the Virgin of Chiquinquirá, New Kingdom of Granada, 1587 to 1694'. *Colonial Latin American Review* 28, no. 3 (2019): 396–423.

Crewe, Ryan Dominic. *The Mexican Mission: Indigenous Reconstruction and Mendicant Enterprise in New Spain, 1521–1600*. Cambridge Latin American Studies. Cambridge: Cambridge University Press, 2019.

Cuéllar, Andrea M. 'The Archaeology of Food and Social Inequality in the Andes'. *Journal of Archaeological Research* 21, no. 2 (2013): 123–174.

Curatola Petrocchi, Marco, and José Carlos de la Puente. 'Contar concertando: Quipus, piedritas y escritura en los Andes coloniales'. In *El quipu colonial: Estudios y materiales*. Edited by Marco Curatola Petrocci and José Carlos de la Puente, 193–243. Lima: Pontificia Universidad Católica del Perú, 2013.

References

Dean, Carolyn. *Inka Bodies and the Body of Christ: Corpus Christi in Colonial Cuzco, Peru*. Durham, NC: Duke University Press, 1999.

Deardorff, Max. 'The Politics of Devotion: Indigenous Spirituality and the Virgin of Chiquinquirá in the New Kingdom of Granada'. *Ethnohistory* 65, no. 3 (2018): 465–488.

Dehouve, Danièle. *Relatos de pecados en la evangelización de los indios de México (siglos XVI–XVIII)*. Mexico City: Centro de Estudios Mexicanos y Centroamericanos, 2010.

DeMarrais, Elizabeth, Luis Jaime Castillo, and Timothy Earle. 'Ideology, Materialization, and Power Strategies'. *Current Anthropology* 37, no. 1 (1996): 15–31.

Departamento Administrativo Nacional de Estadistica. 'Lenguas y dialectos indígenas'. In *Ayer y hoy de los indígenas colombianos*, 45–49. Bogotá: Departamento Administrativo Nacional de Estadistica, 1971.

Dery, David. '"Papereality" and Learning in Bureaucratic Organizations'. *Administration & Society* 29, no. 6 (1998): 677–689.

Dierksmeier, Laura. *Charity for and by the Poor: Franciscan and Indigenous Confraternities in Mexico, 1527–1700*. Norman: University of Oklahoma Press, American Academy of Franciscan History, 2020.

Ditchfield, Simon. 'Romanus and Catholicus: Counter-Reformation Rome as Caput Mundi'. In *A Companion to Early Modern Rome, 1492–1692*. Edited by Pamela M. Jones, Barbara Wisch, and Simon Ditchfield, 131–147. Leiden: Brill, 2019.

'Tridentine Catholicism'. In *The Ashgate Research Companion to the Counter-Reformation*. Edited by Alexandra Bamji, Geert H. Janssen, and Mary Laven, 15–31. Farnham: Ashgate, 2013.

Dougnac Rodríguez, Antonio. *Manual de Historia del Derecho Indiano*. Mexico City: Universidad Nacional Autónoma de México, 1994.

Drennan, Robert D. 'Chiefdoms of Southwestern Colombia'. In *The Handbook of South American Archaeology*. Edited by Helaine Silverman and William Harris Isbell, 405–428. New York: Springer, 2008.

Dümmler, Christiane. 'La Nueva Granada como campo de labor lingüístico-misionera: presentación y análisis de varias obras de la época colonial'. In *La descripción de las lenguas amerindias en la época colonial*. Edited by Klaus Zimmermann, 413–431. Frankfurt; Madrid: Vervuert Iberoamericana, 1997.

Durston, Alan. *Pastoral Quechua: The History of Christian Translation in Colonial Peru, 1550–1650*. Notre Dame, IN: University of Notre Dame Press, 2007.

Dussel, Enrique. *El episcopado latinoamericano y la liberación de los pobres, 1504–1620*. Mexico City: Centro de Reflexión Teológica, 1979.

Duve, Thomas. 'La condición jurídica del indio y su consideración como persona miserabilis en el derecho indiano'. In *Un giudice e due leggi: pluralismo normativo e conflitti agrari in Sud America*. Edited by Mario G. Losano, 3–33. Milan: Dipartamento Giuridico-Politico dell'Università deglo Studi di Milano, 2004.

'Legal History as a History of the Translation of Knowledge of Normativity'. *Max Planck Institute for Legal History and Legal Theory Research Paper Series* 2022, no. 16 (19 September 2022).

'Pragmatic Normative Literature and the Production of Normative Knowledge in the Early Modern Iberian Empires (16th–17th Centuries)'. In *Knowledge of the Pragmatici: Legal and Moral Theological Literature and the Formation of Early Modern Ibero-America*. Edited by Thomas Duve and Otto Danwerth, 1–39. Leiden: Brill, 2020.

Duve, Thomas, and Heikki Pihlajamäki, eds. *New Horizons in Spanish Colonial Law. Contributions to Transnational Early Modern Legal History*. Frankfurt: Max Planck Institute for European Legal History, 2016.

Duviols, Pierre. *La lutte contre les religions autochtones dans le Pérou colonial; 'l'extirpation de l'idolâtrie' entre 1532 et 1660*. Lima: Institut français d'études andines, 1971.

Earle, Rebecca. 'Indians and Drunkenness in Spanish America'. *Past and Present* 222, suppl. 9 (2014): 81–99.

Egío, José Luis, and Christiane Birr. 'Before Vitoria: Expansion into Heathen, Empty, or Disputed Lands in Late-Mediaeval Salamanca Writings and Early 16th-Century Juridical Treatises'. In *A Companion to Early Modern Spanish Imperial Political and Social Thought*. Edited by Jörg Tellkamp, 53–77. Leiden: Brill, 2020.

Errington, Joseph. *Linguistics in a Colonial World: A Story of Language, Meaning, and Power*. Oxford: Blackwell, 2008.

Estenssoro Fuchs, Juan Carlos. *Del paganismo a la santidad: la incorporación de los indios del Perú al catolicismo 1532–1750*. Translated by Gabriela Ramos. Lima: Pontificia Universidad Católica del Perú, 2003.

'El simio de Dios: Los indigenas y la Iglesia frente a la evangelización del Peru, siglos XVI–XVII'. *Bulletin de l'Institut Français d'Études Andines* 30, no. 3 (2001): 455–474.

'Las vías indígenas de la occidentalización. Lenguas generales y lenguas maternas en el ámbito colonial americano (1492–1650)'. *Mélanges de la Casa de Velázquez* 45, no. 1 (2015): 15–36.

Estrada de Gerlero, Elena Isabel. 'Nota preliminar'. In *Instrucciones de la fábrica y del ajuar eclesiásticos [Instructiones fabricae et supellectilis ecclesiasticae Caroli S. R. E. Cardinalis Tituli S. Praxedis]*. Edited by Bulmaro Reyes Coria. Mexico City: Universidad Nacional Autónoma de México, Impr. Universitaria, 1985.

Eugenio Martínez, María Angeles. *Tributo y trabajo del indio en Nueva Granada (de Jiménez de Quesada a Sande)*. Seville: CSIC, 1977.

Fabian, Johannes. *Language and Colonial Power: The Appropriation of Swahili in the Former Belgian Congo, 1880–1938*. Cambridge: Cambridge University Press, 1986.

Fals Borda, Orlando. 'Indian Congregations in the New Kingdom of Granada: Land Tenure Aspects, 1595–1850'. *The Americas* 13, no. 4 (1957): 331–351. doi:10.2307/979439.

Farriss, Nancy. *Maya Society under Colonial Rule: The Collective Enterprise of Survival*. Princeton, NJ: Princeton University Press, 1984.

Tongues of Fire: Language and Evangelization in Colonial Mexico. Oxford: Oxford University Press, 2018.

Fernández Terricabras, Ignasi. *Felipe II y el clero secular: la aplicación del Concilio de Trento*. Madrid: Sociedad Estatal para la Conmemoración de los Centenarios de Felipe II y Carlos V, 2000.

References

Flynn, Maureen. 'Charitable Ritual in Late Medieval and Early Modern Spain'. *The Sixteenth Century Journal* 16, no. 3 (1985): 335–348.

Sacred Charity: Confraternities and Social Welfare in Spain, 1400–1700. Basingstoke: Macmillan, 1989.

Francis, J. Michael. *Invading Colombia: Spanish Accounts of the Gonzalo Jiménez de Quesada Expedition of Conquest*. University Park: Penn State University Press, 2007.

'"La tierra clama por remedio": la conquista espiritual del territorio muisca'. *Fronteras de la Historia* 5 (2000): 93–118.

'Población, enfermedad y cambio demográfico, 1573–1636. Demografía histórica de Tunja: una mirada crítica'. In *Muiscas: Representaciones, cartografías y etnopolíticas de la memoria*. Edited by Ana María Gómez Londoño, 74–151. Bogotá: Editorial Pontificia Universidad Javeriana, 2005.

'The Muisca Indians under Spanish Rule, 1537–1636'. PhD dissertation, University of Cambridge, 1998.

'The Nature and Quality of Early-Colonial Tribute Records in Colombia's Eastern Highlands, 1560–1636'. *Jahrbuch Für Geschichte Lateinamerikas* 49, no. 1 (2012). doi:10.7767/jbla.2012.49.1.285.

'The Resguardo, the Mita, and the Alquiler General: Indian Migration in the Province of Tunja, 1550–1636'. *Colonial Latin American Historical Review* 11, no. 4 (2002): 375–406.

Frassani, Alessia. 'La Virgen de Chiquinquirá y la religión muisca'. *Historia y sociedad* no. 35 (2018): 61–86. doi:10.15446/hys.n35.70319.

Frassani, Alessia, and Patricia Zalamea. 'El templo doctrinero de Sutatausa y su pintura mural'. In *El patrimonio artístico en Cundinamarca. Casos y reflexiones*, 72–87. Bogotá: Gobernación de Cundinamarca, Universidad de los Andes, 2014.

Friede, Juan. 'Los franciscanos en el Nuevo Reino de Granada y el movimiento indigenista del siglo XVI'. *Bulletin Hispanique* 60, no. 1 (1958): 5–29. doi:10.3406/hispa.1958.3561.

Vida y luchas de don Juan del Valle, primer obispo de Popayan y protector de indios. Popayán: Editorial Universidad, 1961.

Friedrich, Markus. 'Circulating and Compiling the Litterae Annuae. Towards a History of the Jesuit System of Communication'. *Archivum Historicum Societas Iesu* 77 (2008): 3–39.

'Communication and Bureaucracy in the Early Modern Society of Jesus'. *Schweizerische Zeitschrift für Religions- und Kulturgeschichte* 101 (2007): 49–75.

Gálvez Piñal, Esperanza. *La visita de Monzón y Prieto de Orellana al Nuevo Reino de Granada*. Seville: Escuela de Estudios Hispano-Americanos, 1974.

Gamboa, Jorge Augusto. 'Caciques, encomenderos y santuarios en el Nuevo Reino de Granada: reflexiones metodológicas sobre la ficción en los archivos: el proceso del cacique de Tota, 1574–1575'. *Colonial Latin American Historical Review* 13, no. 2 (2004): 113–145.

El cacicazgo muisca en los años posteriores a la Conquista: del sihipkua al cacique colonial. Bogotá: Instituto Colombiano de Antropología e Historia, 2010.

'Los caciques en la legislación indiana: una reflexión sobre la condición jurídica de las autoridades indígenas en el siglo XVI'. In *Juan de Solórzano y Pereira:*

References

pensar la colonia desde la colonia. Edited by Diana Bonnett Vélez and Felipe Castañeda Salamanca, 153–190. Bogotá: Universidad de los Andes, 2006.

Los muiscas y su incorporación a la monarquía castellana en el siglo XVI: Nuevas lecturas desde la Nueva Historia de la Conquista. Tunja: Universidad Pedagógica y Tecnológica de Colombia, 2016.

'Presentación'. In *Gramática en la lengua general del Nuevo Reino, llamada mosca*, 13–57. Bogotá: Instituto Colombiano de Antropología e Historia, 2010.

García Gallo, Alfonso. 'La ley como fuente del derecho en Indias en el siglo XVI'. *Anuario de historia del derecho español* 21–22 (1951): 607–730.

García García, Antonio. 'Los privilegios de los franciscanos en América'. *Archivo Ibero-Americano* 48, no. 48 (1988): 369–390.

García Icazbalceta, Joaquín. *Bibliografía mexicana del siglo XVI; primera parte: catálogo razonado de libros impresos en México de 1539 a 1600 con biografías de autores y otras ilustraciones, precedido de una noticia acerca de la introducción de la imprenta en México*. México: Librería de Andrade y Morales, 1886.

García León, Javier, and David García León. 'Políticas lingüísticas en Colombia: tensiones entre políticas para lenguas mayoritarias y lenguas minoritarias'. *Boletín de filología* 47, no. 2 (2012): 47–70.

Garrain Villa, Luis José. 'Documentos sobre Fray Luis Zapata de Cárdenas y otros evangelizadores llerenses en los archivos de Llerena'. In *Extremadura en la evangelización del Nuevo Mundo, actas y estudios: congreso celebrado en Guadalupe durante los días 24 al 29 de octubre de 1988*, 379–400. Colección Encuentros. Serie Seminarios. Madrid: Turner, Junta de Extremadura, 1990.

Garriga Acosta, Carlos Antonio. 'La expansión de la visita castellana a Indias: presupuestos, alcance y significado'. In *XI Congreso del Instituto Internacional de Historia del Derecho Indiano: Buenos Aires, 4 al 9 de septiembre de 1995. Actas y estudios. Vol. 3*, 51–80. Buenos Aires: Instituto de Investigaciones de Historia del Derecho, 1997.

'Las audiencias: Justicia y gobierno de las Indias'. In *El gobierno de un mundo: Virreinatos y audiencias en la América Hispánica*. Edited by Feliciano Barrios, 711–794. Cuenca: Ediciones de la Universida de Castilla-La Mancha, 2004.

Germeten, Nicole von. *Black Blood Brothers: Confraternities and Social Mobility for Afro-Mexicans*. Gainesville: University Press of Florida, 2006.

Gil, Fernando. 'Las juntas eclesiásticas durante el episcopado de Fray Juan de Zumarraga (1528–1548): Algunas precisiones históricas'. *Teología: Revista de la Facultad de Teología de la Pontificia Universidad Católica Argentina* no. 54 (1989): 7–34.

Glave, Luis Miguel. 'Propiedad de la tierra, agricultura y comercio, 1570–1700: El gran despojo'. In *Compendio de historia económica del Perú, II: Economía del período colonial temprano*. Edited by Carlos Contreras, 313–446. Lima: Banco Central de Reservas del Perú, Instituto de Estudios Peruanos, 2009.

González, Margarita. *El resguardo en el Nuevo Reino de Granada*. Bogotá: Universidad Nacional de Colombia, 1970.

References

González Alonso, Benjamín. *El corregidor castellano (1348–1808)*. Madrid: Instituto de Estudios Administrativos, 1970.

González Dávila, Gil. *Teatro eclesiástico de la primitiva iglesia de las Indias Occidentales, vidas de sus arzobispos y obispos, y cosas memorables de sus sedes*. Valladolid: Universidad de León, Junta de Castilla y León, Consejería de Educación y Cultura, 2001.

González de Pérez, María Stella. *'Diccionario y gramática chibcha': manuscrito anónimo de la Biblioteca Nacional de Colombia*. Bogotá: Instituto Caro y Cuervo, 1987.

Trayectoria de los estudios sobre la lengua chibcha o muisca. Bogotá: Instituto Caro y Cuervo, 1980.

Graff, Gary Wendell. 'Cofradias in the New Kingdom of Granada; Lay Fraternities in a Spanish–American Frontier Society, 1600–1755'. PhD dissertation, University of Wisconsin, 1973.

Graubart, Karen B. 'Learning from the Qadi: The Jurisdiction of Local Rule in the Early Colonial Andes'. *Hispanic American Historical Review* 95, no. 2 (2015): 195–228.

'"So color de una cofradía": Catholic Confraternities and the Development of Afro-Peruvian Ethnicities in Early Colonial Peru'. *Slavery & Abolition* 33, no. 1 (2012): 43–64.

Greer, Margaret Rich, Walter Mignolo, and Maureen Quilligan, eds. *Rereading the Black Legend: The Discourses of Religious and Racial Difference in the Renaissance Empires*. Chicago: University of Chicago Press, 2007.

Groot, José Manuel. *Historia eclesiástica y civil de Nueva Granada*. Bogotá: Ministerio de Educación Nacional, Ediciones de la Revista Bolívar, 1953.

Historia eclesiástica y civil de Nueva Granada: Escrita sobre documentos inéditos. Bogotá: Casa Editorial de M. Rivas, 1869.

Groupe de La Bussière. *Pratiques de la confession. Des Pères du désert à Vatican II. Quinze études d'histoire*. Paris: Cerf, 1983.

Guevara Gil, Armando, and Frank Salomon. 'A "Personal Visit": Colonial Political Ritual and the Making of Indians in the Andes'. *Colonial Latin American Review* 3, nos 1–2 (1994): 3–36.

Hampe Martínez, Teodoro. 'La encomienda en el Perú en el siglo XVI (ensayo bibliográfico)'. *Histórica* 6, no. 2 (1982): 173–216.

Hanke, Lewis. *The Spanish Struggle for Justice in the Conquest of America*. Boston; Toronto: Little, Brown and Company, 1949.

Harvey, Penelope. 'Language States'. In *A Companion to Latin American Anthropology*. Edited by Deborah Poole, 193–213. Malden, MA: Blackwell, 2008.

Henderson, Hope, and Nicholas Ostler. 'Muisca Settlement Organization and Chiefly Authority at Suta, Valle de Leyva, Colombia: A Critical Appraisal of Native Concepts of House for Studies of Complex Societies'. *Journal of Anthropological Archaeology* 24, no. 2 (2005): 148–178.

Henningsen, Gustav. *El abogado de las brujas: brujería vasca e Inquisición española*. Madrid: Alianza Editorial, 1983.

Heredia Herrera, Antonia, ed. *Catálogo de las consultas del Consejo de Indias (1529–1591)*. Madrid: Dirección General de Archivos y Bibliotecas, 1972.

Hernández Rodríguez, Guillermo. *De los chibchas a la colonia y a la República; del clan a la encomienda y al latifundio en Colombia*. Bogotá: Universidad Nacional de Colombia, Sección de Extensión Cultural, 1949.

Herrera Ángel, Marta. 'Milenios de ocupación en Cundinamarca'. In *Los muiscas en los siglos XVI y XVII: Miradas desde la arqueología, la antropología y la historia*. Edited by Jorge Augusto Gamboa, 1–39. Bogotá: Universidad de los Andes, 2008.

'Ordenamiento espacial de los pueblos de indios: dominación y resistencia en la sociedad colonial'. *Fronteras de la Historia* 2 (1998): 93–128.

Herzog, Tamar. *Defining Nations: Immigrants and Citizens in Early Modern Spain and Spanish America*. New Haven, CT: Yale University Press, 2008.

Ritos de control, prácticas de negociación. Madrid: Fundación Ignacio Larramendi, 2000.

Upholding Justice: Society, State, and the Penal System in Quito (1650–1750). Ann Arbor: University of Michigan Press, 2004.

Horton, Robin. 'African Conversion'. *Africa: Journal of the International African Institute* 41, no. 2 (1971): 85–108.

'On the Rationality of Conversion: Part I'. *Africa: Journal of the International African Institute* 45, no. 3 (1975): 219–235.

'On the Rationality of Conversion: Part II'. *Africa: Journal of the International African Institute* 45, no. 4 (1975): 373–399.

Hsia, R. Po-Chia. *The World of Catholic Renewal, 1540–1770*. Cambridge: Cambridge University Press, 1998.

Itier, César. 'Lengua general y quechua cuzqueño en los siglos XVI y XVII'. In *Desde afuera y desde adentro: ensayos de etnografía e historia del Cuzco y Apurímac*. Edited by Luis Millones Figueroa, Hiroyasu Tomoeda, and Tatsuhiko Fujii, 47–59. Osaka: National Museum of Ethnology, 2000.

'What Was the "Lengua General" of Colonial Peru?' In *History and Language in the Andes*. Edited by Adrian J. Pearce and Paul Heggarty, 63–85. Basingstoke: Palgrave Macmillan, 2011.

Jaimes Rodríguez, Jerson Fidel, and Santiago Mendieta Afanador. 'Devociones católicas, prácticas religiosas, y cofradías – hermandades en Colombia (siglos XVI–XIX): Una aproximación bibliográfica'. *Anuario de Historia Regional y de las Fronteras* 25, no. 1 (June 2020): 173–203.

Jaque Hidalgo, Javiera, and Miguel A. Valeiro, eds. *Indigenous and Black Confraternities in Colonial Latin America*. Amsterdam: Amsterdam University Press, 2022.

Jaramillo Uribe, Jaime, ed. *Manual de historia de Colombia*. 3 vols. Bogotá: Instituto Colombiano de Cultura, 1976.

Jones, Christopher P. *Between Pagan and Christian*. Cambridge, MA: Harvard University Press, 2014.

Kamen, Henry. *The Phoenix and the Flame: Catalonia and the Counter Reformation*. New Haven, CT: Yale University Press, 1993.

Kaser, Max. *Ius gentium*. Translated by Francisco Javier Andrés Santos. Granada: Comares, 2004.

Kruschek, Michael H. 'The Evolution of the Bogotá Chiefdom: A Household View'. PhD dissertation, University of Pittsburgh, 2003.

References

Lamana, Gonzalo. 'Of Books, Popes and Huacas; or, the Dilemmas of Being Christian'. In *Rereading the Black Legend: The Discourses of Religious and Racial Difference in the Renaissance Empires*. Edited by Margaret Rich Greer, Walter Mignolo, and Maureen Quilligan, 117–149. Chicago: University of Chicago Press, 2007.

Lane, Kris E. *Colour of Paradise: The Emerald in the Age of Gunpowder Empires*. New Haven, CT: Yale University Press, 2010.

Langebaek, Carl Henrik. *Arqueología regional en el valle de Leiva: Procesos de ocupación humana en una región de los Andes orientales de Colombia*. Bogotá: Instituto Colombiano de Antropología e Historia, 2000.

'Buscando sacerdotes y encontrando chuques: de la organización religiosa muisca'. *Revista de Antropología y Arqueología* 6, no. 1 (1990): 77–100.

'Competencia por el prestigio político y momificación en el norte de Suramérica y el Itsmo, siglo XVI'. *Revista Colombiana de Antropología* 29, no. 1 (1992): 4–27.

'De las palabras, las cosas y los recuerdos: el Infiernito, la arqueología, los documentos y la etnología en el estudio de la sociedad muisca'. In *Contra la tiranía tipológica en arqueología: una visión desde Suramérica*. Edited by Cristóbal Gnecco, Axel E. Nielsen, and Carl Henrik Langebaek, 215–270. Bogotá: Universidad de los Andes, Facultad de Ciencias Sociales-CESO, 2006.

'Fiestas y caciques muiscas en el infiernito, Colombia: un análisis de la relación entre festejos y organización política'. *Boletín de Arqueología* no. 9 (2005): 281–295.

Los herederos del pasado: indígenas y pensamiento criollo en Colombia y Venezuela. Bogotá: Universidad de los Andes: Ediciones Uniandes, 2009.

Mercados, poblamiento e integración étinca entre los muiscas: Siglo XVI. Bogotá: Banco de la República, 1987.

Regional Archaeology in the Muisca Territory: A Study of the Fúquene and Susa Valleys [Arqueología regional en el territorio muisca: estudio de los valles de Fúquene y Susa]. Pittsburgh: University of Pittsburgh; Bogotá: Universidad de los Andes, 1995.

'Resistencia indígena y transformaciones ideológicas entre los muiscas de los siglos XVI y XVII'. In *Muiscas: Representaciones, cartografías y etnopolíticas de la memoria*. Edited by Ana María Gómez Londoño, 24–71. Bogotá: Editorial Pontificia Universidad Javeriana, 2005.

'Santuarios indígenas en el repartimiento de Iguaque, Boyacá: Un documento de 1595 del Archivo Histórico Nacional de Colombia'. *Revista de Antropología* 4, no. 2 (1988): 201–227.

Langebaek, Carl Henrik, Marcela Bernal, Lucero Aristizabal, María Antonieta Corcione, Camilo Rojas, and Tatiana Santa. 'Condiciones de vida y jerarquías sociales en el norte de Suramérica: el caso de la población muisca en Tibanica, Soacha.' *Indiana* no. 28 (2011): 15–34.

Leal del Castillo, María del Rosario. 'El purgatorio en la plástica neogranadina'. *Alarife: Revista de arquitectura*, no. 18 (2009): 85–95.

Lee López, Alberto. 'Clero indígena en el Arzobispado de Santafé en el siglo XVI'. *Boletín de Historia y Antigüedades* 50, nos 579–581 (1963): 3–86.

'Gonzalo Bermúdez, primer catedrático de la lengua general de los Chibchas'. *Boletín de Historia y Antigüedades* 51, nos 594–597 (1964): 183–217.

References

Lleras Pérez, Roberto. 'Las estructuras de pensamiento dual en el ámbito de las sociedades indígenas de los andes orientales'. *Boletín del Museo del Oro* no. 40 (1996): 3–15.

'Los Muiscas en la literatura histórica y antropológica. ¿Quién interpreta a quién?' *Boletín de Historia y Antigüedades* 92, no. 829 (2005): 307–338.

Lockhart, James. *The Nahuas after the Conquest: A Social and Cultural History of the Indians of Central Mexico, Sixteenth through Eighteenth Centuries.* Stanford, CA: Stanford University Press, 1992.

Lohmann Villena, Guillermo. *El Corregidor de indios en el Perú bajo los Austrias.* Lima: Fondo Editorial PUCP, 2001.

Londoño, Eduardo. 'Documento sobre los indios de Fontibón y Ubaque: Autos en razón de prohibir a los caciques de Fontibón, Ubaque y otros no hagan las fiestas, borracheras, y sacrificios de su gentilidad'. *Revista de Antropología y Arqueología* 7, nos 1–2 (1991): 130–156.

'El lugar de la religión en la organización social muisca'. *Boletín del Museo del Oro* no. 40 (1996): 63–87.

'El proceso de Ubaque de 1563: La última ceremonia religiosa pública de los muiscas'. *Boletín del Museo del Oro* no. 49 (2001): 1–12.

'Memorias de los ritos y ceremonias de los muiscas en el siglo XVI'. *Revista de Antropología y Arqueología* 6, no. 1 (1990): 229–250.

López Rodríguez, Mercedes. 'La memoria de las imágenes: Donantes indígenas en el Lienzo de las Ánimas de San Nicolás de Tolentino'. In *Historia e imágenes: Los agustinos en Colombia, 400 años.* Edited by José Antonio Carbonell Blanco, 29–39. Bogotá: Museo Nacional de Colombia, 2002.

Lotz-Heumann, Ute. 'Imposing Church and Social Discipline'. In *The Cambridge History of Christianity. Vol. VI: Reform and Expansion, 1500–1660.* Edited by R. Po-Chia Hsia, 244–260. Cambridge: Cambridge University Press, 2007.

Lozada Mendieta, Natalia. *La incorporación del indígena en el Purgatorio cristiano: estudio de los lienzos de ánimas de la Nueva Granada de los siglos XVI y XVII.* Bogotá: Ediciones Uniandes, Universidad de los Andes, 2012.

Lucena Salmoral, Manuel. 'El indofeudalismo chibcha como explicación de la fácil conquista quesadista'. In *Estudios sobre política indigenista Española en América. Vol. 1,* 111–160. Valladolid: Seminario de Historia de América, Universidad de Valladolid, 1975.

Luscombe, David E. 'Natural Morality and Natural Law'. In *The Cambridge History of Later Medieval Philosophy: From the Rediscovery of Aristotle to the Disintegration of Scholasticism, 1100–1600.* Edited by Norman Kretzmann, Anthony Kenny, and Jan Pinborg, 706–719. Cambridge: Cambridge University Press, 1982.

'The State of Nature and the Origin of the State'. In *The Cambridge History of Later Medieval Philosophy: From the Rediscovery of Aristotle to the Disintegration of Scholasticism, 1100–1600.* Edited by Norman Kretzmann, Anthony Kenny, and Jan Pinborg, 757–770. Cambridge: Cambridge University Press, 1982.

MacCormack, Sabine. 'Limits of Understanding: Perceptions of Greco-Roman and Amerindian Paganism in Early Modern Europe'. In *America in European Consciousness, 1493–1750.* Edited by Karen Ordahl Kupperman, 79–129. Chapel Hill: University of North Carolina Press, 1995.

Religion in the Andes: Vision and Imagination in Early Colonial Peru. Princeton, NJ: Princeton University Press, 1991.

MacLeod, Murdo J. 'Confraternities in Colonial New Spain: Mexico and Central America'. In *A Companion to Medieval and Early Modern Confraternities.* Edited by Konrad Eisenbichler, 280–306. Leiden: Brill, 2019.

Majer, Michael. 'Confession and Consolation: The Society of Jesus and Its Promotion of the General Confession'. In *Penitence in the Age of Reformations.* Edited by Katharine Jackson Lualdi and Anne T. Thayer, 184–200. Aldershot: Ashgate, 2000.

Maldavsky, Aliocha. 'De l'encomendero au marchand: charité et évangélisation dans le Pérou colonial, xvie-xviie siècles'. *Cahiers des Amériques latines* 2011, no. 67 (2012): 75–87.

'Encomenderos, indios y religiosos en la región de Arequipa (siglo XVI): Restitución y formación de un territorio cristiano y señoril'. In *Invertir en lo sagrado: salvación y dominación territorial en América y Europa (siglos XVI-XX).* Edited by Aliocha Maldavsky and Roberto Di Stefano. Santa Rosa: Universidad Nacional de la Pampa, 2018.

'Giving for the Mission: The *Encomenderos* and Christian Space in the Late Sixteenth-Century Andes'. In *Space and Conversion in Global Perspective.* Edited by Giuseppe Marcocci, Wietse de Boer, Aliocha Maldavsky, and Ilaria Pavan, 260–284, Leiden: Brill, 2014.

'Les encomenderos et l'evangélisation des Indiens dans le Pérou colonial: "Noblesse", charité et propagation de la foi au XVIe siècle'. In *Le Salut par les armes: Noblesse et défense de l'orthodoxie (XIIIe–XVIIe siècle).* Edited by Ariane Boltanski and Franck Mercier, 239–250. Rennes: Presses Universitaires de Rennes, 2011.

'Teología moral, restitución y sociedad colonial en los Andes en el siglo XVI'. *Revista Portuguesa de Filosofia* 75, no. 2 (2019): 1125–1148.

'The Problematic Acquisition of Indigenous Languages: Practices and Contentions in Missionary Specialization in the Jesuit Province of Peru (1568–1640)'. In *The Jesuits II: Cultures, Sciences, and the Arts, 1540–1773.* Edited by John W. O'Malley, Gauvin Alexander Bailey, Steven J. Harris, and T. Frank Kennedy, 602–615. Toronto: University of Toronto Press, 2006.

Vocaciones inciertas: misión y misioneros en la provincia jesuita del Perú en los siglos XVI y XVII. Seville; Lima: Consejo Superior de Investigaciones Científicas; Instituto Francés de Estudios Andinos; Universidad Antonio Ruiz de Montoya, 2012.

Mann, Michael. *The Sources of Social Power.* Cambridge: Cambridge University Press, 1986.

Mantilla, Luis Carlos. *Historia de la arquidiócesis de Bogotá: Su itinerario evangelizador, 1564–1993.* Bogotá: Arquidiócesis de Bogotá, 1994.

Los franciscanos en Colombia (1550–1600). Bogotá: Editorial Kelly, 1984.

Manzano Manzano, Juan. *Historia de las recopilaciones de Indias: siglo XVI.* Madrid: Ediciones Cultura Hispánica, 1950.

Marín Taborda, Jorge Iván. *Vivir en policía y a son de campana: El establecimiento de la república de indios en la provincia de Santafé, 1550–1604.* Bogotá: Instituto Colombiano de Antropología e Historia, 2022.

References

Marín Tamayo, John Jairo. 'La convocatoria del primer Concilio neogranadino (1868): Un esfuerzo de la jerarquía católica para restablecer la disciplina eclesiástica'. *Historia Crítica* 36 (2008): 174–193.

Martínez, María Elena. *Genealogical Fictions: Limpieza de Sangre, Religion, and Gender in Colonial Mexico*. Stanford, CA: Stanford University Press, 2008.

Martínez Martin, Abel Fernando, and Andrés Ricardo Otálora Cascante. 'Una tradición de larga duración: la Semana Santa en Tunja'. *Historia y Espacio* 17, no. 57 (2021): 75–114.

Massing, Jean Michel. 'Jerome Nadal's *Evangelicae Historiae Imagines* and the Birth of Global Imagery'. *Journal of the Warburg and Courtauld Institutes* 80, no. 1 (2017): 161–220.

Masters, Adrian. 'A Thousand Invisible Architects: Vassals, the Petition and Response System, and the Creation of Spanish Imperial Caste Legislation'. *Hispanic American Historical Review* 98, no. 3 (2018): 377–406.

Matthew, Laura E. *Memories of Conquest: Becoming Mexicano in Colonial Guatemala*. Chapel Hill: University of North Carolina Press, 2012.

Mayorga García, Fernando. *La Audiencia de Santafé en los siglos XVI y XVII*. 2nd edition. Bogotá: Imprenta Distrital, Secretaría General de la Alcaldía Mayor de Bogotá, 2013.

Medina, José Toribio. *La imprenta en Bogotá, 1739–1821*. Amsterdam: N. Israel, 1964.

Meiklejohn, Norman. *La iglesia y los Lupaqas de Chucuito durante la colonia*. Cuzco: Centro de Estudios Rurales Andinos "Bartolomé de las Casas", Instituto de Estudios Aymaras, 1988.

Mesa Gómez, Carlos Eduardo. 'Creencias religiosas de los pueblos indigenas que habitaban en el territorio de la futura Colombia'. *Missionalia Hispanica* 37, nos 109–111 (1980): 111–142.

Mills, Kenneth. *Idolatry and Its Enemies: Colonial Andean Religion and Extirpation, 1640–1750*. Princeton, NJ: Princeton University Press, 1997.

Miramón, Alberto. *El doctor Sangre*. Bogotá: Academia Colombiana de Historia/ Editorial ABC, 1954.

Moran, J. F. *The Japanese and the Jesuits: Alessandro Valignano in Sixteenth-Century Japan*. London: Routledge, 1993.

Morris, Colin. *The Papal Monarchy: The Western Church from 1050 to 1250*. Oxford: Clarendon Press, 1989.

Morris, Craig. 'Storage, Supply and Redistribution in the Economy of the Inka State'. In *Anthropological History of Andean Polities*. Edited by John V. Murra, Nathan Wachtel, and Jacques Revel, 59–68. Cambridge: Cambridge University Press, 1986.

Muldoon, James. *Popes, Lawyers and Infidels: The Church and the Non-Christian World, 1250–1550*. Philadelphia: Penn State University Press, 1979.

Mumford, Jeremy Ravi. *Vertical Empire: The General Resettlement of Indians in the Colonial Andes*. Durham, NC: Duke University Press, 2012.

Muñoz Arbeláez, Santiago. *Costumbres en disputa: Los muiscas y el Imperio español en Ubaque, siglo XVI*. Bogotá: Universidad de los Andes, Facultad de Ciencias Sociales, Departamento de Historia, 2015.

References 329

'The New Kingdom of Granada: The Making and Unmaking of Spain's Atlantic Empire, 1530–1620'. PhD dissertation, Yale University, 2018.

Nalle, Sara Tilghman. *God in La Mancha: Religious Reform and the People of Cuenca, 1500–1650*. Baltimore: Johns Hopkins University Press, 1992.

Ojeda Pérez, Robert, Adriana Castellanos Alfonso, and Sebastián Torres. 'Incendio del palacio virreinal en Santafé: Resonancia histórica y patrimonial'. *Módulo Arquitectura CUC* 12 (2013): 163–181.

Olaechea Labayen, Juan Bautista. 'Las instituciones religiosas de Indias y los mestizos'. *Cuadernos de investigación histórica* 16 (1995): 233–248.

O'Malley, John W. 'The Council of Trent: Myths, Misunderstandings, and Misinformation'. In *Spirit, Style, Story: Essays Honoring John W. Padberg*. Edited by Thomas M. Lucas, 205–226. Chicago: Jesuit Way/Loyola Press, 2002.

The First Jesuits. Cambridge, MA: Harvard University Press, 1993.

Trent : What Happened at the Council. Cambridge, MA: Harvard University Press, 2013.

Orique, David Thomas. *To Heaven or to Hell: Bartolomé de Las Casas's Confesionario*. University Park: Penn State University Press, 2018.

Ortega Ricaurte, Carmen. *Los estudios sobre lenguas indígenas de Colombia: notas históricas y bibliografía*. Bogotá: Instituto Caro y Cuervo, 1978.

Ospina Suárez, Pedro Antonio. *Hernando Arias de Ugarte (1561–1638): El criollo arzobispo de las tres sedes sudamericanas*. Rome: Pontificia Universitas Gregoriana, 2004.

Oss, Adriaan C. van. *Catholic Colonialism: A Parish History of Guatemala, 1524–1821*. Cambridge: Cambridge University Press, 1986.

Ostler, Nicholas. 'Fray Bernardo de Lugo: Two Sonnets in Muisca'. *Amerindia: Revue d'ethnolinguistique Amérindienne* 19–20 (1995): 129–142.

Owensby, Brian Philip. 'The Theater of Conscience in the "Living Law" of the Indies'. In *New Horizons in Spanish Colonial Law: Contributions to Transnational Early Modern Legal History*. Edited by Thomas Duve and Heikki Pihlajamäki, 125–149. Frankfurt: Max Planck Institute for European Legal History, 2016.

Pacheco, Juan Manuel. *La consolidación de la iglesia, siglo XVII. Historia extensa de Colombia*. Vol. *13, part 2*. Bogotá: Academia Colombiana de Historia, 1975.

La evangelización del Nuevo Reino, siglo XVI. Historia extensa de Colombia. Vol. *13, part 1*. Bogotá: Academia Colombiana de Historia, 1971.

Pachón, Ximena, and François Correa. *Lenguas amerindias: Condiciones sociolingüísticas en Colombia*. Santafé de Bogotá: Instituto Colombiano de Antropología, 1997.

Padden, Robert Charles. 'The Ordenanza del Patronazgo, 1574: An Interpretative Essay'. *The Americas* 12, no. 4 (1956): 333–354.

Pagden, Anthony. *The Fall of Natural Man: The American Indian and the Origins of Comparative Ethnology*. Cambridge: Cambridge University Press, 1982.

Pardo, Osvaldo F. *The Origins of Mexican Catholicism: Nahua Rituals and Christian Sacraments in Sixteenth-Century Mexico*. Ann Arbor: University of Michigan Press, 2004.

Penry, S. Elizabeth. *The People Are King: The Making of an Indigenous Andean Politics*. Oxford: Oxford University Press, 2019.

330   *References*

Pérez Riaño, Pablo Fernando. *La encomienda de Chita, 1550–1650.* Bogotá: Academia Colombiana de Historia, 2021.

Phelan, John Leddy. *The People and the King: The Comunero Revolution in Colombia: 1781.* London: University of Wisconsin Press, 1978.

Pinilla Monroy, Germán, and Juan Carlos Lara Acosta. 'El aporte de la Arquidiócesis de Santafé a la educación, siglos XVI, XVII y XVIII'. In *Arquidiócesis de Bogotá, 450 años: miradas sobre su historia.* Edited by Jaime Alberto Mancera Casas, Carlos Mario Alzate Montes OP, and Fabián Leonardo Benavides Silva, 133–162. Bogotá: Universidad Santo Tomás, Arquidiócesis de Bogotá, 2015.

Piras, Giuseppe. 'El P. Diego de Torres Bollo: Su programa, su partido y sus repercusiones'. In *Sublevando el virreinato: documentos contestatarios a la historiografía tradicional del Perú Colonial.* Edited by Laura Laurencich Minelli and Paulina Numhauser, 125–156. Quito: Abya-Yala, 2007.

Martin de Funes S. I. (1560–1611) e gli inizi delle riduzioni dei gesuiti nel Paraguay. Rome: Edizioni di Storia e letteratura, 1998.

Plata, William Elvis. 'Frailes y evangelización en el Nuevo Reino de Granada (s. XVI). Vicisitudes de un proceso conflictivo y no muy exitoso'. *Franciscanum* 58, no. 165 (2016): 263–302.

Pollock, Sheldon. 'Cosmopolitan and Vernacular in History'. *Public Culture* 12, no. 3 (2000): 591–625.

Poole, Stafford. *Pedro Moya de Contreras: Catholic Reform and Royal Power in New Spain, 1571–1591.* Berkeley: University of California Press, 1987.

Porras Collantes, Ernesto. 'Historia del primer templo mayor de Tunja, nombrado de Nuestra Señora de Guadalupe'. *Anuario Colombiano de Historia Social y de la Cultura* no. 31 (2004): 33–44.

Rafael, Vicente L. *Contracting Colonialism: Translation and Christian Conversion in Tagalog Society under Early Spanish Rule.* 2nd edition. Durham, NC: Duke University Press, 1993.

Ramos, Gabriela. *Death and Conversion in the Andes: Lima and Cuzco, 1532–1670.* Notre Dame, IN: University of Notre Dame Press, 2010.

'Pastoral Visitations: Spaces of Negotiation in Andean Indigenous Parishes'. *The Americas* 73, no. 1 (2016): 39–57.

Ramos, Gabriela, ed. *La venida del reino: religión, evangelización y cultura en América, siglos XVI–XX.* Cuzco: Centro de Estudios Regionales Andinos "Bartolomé de las Casas", 1994.

Rappaport, Joanne. 'Letramiento y mestizaje en el Nuevo Reino de Granada, siglos XVI y XVII'. *Diálogo andino* no. 46 (2015): 9–26.

The Disappearing Mestizo: Configuring Difference in the Colonial New Kingdom of Granada. Durham, NC: Duke University Press, 2014.

Rappaport, Joanne, and Thomas B. F. Cummins. *Beyond the Lettered City: Indigenous Literacies in the Andes.* Durham, NC: Duke University Press, 2012.

Real Cuesta, Javier. 'Política lingüística en el Nuevo Reino de Granada durante los siglos XVI y XVII'. In *Estudios sobre política indigenista española en América. Vol. 1,* 279–302. Valladolid: Seminario de Historia de América, Universidad de Valladolid, 1975.

References

Real Díaz, José Joaquín. *Estudio diplomático del documento indiano*. Seville: Escuela de estudios hispanoamericanos, 1970.

Reff, Daniel T. *Plagues, Priests, and Demons: Sacred Narratives and the Rise of Christianity in the Old World and the New*. Cambridge: Cambridge University Press, 2005.

Resines, Luis. *Catecismos americanos del siglo XVI*. Salamanca: Junta de Castilla y León, Consejería de Cultura y Turismo, 1992.

Restall, Matthew. *Seven Myths of the Spanish Conquest*. Oxford: Oxford University Press, 2004.

Restrepo, Luis Fernando. *El estado impostor: Apropiaciones literarias y culturales de la memoria de los muiscas y la América indígena*. Medellín: Editorial Universidad de Antioquia, 2013.

'The Ambivalent Nativism of Lucas Fernández de Piedrahita's Historia general de las conquistas del Nuevo Reyno de Granada'. In *Creole Subjects in the Colonial Americas: Empires, Texts, Identities*. Edited by Ralph Bauer and José Antonio Mazzotti, 334–354. Chapel Hill: UNC Press Books, 2012.

Rey Fajardo, José del. *Biblioteca de escritores jesuitas neogranadinos*. Bogotá: Editorial Pontificia Universidad Javeriana, 2006.

Rodríguez, Diana Farley. '"Y Dios se hizo música": la conquista musical del Nuevo Reino de Granada. El caso de los pueblos de indios de las provincias de Tunja y Santafé durante el siglo XVII'. *Fronteras de la Historia* 15 (2010): 13–38.

Rodríguez-Salgado, M. J. 'Christians, Civilised and Spanish: Multiple Identities in Sixteenth-Century Spain'. *Transactions of the Royal Historical Society* 8 (1998): 233–251. doi:10.2307/3679296.

'"How Oppression Thrives Where Truth Is Not Allowed a Voice": The Spanish Polemic about the American Indians'. In *Silencing Human Rights: Critical Engagements with a Contested Project*. Edited by Gurminder K. Bhambra and Robbie Shilliam, 19–42. Basingstoke: Palgrave Macmillan, 2009.

Rojas, Ulises. *El cacique de Turmequé y su época*. Tunja: Departamento de extensión cultural de Boyacá, 1965.

Romero, Mario Germán. *Fray Juan de los Barrios y la evangelización del Nuevo Reino de Granada*. Bogotá: Academia Colombiana de Historia, 1960.

Romero Sánchez, Guadalupe. *Los pueblos de indios en Nueva Granada*. Granada: Editorial Atrio, 2010.

'Los pueblo de indios en Nueva Granada: Trazas urbanas e iglesias doctrineras'. PhD dissertation, University of Granada, 2008.

Rosenblat, Ángel. 'La hispanización de América. El castellano y las lenguas indígenas desde 1492'. In *Presente y futuro de la lengua española: actas de la asamblea de filología del I Congreso de Instituciones Hispánicas*. Vol. II, 198–216. Madrid: Ediciones Cultura Hispánica, 1964.

Rubin, Miri. *Corpus Christi: The Eucharist in Late Medieval Culture*. Cambridge: Cambridge University Press, 1991.

Rubio Merino, Pedro. 'El presidente Francisco de Sande y don Bartolomé Lobo Guerrero, arzobispo de Santa Fe'. In *Andalucía y America en el siglo XVI: actas de las II Jornadas de Andalucía y América*. Vol. 2. Edited by Bibiano Torres Ramírez and José J Hernández, 67–114. Seville: Escuela de Estudios Hispanoamericanos, 1983.

References

Ruiz Rivera, Julián Bautista. *Encomienda y mita en Nueva Granada en el siglo XVII*. Seville: CSIC, 1975.

Ryan, Magnus. 'Bartolus of Sassoferrato and Free Cities. The Alexander Prize Lecture'. *Transactions of the Royal Historical Society* 10 (2000): 65–89.

Salomon, Frank, and Stuart B. Schwartz. 'New Peoples and a New Kind of People: Adaptation, Readjustment and Ethnogenesis in South American Indigenous Societies (Colonial Era)'. In *The Cambridge History of the Native Peoples of the Americas. Vol. 3: South America, part 2*, 443–501. Cambridge: Cambridge University Press, 1999.

Sánchez Bella, Ismael. *Iglesia y estado en la América española*. Pamplona: Ediciones Universidad de Navarra, 1991.

Schäfer, Ernst. *El consejo real y supremo de las Indias: Su historia, organización y labor administrativa hasta la terminación de la Casa de Austria*. Seville: Imprenta M. de Carmona, 1935–1947.

Schwaller, John Frederick. 'The *Ordenanza del patronazgo* in New Spain, 1574–1600'. *The Americas* 42, no. 3 (1986): 253–274.

The Church in Colonial Latin America. Lanham, MD: Rowman & Littlefield Publishers, 2000.

Sicroff, Albert A. *Los estatutos de limpieza de sangre: controversias entre los siglos XV y XVII*. Madrid: Taurus, 1985.

Sidbury, James, and Jorge Cañizares-Esguerra. 'Mapping Ethnogenesis in the Early Modern Atlantic'. *The William and Mary Quarterly* 68, no. 2 (2011): 181–208.

Smith, Thomas William. *Curia and Crusade: Pope Honorius III and the Recovery of the Holy Land: 1216–1227*. Turnhout: Brepols Publishers, 2017.

Solano, Francisco de. *Ciudades hispanoamericanas y pueblos de indios*. Madrid: Consejo Superior de Investigaciones Científicas, 1990.

Sotomayor, María Lucía. *Cofradías, caciques y mayordomos: Reconstrucción social y reorganización política en los pueblos indios, siglo XVIII*. Bogotá: Instituto Colombiano de Antropología e Historia, 2004.

Stevens-Arroyo, Anthony M. 'The Evolution of Marian Devotionalism within Christianity and the Ibero-Mediterranean Polity'. *Journal for the Scientific Study of Religion* 37, no. 1 (1998), 50–73.

Strathern, Alan. *Unearthly Powers: Religious and Political Change in World History*. Cambridge: Cambridge University Press, 2019.

Stroumsa, Guy G. *A New Science: The Discovery of Religion in the Age of Reason*. Cambridge, MA: Harvard University Press, 2010.

'The Scholarly Discovery of Religion in Early Modern Times'. In *Cambridge World History. Vol. 6, part 2*. Edited by Jerry H. Bentley, Merry E. Wiesner-Hanks, and Sanjay Subrahmanyam, 313–333. Cambridge: Cambridge University Press, 2015.

Tau Anzoátegui, Víctor. *Casuismo y sistema: Indagación histórica sobre el espíritu del derecho indiano*. Buenos Aires: Instituto de Investigaciones de Historia del Derecho, 1992.

Tavárez, David Eduardo. *The Invisible War: Indigenous Devotions, Discipline, and Dissent in Colonial Mexico*. Stanford, CA: Stanford University Press, 2011.

References 333

Taylor, Gerald. 'Un documento quechua de Huarochirí-1607'. *Revista andina* 5, no. 1 (1985): 157–185.

TePaske, John J. *A New World of Gold and Silver*. Edited by Kendall W. Brown. Leiden: Brill, 2010.

Terpstra, Nicholas. *Lay Confraternities and Civic Religion in Renaissance Bologna*. Cambridge: Cambridge University Press, 1995.

The Politics of Ritual Kinship: Confraternities and Social Order in Early Modern Italy. Cambridge: Cambridge University Press, 2000.

Therrien, Monika, and Lina Jaramillo Pacheco. *Mi casa no es tu casa: procesos de diferenciación en la construcción de Santa Fe, siglos XVI y XVII*. Bogotá: Alcaldía Mayor de Bogotá, Instituto Distrital de Cultura y Turismo, 2004.

Torres Moreno, James Vladimir. *Minería y moneda en el Nuevo Reino de Granada: el desempeño económico en la segunda mitad del siglo XVIII*. Bogotá: Instituto Colombiano de Antropología e Historia, 2013.

Tovar Pinzón, Hermes. 'Apéndice documental: Estado actual de los estudios de demografía histórica en Colombia'. *Anuario Colombiano de Historia Social y de la Cultura* no. 5 (1970): 115–140.

Tovar Zambrano, Bernardo. 'La historiografía colonial'. In *La historia al final del milenio: ensayos de historiografía colombiana y latinoamericana*, 21–134. Bogotá: Editorial Universidad Nacional, 1994.

Traslosheros, Jorge E. 'Audiencia Episcopal (Episcopal Court)'. *Max Planck Institute for Legal History and Legal Theory Research Paper Series 2021* no. 12 (2021).

Iglesia, justicia y sociedad en la Nueva España: La audiencia del arzobispado de México, 1528–1668. Mexico City: Editorial Porrúa; Universidad Iberoamericana, 2004.

Trexler, Richard C. 'From the Mouths of Babes: Christianization by Children in 16th Century New Spain'. In *Religious Organization and Religious Experience*. Edited by J. Davis, 115–135. London: Academic Press, 1982.

Triana y Antorveza, Humberto. 'Factores políticos y sociales que contribuyeron a la desparición de lenguas indígenas (Colonia y Siglo XIX)'. In *Lenguas amerindias: condiciones sociolingüísticas en Colombia*. Edited by Ximena Pachón and François Correa, 85–154. Santafé de Bogotá: Instituto Colombiano Antropología, 1997.

Las lenguas indígenas en el ocaso del imperio español. Santafé de Bogotá: Instituto Colombiano de Antropologia, 1993.

Las lenguas indígenas en la historia social del Nuevo Reino de Granada. Bogotá: Instituto Caro y Cuervo, 1987.

Turbay Ceballos, Sandra. 'Las familias indígenas de Santafé, Nuevo Reino de Granada, según los testamentos de los siglos XVI y XVII'. *Anuario Colombiano de Historia Social y de la Cultura* 39, no. 1 (2012): 49–80.

Vargas Murcia, Laura Liliana, and Eduardo Valenzuela. 'Kerigma en imágenes: El programa iconográfico de los muros de la iglesia de Turmequé en el Nuevo Reino de Granada (Colombia)'. *Artefacto Visual: Revista de Estudios Visuales Latinoamericanos* 3, no. 4 (2018): 81–109.

Villamarín, Juan A., and Judith E. Villamarín. 'Chiefdoms: The Prevalence and Persistence of "Señoríos Naturales", 1400 to European Conquest'. In *The*

Cambridge History of the Native Peoples of the Americas. Vol. 3: South America, part 1. Edited by Frank Salomon and Stuart B. Schwartz, 577–667. Cambridge: Cambridge University Press, 1999.

'Epidemic Disease in the Sabana de Bogotá, 1536–1810'. In *Secret Judgments of God: Old World Disease in Colonial Spanish America*. Edited by Noble David Cook and W. George Lovell, 113–141. Norman: University of Oklahoma Press, 1991.

'Kinship and Inheritance among the Sabana de Bogotá Chibcha at the Time of Spanish Conquest'. *Ethnology* 14, no. 2 (1975): 173–179.

Villegas, Juan. *Aplicación del Concilio de Trento en Hispanoamérica, 1564–1600: Provincia eclesiástica del Perú*. Montevideo: Instituto Teológico del Uruguay, 1975.

Wandel, Lee. 'The Reformation and the Visual Arts'. In *The Cambridge History of Christianity. Vol. 4: Reform and Expansion, 1500–1660*. Edited by R. Po-Chia Hsia, 343–370. Cambridge: Cambridge University Press, 2007.

Wasserman-Soler, Daniel I. *Truth in Many Tongues: Religious Conversion and the Languages of the Early Spanish Empire*. University Park: Penn State University Press, 2020.

Webster, Susan Verdi. 'Research on Confraternities in the Colonial Americas'. *Confraternitas* 9, no. 1 (1998): 13–24.

Wheat, David. 'The First Great Waves: African Provenance Zones for the Transatlantic Slave Trade to Cartagena de Indias, 1570–1640'. *Journal of African History* 52, no. 1 (2011): 1–22.

Wilde, Guillermo. 'Regímenes de memoria misional: Formas visuales emergentes en las reducciones jesuíticas de América del Sur'. *Colonial Latin American Review* 28, no. 1 (2019): 10–36.

Religión y poder en las misiones de guaraníes. Buenos Aires: Editorial SB, 2009.

Zavala, Silvio. *La encomienda indiana*. 3rd edition. Biblioteca Porrúa 53. Mexico City: Editorial Porrúa, 1992.

Zuretti, Juan Carlos. 'Un precursor de los derechos humanos en el Tucumán del siglo XVI: El padre Diego de Torres Bollo SJ'. *Teología: revista de la Facultad de Teología de la Pontificia Universidad Católica Argentina* 57 (1991): 13–22.

Zutshi, Patrick. 'Petitioners, Popes, Proctors: The Development of Curial Institutions, c. 1150–1250'. In *Pensiero e sperimentazioni istituzionali nella Societas Christiana, 1046–1250: Atti della sedicesima Settimana internazionale di studio, Mendola, 26–31 agosto 2004*. Edited by Giancarlo Andenna, 265–293. Milan: Editrice Vita e Pensiero, 2007.

Index

Acosta, José de, 148, 182, 194, 199, 207–208, 211
Acquaviva, Claudio, 200, 213
Aguado, Pedro de, 27, 66, 94, 115
Alcalá, Diego de, 150
Alias felicis recordationis (1521), 74
Almansa, Bernardino de, 302
Alonso Saqueypaba, captain of Fontibón, 287
Alonso, *cacique* of Chocontá, 163
Alonso, *cacique* of Fontibón, 54, 59, 287
Alonso, *cacique* of Sogamoso, 105
Alonso, *cacique* of Tausa, 163
Alonso, Diego, 131
Alonso, Rodrigo, 256
Álvarez de Paz, Diego, 190, 196
Anbarja, *cacique* of Soracá, 111
Andrés, *cacique* of Machetá and Tibirita, 296
Andrés, captain of Suta, 300
Andrés, carpenter and part-time catechist, 108
Angulo de Castejón, Diego, 109
Antonio Saquara, leader of Teusacá, 45
Antonio, *cacique* of Pausaga, 43
Antonio, *cacique* of Somondoco, 107
Aquinas, Thomas, 23, 147, 165, 168, 220
Arendt, Hannah, 161
Arias de Monroy, Cristóbal, 160
Arias de Ugarte, Hernando, 237, 251, 255–258, 267–270, 272, 274, 276–278, 285, 291–293
Arias Torero, Hernando, 268
Armendáriz. *See* Díez de Armendáriz, Miguel
Arriaga, Pablo José de, 190, 196

Atunguasa, *cacique* of Mama, 52
Audiencia of Santafé, 7, 12, 15, 26, 30, 35–36, 46, 51, 53–55, 58, 63, 73, 76–77, 79–80, 84, 86–90, 93, 96, 100–102, 109, 112–114, 118–124, 126–128, 135, 142, 144–146, 148–149, 151, 153–154, 156–157, 160–162, 169–170, 173, 175–176, 178–180, 185–186, 236, 238–239, 241, 245, 248, 252, 258, 262, 265, 283, 287, 300, 305, 307
Augustine of Hippo, 23, 33, 37, 220, 308
Augustinian Recollects, Order of, 267
Augustinians (Order of St Augustine), 3, 75, 90–91, 110, 132, 144, 153, 245, 249, 266–267, 284
Auncibay, Francisco de, 154, 156–157, 160, 162, 169
Ávila, Francisco de, 190

Bagajique, 110
Bagajique, *cacique* of Bagajique, 110
Banesta, Juan, 294
baptism, 111, 133–134, 150, 204, 216, 230, 258, 301
Baronio, Cesare, 195
Barrera, Juan de la, 132
Barrios, Juan de los, 36, 75, 77, 79, 90–91, 95–100, 107–109, 112, 127–128, 133, 135, 137–140, 146, 191, 230, 268, 273
Bautista, Juana, 290
Bejarano, Lucas, 51
Belalcázar, Sebastián de, 84

336   *Index*

Benítez, Tomás, 254
Bermúdez, Bartolomé, 117
Bermúdez, Gonzalo, 155, 157, 160, 170,
    239–241, 244, 246–248, 252–254
Betancur y Velosa, Juan de, 258
Betéitiva, 159
Bobasé, 297
Bochica, 54, 67
Bogotá, 35, 149, 154, 156, 243, 262, 275,
    303
Bohorques, Ana de, 290
Bohorques, Juan de, 289
Bojacá, 297, 299
Borgia, Francis, 193
Borja y Armendía, Juan de, 14, 172, 191,
    193, 196, 199, 201, 208, 218–219,
    223, 241, 248–250, 261, 266, 270,
    308–309
Borromeo, Carlo, 209, 272, 309
Borromeo, Federico, 195
Bosa, 113, 155–156, 180
Boyacá, 105, 110–111
Bravo de Ribera, Pedro, 106, 113–114
Briceño, Francisco, 94–95, 97, 100, 120, 156

Cabra, Pedro, governor of Tibaguyas, 301
Cajicá, 35, 48, 128, 155, 199, 208, 212,
    214–217, 248, 273, 286, 291, 299, 303
Calatayud, Martín de, 79
Camacho, Bartolomé, 107
Cardoso, Luis de, 154–155, 169
Carrera, Gonzalo, 134
Cartagena de Indias
    city and province of, 9, 21, 80, 128
    diocese of, 80, 135, 251, 270
Carvajal, Francisco de, 128
Carvajal, Gabriel de, 165, 258, 266, 289,
    296, 299–300, 303
Carvajal, Gerónimo de, 108, 116
Catalina, servant of Sebastián Duarte, 277
Catechism of 1576, 143, 149, 168, 238,
    244, 271
Cepeda. *See* López de Cepeda, Juan
Cerinza, 159
Céspedes, Juan de, 117–118
Cetina, Antonio de, 155–157, 162
Chaine, 106
Charles V, 227
Chía, 155
Chipa, 130
Chipatá, 292

Chiquinquirá, 275
    Virgin of. *See* Virgin of the Rosary of
    Chiquinquirá
Chiscas, 130
Chita, 105, 129, 131–133, 275
Chitagoto, 107–108, 184
Chivatá, 106, 113–114, 275
Choachí, 115–117, 275
Chocontá, 163, 179, 285, 298, 303
Chugame, *cacique* of Chita, 129
Ciénaga, 275
Cifuentes, Cristóbal de, 257
Clavijo, Bartolomé de, 155–156, 158
Clement VIII, 195
Cocuy, 275
Cofradías. See Confraternities
Cómbita, 1, 3, 18, 292, 297
Composiciones
    of *encomiendas*, 174, 177
    of land titles, 177, 187, 287
confession, 99, 116, 132–133, 202–203,
    205–206, 216, 241, 258, 274, 278,
    283, 288, 291, 301
confraternities, 15, 265, 280, 284, 290–299,
    302, 304
Confraternity
    of the Blessed Sacrament of Cajicá, 291, 299
    of the Blessed Sacrament of Chocontá, 298
    of the Blessed Sacrament of Santafé, 283
    of the Blessed Sacrament of Sopó, 299
    of the Blessed Sacrament of Sutatenza, 295
    of the Christ Child of Fontibón, 286, 291
    of the Christ Child of Santafé, 283
    of Corpus Christi of Tópaga, 292
    of the Immaculate Conception of Santafé,
    283
    of the Immaculate Conception of
    Tibaguyas, 293
    of the Immaculate Conception of Tópaga,
    292
    of Santiago of Tunja, 285
    of the Souls of Purgatory of Chocontá, 298
    of the Souls of Purgatory of Cómbita, 3, 292
    of the Souls of Purgatory of Ubaque, 285
    of St Agatha of Cocuy, 285
    of St Anne of Tibirita, 296
    of St Barbara of Tibirita, 296
    of St Jacinto of Pesca, 292
    of St John the Baptist of Bojacá, 297
    of St Lucy of Bojacá, 297, 299
    of St Lucy of Machetá, 296

Index

of St Lucy of Santafé, 262, 264, 280, 284
of St Lucy of Tibirita, 296
of St Peter of Pesca, 292–293
of St Peter of Tenjo, 299
of St Peter of Tópaga, 292
of the True Cross of Chocontá, 179, 285
of the True Cross of Santafé, 283
of the True Cross of Tópaga, 292
of the True Cross of Tunja, 285
of the Virgin of the Rosary of Chocontá, 298
of the Virgin of the Rosary of Guasca, 304
of the Virgin of the Rosary of Santafé, 283–284
of the Virgin of the Rosary of Tabio, 299
of the Virgin of the Snows of Pesca, 292
of the Virgin of Solitude of Santafé, 284
of the Virgin of Solitude of Tunja, 285
Conquest. *See* Spanish invasion
Córdoba, Andrés de, 255–256
Cormechoque, 106, 108
Corpus Christi, feast of, 157, 217–218, 262, 289
Corregidores, 11, 93, 175–176, 178, 180, 188, 303
Cortázar, Julián de, 268, 291
Cortés de Mesa, Luis, 94, 157–159, 162
Cota, 95–96, 115, 118, 154–155
Cota, *cacique* of Cota, 95
Council of Trent, 1, 4, 8, 136–138, 140, 143, 181, 203, 205, 214, 217, 219–220, 229, 255, 265, 273, 309
Cristóbal, *cacique* of Pesca, 292
Cubia, 150, 297
Cucaita, 96, 107, 130–131
Cuchitamga, Andrés, 303
Cucunubá, 164
Cupachilagua, *cacique* of Suta, 119
Cuyacucha, guardian of the *cacique* of Suta, 105
Cuyiava, *cacique* of Chaine, 106

Dadey, Joseph, 213, 249
Delgado, Francisco, 258
Demora. See Tribute: to encomenderos
Díaz, Brígida, 134
Díaz Venero de Leiva, Andrés, 135, 142
Diego, *cacique* of Fontibón, 208
Diego, *cacique* of Guáneca, 62
Diego, *cacique* of Tota, 60, 63
Diego Neamenguya, captain of Suta, 163
Diego Tenasichiguya, captain of Tausa, 163

Diego Tenentiba, captain of Pausaga, 164
Díez de Armendáriz, Miguel, 85, 92–93
Díez de Aux y Armendáriz, Lope, 162
Doctrinas, 107, 142–144, 173, 180, 190, 192, 194, 198, 200, 202, 205, 210, 217, 219, 221, 232, 238, 244–245, 247, 252, 255, 257–258, 265, 267, 269, 271, 274, 280, 295, 306
Domingo, *cacique* of Suta, 300
Domínguez de Medellin, Alonso, 185
Dominicans (Order of Preachers), 39, 73, 76, 88, 90, 92, 107, 111, 127, 131, 133–134, 137, 144, 239–240, 245, 249, 252, 254, 266–267, 283, 306
Duarte, Sebastián, 277
Duitama, 158–159, 200, 213, 223, 286

Egas de Guzmán, Andrés, 177–179, 183
encomienda, 11, 30, 79, 84–86, 96, 98–99, 116–120, 135, 174, 177, 186–188
Enríquez, Luis, 182–187, 266, 303
Enríquez, Martín, 138
epidemics, 241, 290, 303
1558, 109–111, 133
Epítome de la conquista del Nuevo Reino de Granada, 21, 46, 48, 61
Escobar, Florentina de, 118
Espejo, Miguel de, 150, 153–154, 169
Eucharist, 4, 206–207, 216, 271, 278–279, 286, 288, 302
Extreme Unction, 241, 279

Federmann, Nikolaus, 84, 90
Felipe, *cacique* of Chipa, 130
Felipe Queasocha, commoner of Guáquira, 164
Fernández de Angulo, Juan, 78
Fernández de Lugo, Alonso, 78, 85, 88
Fernández de Lugo, Pedro, 78, 85
Fernández de Oviedo, Gonzalo, 83
Fernández de Piedrahita, Lucas, 23–24, 27, 32, 49, 67, 305–308
Fernández Terricabras, Ignasi, 137
Fernández de Villavicencio, Nuño, 291, 293
Figueroa, Bernardino de, 134
Figueroa, Francisco de, 191, 193, 245, 287
Figueroa, Gaspar de, 1–2, 18, 293
Firavitoba, 106, 108
First Provincial Council of Santafé (1625), 250–252, 255, 270, 278–279

338   Index

First Synod of Santafé (1556), 91, 100,
   107–109, 133, 212, 230, 266
Foacá, 132
Fontibón, 35, 45, 47, 49, 56–57, 59, 63,
   128, 149, 154, 156, 200, 208, 210,
   212–213, 216, 218–219, 221, 266,
   273, 286–287, 289–291
Fosatiba, *cacique* of Choachí, 117
Fosca, 275
Fosquiraguya, *cacique* of Tausa, 119
Francis, Michael, 109, 303
Franciscans (Order of Friars Minor), 66–67,
   73, 75, 88, 90, 92, 106, 111, 115,
   127–128, 131–132, 137, 139–140,
   144, 154, 180, 184, 239–240, 243,
   245, 266–267, 283–284, 296
Francisco, *cacique* of Bogotá, 154
Francisco, *cacique* of Chitagoto, 107
Francisco, captain of Chita, 132
Francisco, governor of Tabio, 165
Francisco Chicaguentiba, captain of
   Tibacuy, 164
Fuentes, Juan de, 184
Funes, Martín de, 14, 195–196
Funza. *See* Bogotá
Fúquene, 160, 257, 275, 277–278, 294
Fusagasugá, 118, 150, 306

Gacha, 131, 134
Gachancipá, 115–116, 119
Gachetá, 159
Galarza, Juan de, 94, 102
Gamboa, Jorge, 28, 260
Gámeza, 297
Garagoa, 62
García, Gerónimo, 277–278
García, Sebastián, 134
García Matamoros, Pedro, 78, 92
García Vásquez, Gerónimo, 257
García Zorro, Gonzalo, 118
Gómez, Leonor, 170
Gómez de Córdoba, Juan, 89
Góngora, Beltrán de, 94
González, Antonio, 174–175, 177, 179,
   181, 183, 187, 287
González de Piña, Lope, 176
Gonzalo, captain of Chita, 132
Gonzalo Niatonguya, 63
Gordillo, Fernando de, 256, 279
Gótamo, 292
Grajeda, Alonso de, 110

Gregory I, 1
Gregory XV, 269
Guabatiba, Juan, 262–263, 265, 284
Guacamayas, 257
Guachetá, 129
Guamanga, Domingo de, 284
Guanecipa, *cacique* of Choachí, 117
Guáquira, 114, 130–131, 164
Guasca, 128, 304
Guascaryara, *cacique* of Chiscas, 130
Guateque, 108, 275
Guayquen, *cacique* of Támara, 130
Guecha, *cacique* of Gachancipá, 153
Guevara, Domingo de, 160
Guevara, Juan de, 256
Gutiérrez, Nicolás, 38, 40, 43, 46, 153
Guyamuche, Pedro, 57

Herrera, Jorge de, 298
Hidalgo de Montemayor, Diego, 157–160
Holy Orders. *See* Ordination

Ibarra, Miguel de, 49, 55, 170, 177–178,
   180, 183, 285, 289, 303
Icabuco, 105, 129, 131
Iguaque, 56–57, 60, 62, 71
In Supereminenti (1621), 269
Indigenous parishes. *See Doctrinas*
Inter caetera (1493), 5
Itier, César, 235

Jesuits (Society of Jesus), 14–15, 48,
   189–201, 207–223, 242–243,
   245–250, 259, 261, 264, 267, 269,
   274–275, 283–285, 293, 306, 308
Jiménez de Quesada, Gonzalo, 21–22, 30,
   78, 84, 86, 88, 129
Juan, *cacique* of Betéitiva, 159
Juan, *cacique* of Duitama, 159
Juan, *cacique* of Fontibón, 126, 288
Juan, *cacique* of Fúquene, 294
Juan, *cacique* of Guasca, 304
Juan, *cacique* of Lenguazaque, 59
Juan, *cacique* of Soatá, 130, 132
Juan, *cacique* of Sogamoso, 63
Juan, captain of Usaquén, 169
Juan Coruta, captain of Suta, 300
Juan Neaetariguia, captain of Suta, 300
Juan Neaquenchía, 60, 62
Juan Quechantocha, *cacique* of Suta, 163
Juan Quigacha, *cacique* of Pesca, 164

Index

Juan Sachigua, *cacique* of Cajicá, 208
Junta eclesiástica of 1546, 98–99

language materials, 193, 197, 201–202,
   223–224, 226, 234, 238–240, 242,
   244, 247–248, 250–251, 255–257,
   264, 271
   1606 official translations, 248, 250
language policy, 14–15, 141, 145, 192,
   223–232, 235–236, 257–261, 265
Lara, Juan de, 154, 160
Las Casas, Bartolomé de, 20, 117, 148
Las Casas, Domingo de, 88
Laws of Burgos-Valladolid (1512–1513),
   211, 227
Lázaro, captain of Suta, 300
Lebrija, Antonio de, 21, 32, 48, 78
Lebrón, Jerónimo, 78, 90
legal translation, 83, 173, 203, 219, 224,
   308–309
Lenguazaque, 57, 59, 71, 254
León, Francisco de, 252
León, Gonzalo de, 119
Leonor, commoner of Sutatenza, 295
Lima III. *See* Third Provincial Council of
   Lima (1582–1583)
Limpias, Gabriel de, 154
Loayza, Jerónimo de, 138
Lobo Guerrero, Bartolomé, 14, 172,
   181–182, 184–186, 188–192,
   195–196, 199, 203, 207, 209, 219,
   223, 242, 244–245, 247–248, 250,
   252, 254, 261, 267, 269–271, 274,
   280, 287, 291, 293–294, 308
López, Mercedes, 3, 293
López de Cepeda, Juan, 51–52, 128–134,
   167, 169
López Medel, Tomás, 102–106, 108–110,
   112–114, 116, 118, 121, 129, 131,
   146, 178, 187, 303
Lorenzo, captain of Fontibón, 63
Lorenzo, Francisco, 39, 46
Lugo, Alonso. *See* Fernández de Lugo, Alonso
Lugo, Bernardo de, 242, 249
Lugo, Pedro. *See* Fernández de Lugo, Pedro
Luis, *cacique* of Soracá, 294
Luisillo, interpreter and blackmailer, 159
Lyra, Gonzalo de, 220, 243, 247, 258

Machetá, 180, 296
Macías, Alonso, 252

Maldavsky, Aliocha, 98, 194–195
Maldonado, Alonso, 159
Maldonado, Francisco, 262
Maldonado, Leonor, 119
Mallol, Vicente, 249
Malo de Molina, Diego, 243
Marcos, brother of the *cacique* of Chocontá,
   298
Maria of Austria, 193
Mariquita, 185
marriage, 204, 258
Martinico, captain of Usaquén, 169
Medina, Francisco de, 134
Medrano, Alonso de, 192, 245, 287
Mendoza, Francisca, 290
Mexico III. *See* Third Provincial Council of
   Mexico (1585)
Miguel, *cacique* of Chita, 105, 132
Miguel, commoner of Sutatenza, 295
Millán, Andrés, 297
Mogrovejo, Toribio de, 138
Mona, 132
Monguí, 253, 275, 302
   Virgin of. *See* Virgin of Perpetual Succour
   of Monguí
Moniquirá, 71, 96, 106, 109–110, 132,
   184, 256, 277
Moniquirá, *cacique* of Moniquirá, 58
Montañez, Diego, 106, 114, 116–117, 122, 130
Montaño, Juan de, 94–95
Montesclaros, Juan de Mendoza y Luna,
   3rd Marquis of, 190
Montúfar, Alonso de, 138
Monzón, Juan Bautista, 159, 162
Motavita, 3, 111, 292
Moya de Contreras, Pedro de, 138
Muisca, 21–22
   languages, 236–244, 250–255, *See also*
   language materials and language policy
   pre-Hispanic leadership, 40, 42, 45–46,
   163–165, 169, 308
   pre-Hispanic political organisation, 28,
   30–34
   pre-Hispanic religious practices, 12–13,
   49–65, 70–71, *See also* Santuarios
   pre-Hispanic ritual economy, 13, 37–45,
   49, 120, 124–127, 163–165, 289
   Spanish ethnology, 11, 22–26, 65–66,
   306–307
   xeques, 47–48, 50, 55–59, 148, 154, 169,
   197, 208

340 *Index*

Muñoz Arbeláez, Santiago, 27, 42–43, 118, 246
Muzo, 8

Nadal, Jerónimo, 213
natural law, 13, 165, 167
natural lords, 39, 126, 165–169
Navarro, Jerónimo, 223–224, 243
Navarro, Juan, 284
Neamuechequa, *cacique* of Tenza, 108
Neausipa, *cacique* of Chivatá, 106, 114
Nemchía, *cacique* of Samacá, 110
Nemocón, 243
Nemusa, 129, 132
Neubasia, captain of Tunquirá, 111
New Laws, 79–80, 85–87, 92–94
Nimpiqui, captain of Moniquirá, 110
Núñez, Gaspar, 161

Ocavita, 184
Oicatá, 129, 131–134, 275, 280, 293, 297, 301, 303
Ojeda, Bartolomé de, 107
Olea, Francisco de, 128, 140
Onzaga, 131
ordination, 74, 92, 135–136, 143–145, 180, 190, 232, 238, 243, 268, 272
Ordóñez y Flórez, Pedro, 270, 274
Orencipa, *cacique* of Ubaté, 115
Oss, Adriaan van, 16

Pablo, *cacique* of Chita, 132–133
Páez, Esteban, 191, 195
Paipa, 158, 252–253, 255, 275, 306
Palomino, Pedro, 131–132
Pánqueba, 107, 280
Paredes, Diego, 108
Parra, Juan Sebastián de la, 190, 195–196
Patronato. See Royal Patronage
Pausaga, 42, 45, 164
Pedro, *cacique* of Chocontá, 163
Pedro, *cacique* of Fúquene, 160
Pedro, *cacique* of Suba, 40, 124, 126, 168
Pedro, *cacique* of Subachoque, 160
Pedro, *cacique* of Ubaté, 45, 168
Pedro, commoner of Sutatenza, 295
Pedro Cabra, governor of Tibaguyas, 258
Pedro Conbafurguya, captain of Sisatiba, 164
Pedro Neachasenguya, *cacique* of Cucunubá, 164

Pedro Pirascosba, *cacique* of Pesca, 291–292
Penagos, Juan de, 100
penance. *See* confession
Peralta, Luis de, 50
Pérez de Arteaga, Melchor, 35–37, 39, 45, 49, 54, 305
Pesca, 164, 291–293, 297
Philip II, 8, 136–139, 141, 174, 177, 232
Philip III, 170
Piedrahita. *See* Fernández de Piedrahita, Lucas
Pisba, 51, 61, 130–132
Pius IV, 135
policía, 146, 179, 204–205, 207, 211, 228, 230
Popayán
city and province of, 21, 94, 103–104
diocese of, 80, 135, 250–251, 270
population estimates, 6, 103, 109–110, 133, 170, 177–178, 183, 188, 208–209, 303
Porras Mejía, Francisco de, 179
Prieto de Orellana, Juan, 162, 173

Queca, 150
Quecamucha, *cacique* of Icabuco, 105
Quesmecosba, captain of Tabaquita, Pisba, 52
quinto. See Tribute: royal fifth
Quito, archdiocese of, 135

Ramiriquí, 96, 131, 134
Rasgón, 106
reducciones, 11, 56, 113, 118, 149, 169, 176–178, 181, 184, 187, 208, 260, 292, 300
Requejada, Vicente de, 90, 110, 132
requinto. See Tribute: *requinto*
rescript government, 11, 13, 81–82, 121–122, 140
resettlement. *See Reducciones*
resguardo, 178, 184, 285
restitution, 96, 100, 112–113, 116
Río, Bartolomé del, 294, 297, 304
Rioja, Lope de, 150, 153
Roa, Cristobál de, 108
Robles, Francisca, 283
Robles, Gabriel de, 134
Rodríguez Freyle, Juan, 23
Rodríguez de Mora, Juan, 162
Rodríguez Salamanca, Pedro, 105

Index

Rodríguez de Valderas, Diego, 116
Rojas, Diego de, 291
Romero de Aguilar, Alonso, 73, 75, 87, 145, 240
Romero de Aguilar, Diego, 249
royal fifth. *See* Tribute: royal fifth
royal patronage, 79, 141–142
   Cédula magna of (1574), 141, 148, 231, 238, 268
Ruiz de Orejuela, Juan, 93–94

Saacha, captain of Motavita, 111
Saboyá, 256, 277
Sáchica, 130–131
Salazar, Casilda de, 151
Saldierna de Mariaca, Andrés, 186
Samacá, 132, 258
San José de Pare, 256, 279
San Martín, Juan de, 21, 32, 48, 78
San Miguel, Jerónimo de, 88, 90–91
Sanabria, Diego de, 252–254, 299
Sanabria, Luis de, 106, 108
Sánchez Ropero, Martín, 109
Sande, Francisco de, 180–182, 186–187, 203, 245, 274
Santa Marta
   city and province of, 21, 78, 80
   diocese of, 78, 80–81, 251, 270
   governorship of, 7, 78, 82, 85
Santafé de Bogotá
   archdiocese of, 135, 191–192, 256, 264, 266–268, 273, 280, 296, 300
   Audiencia (High Court and Chancery) of. *See Audiencia* of Santafé
   cabildo of, 82, 86, 100, 136, 172, 249
   cathedral chapter of, 89, 91, 97, 156, 159, 179–180, 253–254, 267–268, 306
   cathedral church of, 36, 97, 140, 159, 262, 269, 283–284
   cathedral parish of, 284
   city of, 4, 7, 12, 21, 30, 35, 78, 82, 88–89, 92, 135, 154, 157, 160, 180, 182, 197, 218, 221, 226, 236, 247, 258, 262–263, 268, 270, 280, 283, 290, 296, 306
   diocesan seminary of, 143, 145, 179, 197, 238, 269–270, 306
   diocese of, 80, 135
   parish of Las Nieves, 284–285
   parish of San Victorino, 284
   parish of Santa Bárbara, 284–285

province of, 77, 89, 102, 110, 112, 114, 120, 128–129, 144, 154, 160, 164, 170, 174–175, 177, 183–184, 208, 248, 254, 258, 261, 263, 265, 267–268, 275
Santafé I. *See* First Provincial Council of Santafé
Santana, Antón de, 105
Santo Domingo, 7, 85, 109
   archdiocese of, 135
Santo Filiberto, Juan de, 90, 92
Santo Tomás, Domingo de, 231, 234
Santuarios, 13, 54–65, 149–155, 157, 160–161, 165, 170, 173, 209, 237, 286, 304
Sanz, Alonso, 253
Sanz Hurtado, Juan, 170, 172, 176, 184, 188, 193, 197
Saquencipá, 131
Sasa, 132
Sasa, captain of Pisba, 52
Sastoque, *cacique* of Moniquirá, 106
Sátiva, 184
Second Synod of Santafé (1606), 201–208, 214, 250, 255, 269, 271–272, 274, 293
Sepúlveda, Juan de, 253–254
Sepúlveda, Nicolás de, 116, 119
Siachoque, 252, 297
Sichabón, *cacique* of Boyacá, 110–111
Sierra, Francisco de, 106
Simbaumba, commoner from Tunquirá, 111
Simijaca, 115, 119
Simón, Pedro, 67
Sisatiba, 164
Soacá, 292
Soatá, 111, 130, 132
Socha, 108, 110, 116
Socotá, 109
Sogamoso, 63, 103, 105–106, 159, 252, 254
Somondoco, 107
Sopó, 155, 299
Sora, 131
Soracá, 110–111, 129, 255, 275, 278, 294
Sotaquirá, 297
Sotelo, María de, 107
Spanish invasion, 21, 29
Strathern, Alan, 69–70
Suárez, Gregorio, 107, 130
Suárez Rendón, Gonzalo, 105, 120, 131
Suba, 35, 43, 46, 56, 124, 154–155, 168
Subachoque, 160
Suesca, 96, 115, 243

Súnuba, 108
Susa, 299
Susa, leader of Susa, 46
Susaba, captain of Rasgón, 106
Susacón, 111
Suta, 3, 105, 115, 119, 163, 184, 275, 292, 297, 300
Sutatausa, 299
Sutatenza, 295
Synods of Santafé. *See* First Synod of Santafé (1556) *and* Second Synod of Santafé (1606)

Tabaco, Pedro, *cacique* of Cómbita, 3, 15, 18, 293
Tabio, 165, 253, 299
Támara, 130
Tasa. *See* Tribute, standardisation of
Tausa, 115, 119, 163, 275, 300
Taxation. *See* Tribute
Taylor, Gerald, 235
Tecasquirá, 129
Techo, 266
Tenjo, 116, 118, 299
Tenza, 108
Third Provincial Council of Lima (1582–1583), 138, 197, 201–206, 208, 212, 214, 217, 219, 244, 248, 250, 255, 270, 272
Third Provincial Council of Mexico (1585), 272
Tibacuy, 164
Tibagüenza, captain of Suta, 105
Tibaguyas, 155, 258, 293
Tibaná, 105, 120, 129, 131
Tibasuso, 290
Tibirita, 296
Tinjacá, 131
Tobagia, *cacique* of Socha, 110
Tocavita, captain of Susacón, 111
Toisaga, Isabel, 303
Toledo, Francisco de, 138, 192, 199, 231
Tolosa, Miguel Jerónimo de, 251, 275
Tópaga, 200, 213, 275, 278, 292, 294
Tordehumos, Francisco de, 95, 154
Torres, Alonso de, 111
Torres, Cristóbal de, 4, 276, 279–280, 294, 297–298, 302
Torres, Diego de, *cacique* of Turmequé, 48, 162

Torres, Juan de, 90, 111–113
Torres Bollo, Diego de, 14, 193, 195–196, 199, 207, 219–220, 247, 269
Torres Rubio, Diego de, 246
Tota, 47, 52, 58, 63, 71, 114, 116–117, 130
Tota, *cacique* of Tota, 71
translation, 51, 159, 197, 202, 223, 235, 239–242, 244, 246–251, 256–257, 259, 264, 271
legal. *See* Legal translation
Trent. *See* Council of Trent
tribute, 11, 93, 97, 99, 103–104, 112, 114, 116, 119, 142, 153, 160, 163, 171, 176, 187
to *encomenderos* (*demora*), 30, 84, 86, 92, 95, 98, 104, 107–108, 119, 126, 142, 165, 176, 262, 302, 304
to Indigenous leaders (*tamsa*), 30, 40, 44, 164–165, 168, 287, *see also* Muisca: pre-Hispanic ritual economy
requinto, 177, 188, 262, 304
royal fifth, 126, 150, 161
standardisation of, 43, 92–93, 95–97, 101, 109, 112, 114, 119, 146, 151
Tridentine reform. *See* Council of Trent
Tuna, 35, 46, 56, 154–155, 169
Tunja
cabildo of, 129, 136, 172
city of, 12, 89–90, 92, 103, 105–106, 108, 134, 221, 253, 258, 285, 304
province of, 77, 94–95, 102–103, 109, 120, 128, 143–144, 158, 174–175, 177, 183, 185, 252, 258, 261, 263, 265–267, 275, 295
Tunjuelo, 96, 115, 200
Tunjuelo, leader of Tunjuelo, 115
Tunquirá, 111
Tupachoque, 176, 184
Tupia, 292
Turmequé, 111–112, 129, 158, 297, 299
Tuta, 297

Ubaque, 43, 45, 60, 115, 118, 297, 305, 307
Ubaque, *cacique* of Ubaque, 35, 38, 50, 54, 67, 71, 117–118, 305
celebration of 1563, 39–40, 117–118, 305–307
Ubaté, 45, 96, 115–116, 119, 168, 180, 275, 297, 303

Ubatoque, 42
Ucarica, captain of Moniquirá, 58
Une, 150
Unecipá, 150
Usaquén, 154, 169
Usme, 153

Valcárcel, Juan de, 258, 266, 296, 300, 303
Vargas, Francisco, 216
Vásquez, Hernando, 253
Velandia, Francisco de, 107–108
Velasco, Luis de, 231
Venero. *See* Díaz Venero de Leiva, Andrés
Venezuela, 21
Verdero, Juan Esteban de, 89
Vergara, Diego de, 150
Vilches, Juan Antonio de, 157–158, 160, 170
Villa de Leyva, 267
Villafañe, Diego de, 103, 112, 114–115, 117–118, 121, 167
Virgin of Perpetual Succour of Monguí, 302
Virgin of the Rosary of Chiquinquirá, 299, 302

visitations, 11, 30, 42, 51–52, 93, 95, 123, 128–136, 149, 155, 158, 160, 163–164, 167, 170, 178–179, 183–187, 192, 198, 208, 251, 258, 266, 270, 273–281, 291, 296, 300, 302

Xaguara, leader of Tuna, 50

Yuramico, captain of Pisba, 52

Zamora, Alonso de, 88
Zapata de Cárdenas, Luis, 12, 14, 73, 127, 138–140, 142–146, 148–149, 153–154, 157, 159–160, 168–169, 173, 179–181, 187, 191, 203–204, 206, 209, 212, 237–238, 241–245, 247, 259, 266, 268, 270, 273, 283, 286, 309
  Catechism with Rules and Documents for the Priests of Indians. See Catechism of 1576
Zapata de Lobera, Rodrigo, 265, 267, 296
Zipaquirá, 155, 275
Zumárraga, Juan de, 138, 234
Zúñiga, Juan de, 107

Other Books in the Series (continued from page ii)

130 *A Tale of Two Granadas: Custom, Community, and Citizenship in the Spanish Empire, 1568–1668*, Max Deardorff

129 *A Colonial Book Market: Peruvian Print Culture in the Age of Enlightenment*, Agnes Gehbald

128 *Veracruz and the Caribbean in the Seventeenth Century*, Joseph M. H. Clark

127 *We, the King: Creating Royal Legislation in the Sixteenth-Century Spanish New World*, Adrian Masters

126 *A History of Chile 1808–2018*, second edition, William F. Sater and Simon Collier

125 *The Dread Plague and the Cow Killers: The Politics of Animal Disease in Mexico and the World*, Thomas Rath

124 *Islands in the Lake: Environment and Ethnohistory in Xochimilco, New Spain*, Richard M. Conway

123 *Journey to Indo-América: APRA and the Transnational Politics of Exile, Persecution, and Solidarity, 1918–1945*, Geneviève Dorais

122 *Nationalizing Nature: Iguaza Falls and National Parks at the Brazil-Argentina Border*, Frederico Freitas

121 *Islanders and Empire: Smuggling and Political Defiance in Hispaniola, 1580–1690*, Juan José Ponce-Vázquez

120 *Our Time Is Now: Race and Modernity in Postcolonial Guatemala*, Julie Gibbings

119 *The Sexual Question: A History of Prostitution in Peru, 1850s–1950s*, Paulo Drinot

118 *A Silver River in a Silver World: Dutch Trade in the Rio de la Plata, 1648–1678*, David Freeman

117 *Laboring for the State: Women, Family, and Work in Revolutionary Cuba, 1959–1971*, Rachel Hynson

116 *Violence and the Caste War of Yucatán*, Wolfgang Gabbert

115 *For Christ and Country: Militant Catholic Youth in Post-Revolutionary Mexico*, Robert Weis

114 *The Mexican Mission: Indigenous Reconstruction and Mendicant Enterprise in New Spain, 1521–1600*, Ryan Dominic Crewe

113 *Corruption and Justice in Colonial Mexico, 1650–1755*, Christoph Rosenmüller

112 *Blacks of the Land: Indian Slavery, Settler Society, and the Portuguese Colonial Enterprise in South America*, John M. Monteiro, James Woodward, and Barbara Weinstein

111 *The Street Is Ours: Community, the Car, and the Nature of Public Space in Rio de Janeiro*, Shawn William Miller

110 *Laywomen and the Making of Colonial Catholicism in New Spain, 1630–1790*, Jessica L. Delgado

109 *Urban Slavery in Colonial Mexico: Puebla de los Ángeles, 1531–1706*, Pablo Miguel Sierra Silva

108 *The Mexican Revolution's Wake: The Making of a Political System, 1920–1929*, Sarah Osten

107 *Latin America's Radical Left: Rebellion and Cold War in the Global 1960s*, Aldo Marchesi

106 *Liberalism as Utopia: The Rise and Fall of Legal Rule in Post-Colonial Mexico, 1820–1900*, Timo H. Schaefer

105 *Before Mestizaje: The Frontiers of Race and Caste in Colonial Mexico*, Ben VinsonIII

104 *The Lords of Tetzcoco: The Transformation of Indigenous Rule in Postconquest Central Mexico*, Bradley Benton

103 *Theater of a Thousand Wonders: A History of Miraculous Images and Shrines in New Spain*, William B. Taylor

102 *Indian and Slave Royalists in the Age of Revolution*, Marcela Echeverri

101 *Indigenous Elites and Creole Identity in Colonial Mexico, 1500–1800*, Peter Villella

100 *Asian Slaves in Colonial Mexico: From Chinos to Indians*, Tatiana Seijas

99 *Black Saint of the Americas: The Life and Afterlife of Martín de Porres*, Celia Cussen

98 *The Economic History of Latin America since Independence*, third edition, Victor Bulmer-Thomas

97 *The British Textile Trade in South American in the Nineteenth Century*, Manuel Llorca-Jaña

96 *Warfare and Shamanism in Amazonia*, Carlos Fausto

95 *Rebellion on the Amazon: The Cabanagem, Race, and Popular Culture in the North of Brazil, 1798–1840*, Mark Harris

94 *A History of the Khipu*, Galen Brokaw

93 *Politics, Markets, and Mexico's "London Debt," 1823–1887*, Richard J. Salvucci

92 *The Political Economy of Argentina in the Twentieth Century*, Roberto Cortés Conde

91 *Bankruptcy of Empire: Mexican Silver and the Wars between Spain, Britain, and France, 1760–1810*, Carlos Marichal

90 *Shadows of Empire: The Indian Nobility of Cusco, 1750–1825*, David T. Garrett

89 *Chile: The Making of a Republic, 1830–1865: Politics and Ideas*, Simon Collier

88 *Deference and Defiance in Monterrey: Workers, Paternalism, and Revolution in Mexico, 1890–1950*, Michael Snodgrass

87 *Andrés Bello: Scholarship and Nation-Building in Nineteenth-Century Latin America*, Ivan Jaksic

86 *Between Revolution and the Ballot Box: The Origins of the Argentine Radical Party in the 1890s*, Paula Alonso

85 *Slavery and the Demographic and Economic History of Minas Gerais, Brazil, 1720–1888*, Laird W. Bergad

84 *The Independence of Spanish America*, Jaime E. Rodríguez

83 *The Rise of Capitalism on the Pampas: The Estancias of Buenos Aires, 1785–1870*, Samuel Amaral

82 *A History of Chile, 1808–2002*, second edition, Simon Collier and William F. Sater

81 *The Revolutionary Mission: American Enterprise in Latin America, 1900–1945*, Thomas F. O'Brien

80 *The Kingdom of Quito, 1690–1830: The State and Regional Development*, Kenneth J. Andrien

79 *The Cuban Slave Market, 1790–1880*, Laird W. Bergad, Fe Iglesias García, and María del Carmen Barcia

78 *Business Interest Groups in Nineteenth-Century Brazil*, Eugene Ridings

77 *The Economic History of Latin America since Independence*, second edition, Victor Bulmer-Thomas

76 *Power and Violence in the Colonial City: Oruro from the Mining Renaissance to the Rebellion of Tupac Amaru (1740–1782)*, Oscar Cornblit

75 *Colombia before Independence: Economy, Society and Politics under Bourbon Rule*, Anthony McFarlane

74 *Politics and Urban Growth in Buenos Aires, 1910–1942*, Richard J. Walter

73 *The Central Republic in Mexico, 1835–1846, 'Hombres de Bien' in the Age of Santa Anna*, Michael P. Costeloe

72 *Negotiating Democracy: Politicians and Generals in Uruguay*, Charles Guy Gillespie

71 *Native Society and Disease in Colonial Ecuador*, Suzanne Austin Alchon

70 *The Politics of Memory: Native Historical Interpretation in the Colombian Andes*, Joanne Rappaport

69 *Power and the Ruling Classes in Northeast Brazil, Juazeiro and Petrolina in Transition*, Ronald H. Chilcote

68 *House and Street: The Domestic World of Servants and Masters in Nineteenth-Century Rio de Janeiro*, Sandra Lauderdale Graham

67 *The Demography of Inequality in Brazil*, Charles H. Wood and José Alberto Magno de Carvalho

66 *The Politics of Coalition Rule in Colombia*, Jonathan Hartlyn

65 *South America and the First World War: The Impact of the War on Brazil, Argentina, Peru and Chile*, Bill Albert

64 *Resistance and Integration: Peronism and the Argentine Working Class, 1946–1976*, Daniel James

63 *The Political Economy of Central America since 1920*, Victor Bulmer-Thomas

62 *A Tropical Belle Epoque: Elite Culture and Society in Turn-of-the-Century Rio de Janeiro*, Jeffrey D. Needell

61 *Ambivalent Conquests: Maya and Spaniard in Yucatan, 1517–1570*, second edition, Inga Clendinnen

60 *Latin America and the Comintern, 1919–1943*, Manuel Caballero

59 *Roots of Insurgency: Mexican Regions, 1750–1824*, Brian R. Hamnett

58 *The Agrarian Question and the Peasant Movement in Colombia: Struggles of the National Peasant Association, 1967–1981*, Leon Zamosc

57 *Catholic Colonialism: A Parish History of Guatemala, 1524–1821*, Adriaan C. van Oss

56 *Pre-Revolutionary Caracas: Politics, Economy, and Society 1777–1811*, P. Michael McKinley

55 *The Mexican Revolution, Volume 2: Counter-Revolution and Reconstruction*, Alan Knight

54 *The Mexican Revolution, Volume 1: Porfirians, Liberals, and Peasants*, Alan Knight

53 *The Province of Buenos Aires and Argentine Politics, 1912–1943*, Richard J. Walter

52 *Sugar Plantations in the Formation of Brazilian Society: Bahia, 1550–1835*, Stuart B. Schwartz

51 *Tobacco on the Periphery: A Case Study in Cuban Labour History, 1860–1958*, Jean Stubbs

50 *Housing, the State, and the Poor: Policy and Practice in Three Latin American Cities*, Alan Gilbert and Peter M. Ward

49 *Unions and Politics in Mexico: The Case of the Automobile Industry*, Ian Roxborough

48 *Miners, Peasants and Entrepreneurs: Regional Development in the Central Highlands of Peru*, Norman Long and Bryan Roberts

47 *Capitalist Development and the Peasant Economy in Peru*, Adolfo Figueroa

46 *Early Latin America: A History of Colonial Spanish America and Brazil*, James Lockhart and Stuart B. Schwartz

45 *Brazil's State-Owned Enterprises: A Case Study of the State as Entrepreneur*, Thomas J. Trebat

44 *Law and Politics in Aztec Texcoco*, Jerome A. Offner

43 *Juan Vicente Gómez and the Oil Companies in Venezuela, 1908–1935*, B. S. McBeth

42 *Revolution from Without: Yucatán, Mexico, and the United States, 1880–1924*, Gilbert M. Joseph

41 *Demographic Collapse: Indian Peru, 1520–1620*, Noble David Cook

40 *Oil and Politics in Latin America: Nationalist Movements and State Companies*, George Philip

39 *The Struggle for Land: A Political Economy of the Pioneer Frontier in Brazil from 1930 to the Present Day*, J. Foweraker

38 *Caudillo and Peasant in the Mexican Revolution*, D. A. Brading, ed.

37 *Odious Commerce: Britain, Spain and the Abolition of the Cuban Slave Trade*, David Murray

36 *Coffee in Colombia, 1850–1970: An Economic, Social and Political History*, Marco Palacios

35 *A Socioeconomic History of Argentina, 1776–1860*, Jonathan C. Brown

34 *From Dessalines to Duvalier: Race, Colour and National Independence in Haiti*, David Nicholls

33 *Modernization in a Mexican Ejido: A Study in Economic Adaptation*, Billie R. DeWalt

32 *Haciendas and Ranchos in the Mexican Bajío, León, 1700–1860*, D. A. Brading

31 *Foreign Immigrants in Early Bourbon Mexico, 1700–1760*, Charles F. Nunn

30 *The Merchants of Buenos Aires, 1778–1810: Family and Commerce*, Susan Migden Socolow

29 *Drought and Irrigation in North-east Brazil*, Anthony L. Hall

28 *Coronelismo: The Municipality and Representative Government in Brazil*, Victor Nunes Leal

27 *A History of the Bolivian Labour Movement, 1848–1971*, Guillermo Lora

26 *Land and Labour in Latin America: Essays on the Development of Agrarian Capitalism in the Nineteenth and Twentieth Centuries*, Kenneth Duncan and Ian Rutledge, eds.

25 *Allende's Chile: The Political Economy of the Rise and Fall of the Unidad Popular*, Stefan de Vylder

24 *The Cristero Rebellion: The Mexican People between Church and State, 1926–1929*, Jean A. Meyer

23 *The African Experience in Spanish America, 1502 to the Present Day*, Leslie B. RoutJr

22 *Letters and People of the Spanish Indies: Sixteenth Century*, James Lockhart and Enrique Otte, eds.

21 *Chilean Rural Society from the Spanish Conquest to 1930*, Arnold J. Bauer

20 *Studies in the Colonial History of Spanish America*, Mario Góngora

19 *Politics in Argentina, 1890–1930: The Rise and Fall of Radicalism*, David Rock

18 *Politics, Economics and Society in Argentina in the Revolutionary Period*, Tulio Halperín Donghi

17 *Marriage, Class and Colour in Nineteenth-Century Cuba: A Study of Racial Attitudes and Sexual Values in a Slave Society*, Verena Stolcke

16 *Conflicts and Conspiracies: Brazil and Portugal, 1750–1808*, Kenneth Maxwell

15 *Silver Mining and Society in Colonial Mexico: Zacatecas, 1546–1700*, P. J. Bakewell

14 *A Guide to the Historical Geography of New Spain*, Peter Gerhard

13 *Bolivia: Land, Location and Politics Since 1825*, J. Valerie Fifer, Malcolm Deas, Clifford Smith, and John Street

12 *Politics and Trade in Southern Mexico, 1750–1821*, Brian R. Hamnett

11 *Alienation of Church Wealth in Mexico: Social and Economic Aspects of the Liberal Revolution, 1856–1875*, Jan Bazant

10 *Miners and Merchants in Bourbon Mexico, 1763–1810*, D. A. Brading

9 *An Economic History of Colombia, 1845–1930*, by W. P. McGreevey

8 *Economic Development of Latin America: Historical Background and Contemporary Problems*, Celso Furtado and Suzette Macedo

7 *Regional Economic Development: The River Basin Approach in Mexico*, David Barkin and Timothy King

6 *The Abolition of the Brazilian Slave Trade: Britain, Brazil and the Slave Trade Question, 1807–1869*, Leslie Bethell
5 *Parties and Political Change in Bolivia, 1880–1952*, Herbert S. Klein
4 *Britain and the Onset of Modernization in Brazil, 1850–1914*, Richard Graham
3 *The Mexican Revolution, 1910–1914: The Diplomacy of Anglo-American Conflict*, P. A. R. Calvert
2 *Church Wealth in Mexico: A Study of the 'Juzgado de Capellanias' in the Archbishopric of Mexico 1800–1856*, Michael P. Costeloe
1 *Ideas and Politics of Chilean Independence, 1808–1833*, Simon Collier

For EU product safety concerns, contact us at Calle de José Abascal, 56–1°,
28003 Madrid, Spain or eugpsr@cambridge.org.